THE DIVISION
IN
BRITISH
MEDICINE

'. . . Every doctor will tell you that the doctor who has the luck to be on the staff of a hospital has great advantages, because the hospital is the very centre and spring of all medical knowledge. Books, medical meetings, lectures are all very well in their way, but nothing can take the place of the hospital. There the doctor can use many methods of treatment which cannot be carried out at his surgery or in his patients' homes; there he is in contact with his colleagues and nothing is so likely to keep him up to the mark; there he is under the critical observation of the nurse, who is a very good judge of what a doctor should be; and there he can get the advice of specialists who are at his call when required. I wish every district in this country could follow the example of Mitcham and provide for its doctors a place in which their education could be continued, in the only place that it *can* be carried on properly — namely in a hospital. And obviously the knowledge and skill they acquire there is available in their daily work for people who may never see the inside of a hospital.'

From an address by Dr Alfred Cox, Medical Secretary of the British Medical Association (1912-32), at the opening of the extension for GPs at the Wilson Hospital, Mitcham, in 1935. *The Lancet,* 1935, 1, p.1521

The Division in British Medicine

A history of the separation of general practice
from hospital care 1911-1968

Frank Honigsbaum

**Kogan
Page**

First published 1979
by Kogan Page Ltd
120 Pentonville Road, London N1

Copyright ©1979 Frank Honigsbaum

Printed in Great Britain by
Redwood Burn Limited
Trowbridge Esher

ISBN 0 85038 133 9

To my wife Naomi,
for her unfailing support
and her uncompromising
criticism

Abbreviations

AMA	American Medical Association
BMA	British Medical Association
COS	Charity Organisation Society (now Family Welfare Assn.)
LCC	London County Council
LGB	Local Government Board
LRD	Labour Research Department
MOH	Medical Officer of Health
MPA	Medical Policy Association
MPU	Medical Practitioners' Union
NHI	National Health Insurance
NMU	National Medical Union
PEP	Political and Economic Planning
SMA	Socialist Medical Association
SMSA	State Medical Service Association
TUC	Trades Union Congress

Guide to Text

Letters (a,b,c,d, etc) refer to footnotes appearing on the same page.

Numbers (1,2,3,4, etc) refer to source references appearing at the end of the text.

Acknowledgements

This study has taken many years to complete and I have incurred many debts along the way. Unfortunately, it is not possible to mention every one but I have received particular assistance from the following: the staff of the old Middlesex Executive Council, civil servants from the legal and regional medical departments of the old Ministry of Health, Sir Jack Bailey, Sir William Bowen, Dr Charles W. Brook, Dr Bruce Cardew, Mrs Margaret Cole, Mr L. S. Cottee, Mr Frank Crump, Sir Guy Dain, Mr C. R. Dale, Sir Allen Daley, Dr T. R. Davies, Mr Walter Davis, Lady Eccles, Dr J. C. G. Evans, Dr Hugh Faulkner, Dr Harvey Flack, Mr Edward Franks, Dr Frank Gray, Mr Denis Gordon, Mrs Patricia Gordon, Mr Henry D. Harben, Mr Somerville Hastings, Mr A. G. Herbert, Dr Leslie T. Hilliard, Sir Wilson Jameson, Mr F. T. Jordan, Dr David Kerr, Mr R. E. Kennedy, Dr W. P. Kennedy, Mr Donald Kershaw, Mr Phillip Knightley, Mr Henry Lesser, Mr H. Mathieson, Dr David Stark Murray, Mr Thomas Scrafton, Dr Aubrey Sheiham, Mr Austin Spearing, Mr Joseph A. Speed, Mr S. R. Speller, Dr Derek Stevenson, Lady Mary Stocks, Sir Barnett Stross, Dr Herbert W. Swann, Mr H. W. Townley, Dr Gordon Ward, Dr Alfred Welply, Dr Allan J. Whitaker, Mr J. W. Yerrell.

Most of the research for this work was carried out at the British Museum, the Public Record Office and the Library of the London School of Hygiene and Tropical Medicine. To the staffs of each, I am deeply grateful for their unfailing assistance. I also wish to thank the following for permission to see and/or quote from private material: Beaverbrook Library (Lloyd George and Bonar Law Papers), British Library of Political and Economic Science (Braithwaite and Passfield Papers), Socialist Medical Association (Minute Book of State Medical Service Association), Labour Party, London Local Medical Committee. I apologize to any holder of copyright that I have failed to contact or trace. I also wish to thank the Controller of Her Majesty's Stationery Office for permission to reproduce Crown copyright material.

Funding for this study came largely from my own sources and, for this, I owe everything to my late father. Without his encouragement and support, a study of this prolonged nature would not have been possible. I did, however, also receive aid from the US Government under the terms of a Fulbright Grant and from the (American) Health Information Foundation which enabled me to spend one year as a Senior Research Officer at the

London School of Economics. For that appointment as well as for advice and counsel extending over many years, I am indebted to the late Professor Richard Titmuss.

Above all, I am indebted to Professor Brian Abel-Smith. He has read each draft meticulously and made many valuable suggestions and criticisms. All of this was particularly helpful since his own analysis of present problems and possible solutions differs from mine. The book was greatly strengthened as a result of the comments he made.

I also received much valuable criticism from Professor Maurice Kogan and his assistant, Miss Nancy Korman. Miss Korman undertook the herculean task of editing the manuscript through successive drafts and helped to give the book a clearer form than it originally presented. I cannot thank her enough for her assistance. Neither she nor others who offered criticisms, however, bear any responsibility for the validity of the historical material or for its interpretation.

Lastly, I wish to pay tribute to my sister, Mrs Judith Husten, for her continuous support, and to my wife, Naomi, for her constant aid and criticism. Only they know the agonies the author went through before this work was completed.

Contents

Foreword

by

Professor Brian Abel-Smith

In most industrialized countries the role of general practice has been rapidly declining during this century. The continuous growth of medical knowledge and the associated development of new techniques of diagnosis and treatment have made it impossible for any doctor to know all that can be known about medical practice. By specializing, a doctor can choose a particular field of practice in which he can aspire to become expert and remain expert in the face of new developments. Specialization can provide the doctor with the security of being master of his subject.

Where patients have been free to choose between a general practitioner and a specialist under health insurance, increasingly they have gone direct to the specialist. Patients have taken the view that the specialist is the better doctor. This has been the trend in America and most of continental Europe. It has also been the trend in countries which limit the number of doctors with rights to practise in hospital. In such countries as France and Germany, there are large numbers of specialists practising in the community who have no rights to treat their patients inside hospital. These 'community specialists' have been gaining at the expense of community general practitioners.

The United Kingdom is therefore one of a minority of industrial countries where the general practitioner is still the normal point of entry to the medical care system. Moreover, the general practitioner does not usually play any role in the care of his patients if they are admitted to hospital. Specialists at the hospital take over total responsibility for the clinical care of in-patients. Thus there is a virtually complete separation between doctors who work in the community and doctors who work in hospital. Doctors who enter general practice stay in general practice. And once a general practitioner has his own list of patients he normally stays in the same neighbourhood for the whole of his working life. No longer do we have doctors who practise partly as general practitioners and partly as hospital specialists.

The British system of general practice is also to be found in Ireland, Denmark, the Netherlands, Spain and Italy. While the USSR has a strong system of primary care it differs from the British pattern in a number of important ways. First, the polyclinics which provide primary care are closely associated with the district hospital. Secondly, children are looked after by paediatricians and not by general practitioners. Thirdly, work in primary care is seen as a stepping stone to hospital practice.

Britain is less untypical in having a hospital system which is 'closed' in the sense that doctors working in the community do not have the right to admit their patients and continue their care of their patients in this setting. This is the typical pattern of Western Europe, though there are exceptions. For example, a variety of arrangements are to be found in France, and in Finland health centres have beds attached to them — the model which the Dawson Report recommended for Britain in 1920. But the stronghold of the open hospital is the United States: virtually all doctors in clinical practice have access to hospital beds. The extreme development of open access is to be found in Japan where it is common for the doctor to have his own little 'hospital' at his place of practice.

Despite the evidence that, given free choice, patients increasingly choose to go direct to specialists, the British system of primary care has been resolutely defended on a number of grounds. First, it is argued that the general practitioner should decide whether referral to a specialist is necessary and if so in which specialty. This role of the general practitioner has been aggrandized as 'the conductor of the medical orchestra'. Secondly, it is argued that the general practitioner obtains special diagnostic insights by continuity of relationship not only with the patient but with his family and by knowledge derived from it of the patient's home and work. This enables him to become familiar with the patient's social and medical history at a much deeper level than can be obtained by a doctor questioning a patient whom he has met for the first time. This knowledge can be passed on to any specialist to whom the patient needs to be referred. Thirdly, the general practitioner is well placed to give general health advice and encourage preventive action. Fourthly, it is argued that access to the medical care system through the general practitioner is more economical. The general practitioner can distinguish and treat conditions which are self-limiting and only refer for costly investigation those patients for whom such a use of resources is justified. He can also delegate health care responsibilities to other members of the primary care team. The team as a whole can enable certain patients to be treated satisfactorily at home rather than in hospital and facilitate early discharge. It is this fourth claim in favour of general practice which has led to moves in North America and more recently in continental Europe to try and revive the system of general practice.

Parallel to the defence of general practice has been the defence of the system of closed hospitals. By concentrating his work on referred out-patients and on in-patients it is argued that the hospital-based doctor can best maintain and develop his standards of professional practice. Specialization both by area of medical interest and by only handling pre-selected patients is viewed as a major contribution to the quality of care. Anxiety is expressed about the standards of care provided by the doctor who undertakes a particular medical procedure occasionally rather than regularly.

While the specialist without access to hospital beds has only a limited field in which to keep up-to-date through professional conferences and professional journals, the task facing the general practitioner is much more formidable. He is expected to learn of new techniques of diagnosis and treatment he can use himself. At least in the case of pharmaceuticals the industry ensures at vast cost that he is aware of new products: indeed the risk is that new products will be over-used rather than under-used. But he is also expected to identify those patients for whom specialist care would be helpful.

This problem of enabling general practitioners to acquire such new knowledge as is necessary for the quality of the service they provide has long been recognized. Certain medical journals have consciously attempted to meet the need. An extensive system of continuing education has been developed. Incentives have been built into the British system of payment to encourage general practitioners to work together in groups and to form teams with nurses and health visitors partly to encourage the discussion of cases with the different professionals involved. Domiciliary visits by consultants have been encouraged and in a few health centres consultant services have been introduced.

But still 17 per cent of general practitioners practise alone and some partner-ships involve little professional communication between the partners. Nearly one-third of practices have no attached nurses. Rarely does the general practitioner meet the consultant at a domiciliary visit. And a considerable minority of general practitioners take no part in the continuing education which is provided and spend little time reading professional journals. What is not known is the extent to which general practitioners currently in practice lack important and relevant up-to-date knowledge or are practising out-of-date medicine and how serious this is for their patients.

By the crude criteria of age specific mortality rates, countries where direct access to specialists is allowed and where virtually all clinical doctors have access to hospital beds do not appear to have better health status. But this can be due to environmental reasons or the generic or behavioural characteristics of the different populations rather than to any feature of the organizing and financing of the health care system. One fact about the British system of organizing and financing health care is beyond dispute. It is cheap. The proportion of gross national product spent on health service is one of the lowest among highly industrialized countries. And the strong role of general practice undoubtedly contributes to this low cost.

In the nineteenth century the distinction between the specialist and the general practitioner was mainly one of social class — originating in the distinction between the apothecary and the physician or surgeon. In the inter-war period there were signs that the distinction was breaking down. But rigidity in the present distinction between hospital and general practice was introduced by the National Health Service in 1948. Foreign observers often assume that the creation of this Service was a revolutionary step — the imposition of some socialist blue-print by the post-war Labour Government on a protesting medical profession. While the abolition of the money barrier and the removal of any insurance eligibility test to receive medical care were radical steps by the standards of the time, the actual organization of the Service was evolutionary rather than revolutionary. It extended to the rest of the country the pattern of medical organization which had evolved in the main cities: it was the more prestigious city hospitals which had been able to refuse to allow any general practitioners to practise in them.

The primary reason why this pattern of medical organization was selected for extension was because it was what the leaders of the medical profession wanted. Nor was this merely because they wanted no competition from general practitioners acting as part-time specialists in what would remain of private specialist practice. They wanted to raise the standard of care given in out-lying hospitals up to that of the city hospitals. In particular they wanted to eliminate rather than up-grade the surgery done by general practitioners. And the bulk of general practitioners were by 1948 prepared to accept exclusion from hospital work. It was only a minority who had and wanted to retain a foot in both camps and their interests were sacrificed by the majority. They were forced to choose which side to enter. The door was wide open for a retreat into general practice. But if they chose to become specialists, they risked the possible humiliation of failing to be selected for the level of post to which they aspired.

Such was the settlement after World War II. After World War I it was by no means certain that the profession would wish to polarize itself in this way. This is where the Dawson Report of 1920 was so important because it envisaged a bridge between hospital practice and general practice. It is conceivable that if Britain's economic fortunes in the 1920s had been different and increases in public spending had been acceptable we might have acquired a radically different pattern of medical organization today.

What was the process by which the medical profession decided to turn the ancient class division of the profession into a distinction between hospital-based specialist practice and community-based general practice? Why did consumers and their political representatives accept this? These are the questions Frank Honigsbaum seeks to answer from a meticulous study of the vast documentary evidence which he has assembled. He provides us in this volume with the most comprehensive and fascinating interpretation of the politics of medical organization that has ever been published.

Introduction
The Division in British Medicine

To the world outside, the medical profession appears to form a unitary whole but within its ranks there exists a deep schism. Doctors nearly everywhere are divided into two main classes — general practitioners and specialists — and the gap between them grows wider each year. For this, the advance of knowledge is mainly responsible: no one can hope to master the whole of medicine and new specialties or sub-specialties appear as soon as new techniques develop.[1] But, in Britain, the division is wider than in most countries because of the way medical care is organized: for the most part, GPs do not work in hospital and specialists (or, as they are called in Britain, 'consultants') do not work in the community.[2] The two doctors live in different worlds and rarely meet.[3] 'Only by analogy to a rigid caste system', wrote the dean of an American medical school in 1951, 'can one make clear to the layman the great difference which came to exist in Britain between the specialist consultant and the general physician.'[4] (By the latter, he meant 'general practitioner'. In America, all doctors are called physicians but, in Britain, the term is reserved for those who practise medicine at a specialist level; in America, the latter are called 'internists'.[5])

The patient becomes aware of this gap mainly when he enters a hospital bed. During his whole stay there, he will rarely see the doctor who cares for him throughout the rest of the year. Even after the patient goes home, he may not see his GP unless he lets the doctor know that he has been discharged. If the patient waits for the GP to contact him, he may wait forever since the reports that hospitals send may take weeks to arrive and, by then, his doctor is likely to assume that the need for his services has ended.

No one has described this situation more graphically than Dr Mark Hodson, a well-known GP before his death in 1967. Together with a psychiatrist and another GP, he conducted a detailed examination of 500 letters which consultants sent to GPs and, after the study was concluded, he made the following observation:

'Sometimes a patient will appear in a surgery and announce, "Johnny's doing fine." By the time the GP has worked out which Johnny and how old, and whether he has won a scholarship or gone to a holiday home, the mother will say, "Surely the hospital told you he was operated on for his kidney last week?" It is extremely unlikely that the doctor will know, and he will either mumble deceitfully, "Of course", or attempt, unkindly, to disillusion her and tell the incredulous mother that hospital doctors don't usually write and tell the family doctor that operation is proposed shortly on one of his patients. Fifty-one of the 500 cases were operated on in connection with conditions for which they had been referred, and in only 20 (39%) of these was the GP informed that operation was proposed. On only one case was he actually informed just beforehand that the patient was about to undergo an operation.'[6]

British medicine — in contrast particularly with American — prides itself on the extent to which it offers continuity of care and, for the provision of this benefit, the profession has looked to its huge corps of GPs.[7] But can any system be described in such terms when it contains breaks in delivery like the one cited above? British patients receive continuous care only so long as they remain at home; whenever they enter hospital, they undergo a change greater than that which most patients experience elsewhere. Some may argue that the continuity which the British system provides is more beneficial since most illnesses do not require hospitalization[8] — but, against this, it must be noted that the outcome may be more vital where major illness is concerned. The patient who enters the hospital world may find that his life depends on the extent to which GPs establish contact with consultants. Why, in any case, should a choice have to be made? The aim of every medical system ought to be to provide continuity throughout — no matter where the patient receives care.

Nor are breaks in care the only consequence of the distance between consultants and GPs: even more damaging is the effect it has on the quality of general practice. Doctors who work in hospital have the facilities at hand to keep abreast of medical developments; those who do not tend to slip into repetitive routine. Not many patients understand — or even sense — the connection here. Gaps in delivery are immediately apparent but the slow, insidious effect on quality caused by isolation from the hospital world can be detected only by those intimately familiar with medical affairs.

The problem is largely one which the doctors have themselves created. As a leading hospital administrator (James Elliott) put it in 1969:

'... there exists in Britain a terrible gulf between hospital doctor and community doctor — a gulf not due to the operation of the [National Health Service] statute or to the wiles of the Government of the day, but due almost entirely to the past history, present attitudes, and the future attitudes of British doctors themselves.'[9]

This division has a long history in Britain, stretching back almost to the period when the medical profession was formed.[10] For our purposes, we need only take note of the influences at work at the start of the nineteenth century when the modern development of the profession began. By then, three main types of medical men had emerged — physicians, surgeons, apothecaries — and it was from the latter that the modern corps of GPs arose.[11] This, automatically, put them at the bottom of the profession because apothecaries had originally been grocers and something of the same tradesman stigma still attached. The bulk of their income came from the dispensing of drugs and not until 1829 were they allowed to levy a charge for the giving of medical advice. Previously they had charged for their services by an all-inclusive fee. As a result, patients continued to expect drugs from them long after apothecaries were allowed to charge for advice alone.

Apothecaries, nonetheless, acted as GPs for the mass of the population, rarely finding it necessary to seek the aid of other doctors because medical science was only in its infancy. Physicians provided the same GP function for the upper class and, since they came from the upper class, too, that produced a sharp division within the profession that matched the one among patients. Surgeons also served the upper class but, because of the messy, painful and hazardous nature of their work, they did not enjoy the same status as physicians. Surgeons, like surgery itself, did not become respectable until the end of the nineteenth century when the development of anaesthesia and antiseptic technique made it possible for operations to be performed with less risk and pain.

The main division within the profession was thus between physicians and apothecaries but it cannot be said that the higher social status accorded to physicians derived from the treatment they gave. Since medical science then had little to offer, all doctors tended to employ the same procedures and drugs. The main difference came in the way drugs were supplied. Physicians, who received a classical education traditional to their class, wrote their prescriptions in Latin and left dispensing to others — whereas apothecaries, who underwent only a limited, apprenticeship type of training, supplied the drugs themselves. In this way, the extent to which a doctor freed himself from dispensing became the hallmark of professional status, paralleling the class division that existed in medical ranks.

As the science of surgery progressed, however, drug treatment alone no longer sufficed and apothecaries found it necessary to perform more and more operations in order to supply their patients with a full range of care. This led some to take a double qualification — in surgery as well as medicine — and it was from the ranks of these surgeon-apothecaries that the main body of general practitioners arose. By the middle of the nineteenth century, a sufficient number had emerged to warrant making a legal distinction and, in 1858, Parliament passed a Medical Act which enabled the public to distinguish between those who were qualified and those who were not. All doctors — GPs and apothecaries as well as physicians and surgeons — were entitled to have their names placed on the new Medical Register.

Theoretically, this statute made all doctors equal but, in practice, the old distinctions remained. Physicians and surgeons continued to treat the upper class and they even began to secure a hold over the rest of the population as medical science advanced. Here the way was opened by the growing importance of surgical operations and hospital care. Hospitals grew slowly in Britain until the middle of the nineteenth century but, thereafter, they spread rapidly due to the advance of medical science.[12] The new techniques that appeared were concentrated in the hospital world and only there could major illness be treated adequately. For the first time, a distinction was created between those who practised medicine generally and those who specialized.[13] Physicians were used not merely as GPs for the upper class but, along with surgeons, as specialists for the whole population. Other doctors found it increasingly necessary to consult them and the other specialists that appeared. Because of the growing importance of hospital care, this applied particularly in those areas where GPs did not have access to beds.

To the old class division in the medical world was thus added a new one based on access to hospital facilities. The latter, in fact, tended to reinforce the former because, due largely to the charitable nature of the hospitals in which medical students were trained, young doctors had to go through a long, largely unpaid, apprenticeship before they could hope to become consultants. Not many medical students could afford the process and those that could not had, of necessity, to become GPs. This tended to reserve consultant posts to doctors who came from a higher social class.

Until the end of the nineteenth century, the new division created by the hospital world produced only a limited effect because of the imbalance that existed within the profession. Britain had too few consultants to meet its needs and only the older, more prestigious hospitals in the capital cities of London, Edinburgh and Dublin could hope to attract a sufficient number of pure specialists.[14] The newer hospitals that were built in provincial towns after 1850 had to admit doctors who combined specialism with general practice. Only as the ranks of the profession expanded did the situation change and that led to increasing tension between those who had access to hospital beds and those who did not.[15]

From all of this it can be seen that the division in British medicine preceded the advent of state intervention but the gap was not immutable and forces were at work at the end of the nineteenth century which were tending to close it.[a] Had the profession chosen to do so, it could have used state intervention to complete the process. The doctors, however, did the opposite. Our study therefore, is concerned with the way in which the profession made use of a developing public service to widen the gulf that existed between consultants and GPs.

I shall start with the year when state intervention in the GP sector began — 1911, with the formation of the panel system under the National Health Insurance (NHI) Act. After explaining the operation of that system and how it came into being, I shall examine the administrative structure in which the service operated, tracing the forces that led to the creation of the Ministry of Health in 1919. All of this is needed to supply the background information required to follow the many factors that led to the separation of GPs from the hospital world, starting with the rejection of the type of health centre proposed by the Dawson Report in 1920 and ending with the emergence of an entirely different kind of health centre after the National Health Service was formed in 1948.

Throughout the study, I shall make frequent comparisons between developments in Britain and the United States. The two countries offer a sharp contrast

a   See p.14 below.

which highlights factors that might otherwise be missed. In Britain, GPs are too remote from the hospital world but, in America, they are too closely involved. This difference owes much to the fact that one country has a fully developed public health service, while the other has remained largely under a system of private enterprise. In both respects, the countries stand at opposite extremes and much can be learned from comparing the two. To this I must add a personal note: I am an American who came to Britain in 1957 with the deliberate aim of finding out what my country could learn from the British example. Since America intends to start its own national health insurance system in the 1980s, the moment for such a study is timely and apt.

Part 1
Foundation of the
General Practitioner Service
1911-1919

Extensive public provision of GP care began with the formation of the panel system under the National Health Insurance Act of 1911. The system was based on the club practice started by friendly societies in the nineteenth century but changes were made to make it compatible with the advance of medical science. By covering all employed members of the working class, the 1911 Act made free GP care available to one-third of the nation. Wives and children, however, were largely excluded and this, combined with high infant mortality rates and the reform fever generated by the First World War, produced a demand for extended coverage which led to the creation of the Ministry of Health in 1919.

1
The Panel System

State intervention in the field of medical care in Britain began with the Poor Law.[1] Throughout most of the nineteenth century, local boards of guardians offered free GP service to those who could pass a means test. The degrading nature of the system, however, deterred many from using it and, therefore, public provision of GP care in any real sense did not begin until the NHI Act passed through Parliament in 1911. Then, for the first time in British history, a large proportion of the population had the right to free GP treatment under the panel system. This chapter explains how that system operated.

The NHI Act

The NHI Act was designed to provide general medical care and cash sickness benefits for the manual workers of the nation. It covered *all* engaged in manual labour without regard to the money earned but those in non-manual labour were included only insofar as their income fell below the threshold set for income tax. This figure was raised progressively from £160 in 1911 to £250 in 1920 and then, finally, to £420 in 1942.[2]

When the Act began, only those above age 16 were covered but, in 1937, this was lowered to 14 so as to bring in juvenile contributors as well. As a result of this and other changes (mainly designed to cover many of those who were unemployed), the number of people protected by the Act rose from about 15 million in 1913 to 25 million in 1942, thereby increasing the proportion of the population covered from one-third to one-half.[3] Nevertheless, it still left out the dependants of insured workers — their non-working wives and children — as well as most of those who were unemployed or who were engaged in non-manual occupations. The Act was thus one designed specifically for employed members of the working class; the middle and upper classes were almost entirely excluded.

Those covered by the Act were called 'insured persons' (or 'panel patients' when they were in receipt of medical care) and to establish their right to its benefits, they made weekly contributions which were automatically deducted from their wages. In 1913, when the Act first came into operation, these benefits fell into 2 categories — cash and services (or treatment).[4] The first monetary benefit was called 'sickness benefit' and it offered 10s. a week to men (7s. 6d. to women) for the first 26 weeks of illness. After that, it was changed to 'disablement benefit' and the rate for both sexes was cut to 5s. per week, payable as long as the disability lasted. The other monetary benefit was called 'maternity benefit' and it offered 30s. on the birth of a child to the wife of an insured person or double that amount if she were insured herself.

On the treatment side, the Act provided general medical care and drugs without limit and without charge. Furthermore, whereas the cash benefits ended when the insured person reached the age of retirement (70 in 1911, 65 after the Contributory Pensions Act became law in 1925), medical benefit continued throughout life. The range of care offered, however, was narrow since it covered, for the most part, only what could be provided within a doctor's surgery.

Hospital and specialist treatment was thus generally excluded from the Act. The only type that could be obtained came under the heading of 'sanatorium benefit': this applied only to one disease — tuberculosis — and it could be secured only by accepting confinement, usually for a prolonged period, within a sanatorium located in the countryside. In 1911, only 5,500 beds were available for treatment of this illness in England and Wales and this did not begin to cover the number of people who needed such care. Only after the benefit was removed from NHI in 1920 and placed in the hands of local authorities did accommodation become adequate. By 1929, 22,500 beds were available and no less than 15,000 of these were provided by local authorities (the rest being located in private or voluntary institutions).[5]

No other forms of treatment were available under NHI until 1921, and then these were offered only in the form of 'additional benefits' to insured persons who belonged to societies rich enough to provide them. Such benefits did not normally cover hospital or specialist care; they embraced services mainly in the dental or optical sphere.[6]

The only substantial provision made in the Act for medical care, then, was GP treatment. If an insured person wanted further service, he had to consult a specialist privately. Over the country as a whole, however, less than 3,000 fully-qualified specialists existed and as many as one-third practised in London.[a] Patients in the provinces had to rely on GP-specialists for specialist services and this could create problems if the particular doctors they consulted also served them as panel practitioners under NHI. At what point did the range of free care under NHI end and the area of fee-charging specialist service begin? This was a problem that was to plague the authorities throughout the whole course of the NHI Act.[b]

Before the First World War, many serious cases of illness were treated at home but, if a paying patient needed hospital facilities, he could enter one of the growing number of nursing homes and cottage hospitals in England and Wales. By 1921, the nursing home sector alone contained 26,000 beds and, by the 1930s, some 10,000 more were available in the 600 cottage hospitals that dotted

a   This estimate — the best available before the start of the Health Service in 1948 — applied to the corps existing in the 1930s. A somewhat larger figure — 4,250 consultants and specialists — was cited by one medical leader in 1913 but this was only a rough guess and he probably included in his estimate a number of specialists who were not properly qualified.[7]

b   For more on this, see pps 152-3 and 162-3 below.

the land.[8] From the end of the nineteenth century, even some of the larger voluntary hospitals had begun to offer facilities for paying patients but most of their services were provided without charge.

The larger voluntary hospital, then, was the one place where an insured person could be certain of obtaining free hospital and specialist treatment. To do so, however, he had to undergo the indignity of being labelled a 'charity case' since these hospitals operated as charitable institutions with their own management committees. Only where they were linked with a contributory scheme might a member of the working class establish a 'right' to care by paying, on a voluntary basis, a small weekly contribution. Not until after the First World War, however, did many such schemes come into operation.[9] In 1911 England and Wales had as many as 530 voluntary hospitals with 43,000 beds[10] but few had contributory schemes and a large number of such hospitals were of the small cottage hospital type.

Such was the pattern of care that applied to insured persons. Their dependants had to pay privately for all their medical care or else seek treatment as a charity case from a voluntary hospital. Alternatively, they might obtain the full range of care from the Poor Law authorities, thereby receiving GP treatment from the 3,700 GPs who practised part-time as district medical officers[11] — but to do so, they had to pass the harsh means test imposed. Nor was that all: if they needed hospital care, they ran the risk of having to enter a mixed workhouse (containing able-bodied paupers as well as sick patients) and the doctor who attended them was more likely to be a GP than a consultant. Only in a separately-administered Poor Law infirmary might the services of a fully-qualified specialist be secured. Some 75 infirmaries existed by 1911, containing 30,000 beds in all (as compared with 43,000 in the voluntary sector), and an upgrading process had begun which transformed a number into hospitals of high standard. But the largest amount of hospital accommodation was still to be found in the mixed workhouses — a total of no less than 80,000 beds — and in them were placed most of the chronically ill.[12]

Dependants thus enjoyed even less protection than insured persons and it was to fill this void that local authorities began to provide free services of their own, starting first with infant care (because of the high infant mortality rates prevailing before the First World War) and then extending outwards to a more general maternity and child welfare sector. Beyond that, local authorities had long provided free care in isolation hospitals to deal with infectious diseases like smallpox and scarlet fever (by 1913, as many as 1,118 of these hospitals existed with 32,000 beds)[13] and this was extended, after NHI began, to cover the twin scourges of tuberculosis and venereal disease. By the end of the war many people had the option of attending a free municipal clinic, dispensary or hospital rather than having to pay a private doctor; it all depended on the extent of the provision made by the local authority where they lived.

The number of insured persons thus covered represented as much as 80% to 90% of the population — or some 38 million out of 45 million people. To treat them, about 15,000 GPs (out of a total of 20,000) were available, nearly all of whom joined the panel. With about 15 million (including Scotland) covered by NHI, this meant that the average GP practising in a working-class area had about 1,000 panel patients to tend, plus about 1,500 dependants, making a total workload of some 2,500 in all.[14]

In treating insured and non-insured, it should be made clear, the same doctor was usually employed: he merely acted in a panel capacity at one moment and in a private capacity the next. Only in middle and upper-class areas, for the most part, did GPs find it feasible to practise apart from NHI: there, many patients had to pay fees and the doctors who treated them tended to act solely in a private capacity. This gave them, also, an incentive to extend the range of care they provided far beyond the limits set in working-class areas — and, with the smaller workloads they handled, they had the time to do it. Some 5,000 doctors remained off the panel and, with a population of only 7 million to treat, their list size amounted to only about 1,400 patients on average.

It was from the ranks of the non-panel doctors, therefore, that the main corps of GP-specialists arose. They were the ones who held hospital appointments in provincial towns, thereby making up for the deficiency of consultants that existed before 1948. The panel system thus tended to create a division not only between the social classes but within British medicine. Most of the 15,000 GPs who entered NHI found themselves increasingly cut off from their colleagues in hospital.

Its origins in club practice

The panel system itself was not so much an innovation of 1911 as an offshoot of existing voluntary efforts to offer GP treatment. For a century before NHI began, a rudimentary form of medical care had been provided through what were called 'friendly societies'.[15] These were simply clubs of working men who, originally coming together for social purposes, decided to offer an element of insurance protection for their members against the risks, mainly, of sickness and death. For the former, they offered a small cash payment similar to the one that came to be incorporated in NHI and, in order to make sure that claims were not abused, they hired a doctor to certify incapacity for work.

This doctor became known as the 'club doctor' and he was paid for his services by an all-inclusive capitation fee — or so much per member per year whether the member had reason to seek his services or not. In return for this fee, the doctor was expected to provide not only certificates of incapacity (when warranted) but as much medical care as a general practitioner could offer, working within his own surgery. Since it was customary then for doctors to supply drugs,[a] this vital element of medical care came to be included in the range of services the societies expected.

When club practice began in the 1820s, many doctors found it possible to live with this arrangement since drugs were not a costly item and they needed the financial payments the societies offered to build up a list of patients on the

a   See pp. 2-3 above.

private side. Once the latter reached a sufficient size, the doctor could drop his club appointment and concentrate on private clients. Club practice was thus especially welcomed by young men starting out in practice and they tended to regard it much as a consultant would an honorary (unpaid) appointment in a voluntary hospital.[16]

As the century progressed, however, the movement grew too large for the profession's comfort. Friendly societies spread throughout the country until they covered roughly one-third of the adult working class (wives and children generally being excluded) — or 4 to 5 million out of 15 million people.[17] Their success, furthermore, inspired competition from others so that more and more organizations began to offer medical benefit as a way of recruiting members (or customers). An ever-increasing number of doctors were drawn into the work — while other medical men found it necessary to start clubs of their own in order to retain patients. By the time NHI began, at least half the GPs in Britain — or some 10,000 out of 20,000 [a] — were thought to be engaged in contract practice in one form or another and for a quarter of them (some 4,000 to 5,000 doctors), the number of patients involved was so large that the rates of pay offered had become crucial to their subsistence.

Yet these terms were niggardly in the extreme. When club practice first started in the 1820s, the friendly societies offered capitation fees of 2s. to 3s. per year and, despite the ever-increasing cost of drugs throughout the nineteenth century, they raised the rate to only about 4s. by the time NHI began.[20] For this small fee, they expected the club doctor to provide everything a patient needed in the way of general medical care and drugs for a whole year. Neither party, furthermore, had any choice in the arrangement. Each club tended to employ only one doctor and all its members had to consult him if they wished to establish their right to draw the weekly cash sickness benefit.[21] The only way a dissatisfied patient could change the doctor was to have the club sack him — which meant that the doctor who was discharged lost *all* the members of the club and not just the aggrieved party.

Moreover many friendly societies administered their clubs in the most despotic way and did not allow doctors any voice in management.[b] In some areas, they even established surgeries of their own — called 'medical aid institutions' — in which they not only employed doctors on a salaried basis but subjected them to interference on the treatment they gave. Thus, at one in Birmingham, a doctor was allowed only 1 minute to see a patient and, if

a   This estimate is based on the number of forms which the BMA sent out in 1905 in order to prepare its report on contract practice. The total number was 12,000 but some were sent to doctors who were not engaged in the work. Only 1,548 doctors replied and as many as 692 indicated that they were not involved in any form of contract practice.[18] Better figures, however, are available where the militants of the profession are concerned: as many as 4,000 doctors belonged to the 40 local medical trade unions (or societies) that were formed at the end of the nineteenth century and it was they who led the movement for the reform of club practice.[19]

b   Today, it is ironic to note, we might be tempted to call this a 'democratic' form of administration as it would be one in which the consumers exercised control.

he exceeded that time, 'a loud knocking at the surgery door brought the consultation to a close.'[22]

Near the end of the nineteenth century, the doctors resorted to trade union action in an attempt to persuade the friendly societies to mend their ways but they were frustrated by the lack of solidarity in their ranks. Whenever local doctors tried to boycott a club post, the friendly societies managed to find a doctor elsewhere who would fill it. The nation had too many GPs available in the Edwardian era for a medical strike to hold.[23]

Even stronger competition arose from the ranks of consultants. They had been threatened at the end of the nineteenth century by the intrusion of GPs into specialist work. The development of anaesthetics and antiseptic technique had made it possible for GPs to perform a variety of operations formerly left to consultant surgeons or not performed at all. This prompted the surgeons to retaliate, usurping after-care treatment from GPs and fusing the various branches of the profession to the point where few 'pure' consultants were left.[24] In one way or another, nearly all the specialties were affected, transforming consultants into 'specialist GPs' and GPs into 'general specialists'.[25]

Thereafter, the referral system — which barred consultants from seeing patients except upon referral from GPs — almost completely broke down.[26] Relations between the two branches of the profession reached a critical point when, having won appointments to provincial hospitals as surgeons, GPs demanded the same rights as physicians. From there, the issue spread to the more general one of whether GPs should have open access to hospitals.[27]

The effects of this tension were felt whenever GPs tried to boycott club posts. Their efforts were frustrated not only by the importation of what they called 'six-penny scabs' (i.e. low-class GPs) but by consultants as well. Here was the way one angry GP-specialist put it: '. . . when those of us who were constantly called into consultation refused, there was no lack of material from neighbouring places, and the larger the place and the more prominent the consultant, the more ready he appears to join them [i.e. the "six-penny scabs"] in their cases, and often inconvenience himself to aid them in their difficulties.'[28]

From this it was clear that consultants had developed a vested interest in club practice since it protected them from competition. Friendly society work, by excluding major surgery and specialist procedures, confined GPs within a narrow sphere — so much so that a club post was often enough to disqualify a doctor from a hospital appointment no matter how wide the care he rendered otherwise.[29] Consultants made their interest most evident through the medium of the British Medical Association (BMA). Throughout the nineteenth century, they frustrated all efforts of club doctors to use that organization to break the hold of the friendly societies.[30]

In 1902, however, a well-organized group of club doctors, led by Dr (later Sir) James Smith Whitaker and Dr Alfred Cox, [a] managed to reform

a   For profiles of Cox and Whitaker, see pp. 326 and 338 below.

the BMA's Constitution.[31] Still, they could not carry all their demands and the BMA was split into rival camps — the 'unionists' (or the trade-union-minded club doctors) and the 'scientists' (or consultants).[32] Over the next 9 years, the 'scientists' frustrated all efforts of the 'unionists' to turn the BMA into a fighting organization. What the 'unionists' wanted most was the right to strike but that was barred by the BMA's Memorandum of Association.[33] This, in fact, had been 'the whole issue of the reconstitution' in 1902.[34] But, in 1908, when the 'unionists' tried to obtain the power by means of a Royal Charter, the 'scientists' blocked the move,[35] thereby forcing the BMA 'to undergo the humiliation of the refusal of a State recognition often granted to bodies of a smaller membership and far less importance to the welfare of the State'.[36] Here, in effect, was the profession's 'Taff Vale' judgment.[a]

By 1911, then, it was clear to Whitaker and his colleagues that the only way they would be able to break the hold of the friendly societies was through a state system. They therefore accepted the NHI Bill which Lloyd George[b] introduced and did their best to mould it in the profession's favour. In the eyes of many doctors, however, their efforts did not go far enough and the BMA ended up opposing the introduction of the Act.

Nevertheless, the panel system that emerged did much to strengthen the position of club doctors.[38] It resulted, first, in a vast improvement in their financial condition. NHI almost doubled the capitation fee club doctors received (from 4s. to over 7s.) and relieved them of the need to supply drugs at their own cost where insured persons were concerned.[39] Prescriptions, henceforth, were filled increasingly by chemists — who in turn were paid directly by the state. All the typical panel doctor had to do was sign a form for the patient to present.

Equally beneficial was the way in which the system altered the relationship between the friendly societies and the doctors. No longer were the doctors subject to hire and fire by a club committee: in future, each doctor decided for himself whether he wished to work for NHI. All he had to do was put his name on the panel list maintained by the local administrative agency for his area (which was called the 'insurance committee'). Thereafter, the doctor was free to build up his list of panel patients to any size he desired (maximum limits on list size were not imposed until 1920) and he also enjoyed the same freedom of action where private patients were concerned. Each doctor made his own decision on the extent to which he wished to participate in NHI. He could, if he liked, treat only one insured person, leaving the rest of his time free for private patients. The only real difference in the 2 halves of his practice came in the way he was paid. The state paid for the insured person whereas the private patient had to meet the medical fee himself.

Furthermore, a panel doctor could refuse to accept any patient on his list

a   This famous judgment, delivered by the Law Lords in 1901, exposed the trade unions to damages from strike action, and though that handicap was removed by the Trade Disputes Act of 1906, another restriction (this time on political action) was imposed by the Osborne judgment in 1909. The doctors were more concerned about strike action, but they thought the Osborne judgment would also have to be reversed before the BMA could secure the powers they desired.[37]

b   For a profile of Lloyd George, see p. 332 below.

without losing the patronage of the club as a whole. Free choice operated within the framework of the panel system much as it did outside in private practice. Panel doctors might still lose their right to practise under the system but this could be done only where serious infractions were concerned and the doctor had the right to go through a long appeal procedure before expulsion was decided. The capricious rule of the club committee ended with the passage of the 1911 Act.

Such was the essence of the panel system. It was the closest anyone could come to private practice within the framework of a service financed by the state and that was why the profession became so fond of it. Even the right to buy and sell practices was not disturbed; the panel, in fact, increased the amount doctors could receive because insured persons, under the capitation method of payment, tended to stick to the surgeries they attended no matter how often the doctor changed.[40]

Lastly, the doctors continued to work in their own surgeries[a] and there was hardly any interference in the way they practised. Each doctor decided, from the funds available to him, what sort of equipment his surgery would contain. The range of care offered under NHI tended to be determined by the doctors themselves rather than by the authorities.

Role of approved societies

The profession thus had good reason to be satisfied with the panel system but it was not without its problems and these arose mainly from the presence of the other parties involved in the Act — the 'approved societies'. For just as the state left the doctors free to provide medical care as they pleased, so it left the payment of cash benefits to largely autonomous institutions operating in much the same manner as the old friendly societies. At first this role was to be confined to the friendly societies but Lloyd George brought so many of the working class within NHI that the other organizations catering to them demanded the right to participate. In this way, the industrial insurance offices and the trade unions came to share in the administration of the Act.

The role of all these organizations after 1911, however, was supposed to be confined to the payment of cash benefits — not, as in the case of the old friendly societies, to the administration of medical benefit as well. When the Bill was first introduced, Lloyd George had to leave the approved societies in control of the doctors in order to persuade the friendly societies to accept the measure. But he seems to have intended, ultimately, to bring the doctors into a municipal service,[41] thereby building up a unified system of medical care that would cover everyone: dependants as well as insured persons; specialists as well as GPs; voluntary, municipal and Poor Law hospitals as well as GP surgeries.[b] The main way he hoped to do this was through the medium of sanatorium benefit because provision was written into the Act for it to be extended not only to other diseases (besides tuberculosis) but to the dependants of insured persons. As one legal guide to NHI put it: 'The terms of the Act are wide

a   In America GP surgeries are known as doctors' offices.
b   See p. 30 below.

enough to allow of indefinite extension so that sanatorium benefit might eventually become a general hospital benefit.' [42]

Once this was accomplished, the nation would have a single system of medical care instead of the 3 that existed — private, Poor Law and municipal. But such was not to be: before the Bill went through Parliament, the friendly societies made it clear that they would not accept complete loss of control over medical benefit [43] — and the doctors, on their side, baulked at the prospect of municipal employment. [44]. The profession did not think the heavy hand of the local authority's chief medical officer — the medical officer of health (MOH) — represented any gain over the capricious control of the club committee. Lloyd George, therefore, had to construct a half-way house in the form of an insurance committee on which all 3 parties were represented — the approved societies and the doctors as well as the local authorities. Furthermore, because the friendly societies were most annoyed at the change, he had to give them and their approved society colleagues a 60% majority on the body.

This, for the doctors, seemed to resurrect the spectre of friendly society control and that largely accounts for their opposition to the Act. But the more astute among them recognized the difference between the restricted powers given to the new insurance committee and the unlimited control possessed by the old club committee. Even pay questions, at the profession's insistence, were removed from insurance committee hands and entrusted to the administrative authorities on the national level.

Roots of conflict

Nevertheless, through the local insurance committees as well as through their influence on the national level, the approved societies did manage to make life difficult for the doctors and much of the tension between them arose from the way NHI was financed. The funds came mainly from weekly insurance contributions and, to these, not only insured persons but their employers and the state contributed. This enabled the worker to obtain what Lloyd George called '9 pence for 4 pence' — because employers and the state added 5d. to the 4d. exacted from insured persons. [45] Under club practice, the rate imposed on members had been somewhat higher — 6d. to 7d. in the larger friendly societies [46] — and this tended to restrict the number of workers who could join. By 'cutting' the contribution to 4d., Lloyd George enabled NHI to extend its limits far beyond the borders of club practice, bringing not only all manual workers but even some of the non-manual class inside. But the amount of cash sickness benefit they received was generally the same as the friendly societies had given before — 10s. or 12s. per week for shorter spells of illness. Only in the case of medical and maternity benefits did a more liberal provision emerge.

It was the doctors (and midwives), then, who seem to have benefited the most from the higher contributions NHI imposed. This was a constant source of irritation to the approved societies and remained a bone of contention between them and the doctors during the first decade of the Act. Every time the doctors lodged a pay claim the approved societies made their dissatisfaction known. [47]

A more persistent source of tension arose from the belief, widespread among the approved societies, that they 'owned' the funds which were used to pay the doctors. Many society leaders saw the scheme as a national one only in the sense that the mechanism of the state was used to collect contributions; otherwise, they thought, control resided in the hands of voluntary organizations just as it had done under club practice.[48] This flowed naturally from the decision Lloyd George made in 1911 to base NHI on friendly society practice[49] — but the curious thing is that the belief was unaffected by the size of the Exchequer grant (which had been set at a much higher figure in Britain than under the earlier German system).[50] No doubt it was the absence of a state guarantee of benefits which did much to nullify the belief and an even greater influence was exerted by the method under which NHI was funded. Instead of the pay-as-you-go system used elsewhere, the authorities in Britain put NHI on a fully-funded basis.[51] This made the Act appear more as a self-contained insurance system than one which depended on Government aid.

During the early twenties, the new Ministry of Health deliberately tried to foster this image in an attempt to improve the range and quality of medical benefit. Ever since NHI began, the authorities had sought to raise the tone of panel care to match approved society expectations but they found the job of policing the doctors difficult and distasteful. Perhaps, those in charge thought, the societies themselves could act with more vigour, and the Ministry tried to turn the task over to them, leaving itself the more comfortable role of arbitrator.[52]

The nature of the approved society system lent itself to Ministry attempts to effect this transfer, since the approved societies were encouraged to show the same concern for sick claims as the friendly societies had done. To do that, the state gave each society the chance to earn a surplus so that it could offer its members a store of additional benefits beyond those required under the Act. The extent to which a society did so largely determined its appeal to the public; the principle of free choice operated as much on the money side of NHI as it did on the medical. Each insured person had the right to join the approved society he liked best (providing the society agreed to accept him) and he was attracted to the society that offered the largest store of additional benefits. Each society, furthermore, operated largely on its own so that the extent to which it controlled sick claims determined the amount of its surplus and the range of its additional benefits.

For such a system to work fairly, all the societies had to be put on an equal footing when the Act began, and the state did try to do this where age was concerned. The older the insured person, the more likely he was to have need for sickness benefit and a special subsidy (in the form of 'reserve values') was provided to cover such claims.[53] But the same concession was not made where sex and occupation were concerned. Women, generally, and men engaged in dangerous occupations like coal-mining, tended to suffer more frequent spells of illness, yet the Government made no allowance for this. Two large groups of approved societies, therefore, found themselves handicapped in the race to earn additional benefits: the industrial insurance offices, because they organized most of the women workers; and the trade unions (or at least some of them), because they included in their ranks workers engaged in occupations danger-ous to health. (The friendly societies largely kept their rolls free of insured persons prone to illness just as they had done before 1911.) Whereas the insurance offices, however, managed to overcome their handicap by (among other factors) keeping a tight rein on claims, the unions did not, thereby setting the stage for a division in the approved society world which eventually decided the fate of the Act.[a]

Such a development, however, could not be foreseen when the approved society system began and, to the civil servants who conceived it, it seemed ideal since it left the state free from the details of daily operation. Even more important, the Government's financial obligations were limited since no state guarantee was provided, not even of the statutory benefits provided in the Act. All the Treasury had to do was make its 'two-ninths' contribution to the NHI fund; after that, its financial responsibilities ceased. The sole obligation the state retained was to act as policeman, making sure that all parties adhered to the self-governing rules laid down.

Nevertheless, in the chance to earn additional benefits lay the roots of conflict because it was the doctors, to a large extent, who determined whether an approved society produced a profit. If the doctors failed to treat patients adequately, or if they issued certificates too freely, the sickness claims a society had to meet might consume all its funds and it would have nothing left for additional benefits.

The tension between the parties was further heightened by the inclusion of disablement benefit in NHI — a provision which, as we saw, called for the payment of 5s. a week (after the first 26 weeks) for as long as the disability lasted, ceasing only when the insured person reached the age of retirement (70 until 1925, 65 thereafter). An approved society might thus be obliged to pay this benefit for as long as 54 years, if the worker involved became permanently disabled at the age of 16.

Such a prolonged payment was similar to a pension and, ideally, it would have been better to have included permanent disability in a pension programme financed by the state as had been done in Germany.[54] But because the friendly societies had provided disablement benefit before 1911, it was impossible to take it from them when NHI began. The Act, in fact, compounded the problem by raising the amount the societies paid from 2s. 6d. to 5s. per week. There was, however, one important exception to this procedure. If incapacity arose from occupational causes, then it became the responsibility of the employer under the Workmen's Compensation Act. This gave the societies a strong incentive to shift the burden wherever possible. The same rule, however, did not apply to medical benefit. It continued throughout life no matter which agency paid the cash benefit.

For these as well as other reasons, the kind of care meted out by panel doctors was much more important to the approved societies than it was to the old friendly societies. An exact diagnosis of occupational disability or the detection and treatment of diseases like tuberculosis before they became

---

a   For more on this, see Chapter 22 beginning on p. 217 below.

permanently disabling offered enormous financial relief to the societies — yet the scheme failed to provide panel doctors with the specialist services they needed.[55] It had been found under the Workmen's Compensation Act that it took a specialist, possessing the full range of diagnostic equipment, as much as 30 minutes to detect a malingerer — yet the approved societies expected unaided GPs to do the same within the short 3 to 6 minute periods normally available for each consultation.[56]

In this and other ways, the stage was set in 1911 for a series of clashes between the approved societies and the doctors. Until 1923, the societies managed to hold their own but in that year a pay dispute occurred which tipped the scales in the doctors' favour. Cox, the Medical Secretary of the BMA, at that point made the profession's preference clear:

> '. . . I would rather see the State provide the money. Our Civil Service is incorruptible. I would rather see the Government standing between the insured persons and the medical profession than the approved societies, some of which want the Government to stand aside.'[57]

In making this declaration, the doctors were not alone: to their astonishment, they found an ally in the midst of the approved society world itself. The trade unions, embittered by their failure to enrol as many members as their rivals, or to offer the same array of additional benefits, also came down against the approved society system. Thereafter, in alliance with the doctors, they demanded the creation of a new network of social insurance under which everyone would be treated equally.

Eventually, as we shall see, such a system was formed. Under it, the approved societies were eliminated and managerial control did pass into the hands of the state. At that point, also, medical benefit was separated from the administration of cash benefits and expanded into a National Health Service under which hospital and specialist care were added to the panel system. But none of this took place until 1948 — 37 years after NHI had been established. During that whole period, the only kind of hospital or specialist treatment offered to insured persons came by way of additional benefits and it was meagre in the extreme.[a] Only 1% of the total amount spent by the approved societies on additional treatment benefits took this form; the bulk of the cash went on dental and optical care.[58]

What this meant, therefore, was that throughout the whole NHI period, only general medical care was available to insured persons and the doctors who supplied it had to do so within their own poorly-equipped surgeries. Few had hospital privileges and those who did were generally not expected to offer hospital or specialist treatment as part of the panel service. That need was met by agencies operating outside the Act — the private sector on the one hand and the municipal (or Poor Law) sector on the other.

Though beneficial to club doctors in an economic sense, the panel system thus tended to reinforce the restrictions previously imposed on clinical work. NHI may have freed GPs from the control of the friendly societies but it did not release them from the inhibitions applied by

a   For just what this hospital benefit offered, see p. 158 below.

consultants. The panel system, in fact, deepened the division in the profession by extending club practice over a wider front. Whereas the friendly societies before 1911 covered only 4 to 5 million people, NHI embraced 15 million — and this meant that many more GPs found themselves confined within the narrow bounds of 'club care'. To break free, they had to be given more facilities than the panel system provided but that, as it turned out, could not be considered until a new administrative structure was formed. Reform in practice organization had to await the creation of a Ministry of Health.

2
The Division
in Health Administration

'. . . the first consideration of a minister should be the health of the people.
A land may be covered with historic trophies, with museums of science and
galleries of art, with universities and libraries; the people may be civilised
and ingenious; the country may even be famous in the annals and action of
the world, but, gentlemen, if the population every ten years decreases, and
the stature of the race every ten years diminishes, the history of that country
will soon be the history of the past.'

Disraeli in his famous, *'Sanitas sanitatum, omnia sanitas'*, speech, delivered at Manchester,
3 April 1972.

Of all the departments of state, none in a sane society would rank higher than
the Ministry of Health, for what is more precious than life itself? Disraeli, in
1872, said 'it is impossible to overrate the importance of the subject'[1] — yet not
until 1919 was a durable department established. Attempts were made earlier
— in 1848 with the General Board of Health and in 1871 with the Local
Government Board (LGB) — but both, after a few years, collapsed.[2] The
former disappeared entirely in 1858 while the latter lived on only as a shadow
of what was intended. With few exceptions, the LGB's Poor Law functions
smothered its concern for public health.[3]

For this delay in the creation of a durable department, the doctors
themselves were partly to blame. From the middle of the nineteenth century,
they had called periodically for a Ministry of Health and some public-spirited
practitioners were to be found in every campaign waged down to 1919. But the
bulk of the profession showed interest in the subject only when it held out hope
of strengthening their economic position. What they wanted most of all was
protection against the competition of unqualified practitioners. Here, however,
the 1858 Medical Act and the 1911 NHI Act satisfied much of their needs —
the former, by confining friendly society (as well as public) posts to registered
doctors; the latter, by extending this protection from one-tenth to one-third of the
population.[4] After 1911, medical interest in a Ministry of Health weakened
and it revived in 1918 only after the profession saw how such protection could
be extended without running the risk of bureaucratic control. The Ministry of
Health, as the doctors' leading spokesman on the subject (Bertrand Dawson)
once admitted, 'was brought about by public opinion and not, unfortunately, by
medical opinion.'[5]

If, however, the public was the moving force, why did it wait until 1919 to
act? The answer lay in the primitive state of medical science until the end of the

nineteenth century. Medicine, except for Jenner's vaccine (offering protection against smallpox), had little to offer and therefore the attempts to create a Ministry of Health in 1848 and 1871 were concerned almost entirely with environmental reform. Sewers and drains were not a subject about which public passion could be aroused or a durable department founded. Disraeli might cry *'Sanitas sanitatum, omnia sanitas'* ('Health for all, all for health') but the Liberals were able to dismiss it as a 'policy of sewage'.[6]

By 1911, however, it was clear that medicine did have something to offer and that its benefits were accruing at a rapid rate. The NHI Act of that year was designed to remove the friendly society impediment on the advance of science and it at last brought into public health 'a wholly new element, a leaven' which freed it from its association with sewers and drains. 'The one vital thing in the Insurance Act', wrote the civil servant charged with administering it (Sir Robert Morant), 'was (in my view in 1911) the organisation of medical treatment for all wage-earners.'[7] Its benefits, however, were put at the disposal of only one-third of the nation. The groups that needed medical care most — working-class women and children — were almost entirely excluded and it was on their behalf that a demand for a Ministry arose. The 1914 War, with its long death rolls and low birth rate, dramatized the need, for it showed the nation that it could no longer afford the high infant and maternal mortality it had experienced.

Even before the war, the infant mortality rate had caused concern; almost alone among the indices of public health, it failed to fall in the nineteenth century. In 1899, in fact, it rose to a record height of 163 deaths per 1,000. Thereafter, it started to decline but, as late as 1906, the Prime Minister (Sir Henry Campbell-Bannerman) was so alarmed that he thought the country 'could hardly look the world in the face'.[8][a] Not until 1917, however, did the public share his concern; then, the cost of infant mortality was driven home with some force. No less than 1,000 babies still died each week, a rate that exceeded even the heavy war toll: for every 9 soldiers killed in the trenches, 12 babies died at home.[10] How, the leaders of the infant mortality movement asked, could the nation afford to waste such precious lives? Like Disraeli, they coined a slogan: 'It was more dangerous to be a baby in England than a soldier in France.'[11] But, unlike him, they did manage to stir the public.

To arouse the public was one task — actually to create a Ministry was another and this proved to be far more difficult than anyone imagined. By 1914, 3 central departments and 8 local agencies had become involved in the administration of maternity and child welfare services alone (see chart on page 24). The LGB offered care through 630 boards of guardians and 1,800 sanitary authorities — while the Board of Education used as its arm 317 education authorities. Both, in addition, employed some 300 voluntary societies — the same society sometimes acting in the same capacity for both departments. The NHI Commission, on the other hand, provided its benefits by means of over 20,000 approved societies and 238 insurance committees —

a It should be noted, however, that only 4 countries in Europe at the time had a lower rate.[9]

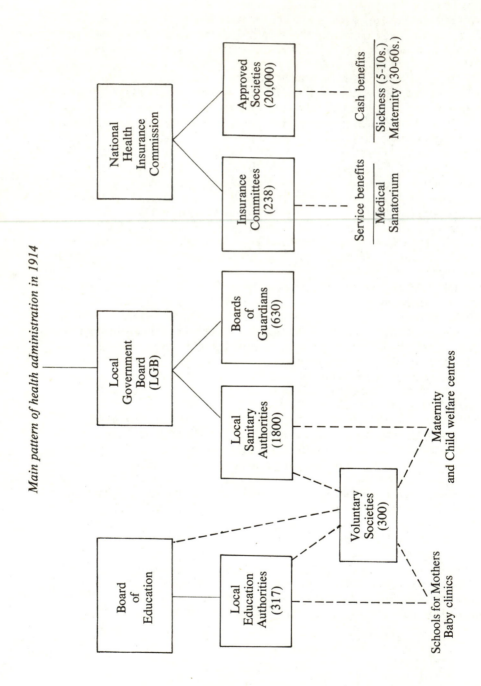

Main pattern of health administration in 1914

and to these must be added the gratuitous services of some 530 voluntary hospitals.

Nor was that all. Even more departments were involved outside the field of maternal and child welfare.[12] One working-class family might receive care from as many as 9 different doctors working under 5 different departments. Exactly how this could happen was spelled out in 1917 by the Secretary of the BMA, Dr Alfred Cox:

> 'Father, in all illnesses (except tuberculosis) attended by his insurance practitioner; mother, in all illnesses (except those connected with childbirth and tuberculosis) if an insured person, attended by her panel doctor (probably also her husband's); if not an insured person attended (when she can afford it) by private practitioner (probably her husband's panel doctor), when she cannot afford it, either by the parish doctor or by some medical charity; during pregnancy consults the maternity centre doctor; at her confinement attended by a midwife or a doctor provided by the maternity centre; if affected by tuberculosis, by a tuberculosis officer. Infants and young children up to school age attended by maternity centre doctor; after school age attended for "school diseases" by school medical officer and by private doctor (probably father's panel doctor) when too ill to go to school; after school age and up to 16 attended by private doctor; after 16, attended by panel doctor — probably the same practitioner; if affected by tuberculosis, the tuberculosis officer is introduced.'[13]

The tendency had been to form separate staffs to administer each service and this was done even within the framework of the same department. Worst of all, the oldest medical system in the country was isolated; those who headed the medical department of the LGB wanted nothing to do with the Poor Law.[14] The medical services provided by the Poor Law fell under LGB supervision and so did the 'free' municipal services (covering mainly infectious disease) that developed under the Public Health Act of 1875. But no attempt was made to co-ordinate the two systems. Boards of guardians had long employed their own corps of Poor Law doctors (some part-time, some full-time) but, instead of using them, local authorities created an entirely independent network of medical officers — and this, in turn, was further divided by disease categories (e.g. tuberculosis, measles, those associated with maternity, venereal disease) as the years passed.[15]

The nation, in 1914, thus had three distinct bodies of doctors as far as public health administration was concerned: Poor Law, municipal and panel. Theoretically, it was possible for a private practitioner to serve all three systems on a part-time basis but the tendency in the Poor Law and the municipal sectors (particularly the municipal) had been to employ doctors on salary. The private practitioner thus came to identify his interests with NHI and, from 1911 on, he often saw the extension of the panel system as a way of protecting himself against the encroachments of municipal medicine.

It was from the 'hated' municipal sector, however, that the best chance of creating an integrated service arose. At the time none of the 3 public systems offered an opportunity for GPs and consultants to work together. This applied as much to the municipal and Poor Law sectors as it did to the panel system.

Though some GPs worked in mixed workhouses, few gained entry to municipal hospitals or to the modern Poor Law infirmaries that arose. Under the Poor Law, in fact, a rigid demarcation was set between community and hospital care (called, respectively, 'outdoor' and 'indoor' medical relief) in order to lessen the chance of abuse. By 1909, LGB officials had even come to see hospital treatment as a kind of workhouse test for medical relief.[16]

But the medical officer of health (MOH) who was charged with the duty of administering municipal health services had the potential to change this. Once all health services provided by the state passed under local authority control, he would have the facilities needed to give GPs access to municipal hospitals. With the privilege, however, was likely to go some loss of clinical or vocational freedom and not many GPs were willing to sacrifice that. The hopes of creating an integrated service thus tended to conflict with the profession's desire to be master of its own fate.

From all of this, we can see that the task of those who wished to create a Ministry of Health was formidable. They did not have a clear field in which to operate but had to pick their way amidst a welter of competing interests. This chapter and the one that follows attempt to show how they did it.[a]

Strategy of reformers

I shall start by analysing the strategy of those who led the movement for a Ministry of Health. The key figures emerged from the campaign waged in the first decade of this century to humanize the administration of the Poor Law — a system that offered benefits to individuals only if they could pass harsh means tests. Why was Poor Law reform of such interest to those who wished to create a Ministry of Health? Mainly because of what had happened to the LGB. Health, it was thought, had to be separated from welfare (meaning here cash relief and related means-tested assistance) before a durable department could be established.[17] The leadership in the Ministry fight, however, was not supplied by the two eminent Fabian socialists who led the overall campaign for Poor Law reform — Sidney and Beatrice Webb. Rather, it came from one of the great civil servants of this century — Sir Robert Morant.[b] Morant, until 1911, made education his specialty, serving as Permanent Secretary of the Board of Education for 8 years. But out of his experience there, he came to see that the health of the nation demanded even more attention and, in 1904, he began to search for ways to extend public provision.

Here, he ran up against the barrier formed by the 1875 Public Health Act. That Act, except for infectious disease, permitted state aid only through the Poor Law and the department that administered it — the LGB — wanted to restrict even that provision.[c] The country, as a result, had

a   The account given here is a highly condensed version of the events leading up to the creation
     of the new department. For the full story see my study. 'The Struggle for the Ministry of
     Health', *Occasional Papers on Social Admin.* No. 37, G. Bell, 1970.

b   For a profile of Morant, see p. 335 below.

c   Section 131 of the Act did give local authorities the power to build any hospitals (not ceased to lead in the field of public health, falling far behind other European countries in the development of personal care programmes. The only way out of the impasse was to extend the service through the medium of other departments and Morant made use of the one nearest at hand, the Board of Education. In 1907, he — or, rather, his President — slipped a Bill through Parliament which, though calling only for the medical inspection of schoolchildren, soon led to treatment as well.[19] This was only a modest start but 4 years later Lloyd George followed suit with a more grandiose scheme. His NHI Act not only extended GP and drug care to one-third of the population but foreshadowed further expansion across a broad front. Even the LGB, roused by the competition the new schemes engendered, began to take an interest in public health. By 1914, health services were expanding in all directions. The barrier of the 1875 Act had been broken.

Up to this point, 'extension' had been the overriding consideration but now another subject began to receive attention, and again it was Morant who raised it. He lost his post at the Board of Education in November, 1911, but immediately afterwards Lloyd George made him Chairman of the English NHI Commission, the most important of the 4 established. Morant accepted the appointment for only one reason — he wanted to unify the public health services:

'. . . It has always seemed to be very strange that we English people are so unthinking that we should have gone ahead as far that we did in Education for so many years without giving adequate thought to Health . . . I remember saying in 1911-12 to the then Chancellor of the Exchequer that there would be a great danger, if we were not careful in developing the new health service, of increasing the difficulties of the necessary unification that must some day come if the health of the people was ever to be dealt with properly as a whole . . . There must be real unification of health services so that the day should come when Health should be recognised as one of the great public responsibilities just as Education came to be recognised as a public duty, and a Ministry was established away back in 1899, called the Board of Education, with the whole field of education as its province.'[20]

Long before he arrived at the NHI Commission, Morant had studied the subject. This was what had brought him into alliance with the Webbs. They, in contrast to Lloyd George, wanted to unify the public health service first and worry about extension later. No other policy was possible within the context of a debate centring on the reform of the Poor Law. Only by stressing the cost savings to be gained by co-ordination could the Webbs hope to convert the stern critics of outdoor relief to their point of view. So far did they go in this respect that they even excluded the friendly society class of worker from the public sector.[21] Their aim, simply, was to lift health out of

just for infectious disease) and Section 133 even permitted them to supply drugs on a temporary basis to the 'poorer' inhabitants of the neighbourhood. But little use was made of either provision and costs, in any case, were supposed to be recovered from patients outside the Poor Law if they did not have infectious disease. Only as the definition of infectious disease widened did public health services become more freely available.[18]

the Poor Law and combine it with other public health services already in existence.

At no point was the Poor Law more vulnerable. By 1909, even the Poor Law staff of the LGB had begun to wonder whether medical care should be offered more freely.[22] Once medical relief was transferred to local authorities, it was only a matter of time before cash relief went too — particularly since so much food was handed out in the form of 'medical extras'.[23] For the Webbs then, public health was the key to the break-up of the Poor Law and that was the main reason why they devoted so much time to it.

Lloyd George, on the other hand, wanted (like the doctors themselves) to break up club practice, not the Poor Law. His interest in social reform embraced the working class as a whole and could not be satisfied through a programme confined to those below the poverty line. Lloyd George wanted to reach a larger segment of the population than the Webbs and this made him concerned, above all else, with 'extension'. So when Morant arrived at the NHI Commission, he found himself torn between Lloyd George's drive for 'extension' and the Webbs' call for 'unification'.

How could the 2 aims be reconciled? The answer came from the 2 influential MOHs who had helped the Webbs prepare the public health proposals in their Poor Law reform programme — Dr (later Sir) Arthur Newsholme and Dr (later Sir) George Newman.[a] Morant was closer to Newman but Newsholme, besides being older, was the recognized leader of the public health world. From them, Morant learned that the most progressive elements in that world came from whole-time MOHs like themselves. Since they operated on the local rather than the national level, why not push ahead with local unification first?[24] The LGB might resist all reform but, through the medium of MOHs, the groundwork could be laid for reorganization at the top. Together with the Webbs, Morant and his MOH friends developed a plan of action as early as 1907: first, the school medical service and then the Poor Law medical system would be brought under MOH control; after that had been accomplished, consolidation at the centre would follow and the LGB would be transformed into a bona fide Ministry of Health.

LGB versus Board of Education

Newman went to the Board of Education in 1907 with this plan very much in mind. He was appointed Chief Medical Officer over the head of the leading contender for the job (Dr James Kerr, head of the school medical service in London) mainly to ensure MOH control. Most education authorities followed his advice but the influential London County Council (LCC) did not. It put Kerr in charge of a separately-administered school medical service and thereby threatened to upset the pattern of local unification. Not until 1911 was the issue settled as Newman desired. Then Kerr lost his post and the education committee of the LCC surrendered supervision to the public health committee.[25] Thereafter, in London as elsewhere, the school medical service was under MOH control.

a   For profiles of Newman and Newsholme, see pp. 336-7 below.

Once unification was secure, extension followed. Exchequer aid to the local authorities and voluntary societies that provided health care for children began in 1912 and the Board of Education sought to enlarge its treatment powers early in 1914 so as to cover not only schoolchildren but infants from birth, providing home visits as well. This at last aroused the LGB and it countered with an all-embracing programme, laying claim to the whole field of medical treatment for mothers and children — from the moment a woman became pregnant until the child she delivered was old enough to enter school.[26] The time for the Board of Education to abdicate the health sphere seemed near.

But then the unexpected happened: the voluntary societies which provided infant care did not want the Board of Education to let go. The societies had done yeoman work in the past, supplying health visitors as well as an array of services through the maternity centres which they themselves had opened.[27] Local authorities, furthermore, had relied greatly on their aid in order to avoid the free care restrictions contained in the 1875 Public Health Act. But since the societies operated on their own, the work they did was not easy to control and, by 1914, many MOHs as well as the LGB itself felt that they had outlived their usefulness. Newman, in accordance with his own preference for local unification, might have been expected to accept this view but he was reluctant to see the societies disappear until he was sure that something better was going to be put in their place. Under his lead, then, the Board of Education arose as the defender of the voluntary society against local authority and LGB encroachment.

The clash between the 2 boards came to a head in the spring of 1914 when Lloyd George reserved a place for maternity and child welfare in his Budget. Which department should administer the grant? For 3 years the dispute dragged on and not until February 1917 was it settled. Then the Presidents of both boards — Lord Rhondda for the LGB, Herbert Fisher for Education — agreed to turn all maternity and child welfare services over to a new Ministry of Health as soon as one could be created. This was done, however, with the understanding that the new department would be based on the LGB. Why did the Board of Education acquiesce? Partly because it was allowed to keep the school medical service, an arrangement that survived until the National Health Service itself was reorganized in 1974. But there was a more important reason: Newman wanted to push Rhondda behind the movement for a Ministry of Health. No sooner, however, did the Board of Education drop out of the struggle than a new competitor appeared — the NHI Commission. To understand how this happened, we need to go back and trace the work of that other influential MOH, Sir Arthur Newsholme.

LGB versus NHI Commission

Newsholme went to the LGB in 1908 with even higher hopes than Newman since his department was on line to become the Ministry of Health and he, as Chief Medical Officer, would be in charge of a unified service. But only 3 years after he arrived he received a shock from which he never recovered. Newsholme wanted Lloyd George to leave medical benefit out of NHI and create a comprehensive salaried state medical service that would cover dependants as well as insured persons.[28] Lloyd George, however, not only found that impossible to finance: he was forced to establish an entirely new department in order to give the various interests involved a place in administration. Hence arose the 4 NHI Commissions, one for each 'country' in the British Isles — England, Wales, Scotland and Ireland. (There was also a joint committee to lay down common policy for the U.K. as a whole but, for the purpose of this study, we need to deal only with the English Commission.)

Now the LGB also had the English Commission as a competitor and it, unlike the Board of Education, entered the health field *en masse*. Not only did it provide GP and drug care but sanatorium treatment for tuberculars. Furthermore, though its sickness and maternity benefits were paid in cash, they could be used to purchase additional health services. The total expenditure on these benefits in 1914 came to £14.4 million and, of this amount, as much as £5.6 million was due to medical care.[29]

How, once it was created, could this huge system be absorbed? Newsholme attacked the problem even before the NHI Bill passed through Parliament. He persuaded Lloyd George to insert provisions which would lead to local authority control. This was to be done in 2 stages. In the original Bill, medical benefit stayed where it had been for a century — under the control of the friendly (and other 'approved') societies.[a] The first stage called for the transfer of medical benefit to the new *ad hoc* insurance committees on which the local authorities as well as the societies were represented. Once that had been accomplished, financial pressure would be applied to ease the societies out.[30]

In practice, however, only the first stage of this process was ever completed. The second was frustrated not only by the friendly societies but by the local authorities as well: they did not want to shoulder the financial burden the move required. Newsholme's dream of local unity was thus shattered by his own constituents but there still remained the possibility of consolidation at the national level. Why not merge the 2 central departments and worry about local unity later? That, as in 1871, seemed the wiser place to start. Too many vested interests were involved at the periphery and they would be more likely to respond to a plea for national, as opposed to local, welfare.[31]

By 1914, then, the idea of securing local unity first had been dropped and this decision meant that the hopes of a unified service would have to be deferred until a Ministry of Health was created. Local authorities, insurance committees and boards of guardians were to go their separate ways, each providing the network of services that fell under their care. Such services, meanwhile, might be extended and that could arouse opposition from groups adversely affected by the move, thereby making the ultimate task of merging them more difficult. But this risk would have to be run. These who wished to unite the profession would have to wait until the question of central administration was resolved.

a   See p. 16 above.

3
Unification or Extension?

By 1914, the need for the eventual merger of the LGB and the NHI Commission was recognized but there still remained the problem of how it should be done. At that time, only one answer seemed possible: despite its disastrous history, the LGB had to predominate. Let us see why this view prevailed.

The NHI system offered certain advantages. It was not 'tainted' by the Poor Law, it gave the parties involved a place in administration (a matter of much importance to the doctors) and it provided a good deal of central control. The latter, in particular, was valued. Since they did not have rate-making power, insurance committees could not frustrate national plans the way local authorities and boards of guardians did.

But the representation of so many conflicting interests in administration did create a problem. It made the whole structure unwieldy and nullified many of the advantages of central control. Furthermore, the insurance basis of the system constituted a barrier to unification, for how could everyone be covered if they had to pass employment tests? The LGB already made provision for those below the poverty line and, through the creation of free municipal services, was beginning to reach above it. Its environmental duties, moreover, were inextricably interwoven with its medical side — then much more than now. How, for example, could the problems of tuberculosis or infant and maternal mortality be separated from that of slum housing?[1] Only later, as new drugs developed, did clinical medicine breed a life of its own.

Nevertheless, the LGB was 'tainted' by its association with the Poor Law and it was this, more than any other factor, that made people turn against it. For that, however, its defenders also had an answer. Health and welfare, they pointed out, had been administered under the Poor Law for a century and, in view of the failure of the Webb campaign, it seemed impossible to divide them. Some even thought it wrong to do so for a department devoted to one subject alone (i.e. health) 'would tend to be guided too much by expert advice, and would be apt to lose sight of a variety of extraneous considerations which statesmanship cannot overlook'.[2] All the experts agreed that it would be harder to separate 'health' from the LGB than to bring NHI within the LGB orbit.

John Burns, however, was President of the LGB and, as long as he remained in office, no merger seemed possible. He came from the ranks of the working class but few men applied the Poor Law more harshly than he.[3] Not until Burns left the LGB early in 1914 was it possible to merge the 2 departments but then prospects appeared hopeful because his successor turned out to be a humane and imaginative administrator named Herbert (later Lord) Samuel. The initiative, however, had to come from someone acceptable to the NHI world and, for this purpose, Lloyd George turned to Dr Christopher (later Lord) Addison.[a] He was a doctor and everyone thought such qualifications were needed to reform the creaky panel system. How should GPs be paid? This remains, even today, one of the unsolved problems of public health administration. Morant, in common with the Webbs and the MOH world, preferred salary but the doctors, in 1912, were reluctant to accept even capitation. The only chance of securing their assent to change was to put a medical man in charge. Therefore, early in 1914, Lloyd George decided to move the NHI Commission from the Treasury (where it had been lodged for finance purposes) to the LGB as a sub-department under Addison.[4]

No sooner, however, did the planning over the 1914 Budget begin than the approved societies made it clear that they had no intention of letting 'their' Commission be swallowed by the LGB. Now, for the first time, Lloyd George became aware of the vigour of the vested interests he had created. He therefore decided to drop unification and go ahead, as Addison advised, with the extension urgently needed in the health services: the LGB and local authorities were to be given the new maternity and lab-testing programmes while the NHI Commission and insurance committees were to receive control over the proposed nursing and specialist clinics.[5]

Lloyd George thought he had divided the schemes fairly but still the approved societies objected. However, they did not protest because they lost the lab-testing programme which was so crucial for the development of effective GP and drug care. Rather, they were in a panic over the projected maternity service. Under NHI, the approved societies had two benefits to offer: cash following sickness (or permanent disability) and maternity. The latter was not paid out per week like the former but it was larger in amount (30s. or 60s. as compared with 5s., 7s. 6d. or 10s.) and much easier to administer. Unlike sickness benefit, it did not depend on a difficult determination of incapacity but a readily ascertainable event — the birth of a child — and one associated more with health than sickness. Of all the benefits under NHI, the payment for maternity was the most popular with insured persons. Even more important, though the money was intended to meet the costs of confinement, the approved societies found it useful for other purposes. This applied particularly to the industrial insurance offices which were surprised by the way it stimulated the growth of life assurance policies. With over 50% of the women covered by the Act in their approved societies (as much as 75% of married women),[6] the agents employed by the offices were well-placed to exploit the arrangement.

The approved societies thus had a large stake in the preservation of maternity benefit. A modest extension in maternity services might not have bothered them but they were frightened by the scale of Newsholme's programme. It was to cover ante-natal as well as confinement and post-natal

a   For a profile of Addison, see p. 323 below.

care; domiciliary as well as institutional treatment; insured as well as non-insured persons; infants and children up to school age as well as mothers.[7] Nothing more comprehensive could have been imagined and the insurance offices feared that this would not only spell the end of NHI's maternity benefit but threaten the existence of the approved society system itself.

Maternity services

Underlying this dispute was a basic issue that became the focal point of the controversy that followed over the next 4 years: should provision for maternity be made by means of an insurance system or a municipal service? There was much to be said for the insurance method. It did not depend on local initiative but came into operation swiftly from one end of the country to the other. The approved societies could rightly claim that maternity benefit had helped to raise the standard of medical care, stimulate the demand for institutional confinements and provide financial aid to people who would not or could not apply for assistance under the Poor Law.[8]

But the fact that maternity benefit was provided under NHI did create problems. Only those covered by the Act received it, which meant that 1 million out of 7 million married women were excluded.[9] Medical and sickness benefits were even more restricted since they applied only to the 700,000 women who were insured in their own right. Furthermore, the range of care offered was far from complete. Not only was the confinement period (labour and 10 days after) excluded but no provision was made for children. Local authorities had begun to fill this void but their attempts to reduce mortality had been thwarted in the ante-natal field. NHI, theoretically at least, covered that period and local authorities felt free to start their work only from birth. Spurred by Newsholme, however, the LGB conquered that inhibition in 1915 and fostered the growth of ante-natal clinics housed in maternity centres offering the full range of care to all, whether insured or not.[10]

To working-class women like those represented by the Women's Co-operative Guild, there was only one answer to the question: maternity services should not be provided by the insurance method.[11] The voluntary societies involved in the campaign to reduce infant mortality agreed [12] and they were joined by the Webbs and the Fabian Society.[13] The time, in 1914, had come to lift maternity out of insurance and provide a comprehensive service through the medium of local authorities.

Whatever the insurance offices might think, then, Lloyd George was prepared to go ahead with the maternity programme. The outbreak of war only temporarily delayed the Budget grant. Within a year (July, 1915), Walter (later Lord) Long, who had succeeded Samuel at the LGB, introduced a Bill designed to stimulate the development of municipal maternity services as well as to remove any doubt about legality. The Bill passed but not before England and Wales were struck out. Only in Scotland and Ireland was it possible to go ahead because the LGB was then involved in its dispute with the Board of Education.[14]

A year and a half later, however, that dispute was settled and Rhondda (who had succeeded Long) came back with a similar Bill for England and Wales.[15] His position, in 1917, was strong. By then the public had become alarmed by the long death rolls and the failure to reduce infant mortality, and social reformers like Benjamin Broadbent (who led the campaign to reduce infant mortality) were demanding action. The approved societies were thrown sharply on the defensive. Consequently they were even ready to accept municipal management of treatment services, provided they could retain the right to pay NHI's cash benefits.[16]

LGB call for a Ministry of Health

At this point, however, Addison intervened. He and Morant now saw more clearly than before the danger involved in extending the health services before they were unified. Vested interests would multiply and it would become harder than ever to persuade them to give way. Even worse, the public might lose all interest in a Ministry of Health if its appetite for extended care were satisfied through existing channels. This applied particularly to maternal and child welfare. Broadbent and his group were the driving force behind the Ministry movement, but the steam might go out of their campaign if Rhondda's Bill passed.[17] No, Addison and Morant agreed, extension must wait; unification came first. Somehow Rhondda had to be deflected from his narrow concern for infant mortality into the larger prospect of a Ministry of Health.[18]

The doctors, almost without their realizing it, supplied the way. For months, the medical correspondent of *The Times* (Dr Robert MacNair Wilson) had tried to rouse their interest in a Ministry of Health by presenting it as a way of fighting quackery and other social evils. The 1911 Act, he argued, had only partly solved the problem; the need now was to extend the process it had started through better organization.[19] That, to his mind, meant not only a Ministry but a salaried service — and he was not alone in linking the 2 concepts. As early as 1913, the State Medical Service Association (SMSA), the forerunner of the Socialist Medical Association (SMA), had seen the setting up of a Ministry 'as an absolutely necessary preliminary to the establishment of a State Medical Service'.[20]

The leaders of the BMA, however, knew better — and that applied particularly to Cox and Dr (later Sir) Henry Brackenbury.[a] If the establishment of a Ministry meant a salaried service, then the profession would never accept it.[21] Newsholme had made the mistake of describing in public just what such a system under MOH control implied. A doctor who persistently treated tuberculosis as chronic bronchitis, he told the Royal Commission on the Poor Laws in 1908, 'would certainly get his knuckles rapped'.[22] With private practitioners, he admitted, he had to be more delicate, but that was partly why he wanted to bring them under municipal control.

BMA leaders wanted a Ministry, too, but they knew it would never come on Newsholme's terms. The way to arouse medical interest in the subject was to

---

a   For a profile of Brackenbury, see p. 325 below.

present the proposed Ministry as a way of stopping salary, not starting it [23] —
and Newsholme gave them the opportunity. He had not waited for a new
department to begin but had fostered the growth of salaried schemes in
municipal clinics falling under LGB supervision — first in those covering
tuberculosis, later in maternity and child welfare.[24] The doctors did not worry
greatly about the former since tuberculosis was covered by the panel system
(which meant that GPs were paid for much of the work whether they did it or
not).

But the maternity centres were another matter. Midwifery was then a vital
part of GP work and the confinement period had been excluded from the panel,
leaving it entirely in the area of private practice. This exposed GPs to the full
force of midwife competition and now Newsholme added a new threat. Ever
since 1915, when the LGB launched its maternity programme, Brackenbury
had urged the use of part-time practitioners in municipal clinics so that private
GPs would have the chance to participate in local authority work. But
Newsholme had not listened — he encouraged the employment of whole-time
salaried officers instead.[25] In 1916, he even managed to go further when the
new VD centres were formed: they were established entirely on a whole-time
basis. Yet, oddly enough, the BMA had agreed where VD was concerned.[26]
Several factors were involved but the main reason for the difference in the
profession's attitude was the complete protection it received against unqualified practice in the field of VD.[27]

This seems to have raised a thought in Newsholme's mind: perhaps by
offering such protection over the whole range of medicine, the profession would
agree to a salaried service. The opportunity to press such a proposal soon
arose. When Rhondda sought his advice on a maternity Bill, Newsholme
countered with a scheme that would cover the nation for everything. The time,
in his view, had come to create the state medical service which Lloyd George
had rejected in 1911.[28]

This threat at last aroused the profession and, soon after Rhondda made
public his plans for a maternity scheme, the BMA leaders objected, urging
the creation of a Ministry of Health instead.[29] Through such means, they hoped
to secure a sufficient voice in government planning to prevent the start of a
salaried service.[30] Rhondda (who was more interested in creating a Ministry of
Health than in starting a salaried service) [31] endorsed the idea and it received
wide support. But the proposal generated so much opposition from the
approved societies (which did not want the Ministry based on the LGB) that
it had to be shelved and Rhondda left the LGB to become Food Controller.[32]

Rhondda was succeeded by his Parliamentary Secretary, William Hayes
Fisher (later Lord Downham), and he decided to return to the Maternity Bill
originally considered by Rhondda. The measure he prepared, however, was
much weaker than the one Rhondda had earlier proposed. It made no provision
for domiciliary care and it did not require the local authorities to provide
anything in the way of new clinic services. All it compelled them to do was
establish maternity and child welfare committees. Otherwise, they were left on
their own to decide how much provision they wished to make and, because of
the war, little aid from the Exchequer was envisaged.[33]

NHI call for a Ministry of Health

Weak as it was, the LGB Bill posed enough of a threat to maternity benefit to
force the NHI world to act and, in the summer of 1917, the insurance offices
felt that the way to meet it was to draft a Ministry of Health scheme of their
own.[34] Their answer to the extension threat raised by Hayes Fisher, then, was
'unification' along the same lines that Rhondda had proposed but, unlike him,
they wanted the new Ministry to arise from the NHI Commission rather than
from the LGB. In order to make this clear, they had the solicitor who drafted
their scheme, Mr (later Sir) Kingsley Wood,[a] launch an attack on the point at
which the LGB was most vulnerable — its association with the Poor Law.
While Wood's plan called for the unification of public health services, it
demanded the exclusion of the Poor Law; consequently, if health could not be
separated from welfare, some unification on the health side would have to go,
too. With 70% of LGB work taken up with the Poor Law, there was clearly no
place for it in the insurance office plan.

Until then, the approved society world had not been united on the issue but
this attack on the Poor Law appealed greatly to the friendly societies as well as
to the trade unions. No one in their ranks wanted anything to do with the boards
of guardians and, since these bodies came under the LGB, it was stigmatized,
too. Indeed, due to its association with the Poor Law, the LGB had become the
most 'horridly unpopular' of all government departments.[35]

Yet, distasteful as the LGB was, one figure from the trade union world had
misgivings about forming an alliance with the insurance offices. This was Fred
(later Lord) Kershaw, an administrator for an approved society covering
women workers which had suffered greatly from the competition posed by the
offices.[b] Some in the trade union world were attracted by the office scheme, too,
but Kershaw's concern was directed mainly at his brothers in the friendly
society movement, and to them he issued a prophetic warning: '. . . A powerful
force is arising which, aghast at the unholy alliance, is determined to save the
working class organizations, and unless the present leaders of the movement
recognise that the ultimate fate of the movement depends upon action now,
they will find themselves in the unenviable position of fighting their brethren
with the Industrial Companies as their allies.'[36]

Kershaw's warning went unheeded: not only the friendly societies but even
some trade unions endorsed the insurance office plan. Nevertheless, the offices
had no more success with their call for a Ministry of Health than Rhondda had
with his. This time, opposition arose from the leader of the infant mortality
campaign (Broadbent) who denounced the office plan as an attempt to keep the
'blood money' in NHI.[37] He was incensed at the way their agents had abused
maternity benefit, using it to persuade mothers to purchase industrial
insurance policies instead of spending the money on services that might help to
reduce Britain's high infant mortality rate. Once again Lloyd George (who had
become Prime Minister in 1916) found the proposal too controversial to

a   For a profile of Wood, see p. 340 below.
b   For a profile of Kershaw, see p. 331 below.

pursue in wartime and that left Hayes Fisher with a clear field for his Maternity Bill.[38]

At this point, a dangerous breach appeared in the ranks of the Ministry movement. The Broadbent group was furious at the delay and would wait no longer. Their concern for infant mortality had always led them to consider 'extension' more important than 'unification', believing (in contrast to Addison) that more deaths were due to gaps in coverage than to lack of co-ordination.[39] They threw their weight strongly behind the Bill sponsored by Hayes Fisher, even though it was weak. What Addison so feared had happened: the steam was going out of the Ministry movement, leaving the country with nothing more than an inadequate maternity programme.

From this, and from his behaviour during the months that followed, it became clear that Hayes Fisher did not want to see a Ministry of Health created. He was closely allied with a key figure in the Conservative Party, Walter Long (under whom Hayes Fisher had first served at the LGB), and the two seem to have been intent on repairing the defeat they had suffered in 1911 when the NHI Bill passed through Parliament.[40] Eventually, it appears, they not only hoped to repeal NHI but also to revoke much of the other social legislation passed by the Liberals before the war.[a]

Morant was the first to sense the danger and, on 19 November 1917, he wrote Lloyd George an impassioned letter, begging him to kill Hayes Fisher's 'villainous maternity bill'.[41] Only three years earlier he had pursued the opposite course, defying his political chief (then Charles Masterman) in an attempt to push the LGB's maternity scheme through. Now, Morant must have wondered, was Masterman right after all? In an imperfect world one had to choose, and the insurance offices made better allies than the reactionary forces allied with Hayes Fisher. Though their commercial interests were distasteful, the offices had a vested interest in life insurance which put them on the side of longer life expectancies.

Morant now saw, as Lloyd George did in 1911, that he would need the power of the industrial insurance industry to push a health Bill through Parliament. He therefore abandoned all hope of basing the Ministry on the LGB: either a new department had to be created or none would be created at all. This decision marked the final break of the old alliance with Newsholme. Even before this, Newsholme had been drifting away but now, in an ironic reversal of roles, he showed himself ready to accept 'extension' at any price (partly because he did not understand Hayes Fisher's tactics). He was therefore guilty of pursuing the same policy for which he had condemned Lloyd George in 1911.

It was almost too late — the chance for a new department nearly died. But the doctors saved the day. Hayes Fisher had tried to pacify them by excluding domiciliary attendance but this, argued Cox, made the Maternity Bill meaningless. In a letter to the War Cabinet, he asked the Government to postpone the programme until the Ministry was established.[42] The profession, by then, seemed ready to extend the panel to dependants [43] and Cox wanted to do that before the municipal clinic pattern hardened. Like the approved

a   For more on this, see pp. 75-6 below.

societies, the doctors wanted unification first and extension later — with the Ministry to come by way of the NHI, rather than the LGB, pattern of administration.[44]

In making this choice, the doctors showed clearly that they did not wish to be absorbed into a municipal service. If private practice could not be preserved, then they wanted the extension of the public sector to come by way of the panel system in which they enjoyed much freedom. Integration with the hospital world was not a matter that concerned them at the moment. All their energy was reserved for restricting the growth of the municipal sector and establishing a national system of administration in which they would have a voice.

The race for the statute book

Such was the state of affairs when the year 1918 opened and the race for the statute book began. Which would pass first — the Maternity Bill presented by Hayes Fisher or the Ministry of Health scheme desired by the NHI world?

The doctors' intervention delayed the progress of the Maternity Bill long enough to permit Addison to develop a Ministry Bill. Between November 1917 and January 1918 he conducted furious negotiations with the approved societies in an attempt to secure agreement. The main obstacle was presented by the Poor Law: it, the approved societies insisted, must not be allowed to 'taint' the new department. A way to do so was offered in January by a report prepared by an official committee on which Morant served and which was chaired by the Liberal leader, Sir Donald Maclean. This assumed that a new department would be created and, after that was done, it called for the abolition of the boards of guardians and the creation of a comprehensive medical service under the control of local authorities.[45] This promised to produce the eventual break-up of the Poor Law and, as soon as the Government accepted the report in February, Addison was able to work out a Ministry Bill along the lines of the scheme which the insurance offices had drafted. By March, the Bill was ready for presentation to Parliament.[46]

This attack on the Poor Law was aided by the reform fever generated by the war as well as by the provision of free VD treatment in 1916. If, key members of the Maclean Committee asked, a person could not be blamed for contracting VD, should he be punished for incurring any other disease?[47] The time had come, in the Committee's view, to make health care free and open to all. Nevertheless, despite the appeal of this argument, it did not move those forces anxious to preserve the Poor Law, and they still had considerable strength.[48] Drawing on their support, Hayes Fisher managed to delay the Ministry Bill and, thereafter, nothing could stop him from putting his Maternity Bill on the statute book. What made it easy for him to do so was the failure of Addison (and others) to understand the implications of the maternity programme when it was first presented in the summer of 1917. At that time, Addison even supported the measure because he had hopes of creating a Ministry of Health before any maternity programme passed. Only later did he realize his mistake but this led him into a mass of contradictions which made it impossible to stop Fisher.[49] The Maternity and Child Welfare Act became law in August 1918.

Once that was accomplished, Hayes Fisher revealed his true aim for he now did all he could to stop the Ministry Bill. The main tactic he employed was to persuade the Cabinet to revoke the pledge it had given on the Maclean Report. In place of a definite timetable for the removal of Poor Law duties from the new department, the Government inserted only a vague promise in the Ministry Bill.[50]

This alteration aroused the fury of the friendly societies and they refused to have anything more to do with the measure. But the insurance offices understood political realities enough to see the need for compromise. By then, the momentum generated by the infant mortality campaign had gone too far to stop. The Government was ready to remove maternity benefit from NHI and pay a bonus to every mother through the LGB. Once that happened, who knew where the process would end? Hayes Fisher, it seemed, was waiting for the chance to dismantle NHI benefit by benefit and it was only within the framework of a new department that he could be contained. This was why the *National Insurance Gazette* (an approved society journal which reflected the viewpoint mainly of the insurance offices) said: '. . . we want a Ministry of Health more than we fear the Poor Law "taint".'[51]

Soon not only the doctors but most of the trade unions had come to the same conclusion and that, combined with an influenza epidemic that frightened the nation, enabled Addison to push a Ministry of Health Bill through Parliament after the Armistice and the General Election that followed.[52] It became law in June 1919. From this, it was clear that Hayes Fisher had miscalculated. He had counted on the extension contained in the maternity programme to be sufficient to forestall unification, but the measures were not ample enough. Therefore, the nation — aroused by the millions of women who voted for the first time in the 1918 General Election — demanded the creation of a Ministry of Health to pave the way for further action.

The Bill passed through Parliament just in time. Had it come later, it might have been defeated by a host of forces led by the anti-vivisectionists. The latter were the strongest anti-science group in the country and they opposed any development in the field of public health which might encourage medical research since that entailed experiments on animals. This put them on the side of those who favoured preventive medicine or environmental reform, but any innovation in the field of health tended to make them nervous because they could never be sure where it would lead. NHI, in particular, had aroused their anger because it increased the amount the nation spent on research from £2,000 to £60,000 a year.[53] What worried them most was the fear that under the new Ministry it would rise still further.

As far back as 1876, the anti-vivisectionists had managed to place restrictions on the way animal experiments were conducted in Britain, but they had not been able to stop them completely. After the 1911 Act increased the amount spent on research, they made an attempt to have dogs removed from medical laboratories and, in 1914, they almost succeeded. Through their spokesman in Parliament, Sir Frederick (later Lord) Banbury, they nearly won approval of a Bill that would have ended all experiments on dogs.[54]

Addison, therefore, took no chances with the Ministry Bill: to the surprise of

Parliament, he left medical research out of the new department, arranging for the function to pass to the control of an autonomous Medical Research Council that would be responsible only to the Privy Council.[55]Nor was that the only precaution he took: he let another Bill banning vivisection on dogs go through its second reading in March 1919 without one word of protest.[56] Only after the Ministry Act was safely on the statute book did Addison feel it safe to kill the measure.[57] The anti-vivisectionists howled in anger but it was too late to stop the new department.

A Ministry of Health is created

The Ministry of Health was thus formed in the summer of 1919. All the functions of the LGB and the NHI Commission passed to it, as well as most of the health duties formerly exercised by the Board of Education. Only the school medical service remained with the Board under an arrangement provided in the Act which allowed the duty to stay there if the Minister of Health saw fit. Some other health duties also fell outside the Act — those associated with medical research, and the factory medical service (which then came under the Home Office) — but by and large, unification had been achieved at the centre. The 3 main sectors of state medicine — Poor Law, municipal, panel — had at last been put under one department. Only the local bodies that administered them — boards of guardians, local authorities, insurance committees — remained separate. The next task was to achieve unity on that level, too.

Within the new Ministry, some familiar faces appeared but they were not those associated with the LGB. All the key posts went to NHI figures: Addison became Minister; Waldorf Astor (Addison's chief Conservative ally during the Ministry struggle), Parliamentary Secretary; Kingsley Wood, Private Parliamentary Secretary; Morant, Permanent Secretary. Not only the LGB's Permanent Secretary (Sir Horace Monro) but even its Chief Medical Officer was forced to retire. Newsholme, in addition to his other mistakes, had shown himself to be impervious to the realities of medical politics. His incessant promotion of salaried schemes made him unacceptable to the profession. He also was unpopular with other medical officers at the Ministry because he had been too much under lay control at the LGB.[58] Though he had spent 10 years in office, he had not been able to bring the Poor Law medical service under his supervision — which makes one wonder how far he would have progressed with any form of unification.[59]

Newman, as a result, was appointed Chief Medical Officer while continuing to hold the same office at the Board of Education. This eased the tension caused by the separation of the school medical service, and it also enabled Newman to elevate the status of the Ministry post far above the level which Newsholme and his predecessors had enjoyed.[60]

The status of the Chief Medical Officer, however, was not the only issue with which NHI forces were concerned. More important was the question of central control, and here they managed to influence policy through the consultative councils that were created. One each was set up for the local authorities, the public, the doctors and the approved societies, but it was with the latter 2 that the NHI world was mainly concerned. The councils, in Morant's own words, were intended to be 'the 1920 counterpart of the special elements which Lloyd George had in mind in 1912 in forming the NHI Commission'.[61] Now, however, the 'special elements' were not mixed together as on the commissions but segregated within their own councils. This was done mainly to please the doctors who did not want the approved societies to interfere in medical affairs.[62] Once the Ministry was established, therefore, a Medical Consultative Council was formed and it was this body which produced a report in which the doctors had the chance to make known their views about medical organization.

Throughout the struggle for the new department, the doctors had said little about the kind of service they wanted, preferring to wait until the administrative issue was settled before the question of practice organization was discussed. No group involved in the struggle, however, showed a greater awareness of political realities than the leaders of the profession. Though they wanted nothing to do with the LGB, they posed no objection to the incorporation of the Poor Law within the new department. In fact, as far as its medical side was concerned, they positively desired its inclusion. Unification at the centre, medical leaders recognized, would have to come first; only after it had been secured would it be possible to achieve reform at the local level. Through the medium of the Medical Consultative Council, they turned their attention to what should come next.

Part 2
The Fight Against Salary
1919-1921

Women and Labour led the movement for a salaried service that emerged during the First World War. It was linked in the public mind with the extension of public provision. The doctors responded by calling only for the development of institutional facilities and they firmly rejected any thought of salary. The Minister of Health, nevertheless, had hopes of unifying local health administration and of extending free care to the dependants of insured persons. All he managed to do was secure minor changes in the panel system. The economy campaign (led by defenders of the Poor Law), together with the depression that began in 1921, destroyed all chance of significant reform during this period. In the process, however, an accommodation occurred which set the stage for the creation of the National Health Service 25 years later. Labour came to see that the doctors might accept extended coverage if the Party would drop its demand for a salaried service.

4
Movement for a Salaried Service

The movement for a salaried service loomed large during the struggle for a Ministry of Health and it did not die with the creation of the new department. It remained in the clause of the Ministry of Health Act which gave the Minister power to start a service of whatever form he desired. In contrast to the 2 Acts passed in 1918, which banned domiciliary care for mothers and children, the 1919 Act left (or seemed to leave) the Minister free to introduce a salaried service by regulation — and that power remained on the statute book until 1949 when the BMA forced the Government to amend it.

To understand the effect of the different provisions here, we need to take a closer look at the statutes involved. The 2 Acts passed in 1918 were the Education Act and the Maternity and Child Welfare Act. Before 1918, local authorities were merely empowered (not required) to provide treatment for schoolchildren; no obligation was imposed until the Education Act passed in 1918 (and that did not take effect until 1 April 1920). The BMA opposed the change *in toto,* seeking to leave treatment in the hands of private practitioners. The Act, however, merely banned domiciliary care and restricted the kind of ailments that could be treated at the clinics which local authorities established.[1] A similar ban was inserted in the Maternity and Child Welfare Act which Hayes Fisher pushed through in the same year.[a]

It is important to recognize, however, that both bans applied only to a *general* domiciliary service.[2] Local authorities were free to provide treatment at the clinics and even on occasion, it seems, in the homes of the patients attending them. Many clinics no doubt did provide such treatment between the wars. Furthermore, the 2 Acts taken together covered only children up to school-leaving age; otherwise, they left local authorities (and the Ministry) free to do whatever they liked. The rest of the population could have been covered by a free domiliary service at any time before 1948.

This is where the Ministry of Health Act comes in. Clause 2 of that Act read as follows:

'It shall be the duty of the Minister . . . to take all steps as may be desirable to secure the preparation, effective carrying out and coordination of measures conducive to the health of the people, including measures for the prevention and cure of disease . . .'[3]

a   See pp. 35 and 37 above.

This innocent-sounding clause, in the opinion of one medical leader, seemed to give the Minister power to start a salaried service[4] and he also derived such authority from the NHI Act itself.[5] The latter, however, was in a more restricted form: it gave the department power to start a salaried service only in selected areas — wherever a sufficient number of doctors failed to join the panel — and was designed to cope with a medical strike. It was exercised only once during the NHI period (1911-48)[6] and was not intended to be a general enabling power. On the contrary, the right of free choice (and its associated grant of free entry to the panel) had been written into the 1911 Act itself, thereby presenting a bar to the creation of a salaried service throughout the country as a whole.[7] Though that right continued after 1919, the wide enabling power in clause 2 of the Ministry of Health Act seemed to supercede it. Since the authority was never exercised, it is hard to determine the exact position.

Questions of legality, in any case, did not deter those who wished to start a salaried service; they knew that Parliament could grant the necessary power whenever it deemed appropriate. Even before the Ministry of Health Act passed, they began to agitate for salary, and their influence was reflected in the spread of municipal clinics, particularly those catering for women and children. From 650 in 1915, the number of maternity and child welfare centres had risen to 1,278 in 1918[8] and, though weak in conception, the Maternity and Child Welfare Act which passed in that year seemed to foreshadow further expansion.[a]

Union support for a salaried service

The movement for a salaried service was thus linked with the demand for wider public coverage and it received support from trade unions who desired a national service in order to bring the voluntary hospitals under state control. This, the unions believed, was needed both to extend the range of care provided by the panel and to offset the influence of the accident insurance companies on workmen's compensation claims.[b] Too many hospitals were dependent on employers for charity — and too many doctors were receiving payments from the insurance industry — for reports favourable to the employee to be returned by the inquiries. Only by removing medical care from outside influence, the unions believed, could the injured worker hope to receive just compensation.

The trade unions and the Labour Party had shown interest in this subject even before the war. Resolutions calling for the nationalization of the hospitals were passed at Labour Party conferences in 1909 and 1910, — while the demand for a comprehensive state medical service was

a   As a matter of fact, the number rose to over 3,000 by 1937, and to these we must add, 1,592 ante-natal clinics, 560 post-natal clinics, over 2,000 clinics for schoolchildren, 482 TB dispensaries and 186 VD centres.[9]

b   The Workmen's Compensation Acts (first passed in 1897) were administered by employers and insurance companies. Not until 1946 did the state assume control under the Industrial Injuries Act.

approved in 1911 and 1913.[10] Not until later, however, did it develop into a strong movement, led by unions like the National Union of Railwaymen whose members had suffered greatly from a compensation system run by private insurance companies and employers.[11]

This was revealed most clearly at the annual conference of the TUC in 1912. Then, a delegate from the railroad industry accused the honorary medical staff in the voluntary hospitals of being 'themselves in the pay of these great insurance concerns'. As a result, he claimed, workmen's compensation cases are 'adjudicated beforehand in the hospital, when possibly the injured worker is unconscious.'[12] Since the compensation system was administered by private enterprise, the remedy, as he saw it, was not only to turn control over to the state, but to create a national medical service under which the Government, rather than private firms, would pay hospital doctors.[a]

The unions demanded such a service despite the fact that it might force them from the health field. In their case, the sacrifice would not be great since they had managed to enrol only a small proportion (11.4% in 1912)[13] of the NHI world.[b] Their main function was still to represent the worker as a producer rather than a consumer.

But the friendly societies were in a different position. No other type of approved society had a larger stake in NHI. They not only had the largest proportion of members (46.5% in 1912 compared to 41.6% for the insurance offices)[13] but they had few other benefits to offer the public. Health insurance had long been their main attraction and NHI, since 1911, had become the most important part of their work.

It was, therefore, surprising to find the friendly societies leaning in the direction of a state-run service. What tempted them in 1918 was the need to secure protection for the families of their members. Dependants were not covered by NHI — nor were they, for that matter, protected by private insurance to any significant extent — so the creation of a state medical service seemed to offer the surest way of rescuing them from the incessant rise in medical fees. At a thinly attended meeting of the National Conference of Friendly Societies in 1918, the vote in favour of either a state medical service or the extension of NHI to the dependants of insured persons was 29 to 5.[14]

Women and a salaried service

Nevertheless, as the slight vote suggests, friendly society support for such a service was hesitant, and the unions were too preoccupied with other matters to push it strongly. The driving force behind the campaign for extended coverage came, rather, from those who were most likely to benefit — women. By 1918 they had developed an array of organizations

---

a   For the way this demand later shaped union interest in the Health Service, see p. 227 ff. below.

b   Later, the insurance offices not only reduced still further the small proportion held by the unions but they even overtook and passed the larger percentage enrolled by the friendly societies. See p. 221 below.

to promote their interests in every field of endeavour, but the strongest of these had concentrated on the fight for female suffrage. In that year, however, women finally won the right to vote (at least at the age of 30) and this turned the thoughts of some suffrage leaders to other problems. They made the promotion of public health one of their chief concerns.[15] This applied particularly to the Women's Freedom League and the National Union of Women's Suffrage Societies. In March 1919 the latter changed its name to indicate its new orientation: henceforth, it was known as the National Union of Societies for Equal Citizenship.

Why did women show such interest in health problems? It was not simply because women (along with children) had largely been excluded from NHI. More important was the concern that stemmed from their key role in society. As Sir Donald Maclean put it to Parliament in 1919:

> '... women are the public health officers of the home. The questions of
> health or sickness in the home affects them more directly than it affects men.
> They are the special guardians of the physical as well as the moral well-
> being of the future citizens of the country.'[16]

Those who had been involved in the administration of the Poor Law did not need to be told of the special concern women felt for health. Ever since 1894, when married women first became eligible to serve on boards of guardians, the quality of care given in the infirmaries had improved markedly and, along with the medical department of the LGB, the female contingent of members deserved credit for this. Yet many of them came from a higher social class than the men with whom they sat,[17] so it seems strongly arguable that the sex of the member involved had a greater influence on softening the Poor Law than the social class to which he or she belonged.

Nowhere was the concern women felt for health more evident than in the campaign to reduce infant mortality. Women were far more aroused by the problem than men and, here again, feeling was not confined to a few militants but pervaded all social classes and political groups. The most intense statement on the subject, in fact, came from a leading member of the Conservative and Unionist Women's Franchise Association and she made it long before the First World War alerted men to the same danger. This is what she had to say in July 1914:

> '... The subject of infant mortality bears very strongly on the question of
> votes for women, for women are more intimately and personally affected by
> these things than men. The tables of birth and death statistics — those
> bewildering columns of small print — are to many men just so many rows of
> figures like any others, signifying no doubt great national loss and waste; but
> to women they mean not so much the useless sacrifice of many lives and
> much economic loss, as the most pitiful of human tragedies involved in the
> individual suffering of each one of the hundreds of thousands of women
> concerned. Never let it be said that women are indifferent to these things.
> They are the things that lie at the root of the demand of women for a voice in
> the ordering of the world they have to live in.'[18]

The writer was Lady Julia Chance, wife of the man who fought hardest to preserve the Poor Law, Sir William Chance. He was virtually the only prominent person during the war to call for the preservation of the boards of guardians. On that subject even the hard-hearted group that dominated the Charity Organisation Society (COS) had begun to weaken but, when it actually entertained a motion to abolish the guardians, Chance rose to the board's defence: 'To his mind the greatest compliment that could be paid to a Public Assistance authority was to say . . . that it was unpopular. He would certainly leave the C.O.S. if it became popular'[19]. Nor was that the only issue on which Chance's reactionary stance appeared: he was also among those who strongly opposed the creation of the Ministry of Health.[20] Yet his wife did much to bring the new department into being by the concern which she and hundreds of others from her social class displayed for infant mortality.

The influence of women on the Ministry of Health

In the face of such feeling, the Government found it hard to resist the demands of women once they secured the vote. This was evident in the closing phase of the struggle for the Ministry of Health. The pressure applied by women on the eve of the 1918 election did much to blunt opposition in the Cabinet so that the Bill finally went through. Some sense of this can be obtained from a statement issued by the Women's Freedom League, one of the more militant women's organizations in the health field:

'. . . Women are angry because of the perpetual dilly-dallying of the authorities in regard to the establishment of a Ministry of Health. They have no kind of patience with the petty jealousies of the heads of Government Departments who have delayed it; they openly demand that there shall be a woman Minister of Health, appointed from women members elected to the House of Commons.'[21] [a]

Women did not secure their female Minister in 1919 but they did see one of their own sex appointed to the head of the maternity and child welfare section of the new Ministry. She was Dr (later Dame) Janet Campbell who contributed so much between the wars to the fight to reduce maternal mortality.[23]

Even more important, pressure from women led Addison to add a fourth consultative council to the 3 he had included in the Bill. These were designed to carry out the important function of advising the Minister on major points of policy and none had been created for patients as such — only for doctors, approved societies and local authorities. This infuriated the leaders of the women's health movement and, under the guidance of Lady Rhondda (daughter of Lord Rhondda), they formed a Ministry of Health Watching Council in January 1919, just before the Bill was presented to Parliament. Lady Rhondda, who was herself an efficient business administrator, told Addison[b] to add two consultative councils for patients: one

a   Another indication came from a pamphlet written by Dr Robert MacNair Wilson, medical correspondent of *The Times*. In it the claimed: 'The underlying idea of a Ministry of Health is to cement the alliance between the mother and the doctor.'[22]

b   Addison was always anxious to accommodate women. Not only did he address the first consisting of experts, the other of 'ordinary wives and mothers'.[25]

Labour women, however, objected to the proposal. They wanted only working-class wives to represent patients, not middle-class experts, and they demanded the right to make their own appointments rather than leave the selection to the Minister as was the case with the other consultative councils.[a] Labour women also wanted females appointed to every council, not segregated on one for 'ordinary wives and mothers' alone. On the patients' council however, they did want women to have the majority.[26]

Addison was able to meet these demands only in part. Parliament authorized only one council for patients — called the Consultative Council on General Health Questions — and Addison could not grant the right of direct representation without undermining his control over the other councils. But he did give women the majority (12 out of 19) and he made Lady Rhondda the Chairman. Assisting her as Vice-chairman was Arthur Greenwood, Addison's Assistant Secretary at the Ministry of Reconstruction and a long-standing Fabian. His appointment was designed to give Labour status on the council.[27]

Women and Labour — in the main, the council represented a coalition of these two interests. But it was more than that: it became the instrument through which everyone who wanted a state medical service hoped to realize his dream. As Greenwood so eloquently put it:

'. . . We hold strongly that the nation cannot afford to be without an effective public health service, that the preservation of human life and the conservation of human powers and energy, and the abolition of preventable disease and unnecessary suffering are essential to the well-being of the community. What the nation cannot with impunity allow are the far-reaching effects of physical inefficiency and incapacity which reach upon every side of its social and economic life. The exercise of the responsibility of citizenship, motherhood, and employment are bound up with the health and vigour of the people. Our educational system can yield its full fruits only when the school population is healthy. The ends of economy will be served, not by crippling the public health service, but by a wise and generous expenditure devoted to the provision of adequate health services which will conserve and develop the physical powers and energy of the people. To withhold financial resources from the public health service is a short-sighted policy striking at the foundation of the national welfare. The adoption of a comprehensive public health programme, on the other hand, will be abundantly justified by the immeasurable gains which would accrue in the social efficiency of the whole population.'[28]

public demonstration organized by Lady Rhondda on behalf of a patient's council but one of his civil servants (Michael Heseltine, who later married Janet Campbell) worked closely with women in order to overcome the opposition of the House of Lords. Opposition to the patient's council was strong — so strong, in fact, that one was created only in England, not in Scotland, Ireland or Wales.[24]

a   Here, they cited the precedent established by the Ministry of Food when it created its own consumer's council. The Food Ministry did grant the right of direct representation (to various labour organizations) but, as a result, the consumer's council could not be given statutory status.[26]

5
Doctors Attempt to Influence Ministry Policy

How were the doctors in 1919 to offset the pressure of those who wished to create a salaried service? The question demanded immediate attention because, with the creation of the Ministry of Health, power had been concentrated in the hands of one man (the Minister) and no one could be sure which way Addison or his successors would turn.[1] No fewer than 8 people, by contrast, had been responsible for NHI in England (as members of the NHI Commission) before the Ministry was created.

The idea of a central medical board

To meet this challenge, a new figure arose in the medical world — the physician, Sir Bertrand (later Lord) Dawson.[a] Though he tended to reflect consultant opinion, he had strong views of his own and, during this period, he shared with BMA leaders the task of moulding medical policy. Even before the new department was formed, the BMA had tried to forestall the threat of ministerial control by suggesting that clinical services be placed under the control of a central medical board, composed entirely of medical administrators.[2] Dawson was at first sympathetic to the idea; like the BMA, he objected strongly to the degree of lay control under NHI. Not only did the approved societies have a 60% majority on insurance committees[b] but they also seemed to possess more influence than the doctors at the centre (on the NHI Commission) where policy was decided. The uninformed nature of their demands had become all too evident where sanatorium benefit was concerned. Contrary to the best medical opinion, the approved societies thought *all* tubercular cases should be sent to sanatoria for treatment.[3]

This situation made Dawson furious and he gave vent to his feelings in a Cavendish Lecture which he delivered in the summer of 1918. 'The practice of putting the skilled under the control of the unskilled', he angrily declared, 'must cease'.[4] All the places where doctors worked, he maintained, should be under the direction of doctors, and appeals from their decisions should be allowed

---

a   For a profile of Dawson, see p. 326 below.

b   The local authority and NHI Commission appointees (some 20% of the total) were also composed largely of laymen but, throughout the entire NHI period, they were considered 'neutral' in the struggle for control of medical benefit, and the doctors did not worry unduly about their presence.

'only to people who know, not to amateurs':

> '. . . There should be a system of administration and appeal right up to the
> Central Medical Board, which will advise and have direct access to the
> Minister. Either the permanent under secretary should be a medical man or
> the professional Chairman of the Central Medical Board should have
> executive powers. On the administrative side there should be a mixture of
> doctors and trained laymen, but on strictly health matters the men who know
> must be in control throughout . . .'[4]

According to one report, the idea of having a purely medical Ministry
controlled by doctors was actually considered by the Government and was
rejected only because (apart from the costs involved) it might establish
another form of *ad hoc* administration.[5] But there was a more important
reason why all such proposals were bound to be dismissed: neither the
approved societies nor the local authorities would have allowed the health
services to pass under medical control, no matter how the doctors in
charge were appointed. The profession itself soon recognized that, for as early
as January 1918 the Council of the BMA dropped its demand for an administrative board and called only for the creation of a medical body with advisory
powers.[6]

Dawson, however, was new to medical politics and he resurrected the
administrative board idea when he delivered his Cavendish Lecture in
July. Not until later did he change his mind and then he did so, it seems,
as the result of a warning from a most unlikely quarter — Sidney Webb,
then actively engaged in the reconstruction of the Labour Party. As early
as September, 1917, Webb had warned the profession against the creation
of a salaried board, even one composed entirely of doctors. Speaking through
the *New Statesman* he (or some writer who reflected his views) told the
profession that its representatives must remain

> '. . . 'outsiders' so far as the Ministry is concerned, and not be transformed
> into salaried bureaucrats themselves. As had been abundantly demonstrated
> by the Insurance Commissioners, the whole-time salaried representatives of
> outside interests inevitably become worse than useless for the legitimate
> functions of a public Advisory Council. A whole-time, salaried medical
> bureaucrat on a Board no more serves as a representative of the medical
> profession than does the medical officer of the department.'[7]

This advice must have appeared odd, coming as it did from a leading
Fabian socialist. Before the war, he and his wife, Beatrice, had shown
little concern for medical interests during the course of their campaign to
reform the Poor Law. At one point, they did consult BMA leaders and
were surprised to find them receptive to their programme.[8] Sir Victor
Horsley, the radical surgeon active in BMA politics, even helped them to
prepare the Minority Report.[9] But the only place in that Report where the
Webbs actually showed concern for medical interests was in the provisions

they suggested should be made for the protection of private practice.[a] Otherwise, following Newsholme's lead, they put the profession under the direct control of that medical bureaucrat *par excellence,* the MOH. Only the Majority Report had the discretion to give the doctors a place in administration: it offered the BMA a seat on the medical assistance committees to be set up under the wing of the new public assistance committees.[12] The Webb-dominated Minority Report, on the other hand, left administration solely in the hands of local authorities — and there the doctors were not even offered an advisory committee of their own.[13]

Why, then, did the Webbs change their views during the war? The initial cause stemmed from a radical change in public opinion. Before the war, everything had to be done with an eye toward efficiency and cost control — which was the main reason why the Webbs had confined their Poor Law programme to a small segment of the population. But the sacrifices demanded by the war effort forced the Government to hold out hope of a better world to come and, in the debate on the health services, this produced a change in emphasis from cost control to extension of coverage. The Webbs then saw the chance of securing medical support for a wider public health service if they dropped their demand for salaried employment under MOH control. This was ironic because, had their Poor Law programme been implemented before the war, the principle of universality might never have evolved: Britain, today, would not have a National Health Service.[14]

There was, however, an even more important factor behind the Webb conversion which stemmed from Sidney's involvement in the reconstruction of the Labour Party. Until the war, Labour had been dominated by the unions and working-class attitudes. This had prompted *The Times,* as a result of the growing power of the Labour Party in 1917, to produce a series of scare-mongering articles called 'A Ferment of Revolution'.[15] In them, organized labour was described as a separate class intent on overthrowing the existing order. Against it were pitted the propertied classes, the professions and everybody else. These, the articles claimed, were the 'two nations' into which Britain had been divided in the twentieth century.

If Labour was ever to gain power, Webb recognized, it would have to destroy this image and enlarge its vision so that it represented the nation as a whole. To do that, it would not only have to attract middle-class support but provide a home within its ranks for 'workers by brain as well as by hand'. 'Nothing is more marked', declared the *New Statesman* in its appeal to the professions in 1918, 'than the growing tendency of the

---

a   Thus, the Minority Report set the income limit for free treatment so low that only the very poor could qualify — and it denied to all who used the public health service the right to choose their own doctor.[10] This was obviously designed to win medical support for their programme, but it also reflected the strong streak of paternalism underlying the Webbs' thought. The Webbs really did believe the poor should be denied free choice in order to give the profession power to wean them from unhealthy ways of living. Newsholme argued this strongly too,[11] and here again the Webbs slavishly followed his lead.

"black-coated" workers toward more or less avowed forms of trade union organisation and action':

> 'The professional classes have need of the Labour Party; and the Labour Party has need of the professional classes. Only by their closer co-operation and interaction can a really national party of social emancipation and construction be constituted.'[16]

What Webb had in mind, as far as the doctors were concerned, was best expressed by Dr Peter Macdonald, himself a Labour candidate for Parliament and destined to become one of the BMA's main policy-makers between the wars.[a] At the time, however, Macdonald was active in a rival medical organization which eventually came to be known as the Medical Practitioners' Union (MPU), and we need to take a closer look at the nature of that body if we are to understand the attempt made by Webb and Macdonald to establish a rapport between Labour and the profession.

Formation of the MPU

The MPU was established in July 1914, but the movement which gave rise to its birth went back earlier to 1908 when a Socialist Medical League was formed in conjunction with the Fabian Society. It was created by Dr M.D. Eder and attracted among its tiny corps of 70 members the doctor, who, 4 years later, became Medical Secretary of the BMA, Dr Alfred Cox.[17] (Cox, then a committed socialist, had been a member of the Independent Labour Party for years and was active in Fabian as well as BMA circles.)[18] The main purpose of the League was to rally medical support behind the Webbs' programme for the reform of the Poor Law, but the organization collapsed when differences arose over the policies in the Minority Report dealing with diet and unemployment.[19]

The impulse that gave rise to the League — the desire to extend public provision for medical care, no matter how it was done — did not die. This feeling embraced people of all political persuasions and not just those who belonged to the Fabian Society. In the wake of NHI, therefore, another attempt was made to enlist medical support through an organization we have already encountered, the SMSA.[20] It, too, was formed largely by Fabians (Sidney Webb was one of the vice-presidents)[21] and, as its name implied, it leaned in the direction of the Webb-Newsholme formula of a salaried service under municipal control. But, in contrast to the Socialist Medical League, the SMSA did not confine itself to socialists: Liberals as well as radicals joined it, and an attempt was made to enrol Conservatives. (Thus Balfour and Neville Chamberlain were both asked to serve as vice-presidents but they declined.)[22]

This flexibility, however, failed to attract many more doctors than the League had done (145 as opposed to 70)[23] and the Liberals in the ranks of the SMSA did not stay long. In January, 1913, they managed to defeat a motion for a salaried service by a thin vote of 13 to 9[24] but, thereafter, the policy of the organization turned increasingly in the opposing direction,

---

a   For a profile of Macdonald, see p. 333 below.

and many Liberals resigned.[25] By 1914, the socialists in the SMSA — led by Professor Benjamin Moore, its President, and Dr Charles Parker, its Secretary — were in full control and, taking care not to violate the SMSA's nominal non-party status, they (together with the leaders of the National Association of Trade Union Approved Societies) formed a War Welfare Group to work with the Labour Party.[26] That Group, in turn, persuaded the Party to establish a Public Health Advisory Committee and it was through this medium that the SMSA tried to push Labour towards a salaried service.

Meanwhile, the Liberals who left the SMSA were not inactive. They were led by Dr H. H. Mills and he, together with a prominent Liberal member of the BMA's Council, Dr Lauriston Shaw, formed a National Insurance Practitioners' Association in December 1912, when the BMA made its decision to boycott the Act.[27] (Shaw resigned from the Council at that time, along with several other members who were sympathetic to NHI.)[28] The new Association, however, did not last long: it could not because its leaders were branded as 'traitors' and 'blacklegs' by those in the profession who tried to resist the introduction of the panel system.[29] When, therefore, in the summer of 1914 NHI was threatened with an attempt to end its compulsory status,[30] a new 'progressive' medical organization was needed to resist it.

This was to be the MPU. It was started by the same doctors who established the National Insurance Practitioners' Association[31] but they had to put new faces in front to avoid the stigma that attached to the earlier organization. They intended, furthermore, to make the MPU into a political rather than an economic instrument; that, indeed, was why they originally called it the Panel Medico-Political Union. Their main object was to use the organization to promote legislation that would extend the medical care offered by the state beyond the narrow limits set by NHI. On this, they agreed with their more extreme colleagues in the SMSA. But where they differed was on the method by which extension was to take place: on no account did Shaw and his colleagues want the new system to evolve in a salaried direction, at least as far as GPs were concerned. In order to promote that view, as well as to increase medical influence on legislation, they decided to sponsor candidates for Parliament.[32]

Dr Peter Macdonald was among the first to try and he did his best in 1918 to steer the MPU in the direction of the Labour Party:

'... Now, whatever our various political prejudices and sympathies may be, it would be wise for the medical profession to remember that the Labour party will have a great influence in shaping schemes which have a relation to the social welfare, whatever party is in power; and in the near future it is not unlikely that the influence of the Labour party may become dominant. The signs of the times almost point to this as a probable eventuality. This being so, it is policy for the medical profession to endeavour to shape Labour medical politics from within. The views of the Labour party on medical politics are not yet determined. This condition, however, will not long continue, and a time will shortly come when a crystallization of its views will render its receptivity of the views of the profession less likely. The time to guide the Labour party is now. There is a distinct danger that this crystallization of its views may set in the direction of a crude "State medical service". There are influences at work tending in this direction.'[33]

To make its influence felt, Macdonald and Major John Kynaston (another politically-minded doctor active in MPU circles) urged the MPU to affiliate with the Labour Party[34] but, though that move failed, they and two other MPU leaders (Drs Alfred Salter and E.H.M. Stancomb) did stand as Labour candidates in the 1918 election. None, however, succeeded and this prompted Macdonald to draw the following moral for the profession as a whole: 'Medical practitioners have not yet progressed far enough to vote for a Labour candidate. They do not yet recognise that their interests coincide, not with Capital and the propertied classes, but with Labour and the class to which the vast bulk of their patients belong, and that a satisfactory reconstruction of medicine can come only from the Labour party.'[35]

Why did the doctors fail to agree? Class differences lay at the root of their attitude. Most doctors came from the middle class and they had no reason to believe that Macdonald was right. Club practice, in fact, had taught them to lean in the opposite direction. As one doctor put it in July, 1918:

'... Unfortunately, Labour has never shown itself sympathetic to claims of doctors for reasonable payment, and the moment questions of remuneration crop up the medical labourer is deemed anything but worthy of his hire. Indeed, the ferocious hostility displayed by the Socialist wing towards the professional classes is enough to show that we shall do well to expect little justice and less generosity from that quarter.'[36]

Where South Wales was concerned, there was some justice to these remarks: the medical clubs run by coal miners were undoubtedly harsh on the doctors.[37] But throughout the rest of the country, the unions could not be blamed since club practice was dominated by the friendly societies, and they were not affiliated to the Labour Party. The societies were supposed to steer clear of politics and they did, in the main, manage to avoid involvement. As for the sympathies of their members, they tended to vote Liberal or Conservative. Most were skilled artisans, belonging to that section of the working class which always (particularly in Britain) preferred to identify itself with those higher in the social scale.

The doctors, however, refused to make fine distinctions between working-class organizations.[38] They blamed labour as a whole for the conditions of club practice and they tended to attach the same stigma to the Labour Party after it was formed. Feeling in the profession was so strong that doctors who were sympathetic to labour often found it hazardous to make their views known. As one of them (Dr H.B.W. Morgan, later a Labour MP and medical adviser to the TUC) once indicated: 'It is not generally recognized by the workers and Trade Unions how difficult it is for *any member of the medical profession (or indeed any applicant) who is known to be in sympathy with Labour to secure an appointment, even in a minor capacity, on the Hospitals.'*[39]

Webb thus faced a formidable task in trying to gain the support of the doctors and it was this that made him so flexible on medical policy. Furthermore, he had a personal stake in the subject: in the 1918 election, he contested the first university seat fought by a Labour candidate. These seats, which had risen in number over the years (from 9 to 15), were strongly influenced by the votes of medical graduates, nowhere more so than at the University of London. Unable to find a doctor willing to stand in the labour cause there, Webb had to assume the task himself. He lost, but the campaign did give him the chance to place his views on medical administration before the profession.[40]

Thus, in a letter dated 10 July 1918 — only 6 days after Dawson delivered the first part of his Cavendish Lecture[a] — Webb warned the medical graduates of the university against medical bureaucrats. In place of them, he argued, there should be established an advisory committee, created on a statutory basis, which would be 'composed not of the Medical Bureaucracy inside the office, nor yet of the nominees of the Royal Colleges, but of the duly chosen representatives of the profession outside the Government service'. This committee 'ought to have no executive power (because we do not want it to become itself part of the bureaucracy). . . '[41] Its sole function would be to advise and criticize. In an address he had delivered to the approved societies a few months earlier, he had stressed this point even more. The advisory committee, he then said, 'should not have any power over the Minister of Health, who must be absolutely responsible to Parliament for the orders he gives.'[42]

These views, brought so directly before the profession, apparently made a strong impact on Dawson[b] for, soon after Webb presented them, he all but dropped the administrative board idea. When his Cavendish Lecture was published (for the benefit of the lay public) in September 1918, Dawson did not alter the text but he did add a new introduction in which he called only for the appointment of a medical advisory council as a permanent part of the organization of the Ministry of Health.[46]

Though Dawson thus dropped the administrative board idea, neither he nor Webb adhered strictly to the principle of representation through advisory bodies where local administration was concerned. Both called for the creation of advisory bodies here, too, but neither thought that they alone would suffice; in addition, they wanted the profession to be directly represented on local authority health committees. Dawson thought this was necessary to counter the evils of local politics[47] — while Webb saw it mainly as a way of extending the profession's advisory role.[48]

a   Dawson delivered the lecture in 2 parts — on 4 July and 11 July.

b   Webb may even have put his views directly to Dawson for we know that Dawson had discussions with Labour spokesmen in 1918.[43] Cox — who as we saw (see p. 54 above) had once been active in socialist circles — also came into close contact with the Webbs: in 1916, he helped Beatrice prepare a report on medical organization for the *New Statesman*.[44] At the end of his life, he also recalled an occasion when Mrs Webb invited him to her house to meet a group of labour leaders and introduced him as, 'the Secretary of the strongest Trade Union in the country'.[45]

Representation of doctors on a medical advisory council

On the national level, however, no such exception was made: there, Dawson now agreed, the profession should have the right only to offer advice. Still, a vital question remained: how were the doctors to select the members of their consultative council? Both Webb and the BMA[49] had come out for the principle of direct representation — mainly, they argued, in order to secure the co-operation of those employed in the service. Dawson, however, objected strongly to the idea. Such a system, he believed, would produce conflicts of interest in which that of the public might be lost. The profession, he argued, did not have the civic sense needed to exercise direct responsibility for the conduct of its affairs. It would have to go through a long educational process of participation in local as well as national government before it could hope to show the necessary restraint.[50] Until then, the medical council would have to be a small and effective working body, not 'an aggregate of individuals who might not co-operate fully with each other'.[51]

As spokesman for the consultants and the Royal Colleges, Dawson had good reason to object. GPs, at the time, outnumbered consultants by more than 4 to 1 (over 20,000 GPs as opposed to less than 5,000 consultants)[a] and any system of direct representation would have entailed election by the profession as a whole. In such a contest, consultants were sure to lose. Dawson, therefore, did not want the council to be 'representative of the profession in the parliamentary sense. Its members must not only be individually excellent, but such as will together constitute a good council of advisers.'[52] Due weight, he conceded, must be given to bodies of opinion but 'greater regard should be paid to the representation of varieties of knowledge and experience than to representation of interests, organisations and localities. Such a Council would not work effectively if it were a mere congeries of varied and possibly competing interests.'[53]

GP demands for direct representation, however, were too strong to ignore. They came from doctors who did not trust their own leaders. Suspicions — always rife in the medical world — rose to fever pitch during the war as the result of the close relationship that developed between the BMA and the NHI Commission. Through its Central Medical War Committee, the BMA was given the job of calling up doctors for the armed forces. 'Gradually as time went on', Cox later recalled, 'we interlocked our machinery to such an extent that I sometimes did not know whether they [the NHI Commission] were a Department of our Central Medical War Committee or whether we were a Department of the National Health Insurance Commission.'[54]

This inevitably aroused criticism, particularly after the Committee received compulsory conscription powers in June 1916. Doctors who boycotted NHI accused the Committee of trying to force them on the panel[55] — while those already enrolled believed it was discriminating against practitioners who belonged to organizations critical of BMA policy. The most controversial instance concerned the fiery General Secretary of the MPU, Dr Alfred

a   See pp. 10-11 above.

Welply. Despite the fact that he was suffering from an arthritic hip, Welply was taken into the army on 29 January 1918. Within a few weeks he was sent home, but nevertheless suffered domestic problems as a result of the disruption. This led the President of the MPU (Dr William Coode Adams) to comment: 'My own personal view is that a great injustice has been done and I wonder whether this injustice would have arisen had he not been the Secretary of the Panel Medico-Political Union.'[56]

How much truth there was in these charges cannot now be determined. What is clear is that the BMA did show the utmost concern for the interests of non-panel doctors when the time came for demobilization. Much effort was made to protect them from the competing claims of the NHI Commission and the military authorities.[57] This, however, was not enough to shield the leaders of the BMA from criticism. Even the *British Medical Journal* later had to admit that 'the work was often of an invidious nature and might easily have been dangerous to the prestige of the Association'.[58]

The danger appeared most strongly on the NHI side of BMA work. As a result of their close relationship with the Government, BMA leaders found it difficult to promote the profession's economic interests as vigorously as they had done before the war. Something like a shop steward's movement arose within the medical world and the initiative on money matters passed to the MPU.

Two instances, in particular, should be noted. The first was in 1916 when the profession suffered a cut in the notification fee for infectious diseases. Though the amount was small (from 2s. 6d. per case to 1s.), it was the only instance of a reduction in pay for any class of worker during the war.[59] The second came in 1918 when BMA leaders responded to the Government's 'appeal to their patriotism' by forgoing a general pay increase to cover the sharp rise in the cost of living. In its place, they accepted a modest bonus restricted to hardship cases. Since this occurred at a time when many workers were securing substantial gains, it drew sharp fire from MPU quarters, directed at the BMA committee which did the bargaining for panel doctors: 'The Insurance Acts Committee did not possess any real driving force, and in consequence they received a reply from Sir Edwin Cornwall [the Chairman of the NHI Commission who dismissed the profession's pay claim] that would not have been given to a bricklayer's union.'[60]

Such criticism struck home. The MPU attracted much support during the war and became the main source of demands for direct representation on medical bodies dealing with the Government. So strong did this pressure become that BMA leaders had to satisfy it within the framework of their own committee structure. During 1917, they were forced to grant panel practitioners a majority of places on the central body which they had set up to deal with the NHI Commission.

That body was the Insurance Acts Committee mentioned above, and it contained an amalgam of members drawn from the main policy-making centres of the profession: the Council and Annual Representative Meeting of the BMA, the Conference of Local Medical Committees, and several specialized medical groups like the Society of MOHs. Even before the war, most of the doctors who served on the Committee happened to be on the panel, but they were not directly elected by the chief representative bodies of panel practitioners — the local medical committees and their annual conference.[a] These bodies merely had the chance to suggest names to the Council of the BMA which made the final choice. During the war, however, local medical committees demanded and won the right to make their own selections, largely as the result of pressure exerted by the MPU. By 1917 they had secured a majority of places (even though they were allowed to select only doctors who were members of the BMA).[b]

Dawson and his colleagues were subjected to the same pressure and they too, found it impossible to resist. In March 1919 they finally gave in to BMA demands and agreed to propose that 7 out of 24 members on the Medical Consultative Council should be selected by direct representation.[62] This concession, as one of the consultants involved (Sir George Makins) admitted, was based solely 'upon a recognition of the desirability of securing the confidence of the mass of the profession in the composition of the Council'.[63]

Addison was still cool to the proposal. He was willing to accept it only if the profession could solve its organizational problem.[64] In 1911 Lloyd George had said: 'The greatest difficulties I have had with the negotiations have been due to the conflicts of interests in the profession itself.'[65] (Bevan, no doubt, came to the same conclusion in 1946.) If Addison was to avoid a repetition of the problem, then he had to have a body that could speak for the profession as a whole. The BMA, in his view, did not fill that role: it had too many committees and too narrow a vision to suit him. That was the main reason for his backing the MPU when it was formed in 1914[66] — but it, too, soon developed an obsession with money matters.[c] Still, the need was great and Addison revealed its extent when he indicated his willingness to accept direct representation on the Medical Consultative Council if the profession could create a body from which proper selections would flow.

Even then, however, he feared the effect such a concession would have

a   Strictly speaking, this was called the conference of local *panel* committees before 1948 because, under NHI, separate committees had been formed in most areas for panel doctors. The term 'local *medical* committee' was thus reserved for committees which embraced all doctors in the area, not just those who practised under NHI. In time, however, so many doctors joined the panel that the difference between the 2 became meaningless and throughout this study we have ignored it, using the single term 'local medical committee' to describe the bodies which the profession organized on the local level before as well as after 1948.

b   Resolutions passed by the committee, furthermore, were still subject to veto by the BMA's Council and not until 1919-20 were both restrictions removed.[61]

c   In 1918, Addison made another attempt at medical organization when he gave his blessing to the formation of a Medical Parliamentary Committee to help him push the Ministry of Health Bill through.[67] This time, the effort was more successful — the Committee *did* stick to politics — but that made it difficult to attract doctors and it had to enrol other workers to survive. In the process it changed its name to the British Federation of Medical and Allied Societies (later the last word was changed to 'Services'), and lingered on for a few years into the 1920s before it died.[68] Nothing like it has been attempted since.

on the other consultative councils. If he gave the privilege to one, how could he deny it to the others? Had not Labour women already made the same demand for representation on the patients' council?[a] Once the principle was conceded, furthermore, it would undermine the whole concept of ministerial responsibility. As Addison put it to one medical deputation: 'He could not admit that any Society or individual had an absolute right to representation upon any of the Councils, for the principle upon which the Councils were to be formed was that the Minister should be responsible for selecting as members of the Councils those persons whom he thought best fitted to advise him on the work of each Council.'[69]

Fortunately for Addison, he never had to resolve these doubts because the profession failed to create a unified organization. Brackenbury thought it never would: he believed unity to be an 'unattainable goal' because the profession was split into too many factions.[70] Beyond that, he really did not want a new body to be formed since he was afraid it might undermine the influence he exercised through the BMA.

For the same reason, Brackenbury had reservations about the desirability of the Medical Consultative Council itself. It, he feared, might fall under the control of the Ministry or, even worse, lapse into disuse because it antagonized the civil service. The profession needed at least one strong organization that kept its distance from the Government, and this was a lesson he had had to learn the hard way. No sooner were the new panel regulations published in 1919 than Brackenbury and his colleagues were denounced as 'liars and traitors'.[71] The charge, as always, came from the MPU. Nor was that the extent of the abuse. Welply and his cohorts also reminded the profession of the occasion in 1911 when the Medical Secretary of the BMA resigned in order to take a post with the NHI Commission: *'No greater betrayal has occurred since 1912, when Dr Smith Whitaker went over to the enemy.'*[72]

The profession thus failed to fulfil Addison's condition for direct representation and the Minister proceeded to appoint a council of his own. Though the BMA, the Royal Colleges and other medical organizations were given the privilege of recommending names, the final choice rested with the department.[b] In this way, Addison sought to impress on those chosen that 'they did not sit upon the Council in a representative capacity, and he hoped that he might rely upon receiving from them the best advice they could furnish as independent individuals'.[74]

Addison thus made it clear that the council was to be his body and not the profession's. Its purpose was to justify ministerial policy to the public, not alter it to suit the profession. Dawson himself was ready to accept this role and he also thought the council could help the department to implement policy. Here, he believed, the profession would be able to render great service since the original intention was to create consultative councils on the local level as well: 'I know that the Ministry of Health

a   See p. 50 above.

b   Brackenbury himself was not appointed despite the fact that his name was put forward by the BMA.[73]

cannot exercise too close a control over details or at any rate had to do it very tactfully, but that is where the local Medical Councils come in and where our Council comes in.' These words were contained in a letter Dawson wrote to the Permanent Secretary of the Ministry in September 1921, and although he crossed out the last 6 words, thereby excluding the central council from this role, he evidently once envisaged some part for it to play, too.[75]

Role of a medical advisory council

Had that been the extent of Dawson's design then the consultative council on which he pinned such hopes might have survived, but he made the mistake of wanting it to exercise too much influence over policy. The main purpose of the council, as Dawson saw it, was to give the department the benefit of outside experience, not have it rely solely on advice from the civil service. To do this effectively, it would have to become 'an integral part of the office staff'; it would need to know 'all that is going on' and have a say on nearly all questions of policy.[a] Differences would inevitably arise and Dawson did not indicate how he expected them to be decided — but many doctors were optimistic about the outcome because, like some American businessmen today, they did not see how their interests could clash with those of the nation. As *The Lancet* put it at the time: '. . . in the long run, what is best for medicine is best for the public.'[77]

Not surprisingly, the civil servants at the Ministry failed to agree. They objected strongly to Dawson's conception and Sir George Newman, as Chief Medical Officer, was the one most particularly alarmed. Not only did the role Dawson envisaged for the council threaten Newman's own position but it went far beyond the point he considered possible or desirable. How, he asked, did Dawson expect to find the time to participate in Ministry affairs? He would have to be in constant attendance to influence policy for it could not, as Dawson so naively assumed, be separated from the task of administration: 'A Minister really settles his policy at no given point, it emerges and grows as he considers it, and is necessarily modified day by day owing to political, social or administrative exigencies . . .'[78]

Nor, Newman contended, could such policy be decided on medical grounds alone. Much else was involved which Dawson and his colleagues did not have the competence to consider. They were not experienced in 'communal' medicine; all their work had led them to view medical problems 'from an individualistic point of view'. They were not 'in the same position to advise a Government department as a group of medical men and women who have devoted the best part of their lives to the Public

---

a   These quotations, and the ones that follow, are taken from internal Ministry minutes prepared by Sir George Newman, the Chief Medical Officer of the department, after discussions with Dawson about how the council should operate. The words attributed to Dawson may not have been the actual ones he used. In the minutes, Newman merely paraphrased or interpreted what Dawson said and that is what has been quoted here.[76]

Health service'.[79] All the council could offer was some indication of 'the mind of the medical profession in practice'[80] — and even that contribution was limited because the Minister could learn all he needed to know from his own medical staff: 'We are in day by day contact with private practitioners and know in some ways quite as well as Lord Dawson, and in some ways better, what the general atmosphere and temper [a] of the profession is.'[81]

The Minister, Newman argued, not only had little to gain from the council — he had much to lose. To interpose the council between him and his staff would delay decisions and complicate relations: '... only disaster could ensue.'[82] It would also jeopardize the confidentiality of Ministry affairs. How could 20 doctors living in different parts of the country resist the temptation to tell others what they had learned in secret at the department? A man could not be both a civil servant and a freelance. If the Minister gave Dawson all he asked, 'I think we should soon find ourselves in an impossible position and the tail would begin to wag the head.'[83]

The Minister, in any case, never intended the council to operate in this way. Dawson, Newman contended, 'is reading into his position large (and to him, entirely novel) duties.'[84] The council was not asked to provide 'complete and all-round advice'[85] on the subjects referred to it. Rather, it was meant to give only an informed reaction from a sample of doctors in active practice. In that way, the Minister could make more practicable decisions and, hopefully, secure the profession's support for the policies he adopted. But to fulfil this function, Newman stressed, it was not wise for the council to work too closely with the department. In fact, the opposite applied: 'The council is really of value to us and the profession in the degree by which it is untied and untrammelled by association with the office.'[86]

It did not take the leaders of the BMA long to realize the implications of this argument. What was the point of having any body between themselves and the Minister if the council was to have only the limited scope Newman assigned to it? The BMA could do a far better job of representing the views of the profession — and, at least in it, the doctors had an organization over which they could exercise democratic control. The council, whether anyone realized it or not, was doomed from the day Addison denied the doctors direct representation. Though it managed to hold periodic conferences with the Ministry staff until February 1924, it did not do any work on its own after July 1921.[87]

a   Newman originally wrote the word 'temperature' here but he changed it to read 'temper'.

6

The Dawson Report

Before the Medical Consultative Council died, it managed to produce a plan which has gone down in history as the Dawson Report — the first to give official sanction to the idea of health centres. This chapter explains the origin of the report and the meaning of its proposals.

Original purpose of Dawson's plan

As soon as the new department was established, Addison appointed the members of the Medical Consultative Council and asked them 'to tell him what in their view should be the ideal system of medical and allied services toward which the Ministry should work'.[1] The council held its first meeting in October· 1919 and produced an interim report in May 1920.[2] No other report followed. It was this interim report which became known as the Dawson Report.[3] Dawson deserved to have his name associated with it not only because he was chairman of the council but because he drafted the report himself[4] and put in it the ideas he had outlined in his Cavendish Lecture. In order to understand the origin of the Dawson Report, then, we must first see how Dawson came to deliver that lecture in the summer of 1918.

This was the time when the fate of the whole new department was in doubt as a result of the Maternity and Child Welfare Bill that Hayes Fisher had introduced in Parliament.[a] Until then, the doctors had shown little enthusiasm for a Ministry of Health because they thought it would arise from the LGB and that, for them, meant a salaried service. *Dawson's plan was designed to show them how the two concepts could be separated.*[5] He outlined an exciting scheme of clinical organization free from the stigma of a salaried service.[b]

In the hopes of winning support for his views, Dawson first presented them (in April and May 1918) to a select group at the Royal Society of Medicine.[6] Then, in July, he expanded his theme into a formal paper which he delivered to the West London Medico-Chirurgical Society as the Cavendish Lecture for the year. Though this was not the most prestigious platform a doctor could command, the lecture was regularly reported in the medical press and that brought the subject prominently before the profession. Morant, who attended the lecture, said publicly that it was

a   See p. 37 above. For the background to what follows here, see pp. 34-9 above.

b   For the details, see pp. 67-8 below.

intended to rouse the doctors against the Maternity and Child Welfare Bill[7] but this aim was only partly realized. Indeed, the leading hospital journal of the day went so far as to say: 'To be quite frank, the Cavendish Lecture this year cannot be regarded as a brilliant success.'[8] (A similar reception was later accorded to the Dawson Report itself. When it appeared in May 1920 it aroused hardly any correspondence in the medical press.)[9]

This strange lack of medical interest forced Dawson to direct his ideas to the public instead and, in the process, he changed the title of his lecture from 'The Future of the Medical Profession' to 'The Nation's Welfare'.[10] By then (September 1918), however, the Maternity Bill had passed onto the statute book and sentiment for a salaried service continued to grow.[11] As far as the doctors were concerned, therefore, the main effect of Dawson's plan was to harden their attitude against salary in any form.

Dawson's proposals

Still, this did not mean that the doctors were opposed to state intervention. On the contrary, they were inclined to welcome it as a means of accomplishing things they were unable to do themselves. Dawson left no doubt of his own feelings on the subject. By 1918, he could see that it was neither possible nor desirable to stop the spread of public provision: medical care had become too expensive for that. It required increasing amounts of costly equipment which the profession itself was unable to provide entirely from its own resources. The state had to help, but Dawson wanted it to interfere as little as possible. All he wanted the Government to do was provide the equipment. 'Collectivism' was to be used to build the institutional framework of medicine; where human relationships were concerned, 'individualism' would reign.[12]

How would the panel system fit into this scheme? To Dawson as to many doctors, the panel had become an acceptable form of practice — not offering the ideal of private practice, but still far from being a service run directly by the state. The money to fund it came largely from insurance contributions rather than the Exchequer, and the administration of the system left the profession enough freedom to make it resemble private enterprise. To Dawson, the choice lay only between the panel and a salaried service run directly by the state. Dr Alfred Cox himself held this view in 1913[13] and it was reiterated by Dr Peter Macdonald in 1919:

'. . . the time was past for them to make the choice between panel practice and private practice. There was no such choice left. The choice was between panel practice with accessory services or a State Medical Service.'[14]

Dawson therefore urged the profession to throw its weight behind the system Lloyd George had created in 1911: 'Surely the wise course is to fit and mould the insurance organisation into the larger scheme of systematised medical service which, if the health of the people is to be secured, must be set up and made available for all sections of the community.'[15]

NHI covered only the wage-earning members of the working class but everyone expected it to be extended so that it covered dependants as well. That would bring in over 80% of the population, and some members of the middle class, it was thought, might also be added. But, in presenting his views to the profession, Dawson held out hope of saving the middle class for private practice if only the doctors would agree to let the state provide the equipment.[16]

Under Dawson's proposal, everyone would receive the same services in the same buildings but, while most patients would have their bills covered by NHI, some would continue to pay themselves. Dawson's answer to the threat of salary, then, was to extend the panel and make it strong by adding the necessary physical support. His scheme, however, did not entirely exclude salary; Dawson made provision for whole-time as well as part-time appointments in local authority clinics and other similar posts. Furthermore, he fully expected an increase in the proportion of earnings coming from salaried sources. This, he thought, was needed to extend medical interest in the direction of prevention: patients were more willing to pay for care when they were ill than when they were well. To encourage them to seek attention before they became ill, they would have to receive the preventive services free of charge, and the doctors who provided such attention would have to be paid by salary.

Here was the way one member of Dawson's consultative council, Dr (later Sir) Guy Dain, a leading figure in BMA circles from the First World War until his retirement in 1960, described the policy:

'. . . While in most cases they [ie., patients] should still pay all or part of his [ie., the doctor's] fee for attendance on them in sickness, the Local Health Authority should pay for his preventive services and he should come to look more to preventive work for his income. The public would not be slow to appreciate the altered position of the doctor "free when well, pay when ill".'[17]

Some medical policy-makers wanted to go further and make the curative services free as well. This was true of some BMA leaders — notably Dr Charles J. Bond of Leicester. In 1919, he became Dawson's vice-chairman on the Medical Consultative Council and he used that position to argue strongly for a free service.[18] But Dawson himself opposed the idea and the majority of the council agreed with him. The profession was not ready for such a sweeping proposal. All it might accept was an extension of the panel to dependants in the hope that such a move would be sufficient to satisfy the public demand for freer care. But even medical approval of that was uncertain because of the fear, widespread within the profession, that any substantial extension of the panel would lead straight to a salaried service.[19]

Dawson, therefore, thought it wise to steer clear of the issue and he managed to carry his colleagues on the council with him. All they said in their report was that the medical services should be 'available' and by that they did not mean they should be 'free': 'we exclude for the moment the question of how they are to be paid for.'[20]

They did expect a decline in direct fee payments as treatment became more costly: public aid and private insurance would absorb an ever-increasing proportion of the medical bill. This process, in the council's view, was to apply first to hospital treatment. After continual prodding from Bond, the council agreed to recommend that this be made free to all. The decision was taken in December 1920, 7 months after the council issued its interim report (i.e. the Dawson Report) and 7 months before its meetings terminated in July 1921.[21] Coming as late as it did, the Ministry chose not to publish the recommendation, but notice of the council's action was taken in a journal distributed by the Labour Party.[22]

However fee payments might shrink, Dawson left no doubt that he himself expected private practice to continue, certainly as far as the middle class was concerned. *His main aim, therefore, in presenting his proposals was to change the way in which medical practice was organized rather than the way in which it was funded.* Medicine, he felt, had become too vast for one man to comprehend and too expensive for single-handed doctors, or even partnerships, to afford. As a Major-General during the war, he had seen doctors in the armed forces do inspired work: working in teams, they had had more equipment at their disposal than ever before. Dawson wanted to give them the same opportunities when they returned home. For this purpose, he thought it advisable to organize civilian practice on military lines — through an interlocking network of health centres, starting with a form of 'first-aid' treatment at or near the patient's home (cf. the 'battle-field') and becoming increasingly more elaborate as the patient was transferred 'inwards' towards the best-equipped and most specialized hospitals.

As Dawson's plan finally evolved, simpler treatment was to be provided by GPs in small (or primary) health centres located near the homes of patients; while more complex services would be supplied by consultants in larger (or secondary) health centres sited at a greater distance. The small centres, however, would contain not only GP consulting rooms but diagnostic facilities (laboratory and X-ray equipment) and local authority clinics as well. All health centres, furthermore, would have beds — the small ones only about 16 or 32, the larger ones the same number (usually 100 or more) as were found in the specialized hospitals of the day. Patients, initially, might be seen in the smaller centres but, if they required more complex treatment, they would be passed along to the larger ones. To facilitate this process of referral (as well as to give GPs the specialist aid they needed) consultants would work in both the small and the large centres. The 2 sections of the profession, then, would not work apart; on the contrary, they would be united as never before through the health centre network that Dawson envisaged.[23]

When Dawson first outlined his scheme in July 1918 he did not use the term 'health centre',[24] but referred to 3 separate (and already existing) units of organization: common (or group) surgeries, local authority clinics, and hospitals. All were to be located near each other, but at that time

Dawson did not consider that they should be housed in the same building.[a] This idea did not emerge until the Labour Party produced a report on medical organization in 1919 in which it said: 'Public hospitals when established should become *the health centre* or institute of each local authority, and should provide accommodation within their walls for all medical activities.'[25]

This, apparently, was the first time anyone employed the term 'health centre' in Britain although it had been used earlier in America. There, the term had a different meaning than it did here and we must pause to explain it. In America, the concept of a health centre was originally close to Britain's as far as the range of care was concerned: hospital, GP and local authority services were all to be housed within the same building. (Only home treatment was missing from the American concept.) But the 2 concepts differed greatly in terms of administration and control. The American centre was seen mainly as an extension of municipal medicine — whereas the British centre (at least as conceived by Dawson) was designed to thwart it. Dawson saw the health centre as the place where the 3 main streams of British medicine would meet — not the instrument through which local authorities would make up for deficiencies in the private sector. The latter was traditionally the American aim and it was no accident that the term (until recently) was always used there to describe the buildings in which municipal health departments were housed.[26]

How did Dawson's council make use of the health-centre concept that appeared in the Labour report? In accepting the idea they added a distinction between *primary* and *secondary* health centres. This, they hoped, would enable them to keep separate not only hospitals for GPs and hospitals for consultants but also those which were publicly owned and those in the private sector. If municipal and Poor Law hospitals could be persuaded to accept a primary health centre status, that would leave the more prestigious secondary-centre role free for the voluntary hospitals if they were willing to accept it. No one had thought of making this kind of distinction before, and that was what made Dawson's use of the term 'health centre' unique.

Even in 1918 Dawson had made the same distinction — only then he used the words 'local' and 'central'. Other elements of the health centre idea, however, were not unique to Dawson or, for that matter, to the Labour Party. Rather, they had been anticipated by various medical reformers, particularly by those who were active in SMSA circles. Their ideas took the form of 'polyclinics', 'receiving stations', 'central depots' or 'clinical centres' — all variations of the group-practice concept. What distinguished the health-centre term from these precedents was the idea of concentrating *all* medical activities in one building and, for this, the Labour Party deserves the credit.[27]

Health centres and GPs

How did Dawson want GPs to fit into this framework? From the beginning, he did not expect them to work exclusively in health centres. He thought they

---

a The collection of buildings so formed Dawson called a 'settlement'.

would continue to maintain their own surgeries and, from there, make home visits as they had done in the past. But Dawson did expect the value — and, hence, the frequency — of home visits to decline as medical technology advanced. Since the latter would be concentrated in health centres, this meant that GPs, as well as patients, would have to spend an increasing amount of time there if they were to obtain the best that medical science had to offer.

Once in health centres, furthermore, GPs would be expected to practise in groups. Later, however, Dawson was forced to modify this view as the profession became concerned about the amount of state interference that group practice might entail.[a] He and his council then decided that GPs should enter health centres only when they had to make use of equipment not available in their surgeries.[28]

All this was designed mainly to alter the organization of practice. No major change — apart from free hospital treatment or the possible addition of dependants to NHI — was contemplated on the funding side. In Dawson's view, these points were inter-related: free treatment implied salary, and he did not see how one could be introduced without the other. He said this explicitly when he was confronted with a demand for a free service from the consultative council representing the public: 'The universal provision of free medical attendance would in his view imply the establishment of a whole-time salaried medical service which would be open to the objections in para. 52 of his Council's Report.'[29]

For this reason, too, he wanted GPs to pay for the use of health centres —not to have free use of the equipment. Here, he was striving to avoid the pattern set by the voluntary hospitals where everything was freely provided.[b] Only where local authority clinics were concerned did Dawson permit any element of free care and salaried service to enter. But by placing the clinics at the health centres, Dawson hoped to encourage the use of part-time GPs in place of whole-time medical officers and contain the threat of salary in that way.[c]

Hospital treatment

Dawson introduced similar safeguards for consultants, since their position had been endangered by the upgrading of Poor Law infirmaries employing whole-time staff. As this process was bound to accelerate once the infirmaries passed under municipal control, Dawson aimed to transform those which had not yet been modernized (the bulk of them) into primary health centres, leaving the voluntary hospitals to serve as secondary health

a   For more on this, see Chapter 10 beginning on p. 101 below.

b   According to tradition, voluntary hospitals made no charge for services and, as a result, they offered no payments to the consultants who supplied them. There were, however, many exceptions to this practice. At St. Bartholomew's, for example, the medical staff was always paid — even before charges were imposed on patients.[30]

c   The clinics at Dawson's health centre were to offer services in the fields of maternity and child welfare, medical inspection and treatment of schoolchildren, tuberculosis and occupational diseases, physical culture, nursing and dentistry. Only VD clinics were to be kept separate. Because of the stigma attached to the disease, the public did not want them to be located in health centres.[31]

centres, with their traditional pattern of part-time consultant staffing intact.[32] This meant that their custom of free care would continue, but state intervention could be expected to change that. If the voluntary hospitals opened their doors to some patients who paid, how could they refuse others?[a] Public patients would thus lead the way for private patients, and state intervention, ironically, would provide the medium through which a charity would be transformed into a fee-paying (or, rather, a fee-receiving) institution.

What were the implications for private patients of the major change in policy which the Medical Consultative Council adopted after the Dawson Report appeared? In December, 1920, it will be recalled, the council voted to make hospital treatment free to everyone.[b] Would this have ruled out a place for private patients in voluntary hospitals, and have forced their consultants into whole-time employment? Dawson apparently did not think so and we can see, from what happened in 1948, that neither result necessarily followed. Far more important, from Dawson's point of view in 1920, was the need to rescue the voluntary hospitals from financial plight. Charity no longer seemed sufficient to cover rising costs and the hospitals needed payments from patients, even if the money came through public agencies. In March 1920, only 2 months before the Dawson Report appeared, the London Hospital not only imposed charges on patients but its chairman, Lord Knutsford, actually appealed for state aid. By the end of the year, nearly all the leading hospitals in London had either adopted a pay system or were on the brink of doing so.[34]

In the process, the charitable status of consultants was bound to change too. How could anyone expect them to give service free if the hospitals in which they worked did not do so? In the past, opposition to the prospect of payment for consultants working in the hospitals had come not only from GPs but, surprisingly, from some consultants themselves. The opposition of the first group was understandable: GPs were largely excluded from the hospital world (particularly in urban areas) and they feared the loss of fee-paying patients if the practice of pay beds spread. But many consultants did not take kindly to the idea either: they thought payment would deprive them of the monopoly they possessed over hospital work. *Free care, they recognized, was the price they had to pay to keep GPs out.*[c]

The closest any consultant ever came to admitting this in public was the statement made by Mr A. Dickson Wright, a surgeon, just before the Health Service came into being in 1948. Once it did so, he warned a meeting of

---

a   The payments made for public patients would not come directly from them but would be paid by a public authority, as was already done for schoolchildren, servicemen, and patients suffering from tuberculosis and VD. As much as 25% of hospital income came from public sources in 1920. Private patients were also to be found in voluntary hospitals, but mainly in rural areas, and the total payments over the country as a whole did not amount to much. Before the war, they represented only 21½% of income in general hospitals, 12% to 17% in special hospitals.[33]

b   See p. 67 above.

c   For more on this, see pp. 142-3 below.

London consultants, they would lose the influence they had over appointments to the staffs of voluntary hospitals: '. . . by working for our hospitals for nothing — practically the only people who were doing so — we were able to establish a certain control.'[35] a

Dawson, however, wisely took account of these fears in his plan and he also made arrangements to ease the anxieties of GPs. By giving the latter access to beds, he offered them hope of retaining private patients — yet, by confining such access to primary health centres, he also gave consultants the chance of holding on to their monopoly elsewhere.

The need for co-operation among doctors

Such was the essence of the scheme that gradually took shape in Dawson's mind between 1918 and 1920. Many doctors feared it would bring on the very service he wanted to avoid but Dawson argued to the contrary: 'Far from this making for a whole-time salaried service, he ventured to say that it was the sole alternative.'[36] He wanted to stop the field of health going the way of education, and he argued for a different approach on the grounds that doctors gave a more personalized service than teachers:

> '. . . In few callings is there such a wide gap between the minimum and the maximum efforts, efforts which make demands upon heart as well as head. The distinction between the performance of a routine duty and the fixing of the mind on each individual is vital. Liberty of action, the stimulating force of rivalry, and the personal touch are essential. The patient needs not only advice — but confidence — the human being of his own choice, not the official of someone else's choice. Medicine stereotyped under such a salaried service would become a machine without a soul or hope of salvation.'[37]

This did not mean that Dawson opposed all forms of control. On the contrary, he clearly saw the need for some restraints if the profession was to function properly. As he told his colleagues at one BMA meeting: 'There seemed to be a fear amongst some speakers of the danger of State service or State control. But where some had pointed to individualism he saw only intellectual anarchy. If by individualism was meant absence of all control that was something which would not be good for the profession, and something which the community was not in the least likely to concede.'[38]

What Dawson wished to avoid was not state employment but 'intellectual stagnation'. It might come, he feared, not only from a salaried service but from conditions of work which were boring: '. . . the profession could equally be crushed by having mechanical routine so heaped around it that the individual was left with little opportunity to exercise his personal initiative or to put his soul into his work.'[39] This was the great danger of

---

a   Wright's fears proved to be unjustified. After the Health Service began, consultants found that they enjoyed the best of both worlds. Not only did they receive payment for hospital work, but they also managed to retain control of hospital appointments. After 1948, in fact, consultants excluded GPs from the hospital world even more vigorously than before. For more on this, see Chapter 29 beginning on p. 301 below.

the panel system with its endless queues of patients — and even private practice was not immune. Any doctor who worked alone ran the risk of stagnation.

Above all else, therefore, Dawson strove to end the isolation of the profession. Medicine, as an intellectual discipline, required unity of thought, and the growing complexity of its technique made co-operation imperative. The profession could no longer tolerate a situation which barred GPs from hospital and put practitioners into opposing camps — the one, salaried; the other, not. Some way had to be found to bring all doctors together[a] and Dawson, in the primary health centre, thought he had the answer:

> '. . . The Primary Centre would be the home of the health organization and of the intellectual life of the doctors in that unit. Those doctors, instead of being isolated as now from each other, would be brought together and in contact with consultants and specialists; there would develop an intellectual traffic and a camaradarie to the great advantage of the service.'[41]

Such was the rationale underlying the Dawson Report.

---

a   Dawson also wanted to bring GPs into contact with public health doctors — but more for administrative than clinical reasons. Private practitioners, he admitted in 1921, had no civic sense and they needed contact with MOHs to develop it. How did he propose to bring the preventive and curative sides of the profession together? Mainly through the medium of local medical advisory committees which he wanted to create in each area (on the pattern of the local medical committees already established under NHI): 'The opposition to this mainly comes from the MOHs and they have to grow to the idea. The closing of this cleavage is necessary to progress.'[40]

7
The Failure of Reform

The Dawson Report was drafted quickly and the speed with which it was prepared both marred its production and made it vulnerable to attack. It was Addison, however, not Dawson, who was responsible for the pressure under which the council worked.[1] The Minister thought he had to have an ideal scheme in hand before he could proceed with reform at the local level — and that had been seen as the second stage of legislative action from the early days of the Ministry of Health campaign.[a]

Planned pattern of reform

The aim was to put all health services under the unified control of local authorities, and this entailed not only the abolition of insurance committees but the removal from the health field of boards of guardians. The need to uproot the latter, in fact, was more important than the former. With their blind insistence on means tests, the guardians blocked the provision of free services at every turn. As the journal of the Society of MOHs put it in 1918: 'The existence of Boards of Guardians constitutes the obstacle to all reform in public health.'[2]

Once administration was transferred to local authorities, many reformers believed, the nation was sure to move closer to the ideal of a national health service. The reason lay in the nature of municipal administration: once local authorities assumed control they would (as one Poor Law defender warned) 'be so intent on the treatment of sickness that they would forget to consider whether the recipients ought to be in receipt of public treatment at all'.[3] By the time the war ended, some local authorities had already neglected to collect payment from those who used their maternity and child welfare centres.[4]

But the care the authorities could offer was restricted, and the first need in 1919 was to give dependants the GP service they had been denied before the war. Hospital treatment for the population as a whole could come later; extension, in the Ministry's view, had to start with community care.[5] Even *The Times* put this priority first. Later, it joined the movement that arose against all forms of public expenditure but, as late as January 1920, it too wanted women and children added to the spectrum of care covered by NHI: '. . . no other policy', it maintained, 'is consistent with the maintenance of national health on the highest level.'[6]

a   See p. 30 above.

Local unification was thus closely associated in Addison's mind with the extension of NHI to dependants. These were the recommendations he hoped to secure from the medical council. Once the doctors endorsed the plan, pressure for an extended service could be supplied by the patient's council,[7] while the details of local unification were worked out by the Consultative Council on Local Health Administration.[8] This was the way Addison hoped to use the advisory bodies created under the Ministry of Health Act.

The doctors, however, frustrated the plan from the start: Dawson and his colleagues were too preoccupied with the threat of salary to make the recommendations Addison desired. The Dawson Report left the key questions open but the doctors said enough about both to show where their real sympathies lay. Thus, by suggesting only that the service should be 'available',[a] the doctors left the impression that they did not think it should be free. Dawson even had doubts about the desirability of dependant coverage[b] and he told his colleagues on the council why institutional development should come first:

> '. . . Without then prejudging what would be wise after a lapse of years, extension to dependants should not form part of any PRESENT scheme for immediate operation. Nor have we yet sufficient experience of the Panel System to make such large extensions at the present time. It is more pressing first to get money for institutional provisions that would benefit ALL classes.'[9]

Where local unification was concerned, Dawson and his colleagues were even less helpful. Their report reflected the profession's deep distrust of local authority control, devoting far more space to the way in which doctors should be protected than to the method by which unification could be achieved.[10] Had it not been for the intervention of Morant, the doctors would even have declared themselves in favour of a new *ad hoc* authority, devoted to health alone, in order to secure the place they wanted in the administration of the service. They considered only one alternative — a statutory committee of an existing local authority — but they did not like the idea, and it took a personal plea from Morant to persuade the council to leave the question open.

Since he was a civil servant, Morant could not speak too directly but, drawing on his earlier experience in the field of education, he said just enough about the abolition of school boards under the 1902 Education Act to show the doctors why they should not create a new *ad hoc* authority for health.[11] The profession at large, however, still clung to the idea and Dawson, at the BMA's Annual Representative Meeting in July 1920, had to explain why the council had failed to be more specific in its report: 'The Consultative Council had given a great deal of consideration to the matter, and had passed over it with a light touch because they felt it would be improper for them as medical men to decide questions which ought to be left to experts on local government.'[12]

The doctors had merely stated the alternatives — but one point they did make clear: whichever body administered the service, the profession must be represented on it. Nothing could have been more damaging to the prospect of

a   See pp. 66-7 above.
b   The profession generally came to the same view. For the reasons, see p. 125 below.

local unification because such a demand ran directly counter to municipal policy: '. . . it is a principle of local government', local authority spokesmen repeated endlessly, 'that the people who spend public money should be publicly elected.'[13] Co-option, the authorities might tolerate, but under no circumstances would they grant the doctors direct representation.[14]

Patients' council demands extension

Once the Dawson Report began to take shape, then, the outlook for reform weakened. Addison knew what was coming, since he and others in the Ministry received the minutes of council proceedings. How could he minimize the impact of the medical report? The only way, it seemed, was through patients and Addison turned to the patients' council for support. That body had not met at all since it was formed (in September 1919) but in February 1920 Addison suddenly put it into action.[15] It managed to produce its first report in 6 weeks — on 31 March, only a few days after the doctors handed in theirs. The patients' report dealt only with maternity care and deferred until later the question of general medical treatment. But by focusing its attention of the problems of dependants rather than institutions, it gave Addison the sanction he needed to push for wider coverage of the population.[16]

Furthermore, unlike the medical council, the patients' council was not satisfied with an interim report. Eight months later (in November), it produced another which gave Addison all the support he needed to carry out his plans.[17] Anticipating Bevan by 26 years, Greenwood and his colleagues called strongly for the creation of a comprehensive service open to everyone.[a] Not only that — they opposed any suggestion of *ad hoc* administration, demanding that health care be combined with the other services under municipal control. To those who had the imagination to draft such proposals, the end of the Poor Law must at last have seemed in sight.

Economy campaign blocks reform

Such, however, was not to be: the defenders of the boards of guardians saw to that. Outwitted by Lloyd George before the war, they had begun to marshall their forces in 1917, preparing for the day when they could launch an attack on the Acts which he had managed to slip by them. The lead was taken by Geoffrey Drage and other members of the COS. In December 1917 they formed a Public Assistance Committee with the aim of repealing *all* the welfare legislation passed by the Liberals, leaving the country as it was before 1906 — with only the friendly societies and the Poor Law to fall back on.[19] To win support for their programme, they appealed to the pecuniary instincts of the nation, directing criticism at the money spent on social reform.

In carrying out this campaign, Drage worked closely with his friend Hayes Fisher during the 2 years (1917-18) that he presided over the LGB.[20] The main technique they employed was to secure the publication of a Parliament-

---

a   See p. 50 above. Five members of the council, however, dissented from this recommendation.[18]

ary return, showing the growth in the amount of money spent on all forms of social legislation, which they called 'public assistance'.[21] This, they recognized, was the only way that NHI and programmes like it could be attacked, since they were extremely popular with the public. Once the costs were driven home, they hoped pressure would build up to repeal the legislation and hand all social aid back to the guardians — who were to be renamed 'public assistance authorities' in order to remove the stigma of the Poor Law. (Similarly, 'paupers' were to be called 'assisted persons', 'pauper lunatics' to be referred to simply as 'local patients', and 'workhouses' to be dignified with the title of 'institutions'.)[22]

Drage, who began the campaign as early as 1913,[23] was tireless in pursuit of his goal. As late as 1933 he was still writing letters to *The Times* on behalf of the Public Assistance Committee,[24] which occupied a room at Denison House, the home not only of the COS but of other charitable organizations (like the National Anti-Vaccination League)[25] hostile to legislation in the health field.

The movement Drage started before the First World War gathered momentum after 1918, particularly when the economy began to run into transitional problems. At that point, the COS bloc was joined by an array of reactionary forces, ranging from Henry Page (later Lord) Croft and the National Party on the one hand[26] to the Northcliffe-Rothermere press on the other.[27] The attack then developed (in the autumn of 1920) into a full-blown economy campaign, directed against public expenditure generally. At that point, the Conservative MP, Godfrey Locker-Lampson, organized a People's Union of Economy — while Lady Askwith enlisted female support.[28] Nor were the anti-vivisectionists absent: Banbury himself took charge of the campaign in Parliament, hoping thereby to make Addison pay for thwarting his Dog's Bill.[a]

In time, so many interests joined the economy campaign that the Government came under pressure and lost one by-election after another.[29] Even the local authorities — the 'progressive' bodies on which the Webbs had placed such hopes — ranged themselves on the side of those who resisted reform. The authorities were the ones who were supposed to make possible the end of the Poor Law but most of them rejected the challenge outright. 'The attempt which was made to uproot or shake the old Poor-Law system', observed one of their journals in 1921, 'found practically no support amongst the County Councils and the municipalities, some of whom were very emphatic in their refusal to undertake this work.'[30] Even the doctors showed less resistence to reform. The Medical Consultative Council eventually (in December 1920) came out for a free hospital service[b] — but the municipal council, 7 months later, flatly opposed the idea, and prepared a report calling for charges on patients.[31]

Since the Dawson Report recommended the transformation of Poor Law infirmaries into primary health centres, it immediately roused the COS caucus to action.[32] The support of the other groups in the economy campaign was enlisted by calling attention to the vast expenditure the report entailed. Eventually even the most prestigious paper in Northcliffe's stable — *The*

a   See pp. 39-40 above.
b   See p. 67 above.

Times — added its voice to the clamour. When the Dawson Report first appeared, the paper had nothing but praise for primary health centres since they promised to give GPs access to beds.[33] Only the more elaborate secondary centres, it felt, deserved to be attacked. No such fine distinction, however, appeared in the criticisms made by Sir James Barr and other economy-minded doctors from the medical world. After Barr estimated the cost of the scheme at £100 million for the first 5 years and £150 million for the next 5,[34] one of his colleagues denounced all Dawson's health centres as 'nothing more or less than elaborate hospitals' which would bankrupt the nation.[35] This led *The Times,* after it joined the economy campaign in October 1920, to forget the distinction it had earlier made; now, it, too, denounced Dawson's 'fantastically costly schemes' as a whole.[36]

Unfortunately for Dawson, the civil servants at the Ministry of Health shared these fears. Shortly after the report appeared, Newman was swift to point out how the council had failed to consider the 'financial implications' of its programme.[37] Others, no doubt, had expressed the same criticism earlier, but Addison went ahead with publication all the same.[a]

He did not make the same mistake with the more costly schemes prepared by the patients' council: the reports of that body were doomed even before they arrived on Addison's desk. The first contained only modest expense proposals and was suppressed for reasons other than money. It dealt with maternity care and was also prepared quickly[b] — but this was done not so much to accommodate Addison as to have the report ready for presentation to the National Conference of Labour Women in April 1920. The civil servants at the Ministry protested strongly at such tactics and Addison endorsed their stand. The councils were his bodies, and he did not want them to regulate their affairs with reference to outside organizations. Consequently, when Lady Rhondda requested permission to publish the report, Addison refused. As a result she resigned from the council in June.[38]

Greenwood, who succeeded her, had no more success with the report he prepared. This put health care for all above the constraints of finance[c] and its deliberate disdain of cost considerations touched off an explosion at the Ministry. The new Permanent Secretary, Sir Arthur Robinson, did not share Morant's passion for health. He urged Addison not only to reject the report but to disband the patients' council: 'I understand the Council was brought to birth rather by a side wind and if this present report is an indication of its form its termination would not be matter for much regret.'[39]

To this was added the weight of general economic considerations. The country, in adjusting from war to peace, passed through a period of great uncertainty — so much so that Addison had to reject a medical claim for higher pay in terms which suggested that he had no intention of extending the service.[40] This occurred at the start of 1920 — even before the Dawson Report appeared — and the economic situation grew more perilous as the year

a   For more about this, see p. 93 below.

b   See p. 75 above.

c   See p. 50 above.

progressed.[41] By November, when the second report of the patients' council appeared, Addison had no choice: he told the council it would be 'a grave tactical mistake' to publish its call for a complete service.[42] Such a move, he warned, 'would not be practicable for an indefinite period' — and the onset of the depression in 1921 made that period much longer than Addison had foreseen. As a result, the patients' council collapsed and nothing like it has been attempted since.[a]

In the end, all Addison could do was make minor changes in the panel system. When he tried to remove the Poor Law infirmaries from guardian control through the guise of a Miscellaneous Provisions Bill,[b] he raised a storm which, in conjunction with the mistakes he made in the field of housing, drove him from office. Lloyd George found it expedient to force him out in 2 stages — first, in March 1921, by making him Minister without Portfolio, and then 3 months later, by having that appointment terminated at the end of the Parliamentary session. The end, when it came, was done brutally and Addison never forgave Lloyd George. The 2 men, who had been through so much together in 1912, remained bitter enemies for the rest of their lives.[43]

By the summer of 1921, then, all hope of reform had passed, and those who were left at the Ministry had their hands full just trying to preserve what had been gained since 1911.

a   Community health councils were formed in each area when the Health Service was reorganized in 1974 but no national council has yet emerged similar to the one the Ministry created in 1919.

b   This Bill, which was introduced on 16 August 1920, was concerned mainly with housing but Addison added to it a few clauses dealing with hospitals.

8
Doctors Resist Salary

The doctors, in 1919, could not have foreseen the events to come and their main concern, when the Medical Consultative Council held its first meeting in October, was to ward off the threat of a salaried service.[1] This was no slight danger. Lloyd George himself had been strongly in favour of the proposal during the 1912 dispute and had gone so far as to prepare plans for a salaried service in Bradford.[2] Though such action proved unnecessary after medical opposition collapsed, there was no reason to believe that Lloyd George had changed his mind after he became Prime Minister in 1916. According to a report that appeared in a medical journal in December 1918, one Government committee actually prepared a salaried scheme with salaries ranging from £400 to £1,500 per annum.[3]

Though no trace of such action can now be found in the Public Records Office, there is no doubt that feeling for a salaried service was strong within the ranks of the civil service. That had been the dream of top administrators ever since Morant took charge of NHI in 1912. Any kind of salaried service, they felt, was preferable to the costly and complex panel system which the doctors themselves had done so much to devise.

Nor were they alone in this view: many approved society officials felt similarly. Before the war they had been alarmed by the sharp rise in sick claims that had followed the start of NHI, and they saw in salary a way for panel doctors to free themselves from patient pressure.[4] Though claims fell during the war, interest in the subject revived at the start of 1920 when the Association of Approved Societies published a scheme for a state medical service similar to the one the Webbs had devised.[5]

This came as no surprise to those who knew the history of the Association. It was started in 1913 by Alban Gordon, an approved society official who had long been active in the Fabian Society.[6] Gordon then worked closely with the Webbs as well as with another Fabian, George P. Blizard, who later became (in 1918) Secretary of the Labour Party's newly-formed Public Health Advisory Committee.[7] From 1913 on, Gordon's aim was to win acceptance from the NHI world for the salaried scheme outlined by the Webbs and he had managed to secure some support just before the war broke out. In July 1914 a committee which he and the Association created issued a draft report calling for a salaried service.[8]

Though the societies which formed the Association lacked stature in the NHI world (consisting of small friendly societies, trade unions, church groups and other voluntary organizations), the members of the committee who produced the report possessed much influence. They included not only Beatrice Webb and Lord Lytton (who acted as chairman) but the secretaries of the BMA and the Pharmaceutical Society. Cox, by his presence, showed that he intended to maintain the contacts he had made during his socialist days. Though he dissented from the salary proposal contained in the report, he supported its call for wider coverage.

The war, however, prevented further action and Gordon himself entered the armed forces in 1916.[9] Still, the Fabian tradition which he implanted in the Association remained. It was carried on by Dan T. Jenkins, a trade unionist from the iron and steel industry who (during 1920) replaced Blizard as Secretary of Labour's Public Health Advisory Committee.[10] The report which Jenkins and the Association issued in February 1920 startled the NHI world with its call for a salaried service and its severe indictment of the panel system.[11]

Shortly afterwards, the patients' consultative council completed its report calling for wider maternity care but it was suppressed while the one prepared by Dawson was rushed into print.[a] When the latter appeared in May, Cox immediately declared himself for it 'because it gave the public something very much better than the public had at present, and in the second place it enabled the profession to stave off the demand made by academic people and others to nationalise the medical profession'.[12] By 'academic people', Cox meant Professor Benjamin Moore, the President of SMSA, who, through the Labour Party's Public Health Advisory Committee, was trying to push the doctors in the direction of a salaried service.

Even before the report appeared, however, the danger of salary had receded. Public opinion was still ripe for such a service and the department vastly preferred it. But civil servants are nothing if not pragmatic and they recognized that it would be suicidal to introduce a salaried service without medical assent. Their attitude was revealed in a memorandum written for the NHI Commissioners in 1918 on the subject of the development of an extended medical service for insured persons. (The document was not signed but Whitaker, who was responsible for such questions at the Commission, probably prepared it.) At the end of a long statement describing the various reforms needed, the author explained why he had not dealt with the possibility of whole-time service or salaried employment. The main reason, he admitted, was the opposition of the profession:

> '. . . although undoubtedly more doctors are now in favour of a whole-time service than would have been favourable to it in 1911, the great majority are still hostile. An attempt to introduce it might provoke opposition which, even if overcome, might have prejudicial effects on the service lasting for many years and seriously out-weighing any attendant balance of advantage on other grounds. Whereas if opinion is allowed to ripen it may be that working of the service under the new conditions indicated herein will gradually bring about such a change in the doctor's outlook that the introduction of whole-time service will come about as, in their *then* view, a natural inevitable or

a   See p. 77 above.

even welcome step in the evolution of medical practice.'[13]

Charles Masterman, it seemed, agreed with this judgement. Earlier, he had been Chairman of the NHI Commission and one of the main policy-makers during the struggle over the introduction of the Act. Though he left office in 1914, Masterman never lost interest in NHI and, writing as a journalist in May 1919, he said that the creation of a salaried service 'depended largely on the doctors themselves':

> '. . . If there is a strong desire that the doctors shall become civil servants, with salaries, holidays, pensions and conditions appropriate to Government service, the change will be speedily accomplished. If there is a substantial opposition from the profession, an agitation against the 'State doctor' with mysterious and quasi-compulsory powers over whole blocks of the population would probably prevent its passage into law.'[14]

Uncertain medical support for salary

Medical support for salary had grown during the war due to the dislocation of practices. By January 1917 over half the doctors in the country had been called up for military service[15] and, partnerships being less prevalent then, few medical men had colleagues at home to protect them. The profession did set up schemes to preserve practices but nearly all foundered on the rock of medical greed.[a] The doctors who participated found the temptation to add patients too great to resist — and they were reluctant to hand over any of the increased earnings they enjoyed.[17] Doctors who entered the armed forces soon realized that they would have to start afresh once the war ended, and that made many interested in the security of a salaried service.[18]

Feeling for salary reached its height in 1917 when the *British Medical Journal* published an exchange of articles between Dr Gordon Ward (an articulate GP who later played an active role in the MPU) and Brackenbury.[19] Ward argued for salary while Brackenbury took the opposing view. Even then, however, most doctors who were active in the BMA agreed with Brackenbury as reflected in the fact that the organization's 2 main policy-making bodies flatly rejected the idea later in the year.[20] Only one Division (the local unit of BMA organization)[21] and 2 BMA leaders[22] came out openly for it.

No one, however, knew the feeling of the profession at large and in September 1918 the MPU made an attempt to assess the opinion of doctors in the armed forces. This survey was probably carried out with the aid of Dr G. Rome Hall, Deputy Medical Commissioner of the Ministry of

---

a   Non-panel doctors probably suffered even greater losses than panel doctors. The latter were sometimes excused from military service on the grounds that they were needed more at home than at the Front.[16] This induced many non-panel doctors (particularly in London where opposition had been most intense) to abandon their boycott of NHI. The war thus led to an increase in the number of doctors on the panel as well as to greater sympathy within the profession for a salaried service. Similar dislocations and changes in attitude occurred during the Second World War, thereby paving the way for the creation of the National Health Service. See p. 183 below.

National Service. Hall was then a leading advocate of a salaried service (his views, like those of many others, changed in the 1920s) and, before the war, he had been active in the formation of the Socialist Medical League as well as the SMSA.[23][a] In 1914, he designed a salaried service that was intended to remove the profession's fear of bureaucratic control: under it, the doctors themselves would run the service by means of self-governing guilds and group practices.[b]

The plan appeared in *Medical World,* a journal which, when it began publication in August 1913, was meant to provide an outlet for SMSA views.[24] That approach, however, failed to attract a sufficient number of readers and its owner (and editor), Dr Walter Malden of Cambridge,[c] gradually turned the journal into a medium for the panel doctors who formed the MPU in July 1914. Hall's articles appeared shortly after the MPU began[26] and he wrote another in 1918 after the MPU purchased *Medical World* from Malden.[27] This suggests that Hall (who joined the MPU himself in November 1916) had close ties with MPU leaders[28] and he probably arranged the canvass of army opinion.[29] No results, however, were ever published and, since the MPU joined the campaign against a salaried service a few months later, we can safely assume that medical opinion was not favourable. Even before the poll was taken, the MPU protected itself against an adverse result by declaring its opposition to a salaried service for GPs.[30]

What deterred many doctors was the experience of salaried employment in medical aid institutions under friendly society rule.[d] In 1911, the BMA had insisted that they be excluded from NHI and, though that effort failed, the profession did manage to bar the admission of new ones formed after the Act passed through Parliament.[31] In 1919, however, many doctors feared that the state itself would act as a spur to further development. As one of them put it: 'It will be strange indeed if medical aid societies, which the profession abhorred and determinedly fought against in 1911, are to be accepted and adopted in 1919 because they are State-aided and State-supported?'[32]

Support for salary thus did not reach far or high in BMA circles and feeling for it among the rank-and-file did not long survive the end of the war. Though demobilization proceeded faster than BMA leaders desired, flooding some areas with a surfeit of doctors, over the country as a whole they were far from superfluous. The war took its toll of the medical profession as it did of British manhood generally. Fewer doctors, indeed, may have joined the panel after the war than before it. Such was the claim made by the leading

a   For the connection between these organizations and the MPU, see pp. 54-5 above.

b   For more about this idea, see pp. 107-8 below.

c   Though Malden was owner of *Medical World,* apparently he was not responsible for starting the journal. That, rather, was due to a leader of the SMSA who had married into the Cambridge academic community — the Quaker dentist, F. Lawson Dodd. His links with the Fabian Society were as close as the Webbs (he served as Treasurer from 1911 to 1936) but, unlike them, he supported NHI and thus had no reservations about using it as a starting-point for a larger development. Another Fabian, Dr George F. McCleary, felt similarly, and he was the one who told Beatrice Webb about Dodd's role in the formation of *Medical World.*[25]

d   See p. 13 above.

organization of non-panel doctors, the National Medical Union (NMU), where the city of Glasgow was concerned: there, it said, over half the profession failed to enrol.[33] The Ministry, on the other hand, reported a participation rate of over 80% throughout the country as a whole[34] and this certainly applied during the depression years after 1921. Then almost all GPs had to join the panel to survive. But, whatever the facts in the immediate post-war period, one point was clear: it did not take the doctors long to settle back in practice and forget their sympathy for salary. The pendulum swung so far that proposals were heard for a return to the 'attendance system' — or so much per item of service (in America, called 'fee-for-service') — which the profession had preferred in 1911.[35 a]

Only in MOH circles did feeling for whole-time service remain strong. The Dawson Report promised to end the splintering of municipal health care and give MOHs the unified control they desired[36] — but that did not satisfy those in the public health world who doubted the ability of GPs to run local authority clinics.[37] Even worse, MOHs disliked the implied future pattern of care outlined in the Report: all that was needed, it seemed to suggest, was GPs working with consultants. Public health doctors took this to mean that they would eventually be cut out, and their suspicions were heightened by the absence of what they considered to be adequate representation on the medical council itself. Though 2 of its 20 members were MOHs, neither had been recommended by the Society of MOHs and no public health doctor had found a place on any of the other consultative councils, not even the one dealing with local health administration.[38]

MOHs also felt threatened by the Report's call for a large number of medical representatives on the local authority that was to administer the new unified health service. In the medical council's view, three-fifths of the authority were to consist of elected members but as many as two-fifths were to be co-opted, and local doctors (operating through a local medical advisory committee much like the local medical committees that existed under NHI) were to nominate the majority of these.[39] To MOHs, this represented a direct challenge and, in rebuttal, they cast aspersions on how local doctors might act: 'Medical practitioners co-opted upon a local body inevitably and naturally have quite a different view point from that of the medical officer of health. The MOH views everything from the point of the patient and the public good, whereas medical practitioners view it from the point of view of professional interest.'[40]

So angry were MOHs with the Dawson Report that they denounced it as 'the beatification of the GP and the canonisation of the consultant.'[40] According to the leading public health journal, if the report were adopted, 'the public health service as at present exists will be consigned to the scrap heap, and the structure laboriously erected during recent decades will be ruthlessly demolished.'[41]

---

a   This method of payment was permitted under NHI as an alternative to the capitation system but it was surrounded with conditions that it made unacceptable to most doctors. For more on this, see p. 163 below.

BMA alters MOH opinion

BMA leaders thus faced considerable opposition from MOH quarters but they managed to alter opinion by becoming the trade union spokesmen for the public health corps. Some GPs still favoured low public health salaries as a means of discouraging recruitment, thus curbing the spread of whole-time service. This, apparently, was the unspoken reason behind the BMA's failure vigorously to take up MOH grievances before.[42]

But one of the main effects of NHI (and the war) had been to push GP incomes above levels prevailing in the public health sector. Before 1911, the average GP earned nett, after expenses, about £400 a year, while most MOHs received more. By 1919, however, the average GP's income had risen to about £1,200; yet that of most MOHs still remained less than £1,000. Only MOHs located in large towns could match GP incomes: they received £1,200 a year. (Whole-time clinic doctors earned much less — about £700.) It was said in 1922 that a new panel doctor started at a rate equal to the highest-paid MOH and 4 times above the amount paid to a beginner in the public health service.[43]

With panel incomes well above public health levels, the opposite danger for GPs had emerged: if public health salaries remained too low, the Government might find the cost saving too great and introduce a whole-time system. Furthermore, as the 1921 pay cut and the 1923 pay dispute later demonstrated, low salaries in the public health sector acted as a drag on panel incomes.[44]

The full implications of these changes did not become clear until well after the Dawson Report appeared but enough was evident, by 1919, to show the direction in which the BMA should be heading. At the end of the year, therefore, BMA leaders offered the Society of MOHs aid in a salary campaign. The Society accepted.[45] In doing so, it had to descend from the lofty position it had taken previously. The Society had considered salary questions to be beneath its dignity — so much so that it tended to keep its distance from the BMA because of that organization's obsession with economic affairs. Thus, although the Society did appoint representatives to the BMA's Insurance Acts Committee as early as 1915, it preferred to join hands with the Royal Colleges during the dispute over the Ministry of Health.[46]

The BMA had difficulties of its own where co-operation with MOHs was concerned: many GPs simply did not want to do anything to help those who worked in the public-health world, whether it was to their advantage or not. Somehow such opposition had to be overcome and, in an attempt to do it, BMA leaders thought it best to let MOHs take the initiative at the Annual Representative Meeting in 1920.[47] A formal request for aid in a salary campaign thus came from an officer of the Society of MOHs — Dr G.F. Buchan of Willesden — but, since he was the MOH who had most threatened GPs with the spread of municipal services,[48] many doctors baulked. Not until 1923 did they endorse the salary scale which the MOHs had proposed in 1920 and even then the figures had to be lowered before the profession would assent.[49] After that, however, the joint BMA-MOH campaign gathered momentum and scored one success after another.[50]

The way for this co-operation was opened in 1921 by a victory the BMA won for MOHs on the vital question of employment security. Here achievement had been so long delayed that a review of its history is needed in order to appreciate the significance of the changes the BMA secured. Poor Law doctors obtained tenure rights as early as 1844 and Section 191 of the 1875 Public Health Act gave the LGB power to confer the same security on MOHs if it paid part of their salary. Thereafter, protection was extended to MOHs in London, Scotland and Ireland but, despite repeated pleas from the profession and recommendations from Government bodies, nothing was done for the rest of the corps in England and Wales until 1909 when the Housing and Town Planning Act granted tenure to the 62 MOHs employed on the county level.[51]

That still left hundreds of district MOHs exposed to the danger of sudden removal and it was more important to protect them since they were the ones who came in contact with owners of small house property.[a] Herbert Samuel, the President of the LGB, was ready to help in 1914 but the war intervened and nothing was actually done until the new Ministry was created.[52] Then Addison made use of the new local government Consultative Council to issue an order granting tenure. It applied, however, only to new appointees, not to existing office-holders; fresh legislation was needed to cover them. Finally in 1921, the BMA secured the passage of an Act which extended tenure to nearly all whole-timers.[53]

One result — no doubt foreseen by BMA leaders — was to lessen the drive for an extended municipal service emanating from MOH quarters. Until tenure was granted, many MOHs thought they could obtain protection against discharge by increasing the scope of their work. After it was provided, fewer felt the need to do so.

All this gave Newman the freedom he needed to placate GPs and, even before the tenure Act passed, he came out strongly against the whole-time principle. 'The State', he told the Medical Sociology Section of the BMA in 1920, 'should not take out of the hands of the medical practitioner —whether in contract practice or otherwise — the patient whom he is willing and competent to treat on reasonable terms with which the patient can comply.'[54] He then set out to make GPs competent to handle local authority work by changing the pattern of medical education[55] — and this, it was hoped, would also make them interested in undertaking the challenge. Previously, as the Deputy Medical Secretary of the BMA (Dr G. C. Anderson) admitted, they had shown much indifference to the subject: 'Medical men throughout the country had only this previous apathy to blame if they were not at the present time participating in the various clinics they might be doing. They largely neglected the invitation to discuss the matter which was offered to them when the maternity and child-welfare clinics were first mooted.'[56]

The effect of these events on MOH opinion was startling. As early as 1921, a

a MOHs everywhere had difficult duties under the Housing Acts since they were required to enforce sanitary regulations that might impose heavy costs on home-owners. In the smaller areas covered by district councils, their position was more perilous than elsewhere because of the closer ties existing between councillors and rate-payers.

group of influential MOHs, meeting in joint conference with the BMA, declared their willingness to accept the principle of part-time service in local authority clinics.[57] [a] Even Dr Robert Lyster, then the leading figure in the MOH world, did a *volte-face*. When the panel came under sharp criticism in 1921, Lyster rose to the defence of the very system he had earlier condemned as 'rotten' and 'doomed'.[60]

Convergence of medical opinion

Once the tide began to turn against them, even the militant medical socialists in the SMSA showed a willingness to compromise. Until 1917, they had campaigned strongly for salary, believing that the pressures unleashed by the war would make its realization inevitable. As Dr Charles Parker, the Secretary of the Association put it, the current of events 'is flowing slowly, steadily and unalterably toward a State Medical Service, and its strength has been intensified by the war, which has brought so prominently before the nation the importance of health and physical fitness and the urgent necessity for the preservation of child life.'[61]

But as early as April 1918 Professor Benjamin Moore, the President of the Association, announced his readiness to accept part-time salary as a temporary expedient.[62] A few months later, he (and Parker) went even further in an attempt to placate the profession on the question of administration: '. . . the doctors must be left to manage all purely medical matters and must be given the predominating voice in determining the conditions under which they will serve the community.'[63]

Ordinarily, in any struggle over an issue so emotive as that of a salaried service, one would have expected the main opposition to have come from the right wing of the profession, led then by the NMU and its affiliate, the Medical Guild of Edinburgh. But this was not the case. The NMU actually came out for salary where a medical service for the poor was concerned[64] and this, it will be recalled, was exactly what the Webbs advocated in their Minority Report on the Poor Law. How can this curious convergence of views be explained? The answer lay in the desire of each to protect private practice.[b] Both thought the best way to do so was by confining state aid to a narrow sector of the population and then penalizing those who received it with the denial of free choice of doctor. Conceived in such terms, the salaried idea was anything but 'progressive' and it was no wonder that the NMU embraced it.

The main opposition to salary, rather, came from the 'expansionist' wing of the profession — those who wished to extend the helping hand of the state beyond the borders of NHI — and this position was occupied by a centre party

---

a   By the 1930s, some MOHs even wanted GPs to do clinic work in order to ease the burden on assistant medical officers and speed up their promotion to MOH posts.[58] Not all MOHs, however, could act, for as the President of the Society of MOHs (Dr James Fenton) admitted in 1938: '. . . when a doctor entered the local government service he was no longer a free agent, and the degree of co-operation with his colleagues was not always within his control.'[59]

b   For the Webb interest in this subject, see pp. 52-3 above.

which concentrated its policy-making efforts on the BMA. It was led, initially, by Dr Lauriston Shaw but, after he lost his place on the BMA's Council,[a] direction passed into the hands of another Liberal, Dr Henry Brackenbury. This transfer of power was probably no accident; in any case, no better successor could have been found. With a subtlety unrivalled in medical history, Brackenbury — aided by Dawson — headed off the movement towards salary so that it no longer presented a danger to the profession.

In the process, an accommodation occurred which set the stage, 30 years later, for the creation of the National Health Service. The centre party, led by Brackenbury and the BMA, moved left in recognition of the public demand for extended coverage, while the left wing, represented by Moore and the SMSA, shifted towards the centre in recognition of the profession's fear of bureaucratic control.[65] This was reflected in the report prepared in 1919 by the Labour Party's Advisory Committee on Public Health. While proposing a comprehensive service open to all, it left scope for medical influence in administration: '. . . the coming Service must not be bureaucratic, but one more resembling the chapters or lodges of a skilled craft.'[66] Beyond that, it not only ruled out any ban on private practice but sought, through a public service, to widen the area of free choice for everyone: 'The new system must win on its merits, and be judged with perfect freedom by each individual, who will freely take up his own attitude towards it.'[66 b]

On the controversial question of salary, the report was deliberately vague. Only where consultants were concerned did it mention the word: they were to be employed on a whole-time salaried basis 'as far as possible'.[68] GPs, by contrast, were to be given the option of part-time contracts, and nothing was said about how they were to be paid. All the report indicated was that the 'terms of service should be fair and generous'.[68] What this implied was later suggested by Moore. The salary question, he admitted, was secondary: '. . . the important thing was that the service should be well paid.'[69]

Shaw served on the Labour Committee along with Moore and Parker. Even the BMA was allowed to appoint representatives on the understanding that those appointed would be sympathetic to Labour.[70] This, however, failed to satisfy the socialist intellectual, G.D.H. Cole, who served as director of all the advisory committees created by the Party. He resigned in March 1920 after failing to dislodge the non-Labour members. No indication was given as to who the latter were, but Cox himself later served on the committee and defended his appointment on the grounds that he was still a socialist. The BMA, he claimed, had consented to the arrangement in order to keep abreast of Labour's plans.[71] In 1923, he and Brackenbury went so far as to help the Party prepare a report on NHI's

a   See p. 55 above.

b   Earlier the SMSA had played down the importance of free choice in a state service. Patient interests, Parker wrote to Addison in January 1918, would be protected not only by restrictions on medical entry but also by consultant referrals. The latter would give highly qualified specialists a chance to check the efficiency of GPs.[67]

medical benefit. For this assistance — which was given openly — they were severely criticized by the non-panel doctors who belonged to the NMU.[72]

Beatrice Webb was also a member of the advisory committee in 1919 and she no doubt did her best to harmonize the views of the opposing sides. Indeed, just before the committee issued its report on a new service, one BMA leader (Bishop Harman) told the profession that it could trust Sidney Webb (and Dr Peter Macdonald) to lead Labour away from a salaried service.[73] He was not disappointed: the party produced a report which anticipated the document Dawson later prepared for the Medical Consultative Council.[74] Nor was Harman himself silent on the subject. At a conference which the BMA held jointly with the Labour Party in 1924, he indicated what it would take to have the doctors accept state control of the hospital service. Municipal management, he declared, would not do; what was needed instead was a form of 'worker's control':

> '. . . The Chairman and others had used the magic phrase "Guild Socialism". The withdrawal of the hospital service from the routine of statutory committees and the humdrum routine of statutory authority would be one of the greatest experiments in Guild Socialism, which every Fabian should welcome with open arms. The public authority was quite in its right place in dealing with drains and sewers, but in an institution of the intricacy and delicacy of a voluntary hospital, its influence did not make for efficiency, but the reverse. Let there be Guild Socialism for hospitals throughout England and he and his friends would be perfectly satisfied.'[75]

Addison rules out a salaried service

Addison, in a public interview,[76] had ruled out a salaried service as early as January 1919, but that was probably no real guide to the Government's intentions. At that time, the Ministry Bill had not yet passed through Parliament and Addison needed the profession's support. In view of the Prime Minister's long-standing preference for salary, Addison would not have rejected that method of payment if the doctors had forced it on him.

But the profession, through the Dawson Report, made its opposition to salary abundantly clear. It preferred to give the panel time to prove itself. As one member of the medical council (Dr Alfred Linnell) put it: 'We cannot help feeling that the panel system has not been given a fair trial and that judgement should be suspended until the promised improvements are in working order.'[77] Addison therefore dropped all thought of salary and concentrated his efforts on the modest reforms negotiated with the BMA in 1919.

As early as November 1918, one prominent physician — Sir Wilmot Herringham (then a Major General) — not only predicted this would happen but explained why:

> '. . . The Insurance Act was difficult enough to pass but this would be twice as difficult. The Insurance Act resulted in a much-needed and considerable increase in professional incomes, and it relieved doctors from slavery to the clubs. This change would offer no increase of income, and very small

advantage of other kinds. The only grounds on which a Government would take it up would be a general desire for it on the part of the profession, and an obvious advantage to the public by improvement in practice. I think it would be resisted by us, and would not only not improve, but would generally lower the standard of practice. It does not appear to be within the range of practical politics.'[78]

As the threat of salary receded, so did the profession's interest in the Dawson Report.[79] It revived when the Bradford Borough Council, assuming control of a Poor Law infirmary on shaky statutory grounds, began to staff it on a whole-time basis. Even the department seemed to support the move: Addison added a clause to the Ministry's Miscellaneous Provisions Bill which removed doubts about the legality of such transfers and authorized council subscriptions to voluntary hospitals.[a] For a while, the extension of state intervention seemed imminent and no one needed to remind the profession that Bradford had been the place where Lloyd George almost introduced a salaried service in 1912.[80] But the crisis passed when the Lords threw out Addison's clause and Bradford dropped its plans for a whole-time service.[81] The Government made no further attempt at local unification and, in the face of the depression beginning in 1921, dropped its extension plans as well. Addison left office and with him went all thought of the Dawson Report.

a   For more about this Bill, see p. 78 above.

Part 3
Erosion of the
Health Centre Idea
1920-1929

Political pressures arising from the economy campaign and its new
medical record inspection programme prevented the Ministry from
implementing the Dawson Report, but opposition also developed on
policy grounds. Originally conceived as a collective surgery, the health
centre was expanded to the point where it would contain all the health
facilities a patient would require. Dawson did this mainly as a means
of unifying the profession but GPs feared close contact with MOHs
and consultants. Dawson also gave precedence to institutional
development, but a rival school of thought placed community care
first. This led to the gradual erosion of the health-centre idea. By the
time the profession finished with it, all that remained was a hospital
for the exclusive use of GPs.

9

The Ministry of Health Under Attack

The profession's interest in the Dawson Report was clearly related to the question of a salaried service. Once the threat of that receded, the doctors were free to turn their minds elsewhere.

But was this the only reason for the demise of the Report? Why did Dawson and his colleagues never issue any further statements on the subject? The Report, after all, was only an interim one and Dawson never intended it to be more than that. It was designed, he said, to show a trend of thought, not final conclusions, and he was fully aware of its imperfections: 'No one in the world was better able to destroy the Report of the Consultative Council than himself; there was no report ever brought up through which one could not drive a coach and four.'[1] The Report, he expected, would take 20 years to implement, and many aspects would have to be modified in the process. All he wanted, at the start, were 12 experimental health centres. With those established, the ideas he outlined were capable of 'infinite adaptation'.[2]

The Ministry, however, was not disposed to give him even one health centre. Costs were only one consideration. Far more important was the danger posed to the department itself if it showed any signs of moving towards a wider public health service. Here the threat arose from the economy campaign.[a] The civil servants at the Ministry had been frightened by the intensity of the attack launched on them by *The Times* and its medical correspondent, MacNair Wilson. A great admirer of Morant, MacNair Wilson was friendly to the department and generally supported its policies until Morant died in March 1920. But when *The Times* joined the economy campaign the following October, MacNair Wilson abruptly changed front. Week after week, he assailed Addison and his 'boa-constrictor Ministry'[3] for his costly schemes and his attempts to extend administrative control over panel doctors.

The attack opened just before the Miscellaneous Provisions Bill was presented to Parliament and *The Times* devoted much space to the denigration of that measure.[4] But MacNair Wilson did not stop there: after the Lords threw out the Bill in December, he renewed the attack, choosing as his target a subject on which the Ministry was even more vulnerable — its attempts to improve the clinical records kept by panel doctors.

a   See pp. 75-7 above.

Record-keeping by GPs

Record-keeping was the main duty Lloyd George added to the panel when he increased his pay offer to the profession in October 1912.[5] The records introduced then, however, were poorly conceived and badly designed. They came in the form of day sheets which covered no less than 6 square feet of table space.[6] Even worse, they were divided into 2 sections that were eventually separated from each other and sent to different places. The first part contained the name of the patient and a detailed account of the number of times he had seen the doctor during the course of the year; the second part gave only the total number of attendances and a description of the kinds of illnesses treated. The former went to the appropriate insurance committee and was used solely for pay purposes; the latter went to the NHI Commissioners and was intended to provide statistics for preventive medicine.

In the process of operating the Act, however, both purposes were lost. Since the doctors in all but 2 areas chose to be paid by capitation,[a] insurance committees had no need of details of attendance: all they wanted to know was the total number of patients on each doctor's list. Similarly, Whitaker and his staff made little use of the statistics they received as far as the practice of preventive medicine was concerned: the data was too sparse to apply in a methodical sense. The only way they could employ it was during the course of pay negotiations when disputes arose over the amount of work done by panel doctors.

As far as clinical practice was concerned, the records were never of any use since neither section remained with the doctor. At the start of each year, he received a new day sheet, and, if he wanted to know what illnesses appeared on the old one, the Commissioners could not tell him because the section they received had no space for the name of the patient. This strange omission was no accident: it had been necessitated by the political furore which accompanied the introduction of NHI. The patient's name had to be left off the section sent to the Commissioners in order to silence those who said that the Act violated canons of medical secrecy.[7]

Though Whitaker limply defended this anachronistic procedure, he was grateful for the excuse the war gave to suspend it. Everyone in 1919 felt that the time had come for a fresh start and all (including the BMA as well as Newman) [8] were agreed on the need, in future, to emphasize the clinical objects of record-keeping. Negotiations on a new contract for panel doctors began even before the war ended — in February 1918 — and record-keeping was only one of many subjects covered. R.W. Harris — a layman in the Ministry's employ who exercised much influence over the early development of the panel system — wanted to have the duties spelled out before pay questions were settled,[9] but Morant, no doubt because he sensed the trouble ahead, preferred to wait. Only a general obligation was written into the regulations. The details were left to a committee and,

a   See p. 163 below.

recognizing the need to find a chairman the profession would accept, Morant turned to the eminent GP-physician, Sir James Mackenzie.[10]

No finer choice could have been made. Mackenzie was a lowly GP who had risen to the heights of his profession through dint of record-keeping.[11] By 1920 he was a recognized authority on heart disease, but the research which established his reputation was not carried out in a laboratory. It was done in Mackenzie's own surgery, and the tools he used were those available to every GP — his observations of his own afflicted patients. Since no cures were available, this led Mackenzie to focus his attention on the early stages of heart disease in an attempt to ascertain its causes. In the process, he became known as a 'physician' who specialized in the treatment of heart disease but this was misleading: he was, rather, a doctor who specialized in ways of preventing it. His methods had more in common with those who pursued public health and epidemiology than with those who practised in the hospital world.

This explains, no doubt, why Mackenzie failed to obtain a place in a hospital. Despite repeated attempts, he could not interest other heart specialists in his work, and they refused (except for a short period) to give him beds of his own.[12] This forced him to plough a lonely furrow at St Andrew's Clinic in Scotland, an institution of his own making, and the experiment did not long survive his death. One can understand, therefore, Mackenzie's vitriolic hatred of those who excluded him from the hospital world: '. . . specialism', he declared in 1922, 'is a curse, which misdirects every subject in which it is introduced.'[13]

With that judgement many GPs agreed. They, too, had been scorned by those at the top of the hospital ladder and they also felt threatened by the inroads which the new specialties were making into general practice. Mackenzie, in 1920, was the idol of every GP in the land and no one could have done more to instil in them the desire to maintain decent records. Morant was right to have selected him to lead the way.

Despite Mackenzie's obvious qualifications, however, Newman had doubts and they were stirred further by one authority who reviewed Mackenzie's work for the Ministry. This was Dr James Pearse, a GP of high standing who occupied the same position in Ministry circles as Dr Talbot Rogers did in the 1960s and Dr Tony Keable-Elliot does today. According to Pearse, Mackenzie's work tended not so much to early diagnosis as to the unravelling of physical manifestations previously undifferentiated — and, even on this score, it had yielded only meagre results. 'Mackenzie has unravelled the maze of cardiac irregularity', Pearse observed in a memorandum he wrote for the Ministry in January 1920, 'but are we nearer the cause of, say, auricular fibrillation?' [14]

Leaving this aside, the manner of the man apparently left something to be desired: Newman, for one, found him tedious and boring. When Morant, at the end of 1919, finally decided to ask the great man to chair the committee, Newman baulked: he did not relish the prospect of having to listen to Mackenzie 'by the hour'.[15] In the end, however, he was spared the agony for Mackenzie declined the appointment. Mackenzie's interests in record-keeping, it now became clear, were different from those held by the Ministry. He saw them mainly — almost solely — as a tool for medical research; otherwise, he had doubts about their usefulness in the existing state of medical knowledge. Most patients, he told Morant, suffer from ailments in which there are no definite physical signs, or the signs that exist have no relation to ill-health. Hence, he argued, the Ministry would not be able to obtain the records it desired for the purpose of clinical practice.[16]

Morant, in reply, claimed that any records were better than none and BMA leaders agreed with him. Even as late as 1932, when the programme had come repeatedly under attack, the Secretary of the BMA (then Dr G.C. Anderson) defended it in the following terms:

'. . . This is the only record of the diseases of his patients required from the insurance practitioner, and to suggest that he is not capable of keeping such records is clearly absurd; nor can their value either to doctor or to patient, as a continuous record of the health of the individual and the result of the treatment adopted, be overestimated.'[17]

The department, therefore, did not scrap the committee. On the contrary, it appointed a distinguished academic physician — Sir Humphrey Rolleston — to head it and he, together with Brackenbury and Dain (among others), prepared a new system of record-keeping which has been used in general practice ever since.[18] In contrast to the system that came before, this one did provide a continuous record of attendances, diagnosis and treatment for as long as a patient remained on a doctor's list. Even when he changed doctors, the record was not lost for it followed him to the new practice. Though the Ministry still intended to use the records for other purposes, it stressed the clinical object above all. Whitaker himself made this clear in 1918: 'The primary object of the record is to promote the efficiency of the insurance medical service.'[19]

Record inspections

These were not mere words. To show that it meant what it said, the department did not rely on the good faith of GPs alone. It decided to inspect records periodically through a corps of regional medical officers added to its staff in 1920. So much effort did the department put into the programme that even Mackenzie was impressed. Though he declined to serve on the committee, he did agree to lend support with a memorandum that was subsequently incorporated in the Rolleston Report. In it, Mackenzie said he saw great value in a programme which encouraged the panel doctor 'for his own advancement, to keep a record of each individual case, however trivial it may appear to be.'[20] Nor was that all: he hoped in time that it, combined with the better training of medical students, would lead to the realization of those research objects which he so much desired.

As the starting date (January 1921) for the inspections approached, however, medical anxieties mounted — particularly since fines were to be imposed on those who could not meet the minimum standards laid down. Few

GPs, from the time the old system was suspended in 1917, had bothered to maintain records and those that did were not proud of them. The inspection programme, furthermore, took them by surprise. Though it had been approved by the leaders of the profession in March 1919, [21] only a general obligation to keep records had been written into the regulations and nothing was said about the prospect of periodic inspections. MacNair Wilson needed to write only a few inflammatory articles to touch off an explosion; soon *The Times* was filled with letters from angry doctors protesting against the new procedure. [22]

There was no doubt that the attack was politically inspired [23] for, in choosing to criticize the Ministry, MacNair Wilson exposed himself to an embarrassing contradiction. Earlier he had been the advocate not only of a salaried service [a] but of record-keeping duties as well:

> '. . . The community has a clear right to ask its doctors to make such notes of their cases as will be useful in the future. By these records the study of disease will be facilitated and its whereabouts discovered. Both the medical profession and the public have a clear interest in the matter.' [24]

In making this pronouncement, MacNair Wilson was only repeating the maxims he had learned from Mackenzie during the period of the war when he worked under him. [25] From that experience, he had become a fervent supporter of general practice as opposed to specialism, seeing in it a way to realize the preventive medicine ideals which Mackenzie espoused. [26] In the process, MacNair Wilson also developed a religious passion for his master and later wrote the official life of the man under the title, *The Beloved Physician*. Nothing to which Mackenzie had his name appended could have possibly aroused MacNair Wilson's ire. Indeed, when the Rolleston Report first appeared in July, 1920, MacNair Wilson reviewed it sympathetically, noting with approval the extent to which it had been influenced by Mackenzie's ideals. [27]

Yet no sooner did the starting date of the inspection scheme approach than MacNair Wilson launched a vicious attack, condemning it as a violation of medical secrecy and a 'new inquisition'. [28] Later, not only Mackenzie [29] but even the department itself had doubts about the value of the system that evolved. Because of the difficulty of evaluating clinical entries, regional medical officers found it necessary to confine their inspections mainly to statistical counts of attendances and visits, comparing them with 'norms' set for the country as a whole. [30] If the number of 'ticks' kept by a doctor fell much below standard (which rose over the years from an average of $3\frac{1}{2}$ consultations per patient per year to $5\frac{1}{2}$), [31] then he exposed himself to the danger of a fine. The department, however, did give the doctor a sporting chance to correct his deficiency. When the inspections began, they were sometimes conducted without warning but, as the result of protests from the profession, the Ministry decided to give at least one day's notice. [32] Thereafter, all a doctor had to do to bring his 'ticks' up to standard was to stay up all night manufacturing them. [33]

---

a   See p. 34 above.

This, among other factors, led the medical officer at the Ministry in charge of the programme (Dr George F. McCleary) to dismiss the procedure as pointless.[34] In Scotland and Ireland, doubts about its value were always so strong that the inspection routine had never been imposed. The Scottish Board of Health, instead, tried to stimulate better record-keeping on the Mackenzie pattern — by singling out a special disease each year in an attempt to ascertain its cause. It started this research programme in 1930 and, over the next 4 years, produced studies on a number of subjects, ranging from heart disease to tonsillitis.[35]

The MPU, as early as 1926, tried to start a similar programme in England, substituting combined research on rheumatism for the inspection procedure which the profession abhorred [36] — but despite another attack on the system by MacNair Wilson in 1932,[37] the Ministry decided to stick to 'ticks'. It found the consultation figures too useful to abandon: whenever panel doctors complained of over-work (as an argument in support of a pay demand), the Ministry had data on hand to refute it. In 1937, however, the department placed too much reliance on this technique, thereby producing a reaction that doomed the inspection procedure.

It is revealing to recount here exactly how this happened. Workloads had been an issue in the 1923 pay dispute, but then the new record-keeping system had only been in operation for 2 years and neither party could extract much from the data it supplied. The next time a pay claim came under consideration, however, it was a different matter. As a result of the depression this did not occur until 1937, but then the profession decided to make workloads the main — not merely a side — issue in negotiations.[38] The debate that ensued was bitter and prolonged. Before it could be resolved, the claim again had to be referred to a Court of Inquiry, and there the Ministry not only made much use of record-keeping data but presented its evidence through those who conducted the hateful inspections — the regional medical officers.[39] The wave of indignation that arose against the Ministry's medical corps can be imagined. Some doctors went so far as to demand an end of record-keeping itself, not just the inspections.[40]

It was only at this point that the department took heed of a memorandum which McCleary had prepared just before he retired from the civil service in 1932.[41] In it, he recommended the termination of inspections and the Ministry did just that as soon as the Second World War began.[42] Nor have they been revived since: no doctor had been fined for poor record-keeping since 1939.

It is important to recognize, however, that the decision to suspend the programme was not based on the feelings of GPs alone. Even more important was the attitude of those who conducted the inspections: in the face of medical resentment, regional medical officers found them too distasteful to carry out.[43] They preferred to act as 'advisers' rather than 'supervisors' — and that is what their job has tended to become, even in the one area where they still do exercise control over medical work, the excessive prescribing of drugs.[44]

Had the inspections been linked to extra pay, however, the outcome might have been different. This can be seen from the way the profession accepted the heavy burden of record-keeping imposed between 1912 and 1917. Though no inspections were conducted then, the records required were far more onerous and, since they had to be turned in at the end of each year, there was no way that a doctor could avoid doing the job. Yet the doctors silently carried out the task because it was directly linked (by means of a special Exchequer grant) with the extra pay they received in October 1912. Once, however, the 'nexus between work and cash' was broken (by the merging of the grant in the general remuneration in 1920), the profession's attitude changed. As Whitaker himself observed in 1932:

'... Does the protest of the rank and file against the obligation represent much more than the inclination of the natural man, paid on a fixed salary or capitation basis, to whittle away, if he has the chance, work done for his money that he finds irksome? just as the man paid by fees tends to increase items of work to increase his income. All very "sordid" no doubt, but why should we be hypocritical about it? or allow these natural instincts to cloak themselves in fine pretences?' [45]

None of the necessary payments, however, were provided in 1921 and MacNair Wilson had a field day. Nor was that the only point on which he and *The Times* attacked the department. From October 1920 onwards, the paper criticized nearly all its policies and demanded Addison's removal from office. Not even the civil service remained free from MacNair Wilson's pen: he went so far as to single Newman out for abuse and accused him of dictating the policy that eventually brought Addison down.[46]

Chance for health centre experiments

Such were the hazards facing the Ministry in the months that followed the appearance of the Dawson Report. Newman and his colleagues had good reason to postpone the plan. But even that does not explain their almost total opposition to the health-centre idea for, despite the cost (and newspaper) pressures prevailing, there was still a chance that some experiments could have been conducted. Here, ironically, the way was opened — rather than closed — by *The Times*.

When the Dawson Report first appeared, MacNair Wilson had been generally sympathetic. He did criticize its stress on curative treatment, and he also objected to secondary health centres on expense grounds. But MacNair Wilson was much impressed with the parts of the report that dealt with general practice and preventive medicine. Great gains, he believed, could be realized from primary health centres and the opportunities they presented to extend the range of GP work.[47] What made these centres so attractive to him were the similarities they bore to the clinic Mackenzie had established at St Andrew's in Scotland. There a group of GPs worked as a team and strove, through research, to prevent the onset of disease before it required costly hospital treatment.[48] Mackenzie

expected Dawson's primary health centres to operate in the same way [49] —
and so did MacNair Wilson. If they did, the costs involved in setting them
up would be small compared with the gains to be realized from their
operation. The centres even offered hope of freeing the voluntary hospitals
from the financial crisis facing them.

These possibilities fired MacNair Wilson's imagination. He saw no
limits to the benefits that would be won if GPs were given the chance to
work effectively.[50] Such prospects might justify the construction of primary
health centres (at least a few experimental ones) even in the face of the
economy campaign. Though MacNair Wilson did not state this flatly, he
came close to it.[51] He carefully avoided any criticism of primary health
centres during his attack on the department.

This opening gave the Ministry the chance to give experimental shape to
at least part of the Dawson Report's recommendations, but it made no
attempt to do so. Even before the economy campaign began, Newman had
ignored the Report in his public statements, offering a weak excuse for the
omission.[52] [a] Only within the privacy of the department did he reveal his
true feelings. There he told his Permanent Secretary that the Dawson
Report was a 'somewhat disappointing document from the point of view of
practical suggestion and official administration'.[54] Yet, even this was
disingenuous for, as Newman himself had been forced to admit, the
medical council had not been asked for such advice. Its terms of reference
called only for the delineation of an ideal scheme and that Dawson had
proceeded to do.

Underlying Newman's attitude was a more basic objection: he and his
colleagues simply did not like the ideal scheme Dawson projected. Instead
of giving GPs an active role in the hospital world, the civil servants at the
Ministry wanted them to have passive contact. That preference became
evident in the report issued in 1921 by the Athlone Committee (on which
Newman served).[55] It envisaged access only to cottage hospitals;
otherwise, GPs would undergo refresher courses conducted by consultants.
To promote the latter, the report called for the creation of a new central
post-graduate hospital — and one was finally built at Hammersmith in
1934.[b] GPs in urban areas were thus to be deprived of the beds Dawson
hoped to give them in primary health centres.

Newman and his colleagues, however, were not alone in preferring this
line of development: key BMA leaders agreed with them. A close reading
of the medical journals of the period shows that doubts about Dawson's
ideas arose long before the economy campaign began, and that he was
pursuing a programme which neither Ministry nor BMA leaders wished to
follow. To understand the nature of their opposition and the reasons for it,
a closer look should be taken at the proposals contained in the Dawson
Report.

a   To the writer's knowledge, Newman never once referred in public to Dawson's health-centre
     proposal. In 1919 (and again in 1939), he did mention other views advanced by Dawson but
     these had the effect of supporting Newman's own conception of general practice.[53]

b   From this solitary site arose the ambitious refresher-course programme that exists today.

10
Doctors Reject
Collective Surgeries

The key idea in the Dawson Report was that of the primary health centre and it was against it that medical opposition was concentrated. By tracing the evolution of the concept from the time it first appeared in Dawson's 1918 Cavendish Lecture,[1] a clearer understanding of how this happened can be formed.

Health centre originally seen as a collective surgery

The centre, as Dawson originally conceived it, was intended to be solely a collective surgery where GPs would work in groups of 6.[2] Dawson cited that number as an example only, but one of his colleagues on the Medical Consultative Council (Dr A. Fulton) later gave a good reason for keeping the group small: he did not want it to appear to operate like an out-patient department. Fulton hoped it would present a more inviting image, offering patients continuity of treatment and the chance to establish a personal relationship with the doctor of their choice. Such considerations made Fulton feel that even 6 doctors were too many: 2 or 3, in his view, were all that was wanted.[3] Here, however, he came into conflict with cost considerations: the smaller the group, the less it could justify in the way of equipment. GPs who entered groups of the small size he desired would find it difficult to specialize.

Those who harboured specialist ambitions naturally tended to oppose such a proposal: both then and in later years, they wanted groups with more doctors in them. Still other GPs rejected the concept of group practice entirely because of its historic association with the hated medical aid institutions that the friendly societies had created.[a] Not even the excellent group practice clinic established by Great Western Railway employees at Swindon could overcome this opinion.[4]

Despite these dissenters, Dawson had good reason to expect that some form of group practice would prove acceptable to the profession. As already remarked, war-time experience had led many doctors to see the advantage of teamwork, not only as found in the armed forces, but in the collective surgeries which had been created at home.[5] These were designed to cope with the severe shortage of doctors in civilian practice, and even the MPU had supported them. Thus, when a number of them had made

a   See pp. 13 and 82 above.

their impact felt by 1917, its journal observed: '. . . the accidents of War, necessitating a larger supply of Army doctors, seem likely to bring about a revolution in medical service which a century of peaceful development could hardly have effected.'[6]

With the MPU so responsive, the leaders of the BMA had no reason to be cautious. Indeed, those in charge of the Branch in Glasgow went so far in 1915 as to advocate the creation of 'district centres' (i.e. collective surgeries)[a] in these terms:

'. . . In probably no other profession is the waste of time and energy so apparent as in connection with general medical practice. In urban areas at times as many as half a dozen doctors' motors may be seen in the same neighbourhood, and in many country districts two practitioners may travel a considerable distance over the same road to attend two or three patients in the same outlying district.

'. . . the only apparent direction in which economy of time can be effected is by concentrating the work in districts. To attain this end it is proposed to establish district centres . . .'[7]

Following this call, collective surgeries were created in 6 cities — 3 in Scotland (Aberdeen, Dundee, Edinburgh) and 3 in England (Birmingham, Leicester, Nottingham). Attempts were made to do so in other places, including Glasgow, but, despite the medical support cited above, the experiment failed. The blame, however, lay with the public rather than the profession.

The trouble, it seems, began with private patients and spread to the panel sector. The surgeries were designed to cover an area as a whole and, in order to operate them effectively, restrictions had to be placed on freedom of choice as well as on surgery hours (e.g. no mornings, no Sundays). The surgeries, moreover, offered no continuity of treatment. Though the area surrounding the surgery was divided into districts for visiting purposes (with normally only 1 doctor per district), the central surgery was served by all doctors in turn. This meant that the doctor seen at surgery was usually different from the one who visited the home.

Those who paid for medical care themselves objected to such arrangements and they also did not like the unsightly buildings in which the collective surgeries were housed. They refused to use them and their doctors joined the boycott. Only 2 of the 6 collective surgeries operating in 1918, as a result, even attempted to cover private patients; the rest confined their attention to insured persons.

Because of such difficulties, the authorities decided to restrict the operation of collective surgeries to depressed areas and that led the public to associate them with low class — almost Poor Law — treatment. In time, therefore, even the panel patients who used them raised objections and, after the war, all the surgeries still in operation were disbanded.[8]

Before the Armistice, however, Cox and his colleagues were not

a They were also called central, common or combined surgeries, and co-operative, practitioner or GP clinics. Later, in the 1940s, yet another name arose — communal surgeries.

disheartened by the difficulties the experiment encountered. They thought such prejudices could eventually be overcome and Dawson no doubt took their feeling into account when he delivered his Cavendish Lecture. What made BMA leaders so interested in collective surgeries? Certainly not the possibility of paying the doctors who worked within them by salary, although that had been tried at Birmingham and was felt to be the most efficient way of operating the surgeries.[9] BMA leaders were attracted for a different reason: the surgeries held out the prospect of easing the burdens of general practice. Here was a point likely to appeal to the profession as a whole, and Dawson took care to include it in his lecture. In time, he prophesied, the sharing of a common surgery 'would lead to close co-operation in work amongst the doctors and allow them more freedom for recreation and repose'.[10]

Night calls were a major source of medical grievance. Lloyd George had promised to deal with the subject in the 1912 regulations, but had failed to do so.[11] The BMA thereupon tried to impose a small charge on patients for night calls but Parliament refused to sanction it.[12] The issue arose again during the war when some patients failed to secure attention at critical times in the evening — and this produced a call for an organized night service after 1918.[13]

Dawson's health centre would have satisfied that demand as well as afforded relief from the burden imposed by the capitation system. Some doctors considered the 24-hour responsibility so onerous that they were willing to accept a salaried service in order to free themselves from it.[14] Panel doctors practising in poorer areas could then have realized their one great dream — to move their homes and raise their children in pleasanter surroundings. By 1918 at least 171 doctors in London had already done so, leaving a host of lock-up surgeries behind them.[15] In many cases, however, they failed to make adequate arrangements for the treatment of patients outside surgery hours, thereby producing a never-ending source of conflict between themselves and the approved societies.

Despite the difficulties lock-up surgeries created, they nevertheless did lessen the dislike of doctors for practice in industrial areas and that did ease the chronic shortage prevailing there.[16] The BMA, therefore, decided to campaign for a different policy in depressed areas than in the rest of the country. Until then, it had opposed co-operative clinics out of fear that they would undermine the personal relationship that existed between patient and doctor. Now it decided that they would be acceptable in poorer areas because surgery conditions there were overcrowded.[17]

This left the profession still opposed to the universal application of the idea but, even on that score, there was reason to believe that its attitude might change. GPs everywhere were threatened by the advance of specialization and it was only by combining into groups that they could hope to obtain the equipment needed to stem it. Even then, when the sciences of pathology and radiology were only in their infancy, enough was required in the way of facilities to put them beyond the reach of doctors who practised alone or in small partnerships. Thus Dawson, in his

Cavendish Lecture, mentioned not only the special equipment needed for the treatment of TB and VD but also the use of radiography and the electrocardiograph for the care of 'heart affections'.[18] Gastro-intestinal maladies were another area in which the aid of pathology and radiography might be required. Lastly, and perhaps most important in view of his war experience, Dawson cited the 'complete equipment' needed to deal with injured limbs, including orthopaedic appliances and electrical devices. All these facilities, together with an operating room for surgery, were included in the primary health centre contained in the Dawson Report.[19]

Group practice was thus needed to avoid referrals to consultants and, even before the war, the Government had this consideration in mind when it set a small sum aside for the establishment of what it called 'practitioners' clinics'.[20] But even more important was the need both to provide a stimulus to good work and to attract abler men to the panel. Addison stressed this object strongly, and it was he who persuaded Lloyd George to put the clinic provision in the 1914 Budget.[21] Panel doctors, however, did not entirely share Addison's interest. The NHI Commissioners were anxious to appoint outside consultants to deal with specialist cases and panel doctors saw the clinics mainly as an alternative. By promoting clinical consultation among themselves, they hoped to avoid the deductions from fees that would be made if outside consultants were called in.[a] They also saw the clinics as a way to deal with the huge increase in work expected once dependants were added to the panel.[22]

Though the outbreak of war postponed the experiment, the spread of local authority clinics during the conflict kept medical interest alive. Well-equipped collective surgeries offered to GPs the hope of recapturing the work taken by TB dispensaries and VD centres. Newman himself considered this development desirable, though with a different object than the profession. He did not want GPs to become part-time specialists, fearing that this might weaken their role in the community, but he did favour collective surgeries in the treatment of illnesses — like VD and TB — where strong social factors were involved:

> '. . . There was no solution to the venereal problem in this country unless the practitioners were equipped to handle it. Clinics were a palliative provision in the meantime. Venereal disease would never be eradicated until it was handled in private practice.[b] Its roots were deep socially, and involved something far beyond the narrow medical factor. Hardly any problem gave him more anxiety in his official work than the problem of venereal disease. But it all came back to the private practitioners. The same could be said of tuberculosis . . .'[23]

For this purpose part-time specialization was not enough. GPs, in Newman's view, had a truly important role to play: they had to become

a   For more on this, see pp. 118 and 127 below.

b   By this term, Newman meant panel practice as well. He included within it any medicine practised by doctors operating on their own rather than in local authority clinics. Here also, we can see most clearly why Newman came to oppose the spread of a salaried service through local authority clinics.

'missionaries of hygiene', teaching patients how to prevent disease and alter unhealthy patterns of living.[24] Here, collective surgeries had something to offer. How could GPs preach cleanliness when so many worked in surgeries that were unhygienic? Collective premises would be easier to maintain.[25] They would also lessen the fears of some doctors (and their wives) who wished to protect their homes from the kind of children that would enter them after NHI was extended to dependants. As one doctor put it: '. . . no medical man living in a decent neighbourhood and house would like to have a tribe of dirty, unruly children with their mothers crowding his waiting room and behaving as the children of the British labouring class proverbially do.'[26] Some doctors, indeed, made the same complaint about the fathers of such children: 'Many of them were so dreadfully dirty that afterwards all the carpets had to be taken up and the house turned upside down, for it needed much more than an ordinary spring cleaning.'[27]

Dawson extends health-centre concept

Dawson's original concept of a health centre thus had much to commend it. This was true not only from the profession's point of view but even from that of administrators concerned with costs. The attraction for them lay in the simplicity of Dawson's original idea: his health centre was meant to be, purely and simply, a collective surgery. No beds at all would be provided and not even local authority clinics were to be housed within its walls. All the centre would contain was facilities for GPs and these could be financed more cheaply in one building than in an array of separate surgeries scattered indiscriminately around it.[28] Duplication, if nothing else, would be avoided and the saving from that one source alone might be enough to justify the additonal equipment (over and above the type normally kept by GPs) the centre would provide.

The savings, moreover, would have applied to waiting, as well as consulting, rooms. Even then some doctors offered separate waiting rooms for private patients and many others adopted the practice later. By the time the Second World War began, the custom was widespread, thereby casting the stigma of a double standard of treatment over the panel.[a]

Had the collective-surgery idea been implemented in its original simplicity, costs could have been saved and the latter development have been avoided but Dawson, unfortunately, destroyed that possibility by the way he developed it. In time, his health centre came to include not only practice premises but hospital beds, local authority clinics and the whole range of community health services as well: '. . . just as they provided fabric and equipment for education in the shape of the school', Dawson argued, 'so they would need to bring together all their activities in the

---

a   The bombing that followed, however, provided another chance to erase it: many surgeries were destroyed or damaged and health centres, then as earlier, seemed a cheaper way to rebuild. The argument was not overlooked by Dr David Stark Murray of the SMA who pressed it strongly in his campaign for health centres.[29]

health centre.'[30]

Why did Dawson attach such importance to this union of medical care? One obvious factor stemmed from efficiency considerations. Local authority clinics were then located in different buildings and provided by separate staffs with little co-ordination between them. This was due mainly to the method by which they were financed: the funds came largely from central Government sources and were particularized for categories of disease, TB, VD and so on. Until block grants were provided (in 1929), there was no way funds could be shifted from one category to another and this produced a rigid demarcation in clinic administration.

Health centres, Dawson thought, would provide the means by which these widely scattered clinics could be brought together and operated more efficiently. An attempt along these lines had already been made by Dr J. Middleton Martin, the MOH for Gloucestershire: his 'out-station' programme was cited in the Dawson Report to show what was intended.[31] During the 1930s, other MOHs followed Martin's lead so that, by the time the Second World War began, a number of municipal health centres of this type had come into operation.[a] The profession did not object to the arrangement since, through a consolidation of this sort, the doctors found it easier to keep the spreading salaried movement under surveillance.

That, however, was not the main reason why Dawson favoured the union of medical care. Far more important was his search for 'something which would create a motive for bringing men together'.[32] *The health centre was to be the instrument through which the profession would be unified.* It was to be the counterpart at the periphery of the establishment of the new Ministry of Health at the centre.[33] The counterpart, more properly, would have been unification in local administration but, in the absence of that, health centres had to suffice.[b]

Up to this point, there was nothing new about Dawson's concept of a health centre. It had been anticipated in 1913 by Parker of the SMSA and he had based his scheme on one proposed by Dr Milson Russen Rhodes of Manchester. Though elements of the health centre idea had been growing for years,[34] it took the crisis of NHI to make it mature and Rhodes was the one who gave it focus and direction. He had earlier helped to organize the NMU but he became disillusioned with that body's blind opposition to the Act and subsequently joined the SMSA instead.[35] There, as a founder member and vice-chairman, he exercised much influence on SMSA policy — so much so that the plan he outlined in May 1912 became the starting-point for the development of the health-centre idea.[36]

What did the scheme proposed by Rhodes contain? At its heart lay the concept of a 'central depot' in every locality which would serve as a scientific centre for the profession, providing a meeting place, library, nursing home and repository for medical supplies. But this was not

a   For more on these, see pp. 179-80 below.

b   They were regarded in the same way after the Health Service was created in 1946. Then, too, local unification failed to materialize. See pp. 301-2 below.

supposed to be its main function: that, rather, was to give all local doctors access to beds. The depot was thus to serve mainly as a cottage hospital and was seen as a way of linking GPs with the hospital, rather than the local authority, world.

Parker sought to bring in the latter by having the MOH make his headquarters there[37] — and the Labour Party, in its 1919 scheme, wanted to extend the link still further by putting local authority clinics in the health centre as well. (Labour also wanted GPs to move their consulting rooms to the centre, thereby separating their surgeries completely from their homes.)[38]

Dawson, however, was not content with even this more grandiose concept of a health centre. Mindful of the large number of rejects for the armed forces during the war, he wanted the centre 'to convey the idea of health in its active rather than passive conception' and, for this purpose, he made elaborate plans for physical culture and games.[39] It was no wonder that he said: 'The term "health centre" was employed because something bigger and more embracing was desired than the term "hospital".'[40]

In this respect, Dawson was original, going far beyond anything that had been suggested earlier. The Labour scheme of 1919 did call for physiotherapy and health lectures at the centre but it said nothing about physical culture and games.[41] Dawson here struck a responsive chord for this was the only part of his plan implemented between the wars. In 1926 the Pioneer Health Centre opened its doors in Peckham, offering sports facilities and periodic medical examinations to those who were willing to pay its subscription fee. Families were invited to join *en bloc* and the emphasis throughout was on 'positive health'.[42]

No clinical treatment, however, was provided and this, together with a bias towards unorthodox medicine on the part of its founders (Dr G. Scott Williamson and his wife, Dr Innes Pearse, a pathologist at the London Homoeopathic Hospital)[43] probably accounted for its eventual demise. The Centre received little, if any, aid from public sources; most of its funds came from charitable donations and subscription fees. These ran out in 1940 and the Centre managed to reopen for only 5 years after the war. Many years later (1961), it was turned into a diagnostic centre for GPs — for which purpose it was used until 1974 when it had to close down completely as the result of complaints raised by consultants who did not want such services to be offered outside the constraints of the hospital world.[44] [a]

GPs fear MOH supervision

Apart from this one isolated experiment in Peckham, none of Dawson's dreams ever materialized. Had his plan been confined to the original concept of a collective surgery, the outcome might have been different but not

---

a   The Ministry probably also favoured its closure because the building was too small to contain the growing array of equipment needed for diagnostic procedure. It was the advance of science that killed the Centre as much as the complaints of consultants.

only was the final scheme too expensive — it was unacceptable to the majority of GPs. What they disliked most of all was the way health centres were to be linked with local authorities through the medium of MOHs who were to make their headquarters there. This, the profession feared, might tempt MOHs to interfere in the provision of domiciliary services.[45] Nor was the profession happy with the fact that the building in which the health centre was housed was itself to be owned by local authorities. That, they thought, might invite state control of medical fees or deter patients from consulting them.[46]

Dawson tried to anticipate the worst of these fears by isolating MOHs from GPs.[47] Under his scheme, the director of the collective surgery was to be one of the GPs who worked in it and he would be elected by the group in the way that Dr G. Rome Hall had earlier envisaged.[a] But this effort came to nothing when MOHs, throughout 1919 and 1920, raised complaints about the way they had been denied security of tenure.[48] [b] If that was the way local authorities treated their chief medical officers, many GPs had reason to wonder, how will they treat us? The climax of the MOHs' long struggle for security of tenure destroyed whatever sympathies GPs had about employment in the municipal sector.

As a result of all this, the BMA came out against the creation of GP clinics 'under the aegis of the State'[49] even before Dawson's ideas had matured into the form of an official report. BMA leaders were now paying the price for the patriotic way they had co-operated with the Government during the war.[c] Repeated attacks from MPU quarters had placed them under suspicion and they could not afford to support any proposal, however worthy, which might bring their loyalties into question. When Brackenbury, for example, dared to defend one regulation in 1919 which threatened to lower the selling value of practices, one angry doctor asked: 'Does Dr Brackenbury represent the Ministry of Health or does he represent us?'[50]

As negotiations over the new contract proceeded, panel doctors developed a paranoic fear of a salaried service, seeing in every new regulation proposed a Machiavellian attempt to prepare them from the evil day. As one doctor put it: '. . . the new regulations were the thin edge of the wedge for smashing up private practice and introducing a State Medical Service.'[51] By 1920, the profession had all but forgotten the sympathy it had once expressed for collective surgeries. When the BMA polled its Divisions on the subject, it found a large number (52) were opposed to them even if they were established by GPs and the vast majority (108 to only 7 in favour) completely rejected their being developed under local authority control.[52]

In the face of such feelings, BMA leaders had to abandon the collective-surgery idea. Dawson and his council therefore found it expedient to all

a   See p. 82 above.
b   See p. 85 above.
c   See pp. 58-9 above.

but strike the proposal from their report, suggesting that experiments be conducted only where local conditions permitted.[53] None ever did. With the onset of the depression and the growth of competition for patients, the profession lost interest in teamwork, and it took financial considerations to revive any thought of co-operation. When restrictions on fee-charging under NHI were tightened in the 1920s, panel doctors who wanted to treat insured persons privately found it expedient to share premises with non-panel men.[a]

As a result, partnerships grew — by the time the Health Service began, nearly half the profession practised within them[54] — but they were not of the type Dawson envisaged. Clinical consultation, for the most part, was confined to market towns. There, GPs had to specialize (through group practice) in order to meet the severe shortage of consultants in rural areas.[55] Otherwise, however, isolation prevailed. Though many GPs shared premises with others, when it came to attendance on patients, they practised alone.

a   For more on this, see pp. 152-3 below.

11
GPs Exclude Consultants from Health Centres

The Dawson Report was 'an honest and able attempt to reconcile conflicting medical interests for the benefit of the public'.

the judgement of two medical leaders of the period (Dr Fred Warner, a physician at the London Hospital, and Dr James Kerr, a prominent figure in the public health world) cited by Sir Arthur MacNalty in the *British Medical Journal*, 1948, 2, pp. 6-9.

When medical opinion turned against collective surgeries, that might have spelled the end of the health-centre idea. But Dawson did not give up easily. If health centres could not promote teamwork in one way, then perhaps they could in another.

By 1920, Dawson recognized that any attempt to realize group practice by direct methods would fail. GPs were not even ready to share surgery premises with each other, much less patients. Would they, however, feel differently about hospital beds? This occurred to Dawson as another way to 'create a motive for bringing men together'.[1]

Hospital facilities were then wanted by nearly all doctors — but they could not be provided in isolation. Only by joining together in a common building could GPs hope to enjoy the benefits of a service requiring huge expenditure of funds. Once the doctors did so, there was reason to believe that they would find the experience exhilarating. Hospital access could lead step by step to closer co-operation, evolving in time into a form of organization not too dissimilar from group practice. If it did, then the profession might enjoy the best of both worlds for as one group of doctors declared at the time: 'Such a use of hospitals [that is, by granting access to all doctors] . . . would introduce into medicine most of the advantages supposed in some quarters to lie in a State Medical Service; and at the same time leave the freedom of the individual practice so prized by members of the medical profession.'[2]

Dawson did not use the term at the time but this form of professional relationship might have aptly been called 'the associated free practice of medicine'. Such was the name later given to it by an eminent American doctor — Dr S.S. Goldwater — and he also explained why he thought it preferable to the more direct form of group practice:

'. . . All patients do not need hospital or group practice, but it is the family doctor who must select the patient who must be given its benefits and if the family doctor has no connection with a hospital or clinic organization, he will fully understand neither the power nor the decided limitations of group practice. Even if the doctor's judgment is sound, he will be more reluctant to refer his patient to a hospital or diagnostic clinic with which he has no connection than to one with which he is associated and to which he can turn with the knowledge that its staff will loyally collaborate with him and will make no attempt to supplant him.'[3]

For this reason, as well as for the many benefits the hospital world offered, Goldwater saw a hospital connection as the key to the reconstruction of general practice and the more Dawson studied the problem, the more he shared the view. By 1920, he had come to the conclusion that the primary health centre should serve, above all, as a hospital for GPs.[4]

Need to raise quality of GP care

Not only was such a use desirable — it was, in the opinion of many, urgently necessary. The reason for this lay in the dangers facing general practice after the war ended. Though NHI had raised the pay of GPs, it had done little to improve their clinical standards.[a] Because of the capitation method of payment, general practice was being conducted within a much narrower range under the panel system than in the private sector. This was tending to deter the best men from joining the panel and dragging down those that did to the level of the lowest. As the leading hospital journal of the day said: '. . . to put it bluntly, all the "scallywags" in the medical profession are on the panels, and they sometimes swamp the more conscientious and better educated types. The panel service is admittedly bad: probably even worse than the Ministry of Health suspects.'[5]

The Ministry, however, was fully aware of the problem — and no one there more so than the doctor in charge of the insurance section, James Smith Whitaker. Several years later, when the problem of quality was still very much a cause of concern, Whitaker stated the difficulty clearly:

'. . . He agreed that the general practitioner rapidly deteriorated in insurance practice. After leaving the medical school he often improved for a few years by his contact with human nature, but after that, because he lived among his intellectual inferiors, immune from criticism and never having to pit himself against equal brains, he began to go off . . .'[6]

From the moment NHI began, complaints had been raised about the care rendered by panel doctors and the severe shortage of practitioners during the war did not make matters better. By 1917, even newspapers friendly to NHI (like *The Observer*) called panel doctoring 'a sham and a scandal for the most part'.[7] In some places, it was so bad that a few patients eligible for NHI were said to prefer treatment under the Poor Law.[8] Even BMA leaders like Dr Bishop Harman had to admit that panel care left much to be desired: '. . . the practice of the insurance service, as it now is, does not fulfil our medical standards.'[9]

The danger to general practice, then, was clear. Three-quarters of the

a   See p. 15 above.

GPs in the country were already on the panel and more would follow once NHI was extended to dependants. If general practice in Britain was not to go the way of Germany and America, where specialism was displacing it across a broad front, then something had to be done to make it more challenging. What better way than to encourage GPs to pursue their specialist interests as far as possible without abandoning their role as GPs?

Dawson at first thought the solution lay simply in grouping GPs in collective surgeries, linking them through 'settlements' to hospitals and clinics. By 1920, however, he had come to the conclusion that it would be better to bring GPs directly into hospital themselves. For that purpose, he recognized, the primary health centre would have to contain beds. Dawson therefore shifted the emphasis of his centre from a collective surgery to a GP hospital in the hopes of making it more generally attractive.[10]

Mixed GP support for beds in health centres

The success of the plan, however, depended not on the public but on the profession and the question immediately arose: would the doctors accept it? As far as GPs were concerned, there was reason to be hopeful. The horizons of many had widened during the war due to the medical demands that were placed upon them. As their range of care expanded, so did their interest in clinical medicine. A large number of GPs experienced a satisfaction in work they had never felt before and they were anxious to preserve it after the war ended. This applied particularly to those who had entered the armed forces: they, even more than their colleagues in civilian life, had found hospital doors opened to them and the abundant facilities they shared within left them afterwards with the highest expectations. As the President of the MPU (Dr Frank Coke) put it in 1918: 'When one gets accustomed to admitting to hospital the slight cases of bronchitis, etc, from the Army, one realises how very badly off the civil poor are in this respect.'[11]

Panel doctors were also affected by the movement and nowhere was this more clearly indicated than in an address made to the approved societies in 1919 by Welply of the MPU. 'In my humble opinion', Welply said, 'every medical man who undertakes the treatment of insured persons should be prepared to do all and everything necessary for that patient provided he, in his own opinion, is competent to do so.' At that moment, however, Welply complained, he could not do so, whether competent or not, because hospital doors were closed to the ordinary GP: 'Lack of facilities prevents him from giving of his best to the nation. Every medical man should be connected with a hospital.'[12]

Not all GPs, however, agreed. Some preferred to work solely in the community, believing they could render greater service in that way — while others, less idealistic, found life in their surgery too comfortable to risk the danger of criticism outside. The strongest support for the demand came from those doctors who had specialist aspirations since they needed hospital appointments to establish themselves as consultants.[13]

But all GPs, no matter what their inclinations, were being pushed in the direction of hospital work by the pressure of private practice. Doctors who could not offer the full range of care were in danger of losing patients to others who could. This was a long-standing problem, dating back to the nineteenth century,[a] and the creation of NHI had only temporarily eased it. That Act enabled many doctors to abandon specialist (or hospital) work and practise solely in the community. But the panel did not cover dependants, and the expectations of all patients, whether insured or not, had been raised during the war. This applied particularly to those who had enjoyed the benefits of hospital life in the armed forces: they expected their own doctors to provide the same facilities when they returned home. With such pressures at work, Dawson had good reason to expect GPs to want the beds his primary health centre would provide.[14]

Consultants fear wider services by GPs

Where consultants were concerned, however, the prospects were less promising. They had been unnerved by the higher status accorded to general practice during the war, fearful that this would tempt GPs to render services beyond their competence. If GPs did, then the wider interests of the public, as well as the narrower (economic) interests of consultants, would be endangered. For the age was one in which the border between general practice and specialist care had not yet been clearly defined. Many, if not the majority of, consultants had started out as GPs and had graduated to specialist rank only through experience, not by undergoing instruction at the hands of their peers (and passing the examinations of the Royal Colleges). 'Learning by doing' was the time-worn training technique of the day and one which any consultant, when queried about his qualifications, would have been proud to acknowledge as the one he possessed.

However the point had been reached, in some areas of medicine at least, where this state of affairs could no longer be tolerated. The uncontrolled general practitioner presented a danger to the public. At the moment, he was restrained only by the deplorable conditions under which he worked. Practising alone in his own poorly-equipped surgery, he did not have the means to provide many services beyond his competence. But if he were given access to the full range of facilities in the hospital world, then there was no limit to the lengths to which he might go. Dawson himself had seemed to favour this development: 'Though it is quite right that consultants and specialists should be available to help the general practitioner, these are not nearly so important as providing the means for the general practitioner to help himself.'[15]

These words sent a shiver of fear throughout the consultant world. Who, under Dawson's plan, would decide when patients should be passed on? GPs, consultants had good reason to believe, could not be trusted to make that decision themselves; someone had to do it for them. Physicians harboured

a   See pp. 3-4 above.

more fears on the subject than surgeons; they did not have the protection afforded by the scalpel to shield them from GP competition. Major operations involved increasingly technical procedures and the point had been reached where only qualified surgeons could perform them.[16] General medicine, on the other hand, was more a matter of judgment than technique, and it was harder to determine when specialists should be called in.[17]

All of this became painfully evident when the London Clinic (the only pay hospital built in Britain between the wars) opened its doors in 1932.[18] Then, to the anger of GPs with surgical ambitions, the Clinic barred them from the operating theatre but gave them access in all other respects. Earlier in the century, such distinctions made less difference because some operations could still be performed at home.[19] But, by the 1930s, no sane doctor would have dared to do so. As one GP put it in 1938: "In plain English, an average man properly equipped is safer than the most brilliant operator, beloved by the novelist, who performs major operations on kitchen tables."[20]

General medicine, furthermore, did not always require an institutional setting. Then, as now, physicians could treat many patients as safely outside hospital as within. GPs, therefore, did not always need hospital access to infringe on this specialty. This made physicians realize that it was not enough simply to keep GPs out of hospital; on the contrary, the wiser course was to bring them in and then remove all difficult cases from their control. Such, no doubt, was the argument they made to Dawson behind the closed doors of the Royal College of Physicians.

The anxiety physicians felt was increased even more by the impending transfer of Poor Law infirmaries. If that were not done properly, then physicians might find themselves in a situation where GPs were admitted to the infirmaries while they were not. This was no slight danger. As soon as the infirmaries passed under local authority control, they were expected to be upgraded and made fully competitive with the voluntary hospitals. Some 50 infirmaries had already undergone such transformation by the 1920s and 150 more were scheduled to follow once local authorities took over.[21]

In the infirmaries previously upgraded, GPs had not been employed. The guardians, like the committees in charge of voluntary hospitals, preferred to appoint specialists.[22] But the resident officers of the remaining infirmaries were, in reality, GPs and local authorities might be satisfied with the same type of doctor after they assumed control.[23] If they did, then the only problem facing GPs would be the terms on which they were employed: would they be required to serve whole-time as resident medical officers usually did under the conditions applied by the guardians? Or could they, like consultants in voluntary hospitals, attend part-time, bringing their private patients with them?[24]

The BMA argued strongly for the latter course, hoping in this way to secure the advantage of the voluntary hospital staffing system without the financial penalty it normally entailed (that is, no pay for services rendered).[25] But GPs then were so anxious to secure hospital beds that they were ready to sacrifice the freedom of the voluntary hospitals if that was the only way to secure their own. Brackenbury himself took this position in 1922: 'If the free choice of doctor was going to be denied in the case of voluntary hospitals, while it remained a part of the scheme for municipal hospitals, then he preferred the latter.'[26] All, however, depended on the staffing system local authorities employed. GPs hoped to find MOHs responsive to their demands and no one, in 1920, could be sure which way the decision would go.[a]

With Poor Law reform thought to be imminent, the situation demanded immediate attention and Dr (later Sir Robert) Bolam, Chairman of the BMA's Council, made the fears of consultants known. Leading a deputation to the Ministry in March 1920, he told Addison of

'. . . the serious apprehension among his colleagues throughout the country
lest the utilisation of Poor Law hospitals should prejudice voluntary hospital
arrangements. They felt that the best way to approach the matter would be
to graft on to the voluntary hospital system some of the Poor Law hospitals
rather than that a new set of hospitals should spring up which required
staffing *ad hoc.*'[27]

But how exactly should the grafting job be done? Some consultants wanted to bring the infirmaries under voluntary hospital control through the medium of voluntary committees;[28] others preferred to turn them into specialized hospitals for industrial workers as part of an industrial medical service;[29] while still others sought to confine GP participation to out-patient and casualty departments or merely to refresher courses and after-care work.[30]

Dawson tries to ease consultant fears

Dawson had a better idea: why not turn the infirmaries into health centres of the primary or cottage hospital type, leaving the voluntary hospitals as the exclusive preserve of consultants? The 2 centres would be linked through consultation clinics in the primary health centre, thereby enlarging the concept of group practice — or, rather, 'the associated free practice of medicine' — into one embracing consultants as well as GPs. Consultants would pass back and forth between the 2 centres, advising GPs on treatment and selecting those cases which required more specialized attention for transfer to secondary health centres. Dr Charles M. Wilson (later Lord Moran) [b] had already established such a relationship between St Mary's Hospital and the Paddington General Infirmary.[31]

Under this arrangement, consultants alone would determine when patients moved on and, once admitted to the secondary health centres, patients would pass completely 'from the hands of their own doctor'.[32] Some GPs might still enter the secondary health centre in the capacity of consultants, but they would have to have their status established first by a selection committee composed exclusively of specialists.[33] The way in which nursing and laboratory services were organized would also serve as

a   As it turned out, the decision went against GPs: MOHs proved as reluctant to admit
      them as consultants. See p. 138 ff. below.

b   For a profile of Moran, see p. 339 below.

a control on GPs. Both were to be based on secondary, not primary, health centres and this meant, in the case of laboratory examinations, that those 'involving difficulty would either wait for the routine visits of a consultant from the Secondary Centre or materials could be rapidly sent to the latter'.[34]

Dawson's plan thus promised to give consultants more protection against GP competition than they enjoyed before. The hospitals also stood to benefit, particularly those in the voluntary sector. They badly needed relief from the excessive demands being placed on them and the primary health centres, by giving GPs greater ability to treat patients themselves, promised to lighten the hospital burden.[35] Dawson also expected the paid consultation work generated by the health centres to ease the country's severe shortage of specialists. It would do this by giving younger men the assurance of some income at the start of their hazardous careers. That was why Dawson said: 'A great deal depended upon the maintenance of intellectual traffic between the primary and secondary health centres.'[36]

With those in the hospital world expecting to gain so much from the arrangement, one might have thought GPs would lose but, on the contrary, they actually stood to benefit from the restrictions Dawson placed on their work. They needed to have more than access to beds in order to find an interest in work; they also had to have contact with consultants so as to regain the intellectual excitement of their student days. That, furthermore, was the best way the quality of their care could be raised. As Whitaker once put it: 'The risk of having his [i.e. the GP's] treatment of individual cases from time to time overhauled by better men of his own profession would go far to keep him up to the mark.'[37]

From this would flow the solution to the education problem that was disturbing the nation. In a paper published in *The Lancet* in 1919, Dr James Pearse, the Ministry's adviser on general practice,[a] called attention to the accelerating pace of medical advance and then asked his colleagues: 'Who amongst us who graduated even 20 years ago can pretend to an accurate knowledge of late developments?'[38] Few could answer affirmatively because, unlike their colleagues elsewhere, British doctors had not acquired 'the post-graduate habit'.[39]

One BMA leader (Dain) thought the solution to this problem was not to expose GPs to the occasional formal lecture but to put them in continuous contact with consultants through hospital work.[40] That was exactly what the primary health centre promised to do. Through it, therefore, GP horizons would be widened overnight — yet confined within a range that was dangerous neither to patients nor consultants.

Brackenbury, however, had reservations about the plan and he dominated BMA thinking on the subject. He did not want to link the primary health centre too closely with consultants. Here he disagreed profoundly with Dawson. Dawson wanted GPs to become specialists mainly in local authority clinic work;[41] only a few, he thought, would go on to become specialists in hospital and they might eventually have to abandon

a   See p. 95 above.

general practice to do it. Brackenbury, on the other hand, wanted to leave the whole range of medicine open to GPs; otherwise, he feared, they would be considered inferior to consultants, falling to the lower rung of the ladder which Lord Moran made famous nearly 4 decades later.[42]

Brackenbury voiced this fear openly at a debate on medical education in 1920. It was clear, from the tone of the discussion, that many medical leaders were already placing the educational needs of GPs in a lower category than those of specialists and Brackenbury reacted angrily. The GP, he argued, required as good a scientific education as the specialist: 'He could not admit the relegation of the general practitioner to a lower level.'[43] So far did he go in this respect that one prominent consultant (Dr C. O. Hawthorne) even accused him of trying 'to eliminate the consultant'.[44]

This, however, was unfair. Brackenbury was merely trying to loosen the growing barriers between general and specialist medicine. He was aiming not at the extinction of the consultant but at the preservation of the GP, an object which he and Newman considered vital to the well-being of the nation.[45] But, in advancing this view, Brackenbury did display astonishing short-sightedness — perhaps because he fell too much under the spell of Mackenzie's philosophy. Just as Mackenzie over-rated the potential of preventive medicine, so Brackenbury exaggerated the potential of general practice. As a clear example of the former, we have Mackenzie's disciple on *The Times* (MacNair Wilson) envisaging the day when medicine would prevent heart disease in the same manner as it had 'trench feet'.[46] Similarly, in 1920, we find Brackenbury contending that 'it was by no means difficult for a general practitioner to be largely competent in some specialty or another. It was quite common for a general practitioner to be a first-class operative surgeon...'[47]

Brackenbury thus completely failed to anticipate how hard it would be for GPs to straddle both worlds of medicine as technique advanced. He also made no allowance for the dangers facing the public if GPs were permitted to practise the full range of medicine without limit. Could doctors be trusted to restrain themselves? Some, like Welply of the MPU, believed they could. In 1919, Welply declared: 'No doctor would attempt to remove a patient's appendix unless he was competent to do so.'[48] Brackenbury, by his silence on the subject, apparently agreed — but events proved him and Welply wrong. Had GPs been given complete freedom to perform operations, the nation might have suffered the same orgy of surgery that turned the German people against orthodox medicine between the wars.[a]

GPs unwilling to work with consultants

Later, Brackenbury modified his views [b] and he certainly never intended the average GP to be transformed into a part-time specialist. For Brackenbury, the social-work side of general practice always took priority.[c] But whatever his true

a   See p. 313 below.

b   See p. 146 below.

c   See p. 122 below.

feelings on the subject in 1920, he nevertheless argued like a man bent on giving GPs the freedom to pursue their specialist interests as far as they desired. He therefore did not want consultants in the primary health centre at all — not even in the out-patient department which was to be located there.[49] [a] In an important paper he delivered in 1920, setting forth the future development of the GP service, Brackenbury made this point explicit: 'By team work he did not mean the co-operation of the general practitioner with a series of specialists, all working together as a team, but a series of general practitioners working together.'[51] This, in contrast to the combined groups formed in America, became the pattern in Britain ever after.[b]

Here, no dissent was registered by those in charge of Ministry policy: Addison as well as Newman agreed with Brackenbury. As early as 1914, Addison had advocated group practice in similar terms, hoping in this way to extend the range of care provided by panel doctors: '. . . whilst the present definition was "such a service as can be rendered by any man of average competence and skill', they should aim at a service which "should be such that any medical man shall be free to render under it any service which he feels capable of honestly rendering" . . .'[52]

Many GPs endorsed these sentiments. They were ready to extend the range of care provided, especially if they received more money for it, and they did not want any consultants around to inhibit their freedom of action. At the same time, they faced the danger — first raised in 1914 — of having deductions made from their capitation fees if outside consultants were called in.[53] Rather than have that happen, GPs were ready to do the work themselves, whether they were paid extra or not.

The proposal to make such deductions in all probability came from Whitaker: he was obsessed by the danger of abuse if GPs were given unlimited access to specialist services. During 1918, he went so far as to suggest that no referrals be allowed at all without the approval of medical referees. This, however, posed too great a threat to GP freedom and Brackenbury proposed that control be exercised, instead, through the medium of local medical committees, exercising restraint in the same way as they did with excessive prescribing.

Another suggestion raised at the time was to require GP attendance at every consultation but Brackenbury thought this impracticable. The issue was never resolved because specialist services were not added until 1948,

a   Brackenbury did not notice this provision in the Dawson Report. He thought it appeared only in the Welsh Report but he was wrong: Dawson specifically included out-patient departments in primary health centres. The point, however, was made only in Dawson's summary of recommendations, not in the text itself, and that was why Brackenbury failed to notice it.[50] One other matter needs to be explained here. The Dawson Report applied only to England, not to Wales, Scotland or Ireland. Each of those countries had Consultative Councils and reports of their own. Dawson served only on the English medical council. He had nothing to do with the reports prepared by the other councils and they differed in some respects from the Dawson — or English — Report.

b   For other differences in the development of group practice in the two countries, see p. pp. 306-7 below.

when the whole system was recast. Dawson expected this to happen because he did not think the provision of specialist services could be handled satisfactorily outside the hospitals. The two problems, in his mind, were inseparable and the danger of abuse arose only so long as GPs insisted on working apart from consultants. Together, there was no danger since the consultants themselves could exercise control. That was one of the key assumptions implicit in Dawson's health-centre plan and the immediate impetus for the plan, in fact, came from a discussion of the 'abuse' problem, held in February 1918, between medical leaders and officials of the NHI Commission.[54]

The train of dangers raised by this problem, however, was not the only reason why GPs shunned contact with consultants. More important was the fear of having their work inspected by someone able to judge it.[55] This thought had been uppermost in the minds of some GPs ever since the system of medical referee-consultants was first contemplated in 1914. That addition to the panel was to be much more modest than the one proposed after the war. It would provide only advice (not treatment) and then only in cases where disputes had arisen with the approved societies over the question of incapacity to work.

But, despite its limitations, even that system was expected to enhance greatly the ability of the authorities to police the panel:

'. . . It was believed that, through the opportunities which the Referees would thus have of coming into contact with doctors and obtaining an intimate knowledge of the way in which their work was being done, they would be able to exercise great influence, both direct and indirect, over the work, and also to enable disciplinary action to be taken more effectively than can be the case at present.'[56]

If such was the spectre raised by a limited referee-consultant system, then how much greater was the danger embodied in a full consultant service? Some GPs were frightened by the prospect and wanted nothing to do with an arrangement that threatened to bring consultants into intimate contact with them.

Where medical referees (i.e. regional medical officers) were concerned, however, the leaders of the profession were forced to take a different view. The supervisory powers exercised by these officers, they felt, had to be accepted just to give the authorities some alternative to the disciplinary procedure, then strongly influenced in its operation by the desires of the approved societies. As one conference of medical leaders put it:

'. . . The responsible public authorities must have some means other than the drastic course of removing a practitioner from the list, of securing a reasonable standard of efficiency of service, particularly seeing that the statutory right of practitioners to undertake the work of the service precludes the authorities from any rejection of candidates on grounds of serious doubt as to suitability or even of obvious unsuitability.'[57]

Dawson's scheme thus aroused many anxieties among GPs but far greater than those yet mentioned was the fear of losing not only face but patients if they practised in the same health centre as consultants. Many consultants practised no more 'purely' than GPs: they did not wait for referrals but accepted patients independently and were thus in direct competition. As Lauriston Shaw put it: 'Few general practitioners will deny that they are constrained from seeking specialist advice for their patients, on every occasion when they would value it, by the fact that most specialists undertake independent, as well as consultative, practice, and thereby place themselves in competition with general practitioners.'[58] [a]

This consideration applied with much greater force in the provinces than it did in London. There many GPs had managed to gain access to hospital[b] and that made life difficult for those who wished to practise purely as consultants. London, however, was also affected: as the number of GP-specialists in the provinces grew, fewer patients felt the need to travel to Harley Street and this prompted some consultants to become less particular about whom they saw. As early as 1922, they were accused of accepting patients without referral and the charge did not lessen as the depression deepened.[59]

Not all consultants, of course, allowed their ethical standards to fall; much depended on the extent to which the specialty in which they practised was threatened by GP intrusion. Thus, physicians, as we saw,[c] had more to fear than surgeons — but the age of the consultant involved was also a factor. Those who were established in practice obviously could afford to be particular about the patients they treated; younger men could not. Yet the latter were precisely the kind of consultants Dawson hoped to place in health centres [d] — which makes one wonder how carefully he had thought out the implications of his plan.

Ever since the turn of the century, departures from referral customs had led to frequent disputes between consultants and GPs[e] — but about one thing, they were agreed: the inhibitions it caused were not good for patients. Nowhere was this more evident than in the operation of TB dispensaries.[60] Despite the obvious dangers involved, GPs were reluctant to refer patients to the dispensaries out of fear of losing them. Patients, however, were not dependent on GP sufferance where TB (or VD) was concerned. They could take themselves to the dispensaries local authorities operated (as well as to the VD centres) since, as far as these institutions were concerned, they had been given the right of direct access. But that only prompted GPs to seek additional protection. They opposed the employment of rival doctors in dispensary and clinic posts, thereby giving MOHs good reason to resort to the whole-time principle. Yet that, as we saw, only exacerbated the profession's fear of a salaried service.[f]

a   For Shaw's particular interest in this subject, see pp. 303-4 below.

b   See pp. 141-2 below.

c   See pp. 113-14 above.

d   See p. 116 above.

e   See p. 14 above.

f   See pp. 34-5 above and pp. 139-40 below.

GPs serving under NHI harboured an additional concern: this was the possibility that non-panel doctors — many of whom straddled both wings of the profession — might one day be willing to participate in NHI as consultants even though they had refused to do so as GPs. If they did, panel doctors feared, they might 'pose as persons superior to their rival practitioners who were serving the panel'.[61]

It was partly this fear, no doubt, that later led the Royal Commission on NHI to recommend that specialist services be added to the panel through an independent network of clinics rather than by more traditional means — that is, through the out-patient departments of voluntary hospitals.[a] In the latter, GPs ran the danger of losing patients to consultants, whereas, in the clinics, they had the chance to render specialist care themselves if they could produce the necessary qualifications.

Dawson, however, failed to devise similar safeguards and his plan, therefore, had little chance of success. He was asking GPs to commit economic suicide by suggesting that they work closely with consultants. Only the elimination of private practice would make such co-operation possible. No one was surprised, then, when the Divisions of the BMA voted overwhelmingly (101 to 12) in 1920-1 against the location of out-patient departments in primary health centres.[62] In effect, they were telling Dawson that they wanted him to hang a sign over his health centre which read:

CONSULTANTS KEEP OUT.

a   For other considerations behind the Royal Commission recommendation and the reasons why it was never implemented, see pp. 156-7 below.

12
Extension of Care
to Dependants or Specialists?

The uneasy relations between consultants and GPs were not the only force eroding the health-centre idea. More damaging was the fear that Dawson's plan would lead the country in the wrong direction — towards a system of care that would weaken, rather than strengthen, general practice. Here we come to the question that stood uppermost in the minds of medical planners between the wars: if the country could not afford a comprehensive health service, free and open to all, then which should be added to the panel first — GP coverage for the dependants of insured persons or specialist services for those already insured? 'Dependants or specialists' was the main issue of the day. It, more than any other question, lay at the heart of the controversy between Brackenbury and Dawson.

Brackenbury versus Dawson

In this dispute, Brackenbury came down strongly on the dependants' side because he considered a comprehensive GP service more important for the health of the nation.[1] Like Newman, Addison, and Lloyd George himself, Brackenbury saw the GP mainly as an instrument of social reform and wanted him to spend the bulk of his time in or near the homes of patients, teaching them how to live healthier and saner lives.[2] This meant that Brackenbury emphasized prevention rather than diagnosis and treatment — the social rather than the clinical (or organic) side of general practice. Periodically, he paid lip service to the latter but that was mainly for reasons of medical politics. His heart was not in it and over the years he did everything he could to steer GPs away from the hospital world.

This tendency appeared as early as 1920 when, leading a BMA deputation to the Ministry, Brackenbury expressed concern about the direction in which health policy was going: 'The deputation were somewhat apprehensive lest, if the Ministry of Health did not make its hand firmly felt, hospital development might get a little out of hand.'[3] These were precisely the views Newman held about the Dawson Report and nowhere does the similarity in their outlook appear more clearly. Between the wars, they worked in tandem — Newman inside the Ministry, Brackenbury outside with the BMA — to push medical development in the direction of a social-work role for general practice. They, more than anyone, prepared the profession for the sharp division made between GPs and consultants under the National Health Service.

Dawson, on the other hand, came down just as strongly on the specialists' side. He had no axe to grind for social reform — his interests were in clinical medicine pure and simple: 'What was wanted above everything else was the power of the general practitioner to do his own work in the best possible way and to his own satisfaction.'[4] That, in his view, meant that GPs would have to be brought closer to, rather than further from, the hospital world. They would have to spend less, not more, time in the homes of patients. 'The essential thing about the primary health centre', he stressed, 'was that it should be staffed by the general practitioners of the district, and that when a patient left his home and went into the clinic [meaning here, hospital] he would be followed there by his own doctor.'[5]

Later (1933), Dawson did come out against GP access to the private wards of voluntary hospitals because of the administrative difficulties it would cause. Nurses would then be subject to 3 separate authorities — consultant, GP, resident staff — and this, he feared, would breed confusion. He also doubted the ability of GPs to keep regular hours of attendance on hospital patients and this worried him because, if they did not, then the burden of work would fall on the resident staff.[6] But, in expressing such views, Dawson was talking only about the institutions which were to serve as secondary health centres in his plan and to these, with minor exceptions,[a] he never intended to give GPs access. It was the primary health centre, rather, to which they would gain entry and that aim Dawson never repudiated, no matter how many administrative problems it caused. In any assessment of risks, hospital access had to hold priority and this, for Dawson, meant that somehow, somewhere, a place had to be found for GPs in the hospital world.

As for the alternative of dependant coverage, that, in his view, offered no solution to the crisis facing general practice. It could even make matters worse, for the demands made by mothers and children might overwhelm GPs with work they could not handle. What they needed, Dawson argued, was more equipment, not more patients. Then they would be in a position to do a better job themselves, as well as to determine when consultants should be called in. Even more important, they would have institutional provision at hand which would benefit the nation as a whole — not, as in the case of the dependant alternative, aid the working class alone.[7][b]

Here Dawson also had the financial plight of the voluntary hospitals in mind. Dependant coverage would require a huge outlay of funds and he was afraid that it might deprive the hospitals of the state aid they desperately needed. But his own preference raised cost problems of its own: hospitals and health centres were also expensive and, if forced to choose between them and dependants, the Treasury might come down on the side of the latter. The fact that the voluntary hospitals provided their care free made such a choice all the more likely. Why, the Treasury might well have asked, should we pay for care which patients can already obtain without charge?[8]

There was, however, a less costly alternative which fitted in with Dawson's

a See p. 115 above.
b See the statement by Dawson quoted on p. 74 above.

priorities — that was to add specialist services alone to the panel. These could be provided outside as well as inside the hospital world and the price, when compared with dependant coverage, was modest: £1.29 million against £9$\frac{1}{2}$ million.[9] The Treasury had already committed itself to the programme in 1914, and it would take only a little prodding by the doctors to remind it of its promise.[a]

The money, furthermore, was needed to relieve the country of its severe shortage of specialists: before the war, they probably numbered less than 3,000 (as compared with well over 20,000 GPs) and the population required some 6-7,000 more to meet its needs.[b] Had they been available in 1911, Lloyd George would almost certainly have included them in the Act and the panel would have not been restricted in the way it was to an inadequate GP service.[12]

Dawson was intensely conscious of the problems this shortage caused. His whole policy, indeed, had largely been designed to ease it for, by bringing GPs into the hospital world, he could relieve consultants of many cases that did not require specialist care.[13] In the process, a whole new corps of part-time specialists might evolve, as it did in America and Germany, thereby enabling Britain to meet much of its specialist needs. The danger in such a development was that the process might go too far and produce the opposite problem — a shortage of GPs. That, unfortunately, did happen later in America and Germany, but Dawson had reason to believe that it could be avoided in Britain. *The panel system provided the restraining force.* Through the medium of its capitation system of payment (which forced British doctors to treat the 'whole' patient), it generated sufficient income to avoid the need to practise excessively as part-time specialists. The majority of GPs in Britain could therefore have been expected to remain GPs even if they were admitted to the hospital world.

With a GP service already in effect, Dawson could muster an impressive array of arguments to support the view that specialist services should be added first to the panel. In 1920, he did not actually take this stand: he still had hopes then of realizing his larger programme. But as the depression deepened, all hope of hospital development disappeared, and those who favoured the Dawson view were forced to concentrate their attention on the addition of specialist services alone.

Which side did the profession favour — Brackenbury's or Dawson's? No one who knew anything about the medical mind could say that the doctors were enthusiastic about either. Their attitude, rather, was one of resignation. As Whitaker put it in 1919: 'They [i.e. the doctors] dread further interference of the State or public authorities with their professional work,

---

a   The programme then admittedly was more limited but the intention was to expand it
     into a complete one as soon as possible.[10] One other anticipation of a specialist
     programme should be noted here. This appeared in Clause 3 of the 1917 Regulations
     and called on panel doctors to refer patients requiring specialist services to the facilities
     open to them. The aim was to link NHI with the specialist services only just made
     available to disabled veterans and VD sufferers.[11]

b   See p. 10 above.

and though they may accept this as good citizens in the interest of a better service for the people, they will regard it as mostly to the bad from their own point of view.'[14]

The doctors and dependant coverage

For years, however, BMA leaders had been in favour of both forms of extension and they managed to carry most doctors with them. In a report which Whitaker (as Medical Secretary) prepared for the BMA in 1911 just before the NHI Bill was introduced in Parliament, he recognized the need for dependant coverage in any satisfactory scheme of health insurance[15] but the consideration he had in mind was different from the one which moved the profession later. Then, it arose mainly from the desire to abolish the medical aid institutions the doctors hated.[a] Since these institutions, unlike club practice generally, covered dependants, and since the friendly societies had bothered to create them only where the pressure for dependant coverage was strong, the profession thought it could destroy them by including dependants in NHI. Though that ploy failed along with a subsidiary attempt to bar the existing institutions from the Act, the BMA did find it possible to stop the creation of new ones and the pressure for dependant coverage from that source gradually subsided.[16]

It did not revive until 3 years after the outbreak of war. Then the profession had cause to regret a generous gesture it had made in 1914. Carried away by a burst of patriotism, the doctors offered to give service free to dependants of servicemen but, by 1917, so many men had entered the armed forces that the profession began to search for some way to extract itself from the commitment.[b] NHI, with its modest but adequate capitation fee, seemed to supply it and, in 1917, the BMA issued a report which suggested that panel doctors were willing to accept dependant coverage only if the approved societies were deprived of their massive majority (60%) on insurance committees.[18] This sentiment was greatly reinforced by the spread of municipal clinics that Newsholme had stimulated.[c]

Once the war ended, however, the medical mood changed. Nearly all dependants thereafter had to pay for treatment and the threat arising from local authority clinics was curbed by the ban on domiciliary care which the BMA managed to insert in the 1918 statutes.[d] The latter, in fact, made such a great impact on the doctors that it revolutionized their attitude to dependant coverage. Whereas before 1911 the doctors thought the inclusion of dependants would stop the spread of a salaried service, now they

---

a   See pp. 13 and 82 above.

b   All the doctors could do, short of terminating the scheme, was to attach so many harsh conditions to usage that no one would want to apply for its benefits. This, in fact, was what the BMA did: through the medium of a relief committee composed of doctors, it operated the scheme in much the same way as the boards of guardians did the Poor Law.[17]

c   See pp. 34-5 and 46 above.

d   See p. 45 above.

feared such a provision would accelerate it.

This view was held by no less a figure than the Medical Secretary of the BMA. Dependant coverage, Cox told the profession in 1921, would put so many patients on capitation that there would be little difference (in terms of flow of income) between the panel system and a salaried service. Once that was realized, the state would turn to salary in an attempt to reduce the substantial costs that dependant coverage entailed.[19]

The converse of this point was also beginning to dawn on panel doctors: without dependants, they would have too few patients to justify employment on a whole-time basis. This was said to be the main reason why the NHI Commissioners failed to start a salaried service in 1912 when they were confronted with a medical strike.[20] By 1919, the meaning of that experience had at last been grasped by many panel doctors: as long as they kept dependants out of NHI, they were safe from salary.

The proponents of a salaried service however, believed the opposite: SMSA leaders thought dependant coverage would strengthen, rather than destroy, the panel and for that reason they too opposed the idea.[21] Earlier they had been more kindly disposed to Lloyd George's creation: right after he pushed his Bill through Parliament, they offered their support in an attempt to overcome medical resistance.[22] But their sympathy disappeared after 1914 and, by 1921, the Secretary of the SMSA (Parker) was opposing even the addition of specialist services to NHI; these, he felt, should now be left to voluntary insurance.[23]

The doctors favour extension to specialists

The rest of the profession did not share this view, and most doctors saw the addition of specialist services as the best way to preserve the system. Their desire for the change had been greatly stimulated by the promise made in the 1914 Budget[a] and it was heightened further by the incessant attempts of the authorities (egged on by the approved societies) to squeeze a wider range of services out of the capitation fee. Ever since the panel began, the societies thought the Government had paid too high a price for medical co-operation and some of them went so far as to favour the funding of specialist services through a cut in pay for panel doctors. That, the authorities recognized, the profession never would accept but they nevertheless saw the possibility of a more subtle way to realize the goal. As the *British Medical Journal* warned in 1916: 'Instead of at one fell swoop reducing the medical fees, which would lead to instant and serious revolt now or after the war, a plan far more likely to succeed would be, gradually and by slight increments at a time, to extend the obligations of panel practitioners without touching the present remuneration.'[24]

These fears were realized when negotiations over the new terms of service began in 1919. The plan proceeded in this way. First the Ministry stated the aim of its programme as one designed to remove any suspicion

a   See p. 32 above.

of double standards of treatment. This was most clearly expressed by one of the civil servants who helped fashion it, R. W. Harris, shortly after he resigned from the department (because of Addison's departure) in 1921:

> '... It was common ground that the insurance practitioner must observe at least the standard to which he would conform if he were, in fact, treating his insurance patients as paying patients — as indeed they really are, the only difference being that their contract with the doctor takes the form of a capitation payment, whether the insured person is well or ill, instead of a special payment for services rendered at the time of illness.'[25]

What this meant, in terms of the range of care offered, left the profession gasping. The department now wanted panel doctors to provide the same services for insured persons as they did for private patients no matter how long the treatment took or how much responsibility (and skill) it entailed. In rural areas, GPs did 'practically everything for their patients even to major operations'.[26] The department now expected panel doctors elsewhere to do the same, for it told the profession that, if any GP did not wish to perform surgery, he would have to pay another doctor to do it out of the funds he received from his capitation fee.[27]

One can imagine the uproar this proposal caused in the medical world. Commented the militant MPU: 'This principle must be nipped in the bud. Anything outside ordinary treatment as now given must be entered on a catalogue of services, then priced, and then duly paid for.'[28] The addition of specialist services to the panel promised to do just that: it would ensure payment to whoever provided the service. The only question it left open was who would actually do the work — GPs or consultants? Within the primary health centre, GPs had the chance, for it would give them the special apparatus and skilled assistance they needed to render such treatment.[29] But even if they lost out to consultants, GPs preferred that to the prospect of having to carry out the work themselves without payment. One doctor went so far as to say that he 'would rather have a State service than go on in the present undefined manner'.[30]

Panel doctors had an even more important reason for wanting to extend the range of services provided under NHI: they needed it to secure an increase in pay. As a result again of pressure applied by the approved societies, the Ministry refused to consider any increase until the service was improved and to do that, the doctors contended, they had to have specialist aid at hand. Quality, in their view, was associated with range and, until the latter had been freed from the restrictions placed on it, there was no hope of ensuring satisfactory treatment.[31] Such action was needed, they felt, to raise the public image of the panel system and thus ease the pressure for whole-time employment.[32]

Once they secured their pay increase in March 1920, the doctors lost interest in extension — but until that key question was settled, they were vitally concerned with the order in which additions were to be made to the panel. Given the choice between dependants and specialists, they would have come down overwhelmingly on the side of the latter. This was evident in the response made by the BMA's Divisions to a poll taken in 1920.

Whereas the primary health-centre idea was approved by an overwhelming majority (106 to 13), the suggestion of dependant coverage was rejected by 76 to 40.[33] The vote on the latter was said to be misleading because some Divisions misinterpreted the wording of the question to mean a salaried service. But the message behind the vote for health centres was clear: above all else, the profession wanted access to beds and expensive equipment.

Cox — in contrast to Brackenbury — heartily agreed with them. He attached the utmost importance to the proposal: nothing, in his view, would do more to make the panel service complete. He also thought it would help to relieve the chronic shortage of doctors in industrial areas. GPs who practised there suffered the most from the absence of specialist (and hospital) services. Their lists were far larger than elsewhere and they could not cope with the demands being made on them. The addition of specialist services would at least bring consultants to their aid and that, in turn, might make the conditions of work in industrial areas sufficiently appealing to attract other GPs there.[34]

These views underlay the support Cox gave to the Dawson Report[a] and, in the decades that followed, he never ceased to preach the value for GPs of hospital work.[b] Here he differed sharply from Brackenbury and, from the way the issue was eventually resolved, we can see who was the stronger figure. By 1938, the BMA had decided to alter its priorities and put dependants before specialists.[c] Cox openly expressed his regret at this decision in 1944,[35] but by then he had lost all influence in BMA circles as a result of his retirement from office in 1932. Brackenbury, on the other hand, managed to hold his key place in BMA affairs right down to his death in 1942.

In producing this reversal, Brackenbury showed that he dominated the making of BMA policy between the wars. But his victory came later: when the Dawson Report first appeared, he did not have the freedom to move the profession in that way. The boards of guardians, for one thing, would not let him. Their existence depended on the maintenance of a means test — but how could such a test be preserved if more and more people won the right to free medical care?

The defenders of the Poor Law, therefore, felt threatened more by the addition of patients to NHI than by the addition of services. The former took people completely out of their hands — whereas the latter only presented a challenge that could be met by improving their own system of medical care. Had they not already done this with the upgrading of their infirmaries? By 1918, these had become the pride and joy of the Poor Law. In the two years that followed, the guardians greatly improved their medical service in a frantic effort to stave off reform. This was one of the main reasons why the Minister who succeeded Addison — Sir Alfred

a   See p. 80 above.

b   For evidence of this, see the quotation at the front of this work.

c   See p. 157 below.

Mond (later Lord Melchett) — decided that the time was not ripe to abolish them. 'There is no doubt', he told a Poor Law conference in 1923, 'that the Poor law infirmary to-day is in many instances really almost a general hospital.'[36]

The guardians were not the only obstacle Brackenbury had to face: even more formidable was the question of finance. Here, too, specialist services held a decided advantage since they could be introduced gradually. When the panel began, this was not so readily perceived. Then, it was thought, dependants could be added in conjuction with specialist services and the year 1915 was actually set as the date when both would begin. Though the war ended those plans, the NHI Commissioners were almost forced to go ahead with dependants anyway (in 1917) just to relieve the profession of the burden of treating the families of servicemen without payment.[37]

Once the war ended, however, all thought of dependant coverage disappeared in the face of deteriorating economic conditions. Only the possibility of specialist services remained, and all Brackenbury could do in 1920 was make sure they did not come in the form Dawson intended. His way of saving general practice was to make every GP a bit of a specialist but, for the plan to work, the profession had to be offered an incentive. Panel doctors had made it clear that they would have nothing to do with additions to NHI that were 'free'. Brackenbury therefore sought a substantial pay increase in 1919 to finance his conception of general practice. Addison, spurred on by his advisers, was inclined to accede but, in the face of the opposition from the approved societies as well as the Treasury, he could not do it. To understand why, a closer look needs to be taken at the pay dispute that raged during the months that preceded the appearance of the Dawson Report.

Dispute over pay for panel doctors

At the time that NHI began in 1913, the doctors received a payment that yielded them a total of 7s. 3d. per insured person per year and by 1919 they had managed to raise this to only 8s. 9d. despite the sharp rise in prices that occurred during the war. In 1917, when they had last presented a pay claim, the doctors sought only 10s.[38] but, 2 years later, their demands knew no bounds. Aroused by the MPU and the obligations placed on them under the new terms of service, panel practitioners raised their sights to 13s. 6d. and some wanted to go even higher.[39] This infuriated the approved societies who, in view of the poor quality of care provided under NHI, did not think the doctors were worth even the 7s. 3d. they received in 1913. Under no circumstances would they tolerate an offer larger than 10s. and they called on the Minister to introduce a salaried service if the profession refused to accept it.[40] Not only the Treasury but Sir James Leishman, the fiery Chairman of the Scottish NHI Commission, agreed with them. Leishman went so far as to denounce the doctors' 13s. 6d. demand as 'a barefaced swindle'.[41]

In the face of such opposition, Addison found it difficult to request more than 10s. from the Cabinet. Morant, however, considered the amount inadequate: even 10s. 6d., in his view, was not enough and he urged Addison to demand more. Uppermost in his mind was the need to win medical support for the vast reforms the department contemplated: 'I will go so far as to say that I believe grave irremediable harm will be done to the development of our intended health services if the remuneration figure is not fixed now high enough to secure the goodwill and contentment of the reasonable portions of the profession. 10s. 6d. won't achieve *that*.'[42]

Whitaker, at first, did not share this view. As late as July 1919 he did not see the need for any pay increase at all. A rise in the capitation fee could only be justified if the department intended to enforce higher standards and, even then, it might do little good. Too many inadequate doctors were in practice for much of a change to be realized. The Ministry would have to wait years, Whitaker maintained, before it could expect to see any significant improvement in quality.[43]

This argument completely overlooked the main consideration Morant had in mind. He wanted higher pay not to ensure efficiency but to secure the profession's support for an extended service. After Morant made that object clear, Whitaker dropped his objections and supported the call for a large pay increase.[44]

Addison, in the end, also accepted this argument and asked the Cabinet to sanction an 11s. figure. It was angrily denounced as 'preposterous' by Austen Chamberlain, then Chancellor of the Exchequer, but with the aid of the other medical man in the Government (Sir Auckland Geddes), Addison managed to squeeze the offer through.[45]

To do this, however, he had to rely on efficiency, rather than expansionist, arguments. By January 1920, when the battle was being fought in the Cabinet, the prospects for reform were fading fast. All that seemed to be left were the minor changes in the regulations which the Ministry had managed to make in 1919. These, Geddes agreed, had been drawn tightly enough to ensure a satisfactory service and Addison argued for the higher (11s.) figure on the grounds that it was needed to enforce stringent conditions. In that way, he contended, the inefficient doctors would be weeded out and the better men drawn into the panel system.[46]

The 11s. offer, however, still failed to satisfy the doctors; they wanted nothing less than 13s. 6d. Negotiations were at an impasse and the only way out seemed to be arbitration, but Addison tried to thwart that by threatening the doctors with a wider investigation: 'The inquiry would open up the question of what were the deficiencies of the service, how they had arisen, and to what extent they would be removed by the new Regulations, or whether any other system would give a better result.'[47] The meaning of this warning was clear — Addison had a salaried service in mind — but Brackenbury was not frightened. He countered with a threat of his own — strike action — and that finally left Addison no choice but to accept arbitration.

Doctors offer to widen range of care

Once they had won that concession, BMA leaders devised an ingenious argument to justify their pay claim: they offered not only to raise the standard of care but to extend its range far beyond the point anyone had imagined. The President of the BMA (then Sir Clifford Allbutt) set the theme with a prefatory statement in which he stressed the need for panel doctors to render better and wider treatment than they had ever done before. To do it, he argued, they would have to double the time spent with patients and that, in turn, meant that their pay would have to be doubled as well.[48]

This gave the BMA the opportunity to repeat the same argument Addison had made to the Cabinet (based on the advice given by his civil servants at the Ministry): 'The remuneration of insurance practitioners must not be based on the lowest level of private practice, but on a relatively high level; otherwise, the better type of practitioner cannot but devote himself to other branches of practice, leaving only the inferior for insurance work. This is not what the State wants.'[49]

The BMA, however, was not content with that. Allbutt, in his statement, had mentioned a specific list of services panel doctors ought to provide, including such items as minor operations, subcutaneous injections and lumbar puncture. The BMA also agreed to have panel doctors render advice on hygiene, conduct research and co-operate with local authorities in public-health work. The list of duties was formidable and the BMA frankly admitted that it would take time to bring all panel doctors up to the level where they could perform them. But the profession, it claimed, was ready to accept the responsibility because of the greater demands being placed on it: 'There can be no doubt . . . that in the minds of both the profession and the public the conception of the sphere of the general practitioner has now greatly widened, and that the performance of the above functions must be encouraged if the Insurance Health Service is to be of proper value to the State.'[50]

Here, in its fullest form, was the line of development for general practice that Brackenbury envisaged in opposition to the Dawson Report. Long before the Report appeared, he had laid the groundwork for this plan. At the Annual Conference of Local Medical Committees in the summer of 1919, Brackenbury did everything he could to persuade his colleagues to accept a wider range of NHI work in order to strengthen their case for a higher capitation fee. The effort was most noticeable — and revealing — where the treatment of VD was concerned. The administration of salvarsan was then the accepted technique and most doctors preferred to leave the job to local authorities. The reason, however, was due not merely to their failure to secure extra pay or adequate equipment. Far more telling was the fact that they did not have the desire, competence or confidence to deal with a dangerous drug like salvarsan.

Brackenbury deplored such attitudes and he gave his colleagues good financial reasons for changing them: '. . . he did not want all their arguments for an increase in the capitation fee to be taken away from them. Even within the last six or seven years the level of the general practitioner's skill has been raised in various respects, and these were arguments for an increased capitation fee.'[51] Here, we have a clear example of the way in which Brackenbury worked in tandem with Newman. Both wanted GPs to treat VD — but whereas Newman raised the public-health arguments,[a] Brackenbury gave the 'trade union' ones. The profession, needless to say, was far more impressed by the latter.

The Minister, on the other hand, was impressed with neither — only here it was likely that he was reflecting the views of the Treasury rather than those of his own department. Addison rejected the proposal out of hand. As a rationale, he sought refuge in the developments expected once specialist (and other) services were added to the panel. These, he claimed, would reduce the burden on panel doctors rather than enlarge it.[b]

Nor was that the only point at which Addison failed to respond favourably. He also did not show enthusiasm for the profession's other offer — its readiness to conduct research and co-operate with local authorities. Here, Addison felt, the profession was proposing an ideal which might never be realized but, in any case, he did not think the time was ripe for such a programme. It would have to await the day when all GPs could be involved — not just panel doctors — through the medium of a public health service that would cover the nation as a whole. Until then, he did not want to do anything that would prejudice future development.[53]

Unfortunately for the doctors, the arbitrators agreed with Addison: they, too, awarded 11s. Brackenbury thus found his conception of general practice undermined by the Government's refusal to finance it. In 1920, it was true, he expressed great regret:

> 'To many of us the main disappointment in the matter is that the Government has missed a magnificent opportunity — one which is not likely to recur, at least in so favourable a form. At the present stage of national health developments the fundamental necessity has appeared to us to be the definition, the establishment, the encouragement of a "GP service" (not with reference to the Insurance Acts alone) of the best type, and with the widest outlook as regards its responsibilities towards both the individual and the community . . . We must accept the lower level of service as what it is now proposed to pay for; we shall no doubt give good and honest value on that level; but once more it is proved that the profession is willing to give practical effect to ideals far in advance of those held by politicians and administrators — even those charged with the care of public health.'[54]

In later years, however, Brackenbury never once returned to this theme: he was content to let general practice develop in an opposite direction. Year by year, the range of panel work narrowed — which suggests that Brackenbury perhaps did not really want the GP in Britain to become a bit of a specialist.

The approved societies, on the other hand, never forgot the words he uttered in 1920. Soon it produced a tendency among them to confuse questions involving the range of service with the quality of care rendered. This was most noticeable during the course of the pay dispute that occurred in 1923 and it was

---

a   See p. 104 above.

b   Addison actually made this point at an earlier stage of negotiations — before arbitration took place. The BMA first presented an outline of its offer in 1919 and it was then that Addison rejected it.[52] Both sides of the argument, however, were spelled out in greater detail before the arbitrators and the points mentioned here are taken mainly from the case presented to them.

Brackenbury who made the discovery. 'I am beginning', he told his colleagues, 'to have to tackle approved society officials who want to get our general practitioner *plus* specialist services all under the capitation fee!'[55] Only at that point did the profession respond to the suggestion he had made in 1919 when he thought the way to avoid such problems was to 'take these services out of the hands of the Panel Practitioner and put them into the hands of a special service'.[56] In 1919, the doctors who heard this proposal cried 'No! No!' but, after the dispute with the approved societies in 1923, many of them were ready to agree.

Part 4
The Deterioration
of the Panel System
1930-1939

Opposition to GP entry to hospital emerged strongly between the wars. MOHs withheld access to the new municipal hospitals — while consultants made it difficult for GPs to secure payment from private patients under the new pay bed and insurance schemes operating in voluntary hospitals. This left most GPs without sufficient facilities to keep abreast of advances in medicine and the panel system failed to make up the deficiency. The result was a narrowing of GP care and a lowering of medical aspirations. Anti-vivisectionists tried to exploit the situation by turning GPs against specialists and orthodox medicine.

13
GPs Excluded from Hospital

By the time the profession finished with the health-centre idea, all that remained was a building containing beds and diagnostic facilities for GPs. As such, there was nothing to distinguish it from the scores of cottage hospitals already in existence — yet, despite all his grandiose plans for the centre, Dawson seemed willing to accept that more modest concept.[1] Cottage hospitals at least gave GPs access to beds.

Once this change in thought took hold, even Brackenbury dropped his opposition to the health-centre idea.[2] What moved him was the need to avert the displacement of GPs from midwifery.[3] In an attempt to save the lives of mothers as well as infants, medical experts had seen fit to recommend deliveries in hospital rather than in homes and, if GPs were not to be uprooted from the field, then they would have to secure beds of their own. Where the specialty of surgery was concerned, Brackenbury, even then, might have been willing to let events take their course but the one area of GP work he wished to preserve was midwifery. Here, above all, was the place where GPs had the chance to transform themselves into family doctors and this was critical for them if they were to play fully the social role Brackenbury desired.

Not many GPs, however, responded enthusiastically to the challenge. GP hospitals, panel doctors feared, would only add to an already over-burdened routine a demand from patients for a host of unnecessary tests.[4] This was the main reason why many GPs actually 'feared having beds in the [health] centres'.[5] Dawson, they claimed, had grossly over-estimated the need for hospitalization,[6] while the Ministry had only just rejected their offer to perform a wider range of services in exchange for higher pay.[a] Before they undertook more work, they wanted more money. Until that was forthcoming, they were content to send their patients directly to the larger hospitals.[7][b]

One point they made clear: under no circumstances would they let hospital treatment come under the cover of their capitation fee. That could have exposed them to the danger against which they had been warned earlier — namely, the gradual extension of their duties without any increase in pay.[c] In

a   See pp. 130-3 above.

b   The Scottish medical consultative council, as a result, decided to omit the health-centre proposal entirely from the separate report it prepared. It called instead for the extension of the panel system so as to cover more services and more people.[8]

c   See p. 32 above.

the years that followed, the doctors protested strongly against the attempts the Ministry made to have hospital treatment included in their terms of service.[9] For the most part, it remained outside. Only in those areas with 'open staff' hospitals (i.e. where the hospital opened its doors to all local doctors) did the department manage to have the duty covered by the capitation fee. Elsewhere, it tried but, except for a brief period in 1935, the profession succeeded in keeping all areas with 'closed staff' hospitals completely free of the obligation.[10] Since no less than 3 out of 4 hospitals operated in this way[11] (including, it is revealing to note, many cottage hospitals)[12] the majority of panel doctors did not have to worry about even the financial implications of hospital care.

MOHs exclude GPs from municipal hospitals

At one point between the wars, the doctors had every reason to change their minds on the subject. The passage of the Local Government Act in 1929 presented them with a magnificent opportunity: at long last it abolished the boards of guardians and put hundreds of Poor Law infirmaries under municipal control. For the first time, MOHs had sufficient beds in hand to satisfy the needs of nearly every GP in the country and a strong plea arose for them to do so. It came from *The Lancet* which, at the time, saw GP access to local authority hospitals as the only way to save general practice from destruction.[13 a]

Despite this warning, the doctors failed to rise to the occasion. Few expressed desire for entry and some even opposed the move out of fear that it would add greatly to their responsibilities under the panel. Nor did they wish their colleagues to have any choice in the matter: the threat of competition ruled that prospect out. When asked by a medical neighbour who desired access to hospital whether he would support the move, the typical GP of the period replied: 'I don't want the privilege, and I therefore don't desire you to have it either.'[15]

MOHs were equally unenthusiastic about admitting GPs to municipal hospitals: they preferred to appoint fully-qualified consultants instead. Only in that way, they felt, could they hope to raise the standard of their hospitals to that of the voluntary sector. The Poor Law stigma was bad enough to live down; if a GP handicap were added as well, then local authority hospitals might never win the respect of the public.

Here, the LCC led the way. It 'ruled over a vast hospital empire', embracing some 77,000 beds (compared with a total of only 14,000 beds in the voluntary hospitals of London).[16] With so many beds to cover, the LCC might have been expected to admit GPs but it relied instead on a corps of part-time consultants to supplement the work of the resident staff. The leaders of the Royal Colleges were greatly impressed. As early as 1933, even Dawson said: 'An academic atmosphere had been gradually introduced into these municipal hospitals.'[17]

a   Today *The Lancet* takes a different view: now it subscribes to the 'social work' conception of general practice. This shift took place in the 1950s while the journal was under the editorial control of Dr (later Sir) Theodore Fox.[14]

Not all local authorities, however, could afford to be so selective. Some had to admit GPs because of the shortage of specialists outside of London[18] — yet those that did often had cause for regret. Too many GPs simply did not have the time, interest, temperament or competence for the work. MOHs only had to remind themselves of the lessons they had learned in the operation of local authority clinics to know this to be so. These had been formed mainly because GPs had failed to supply the care needed. Thus, even infant welfare, simple as it was in a technical sense, seemed to be beyond the ken of many — as Brackenbury himself was forced to admit in 1928: 'Although it was more or less a disgrace to the profession, it was true that a considerable number of private practitioners could not give the required advice.'[19] If this, MOHs asked, were true of a simple subject like child care, then how could GPs be trusted with 'real' specialties?

Even more serious were the failings GPs had shown in the field of obstetrics. Here, MOHs had been given a special role to play because of the high maternal mortality rates prevailing. This problem dominated the public-health world between the wars — so much so that laymen as well as doctors were obsessed with it — yet when the time came (under an Act passed in 1926) to ascertain its causes, the task was given to MOHs rather than obstetricians.[a]

It did not take the public-health world long to discover where the main responsibility for maternal deaths lay. The most outspoken man on the subject was Dr Andrew Topping, later (in 1950) the first full-time Dean of the London School of Hygiene and Tropical Medicine. Topping learned much about the causes of maternal mortality while serving as MOH of Rochdale during the years 1930-2 and, in 1936, he publicly put his views on record: ' . . . it is idle to deny that many avoidable deaths are directly attributable to the lack of knowledge, error of judgment (frequently arising from the foregoing), carelessness, hurry, or unwillingness to call in expert assistance, on the part of a general practitioner.' As a result, he asserted, 'in many cases maternal deaths are nothing short of murder'.[22]

Lack of knowledge, however, was not the only problem GPs presented to those who worked in the public-health world. When MOHs tried to use them in the operation of local authority clinics, they tended to be not only poor timekeepers but 'bad co-operators both amongst themselves and with official bodies'.[23] Also, the work they did varied too much in quality to provide any consistent — or satisfactory — standard of service. This applied particularly where MOHs complied with BMA wishes and appointed GPs on an indiscriminate basis from a rota of local doctors.[24]

Some MOHs tried to avoid these difficulties by using selected GPs but that created more problems than it solved. In the first place, the very act of selection aroused hostility and resentment: MOHs who followed the procedure found

a The obstetricians reacted angrily to the decision[20] and this led many MOHs to appoint GPs (in place of obstetricians) to the advisory panels that were created under the Act.[21] But that did not alter the preference of MOHs for fully-qualified obstetricians when the time came to make appointments to municipal hospitals.

themselves in an invidious position. Some even feared libel action. This became evident in 1938 when the Ministry advised local authorities to create advisory committees (composed of 2 obstetricians, 2 GPs and the MOH as chairman) in order to select GPs for maternity work.[a] At Willesden, the Borough Council could not persuade doctors to serve until it had agreed to indemnify them for damages arising from the choices they made.[25]

Selection caused clinic attendance to suffer as well. Doctors who had been rejected through the selection process flatly refused to use the clinics — and other GPs did the same simply out of fear of losing patients to competitors.[26]

With such problems, it is not hard to understand why MOHs, like local authority members generally,[b] preferred to employ doctors who were willing to work on a whole-time basis. The 1929 Act at last gave MOHs the chance to build the salaried service they desired and they had reason to hope that the younger specialists, hard-hit by a diminution in private practice as a result of the depression, were ready to accept employment on those terms. But GPs clearly were not: they had repeatedly made their opposition to that method of payment known. To remove any doubt on the subject, the BMA had only just issued a statement of policy (under the title, *A General Medical Service for the Nation*) which reaffirmed its faith in the panel system. At a later date perhaps, GP attitudes might change but, for the moment as least, MOHs saw clearly that their attempts to build a salaried service would have to be confined to the hospital world.[28]

Such an approach, furthermore, gave them hope of retaining their own influence on municipal policy. Dawson, in 1920, had issued a direct challenge to their authority by calling for the creation of local medical advisory committees on the NHI model. This proposal was coolly received by the public-health world. Some MOHs saw it as an 'insult' since it implied that they were not competent to deal with medical affairs.[29] In retaliation, they pointed to the dangers involved if vested interests were admitted to the administrative process[30] but this, many MOHs recognized, was only a futile gesture. Their best hope, rather, lay in the easing of consultant fears and what better way to do that than to make hospital appointments in accordance with the wishes of the Royal Colleges? GP involvement, on the other hand, would destroy all chance of dismissing the advisory committee idea. Panel doctors already enjoyed greater protection under NHI and they would certainly not accept less within the framework of a municipal service. Most MOHs thus came to the conclusion that it would be better for all concerned if GPs had nothing to do with the new system of hospitals evolving under local authority control.[31]

Consultants restrict hospital role for GPs

Not surprisingly, the consultants now reached the same conclusion. In 1920,

a   For more about these committees, see p. 155 below.

b   This applied to members of all political parties — Conservative and Liberal as well as Labour. As one MOH put it in 1939: '. . . members of local authorities of all shades of political opinion prefer whole-time salaried servants whose undivided allegiance they can command.'[27]

they had been willing to share some hospital facilities with GPs in the hope of rescuing the voluntary hospitals from the financial crisis facing them. By 1928, however, that crisis had passed and few consultants thereafter showed any enthusiasm for the prospect of GP participation.[32] Consultants preferred to work with doctors who were willing to devote their whole time to the specialist world; GPs, by definition, could not.

Therefore, consultants felt, they could not be trusted with 'serious' medicine; their knowledge was too superficial for that. It was far better to confine them to minor illness (as they were under the panel system) and leave the major cases to those who had the competence for the work. That competence, furthermore, would be endangered if GPs were admitted to hospital work, since consultants would then not have enough patients of their own to develop (and maintain) skills.[33] Merely the thought, therefore, of allowing GPs to enter general wards was 'anathema' to the consultants who had beds there.[34] [a]

This applied particularly to the surgeons: they were outraged by the inroads GPs had made on their specialty since 1920. During the war, they had been forced to accept GP aid in order to cope with the demands being made on them — but they did not expect that relationship to continue afterwards. Surgical technique, they believed, had advanced too far for that; it had been stimulated greatly by military needs and the surgeons thought GPs would abandon the field voluntarily. They did not reckon, however, on the rise of motor transport in the 1920s: this produced a spate of road accidents which kept doctors in cottage hospitals busy.[35] Emergency operations became the order of the day and GPs who had to perform them soon developed an inflated view of their skills. If they were good enough to operate on casualty cases, they asked, then why not on others? GP horizons expanded fast — so much so that, by 1926, the surgeons felt they could no longer remain silent. In that year, they launched a scathing attack on GPs who had strayed into their specialty[36] and it did not take long for other consultants (notably orthopaedists and obstetricians) to join them.[37] By 1929, the surgeons were not only opposing GP entry to Poor Law infirmaries but predicting the end of general practice itself.[38]

Only the physicians held back. This was because, in 1930 as in 1920, their security depended on an accommodation within the profession. Not only were they more exposed to GP competition than surgeons[b] but they needed GP aid just to relieve themselves of convalescent and other care that fell within GP range. The country simply did not have enough 'pure' consultants to go around. Only in London, where so many consultants were concentrated, was it possible to bar GPs from hospital; elsewhere, even in large provincial towns, they had to be used.

It was precisely in such towns that GPs had managed to establish themselves most firmly in the hospital world. There, over a period of two generations, they had won appointments as 'consultands'[39] — a term which, though no doubt

a   GPs could not ignore this hostility and it made many lose interest in hospital appointments. Then as now, consultants attitudes did much to intensify the inferiority complex displayed by GPs.

b   See pp. 113-14 above.

meant to suggest a lower form of consultant life, did not deter GPs from accepting. By the 1920s, according to Brackenbury, they actually comprised the majority of the staffs of voluntary hospitals despite the fact that three-quarters of such hospitals operated on the closed staff principle.[40] The hospital world clearly could not do without GPs and physicians, above all other consultants, had to make use of them.

By the 1930s, however, even the physicians wanted to restrict the way GPs were employed. What altered their attitude was the growth of pay beds in the 1920s. 'Consultands' were acceptable so long as the voluntary hospitals confined their beds to charity cases but now physicians asked whether they could afford to damage their reputation by letting GPs treat those who could afford to pay. Not only Dr Charles Wilson but Dawson himself said no.[41] Wilson, in fact, called for the total exclusion of GPs from pay wards. Even if only a few were admitted, he argued in 1928, they would come to

'. . . occupy in the eyes of the public much the same position as that of the medical consultant. Presently, without the additional years of study and without the unproductive hours in the outpatient department they will reap the same advantages as the consulting staff. This is a state of affairs which is inequitable, and if it came to pass it would not level up but level down the whole standard of medical treatment.'[42]

Some means, Wilson contended, had to be found to pursuade GPs to turn paying patients over to consultants.

The provident schemes that emerged in the 1920s provided the way. Under these, middle and upper-class patients secured insurance coverage for hospital and specialist treatment but not (with a few exceptions)[43] for GP care. Only recognized specialists could participate and this meant that most GPs — probably even many of those holding 'consultand' appointments — were excluded from payment.[44] 'Consultands' had no choice but to turn their 'provident' patients over to 'proper' consultants.

The only chance they had to secure payment was through the contributory schemes designed for the working class. Under these, GP coverage was more common but it could be obtained only at out-patient departments, not in homes.[45] This effectively precluded most GPs from the work and others were barred by the restrictions placed on hospital lists (i.e. the names of doctors to whom the schemes were willing to make payment).[46] Still, some GPs managed to gain entry and, once there, they had a large clientele to serve, much larger than in the case of the more aristocratic provident schemes. The latter covered only a few hundred thousand people in all, whereas the contributory schemes, which had begun as far back as the 1870s, embraced 10 million members.[47]

As far as payments were concerned, however, this huge enrolment did the doctors little good because the contributory schemes, unlike the wealthier provident schemes, collected only small contributions. The amounts, in most cases, were not enough to cover the cost of hospital services, much less medical care.[48] The hospitals concerned with the schemes, therefore, kept the bulk of the funds themselves: in 1930, only 66 out of 353 made payment to doctors.[49]

GPs may have been unhappy with this state of affairs but consultants were not. They were ready — indeed, anxious — to forgo payments from patients below the provident class in order to retain their hold on hospital beds.[50] What better way could they devise to discourage GPs from seeking hospital appointments? All the consultants had to do was to profess a desire to be charitable. The vested interest they were so anxious to protect could thus be hidden under a layer of professional altruism.[a]

Consultants had an additional point to consider: if they did try to widen the area of payment, then hospital governors might insist on subjecting them to closer regulatory control.[51] As it was, no one said a word if they turned up 3 hours late for a ward round.[52] Once consultants received fees for treating a substantial number of patients, the situation would change. By and large, therefore, the consultants wished to confine payments from voluntary hospitals to the small group of patients in the pay-bed and provident-scheme class.

During the 1930s, however, many consultants had to modify this stand as a result of the hardships caused by the depression. The pressure for payment came mainly from the younger consultants in provincial towns rather than their older, established colleagues in London, but they joined the BMA in sufficient numbers to produce a change in policy. Until the First World War, the BMA had opposed any payments to doctors in voluntary hospitals so long as the hospitals catered to charity patients and excluded GPs.[53] This was in accord with GP wishes since GPs did not want the hospitals from which they were barred to invade the area of fee-paying practice.[54] After the war, however, BMA policy changed as a result of the admission of fee-paying patients to voluntary hospitals and the appointment of increasing numbers of 'consultands' to hospital staffs. The latter wanted the same share from contributory-scheme patients as consultants were receiving from pay-bed patients and they made their views known at BMA meetings. By 1924 the principle of payment for the work done by all hospital doctors was formally accepted.[55] It did not progress very far, however, until a substantial corps of consultants supported it. During the 1930s, an increasing number of contributory schemes agreed to make payment.[56]

Between the wars, then, the rigid stand taken by consultants on the pay question had begun to erode but it was not enough to affect the position of most GPs who worked in the hospital world. The situation still left them on the horns of a dilemma: they wanted to be paid in the same manner as consultants but they were only allowed to serve patients whose treatment called for no (or virtually no) charges at all. Their dilemma was even crueller than that, for no sooner did GPs succeed in winning payment from the contributory schemes than the schemes tried to exclude them from the work. As long as the schemes received medical treatment free, they were content to let the hospitals use 'consultands' but, once the doctors demanded payment, the contributory schemes insisted on the same consultants as those used by the provident schemes.[57]

How did GPs respond to this dilemma? Their solution — as expressed in BMA policy in 1929 — was to demand the provision of pay beds in institutions

a   See also pp. 70-1 above.

outside the voluntary hospital world. In addition, they wanted all GPs — whether on hospital staffs or not — to participate in the treatment of private patients while in hospital. This meant that such patients would be presented with two bills rather than one — from the GP who saw them first as well as from the consultant. Neither solution, however, progressed very far; the economic climate between the wars was not conducive to the construction of new hospitals or the payment of superfluous medical bills.[58]

GP access to nursing homes

Only one substantial group of GPs received payment for bed care — those with access to nursing and convalescent homes. The reason for this lay mainly in the restricted nature of the service provided. Specialism, within their walls, had only a limited function to play and it had always seemed natural that GPs, along with other doctors, should have access to them.

The right, however, was no mean one. Though each home was small, so many of them existed that the store of beds in all was far greater than the number of pay-beds available in voluntary hospitals. In London in 1928, it was 3 to 4 times as great — 3-4,000 beds in the homes against 1,000 pay beds in the hospitals. For England and Wales as a whole, no pay-bed figures are available but the total for the nursing-home bloc in 1921 came to 26,000.[59]

Most of the homes lacked operating theatres and few had X-ray or laboratory facilities. It was only a matter of time before the advance of medical science would make them obsolete for the care of the acutely ill. But the fact remains that, as late as the 1920s, they still catered for the bulk of private patients and that GPs, through their access to the homes, managed to receive payment for bed care. The nursing-home bloc thus comprised the only significant group of GPs in Britain with a vested interest in the hospital world.

During the 1920s that interest came under attack from more than one source. Not only was it threatened by the advance of medical science but, more directly, by the regulatory arm of the state. Abuses in the homes were rife and Parliament, in 1927, saw fit to subject the institutions to a Registration Act administered by MOHs anxious to foster the growth of their own hospital service.[60] Many homes managed to survive the onslaught simply by changing their name: after 1927 they called themselves convalescent homes, but did not alter their work in any significant way. This is the main reason why the number of beds listed in convalescent homes doubled (from 13,000 to 26,000) between 1921 and 1938 while those in the nursing-home sector fell from 26,000 to 22,500.[61] But these figures masked a movement which threatened to disrupt completely the pattern of private care. As nursing homes closed, few cottage hospitals rose in their place. Rather, like the district general hospital movement today, bed provision became increasingly concentrated in the larger hospitals falling under municipal control.

The effect on private patients was predictable: they turned to the new pay beds opened by the voluntary hospitals and that stimulated the growth of provident schemes from which GPs were largely excluded. In the process, a ring was formed around hospital practice which threatened to deprive GPs completely of the chance to receive payment for bed care.[62] The nursing-home bloc lost no time in making its plight known and it had, as its spokesman, one of the ablest doctors in the land — Dr E. Rowland Fothergill of Hove.

As the owner of a nursing home himself, Fothergill might have come under suspicion — but no one who knew the man could doubt the purity of his motives. He served on the BMA's Council for an unprecedented 36 years (1902-38) and, during that time, devoted himself unsparingly to its work, striving in every way to promote the welfare of the profession. No one (apart, that is, from Brackenbury and Cox) did more to shape BMA policy toward the panel system and this despite the fact that Fothergill did not (except for a few years after 1911) serve under NHI himself. Among his many innovations, 2 above all should be noted — he originated the idea of holding annual conferences of local medical committees and he inspired the publication of the BMA's *General Medical Service for the Nation.*[63]

BMA leaders do little to secure hospital entry for GPs

BMA leaders thus had good reason to listen when Fothergill spoke and he called unceasingly for GP access to hospital in order to protect the profession from the displacement process set in motion by the closure of nursing homes.[64] Closed staffs,[65] pay beds and provident schemes that excluded GPs,[66] panel restrictions on charges for specialist services[67] — all came under his fire. Year after year from 1926 he raised these points at BMA meetings and the debates he started soon narrowed down into a straight clash between the interests of GPs and consultants.

The dispute put BMA leaders in a difficult position. Most of them were GPs themselves and knew from direct experience how difficult it was to maintain clinical standards in isolation from the hospital world. This, if nothing else, made them sympathetic to the demands of the nursing-home bloc. But, as medical-politicians, they really had no choice: Fothergill and his followers were too vocal to ignore. Even Brackenbury had to appear sympathetic to their demands.[68]

At the same time, however, BMA leaders could not ignore the wishes of consultants. One day, NHI (or some other form of public service) was sure to be extended to the hospital sector and, once discussions with the Government began, the profession had to present a united front if it wanted to secure favourable terms. Ideally, the way to do this was through a single organization but, at the moment, the doctors were divided: though most GPs belonged to the BMA, the leading consultants acted through the Royal Colleges. Not only did this create a division which Cox (among others) deplored, but it encouraged apathy in the specialist sector, since the Colleges took little interest in economic and political affairs.[69] BMA leaders wanted to wean consultants away from the Royal Colleges but many consultants were deterred from joining the BMA because of its domination by GPs. One leading surgeon (Sir William Arbuthnot Lane) resigned over the issue in 1926.[70]

Cox and his colleagues hoped to find some way to pacify consultants but they were inhibited by the belief, widely held among GPs at the time, that it was consultants who dominated BMA policy. This was a heritage of the great reform of 1902.[a] Until that year, consultants did dominate BMA policy and it had taken a prolonged constitutional struggle before GPs were able to strengthen their position. The extent to which they had succeeded was reflected in the background of the holder of the most powerful office the organization had — Chairman of Council. Until 1902, the doctor selected had always come from the consultant class but, between that year and 1937, no fewer than 4 out of 6 were GPs.[71]

Lane's resignation, however, finally forced BMA leaders to move in the consultants' direction: through specialty groups, they offered consultants the same kind of autonomy as panel doctors enjoyed on the Insurance Acts Committee. Between 1927 and 1938, 8 such groups were formed, the most important being the Consultants and Specialists Group (created in April 1934) which covered both physicians and surgeons.[72]

How did this development affect the stand taken by BMA leaders on the key issue of GP access to the hospital world? In a word, it left them indecisive since they saw no point in irritating consultants when so few GPs, outside the nursing-home bloc, showed concern for the subject. As the Chairman of the BMA's Hospital Committee (then Dr Peter Macdonald)[b] put it in 1933: 'The hospital staffs were not with the Association yet, but they were gradually approaching that position, and their pace of approach could be accelerated if they were not antagonised.'[73]

For Brackenbury, this need to placate consultants came as a blessing for it gave him the leverage he needed to push the profession in the direction of his conception of general practice. Earlier, in accordance with the dogma of the day, he had argued the case of the GP-specialist[c] but now, he pointed out, medicine had become too specialized for that. Though GPs could still offer a sufficiently broad range of service to avoid the need for excessive referrals, Brackenbury warned them against attempting any which they were not competent to perform. The family doctor's knowledge of patients, he took pains to point out, differed from that of specialists. It could best be described as 'fullness over a wide field' rather than 'depth over a smaller area'.[74] The good GP, he believed, should have 'powers of perspective in disease that are denied to the specialist'; he should strive for a 'more comprehensive outlook than a man whose life is devoted to perfecting himself in the technique and minutiae of one subject'.[75]

How could such a doctor hope to practise in the hospital world, that centre of specialist medicine *par excellence?* Brackenbury, no doubt, wanted him to abandon the attempt completely — but few GPs, at the time, were ready for so bold a move. They had to be given a larger stake in community medicine (e.g. local authority clinics) before they would be willing to accept complete separation from the hospital world. Meanwhile, Brackenbury had to proceed

a   See pp. 14-15 above.

b   Macdonald left the MPU after he lost the 1918 election (see pp. 54-6 above) and devoted himself thereafter to BMA affairs, rising rapidly in the medical hierarchy.

c   See p. 117 above.

slowly and he managed to introduce a subtle shift in BMA policy — altering the GPs role in hospital from curing to caring:

> '... The doctor has, of course, immediately to assist the patient to get over an illness; but it is not the less important that he should help him to combat or avoid any possible sequels or consequences arising out of that illness, to recover complete health, that he should advise how to prevent any recurrence of the morbid condition, and further after considering his whole environment, direct or encourage the patient in a way of life which may improve his average standard of health and enhance his physical and mental powers.'[76]

Henceforth, he argued, the distinguishing factor of a GP case should be home circumstances rather than the severity of the illness. Patients from houses without running water or without relatives to tend them were examples of the kind GPs should treat in hospital; those who required surgical operations were not. Cottage hospitals, he noted (but without comment), were overwhelmed with surgical cases; therefore, new hospitals had to be built in order to give GPs the facilities they would need. They would be called 'home hospitals' and, presumably, they would eventually replace the hundreds of cottage hospitals and nursing homes already in existence. Once that happened, the GP's role as a 'health custodian' would be assured and he would be freed from specialist distractions so that he could devote himself completely to the practice of what we now call community medicine.

The term 'home hospital' was not a new one: it had been used as early as 1877 by Sir Henry Burdett (the layman who led the voluntary hospital world until his death in 1920) simply as a means of designating a hospital for GPs.[77] Such usage was still appropriate during the 1930s because GPs had little access to beds outside nursing *homes* and cottage *hospitals*. Brackenbury's home hospital, however, was intended to serve a different function than either of these institutions: it was meant more as a substitute for home treatment than an addition to it. Thus, it would cater mainly for patients from homes which were not suitable for treatment; it would leave to larger hospitals (and specialists) those patients who were too ill to be treated at home whether their homes were suitable or not. Burdett had the same function in mind, but he conceived the term before the advance of science had made the hospital indispensable for the treatment of serious illness. In this sense, therefore, Brackenbury's home hospital was unique: it marked a major stage in the process under which GPs were transformed from part-time specialists into part-time social workers.[a]

Within the BMA, Brackenbury's 'home hospital' found a receptive audience — so much so that it permitted the organization to drop its long-standing commitment to Dawson's health centre. This change was facilitated — indeed, virtually necessitated — by the swift deterioration in GP-MOH relations that occurred in 1937 as the result of a dispute in Croydon.[b] GPs no longer wished

---

a　For the next stage of this process, see pp. 310-12 below.

b　See pp. 192-4 below.

to enter buildings which, because they contained local authority clinics, MOHs might have reason to enter. In 1929, when the BMA first issued its *General Medical Service for the Nation,* it held fast to the health-centre idea[78] — but, 9 years later, when the statement was republished, all reference to the subject had gone. Home hospitals, by contrast, remained in both — although only the idea (not the actual term itself) was expressed in the 1938 version, probably to quiet the fears of doctors who thought the new institutions might deprive them of the privileges they already enjoyed in cottage hospitals and nursing homes.[79]

Where other hospitals were concerned, however, the BMA remained silent — or nearly so. It did not wish to expand the number of cottage hospitals or nursing homes — nor did it try to secure a place for GPs in the larger hospitals evolving under municipal control. All it did was express (within the confines of a single Council meeting held in 1929, not in the policy statement itself) the pious hope that the 1929 Local Government Act would somehow enable GPs to obtain freer access to 50-100 bed hospitals (most of whom had closed staffs). [80] None, so far as one can tell, ever did — but even if all had done so, it would have made little difference to the bed provision for GPs. Such hospitals contained, in total, about 15,000 beds but, with over 20,000 GPs in the land, this meant that less than one bed on the average would have been made available to each GP.

Pay beds and provident schemes suffered similar neglect within BMA circles. Other than the two weak attempts described above,[a] the organization made no real effort to bring GP care, or payment for hospital and specialist work done by GPs, within their net. Thus, though the BMA (nominally) sought pay for all doctors who worked in voluntary hospitals,[81] it left arrangements so constituted that only consultants and fully recognised specialists would receive it. GPs in such hospitals continued to give services free.

In developing its hospital policy, then, the BMA did little to bring GPs closer to the hospital world. In fact, the gap widened after 1929. This, as we saw, was no accident: it was the result of a deliberate policy fostered by Brackenbury. In so doing, Brackenbury acted from the best of motives: he simply believed GPs had a greater service to perform in the community. That, for the most part, was all that was involved in the BMA's decision. Some GPs, however, interpreted the move differently. They thought the BMA had once again fallen under the sway of consultants[82] and their response, as in 1902, was the same: they began to form cells within the framework of the larger organization. Slowly but surely, the BMA split into rival camps. Thus, when consultants restricted membership of their Consultants and Specialists Group to 'pure' consultants in 1935,[83] the GPs formed a GP Committee of their own and did the same.[84]

Cox, who knew what damage this had done to the doctors in the past, rose in protest: 'The interests of the general practitioner are so closely interwoven with those of other sections of the profession that it is *never* safe to discuss them without the help of other sections of the profession.'[85] For the most part, however, his words fell on deaf ears. Though GPs did agree to add specialists to

a   See pp. 143-4 above.

the committee which they had created, the consultants failed to reciprocate. Here in the 1930s were the beginnings of the split which Aneurin Bevan (the Minister of Health who created the Health Service in 1946)[a] exploited so skilfully a decade later.

a   For a profile of Bevan, see p. 323 below.

14
Range of Care Narrows

With the BMA thus divided, the initiative on hospital policy passed to the MPU, giving it the chance to lead the fight for GP entry to the hospital world. Ready as always to use any excuse to attack the BMA, MPU leaders made the most of the opportunity. From 1921 on, they persistently sought to open hospital doors and repeatedly criticized the BMA for any deviation from that goal.[1] But though its leaders might rant, the MPU had too many panel doctors in its ranks to give the campaign hope of success. Few MPU members expressed desire for hospital beds and, as a result, the demands of their leaders fell on deaf ears. In the end, it failed to secure entry even to Poor Law infirmaries.[2]

Limits on GP-specialists

Most GPs accepted the decision without protest — some, no doubt, even with relief. Others found consolation by splitting fees with consultants.[3] But GPs who wanted to specialize now had to invest heavily in equipment for their surgeries. Significantly, it was only at this point that panel doctors began to press vigorously for state provision of laboratory and radiological facilities[4]— as well as to extol the virtues of home treatment, particularly where maternity care was concerned.

This led Brackenbury (of all people!) to pursue what many regarded as an irresponsible policy: time and again, he praised the advantages of home confinements despite the fact that hospital deliveries carried fewer risks.[5] Until 1936, the latter did hold out the danger of puerperal infection but the discovery of prontosil in that year all but removed the peril.[a] Thereafter, no one who knew anything about medicine could have failed to recognize the revolution that had occurred in maternity practice — but, despite the doubts he must have entertained on the subject, Brackenbury continued to assert a belief in the greater safety of home confinements. As one medical journal put it a few years after his death: 'The late Henry Brackenbury used this plea of safety [for preferring home confinements], but those who knew Sir Henry were not impressed by his argument, and believed that he himself doubted its validity.'[6]

---

a   Prontosil was the first of the sulphonamides — or 'anti-germ' drugs — that marked the start of the chemotherapeutic revolution in medical treatment. It was followed by the discovery of penicillin in 1940.

Midwifery, however, was not the only area in which GPs hoped to stake a specialist claim: they wanted to cover the whole field of medical practice. As one doctor put it in 1938: '. . . the ideal to be aimed at is that every patient should have a panel family doctor and panel specialists.'[7] What he meant by this was that GPs should be given the chance to do specialist work through a scheme offering such services outside hospital walls. Many GPs, including even some who had bitterly opposed the 1911 Act, wanted the scheme to be organized in conjunction with it. The demand for specialist services gathered strength in the medical world as long as it was understood that GPs — and not hospital-based consultants — would be the doctors that provided treatment.

The Government, however, failed to act — and, in the midst of a depression, little could be done through private means. One of the main contributory schemes (the Hospital Savings Association) did start a plan of its own which offered specialist services at a reduced fee — 1 guinea per consultation instead of the 3 guineas usually charged.[8] After some initial wrangling, furthermore, the Association (in 1931) agreed to open its own list of approved specialists to doctors specified by the BMA. In this way, no doubt, some GPs were put in the position where they could hope to receive pay for specialist work.

But the consultants made sure that most were disappointed. They did this, first, by restricting the operation of the Savings Association scheme to London. At the start of negotiations, the BMA scored a major coup for GPs: it persuaded the Association to accept the same liberal criteria that the approved societies used for determining whether panel doctors could charge fees for specialist services rendered outside the range of care covered by NHI. These were hospital experience, postgraduate education or local recognition. To the first 2, the doctor had to add proof that he had 'actual recent practice in performing the service rendered'[9] — but this posed no problem for GPs who held hospital appointments or who had secured admission to the Royal Colleges as Members or Fellows. Most bona-fide GP-specialists established their credentials in one of those ways.

But doctors who relied on local recognition often ran into difficulty and this was where all the trouble with the Savings Association began. Under NHI, approval was a local matter and, in some places, all a doctor had to do to secure it was to 'get one or two friends to say that he was recognized as a consultant'.[10] This may have been good enough for the approved societies but it was not acceptable to the Hospital Savings Association. It insisted on the creation of a central Consultants' Board (composed of 12 members appointed jointly by the BMA and the Royal Colleges) to apply uniform criteria everywhere.[11]

The BMA found that principle easy to accept so long as the Association's activities were confined to London but when, in 1933, it tried to extend the scheme to the provinces, it ran into difficulty. Many doctors in rural areas practised more than one specialty;[12] indeed, they had to since the volume of work available was too meagre to permit them to confine their activity to one specialty alone. But the Hospital Savings

Association scheme did not permit that: 6 headings had been established on its consultants' list (physicians, surgeons, gynaecologists, dermatologists, oto-rhino-laryngologists, radiologists) and no doctor could have his name put under more than one heading. The problem this caused was never resolved: in 1935, the BMA's newly-established Consultants and Specialists Group decided that the Savings Association scheme should not be extended to the provinces.[13]

Even in London, consultants managed to restrict the specialist activities of GPs through the monopoly they held over hospital appointments. With the consent of governing bodies, they introduced another innovation in the voluntary hospital world — the inauguration of paying sessions for private patients in rooms adjacent to out-patient departments.[14] After that, queue-jumping became a simple matter: patients tired of waiting to see hospital doctors no longer had to look elsewhere. All they needed to do was move to the adjoining room with a suitable sum of money in hand. GPs who managed to have their names put on the Association's approved list of specialists thus found themselves with few patients to treat.

How, under such conditions, could GPs hope to develop specialist skills? The only chance they had was through the panel system as it existed — by a gradual widening of care beyond GP range so that it embraced more and more of the specialist sector. The Ministry itself tried to do this in 1919[a] — but it offered no financial incentive for the effort. On the contrary, it expected the doctors themselves to pay for treatment in any instance where they did not feel personally competent. The profession, however, denounced the proposal and insisted on the exclusion of all specialist services from the definition of panel care. Those practitioners who wanted to do more actually found themselves penalized if they made the attempt.

Here the approved societies contributed to the dilemma: due to the pressure they applied, the regulations governing fee-charging were tightly drawn. Until 1934, no panel doctor could levy fees for specialist services given to patients on his own list — and, after that year, he could do so only if he could prove he were a specialist. (Even then, he could not charge for any service provided in an emergency, no matter how intricate or costly the treatment involved.)[15] The profession did its best to liberalize these rules and, for a fleeting moment in 1931, it won the department's assent. But the approved societies refused to accept the agreement and they persuaded Parliament to revoke it.[16] Their victory, nonetheless, did insured persons no good, for the regulations on fee-charging had an effect exactly opposite to the one intended: instead of forcing panel doctors to extend the range of service provided, it induced them to confine it to the minimum necessary.[17 b]

Nor was that the only effect of the panel system: not only did the range of care provided under NHI fail to widen between the wars — it actually narrowed. As

a   See pp. 126-7 above.
b   See also pp. 162-3 below.

specialist work became more costly due to the advance of technique, those doctors who could not charge fees (because they had not been recognized as specialists) were forced to abandon the work and demand restrictions on range. By 1938, some were even ready to give up minor surgery unless they received payment for catgut, silkworm-gut and local anaesthetics. Out-patient departments again became overcrowded.[18] The fall in attendances which had been produced by NHI lasted only from 1911 to 1920. Thereafter, attendances rose incessantly.[19] Yet the profession showed no concern for the burden this imposed on the voluntary hospitals. On the contrary, the doctors became alarmed only when the hospitals began to treat increasing numbers of patients falling in the private sector. Then they raised the same cries of 'abuse' and 'encroachment' that they had voiced before 1911.

Some doctors still managed to charge fees for services despite the safeguards in the regulations. They did so either by flouting the rules outright (thereby becoming known in responsible medical circles as 'the Dodsons and Foggs of our profession')[20] or by practising in partnership with non-panel men through whom the payments could be disguised. But this had no effect on the range of care provided by GPs between the wars: that continued to narrow even when payments were secured because the doctors involved had neither the time nor the amount of work required to maintain skills. Such, for the most part, applied even to doctors engaged solely in private practice. They, like their panel colleagues, lost the art of specialism — or never developed it — because they had too few patients seeking specialist treatment. The only way to preserve (and develop) such competence was to select a limited number of GPs in each area and let them provide the service for everyone.

Problems of selection

Selection, however, was the last thing the doctors wanted. Their reaction to this proposal showed itself most forcefully in 1924 when the department first limited the right of charging fees to those recognized as specialists. Many doctors objected strongly to the restriction. They wanted it to be based on the nature of the service performed, not on the qualifications of the practitioner. Once the service passed into the realm of private practice, they argued, it should not be subject to NHI rules.

The MPU first raised the subject before the Royal Commission on NHI (in 1925)[21] but it was only after GPs lost the fight over hospital policy that Fothergill pressed the point home in BMA circles.[22] Brackenbury, however, refused to support the demand; to the surprise of many doctors, he did not see anything wrong with the restriction. Learning by doing, he felt, had become too dangerous an exercise. Strictly speaking, the services in question *did* fall within the realm of private practice and could have been considered outside the purview of NHI. But Brackenbury made no attempt to protest along these lines; fee-charging continued to be confined to recognized specialists.

Brackenbury thus left his colleagues no choice but selection — yet still they refused to accept it. They preferred to see all GPs give up specialist work rather than have a few stand out above the rest. What made them so obstinate on the issue? Pride, envy, fear and jealousy were all involved. Each GP considered himself to be the best judge of his fitness to render a specialist service — and he feared the consequences if, through a process of selection, he were not chosen. Those singled out as specialists would become known as super-GPs and attract patients. Having rejected selection for the panel in 1911, GPs were in no mood to accept it in 1929 — even if the classification were carried out by medical colleagues. In its place they put one of the great myths of British medicine, one that has dominated the thinking of the profession ever since — namely, the belief that 'all GPs are equal'.[23]

Even more important for understanding GP attitudes was the inferiority complex they developed in the face of advancing specialization.[24] For this, the public was partly to blame: it failed to understand the GP's proper role in medicine and came to attach greater value to the service rendered by consultants. In time, consultants were considered superior even for the treatment of minor ailments. Here, in any rational scheme of medical care, was where the GP should have reigned supreme and British medicine, through the development of a state system, did manage to preserve a larger place for him there than was done in other countries (like America). But though the *number* of GPs in Britain remained higher than elsewhere, their *status* within the profession fell faster due to the increasingly narrow confines in which panel practice was conducted.

Even the language used by GPs in Britain tended to depreciate their status. Unlike hospital doctors, they tried to make themselves understood and this led them to adopt the same terms their patients employed to describe illness — e.g. gastric catarrh instead of dyspepsia. The custom, however, only served to reinforce the impression in the public's mind that GPs were of an inferior order.

Consultants in Britain thus came to provide a wider range of care than elsewhere. But that was not all they were expected to do: because GP standards were distrusted, the public wanted them to pass judgment on the treatment provided by GPs. Here, the role ascribed to consultants had a long history — one rooted in club practice when GPs did little more than provide bottles of medicine. Club members wanted to make sure such prescriptions were proper and that was what they thought a consultation service was for — as the Birmingham Consultative Institute discovered when it opened its doors in 1901:

> 'No one . . . attempted to define what was meant by the term 'consultant', but it was quite clear that the workmen wanted to have someone at their disposal to whom they could bring their medicine, who would smell the bottle, shake his head and prescribe something better. They did not want a real consultant to meet their club medical officer and consult with him, but they wanted a sort of referee who would act as a check over him. They compared their GP to the ordinary workman and thought that it was only right that a foreman should be set over him to keep him in order and to see that he did his work properly. The consultant was evidently destined to play the part of foreman.'[25]

In the face of such attitudes, it was not surprising that GPs developed an inferiority complex. It was this feeling, more than anything else, that made them sensitive to criticism and resentful of review. Here we have the underlying reason for the BMA's failure to preserve the range of GP care and raise its quality. Had British GPs been willing to accept tests of specialist competence, they might have gained hospital privileges the way American doctors did,[a] but by rejecting them in 1928, they undoubtedly destroyed their best chance of securing appointments. Even the liberal criteria applied to fee-charging under the panel were considered too stringent for entrance to hospital work. Only where contributory schemes were concerned did they accept restrictions, and then, only after their demands for self-selection had been rejected.[b] In the maternity sphere, the most they would do was accept review after they had done the work.

The situation here was so revealing that it needs to be looked at more closely. The 1936 Midwives Act established obstetric panels to provide medical aid to midwives who had been brought into municipal employment on a salaried basis. Any doctor was free to have his name put down on such a panel, but he could be removed (or forced to take a postgraduate course) if his work proved unsatisfactory. The public-health world wanted to select suitable doctors for the work and, for this purpose, the Ministry made provision for advisory committees to be created in each area, composed of 2 GPs, 2 obstetricians and the local MOH as chairman.[27]

The profession, however, refused to accept selection in any form and insisted on the right of any doctor to have his name put on the panel. The committees' work was thus limited to a review of work done. On this basis, the formation of the committees went ahead but, in many areas, the profession still refused to co-operate. Few obstetric panels, as a result, were ever created; many MOHs relied, instead, on an informal selection process, operating through the medium of midwives and GPs who could be trusted.[28] All this had important implications when the Health Service was created.[c]

Nowhere were the suicidal tendencies of the profession more evident than in the fight during the 1930s with the workmen's medical club at Llanelly. The club used panel doctors (instead of the more usual device of a medical aid institution) to provide medical care to dependants as well as to insured persons. A wide range of treatment was available — far wider than the services covered by NHI — but it was rendered entirely by GPs. Only one of them had surgical qualifications and he left Llanelly in 1930.[d] Thereafter, club leaders grew increasingly dissatisfied with the way

a   Between 1919 and 1931, the American Medical Association (AMA) secured hospital appointments for 2 out of every 3 doctors (98,490 of 152,500)[26] — thereby, incidentally, giving it the disciplinary powers it needed to control its membership. The BMA was forced to acquire these powers in another way — through the organizational structure created under NHI — but the sanctions it possesses are nowhere as strong as those held by the AMA.

b   See p. 151 above.

c   See p. 177 below.

d   The writer is indebted to Dr T. R. Davies of Llanelly for information regarding the dispute. He himself was involved and his brother was the GP with surgical qualifications who left Llanelly in 1930.[29]

operations were being performed. They tried to reach an accommodation with the doctors involved but none emerged — so, in 1934, the club imported a fully-qualified surgeon and employed him on a whole-time salaried basis. The GPs who had performed the operations thus not only lost the work but had their pay reduced in the process. They resigned *en bloc* and tried to carry on without the club, servicing the same patients through a system of their own. Club leaders replaced them with a full corps of doctors who, like the surgeon hired earlier, were employed on a whole-time salaried basis. Since all the club doctors worked in the same building, the club, in effect, had created a medical aid institution to replace the panel-type service it had formerly run.

Two competing systems thus came into operation, each striving to enrol the same patients. The relations between them were said to amount to a 'state of war'.[30] The struggle went on for 4 years and was settled only with the aid of the TUC. In the end, the club dismantled its salaried service and rescinded the pay cut — but the GPs involved lost out on the issue that started it all. Surgery was taken away from them and given to the fully-qualified surgeon the club had employed (who, however, no longer worked on a whole-time basis). Brackenbury believed the whole dispute could have been avoided if, in the beginning, the GPs involved had been willing to restrict surgery to a select few.[31]

Some suggestion that such a solution would have sufficed had come earlier from Cheshire. There the MOH had proposed to restrict surgical work on schoolchildren to 3 doctors. Local GPs were willing to accept selection but they considered the MOH's proposal unduly restrictive. To induce him to widen it, they agreed to accept the same criteria for these duties as had been applied to fee-charging under the panel.[a] Happily for all, the MOH agreed and threw the work open to a larger number of GPs.[32]

Attempts to expand panel care

We are now in a position to understand more fully why specialist services failed to develop under NHI. In its call for expert out-patient provision, the Royal Commission on NHI (which reported in 1926) made it clear that GPs would be used: '. . . what is wanted is not necessarily the opinion of an expert. The second opinion of any general practitioner of wide experience and good standing will usually serve the purpose equally well.'[33] To facilitate GP participation, clinics were to be created outside the hospitals,[34] and even the consultants had acquiesced since the proposal seemed to offer a way of satisfying GP-specialist aspirations without granting access to beds.[35][b]

Not every GP, however, was to be admitted to the programme: only those who possessed the necessary qualifications would be chosen. Had the proposal progressed very far, this certainly would have aroused the doctors — but they never had the chance to protest because the approved societies wanted more than the opinion of 'a brother panel practitioner'.[36]

Nor was that the only reason why the societies objected: they also disliked the way the programme was to be financed. Before the Royal Commission sat, everyone expected the medical service to be extended through 'normal' means — by raising the money needed through an increase in either weekly insurance contributions or the Exchequer grant. Such hopes were dashed by the passage in 1926 of the Economy Act: it took funds from NHI to help finance the new Contributory Pensions Act. The only way left to extend the medical service was through the pooling of approved society surpluses and the Royal Commission suggested that one-half of such funds be applied for the purpose.[37]

The friendly societies, however, rejected the proposal, not only because they were wealthier than the other approved societies but because they feared that once pooling began, it would — by restricting the chance to earn a surplus — limit the amount of additional benefits a society could offer and thus undermine the rationale of the approved society system.[b] Their action was not well-received by the public and the doctors made the most of the occasion:

> '. . . Thus, the approved societies have been discovered, and unequivocally declared, to be a gigantic obstruction to the main advance, most urgently needed, which ought now to be made in the public health service of the nation. This cannot be forgotten, and should be proclaimed and emphasised at every suitable opportunity.'[38]

Ten years later, however, the doctors found it more difficult to shift responsibility. By then, the outlook for the addition of specialist services looked promising despite the depression. This was due to the incessant rise in claims for disability benefit. They were eating deeply into approved society funds and the addition of specialist services would have done much to restrain them. Through the medium of the insurance committees, the societies approached the doctors in 1935 and discussions dragged on for 3 years. At several points, agreement seemed imminent but, in the end, it foundered on the principle of selection. The societies lost the incentive to provide the funds when the BMA tried to extend the number of GPs allowed to serve as specialists. Brackenbury, no doubt, breathed a sigh of relief because he, as we saw earlier[c], wanted dependants to be added to the panel first. In 1938, he finally managed to terminate the talks: the Council of the BMA decided (but by only one vote) to forget specialist services until dependants could be covered as well.[39]

held out hope of putting specialist provision under insurance committee control. Alternatively, such extension might have come by way of additional benefit schemes financed from the surplus funds of approved societies and, if that had happened, all who supplied specialist services would have been subjected to direct approved society management.

b   For an explanation of the approved society system, see pp. 16-20 above.

c   See p. 122 above.

What all this meant was that no significant additions were made to the panel between the wars. The only extras came in the form of additional benefits financed from approved society surpluses and these, as far as specialist services were concerned, were nowhere near sufficient to cover the costs entailed. They were more in the nature of charitable contributions to the hospitals involved and were not intended as compensation for the hospital staff. Out-patients were not entitled to such benefits at all and the in-patients who were received no better treatment as insured persons than those who were not.[40] The same, in all probability, applied to patients who belonged to contributory schemes: all, from the hospital's point of view, were charity cases or close to them. Only members of provident schemes (and patients in pay beds) were in a position to expect preferential treatment.

Apart from this, the only other attempt worth noting to expand the panel came in 1934 when the Ministry tried to encourage panel doctors to take an interest in ante-natal care. Previously, the subject had been shrouded in uncertainty as far as NHI was concerned. Few doctors wanted to do the work and the BMA itself had claimed that an examination was required 'only if requested' by an insured woman.[41] To remove doubts, the department suggested in 1934 that one ante-natal examination be specified as a duty and, so anxious was it to win acceptance, it even attached a financial incentive (1_4d. on the capitation rate) to the proposal. Despite the money involved, however, BMA leaders had the utmost difficulty persuading their followers to accept it. To do so, they had to employ the bludgeon always reserved for such occasions — the threat of a state medical service.[42] The duty thus became enshrined in the regulations. Even then, many doctors still disclaimed responsibility for the work. Said one doctor: 'In his opinion, pregnancy was a physiological condition, not a pathological one, and the duty of the insurance doctor was to treat pathological conditions.'[43]

Behind this response lay a complex of fears that affected GP attitudes across the whole range of maternity care. Throughout the 1920s and 1930s, GPs were subjected to a stream of criticism (most of it deserved) for the poor work they did where mothers and babies were concerned.[a] All this made the profession very sensitive to review and intensified its feelings of inferiority. During the 1930s GPs undertook major operations with more confidence than normal deliveries.[44] Many abandoned the work completely — while others lost out to midwives who, aided by the revolutionary Minnitt machine[b] and the backing they received from public health officers under the 1936 Midwives Act, took over an ever-increasing share of home confinements.[46] To this was added the toll taken by the trend towards hospital births: in 1927, only 15% of mothers had their

a   See p. 139 above.

b   This machine, developed by Dr R.J. Minnitt in 1932-3 with the support of the National Birthday Trust Fund, enabled gas-and-air to be administered so simply that even a patient could operate it. The doctors, however, managed to delay its use by midwives in any extensive way until after the war.[45] Meanwhile midwives had become salaried employees of local authorities under the 1936 Act and, Minitt machine or not, became responsible for many more deliveries.

babies delivered there; by 1946, the proportion had risen to 54%.[47][a] GPs without access to beds thus found themselves caught in a pincer movement: pressure from two directions was driving them from maternity. By the time the war ended, only about 1 out of 3 still did midwifery.[48]

In Scotland, the pattern was different: there, because of its large rural areas, something like 2 out of every 3 GPs found it necessary to undertake the work.[49] As a result, the Scottish Department did not follow the lead taken in England with the 1936 Midwives Act but channeled normal deliveries through GPs under a different statute passed in 1937.[50] In the end, however, this made little difference in the actual number of cases handled by GPs. The fees set in Scotland were so low (£2 for a normal delivery) that 1 out of 4 GPs refused to work the Act at all.[51] In 1946, the proportion of GPs doing deliveries north of the border amounted to only 26% rural and 18% urban as compared with 20% rural and 12% urban south of it.[52]

Nothing seemed able to stop the incessant erosion of care traditionally provided by GPs. Not only maternity but fracture treatment went. This had long been regarded by GPs as falling within their range — and the increase of road accidents in the 1920s, already noted, reinforced the feeling. GPs with access to cottage hospitals found themselves over-whelmed with orthopaedic cases. But the insurance offices who paid for the work did not like the care GPs gave and they stimulated the development of specialized clinics which took fracture treatment away from cottage hospitals.[5b][a] GPs in rural areas thus lost a large source of interesting work — but their colleagues in the cities showed no sign of regret. The work was very badly paid: as so many in the profession put it at the time, there was 'no money in fractures' outside the hospitals.[56]

Lowering of quality of panel care

Though the approved societies welcomed the development of fracture clinics, they viewed with dismay the growing restrictions on panel treatment. Advances in medicine were not only by-passing NHI but were forcing it into a tighter mould which raised costs and lowered quality. This was most evident in the effects the lack of laboratory facilities had on the panel. By the 1930s specific treatment had become available for a number of ailments which before had been subject only to symptomatic relief — but nearly all required laboratory tests. This was true not only of insulin for diabetes but of anti-sera for diphtheria and liver extracts for pernicious anaemia.[57] Because of the absence of laboratory facilities, panel doctors

a   These figures apply to live births only.

b   One insurance company did even more. The Prudential donated £1,500 a year for 7 years to the London School of Hygiene and Tropical Medicine and this money was used to finance the Chair in Public Health held by Dr (later Sir)Wilson Jameson.[54] Jameson, in 1932, paid tribute to the Prudential for its generosity[55] but that did not stop him, a decade later (after he had become Chief Medical Officer of the Ministry of Health), from devising a health service in which the insurance industry had no place. For Jameson's appointment to the Ministry in 1940, see p. 181 below.

were treating all cases of anaemia with liver extracts because they could not tell which were pernicious.[58] One doctor wasted £200 in this way on a patient who was subsequently discovered to be suffering from anaemia of the haemolytic type.[59] Laboratory facilities were no longer 'a frill' but an absolute necessity for general practice.[60]

Of all the possible additions to the panel, the Ministry considered this the most important. It told the Royal Commission on NHI that it wanted laboratory tests provided even if other specialist services had to be dropped[61] — yet they were lost in 1926-7 along with everything else. Only the few insurance committees which had started such a service before 1928 (from funds drawn out of their administration account) were allowed to continue;[a] otherwise, no panel doctors anywhere had the right to order pathological examinations under NHI. If they wanted them free of charge, they had to turn to the voluntary hospitals or local authorities that offered the service.

The voluntary hospitals had proceeded faster in this respect than the local authorities but, by 1939, no less than 80 local authorities provided some kind of testing facility.[63] This made imperative a link between the 2 since data was being locked up in municipal laboratories which could have aided hospital treatment.[64] GPs were best placed to provide the connection — yet BMA leaders refused to let the Ministry integrate local authority services with the panel. Fear of wider municipal control was only a small part of their objection; more important was their concern for the financial interests of private pathologists. They, along with other specialists, were in the process of being recruited to the BMA and the organization was anxious not to seem to go against their interests.[b] BMA leaders therefore organized their own pathological scheme under which 100 privately-controlled laboratories agreed to accept reduced fees for insured persons and their dependants.[67] This may have pleased the pathologists but it did not meet the needs of the nation. The approved societies thus secured little relief for their funds from the policies adopted by the BMA.

They could, however, find some consolation in the addition of 'pure' specialists to the regional medical staff of the Ministry. Previously, in accordance with the profession's wishes, only GPs had been appointed. Again, it was fear of competition that had dictated GP demands.[c] They did not want the service to obtain second opinions; rather, they saw it as a way of securing relief from importunate patients who demanded certificates entitling them to cash sickness benefits. The MPU accurately reflected the

a   This restriction was due to action taken by the profession itself. As much as the doctors desired laboratory services, they did not want to do anything that would prejudice the formation of a nation-wide system. It was the BMA that insisted on the insertion of a ban in the 1928 NHI Act; only those schemes already in existence were allowed to operate.[62]

b   The BMA created a special Pathologists Group in December 1927.[66]

c   Regional medical officers were also needed to prevent a split in the profession between 'ordinary' panel doctors and the 'super' GPs whom the approved societies had used earlier to settle certification disputes.[68]

feeling of panel doctors in 1919 when it described the kind of regional medical officer who would be acceptable to the profession: 'What is wanted is a sort of super-GP, not in competition with us, a whole-time appointment, elected and nominated by ourselves.'[69] Though the profession never secured the right to elect or nominate regional medical officers, it did see part of its demands fulfilled. Only GPs with 10 years' experience were appointed and part-timers (who were employed as a supplement to the whole-time staff) were not used in the districts where they practised.[70] This was entirely satisfactory to the approved societies at the time since they were more interested in a referee than a consultation service.

Addison, however, felt differently. In 1914, he had fought hard to include specialist services in the Budget and, when all hope passed in 1920, he made the regional medical staff available for second opinions.[71] Even domiciliary consultations were provided until Mond (who succeeded Addison) suspended them in 1921.[72] Panel doctors, however, made little use of the service. They dismissed regional medical officers as 'generalized specialists' who were not suitable for consultation.[73]

The Home Office rejected them for the same reason, in spite of an official recommendation that they should be used to settle disputes under the Workmen's Compensation Act.[74] Furthermore, as medicine became more specialized, they were not always adequate as referees under NHI and, in 1934, the Ministry decided to add eye and heart specialists, a surgeon, a neurologist and a radiologist to the regional medical staff. In the Glasgow Centre, even laboratory tests were provided.[75] The staff, however, was too small to cover the country as a whole and had to be reserved for the purpose GPs always preferred — as referees in certification disputes. In 1932, the regional medical corps amounted to only 82 in all[76] — which, in relation to the 19,000 doctors serving insured persons, meant a ratio of only 1 medical man on the Ministry's staff for every 230 practitioners on the panel.

Addison's dream of a proper specialist service was thus never fulfilled. The panel system entered the Second World War more restricted in range than it had been at any time since it was created in 1911. For this development, it seems, Newman was partly responsible. If dependants could not be added first, then nothing would come: that seems to have been the view he adopted during his long reign at the Ministry (covering the years 1919 to 1935). As a writer in *The Lancet* commented when Newman died in 1948: '. . . he tended to concern himself more with explaining what should be done than with using his powers to do it.'[77] His failure to act cannot be attributed solely to the long depression which began in 1921, for that did not inhibit the growth of social insurance. By 1939 Britain had one of the most fully developed systems in the world — yet, in the provision of medical treatment under public auspices, it lagged far behind. As an official of the International Labour Organization told the Beveridge Committee in 1942: 'In no other country has medical benefit remained the same since 1911.'[78]

15

The Anti-Vivisectionist
Attempt to Divide the Profession

'. . . Modern medicine is materialistic and its whole trend is in the direction of
increasing specialism. The general practitioner is identified with this
movement . . . By allowing himself to be carried along . . . the general
practitioner is losing his own standpoint . . . He should not try to emulate the
specialist but instead endeavour to do something for his patients that the
specialist cannot do . . . In this he would find 'nature cure' and homoeopathy,
which are especially suited to his needs, of great service . . . '

'Has Modern Medicine Failed?', a lecture delivered by the Treasurer of the
MPU, Dr T. T. B. Watson, before the anti-vivisectionist Health Education
and Research Council, 18 May 1939, as reported in *Medical World,* 14
July 1939, pp. 743-9.

By the 1930s, the main line of development for panel practice had been drawn:
it was to be separated from the hospital world and conducted within a range that
only privately-owned facilities would allow. So constituted, it might be
extended to cover the nation as a whole — which gave those concerned with
'quantity' reason to be hopeful. But, from the standpoint of 'quality', the
prospect was less promising: even the most ardent proponents of state medicine
had to admit that the standard of treatment given under NHI left much to be
desired. Nor could its deficiences be confined to the public sphere: the panel
system was too closely involved with private practice for that. As a result, the
bad habits engendered by NHI were leaving their mark on the whole range of
general practice in Britain.

Panel doctors who tried to improve the service they offered succeeded only
in winning the opprobrium of their colleagues. As the MPU's journal put it in
1926: 'The danger always present in health insurance practice is that someone
better able than his colleague to equip himself with special apparatus, may
render a service beyond their reach if not beyond their competence.'[1] In this
way, the fear of losing patients to competitors drew an ever-tighter ring around
the range of panel care, pulling it within the competence of the least able and the
most lethargic.

No uniform national pattern, however, existed: due to the absence of
specialists, GPs in rural areas offered a wider array of services than those in
urban areas. Under NHI, 'range' questions had to be determined locally on a
case-by-case basis. In practice, this led to what Brackenbury called 'counting
heads'[2]: a service was deemed to fall within the range of NHI's medical benefit
only if it were performed by a majority of GPs in the area. With the aid of the
Labour Party, Brackenbury tried to stop the practice in 1923. He drew up two

schedules — one listing in detail all the services that would fall within medical benefit; the other listing those outside. Before a doctor could charge for the latter, he would have to establish his competence more carefully than he had done before. Previously, a GP with specialist ambitions could rely on local recognition;[a] henceforth, he would have to hold a hospital appointment or possess the necessary adademic qualifications.[3]

The Ministry, however, did not feel it could live with the rigidity inherent in Brackenbury's plan. What it was proper for a GP to perform today might not, due to the advance of medical science, be appropriate tomorrow. Specific delineation of GP duties, therefore, would not do; the NHI world would have to live with a general definition of range, leaving disputes to be settled locally.[4] This meant, also, that the department could not tighten the tests for fee-charging; panel doctors would still be able to rely on friends to establish their competence as consultants.

Over the years, a large body of case law built up, but it had an effect exactly opposite to the one which the authorities intended. No sooner was a service ruled within the range of panel treatment than GPs made every effort to give it up. They were anxious to extend themselves only so long as they could charge extra fees for the treatment. It is misleading, therefore, to use the case decisions as a guide to range in the way the Ministry did.[5] They reveal only when fees could be charged, not whether the treatment was customarily provided by GPs under the panel.

In one urban area — Manchester and Salford — the service was wider than elsewhere because of the way panel doctors were paid. The profession there chose the attendance (or fee-for-service) method rather than capitation, and this gave GPs an incentive to extend themselves. Some of the approved societies, as a result, became interested in the system and, before the Royal Commission on NHI in 1925, one group (the Association of Approved Societies) called for its extension across the country as a whole.[6]

The decision, however, rested ultimately with the doctors and, by then, even those who practised in Manchester and Salford had lost their enthusiasm for the attendance system. What made them feel this way were the restrictions placed on the payments they received. No matter which method local doctors chose, the total allowed was fixed — which meant that one doctor's operating fee came out of his colleagues' normal attendance charge. This gave the profession a vested interest in keeping the 'extras' down. By 1926, so many restrictions had been imposed on this method of payment that, as the Royal Commission concluded, it 'really differs in essence very little from the capitation system'.[7] Shortly afterwards, the doctors in Manchester and Salford decided to let it go.[8] From 1928 onwards, the profession everywhere was paid by capitation and the range of services offered in urban areas tended to be uniform.

Appeal of fringe medicine

During the 1930s, only one area of specialist practice remained free of the

a   For what this actually meant in practice, see p. 151 above.

restraints which NHI had placed on it. This was physical medicine, the specialty which offers such services as massage, exercise, whirlpool baths and heat treatment. With minor exceptions,[a] these were not covered by NHI and, due to the weak status of the specialty,[10] GPs found they could charge fees for such services without worrying about specialist tests of competence. To embark on such work the only equipment needed was an inexpensive sun lamp, a device widely prized by the public between the wars.[11] Once this practice began, some GPs found it tempting to add to the services for which they could charge by offering various forms of fringe medicine as well — particularly those like osteopathy and chiropractic which employed methods similar to those used in physical medicine.[12] The value of fringe medicine was difficult to prove but that did not deter GPs since the same applied to much orthodox practice. Even today, the cures that medical science can offer are limited and many patients find the care they receive from cult practitioners to be more beneficial than that from qualified doctors.[13]

The movement in this direction between the wars, however, did not have such an innocent connotation. It was part of a concerted campaign by leading figures in the anti-vivisectionist world to turn GPs against medical science. Physical medicine lay within the bounds of orthodox practice but, like osteopathy and other types of fringe medicine, it did not require the use of drugs or other forms of treatment that depended on animal experimentation. Anti-vivisectionists, therefore, condoned it and used it as a means of weaning GPs from orthodox methods. Specialists, they recognized, would be harder to influence because of their close association with medical research. This led some in the anti-vivisection movement to oppose specialization in any form, urging the profession to treat the patient as a whole rather than the disease. As one leading medical anti-vivisectionist (Dr Howard Fergie Woods) put it in 1941: 'We must get rid of the idea of disease as something to attack.'[14] The aim of anti-vivisectionist propaganda was thus to widen the split that already existed within the profession.

Emergence of anti-vivisectionist influence in the MPU

The campaign the movement conducted during the 1930s was led by a medical anti-vivisectionist who managed to secure a position of influence within the MPU. This was Dr Maurice Beddow Bayly, a panel doctor from Bethnal Green who found the MPU's obsession with economic matters to be an excellent cover for attacks on medical science.[15] In 1923, for example, the MPU resisted the introduction of insulin, not because it was based on animal experimentation but because it involved too much work.[16] Bayly, to make himself popular in MPU circles, did not have to preach kindness to animals; all he had to do was to protest against any

a   Some approved societies did manage to provide some forms of physical therapy (mainly massage) under the cover of additional benefits, like nursing, or by way of donations to charitable institutions, but the number of insured persons involved in such arrangements was always small.[9]

advance in medical science that tended to injure the economic interests of panel doctors.

During the late 1920s, however, Bayly found a way to speak more directly. The opening was provided by a court case won by the leading medical anti-vivisectionist of the day, Dr Walter Hadwen, President of the British Union for the Abolition of Vivisection.[17] Hadwen's case did not involve the disciplinary procedure under NHI but another complaint, almost identical with the one filed against him, did. This was lodged against a panel doctor in London by the name of Harvey who was charged with negligence by the London Insurance Committee.[18] The sub-committee which originally heard the case called only for a fine to be imposed and, had that recommendation been accepted, nothing more would have been heard of the matter. But, since the patient died, the Insurance Committee felt the offence too serious for the doctor to be let off lightly. It therefore called for his removal from the service and this meant that the case was automatically referred to a court of enquiry at the Ministry.

Here Harvey emerged the victor — at least so far as the question of removal was concerned.[19] But the department did not think that he should be absolved completely. Harvey, like Hadwen, had made the wrong diagnosis — yet he was so sure he was right that he refused to take a test for another illness which the patient actually had. There was no question of penalizing him for making the wrong diagnosis, but the Department did think he should be punished 'for omitting to do what any reasonably careful doctor would have done, however certain he might have been in his own mind that the result of the test would be negative.'[20] Since this was only a minor infraction of the terms of service, the Ministry called for the lesser penalty which the sub-committee had originally recommended. Harvey was asked to pay a fine of £20.

Despite the lightness of the penalty, however, the profession did not take kindly to the decision.[21] It came on top of other cases in which similar action had been taken and larger fines imposed. All these decisions, taken together, seemed to fit into a pattern: the Ministry was trying not only to impose a proper line of treatment but to establish a higher standard of care under NHI than that which applied to private practice in a court of law. In a sense, this was true: the department, as the provider of panel pay, could not devolve itself of responsibility for the quality of panel care. Private patients not only had legal sanctions at their disposal — they also had economic sanctions. Insured persons could hope to duplicate these only with the backing of those who actually paid the doctors. The right to change doctors offered some remedy but it was only through action taken under the complaint procedure that insured persons could hope to simulate the financial penalties that private patients possessed. The Ministry, therefore, could not be content with legal tests; it had to employ economic ones as well. The Royal Commission on NHI had itself endorsed this conception of the department's role.[22]

But the Ministry did not intend to apply its powers in the way the profession believed. It had no wish to impose a proper line of treatment; all it wanted to do was to make sure the panel practitioner 'duly applied his mind' and took 'proper care'. Nor was it even consciously seeking to raise panel standards above legal standards; it merely hoped to bring the action taken by 'weak' insurance committees up to the level of 'stronger' ones and establish a uniform pattern of penalties throughout the country.[23]

This, however, was not the way it appeared to the profession. Hadwen and Harvey had both been charged with the same offence but, whereas Hadwen had got off scot-free in the courts, Harvey ended up having to pay a fine. Another case soon afterwards provided an even more direct contrast between 'public' and 'private' justice since it involved only one doctor, not two. A panel practitioner called Tanner found himself cleared in court of the very same offence for which he had earlier been 'convicted' under the complaint procedure.[24] For panel doctors this was a startling reversal of affairs. Ever since NHI began, they had been accused of giving insured persons a service inferior to that which they provided privately; now it seemed, they were to be driven in the opposite direction under the whip of the complaint procedure.[25]

The situation provided a tailor-made opportunity for the MPU, since Harvey belonged to it and not the BMA.[26] Here was the chance it had been waiting for to secure recognition from the Ministry. Ever since it was formed in 1914, it had been searching for ways to displace its larger rival so it could become the spokesman for panel doctors. During the early days of NHI, the MPU did manage to send deputations to the NHI Commissioners but, because of the intemperate attacks it made on civil servants, all that ceased after the new department began.[27]

Now it seized this new opening. The BMA could not claim to represent Harvey when he belonged to the MPU. Welply therefore approached the Ministry hopefully in April 1925, but he received an icy reception;[28] none of the officials at the department could forget the attacks that had been made on them. Robinson (the Permanent Secretary) dismissed the MPU bid for recognition with these words: 'They ought to learn the elementary decencies of controversy before asking to be heard here.'[29] And his deputy — Mr (later Sir) Laurence Brock — made an even angrier response: 'They are impossible people to negotiate with because what they want is not agreement but advertisements.' MPU membership, he noted, had been stationary for years: 'But if they secure recognition they might easily become dangerous.'[30]

For the MPU, this rejection amounted to a call to arms. Welply and his ally in NHI work, Dr Gordon Ward, launched an attack on the way the department administered the complaint procedure. 'At no time in the history of NHI', cried *Medical World* in July 1925, 'has the disciplinary lash been wielded with such remorseless vigour over the profession as at present.'[31] In the months that followed, the MPU mounted a massive assault on the Ministry's powers[32] and soon it was joined not only by the BMA but by *The Times*[33] and the legal profession.[34] The forces converging on the department were formidable and, though it managed to resist the MPU's call for an appeal to the courts (from decisions taken under the disciplinary procedure),[35] it could not withstand the profession's other demands. In 1928, the doctors entered the ranks of the department in force.[36] Had the approved societies not been distracted by other problems, the outcome might have been different but, with no one to stiffen the civil servants at the Ministry, the changes made marked a watershed in the development of NHI. After 1928 the profession no longer had reason to fear the countervailing power of the approved societies and its influence over administration grew stronger year by year.[37]

For Bayly, however, the significance of the occasion lay elsewhere: it rested in the nature of the charge against Hadwen and Harvey. Both were accused of failing to take a swab test for diphtheria — and, hence, of administering antitoxin — in cases that seemed to call for it. From the moment the two doctors went on trial, few in the profession liked the way their clinical treatment was brought under investigation; even to the most orthodox doctor, that seemed to be a violation of professional freedom. One of the most respected GPs in the land — the East End socialist, Dr Harry Roberts — cried out against it in these terms:

> '. . . If we stand this we shall stand anything. We have been subjected to an affront and an injustice which no body of organized workmen in the country would tolerate for a minute. Quite apart from the disregard of the considered verdict of the tribunal, it is nothing short of an outrage that the officials of a Government department should be able with impunity to impose financial penalties for what even they only describe as an error of judgement.'[38]

Hadwen was not content merely to express his feelings; he was so incensed at the fine on Harvey that he declared his refusal in the future either to take swab tests for diphtheria or to administer the antitoxin which he, as an anti-vivisectionist, so much deplored.[39] Nor was Hadwen alone in this reaction: some doctors who had never dared to question the canons of medical science before began to wonder whether swab tests were of any use at all.[40] Initially, it was Hadwen and Harvey who were in the dock but before the incident ran its course, medical science itself went on trial[41] and Bayly, by 1928, found it possible to attack the subject directly.[42] Thanks to the Ministry's innocent and well-intentioned action in the Harvey case, anti-science views found a way to make themselves respectable in MPU circles.

Bayly joined the Council of the MPU in that same year (1928) and soon began to exert an increasing influence on its policy, becoming first Chairman of the Council's Executive Committee in 1930, then Chairman of the MPU's strategic NHI Section in 1931 and, finally, Chairman of the Council itself in 1934.[43] An even more important source of influence came his way in 1936 when he managed to assume *de facto* control of *Medical World*. Welply, in his capacity as General Secretary, still retained nominal authority over the journal, but he could not write well and tended to leave the details of publication to others. Bayly's influence became so pervasive that one of his friends in the homoeopathic world thought it fit to describe him as editor.[44] [a] Within the columns of *Medical World*, however, Bayly tried to hide this fact. Since he was known as an anti-vivisectionist, he did not want to alienate medical readers by having the journal become too closely identified with him. Only in the form of unsigned leaders and book reviews was it possible

a   The only official recognition of Bayly's tie with *Medical World* came in 1943 when he was listed as a member of the journal committee.[45] No committee members were named before this year but it is likely that Bayly held the same position in the 1930s.

to detect his touch. The clearest indication came in July 1936, when only one month after Bayly's own book on cancer research was published,[46] the following leader appeared in *Medical World*:

> '. . . We must insist on a halt being called to mere laboratory work on experimental animals. This leads us nowhere, and is merely a wastage of animal life, not to speak of the entailment of needless pain and suffering to the animals concerned. We are not anti-vivisectionists, but we have humane instincts, and we shall, as members of an honourable profession, continue to decry the infliction of suffering on the lower animals in the name of medical science. Cancer research, as at present conducted, is causing untold suffering to myriads of animals. If it resulted in the cure of cancer there would be some excuse for it, but this is not the case: and, therefore, we submit that it is unnecessary and immoral.'[47]

Bayly did not operate alone in this work. Associated with him in the MPU were a number of doctors who either shared his views or had other reasons for furthering his influence. Behind them lay a vast network of interests, deriving mainly from the close ties Bayly had with the two central figures of the anti-vivisection movement, the Duchess of Hamilton and Miss Lind-af-Hageby, both leaders of the Animal Defence and Anti-Vivisection Society.[48] In 1930, they began a concerted campaign to convert GPs to unorthodox methods of treatment through a Health Education and Research Council on which one respected MPU leader agreed to serve.[49] (This was Dr E. H. M. Stancomb, President of the MPU for 3 terms.[50]) It is not possible, however, to determine how many GPs were influenced by the campaign. Members of the medical profession have always been reluctant to publicize their interest in heretical forms of treatment.

Only in Cheshire did the profession show a willingness to reveal itself. There, led by one of the most energetic GPs in the land, Dr Lionel J. Picton, some 600 doctors allowed their names to be identified with a form of 'treatment' not too far from nature cure. Pure — or chemical-free — food, they declared, was the key to good health and they not only put their names on a testament affirming this belief but they let their own local medical committee (with Picton as secretary and editor) publish a quarterly *Compost News Letter* in which the view was made known.[51]

To overcome medical inhibitions, the anti-vivisectionists had to make fringe medicine respectable and that was difficult to do as long as it was denied state recognition. The osteopaths, with some Labour and union backing,[52] made a concerted attempt to win it in 1935 but Parliament rejected their claim because they had little scientific evidence to support it.[53] Thereafter, all Bayly could do was promote physical medicine, hopeful that through it doctors would find an interest in fringe medicine. From the middle of 1938, *Medical World* devoted a supplement per month to physical medicine and, judging from the amount of advertizing involved, many GPs must have installed heat lamps and similar equipment in their surgeries.[54] Whether they went any further in the direction of fringe medicine, it is impossible to say.

Links with anti-semitism

Bayly, however, did not confine his campaign to clinical subjects: he also tried to win GP support by appealing to their prejudice against Jews. Here, he was following a tactic that had been adopted by the anti-vivisection movement when it began since many of the doctors involved in medical research were Jews.[55] At the end of the First World War, the feelings of some anti-vivisectionists expanded into an attack on Jews generally and one — Dr John H. Clarke, the 'Father of Modern Homoeopathy' — went so far as to form an organization called 'The Britons' which was devoted solely to that purpose.[56] This, no doubt, also explains why so many figures from the world of animal welfare and unorthodox practice joined right-wing political groups between the wars.[57] Indeed, the ties between the leaders of the London Anti-Vivisection Society and the British Union of Fascists were so close that the Society almost acted as its voice in the animal welfare world. The key figures were Wilfred Risdon and Mrs Norah Elam Dacre-Fox. Risdon was Mosley's first Director of Propaganda and Dacre-Fox stood as a Fascist candidate in the 1935 General Election.[58]

Bayly led a similar group within the MPU and how they operated we shall see later on.[a] But the point to note here is that Bayly had much greater success with the campaign he conducted against Jews than with the one against orthodox medicine. Far from falling after 1936 (when the racial campaign began), MPU membership rose — to a height of 5,857 members in 1938 compared with only 2,816 nine years earlier. The largest part of this increase came at the end of 1934

MPU Membership, 1915 to 1950
(as of December 31 each year)

1915	599	1933	3788
1916	982	1934	5204
1917	1372	1935	5304
1918	1539	1936	5434
1919	3154	1937	5575
1920	3295	1938	5857
1921	3134	1939	5622
1922	2750	1940	5101
1923	2973	1941	5372
1924	2832	1942	5659
1925	2995	1943	4523
1926	3009	1944	3913
1927	2941	1945	3973
1928	2886	1946	4246
1929	2816	1947	4547
1930	3604	1948	4534
1931	3847	1949	4608
1932	3896	1950	4691

Source: Annual returns submitted to the Friendly Societies Registry Office (on file at the Public Record Office under the shelf-mark FS 12/232).

a   See pp. 275-8 below.

when the MPU affiliated with the TUC[a] and there is reason to believe part of the increase was deliberately over-stated in order to give the MPU the right to send 2 delegates (instead of 1) to the TUC's annual Congress.[59] But the fact remains that MPU membership rose after the anti-semitic campaign began and that the organization never, at any point in its history, had so many doctors standing for election to its Council as it did in 1938.[60] Furthermore, Welply claimed a readership as high as 15,000 for *Medical World* [61] and, if this was correct, then Bayly's influence extended far beyond the confines of the MPU.

From all of this, the lesson for the nation was clear: general practice had deteriorated in a social as well as a medical sense and the need for its reform was urgent. The panel system had produced great benefits: it preserved general practice and, by restraining the amount of surgery done by doctors, prevented the revolt against orthodox medicine that did so much damage to the Weimar Republic. But the isolation of GPs from the hospital world left them arid in a clinical sense and the anti-vivisectionist campaign may have even created a distaste for medical science and specialist medicine. The Conservative Governments, when they introduced the Midwives Act of 1936 and the Cancer Act of 1939, took care to by-pass GPs. Public-health services, by the time the Second World War broke out, were evolving in a hospital as well as a municipal direction and, if a community service was to be formed, then something had to be done to resurrect general practice. This, above all, was the challenge confronting those who wished to create the National Health Service.

a   See p. 182 below.

Part 5
The Lost Opportunity for an Integrated Health Service 1940-1945

GPs showed little interest in hospital access during negotiations on the Health Service. They were more concerned with the Ministry's proposal of a salaried service in health centres under municipal control. The centres were to contain only GPs and local authority clinics, not beds, and they were intended to give GPs a larger stake in preventive rather than curative medicine. Consultants as well as some GPs welcomed this development but the profession as a whole feared the prospect of municipal control. To protect themselves, the doctors sought a system of administration in which they had a voice but the Ministry failed to satisfy the demand until the chance of forming an integrated service was lost.

16
GP Indifference to Hospital Access

Unlike the First World War, the Second did not expand GP horizons: GP services were not needed in hospital as they had been 25 years earlier.[a] On the face of it, this was surprising since the special services created during the Second World War extended over a wider area than those established in 1914. Then only the needs of wounded servicemen had been covered, whereas the emergency services set up in the Second World War took care of certain categories of civilians as well. The services, in fact, were designed mainly for the treatment of air-raid casualties and, before the war ended, they expanded to the point where they also covered many of the ordinary civilian sick. For the most part, however, GP care was not given — one had to enter a hospital or attend a first-aid post before treatment could be secured. This was why it would have been more proper to call it an Emergency *Hospital* Service rather than, as it was officially named, an Emergency *Medical* Service.[1]

To cope with the demand, the Ministry of Health (which administered the service) had less than 3,000 fully-qualified specialists[b] and, to these, it was only able to add about 500 from the pool of refugee doctors who came to Britain before the war.[2] In such a situation, GP aid seemed essential but the department refused to allow it. All it did was make sure that the available supply of consultant services was spread more evenly across the country.[3] In the process, even hospitals formerly open to GPs were affected since they, too, found it possible to draw on the services of fully-qualified specialists.[4] In any case, after 1940, the Ministry left little room for choice. When complaints arose about the poor quality of treatment in some emergency-scheme hospitals, the department moved swiftly to solve the problem. It created its own regional staff of consultant advisers and gave them power to act on their own. 'There is no doubt', Richard Titmuss has commented, 'that the work of these consultants and advisers was effective.'[5]

In terms of clinical duties, then, the Second World War made little difference to general practice: it left the range of treatment as narrow —and the quality of care as low — as it had been in the 1930s. This applied particularly to the kind of service given under the panel system. Apart from BMA leaders and civil servants involved in NHI administration, no one rose

a   See p. 112 above.
b   See p. 10 above.

to defend it. The strongest indictment came from one of the leading socialists in the country — G.D.H. Cole. In 1942, as Director of the Nuffield Social Reconstruction Survey, he produced a report which claimed that the quality of care given under the panel was far inferior to that provided privately.[6]

Labour concern for quality

Though Cole's survey was based more on opinion than fact, it had a profound effect on the movement to which he had dedicated his life: for the first time in its history, the Labour Party became concerned with quality. Earlier, Labour criticism of the panel system had been confined almost entirely to 'quantity' matters: it did not, Labour spokesmen declared, cover enough services or enough people.[7] Where the standard of GP care was concerned, the Party found it prudent to maintain a stony silence. The reason for this lay in its desire to extend the system. BMA leaders, between the wars, were the Party's main ally in the extension movement[a] and Labour did not want to alienate that support by attacking the care the profession gave.

Quality, however, could not be entirely ignored — the inadequate condition of the average doctor's surgery was too obtrusive for that.[8] But only after hopes of extension faded in the 1920s did Labour spokesmen dare to make their dissatisfaction known. In 1930, Ernest Bevin not only condemned the panel as a 'tragedy of incompetence' but expressed regret that Lloyd George had introduced NHI.[9] Ten years later, the President of the SMA (Somerville Hastings) came to a similar conclusion[10] — so that when Cole's report appeared in 1942, it found a receptive audience in Labour circles.[b] In 1943, the Party's Public Health Advisory Committee (with Hastings as Chairman) issued an important policy statement which denounced the panel because 'it does not provide sufficient guarantee for the *efficiency* of the doctors employed'.[11] Nor were these empty words: at the Party conference in 1945, an SMA stalwart and MP, Edith (later Lady) Summerskill, assured the delegates that Labour would guarantee high quality care in the new service.[12]

Exactly how this was to be done was not revealed but, in 1942, another SMA leader, Dr David Stark Murray, thought the standard of GP care could best be raised by bringing GPs into the hospital world.[13] Few in the profession, however, showed enthusiasm for the suggestion and this applied as much to GPs as to consultants. GPs made their last real effort to enter the hospital world in 1929 when the Poor Law infirmaries passed under municipal control — but local authorities, as we saw, proved no more responsive to their demands than boards of guardians.[c] Thereafter, as the depression deepened, GPs lost interest in the subject. Far more important was the question of survival and their attention turned to the threat posed by the ever-growing number of clinics under municipal control.

a   See pp. 86-8 above.

b   For profiles of Bevin and Hastings, see pp. 324 and 327 below.

c   See pp. 138-40 above.

This shift of interest was most noticeable in the policy of the MPU. In 1929, it led the fight for hospital entry but the subject was not even mentioned in the home treatment scheme the MPU distributed in 1940 and 1942 which called only for the extension of GP care to the nation as a whole. That, it stressed, was 'much more important than the provision of extra specialist and institutional services, which can already be provided by county and borough councils.'[14]

BMA ignores hospital-role for GPs

When the debate on the Health Service began, the question of hospital entry hardly arose. As early as August 1940, the BMA created an independent Medical Planning Commission to determine the kind of service that should exist once the war ended and in May 1942 — seven months before the Beveridge Report appeared — this body produced a working document.[15] Like the Dawson Report of 1920, it was called an interim report and, to stress the tentative nature of their proposals, the doctors issued it only in draft form. But despite the long campaign waged by Fothergill and the nursing-home bloc,[a] the Commission did not feel it necessary to mention the subject of hospital beds for GPs. To understand how this omission occurred, we need to take a look at the way the body went about its work.

Though it was created in August 1940, the Commission did not hold its first formal meeting until May 1941. Dawson opened the proceedings and stressed the need for all doctors to have a place in the hospital world but he played no part thereafter.[16] The lead seems to have passed to the principal public-health representative on the body, Dr George F. Buchan, MOH of Willesden.[b]

From the start, Buchan gave the Commission an orientation towards community care. The main need, he declared, was to plan the domiciliary service and he predicted that the Commission would find the GPs' role the 'toughest nut to crack'.[17] Rather than have GPs come between municipal clinics and hospitals, Buchan envisaged their disappearance altogether —but he was, as a matter of practical politics, willing to carve out a place for them in preventive medicine.[18] In his view, the relationship they should have with the hospital world was not one for the Commission to consider — and no doubt the consultants on the body agreed. This, as far as one can tell, explains why the subject was omitted from the interim report.

It did, however, figure prominently in the articles that followed publication. These appeared in the *British Medical Journal* and were intended as a guide for the discussion groups that considered the document.[19] But except for an occasional paper or comment in the *Journal*,[20] nothing of importance seems to have emerged from the discussions. Had the Commission proceeded to the preparation of a final report, then something might have been said on the subject. But all thought of that disappeared in

a   See pp. 144-5 above.

b   For Buchan's earlier involvement in medical politics, see p. 84 above.

November 1942, when the Beveridge Report fell like a 'thunderbolt' on the profession.[21] Until then, the doctors had proceeded at a leisurely pace, expecting a Royal Commission to be created before any reforms were carried out.[22] Once the Beveridge Report appeared, however, all long-term policy-making in the profession ceased.

Throughout the whole period, only one BMA leader protested strongly at this failure to consider hospital entry. That was Dr Peter Macdonald, then Chairman of the BMA's all-important Hospital Committee.[23] Few GPs, however, shared his concern, displaying the same indifference in 1942 as they had done in 1940 when, during the course of an earlier debate on hospital reorganization, one doctor had observed: 'Even the general practitioner seems to agree that he has no part in a hospital scheme, judging by the absence of any claims put forward.'[24]

This explains why, when negotiations on the Health Service began in 1943, the subject was not listed among the 11 principles enunciated by the profession. All the BMA suggested was that experiments be made with different types of health centres and this was later amended to include the attachment of GP beds to the larger general hospitals.[25] [a] No interest in the idea was shown at the Annual Representative Meeting in 1943 but, due largely to the efforts of one persistent GP-surgeon (Dr Raymond Greene), the doctors did pass a motion in favour of small GP hospitals in 1944 and 1946.[27] However, the consultant who succeeded Macdonald as Chairman of the Hospital Committee, Mr R. L. Newell, opposed the proposal because of the damage GPs had done in the field of surgery[b] and he was in charge of the sub-committee that issued a report on the subject. Predictably, the report managed to evade the issue. Though it paid lip service to the idea of GP hospitals, it stressed the difficulties of constructing them due to the shortage both of building materials and consultants (the latter being needed to help GPs with their work in the hospital world).[28]

Though few GPs complained about the report, concern about their role in the hospital world did arise from a different source. It came from the 'consultand' class[c] — particularly from those GP-specialists on the staffs of the smaller voluntary hospitals (157 in number) in or near London. They were threatened with removal from their hospital posts once the Health Service began and, in 1944, they produced a scheme — called the Volims-Griffiths Plan — which was designed to protect them from the control of the more prestigious consultants in London.

For a period during 1945, they did manage to stir GP interest in the hospital question but they could not sustain it because of the ambivalence of their own attitudes towards the smaller GP hospitals. On the one hand, they needed the support of the doctors working within them to make their

---

a   Only one BMA leader — Guy Dain — went further and that, perhaps, was because he remembered what he had learned on the Dawson Committee in 1920. At a meeting with the Ministry in June 1943, he argued for GP access to hospital as a way of raising quality, suggesting that GPs be required to work there as a condition of payment under the new Health Service.[26]

b   For more about this subject, see pp. 305-6 below.

c   See pp. 141-2 above.

own protest count; on the other, they did not want to push the idea so far that it encroached on their own sphere. In the end, the solution they came to was to confine GPs working in the smaller hospitals to 'common ailments', thus turning such hospitals partly into convalescent homes for the aged and chronic sick.[29] That failed to arouse much enthusiasm among GPs.

GPs and maternity work

Their mood did not change until the prospect of maternity work arose. Under the Health Service as originally conceived, pay for this work was to be confined to selected GPs — those who had both the necessary postgraduate education and the continuing experience needed to maintain competence in obstetrics.[30] Some reform like this had been tried by local authorities before the war but it failed.[a] The start of the new Health Service offered the chance to make another attempt.

The department, however, made the mistake of confining selection to England and Wales; in Scotland and Northern Ireland, too many GPs did the work to make selection practicable. English and Welsh GPs, however, did not appreciate the distinction — and they feared that once selection was allowed in midwifery, it might spread to other areas of general practice.[31] From the moment the idea was mooted, they protested against it and, just before the Health Service began in July 1948, Bevan gave in. GPs everywhere won the right to be paid for midwifery, the only difference being that those who possessed the necessary qualifications received 2 guineas more (7 as opposed to 5) for a complete array of services.[32]

Once Bevan decided to drop the restriction, GP interest in hospital beds mounted.[33] With the trend toward institutional deliveries, GPs required such access to maintain their role in hospital work. Yet, even here, it was probably the chance to earn extra fees, not the clinical excitement of the work, that moved them. The restriction, furthermore, was not removed until just before the Health Service began — which meant that throughout the whole period from 1943 to 1948 when the critical negotiations took place, GPs exerted hardly any pressure to enter the hospital world.

Their attention, in any case, was diverted by a more pressing problem — the threat of a salaried service under local authority control. Such a prospect had been raised before[b] but, this time, it assumed a more ominous form since the proposal came from the Minister of Health himself, then Ernest Brown. In March 1943, at the very start of negotiations on the Health Service, he produced a draft scheme which called for the employment of GPs on a salaried basis in municipally-run health centres.[34]

From that point on, the profession could think of nothing else. The danger dominated discussions with the Ministry and prompted the doctors to make demands to meet it. In the process, any thought of hospital entry was lost. As

a See pp. 139-40 and 155 above.

b See Chapter 4 beginning on p. 45 above.

one medical commentator (Dr T.B. Layton) observed in 1944, the campaign for a salaried service 'had a most unhappy effect. It centred discussion on one single point, and that relatively a small one, instead of stimulating a wide outlook upon the whole subject with its thousand effects.'[35]

In retrospect, we can see that the salaried proposal could not have been introduced at a worse time. In raising it when he did, Brown made a serious tactical error because, as a result, the Health Service developed along more divisive lines than he and his planners intended. GPs, in 1948, found themselves more isolated from consultants than they had been before. The separation of the profession became one of the unintended effects of the new Service. To understand how and why this happened, we need to trace the evolution of policy within the Ministry itself. Fortunately, as the result of the reduction of the period restricting access to public papers from 50 to 30 years, such an analysis is now possible.

17
Ministry Desire
for a Salaried Service

Co-ordinated care had long been the object of official planners[a] and the division that existed in the medical world precluded its realization. But more serious from the Ministry's point of view was the gap that had appeared between GP and local authority services. Contrary to the intent of those who conceived the 1929 Local Government Act,[1] municipal clinics and hospitals had developed apart from the GP sector and this was causing severe problems, particularly in the field of maternity and child welfare.

There, municipal growth had gone the furthest due to the exclusion of dependants from NHI. Yet, because of the ban on domiciliary care, local authorities were limited in what they could do.[b] Their efforts were confined largely to those who felt the need to attend clinics and, even then, the municipal emphasis had to be more on prevention than cure. Health education and welfare foods were the main services local authorities offered; only when a baby was born did they reach very far into the clinical sphere.

Health centres without beds

To be effective at all local authorities had to induce mothers to attend clinics and, for that reason, the Ministry had always insisted that the clinics be kept apart from the hospital world. Fear of infection was much stronger then than it is today and only in the most extreme circumstances could patients be persuaded to enter hospital. Not until the chemotherapeutic revolution began in 1936 did the experience lose its terror for the public.[c]

This, above all, explains why the 'health centres' that developed in the 1930s did not contain beds. During that decade, local authorities became aware of the need to rationalize health operations. Previously, municipal clinics had grown in haphazard fashion, scattered throughout the communities they served. Not only was this inefficient but it bred confusion: patients often did not know which clinic to attend. Should a pregnant mother suffering from TB attend the ante-natal clinic in the city centre or the TB clinic on the periphery?

a   See pp. 27-8 above.

b   See p. 45 above.

c   This probably explains the loosening of Ministry policy just before the war. Then, for the first time, it allowed one municipal health centre to be built on hospital grounds.[2] We do not know, however, how the experiment fared. Did clinic attendances fall? Unfortunately, no record appears to have been made.

Only by bringing the clinics together in one building could the confusion be corrected. The authorities that did so had the problem of finding some term to describe the new institution. The words 'health centre' seemed ideal; they breathed the spirit of 'prevention' which the municipal world wanted to convey. They also served to distinguish the buildings housing clinics from those holding beds. The hated word 'hospital' now came to be reserved for the latter.[3]

New role for GPs

Where did GPs fit into this pattern? Their role, in Ministry as well as municipal eyes, lay with the clinics rather than the hospitals. Within the department this view was universal, but it seems to have been held with particular strength by Sir (Evelyn) John Maude, Permanent Secretary (1940-5) at the start of negotiations on the Health Service.[a] The Minister's views were shaped by him and Maude thought that, with GPs working in them, health centres should 'form an integral part of the personal health services already conducted by local authorities'.[4]

Such an arrangement was needed to enable public health officers to reach patients in their homes. The great weakness of the municipal service lay in its work in the community rather than in the hospitals. As a result of the 1929 Act, local authorities had added greatly to their hospital stock and that enabled them to lay the foundations of an integrated service. Co-ordinated care could be given from the moment patients entered the clinic door since the doctors who attended them often worked in hospital. Medical records, as well as medical traffic, flowed freely between clinic and hospital because the staff employed in both fell under the same authority.

The gap came at the other end: clinic doctors often did not know what had been done for patients before they arrived. How much ante-natal care had a pregnant mother received before she decided to seek clinic attention in her seventh month? This sort of question was frequently raised in the public-health world between the wars. The clinics seemed to be forever handicapped by the ban on domiciliary treatment which the BMA had managed to insert in the 1918 Acts. Only by bringing GPs in close contact with them could that difficulty be removed. The health centre thus became the place, above all else, where GPs would work with local authority clinics.[b] By the 1940s, its original function as a GP hospital had been forgotten.

In the process, the Ministry's attitude toward 'quality' altered, too. During the 1920s, it meant competence in the 'acute' sphere; panel doctors should do more for their patients in the way of clinical care.[c] But by 1940 the view that

a   For a profile of Maude, see p. 334 below.

b   This did not mean, however, that the clinics did not value the links they already had with the hospital. On the contrary, they always gave it priority since hospital was the place where the vital elements of medical care had to be provided. No one in municipal circles, therefore, reacted more strongly to the changes made in 1948 than clinic doctors. When hospitals were removed from local authority control, they made their preference clear: links with hospital, they declared, are more important than links with GPs.[5]

c   See pp. 126-7 above.

Newman had always favoured came to the fore: GPs, the department now felt, should function primarily in the social and preventive sphere. Their place in medicine lay not so much in treating patients after they became ill as in teaching them how to stay well. GP aid was needed at the start of the medical care process rather than at the end. The main thing wrong with the panel was not its isolation from the hospital but its distance from the clinics.

In this way, the department arrived at a new formula for solving the 'quality' problem: all it had to do was change the training of GPs and give them a stake in the clinic world. For such a purpose, they had to be brought into the new municipal-type health centres and work in groups. The kind of health centre Dawson had proposed — essentially, a hospital for GPs where they would work with consultants — was now dead.[6]

The civil servant most responsible for this change was Sir Wilson Jameson, Chief Medical Officer of the department from 1940-50.[a] He was a follower of the Brackenbury school of general practice[7] and Newman's own choice as successor when he retired from the Ministry in 1935.[8] A preventive role for GPs, however, was not the only message Jameson had to offer: once ensconced in the new type of health centre, GPs would have to accept a different method of payment. The reason for this was best expressed by Maude in 1943: '. . . the essence of a health centre is the group and partnership, and there could not be competition for fees. The Government could not agree to provide expensive premises and equipment and leave doctors to run it competitively.'[9] If it did, Maude feared, not only would medical manpower be wasted but prescribing and certification costs would rise. In the race to increase list size, doctors would vie with each other for patients. Some would do better than others, leaving those who were less popular both underworked and overpaid.[10]

How, moreover, could the concept of teamwork be fostered if doctors remained in rivalry with each other? 'Commercial competition among doctors', Maude said, 'is at the root of most of the difficulties of medical practice today.'[11] The problems it caused were restrained by the fact that doctors worked apart; if they were brought together in health centres, the damage resulting from their rivalry would know no bounds. A whole-time salaried service, in any case, was needed to end the double standard of treatment associated with the panel. Once the health service was extended to the nation as a whole, those who administered it would no longer be able to tolerate the stigma attached to panel care. 'This, above everything', the department declared, 'is the one idea we have got to abandon for good.'[12]

a   For a profile of Jameson, see p. 330 below.

18

The Profession's
Deceptive Radicalism

In expressing its desire for a salaried service, Ministry officials sounded surprisingly radical — so much so that there was little to distinguish their scheme from the one that the SMA had been pressing on the Labour Party since 1932.[1] The BMA, however, was a better guide to medical opinion and it had repeatedly made its objections to salary known. What made the department think the profession might change its mind in 1943? The answer lay in a report, prepared by an independent Medical Planning Commission, which made the doctors appear deceptively radical. This chapter explains how that 'radicalism' arose and the proper interpretation of it.

SMA-MPU support for salary

Within the profession support for salary arose during the 1930s but the main impetus behind it was supplied not by the SMA but by the hard-pressed panel doctors who belonged to the MPU. Yet the SMA was also involved because the two organizations worked together. The way for this surprising development was laid by the man who founded the SMA — Dr Charles W. Brook. He had entered the medical-political world in 1928 through a seat on the MPU Council[2] and, from that vantage point, proceeded to establish the SMA in 1930 with the aid of Welply.[3][a]

Thereafter, Brook laid the foundations of the movement that led the profession towards a National Health Service. At first, the panel doctors in the MPU would not accept the idea of salary but, as early as 1934, Brook managed to secure their assent to the principle of universal coverage.[4] In the same year, the SMA won Labour Party support for a salaried service,[5] and the next step was to enlist the aid of the TUC. The MPU, being a trade union, was eligible to affiliate and Brook, with the aid of the TUC's medical adviser (Dr H.B.W. Morgan), arranged for that to be done at the end of 1934.[6][b]

Once this was accomplished, Brook tried to use TUC aid to start a comprehensive public service on the local level. With Labour out of power, there was no hope of a national system but perhaps, Brook thought, there might be a chance in those areas where Labour had control of local government. In that way also, the

a   Somerville Hastings, who had been in charge of the dying SMSA, also joined in. He became President of the SMA as well as a member of the MPU. See p. 259 below.

b   Morgan promptly joined the Council of the MPU[7] and wrote a book called *Trade Unionism and Medicine*, but though extracts appeared in the TUC's journal, it was never published.[8]

MPU would be able to secure the recognition which the Ministry of Health had denied. To promote the campaign, the MPU formed a special section for public-health doctors but the movement did not progress very far.[9] Like the profession generally, MPU members would not accept the prospect of local authority administration. This cost Brook his place in the MPU and taught him a lesson he never forgot: thereafter, unlike other SMA leaders, he dropped all thought of municipal management.[a]

At that point, control of the MPU passed into the hands of the group led by Bayly and they had other objects in mind than the creation of a salaried service.[b] But the financial pressures at work were too strong to resist. In 1937, MPU interest in extension revived as a result of the depression, the spread of municipal clinics, and the long-standing concern among panel doctors in London (many of whom were nearing retirement age) about pensions. Since London doctors formed the mainstay of the MPU, Dr Gordon Ward (who, despite his Conservative political sympathies, had always favoured a salaried service)[c] had no trouble securing approval of a pension proposal.[10] From there, it was but a short step to the endorsement of salary.[11]

Feeling for such a service grew rapidly after the war began. Many MPU members came from the poorer areas of London and their practices were disrupted both by the evacuation programme (which deprived them of fee-paying patients) and by the recruitment of doctors into the armed forces (which aggravated the long-standing medical shortage existing in industrial areas).[12] The profession, moreover, had no more success with the protection of practice schemes it devised in the Second World War[13] than it did in the First.[d] By 1940, MPU members were again ready to work with the SMA. Only one obstacle stood in the way — the question of municipal administration. Throughout the year, the two organizations tried to resolve their differences on this issue but it was not until September that a shaky agreement emerged. Then the MPU issued a memorandum calling for the extension of the GP service to the nation as a whole and, in it, GPs were to receive not only pensions but salaries as well.[14] Unlike the scheme produced earlier by the SMA, however, doctors (as well as patients) were to enjoy as much freedom of choice and protection from bureaucratic control as a state-administered service could allow.

One month later, the SMA followed suit and when its plan appeared, the MPU's journal commented:

> '. . . This scheme is much less harsh and rigid in outline than those which it formerly advocated and there is no doubt that the softening influence is due to some unofficial conferences with our Union which took place after our own scheme had been elaborated but some while before it was published . . . This scheme in its broadest outlines would seem to owe as much to the Medical Practitioners' Union as it does to the Socialist Medical Association, and we do not doubt that these two bodies, representing the best and second best

a   See p. 258 below.

b   See pp. 164-70 above and 275-8 below.

c   See p. 81 above.

d   See p. 81 above.

intelligences in the profession, would be able to elaborate a detailed scheme acceptable to both State and doctors. We hope that this will now be done, for if the responsibility is to pass into the hands of those who dwell in Tavistock Square [i.e. the BMA] we are likely to get a scheme for the protection of our practices and interests as futile as that whose death and obscurity is now unduly protracted.'[15]

Nor was the MPU content to wait for the Government to act: it tried to force the pace by securing TUC approval of a motion calling for the immediate creation of a GP service free and open to all.[16] Shortly afterwards, it sent copies of its plan to every doctor in the country. Despite the war, some 2,000 found time to reply. Two out of 3, furthermore, voted in favour[a] and when the results were announced in 1941, Ward used the columns of *The Lancet* to make their meaning clear:

'... Every doctor knows that the low insurance fee and the ever-increasing encroachment of State services have been powerful factors in turning men's minds towards the advantages of a regular salary with a pension to follow ... There is undoubtedly a widespread revolt against general practice as we know it today.'[17]

This development shook BMA leaders to the core. Ever since the MPU affiliated with the TUC, they had been unnerved by the growth of their smaller rival and had taken action to meet it.[b] But, as in the First World War,[c] the BMA's standing in the profession was undermined by the control it exercised over the revived Central Medical War Committee. Once again, the MPU failed to gain a place on the body and this drew a rebuke from the organization reminiscent of those it had raised before: 'It is a curious result that the more the Minister of Health refuses to recognise the Medical Practitioners' Union, the more the outside public seems to grasp the fact that the British Medical Association is little more than a Government department and the Medical Practitioners' Union the only source from which disinterested suggestions or criticisms are likely to emanate.'[18]

BMA response

The BMA's way of meeting this challenge was to form an independent Medical Planning Commission allied to it. Dr Charles (later Lord) Hill[d] who, as Deputy Secretary of the BMA, had a hand in the move, has since claimed that the Commission was created as a result of the planning impetus generated by the Emergency Medical Service;[19] that, by 1940, had resulted in hospital integration and BMA leaders were afraid GPs would come next. Such a possibility did appear to be imminent but what Hill failed to mention was that the impetus towards GP coverage had come mainly from the MPU.

a   Only about 1,400 of the 2,000 who replied, however, did so in a manner that could be counted. The final tally was 849 for, 444 against.

b   See Chapter 24 beginning on p. 239 below.

c   See pp. 58-9 above.

d   For a profile of Hill, see p. 329 below.

It was the challenge presented by the smaller medical organization, not the Emergency Medical Service, that forced the BMA to create the Commission that led to the National Health Service.[20]

Such a motive was reflected in the composition of the Commission. Though nearly every medical organization was given a place on the body — including even the SMA — the MPU was not.[21] Nevertheless, spurred on by its SMA members, the Commission moved swiftly in the direction of the MPU scheme.[22] It called for the immediate extension of free GP-care to the dependants of insured persons (and others), thereby covering some 90% of the population. Even more important, the report accepted the principle of group practice in health centres, with the GPs who worked there to be paid partly by salary and partly by capitation. Though the majority of the Commission ruled out a whole-time salaried service, they did welcome the prospect of pensions as well as the eventual abolition of the sale of practices. The health centres they envisaged would offer not only GP-care but specialist consultations and the array of services traditionally provided by local authority clinics.

On the hospital side, the report was equally 'radical'. Though it wished to preserve the best features of the voluntary hospital system (namely, clinical freedom and a high standard of care), it did call for the creation of a unified service, embracing voluntary as well as municipal hospitals, in which the doctors would be employed on a salaried or sessional basis. All junior doctors would be required to work whole-time but some consultants would have the right to undertake private practice in addition to their hospital duties.

Only where administration was concerned did the profession betray its old conservatism. The report reflected the doctors' long-standing distaste for municipal control and called for the creation of new regional bodies to administer the service. Even on the national level, the doctors showed anxiety for they not only suggested the use of a corporate body in place of a government department but insisted, no matter which method were employed, that a medical man be put at the head. On every level of administration, furthermore, the profession called for strong medical representation.[23]

The report was an interim one intended only for discussion purposes, but the Ministry must have been deeply impressed by its endorsement of group practice in health centres. Only 4 years before the doctors had expunged the health-centre idea from the BMA's revised General Medical Service scheme.[a] As Jameson saw it in 1942, the Commission's report was 'a realisation on the part of the medical profession that their continued existence as a series of isolated units is in the interests neither of themselves nor of the public they serve'.[24] He took care, however, to make sure that the doctors did not fail to reach this conclusion. Not only did Ministry officials attend all meetings of the Commission[25] but one of its own internal memoranda was made available to the Secretary of the BMA.[26] Not

a   See pp. 147-8 above.

surprisingly, some of the department's most important ideas found their way into the doctors' report.

The profession's 'radicalism', however, was deceptive: it did not spring from any burning desire to raise clinical standards but from the pressing need to protect GPs against the spread of local authority clinics. Only by working together in the same building did the doctors think they could contain the menace.[27] This was why Dr Charles Hill described such arrangements at the time as 'the true health centre'.[28] Others — such as those of the Dawson type (i.e. with beds) — did not interest him. The BMA's concern, then as always, was determined by the economic problems of its members.

The same applied to the MPU but, because the economic pressures on its members were greater, it went further than the BMA in devising policy to fight the clinics. For it, no solution would suffice short of abolition and therefore it endorsed the SMA call for universal coverage. Once GP care were extended to everyone, it reasoned, the need for local authority clinics would disappear. The health centres it proposed, therefore, housed only GPs; public health officers had no place within them.[29] Though the SMA did not like this aspect of the MPU's plan, many doctors within BMA circles did, for, at the Annual Representative Meeting held in 1942, the delegates approved a motion for universal coverage by the vote of 94 to 92.[a] This result took the SMA by surprise since the BMA had never before contemplated a service extending beyond 90% of the population. But though they were pleased by the decision, SMA leaders never realized the reason for it: throughout the negotiations that followed, they refused to deviate from their belief in municipal administration.[b]

Consultants push preventive role for GPs

Behind the radicalism of the profession, then, lay pressing economic problems. In presenting their case for health centres, the doctors stressed the clinical advantage of group practice[30] — but they did so only because they knew they could not show their fear of local authority clinics. Some consultants did their best to convey a different impression. Thus, in 1943, Lord Moran (who by then had become President of the Royal College of Physicians and the main spokesman for consultants during the negotiations on the Health Service) told the House of Lords that he wanted group practice for GPs so that they 'would breathe again the atmosphere of their student days in the hospital wards'.[31] But even he had another motive: by persuading GPs to accept teamwork in health centres, he and his colleagues from the hospital world hoped to dissuade them from seeking access to beds. As one consultant put it in 1944: 'The general practitioner is a specialist in his own line, and should be encouraged not so much to continue with hospital work, but to take more and more interest in the preventive and public health aspects of medicine.'[32]

From the moment the debate on the Health Service began, consultants pressed incessantly on this theme and it was the physicians who took the lead.

a   For more about this key issue, see pp. 282-3 and 286-8 below.

b   For more on this, see pp. 257-8 below.

Thus, taking the reconstruction of medicine as his theme for the Harveian Lecture of 1941, the Regius Professor of Medicine at Oxford (Sir Edward Farquhar Buzzard) stressed the place of GPs within it. They, he declared, should be educated in personal hygiene — while curative medicine should be left to hospitals and specialists. The profession would then be divided into two spheres, each with its own special function to perform: GPs for prevention, consultants for treatment. In an attempt to avoid any denigration of the role he had assigned to general practice, he elevated it: 'Prevention — better than cure.' That was the cry on which he ended his lecture.[33]

Two years later, this division of functions received the sanction of the Royal College of Physicians. It was approved in another interim report which called for more medical education in the field of social and preventive medicine. The main object of the exercise was to equip GPs for the role, and it envisaged their placement in health centres like those contained in the Medical Planning Commission Report. There, GPs would work alongside almoners and psychiatric social workers rather than consultants.[34]

Within this framework, however, the physicians did allow some scope for development in the field of clinical medicine. To satisfy GPs, some form of specialism had to be offered but it had to be one which did not intrude greatly on the hospital world. Industrial medicine was the first to be chosen because, unlike other specialties, it dealt with an area of the environment rather than parts of the body. Whatever expert knowledge was needed could be easily acquired and much of it already fell within the range of GP competence. All GPs had to do was apply the same technique to industry as they employed in the community. No doctor was better placed to bridge the gap between home and work. As one expert in the subject once described the needs of the specialty: 'In the industrial sphere, we can combine the techniques of the research worker and public health specialist with the clinical approach and experience of human problems of the GP'.[35]

It was probably no accident, therefore, that the new *British Journal of Industrial Medicine* made its appearance in 1944. From the start, the physicians lent their prestige to the publication and did all they could to stimulate GP interest in the specialty.[36] The Royal College of Physicians even published a report on the subject, calling for the creation of an industrial medical service under the Ministry of Labour.[a]

Neither then nor later, however, did the physicians arouse much of a response. Industrial medicine has always remained a specialty which has peculiarly failed to interest GPs. Far more attractive to them then was the opportunity offered by the paediatricians. In 1946, the latter — through the medium of the Paediatric Committee of the Royal College of Physicians — issued a report challenging GPs to prepare themselves for the task of child welfare: 'The long-term policy, they hold, should be to make the general practitioner primarily responsible for the care of the child, in both prevention and cure of disease, since he is best fitted to give the service in the home.'[37]

What made paediatricians so anxious to recruit GPs was the dissatisfaction

a   See p. 272 below.

they felt with the operation of municipal clinics. Because of the ban on domiciliary treatment,[a] public-health doctors were cut off from home care and the health visitors with whom they worked did not have the technical knowledge needed to bridge the gap. As one paediatric professor (Dr Charles McNeil) so diplomatically put it in 1940: 'In too many areas the child-welfare medical officers, giving excellent service to the community, live in professional isolation and spend their lives in a monotonous treadmill of baby clinics.'[38] Only doctors who were free to enter the homes of patients could alter this state of affairs, and thus we have the phenomenon of one group of consultants actually anxious to enlist the aid of GPs.

With this attitude, the obstetricians strongly disagreed. Their work was closely allied with that of paediatricians and both types of specialist had reason to be dissatisfied with the way GPs had intruded on their specialty in the past.[b] Furthermore, both depended on the operation of municipal clinics for a free flow of patients and both had encountered difficulties as a result of the ban on domiciliary treatment. But, for obstetricians, these problems had lessened greatly following the passage of the 1936 Midwives Act. Since this had brought midwives into municipal employment and enabled them to work closely with public health officers, it had bridged (to some extent) the gap between clinic and home. Some problems still remained — mainly because too many women failed to attend ante-natal clinics — but obstetricians preferred to live with those rather than involve GPs.[c] Municipal clinics were entirely acceptable to them; for the sake of unified treatment that was where they wanted every prospective mother to be. Only when the post-natal period passed did they think it safe to enlist the aid of GPs.

Despite the difference in their positions, it was clear that at one point the views of the two specialists converged: obstetricians, like paediatricians, were willing to accept GP aid after the new-born child reached the age of 10 days. Indeed, some obstetricians went further — they welcomed the move as a means of weaning GPs from midwifery.[40] Where child care was concerned, then, consultants spoke with one voice: here, as in the field of social and preventive medicine generally, they opened the door to GPs.

GPs welcome preventive role

To the delight of consultants, many GPs welcomed the opportunity and they did so for clinical as well as economic reasons. Here was a field in which they could move without stepping on consultant toes. One BMA member spoke for a number of GPs when he said: 'In planning for health they had repeatedly stated that the general practitioner was both willing and competent to

a   See pp. 45 and 180 above.

b   See p. 139 above.

c   The only GPs excepted were those who could meet the postgraduate requirements laid down by the Royal College of Obstetricians and Gynaecologists in the report it published in 1944 on a National Maternity Service. Needless to say, GPs did not take kindly to the proposal, particularly since the paediatricians had already made it clear that they were willing to use GPs before they had become experts in child care.[39]

undertake his full share in preventive work. It was essential for him to do so to give him complete satisfaction in a job well done.'[41]

By this time, many GPs had abandoned all hope of doing hospital work. This applied particularly to doctors from industrial areas; dependent as they were on panel practice, they had no incentive to feel otherwise.[a] But they were not the only GPs who held these views. Others almost disdained specialist work because of the way they had been treated by the hospital world — and such feelings may have been reinforced by the campaign which the anti-vivisectionists conducted through the MPU.[b]

A significant (and influential) number of GPs, therefore, no longer wanted health centres to provide them with facilities for specialist procedures. Instead, they thought the centres should offer 'a means of clarifying and raising the status of general practice as such'.[42] For them as for the Ministry, the definition of general practice had changed: it no longer could or should cut deeply into the sphere of clinical care. Minor treatment and prevention were the only tasks to which these doctors aspired. One BMA leader — Dr Frank Gray, who inherited the missionary role in medical politics left by Brackenbury when he died in 1942 — even began delivering papers in which he glorified 'the challenge of the trivial case'.[43]

Here was the source from which a new philosophy of general practice grew, one that was to influence greatly those who formed the College (now Royal College) of General Practitioners in 1952. Though the movement gathered strength only after the Health Service began, it made its appearance in force as early as 1942. Then, a group of young doctors led by Dr Stephen (later Lord) Taylor published a report in *The Lancet* through an organization called Medical Planning Research.[44] In it, they made an attempt to define the scope of general practice, something which the Ministry had never dared to do, and they left no doubt about their desire to exclude all significant forms of treatment, particularly major surgery.[c] GPs were to prepare themselves for a different role: they were to become 'home health educators'[45] along the lines that Brackenbury had delineated a few years earlier.[d] Specialist work was to be left to specialists and, on this point, the group took an emphatic stand since they expected much opposition.[46] To their astonishment, however, very little arose[47] — which shows how far GP aspirations had been lowered by the deterioration of the panel system between the wars.

By the time the Medical Planning Commission reported, then, differences within the profession had substantially diminished. Only where the location of diagnostic facilities was concerned did opinions differ and, in deference to the wishes of GP-specialists, the BMA made their inclusion in health centres one of its main themes until the Health Service began. Otherwise, few doctors expected the health centre to approximate to a GP-hospital; if anything, the profession as a whole now saw it as an alternative.

a   See Chapter 14 beginning on p. 150 above.

b   See Chapter 15 beginning on p. 162 above.

c   See also pp. 305-6 below.

d   See pp. 146-7 above.

19
Medical Fear
of Municipal Control

The civil servants at the Ministry welcomed the change that had been wrought in the profession's attitude toward health centres. The centres were now designed to fit GPs for the role Newman had always wanted them to play. Whereas, in 1920, the department had found an array of excuses to put off the kind of health centre Dawson proposed, now in the midst of a war that drained the resources of the nation Jameson and his team tried to persuade the doctors to proceed with the type of health centre their own Commission had suggested.

Costs, it seems, were no longer the consideration they had been in 1920; as soon as the war ended, the department hoped to implement the profession's plan. Indeed, if its early memoranda are to be believed, it expected the centres to be in place before the many doctors in the armed forces returned home.[1] Only after the profession raised objections and insisted on experiments with different types of health centres to take place first did the department recognize the difficulties involved.[2] The moment of truth came in July 1943. Then the Ministry told the Cabinet that health centres would have to wait until the doctors developed a 'health-centre attitude' and that, it admitted, would take as long to evolve as the health centres themselves.[3]

Ministry links health centres to municipal control

Earlier, however, the department did everything it could to arouse medical interest in the innovation: for this purpose, it did not exclude the possibility of letting some GPs pursue specialty interests within the framework of health-centre group practice. But it made the mistake of adding two conditions which destroyed for two decades any chance of medical acceptance: once the health centres were constructed, the department declared, the doctors would have to accept not only a salaried service but municipal control.

Perhaps if salary alone had been involved, the profession might have acquiesced for, even before the war, sympathy for that method of payment had made itself felt in BMA quarters.[4] Though the proposal was defeated at the Annual Representative Meeting in 1942, a poll taken in 1944 showed that it had risen in favour again.[5] To the astonishment of BMA leaders, over half the doctors declared themselves ready not only to work in health centres but to accept salary for all or part of the services they provided there.[6]

Salary, in any case, was implicit in the dichotomy the physicians proposed, for GPs could not play a preventive role until they had been freed from financial

distractions.[7] GPs who worked in local authority clinics had long been accustomed to payment by salary and none expected to be rewarded differently as far
as that part of their day was concerned. Once the clinic approach was expanded
to the point where it covered all (or nearly all) general practice, the profession,
one might reasonably expect, would slip without protest into a salaried service.

The Ministry did not explicitly recognize this possibility at the time but it came
close to doing so in various internal memoranda it prepared.[8] This raises
an intriguing question: did the department foster a preventive role for GPs
mainly in the hope of persuading them to accept a salaried service? If so, it would
help to explain why the Ministry lost interest in prevention after the Health
Service began. In 1943, however, the department did not convey that impression
and the public-health world applauded every move it made. At last, it appeared
to many MOHs, they were going to secure the kind of salaried service they had
long desired.[9] In 1942, their Society produced a plan for a National Health
Service and, though it did not specify the method of payment, it did say enough
about the advantages of salary to show that this was what the MOH world
wanted.[10]

No matter how the doctors were paid, one point did emerge clearly from the
MOH scheme — local authorities, not some new bodies on which the profession
was represented, would be given the task of administering the Service. With that,
also, the Ministry agreed, and here was the point at which its judgement went
completely wrong. Medical fear of municipal control had been only part of the
campaign the profession waged earlier through the Dawson Report. Then the
method of payment had been primary: at the end of the First World War, the
doctors did not want to be paid by salary no matter which body administered the
service.[a] In 1918 the BMA had gone so far as to accept the principle of municipal
control, adding only a demand for separate clinical officers (drawn from the
ranks of doctors in active practice) to handle relations with consultants and GPs.
Later, in response to criticism from the public-health world, the BMA abandoned even that demand and agreed to accept unitary control under the supervision of one chief medical officer — who might be the MOH if he were
recognized as the best man for the job.[11]

But the disputes the profession had with local authorities between the wars
changed all that. By 1943, the doctors cared less about salary than they did
about municipal control. Under no circumstances would they accept a service
under which MOHs might not only grade them for payment but review the
quality, as well as the quantity, of the treatment they provided.[b] This was why, in
the poll taken by the BMA in 1944, the profession as a whole voted overwhelmingly (53%—31%) against local authority control of health-centre practice;
GPs alone by a vote of 63%—23% and consultants alone by 48%—29%. Only
'salaried doctors' (i.e. mainly those already in municipal employ) voted for local
authority control, but even they did so by a surprisingly narrow margin (45%—
39%).[12]

---

a   See Chapter 8 beginning on p. 79 above.

b   For a discussion of the whole quality control issue, see Chapter 21 beginning on p. 203
below.

Brackenbury had done his best to steer the profession in a different direction and he relied on Dr Charles Hill (a public health officer before his appointment to the BMA staff in 1932)[13] to help him. Hill made that clear in December 1936, when, addressing an important group of MOHs, he declared himself in favour of municipal management. Not only did he believe such a development to be 'inevitable' for the creation of a unified service, but he thought his colleagues were ready for the move: '. . . at no time had the private side of the profession been more prepared to submit to the administrative control of the public side.'[14]

The Croydon dispute

Hill, however, was wrong and a dispute arose a few months later that proved it. The controversy grew out of a typhoid outbreak in Croydon in November 1937. Dr Oscar Holden, the MOH for the borough, had long irritated local GPs by using a hospital-based service which deprived them of maternity work.[15] Now he exposed himself to attack by failing to consult the profession during the course of the outbreak. Unfortunately, he also did not trace its source until 329 people had contracted the disease and 42 had died. The tribunal which the Ministry created to investigate the incident exonerated Holden from blame,[16] but the local authority lost the test case in court, thereby exposing itself to damages of £100,000.[17]

In the hope of preventing similar incidents, the Ministry appointed 5 new regional medical officers to keep in touch with MOHs throughout the country.[18] Nor was that all — it urged local authorities to maintain contact with local doctors through the creation of local medical advisory committees and by the co-option of clinicians to public health committees.[19] The Society of MOHs also decided to take precautionary action: it urged MOHs to act quickly in the face of an epidemic to preserve the reputation of the public health department — and it advised MOHs to join one of the medical defence societies to protect themselves against litigation.[20].

During the course of the dispute, the split within the profession became embarrassingly evident and this gave Dawson the chance to strike back at those who had frustrated his ideas on vocational democracy.[21][a] He and Sir Kaye Le Fleming (then Chairman of the BMA's Council) wrote a letter to *The Times* condemning Holden and deploring the absence in Croydon of consultative machinery along the lines suggested in the Dawson Report. Similar defects in medical administration, they asserted, 'were common throughout the country, to the detriment of the public interest'. As a result of this and the growth of local authority services, they declared, the profession had been split asunder: 'There are two groups of doctors in a community, a smaller group running enlarging municipal services and a larger group who practise in the hospitals and homes of the community, and between these groups there is an ever-widening gap.'[22]

There was much truth in the charges the two medical leaders made. Few local authorities had created medical advisory committees and none had co-

a   See Chapter 5 beginning on p. 51 above.

opted doctors to their public health committees.[23] For this, MOHs as well as local councillors were responsible. MOHs saw themselves 'as the official adviser of the local authority in health matters, and that authority cannot well acknowledge the guidance of any other person or body'.[24] Doctors were still eligible for election as councillors and the 1933 Local Government Act had relaxed the ban on those employed in a part-time capacity (e.g. GPs in local authority clinics) by municipalities.[25] But despite the concession, only 150 doctors had been elected to 120 authorities by 1936.[26] Except in London and Cheshire (where no less than 7 gained office), few doctors dared to run the election gauntlet — or succeeded when they did. Nor did the BMA dictate the policy of all who were elected.[27] Drs Hastings, Brook, Rickards and Jeger (all SMA members on the LCC) could hardly have been called representatives of BMA — or even medical — opinion.

Despite the truth in the charges made by Dawson and Le Fleming, Brackenbury did not find the moment opportune to make them. Throughout the 1930s, he and the leading spokesman for the public-health world — Sir George Elliston, editor of *Medical Officer* — had done their best to find an accommodation that would be acceptable to the profession.[28] In this direction, much progress had been made but now, it seemed, the letter which Dawson and Le Fleming had written threatened to throw all their efforts back to square one. 'Unless', Brackenbury told the BMA Council, 'the atmosphere of cooperation and increasing feeling that they were all members of one body, and not two antagonistic sections thereof, could be restored, a great deal of the laborious work of years past would be undone.'[29] The Council, responding to Brackenbury's oratorical powers, promptly disassociated itself from the letter and did so in the manner Brackenbury desired — 'with as little discussion as possible, and that thereafter nothing should be said about the matter'. Even the proceedings of internal committee meetings, it seemed, were suppressed. Before Brackenbury gave this advice to the Council, the subject has been thrashed out in full by the BMA's Public Health Committee but no report of that discussion appeared in the *British Medical Journal.*[30]

Despite these efforts, the incident failed to blow away. Dawson refused to retract one word[31] and, though Le Fleming was more conciliatory (apologizing in public for his indiscretion), it was not long before he returned to the attack. This time, however, he took care to exonerate MOHs from blame. The fault, he said, lay rather with local authorities for failing to rely on MOH advice. Deploring the great gap between GPs and the public health service, he admitted the need for GPs to learn more about preventive medicine. But that, he asserted, was not the main cause of the problem. It lay, rather with the attitude of local authorities: whether GPs were qualified or not, municipal councillors did not want to consult them. 'Why', Le Fleming asked, 'does a local authority call in expert advice to help it in educational matters, and refuse to do so in health?'[32] The remedy, in his view, lay in the creation of administrative machinery through which local doctors could influence both municipal and Ministry policy. At the same time, Le Fleming wanted to have the position of MOHs strengthened — but that alone, he made clear, would not be enough to protect medical interests.

This also was not enough to pacify the public-health world and Elliston, who had always been conciliatory before, rose with rage to Holden's defence: 'It is, we admit, neither usual nor useful for the medical officer of health in times of urgency to confer with representatives of the local medical profession. Such a procedure would be far too dilatory to be of any value.'[33] That, in turn, produced a heated reaction from Croydon GPs and the counsel they hired cross-examined Holden unmercifully at the inquiry held by the Ministry.[34]

Nor was that the only consequence of the dispute: the hard feelings it caused forced the BMA to revise its General Medical Service scheme. When this first appeared in 1929, it left the question of municipal administration open and Brackenbury did his best to persuade the profession to accept it.[35] But now, instead of moving closer to that goal, the doctors shied away. As Dr J. B. Miller (who chaired the committee that redrafted the scheme) put it: 'In 1929 there was a feeling that the administration of National Health Insurance should be taken away from insurance committees and placed in the hands of local authorities. He thought that feeling had disappeared.'[36]

Unification machinery still appeared in the scheme but an independent statutory committee (like the insurance committee), together with the co-option of doctors on it, was now considered essential.[37] The same applied to the local medical advisory committee which was not only to have direct access to the local authority,[a] but was to exclude the MOH from membership.[39] The panel system, in any case, was to remain under central control.[40] Health centres — which had been reduced to diagnostic centres in the 1929 version[41] — completely disappeared.[b] The profession had moved a long way from the Dawson Report when it accepted the need for clinical administration in a unified service.[42 c]

Elliston made one more effort to repair relations between the two sides. This time, a financial crisis facing the Society of MOHs in 1939 provided an opening. In an attempt to save itself, the organization had to move its headquarters into BMA House, and the transfer was accompanied by an agreement — consummated by Elliston and Hill without referral to the branches of the Society — calling for closer co-ordination between the two organizations.[43] Elliston no doubt hoped this would help to repair the damage done by Croydon, but his colleagues in the public-health world did not see it that way. As one of them put it: 'No doubt we have got a bargain at £365 a year for offices in the BMA House, but since they have been given our soul, should we be called upon to pay the BMA for taking our body? Why not cast our disembowelled carcass into the fires of the BMA Public Health Committee?'[44]

In the face of such feelings, how could one historian claim that 'relations between the family doctor and the public service were far better in 1939 than in 1919'?[45] Perhaps he, like the Ministry itself, was so anxious for unification that he refused to recognize the deep split prevailing in the profession when negotiations on the Health Service began.

---

a   This, however, had also been demanded earlier. It was added to the 1929 scheme as the result of an amendment introduced by Fothergill in 1930.[38]

b   See p. 148 above.

c   See p. 191 above.

20
Evolution
of Ministry Planning

The lesson from the Croydon incident was clear — GPs and MOHs were not ready to work with each other. But, when planning on the Health Service began, the Ministry continued to pin its hopes on municipal administration. At one point, the department did give some thought to the idea of a completely centralized service but Ernest Brown threw that out because of the damage it might do to local government.[1]

Idea of a comprehensive health service

With municipal hospitals and clinics already in place, the base for the service the Ministry desired already existed. The problem, as it saw it, was to find some way of extending the salaried pattern to the GP sector.[a] That could best be done by extending the panel system so that it covered dependants and others. At first, the Ministry concentrated its attention on hospital care because of the financial problems bedevilling the voluntary sector [2] but, in the midst of this process, the civil service made a bold leap — one that led straight to the conception of a comprehensive National Health Service. If, one member of the Ministry asked, the panel were to be extended in one direction, why not in the other? Hospitals and specialists could be thrown in with the lot: '. . . it seems worth while thinking whether we can't take the whole business at one gulp.'[3]

The civil servant who suggested this possibility (in January 1941) did not want to wait, and the GP sector seemed the place to start since the Emergency Medical Service covered only hospital care. When BMA leaders were approached, however, they baulked: they did not want to do anything that might force the profession into the 'grip' of a whole-time state medical service.[4] All they were willing to do was to extend the panel so that it covered the dependants of servicemen.

The BMA made this proposal shortly after the beginning of the war as the result of prodding from the MPU.[5] Though the Ministry rejected the suggestion, it did agree (in January 1940) to a scheme which offered domiciliary care on a means test basis to civilians suffering from war injuries. A few months earlier (in October 1939), it also made arrangements for free GP care to be given under the evacuation scheme to schoolchildren in

---

a   Brook faced the same problem in the thirties — which was why he devoted so much time to the MPU. See p. 182 above.

reception areas who had not been accompanied by their mothers. The doctors who participated in both schemes, however, were paid by capitation, not salary,[6] and this no doubt explains why the department failed to respond to suggestions for any further extension along these lines. It preferred to wait until it could make provision for *all* dependants at once since then, it hoped, it would have the chance to persuade the profession to accept a salaried service.[7] Meanwhile, it was content to meet contingencies through the enlargement of hospital care and, as early as October 1941, the Government declared its intention to create a comprehensive hospital service as soon as the war ended.[8]

Not until the Beveridge Report appeared did the department's intentions with regard to GP care come into public view. Then in February 1943, the Government extended the commitment it had earlier confined to hospital treatment to the point where it covered the health field as a whole.[9] On neither occasion, however, did the Government make clear its intent to make the service 'free'. As in the case of the Dawson Report two decades earlier,[a] it put the stress on 'available' instead — which meant that charges might still be imposed on some people (e.g. the middle class) and for some services (e.g. 'hotel expenses' for hospital in-patient care as suggested in the Beveridge Report).[10] In February 1944, however, the Government issued a White Paper that finally removed all doubt: the National Health Service was to be free and open to all.[11][b] In prodding the Ministry to adopt this view, much credit must be given to the MPU (it pushed for free care to all) [12] and the Scottish Department of Health (it opposed the 'hotel' charges for in-patient care).[13]

By this circuitous and almost accidental route, the Ministry arrived at its bold conception of a comprehensive service — but that was never the main point of its plan. Rather, what the department aimed at was a co-ordinated system of medical care. As Brown told a Cabinet committee in September, 1943:

> '. . . A single panel doctor service could no doubt be administered centrally and nationally, as long as it was regarded as a separate and self-contained service. But it can no longer be so regarded. *The essence of reform is to bring together and correlate all stages of medical care as parts of a single process of health treatment.* That is just what has been lacking in the past, and it is one of the main reasons for the changes in prospect.'[14]

As far as the objective alone was concerned, the doctors had no quarrel.[15] They differed from the Ministry only in the use of local authorities to achieve that goal. They wanted it to be done through a central agency with a doctor at the head[c] and, in rejecting that demand, the Ministry might have miscalculated again because, had it carried, the profession might have proven more receptive to other features of the Government's plan.

a See pp. 66-7 above.

b The doctors, however, still had to give their assent and, for that, see pp. 211-13, 282-3 and 286-8 below.

c See p. 185 above.

Doctors call for a regional administration

Even the doctors recognized that everything could not be done from the centre and it was the hospital service that offered a way to avoid municipal administration. Since the voluntary hospitals led an independent existence, new agencies would be needed to co-ordinate their activities with those of their municipal counterparts. These, the doctors argued, should be established on a regional pattern rather than on the smaller county and county borough basis on which local government depended. Only in that way would the area of administration be large enough to organize an efficient hospital service. The existing local authorities, if used at all, should be employed only after they had undergone reform: health functions should be removed from the smaller authorities and placed in the hands of the larger councils. Beyond that, the doctors contended, local government as a whole needed to be reorganized.[16]

Where this demand was concerned, the doctors did find the Ministry more responsive, but for a different reason. In the department's view, regional administration was needed mainly to stop the in-breeding of senior hospital appointments.[17] Before the Health Service began, the situation in some parts of the country had reached scandalous proportions: too many doctors secured hospital posts on the basis of whom they knew rather than what they knew. Many consultants deplored the practice but were reluctant to abandon the existing pattern of administration. As long as local authorities were confined to small areas, they had to turn to the voluntary hospitals for specialist aid.[18]

GPs had a different reason for wanting a regional pattern and, in the process of developing it, they were forced to throw their lot in with the hospital world. But their demand should not be misconstrued: it sprang from a desire to keep MOHs out of health centres, not to bring consultants in. In 1943 as in 1920,[a] GPs wished to practise free from the view of their specialist peers. Beyond that, GPs insisted on the same right of direct representation as they enjoyed under NHI — local medical committees and a place on the regional body that administered the service.[19] Since consultants had not enjoyed the privilege before, they did not attach the same importance to it. But, even here, GPs recognized that their demand could apply only on the regional level, not nationally. As soon as the Government dismissed any thought of a corporate body, the doctors dropped it, too.[20] They were content to work within the framework of a Government department. All they wanted was the chance to exert influence over policy.[21]

Scotland leans toward central control

In Scotland, the department was prepared to meet much of the profession's demands. Thomas Johnston, the Secretary of State, was even ready to give GPs central control despite the damage that would do to health administration. What worried him, rather, was the effect such an arrange-

a   See pp. 119-21 above.

ment would have on links between GPs and the hospital world. How could the two divisions of British medicine establish close links if they were administered by different bodies? The hospitals could not conceivably be managed from Edinburgh (or Whitehall) as long as those in the voluntary sector maintained a separate existence. Only by bringing them, along with municipal hospitals, directly under state control could a common administration be formed with the GP service. Nationalization would have to apply to both before unity could be achieved.

Johnston, however, did not dare to advocate such a bold solution. All he could think of at the time was the use of regional medical officers to bridge the gap and he was not hopeful of their ability to do it. 'In any event', he frankly admitted, 'I personally would rather sacrifice some degree of apparent unity to get our reforms introduced in an atmosphere of goodwill.'[22] To him, it seems, universal coverage held a higher priority than co-ordinated care and, in this respect, he differed sharply from Brown south of the border. His preference, however, conformed exactly with socialist thought — which was not surprising since Johnston, as a leading Labour journalist, had done much to mould it. He founded and edited (for 27 years) one of the most influential socialist journals in Britain: *Forward*, now called *Socialist Commentary*.[23] Brown, on the other hand, was a Liberal. When Bevan came to power, he, not surprisingly, followed in Johnston's rather than Brown's footsteps.[a]

Local authorities want control in England

Brown, in any case, did not enjoy the same freedom of action: local authorities in England held a tighter rein on their health powers than those in Scotland. The latter were more flexible mainly because of the sparsely populated areas they served. To survive, they needed aid from central sources — much more than any local authority in England. One had only to look at the Highlands and Islands Medical Service to see proof of the point. It had long been financed solely from Edinburgh and patients were scattered so far and wide that even the doctors employed in it had seen the necessity of payment partly by salary. Only by combining forces could the Scottish local authorities have raised the funds they needed to administer a Health Service — but they disliked that possibility even more than central control. Glasgow and Edinburgh, in any case, were too large to include in such an arrangement; as much as one-third of Scotland's population fell within their boundaries. In Scotland, then, central control seemed the most sensible solution for all concerned — and the same principle applied to health-centre development alone.[24] When the time came to start the latter, it was conducted directly by the Department of Health.

In England, different conditions prevailed. Local authorities had no claim on the GP service — nor, for that matter, had they shown much enthusiasm for the prospect in the past. In 1929 as in 1911 and 1919, only MOHs had been anxious to bring domiciliary care within the municipal domain: clerks and councillors, for the most part, rejected the idea.[25]

a   See p. 289 below.

But in 1943 the situation was different: for the first time, local authorities were being given the chance to administer a comprehensive service that would cover the nation as a whole. Local government status was bound to rise in the process — and, with it, would follow the salaries of all the officers in its employ. Almost without dissent, the municipal world in England welcomed Brown's plan. The only serious concern it expressed centred on the joint boards. These, it felt, would leave it with too little to do rather than too much. Here, the smaller local authorities had the most to fear since they stood to lose control of some health functions (notably, those dealing with infectious disease hospitals and maternity and child-welfare services) to the larger county councils and joint boards. For this reason, they wanted local government itself to be reformed before the Health Service was created.[26]

Otherwise, no reservations were expressed by the municipal world and its public-health corps even showed enthusiasm for the proposal. The latter, speaking through the medium of *Medical Officer*, went so far as to denounce the doctors' demand for management by means of a public corporation as 'undemocratic' — on 'the principle of fascism'.[27] Equally fervent feelings were expressed where hospitals and health centres were concerned. Since the latter were to house not only GPs but their own clinics as well, MOHs expected to be given the job of administering them. Any proposal to put health centres in England under central control would, in Brown's own words, have been regarded by the municipal world 'as an intrusion into the rightful sphere of local government'.[28 a]

The same applied to the hospitals which the larger local authorities had established. Nothing gave the socialist members of the LCC greater satisfaction than the excellent hospital service they had developed since they assumed control in 1934. Under no circumstances, did it seem before 1945, would they let their hospitals go. When the idea of removing them arose in 1941, Charles (later Lord) Latham, the Labour leader of the Council, left no doubt as to his own feelings on the subject: 'The Fifth-Columnists against democracy are preparing to steal the people's municipal hospitals.'[29]

This reaction had been correctly anticipated by Sir Edward Forber, Deputy Secretary of the Ministry of Health during the years (1925-30) when the Local Government Act of 1929 was being drawn up. In 1941, he told Maude that the strongest support for municipal control of the hospitals would come from Labour-dominated councils.[30] But Forber was wrong in thinking that the majority of county councils would oppose the idea. Their main concern was about the extent to which they would have to delegate powers to the joint boards.

Far from resenting the attitude of the socialist councils, Brown and the Ministry staff welcomed it. Above all, they wanted to build a unified service and municipal demands gave them the rationale they needed to put everything under local authority control. The doctors, however, still had to

---

a This applied even more after Bevan took their hospitals away from them. See p. 290 below.

be satisfied. How could the Ministry persuade them to accept municipal oversight?

Joint boards proposed

The demands of hospital administration offered a partial way out. The doctors, as we have seen,[a] insisted on larger areas for that and even the municipal world recognized the justice of their case. Local government boundaries were still based on the tiny sanitary districts carved out by a Royal Commission in 1869. As a result, not more than one out of 10 authorities was defensible as a self-contained unit: in order to carry out their health duties, some MOHs found themselves in the service of as many as 10 different employers.[31]

In the face of such facts, the municipal world had no defence. Though the local authorities were not willing to turn their hospitals completely over to new regional bodies, they were ready to combine with others to form larger areas of administration.[32] The Ministry had already pushed them in that direction under the Cancer Act of 1939 and the highly centralized organization that emerged made the management of cancer in Britain an example to the world.[33] [b]

Co-ordination of GPs and specialists

As early as March 1942, the department began to lay plans for the creation of joint boards to administer the hospital service.[36] Once the hospitals were put there, the Ministry felt sure, GPs would follow: '. . . it would be almost impossible to defend not having the hospital and general practitioner service in the same hands, since one of the major objects of the scheme is to link up general practitioners with consultant and specialist services based on hospitals.'[37]

At this time (that is, July 1943), the department obviously did feel the need to create closer ties between GPs and the hospital world. The chief reason was probably the severe shortage of specialists then facing the country. At the outset of the Health Service in 1949, there were (in terms of whole-time equivalents) only 3,488 consultants available in England and Wales for a population of 42.2 million.[38] This produced a ratio of only 8.27 whole-time specialists per 100,000 population — whereas in America at that time, the ratio was as high as 42 per 100,000.[39,c]

How could this shortage be overcome? To many (including the SMA),[d]

a   See p. 197 above.

b   In this respect (as in the case of maternity care),[34] the Health Service probably worsened the situation. Before 1948, some local authorities ran cancer clinics and patients did not have to rely on GPs to pick up suspected malignancies.[35] Now they are entirely in GP hands and, as some patients have learned to their cost, referrals are not always made in time.

c   Even if hospital doctors below the consultant grade were added to the English figures, the total came to only 11,735 and that still produced a ratio of only 27.8 per 100,000.

d   See p. 256 below.

the answer seemed to lie with GPs. By working in groups in health centres, they could devote part of their time to specialist work and some would develop sufficient skills to merit consultant appointments. The process, however, would take time and, meanwhile, GPs would have to work closely with consultants in order to develop the necessary expertise.[a]

The shortage of consultants was particularly severe in the case of paediatrics and that partly explains why the doctors who practised in that specialty were receptive to GP aid.[b] The Ministry did not fail to notice their feeling: integration in child care was the point it emphasized in its plan.[40] But that was not the limit of its policy for promoting teamwork within the profession — nor were manpower problems in the hospital world its only consideration. Nearly everyone at the time believed the isolation of GPs to be bad for general practice.[41] Only in the case of surgery did the Ministry (and others) wish to create a clear demarcation.

All this lay behind the development of the joint-board idea and, in order to make unification complete, Brown hoped the clinics would pass under the joint boards, too. But he was prepared to let them stay where they were if the municipal world insisted.[42] That, clearly, was the direction in which he moved after the prospect for health centres weakened. If GPs could not be combined with municipal clinics in the same building, then what was the point of insisting that the clinics come under the joint boards? Politically it was easier to let them stay with local authorities (along with the diminishing prospect of health centres) while GPs joined hands with the hospital world. That, at least, would combine two branches of the service and make it easier to complete the unification process when the doctors were ready to work in health centres on the terms the Ministry desired.

It thus seems likely that Brown assigned a higher priority to the integration of GPs with the hospital world than with local authority clinics. The same, however, could not be said of his advisers. Maude, in particular, always felt the clinic tie to be of greater importance and he, as Permanent Secretary, continued to mould policy after Brown left the Ministry in November 1943 until his own retirement from the civil service in 1945.[43] The man who replaced Maude, Sir William Douglas, Permanent Secretary of the department from 1945 to 1951, seems to have shared his views. Jameson, in any case, was always there (1940-50) to push a preventive role for GPs.

Too much, however, should not be made of this difference between Brown and Maude since it applied more to administrative ties than to working arrangements. Brown, like Maude, wanted GPs to run local authority clinics and, in an address delivered just before he left office, he laid great stress on a preventive role for general practice.[44] The vigour with which he pursued GP and hospital integration probably owed more to tactical considerations than to anything else. With the prospect for health

---

a   Only after the Health Service began did a different possibility emerge: then, in deference to consultant wishes, the new hospital authorities decided to develop their own corps of junior specialists instead (see pp. 294 and 302-3 below).

b   See pp. 187-8 above.

centres fading fast, Brown wanted to preserve what he could of the unification idea.[45] No doubt, Maude concurred with most of this.

GPs tried to balance between these two perilously conflicting objectives: on the one hand, they wished to work in local authority clinics; on the other, they did not want to submit themselves to local authority control. For this reason, they threw their lot in with the hospital service.[a] Once again, that decision was taken solely (or mainly) for administrative reasons. This the doctors suggested in their Medical Planning Commission report: it said nothing about access to GP beds. The report did, however, give space to the clinics; it specifically called for GPs to operate (or replace) them. To make sure that happened, the Commission even preferred to see the new health centres pass under statutory rather than voluntary control.[46]

For the Ministry, this aspect of the report was most encouraging for it suggested that the doctors might be willing to accept the joint-board idea.[47] What else, after all, did 'statutory' control mean? In England, departmental direction of health centres was out: if local authorities did not develop them, then some other body in which they had a hand must. Had not the doctors themselves called for regional authorities or councils to administer the service? What were they but another way of expressing the joint-board concept? Such was what the Ministry allowed itself to believe.[48]

There was, however, a crucial difference between the two ideas: the doctors themselves were to be represented on the regional bodies they envisaged, whereas no similar provision had been made in the Ministry's plan. The department recognized the distinction but, despite a clear warning from Maude, it failed to take sufficient action to satisfy the profession.[b] Here is what Maude wrote in November 1942, four months before negotiations began: 'There are indications that our main difficulty is likely to lie in matters of organisation and, in particular, in the fear of the profession of finding themselves under much closer control than has hitherto existed.'[49]

Here, rather than on the salaried method of payment, was where all the trouble began. As Lord Moran explained the source of the impasse in 1945: 'The crux of the whole problem was the medical profession's fear of interference by local authorities in clinical work.'[50]

a   See p. 197 above.

b   For the reason why, see pp. 207-8 below.

21
Doctors Demand
Direct Representation

'. . . From the point of view of the profession, the essence of administration is that doctors should have an effective voice at all levels of organisation, and that this effective voice should be secured by electing medical men on to the various responsible bodies.'

— from a leader in the *British Medical Journal, 1944, 2, pp. 794-5.*

'It is sometimes suggested that the best method of linking the expert point of view with the direct administration of the service would be to include in the local administrative authorities themselves, and in their committees, a proportion of professional members appointed for the purpose by the appropriate professional organisations, with or without voting powers. Arguments can be adduced both for and against a system of this kind, but on balance the Government feel that the risk of impairing the principle of public responsibility — that effective decisions on policy must lie entirely with elected representatives answerable to the people for the decisions that they take — outweighs any advantages likely to accrue.'

— from the Government's White Paper on 'A National Health Service', HMSO, 1944, Cmd. 6502, p.20.

Much of the profession's fear of municipal control came from direct experience with the public health service. Doctors who worked in local authority clinics or hospitals did not like the way MOHs or medical superintendents supervised the services they gave. Others, whose work was confined to panel or private practice, resented the fact that they had to secure the consent of TB officers before they could administer tuberculin.[1] Beyond that, the profession did not take kindly to the comments made by some MOHs of the work they had done in midwifery.[a] Yet none of these considerations were enough to explain the doctors' almost irrational fear of supervisory control. For that, we have to look to the experience they had before 1911 with the friendly societies under club practice.[2][b]

Unfortunately, the Ministry's plan did nothing to allay the profession's fears. Maude himself recognized that the traditional pattern of municipal employment would have to be modified to accommodate GPs: 'To convert at a stroke one of the oldest and most honourable professions into a public service amenable to all the discipline which public service involves is an operation quite

a   See p. 139 above.
b   See pp. 13-14 above.

without precedent; and the novelty and magnitude of the experiment seems to justify departing somewhat widely from the standard pattern of local government administration.'[3] This applied particularly to 'grouping the existing practitioners in teams and fitting them into salary scales'.[4] Even more thorny was the problem of determining when salary adjustments would be made. Who would decide when a GP had performed well enough to warrant an increase? The department never really came to grips with either problem.[a] Though it tried to introduce safeguards from sources outside local government,[b] it left too much discretion in MOH hands to satisfy GPs.

Underlying the Ministry's reluctance to tackle the problem was the belief, common to so many 'progressive' planners today, that salary by itself would solve everything.[c] Once the doctors agreed to alter the method by which they were paid, the way would be open for them to practise in groups and then they would be able to regulate themselves.[d] Competition was at the root of the profession's problems:[e] remove it and the doctors could be trusted to raise the quality of general practice without regulation.

The doctors, however, entertained no such illusion about themselves — nor, in fact, did the Ministry feel it safe to rely entirely on safeguards flowing from salary.[f] Medicine, among all professions, calls for the highest display of ethical conduct and doctors do feel an obligation to abide by the Hippocratic oath which binds them. But medical men are only human and they could not help but be affected by a change in the economic rules that governed them. Once the discipline of the marketplace was removed, something in the way of administrative supervision would have to be put in its place or the GP service would go completely out of control. Who would exercise that power? The doctors opted for an arrangement similar to that used in the voluntary hospitals.[6] The Ministry, however, took a different view: as long as the service remained in municipal hands, there seemed to be only one answer — the MOH. He — or the deputies under him — were bound to exert a dominating influence over the lives of GPs who worked in health centres.

Arguments for direct representation

How, under such conditions, could the doctors protect themselves? The only safe way, they believed, was through the right of direct representation. That principle had a hallowed history in BMA affairs: its denial in 1919 had led to the demise of Dawson's council.[g] In its place, the Ministry had offered the profession an advisory role — and now local authorities were likely to do the

---

a   In the White Paper, the subject was almost entirely evaded. Nothing specific was said about the role MOHs would play and the problem of adjusting GPs' salaries was buried in an Appendix at the back of the document.[5]

b   See pp. 207-10 below.

c   For the SMA obsession with this idea, see pp. 297-8 below.

d   For an early anticipation of this theory, see pp. 81-2 above.

e   See p. 181 above.

f   See pp. 207-11 below.

g   See Chapter 5 beginning on p. 51 above.

same. But that, as Hill himself pointed out during the course of the dispute, was no substitute: 'It is one thing to be a member of an advisory committee and another thing to be a member of the authority itself: one thing to tender advice by memorandum and another to speak from one's place on a board or committee.'[7]

Dawson now concurred whole-heartedly with this point of view: he had learned the hard way how inadequate an advisory role was. In order to give the doctors a direct voice in administration, he was even willing to sacrifice the principle of (public) democratic control. Technical subjects like health, he maintained in 1942, needed to be managed by experts, and perhaps those who exercised power ought to have a measure of freedom.[8] Dawson therefore proposed the creation of semi-autonomous executive bodies to administer the Health Service — and the profession's demand for a corporate body,[a] no doubt, arose partly from this suggestion.

For the doctors then, this principle of direct representation was central to their position; before any health centres were built, it had to be conceded.[9] But they did not, they claimed, press it solely for their own interest — the public had a stake in the matter, too. As the BMA put it in 1938:

> 'The experience gained from the national health insurance system has shown that the interests of the public are best served in any organized medical service by putting as much responsibility as possible on the doctors giving the service — responsibility, that is, for the quality of the service and for its smooth working. There are no severer critics of delinquent doctors than their own colleagues invested with the control of purely professional affairs. And there is no surer way of securing an efficient service than to enlist the active interest of those whose reputation as a profession is involved in the manner in which they exercise collective responsibility entrusted to them.'[10]

If the right of direct representation had been granted under NHI, the doctors argued, then why should the Government deny it in a service that would cover the nation as a whole? The new system, after all, would affect the whole of their professional lives, not just a part. Few doctors would be able to survive outside the framework of the service established by the state. Therefore, they felt, they ought to have a direct voice within it.

Local authority objections

The doctors knew that local authorities would not take kindly to the idea. The municipal world had continuously promulgated the view that 'the people who spend the money should be publicly elected'.[11] Certainly, where medical salaries were concerned, the argument was irrefutable. How could the doctors sit on a body that determined their pay? Local authorities would inevitably be deprived of bargaining power, leaving them as emasculated as insurance committees. Central control of medical incomes was a necessary counterpart of any service in which the doctors secured seats on the local bodies that administered them.[12]

a   See p. 185 above.

Brackenbury, however, had earlier suggested another way out — representation without voting power[13] — and, in 1943, the Ministry saw this as the most hopeful solution.[14] But many voices in the municipal world rejected even that. Herbert (later Lord) Morrison, speaking for them in the Cabinet, explained why. The mere presence of doctors at municipal meetings, he feared, could upset the balance of the parties: 'Even if they had no vote, their influence might well be considerable.'[15] Their expertise on technical matters made them formidable adversaries and that could prove embarrassing to local authority officials. How would it look if a clerk found it impossible, in the presence of the elected members, to understand a clinical point raised by the medical representatives? The status of the staff would be undermined.

MOHs were even more uneasy about the proposal. Their position in municipal circles had never been secure, and the Croydon incident had made it more perilous. Lay councillors were hard enough to please — what would happen if medical spokesmen were added as well? Under no circumstances did they want to see doctors in attendance at local authority meetings, whether armed with the vote or not. *Medical Officer* expressed their mood well when it said (in 1938): 'We dislike and distrust administration by any body which is not elected by the franchise, particularly if that body has any shred of vested interest in the matters which come before it.'[16] The most MOHs would offer their colleagues was the right to give advice through local medical advisory committees on the pattern proposed by the Dawson Report.[17] But many, even after the Croydon incident, resisted that, too.

Surprisingly, the strongest resistance to medical representation within the municipal world came not from the right but from the left wing of the political spectrum, the section most intimately associated with the SMA and the Labour Party. Though the Webbs had been the first to father the idea of advice by professional bodies,[a] Hastings and his colleagues on the LCC[b] rejected it: it clashed, they claimed, with the democratic basis of local government.[18]

Most doctors, Hastings argued, came from the middle class and had a 'predominantly conservative' outlook: 'At best, therefore, the effect of such an advisory committee would be to hold back a local authority in its administration.' As for the claim that the doctors were able to police themselves, that, Hastings asserted, was patently absurd: '. . . everyone knows that doctors stick together like leeches and defend one another if attacked, as no other profession would do.'[19]

In the face of such feelings, the doctors knew they had little chance of securing a place in local government itself. Besides, they wanted voting power; after the Croydon incident, they would be satisfied with nothing less.[20] Yet their only chance of obtaining it seemed to lie in the formation of new agencies of government, which was why GPs wanted regional bodies to administer the health service as a whole. The joint boards came close to meeting that demand.

a　　See pp. 52-3 and 57 above.

b　　This, however, did not apply to Brook. See pp. 257-8 below.

Though comprised of local authorities, joint boards offered the profession a better chance of securing a place than individual authorities.[21]

The municipal world, however, did not take kindly to the idea — and, unfortunately for the doctors, neither did the Government. Johnston, speaking for Scotland, explained why his department was so hostile:

'If we concede the principle of membership to the medical profession, we may not be able to stop there; similar claims will no doubt come from the organisations representing nurses, dentists, pharmacists and opticians. In my view, we should go no further than to secure that the views of interested bodies can be made known to the health authorities through some statutory machinery for consultation.'[22] [a]

Brown was more conciliatory. He and his civil servants in England tended to be more responsive to the profession's demand because, unlike Johnston, they were intent on building a unified service.[b] Before negotiations began, they even thought the doctors' demand would be easy to satisfy: outside representation on the local authorities (or joint boards) administering the service would, in the department's view, present 'no insuperable difficulty'.[23] Had not similar rights been granted to teachers in the education world?[24] When the time came to press the point, however, the Ministry proved strangely timid. Local authorities found little resistance to the arguments they raised against the medical demand for direct representation.[25] Thus, though Brown at one point did provide a place for the doctors (and voluntary hospitals) without voting power, he swiftly dropped it in deference to Morrison.[26]

Need for supervisory control

Why, in view of the profession's feeling on the subject, did the department abandon it? The answer lay in the failure of the panel system: by 1943, it had gone completely out of control. Not only had the approved societies lost their leverage,[c] but record-keeping inspections were abandoned shortly after the war began.[d] In the department's view, the only hope of restoring restraint over the doctors lay through local government. As Maude presented the Ministry's mood in November 1942:

'... We are satisfied that the continuance of the arrangements under which the panel system is carried out — arrangements which represent a cross between private practice and a public service and in some respects exhibit the weaknesses of both systems — cannot be accepted. They are indeed incompatible with the organisation of publicly provided Health Centres envisaged in the B.M.A. Report. Moreover, it is tolerably certain that the

a   Johnston was also a socialist and, in taking this stand, he was inspired by the same view of local government that moved his Labour colleagues on the LCC. Bevan, on the other hand, came down on the side of 'worker's control': for him, that was more in accord with socialist philosophy. But even he had misgivings about the extent to which he had to go to satisfy the doctors. See pp. 292-3 below.

b   See pp. 196 and 200 above.

c   See pp. 166-7 above.

d   See p. 98 above.

local authorities would decline to accept responsibility for administering a system so lacking in control and organisation.'[27]

The weakness of the panel system stemmed from the right of every doctor to participate in NHI for, once enrolled as a panel practitioner, he was almost impossible to remove. Expulsion could take place only after a series of hearings which had to be initiated, for the most part, by patients rather than administrators.[28] Few doctors lost their place in NHI unless patients dared to file complaints against them. Not many insured persons did. Only about 100 to 500 complaints were heard each year and this compared with the total of 12 to 17 million insured persons covered at various times by the panel system. The highest number of complaints ever recorded — 520 in 1922 — still produced a ratio of only about one complaint for every 24,000 patients.[29] The BMA, in its testimony to the Royal Commission on NHI in 1925, found a way to make the proportion even smaller: 'The number of prescriptions in the year 1924 was 6,856,766, and if you work that out as a percentage of substantiated complaints to attendances, it works out at .00000994.'[30]

Citing statistics like this, the BMA repeatedly pointed with pride to the low volume of complaints as proof of a high standard of service — but everyone involved in approved society administration knew better. Even after he had served as Parliamentary Private Secretary to the Minister of Health, Sir Kingsley Wood maintained (in 1923) that the small number of complaints filed represented 'really no effective test' of quality: '. . . most of us, when we are ill and are attended by a doctor, are not in a mood or have the desire to make a complaint against a doctor at that critical juncture.'[31] Sixteen years later, Hastings — reflecting a view strongly held by SMA members — registered agreement: '. . . a service that is paid for largely by the State must expect from its members more than the mere satisfaction of those who have no means of assessing the value of the services rendered.'[32] Finally, after years of defending the doctors (and the disciplinary procedure) in public, the Ministry itself came to the same conclusion in private in 1942.[33]

One civil servant had anticipated the problem even before the panel was born. This was William J. Braithwaite. In 1911, when he helped Lloyd George draft the NHI Bill, Braithwaite had objected to the provision which gave the profession the right of free entry. He wanted to preserve a measure of selection but Lloyd George, faced with political problems which Braithwaite did not understand, refused to listen. The right of free entry became enshrined in the statute.[34]

Eleven years later, however, an active member of the London Insurance Committee (Mr David Davis) took up the same theme. As chairman of the Committee's complaints-hearing body, he had become aware of the restrictions imposed by NHI's disciplinary procedure. Too many doctors, in his view, were getting away with too much and, by ending the right of free entry to the panel, Davis hoped to forestall such problems before they arose.[35]

Both Braithwaite and Davis paid a high price for their boldness. Braithwaite was whisked out of NHI soon after the Bill passed through Parliament,[36] while Davis lost his place on the London Insurance Committee. The exact reasons for Braithwaite's departure are not known but, in the case of Davis, we have documentary evidence. Shortly after he made his stand against free entry in

1922, the panel doctors in London decided 'they would in the near future get rid of Mr David Davis'.[37] Any second thoughts they had were completely dispelled during the ensuing two years when Davis, as chairman of the complaints-hearing body, cast his vote against the doctors in 8 out of the 10 cases in which he was forced to break a deadlock.[38]

Restrictions on entry, however, were not enough by themselves to solve the quality problem. Not every doctor likely to create difficulties could be detected before he entered the public service. Some way had to be found to correct mistakes after they occurred and the Ministry, in 1940, hit upon an ingenious solution: why not give local authorities the right to hire and fire within their own sphere of operation? Beyond that their power could not go: a doctor would still have the chance to move to a different area if the local authority that employed him decided not to renew his contract. As Maude himself explained the procedure in 1942: 'In our view the right principle is that the employing authority should be master in its own house, but that apart from cases of serious misconduct or incapacity, termination of employment, as in other walks of life, should not be a serious bar to employment elsewhere.'[39]

Under this procedure, a supervising authority would still have to be created on the national level to determine the fitness of a doctor to serve the public as a whole. Such a body was also needed to regulate the supply — and, more important, even out the distribution — of doctors on a larger scale than individual local authorities could do. But the difficulty here could be resolved by the creation of a central medical board composed, as its name implied, of a majority of doctors.[40] On it would rest the duty of determining whether a doctor were fit to serve the state and, like the General Medical Council (with which its duties would overlap), the board would apply tests of character as well as competence. The Ministry even contemplated the merger of the two bodies if insufficient private practice remained after the Health Service began to justify the separate existence of the Council.[41 a]

Under this arrangement, doctors already on the panel might be excluded from the new service. 'It is notorious', wrote one Ministry official in March 1942, 'that there are some panel doctors who are unfit — by reason of age, infirmity, drink, etc. — to take part in a public service.'[45] On this point, however, the department was prepared to bargain. It would insist only on the maintenance of a roll as 'an essential permanent feature of the scheme on which the whole quality of the professional personnel of the service would depend.'[46]

---

a   That process, it seems, was to start with the consolidation of the disciplinary procedure. As early as 1932, the department had begun to refer certain complaints (i.e. irregular or lax certification, unprofessional conduct, canvassing or fraud) to the Council[42] and, in 1944, it added 'negligence' cases.[43] Only established (or substantially supported) charges were thus referred and they tended to be mainly of so serious a nature that they would justify removal not only from NHI but from the Medical Register. The Council's involvement here represented something of a landmark because it had never considered 'negligence' cases before. (Even today, malpractice suits heard in the civil courts are not referred to it.) Though, with the collapse of the idea of a central medical board, all thought of merging the two procedures disappeared, the Council still maintained an interest in the subject. It was the department that made sure of that: to this day, it has continued the process of referral which it started in 1932 despite repeated protests from the profession.[44]

No doctor could be removed from the roll, furthermore, without a board hearing. The intention was to follow the same disciplinary procedure as had evolved under NHI, with the difference — and this was the main point of the plan — that discretion would be allowed to local authorities once doctors passed into their employ. As long as GPs remained there, they had to accept the same rules as other public health officers and be paid in the same manner. Dismissal, therefore, would be far easier to realize at this level of administration. Once a local authority decided to fire a doctor, all it had to do was give three months' notice. No complex and prolonged disciplinary procedure was to operate here. Maude ruled out even the right of appeal which had been given to MOHs and other municipal officials under the 'protected tenure' system. That, he warned the doctors, involved public hearings and the ensuing publicity might lead to the professional ruin of the officer involved.[a] Since most local authority dismissals were for minor offences, it was far wiser, he advised the profession, for the GP concerned to go quietly and let the central medical board find him employment elsewhere. In this way, Maude stressed, 'firing' would not be total; it would apply only to the municipal area in which the doctor was engaged. The board itself had to act before a doctor could be removed from the service as a whole.[47]

Under this arrangement, so much control was left with local authorities that it was doubtful if the doctors would ever have accepted it. What made it certain they would not was the way in which the Ministry proposed to create the central medical board. To be effective, the department said, the board had to be small, numbering only 10 or 12 members. The majority would be doctors but all were to be appointed by the Minister rather than elected directly by the profession itself. 'There would, therefore,' declared a Cabinet committee in 1943, 'be no danger of the Board being composed of elderly doctors nominated by professional bodies who did not represent the more progressive sections of the profession.'[48]

Even worse, from the doctor's point of view, was the need for some members of the board to devote full time to its affairs: '. . . the profession's main fear about the Central Medical Board', one BMA leader (Dr Solomon Wand) told the Ministry in 1943, 'was that it would consist of whole-time members and soon be out of touch with the profession in the field.[49] [b] Moran attacked the board, too, but on different grounds: he was concerned about its directive powers.[51] In the House of Commons, however, Dr Morgan (then a Labour MP as well as medical adviser to the TUC) echoed the same kind of criticisms as those raised by the BMA.[52] Though he had defended municipal administration himself a year earlier when Brown's salaried plan first appeared,[53] he did not

a   Why not then, the profession might well have asked, hold the hearings in private? That, was the procedure followed under NHI and the case for it was even stronger in a service that would cover the nation as a whole. Maude imposed an unnecessary handicap on his plan by denying the doctors the right of 'protected tenure' in municipal employ.

b   Dawson made the same point in the House of Lords in 1944,[50] and here he was only echoing the advice he had received from Sidney Webb in 1917. See p. 52 above.

think it wise to ignore medical feeling on the subject. By late 1944, the very idea of a universal National Health Service was in doubt and Morgan, from his service on the BMA's Council, knew which way the doctors were heading.[a]

Though the department tried to relieve medical anxiety on the 'bureaucratic' danger associated with the central medical board (by confining whole-time service to only a few members), the damage had been done. No matter how many concessions the Ministry made, the doctors could not forget that the board was intended to be a 'camouflage' for the introduction of a salaried service.[54]

Such was the essence of the plan Brown presented to the profession in April, 1943. No sooner was it made public than Hill denounced it as an attempt to translate 'a free profession into a branch of local government service'.[55] Despite his past affinity for municipal control,[b] Hill was aware of the profession's changed mood in 1943 and, as an aspiring BMA official with parliamentary ambitions (he became Secretary of the BMA in 1944 and eventually won a seat as a Conservative),[56] he could not afford to flout it. His words roused the doctors to fury and that forced the department to modify its plan: controls over entry were relaxed, doctors (it was made clear) could practise in or out of health centres and only those inside would be subjected to municipal oversight. The central medical board, furthermore, was made party to health-centre contracts: hiring and firing was not left (as originally conceived) to local authorities alone.[57]

In the process of making these concessions, the Ministry virtually dropped the idea of a roll: all existing practitioners were to be admitted to the new service and the restrictions imposed on new entrants would be applied only to location. 'Squatting' and succession through purchase were barred: before a doctor could set up in a particular area, he would have to obtain the consent of the central medical board.[58] This, however, was designed to even out the distribution of doctors, not to weed out those who were unsuitable for practice in a public service. The profession would thus have virtually the same right to enter the Health Service as it had under NHI.[59] The only new element of control the Ministry tried to introduce was a short period of apprenticeship for newly qualified doctors during which they might be required to devote their full time to the state. This — plus provision for salary in health centres — was all that remained of the Ministry's dream of a whole-time service.[60]

The profession's reaction to the White Paper, 1944

Although the department thus went to great lengths to placate the profession, it did not go far enough when it came to the most important question of all — that of direct representation. Here the Ministry did nothing. In fact, when the White Paper on the National Health Service finally appeared in February 1944,[c] the

a   For more on Morgan's role here, see pp. 239 and 285 below.

b   See p. 192 above.

c   It was supposed to be issued in July 1943 but the date had to be postponed when negotiations broke down.[61] For more about this, see Chapter 27, beginning on p. 274 below.

doctors found themselves deprived of any place in local administration, even one without voting power. (All they were given was the chance to offer advice through local Health Service councils standing outside the existing order.)[62]

The Ministry deferred to municipal wishes on the control of health centres as well: these were put under the direct control of local authorities instead of the joint boards as the department had earlier planned.[63] As a result, when the BMA conducted a poll on the White Paper, it found the profession against the document as a whole. Only doctors already employed on a salaried basis were in favour; the rest were firmly opposed and that made the vote for the profession as a whole 53% to 39% against.[64]

This vote sealed the fate of the Ministry's plan: the profession from now on refused to accept municipal employment on any terms, even if joint boards were created or local government reformed.[65] What the doctors demanded instead were regional councils on which they would enjoy the right of direct representation. To secure it, they were willing to deprive the councils of executive power, leaving them only with planning duties over the areas under their jurisdiction. In this way, administrative control would pass to the centre but, the doctors thought, they would at least have a voice on the regional councils that advised the department.[66] The Ministry, however, rejected this demand on the grounds that local authorities would never take orders from a body on which they were not represented. Joint boards, it claimed, could administer municipal (and voluntary) hospitals; the department by itself could not. In any case, asked *The Lancet*, was it wise to separate planning from administration? The service would work better if both were concentrated in the hands of one agency.[67]

Once their demands on this key issue were rejected, the doctors found it difficult to retain enthusiasm for the health-centre idea. Group practice and local authority clinics, in particular, no longer appealed to them.[68] All they could think about was the danger of municipal control: with that, health centres had now become inextricably entwined. 'They seem to be wanted', declared the *British Medical Journal* in 1944, 'not so much for what they may be as for what they make possible — first steps toward state control and salaried employment.'[69]

Nor were such fears entirely unwarranted, for the public-health world interpreted the proposals contained in the White Paper in the same way. Though MOHs deplored the plans made for municipal hospitals,[a] they anticipated with delight the future held out for general practice:

> '. . . Whereas it may be assumed . . . that practitioners working singly or in
> voluntary groups will be paid by capitation fee, as soon as they join an
> official centre their remuneration will be by whole-time or part-time salary
> and they will enter into a side-contract with the local authority. It appears to

---

a   Here their displeasure was concerned with the proposed transfer of municipal hospitals to joint boards, which would have removed hospital care for TB, infectious disease and mental defectives from the MOHs of most county boroughs as well as some county councils.

be contemplated, therefore, that general practice will sooner or later come under the management of county and county borough councils.'[70]

With the profession holding this image of the White Paper, the man who succeeded Brown as Minister of Health in November 1943 had no choice. Mr (later Sir) Henry Willink found himself forced to retreat step by step from the position the Government had taken. In the end, he agreed to abandon all controls over general practice, even those which were designed to secure a more equal distribution of doctors. The joint boards went, too, and Willink agreed to establish in their place planning authorities similar to those the doctors demanded. The only change he made here was in the number of tiers: two, instead of one, were to be formed — on an area as well as a regional basis. But — and this was most important from the profession's point of view — the doctors were to have representation on both.[71]

Where GPs alone were concerned, Willink also offered a choice of administrative systems: in place of the NHI pattern, they could have one based on the central medical board proposal, but without directive powers. In either case, he agreed to let the sale of practices continue until the Government could conduct an enquiry. If the decision was then to abolish the custom, compensation would be paid to *all* doctors, not just to those (as suggested in the White Paper) who had agreed to enter health centres. This concession was probably the one that pleased the profession most. Many doctors feared that health centres would spread too fast if compensation were limited to those who entered them — while others were worried about a fall in the value of their practices if the Health Service began before the issue was settled.[72] [a] Willink's proposal did much to ease the fears of both.

What all this meant, in terms of administration, was that the doctors were left with the system they had always preferred and had lived with for so long under NHI — that of the panel.[74] Insurance committees, together with their local medical committee counterparts, won a new lease on life, and all Willink sought in return was acceptance of the principle of universal coverage. To that, at long last, the profession grudgingly agreed.[b] The way was clear for the creation of a Health Service that would cover the nation as a whole. In the process, however, the hope of forming a unified administration was lost.

a   This concern was also reflected in the poll the BMA took on the White Paper. There GPs were equally divided (44% for and against) on the question of abolition of the sale of practices (with compensation) when it was limited to 'publicly remunerated practices' — but they voted 53% to 39% in favour when the question was extended to cover *all* practices.[73]

b   For the fight over this issue, see pp. 282-3 and 286-8 below.

Part 6
Trade Unions and Medical Care 1940-1945

Union interest in social insurance was centred mainly on cash benefits and the way the insurance offices won the organizing race. Despite repeated efforts, the unions could not increase the number of insured persons in their approved societies and this, together with demands from disgruntled industrial insurance agents, led them to seek the nationalization of the insurance industry or its removal from social insurance. Union interest on the medical side was dictated mainly by problems arising from workmen's compensation, and this also brought them into conflict with the insurance industry. The unions wanted the voluntary hospitals under state control in order to free them and their specialist staffs from the influence of the employers and insurance companies that administered the Workmen's Compensation Act. Until that could be achieved, the unions looked to GPs for aid in compensation fights and for assistance in extending the list of industrial diseases for which higher benefits were paid. This led the TUC to join forces with the BMA and out of that alliance emerged a movement which produced the Beveridge Report and the removal of the insurance industry from the administration of the welfare state.

22

Trade Unions
versus Insurance Offices

Bevan, when he became Minister of Health in July 1945, did not have to accept the legacy his predecessor had left him. Even the Conservative-led War Cabinet, it was rumoured, felt that Willink had gone too far in making concessions to the profession and wanted to abolish the sale of practices.[a] The new Minister's room for manoeuvre, however, was limited. By 1945, the profession had been driven to make its preference clear and Bevan, in essence, had only two choices before him: he could do what the SMA wanted and return to the municipally-based plan envisaged by the Ministry;[3] or he could take what the BMA offered (or seemed to offer) —the assurance of universal coverage in exchange for 'professional freedom'.

If Bevan chose the former, he could construct the integrated service that modern medicine demanded but he would certainly lose a number of doctors (and patients) in the process. If the latter, then a truncated administration would follow, but Bevan could at least give the nation as a whole the security which the Beveridge Report had promised. At the end of the first road lay 'unification'; of the second, 'extension'. The choice before Bevan was essentially the same as the one that had faced Lloyd George in 1911 and, like his fellow Welshman, he came down on the side of extension. Bevan considered it more important to provide an adequate service for all than an excellent service for a few.

In making this decision, Bevan had the overwhelming support of the Labour Party; from Tawney to Titmuss, socialist policy had been dominated by 'equality' considerations.[b] This applied particularly to the field of medical care. The subject, in the view of most laymen, is too technical to comprehend and, awed by the scientific jargon which surrounds it, they tend to leave decisions regarding practice organization to doctors. 'Free access to medical care' made sense to the average Labour supporter; 'integrated organisation of

a   This suggestion appeared in the *Daily Mirror* and was duly reported in *Medical World* in July 1945,[1] but I have been unable to find corroboration of it in the Cabinet minutes available in the Public Record Office. On the contrary, on 20 March 1945, the Reconstruction Committee of the Cabinet agreed to delay decision until the question had been studied further.[2]

b   This was the general thrust of Titmuss's work as well as Tawney's, but Titmuss did show some concern over the quality of GP care in a paper he delivered to the BMA in 1965. 'The time', he declared, 'is opportune for change and self-appraisal.'[4] He challenged the doctors to take up the task themselves but, thus far, not even the physical premises in which GPs work have been adequately inspected.

the profession' did not. That was why, as *The Lancet* noted in 1942, the Party was 'more concerned with social security than with the details of medical practice'.[5]

The trade unions concurred with this priority: to a large extent, indeed, they helped to mould it. Their members, as insured persons under NHI, already received GP care, and all they really expected from the Health Service was hospital and specialist treatment. This did not apply to the idealists in union ranks (like F. T. Jordan of the Building Trade Workers)[6] — or to the women in the movement. The latter attached high priority to dependant coverage since they never knew when they themselves might need it on account of pregnancy or other reasons.[7]

Otherwise, union members tended to display a callous indifference to the fate of their families, and nowhere was this more evident than in the case of maternity policy. To the horror of the SMA, the TUC in 1938 endorsed the BMA's stand on the subject [a] — which meant that expectant mothers would be removed from the competent hands of municipal specialists and left to the mercies of unskilled GPs. Working women, whose views had not been consulted, protested but the General Council pushed the policy through in the hopes of securing BMA aid on subjects in which men were concerned — like workmen's compensation.[b] Nor was that the end of the TUC's display of a male orientation. Throughout the 1930s, it opposed family allowances out of fear of the damage the benefit would do to wage negotiations. By contrast, the unions showed great concern for pensions because men, like women, could not avoid the dependency hazards associated with old age.[8]

Union hostility to local authorities

Union interest, where the Health Service was concerned, was thus concentrated on the hospital sector, and the TUC did not attach much importance to the administrative method by which it was added. If the SMA's desire for municipal control had to be sacrificed to bring specialists in, then so be it — the unions never had much use for local authorities anyway, particularly MOHs who, in the opinion of the unions, had failed to enforce the industrial health duties with which they were charged. Ever since 1891, administration in this field had been divided: the Home Office, with its factory inspectors, supervised sanitary conditions in the larger factories, while local authorities, through MOHs and sanitary inspectors, assumed responsibility for the smaller workshops. The latter, it seemed reasonable to expect, would be more vigilant in matters where public health was concerned, but the opposite applied: factory inspectors turned out to be far more conscientious than MOHs and sanitary inspectors. The contrast in their behaviour was most noticeable in areas covered by the smaller local authorities: there, employer influence tended to be strong and that made it difficult for MOHs, despite the security of tenure they enjoyed, to carry out their duties.[9]

a   See pp. 219-20 below.
b   For this, see Chapter 23 beginning on p. 227 below.

The unions, however, were not interested in the cause. All they knew was that the smaller workshops were hardly ever inspected, and conditions in some were a disgrace. That put the unions on the side of those who opposed the enlargement of municipal powers. Whenever MOHs, between the wars, tried to extend their duties in the sphere of industrial health, the unions were the first to object and no one expressed their feeling more strongly than the first medical adviser to the TUC, Sir Thomas Legge. In 1930, he described the typical MOH as 'insensitive, grasping, overworked, incapable of research and generally, in fact, no good at all, even at his own job of directing dustmen and supervising plumbers' work'. That being so, Legge had the temerity to tell the Society of MOHs, 'why . . . should the MOH believe himself fit to enter a factory or have contact with the workers there, or even to carry out or supervise the work of the certifying surgeon?'[10][a]

During the debate on the Health Service, the unions no doubt were tempted to carry this indictment further: if MOHs were not capable of administering a medical service covering industry only, then what made them think they could run one for the nation as a whole? But with the Labour Party (as the result of SMA influence) committed to municipal control, the unions could not express such views. Instead, they let the doctors speak for them.

The unions, in return, had to carry the battle against the approved-society system since the doctors were silenced by the threat of municipal control. When the societies received their sentence of death in 1944, the *British Medical Journal* went so far as to feign regret: 'The medical profession has had to criticise the approved societies, but it seems a pity that their special experience in administration should go to waste. The friendly societies have maintained a sense of fellowship and a human touch which has been a distinctive contribution to social progress.'[11]

These soothing words contrasted sharply with the bitter ones the doctors had levelled at the societies 16 years earlier[b] and even during the 1940s some harsh comments were still heard from MPU quarters.[12] But over the intervening period, hostility toward the societies had lessened as a result of the increased control the doctors secured over the administration of medical benefit. That, coupled with the threat of municipal encroachment in the 1930s, persuaded the profession to make its peace with its old enemies. By the time Brown came to propose his salaried plan, the desire of the doctors was clear: they preferred the panel system, approved societies and all, to anything that the local authorities had to offer. Ideally, however, they wanted to dispense with the societies, too, and the Beveridge Report, inspired as it was by the unions' point of view,[c] gave them the chance to do so.

Here were the ingredients for a close alliance and signs of one had appeared long before the debate on the Health Service began. The first clear indication came in 1938 when the TUC endorsed the BMA's maternity

a   Certifying surgeons were mainly GPs who carried out a variety of industrial medical tasks on a part-time basis. See p. 234 below.

b   See p. 157 above.

c   For the TUC's own recognition of this, see p. 248 below.

policy in opposition to the one adopted by the Labour Party.[13][a] The latter, in conformity with SMA views, called for the development of the salaried service already started by local authorities, whereas the BMA pinned its faith, as always, on the less organized care provided by GPs in their usual entrepreneurial way. The dispute thus brought the issue of 'free choice versus salary' sharply before the public and no one could say that the TUC did not know what it was doing. Its General Council was so embarrassed by the question that it approved the BMA's plan without referring it first to the unions' annual Congress. This caused one delegate to remark: 'I am amazed with the General Council for ever allying themselves with the idea that this magnificent local government service should once more be placed in the hands of the private practitioner.'[14]

The SMA was astounded too,[15] and took action to meet it. In November 1938, the SMA persuaded the Labour Party to revive its Public Health Advisory Committee with Hastings as Chairman[b] and, at the Committee's very first meeting, he made sure the TUC was condemned for its action.[16] This forced the TUC to move more cautiously when the debate on the Health Service began but, after the White Paper appeared in 1944, it went so far as to hold direct discussions with the BMA in order to impress its Labour colleagues with the need to secure the profession's co-operation. Perhaps, the TUC hinted, even Labour's commitment to a salaried service should be dropped.[17] Far more important, in union eyes, was the need for the state to take over the voluntary hospitals: under no circumstances (for reasons stemming from workmen's compensation)[c] should they be allowed to remain in private hands.

Unions lose out on benefits and members

Otherwise, the unions had little to say during the debate on the Health Service.[18] Their interest lay more in the financial than the medical side of the welfare state. Above all, they wanted to equalize the benefits provided under NHI even if it meant eliminating the approved societies which they had created. Since 1911, their members had suffered the most under a system which gave the largest benefits to those who needed it least. This was due to the occupational basis on which the unions were organized and it affected most those whose members were employed in trades dangerous to health.

Thus, the Durham miners rarely had the surplus funds needed to provide additional benefits, whereas the unions confined to shop and clerical workers tended to fare as well as those societies which were organized on a geographical basis.[19] In the hope of securing some of the benefits provided by the latter, the miners in the South Wales Federation decided not to form an approved society but to 'pool' their health risk in the friendly societies that were open to them.[20] Many other workers followed a similar course: of the

a   For other signs, see Chapter 25 beginning on p. 255 below.

b   See p. 255 below.

c   See Chapter 23 beginning on p. 227 below.

375 unions affiliated with the TUC in the 1920s, less than 100 had established an approved society[21] and the disparities in the benefits provided by them were far wider than those prevailing in other sections of the approved society world.[22] During the 1930s, the overall performance of the unions improved but this was due solely to a declining membership (members who dropped out because of unemployment left surplus funds behind them) and, even then, the unions had a larger proportion of members in deficiency than any other group.[23]

Here we have one of the main reasons why union rolls failed to grow over the years and, in this respect, they fared much worse than the insurance offices. Both groups, in contrast to the friendly societies, entered NHI without any ready pool of members to draw on. The offices did try to provide sickness benefit before 1911 but they had to give it up because, with their centralized method of operation, they could not control claims as effectively as the friendly societies did.[24] (That was also true after 1911 under NHI but, this time, the offices hung on because of the other advantages offered by the Act.)

The unions also offered sickness benefit before 1911 and, unlike the offices, they persisted with it — but, in contrast to the friendly societies, they did not provide medical benefit at the same time.[25] From this, we may assume that the unions relied solely on a work test to keep claims under control; they were also more interested in providing protection against industrial injuries (as a prelude to a possible claim under the Workmen's Compensation Act) than against general sickness. For the latter, the average union member (if he could afford it) joined a friendly society —and that was where he remained after NHI began.

Insurance offices win organizing race

The unions, as a result, apparently lost most of their men to the friendly societies and most of their women to the insurance offices. Overall, only about 1 out of 3 or 4 members decided to join the approved society created by their union.[26] Whereas the offices managed to organize well over half the total of insured persons (if collecting society figures are included), the unions secured only 11.4% in 1912 and even that small proportion fell to 8.1% by 1938.[27]

One reason for their poor performance arose from the refusal of some trade union approved societies to admit any but union members. That, they maintained, was needed to prove the existence of industrial disease — a condition which, once established, would entitle those claiming such disablement to the higher benefits provided under the Workmen's Compensation Act.[a] But union members attached more importance to the convenience of having all members of a family enrolled in the same approved society no matter what occupation they pursued.[28] Later, many unions modified their rules to take account of this feeling[b] but, by then, it was too late. The insurance offices always stood ready to insure

a   See p. 230 below.
b   In 1924, according to one survey, 64% (26 out of 40 unions) excluded relatives — whereas, in 1933, according to another survey, only 30% (12 out of 39 unions) did.[29]

everyone for everything and that, combined with the secure financial image they presented, appealed strongly to the working class.[30]

But that was not all the offices had to offer: even more important was the home service provided by the thousands of agents in their employ. Not even the friendly societies could match that, and the agents exploited every opportunity to drive the lesson home. From the moment NHI began, they were on the doorsteps of working-class houses, soliciting recruits, and their energy never slackened in the years that followed.[31] Indeed, after 1937, it increased, for that was the year when juvenile contributors were brought into NHI. The unions, not the offices, were responsible for this innovation. Concerned about the plight of young people entering their first job between the ages of 14 and 16, the unions wanted them to have the full range of statutory benefits under NHI, but all they received was medical benefit plus whatever additional benefits their approved society had to offer.[32] This, nevertheless, was enough to arouse insurance agents for some 800,000 teenagers, long known to them, fell into that category. By 1935, over 80 million industrial assurance policies were in force and, on many, payments had been made from the moment of birth.[33]

As far as the unions were concerned, the result was disastrous. As Jim Smyth, the Social Insurance Director of the TUC,[a] put it in 1941: 'Where our Trade Union Movement is at a disadvantage is that our friends in the insurance world cater for children from birth and they know the exact time when they will come into insurance. They are then on the doorstep, in order to obtain membership, whereas we, in the Trade Union Movement, have to wait until the child comes into industry before we can pick it up, and we are placed at a very serious disadvantage from that standpoint.'[34]

Smyth was not exaggerating. Between 1940 and 1944 alone the insurance offices added more members to their rolls than belonged to all the unions affiliated with the National Association of Trade Union Approved Societies.[35] By the time the war ended, the Prudential by itself had nearly 5 million members while the entire trade union movement could muster less than $1\frac{1}{2}$ million.[36]

Such comparisons drove the unions to distraction and bred a hatred of the insurance offices which Lloyd George found hard to understand. Had the industry not done the nation a service by organizing the mass of the working class previously excluded from the friendly societies? The unions could complain all they wanted about the way the offices had 'scooped the pool'[37] of insured persons but it was nevertheless true that they, in 1912, had shown little desire to do the job themselves. On the contrary, still smarting from the contributions Lloyd George had imposed on the working class, many trade unionists hoped the scheme would fail. As one of them admitted two decades later: '. . . the applications for membership forms, which arrived by the thousand, were thrown on the floor into a corner of the office to await the day when the Act would be repealed.'[38]

In taking this action, the unions were strongly influenced by the belief that

NHI represented a plot against them. This idea began, quite innocently, with a campaign aimed solely at the contributory nature of the Bill and was started in June 1911 by George Lansbury and the Fabian Society. (The latter was led in this work by Henry Harben, the socialist grandson of the founder of the Prudential!)[39] Had the campaign remained in Fabian hands, it would have proceeded responsibly but almost immediately the attack was taken up by two controversial figures —Hilaire Belloc, author of *The Servile State*, and A. F. Orage, editor of *The New Age*. Belloc went so far as to start a journal to voice his views, the *Eye-Witness* (later *New Witness*) — and in his hands the campaign took on ugly, anti-semitic overtones.[40] Orage was not slow to follow this lead and that was the form in which the newly-started *Daily Herald* swallowed it. The latter soon became the main newspaper of the labour movement and, throughout the summer of 1912 just as enrolment in NHI began, it warned the unions (as well as the friendly societies) of the 'Insurance Plot' against them.[41]

All this left Lloyd George with few friends to start the Act and he needed the help the insurance offices could give. Later, the offices administered the Act in such a way as to promote their private interests[42] but so did some of the friendly societies and the trade unions. Only when it came to denying insured persons the right of self-government were the offices unique. For years before 1911, the agents had been skilful at manipulating the democratically-organized collecting societies through the trade unions they formed,[43] and the proprietary companies did not want the same tactics applied to them by means of the approved societies they had to establish under NHI. The Prudential, therefore, deliberately flouted the self-governing requirements of the Act: it set up its own 6 (later 4) approved societies on the most autocratic basis, and the other leading offices (particularly those that joined together to form the National Amalgamated Approved Society) followed suit.

Braithwaite, who ardently believed in the value of self-government, never understood the reasons for their action[44] and that was probably the main reason why he, despite the key role he played (as a civil servant) in drafting the 1911 Bill, was forced to leave NHI administration. Sidney Webb also condemned the offices for this reason[45] — but Charles Masterman was wiser. As Chairman of the NHI Commission in 1912, he swiftly approved the constitutions the offices submitted.[46] Thereafter, it was revealing to observe, only the agents complained:[47] insured persons themselves were content to let management rule.

As the years passed, those who knew anything about the internal difficulties created by the agents' trade unions found it difficult to find fault with the way the offices administered NHI and Lloyd George never forgot the aid they had given. In 1933, on the 25th anniversary of NHI, he publicly paid tribute to them.[48] Even the TUC had to admit the justice of such praise: before the Beveridge Committee in 1942, the Director of its Social Insurance Department (Smyth) acknowledged that NHI could not have been started without the assistance of the industrial insurance offices.[49]

Insurance agent influence on labour policy

It was the agents themselves who first made the TUC aware of the good work the offices had done. As members of trade unions, they had the right to speak at TUC conferences and they never lost the opportunity to remind their brothers of the value of the home service they supplied. Before the First World War, their voice carried much weight because of the strategic position they occupied in the life of the working classes. Who but insurance agents could have carried the union message from door to door? Trade councils, in particular, were dependent on their aid and the same applied to the Labour Party after it was formed in 1900. Not until the birth of constituency parties in 1918 did the movement as a whole develop an alternative instrument through which it could canvass.

Though industrial assurance policies were sold as early as the1840s,[50] it was not until the cotton famine of 1862 that the agents formed ties with the trade unions. Then, as a result of the unemployment they suffered, a large number of Lancashire operatives found jobs with the Prudential: some, like Sir George Green and John Moon, rose to high office.[51] During the 1880s, the relationship deepened when the cotton union leaders — James Maudsley, Thomas Birtwistle and Thomas Ashton — helped to form the first trade union for agents, now called the National Amalgamated Union of Life Assurance Workers.[52] The secretary of the Bolton Operative Spinner's Union, John Fielding, even agreed to serve as the first President of the agents' union.[53]

As soon as the agents formed their union, they tried to join the TUC but they were denied admission because of the non-manual character of their work. Not until 1890 did the TUC relent.[54] Once affiliation was won, however, the agents were swift to make their presence felt. Through the branches of their unions, they joined trades and labour councils[55] and many individuals who were politically-minded entered the leading socialist societies of the day, including the Independent Labour Party and the Social Democratic Federation.[56] Keir Hardie (one of the founders of the Labour Party) showed great solicitude for their interests in his journal, *Labour Leader* — and this applied particularly to the agents employed by the Prudential because of Hardie's friendship with David Jones, the socialist leader of the National Association of Prudential Assurance Agents.[57]

As the labour movement turned to political action in the 1890s, it was the agents who led the way. They were the driving force behind the campaign then waged to secure labour representation on local authorities. This we can see from the remarks made by one agent who urged such action at a meeting of the Stockport Trades Council in 1891:

> '. . . if the Trades Council did not take the question up, they would take it up themselves. (Hear, hear.) He considered that agents in connection with industrial and other companies had a greater opportunity for influence than even the members of the Trades Council.'[58]

It was not surprising, therefore, that when the agents feared exclusion from NHI in 1911, they turned to the Labour Party for help. One Labour MP was quick to accommodate them; not surprisingly, he came from a trade union in the cotton trade. This was A. H. Gill, General Secretary of the Cotton Spinners' Amalgamation. Gill spoke up for the insurance industry in Parliament on 25 May 1911.[59]

Agents demand nationalization of industrial insurance

The agents thus did much to ensure office entry to NHI — but the tactics they employed in the organizing race turned their union brothers against them. No one was more incensed than the President of the TUC — Will Thorne of the Gas Workers. As a result of the office (and employer) sweep of insured persons, he told his colleagues in 1912, NHI was 'digging the grave of organized Labour with a vengeance!'[60] In the years that followed, he and his successors searched for ways to retaliate but it was the agents themselves who showed them how. Smarting under the management's threat of rationalization, the Prudential's own agents demanded state control in order to protect their jobs. Like the club doctors who welcomed NHI, they preferred public service to the hard hand of private enterprise and they feared the gradual displacement that might stem from the development of social insurance through employer deductions. Rather than lose their livelihoods bit by bit, they wanted either compensation or public employment. Such was the substance of the motion they submitted to the TUC in 1911.[61]

The initiative was taken by David Jones and his tiny National Association of Prudential Assurance Agents. But though Jones exercised much influence in the labour movement, he did not speak for the majority of agents, not even of those who worked for the Prudential. Most opposed nationalization, the strongest exception coming from the agents of the collecting societies, since they exercised much control over management.[62] Among other privileges, this protected them against instant dismissal. In fact, because of their right to sell 'book interest', they held a position akin to that of 'petty capitalists'.[63] Feeling among them, however, changed once they began to lose their privileges. As the block system (pioneered by the Prudential) spread, so did greater managerial control and this cut into the commission rates of those who worked for the collecting societies. By the 1920s, many were ready for nationalization to protect their book interest.[64]

When Jones first raised the idea in 1911, however, the big unions who dominated the TUC treated it as a 'huge joke'; not until they lost the organizing race the next year did they begin to take it seriously.[65] Before they could progress very far, however, Sidney Webb intervened: why waste money, he asked in 1915, on collecting weekly contributions? It would be cheaper simply to add funeral benefit to NHI.[a] Lloyd George, it seems, had

---

a   This suggestion came at the end of a long (and excellent) report on industrial insurance which Webb prepared for the Fabian Research Department and published in the *New Statesman* (as a special supplement) in March 1915.[66] In it, Webb clearly wanted to go further and bring the whole life insurance industry (ordinary as well as industrial) under state control but the uniqueness of his proposals lay in the stress he placed on funeral benefit and that is why it is stressed here.

the same idea in 1910 but he made the mistake of grossly underestimating the compensation agents would receive. That, together with other considerations, forced the Chancellor to drop the proposal [67] and Webb, in 1915, faced even greater difficulties. Not only did the agents respond coolly to the suggestion[68] but, surprisingly enough, so did the unions: like the insurance offices, they had their own vested interests to consider. Death benefits (covering funeral costs) were so popular with the working class that even trade unions covering low-paid workers found it necessary to provide them.[69]

As one member of the General Council frankly admitted 16 years later when the TUC (along with the Labour Party at its Conference in Margate) was presented with a motion calling for the nationalization of life assurance:

> '. . . It is a much bigger question than appeared, perhaps, to the mover of the resolution both at Margate and at the TUC. We have so many vested interests — not only in these other societies concerned, such as the Prudential — we have so many vested interests in the Trade Unions; and if we are going to make a national monopoly that is going to prevent the Trade Unions administering death benefits, we are up against a number of our unions who have entered their caveat against the nature of the draft we have in hand. As a result we were compelled to re-draft it and leave it over for further consideration.'[70]

Eventually, after three decades of deliberation, the TUC decided to adopt the solution the agents had sought: nationalization, it told the Beveridge Committee, was the remedy it wanted to correct the abuses of the insurance industry. But if that could not be carried out, then it thought the offices should be removed from social insurance, even if the unions had to go in the process. As one TUC spokesman told the Beveridge Committee: '. . . if it is impossible to deal with them [i.e. the industrial insurance offices] separately, we would say we would rather go out ourselves and leave it to the State absolutely, rather than they should be allowed to administer under such a scheme as we put forward here.'[71]

23

Trade Union Interest in General Practice

Before the Beveridge Committee, the unions were not solely intent on the reform of NHI. More important was the reconstruction of workmen's compensation, and in this chapter we shall see how that aim influenced union interest in general practice.

Where the administrative problems posed by NHI were concerned, the unions faced a dilemma. On the one hand, they found it difficult to exercise vigilance over sick claims because of their traditional role as the worker's defender;[1] on the other, they had to fulfil their responsibilities as approved societies, and this led them to rely greatly on medical aid. Panel practitioners, rather than sick visitors, were the unions' main safeguard against a fraudulent claim.

As the depression deepened and sick claims mounted, the unions shared the growing belief in a salaried method of payment to give the doctors the independence needed to resist the demands of patients who had exhausted their right to unemployment insurance benefits.[2] This applied particularly to insured persons seeking disability benefit. It was paid after the first 26 weeks of illness at only half the rate prevailing before for sickness benefit, but it continued for as long as incapacity lasted (that is, until the normal pension ages of 65 for men and 60 for women). Though the amount of benefit was small (7s. per week for men between 1920 and 1942, 5s. or 6s. for women after 1933),[3] it was the only social insurance payment free from a work condition. Many of the unemployed turned to it in desperation.[4]

Workmen's compensation problems for the unions

Such, throughout the 1930s, was the main preoccupation of the approved societies but, unlike their rivals, the unions did not have only NHI to think about. For them, workmen's compensation was more important since they were concerned, above all, with the welfare of the insured person at his place of work. Here they had the freedom to assume their traditional role as the worker's champion; in contrast to their position under NHI, the unions did not occupy an administrative place in the system. That was left to employers and insurance companies — who, it will be recalled, exercised influence over specialists and voluntary hospitals in such a way as to minimize the amount of claims awarded against them.[a]

These tactics, over the years, did not change: they simply assumed a more

a   See pp. 46-7 above.

sophisticated form, directed mainly at the tendency of injured workers to accept miserly lump-sum settlements. By the 1930s, according to one medical witness who was deeply involved in accident work, the insurance companies had found it profitable to offer 'advice and inducements' to doctors 'to lag behind in treatment. . . with a view to forcing a settlement'.[5] The low weekly allowances provided under NHI — together with the restricted nature of medical benefit — tended to have a similar effect.[6] Was this, the unions wondered, another reason why the system had failed to expand?

In most other countries, lump-sum payments were banned[7] but, in Britain, the unions found it difficult to criticize the practice because of its popularity with injured workers. Workers were willing to settle for small sums mainly because they thought compensation was intended to cover earnings lost in the past, not future liability.[8] They also had a fear of company bankruptcy. Many firms went under during the depression and only in the coal industry were employers, beginning in 1934, compelled to insure.[9] Rather than risk losing a weekly allowance, many workers thought it best to take a lump sum. Such settlements also avoided the financial (and other) hazards involved in legal proceedings. It was not surprising, therefore, to find that as much as one-third of the money given in compensation in 1937 went in lump-sum form.[10] Not until the capital sum was exhausted did the disabled worker realize the mistake he had made.

Such considerations made the unions anxious to remove the insurance offices not only from NHI but from all forms of social insurance. They would not compromise on this issue and repeatedly refused to recognize any of the fine distinctions raised by the offices between the operation of their separate sections. The officials in charge of an approved society run by the offices might argue that it was in their interest for the injured worker to win his compensation claim since then he would lose his right to NHI's sickness or disablement benefit.[11] The latter were payable only when they exceeded the amounts allowed under the Workmen's Compensation Act and, since compensation benefits were so much higher, that rarely happened.

The unions, however, thought the offices might still try to find an excuse to withhold NHI benefits before the compensation claim was settled, thus forcing the worker to accept a small lump sum.[12] They also recognized that the different sections of an insurance office had an obligation to work together for the benefit of the whole firm. For this reason, the approved society section might decide not to help the injured worker win his compensation claim. It might be cheaper for the office to have the worker live with his low NHI benefit than to force a lump-sum settlement.[13] Indeed, even before NHI became law in 1911, Mary Macarthur (the famous women's union leader) warned that the Bill 'might tend to prevent the inclusion of additional dangerous trades under the Workmen's Compensation Act and make sick insurance a substitute for compensation'.[14]

Against all of these charges, however, the insurance offices could claim that they had no incentive to 'cheat' since workmen's compensation represented only 8% of their business,[15] and only a few firms in the industrial assurance field handled it.[16] In fact, from the records available, it is not possible to determine how justified any of the complaints raised by the unions were. But that is not the main issue here since this study is concerned with the *beliefs* that moulded union policy and, no matter what the offices said, the unions thought them to be guilty of malpractices in the compensation field.

All this led the unions to conclude that social insurance had to be regarded as a whole. NHI, they felt, should be combined not only with workmen's compensation but with unemployment insurance and contributory pensions as well.[17] Within such a system, there was no room for the insurance industry; 'all-in' insurance, the unions maintained, should be administered by the state — or at least by those who had no interest in private enterprise. As Arthur Hayday (a leader of the General and Municipal Workers, who was the unions' main spokesman on social insurance)[18] told the TUC in 1929: 'I do not care what interest, in the form of approved societies even, has to be sacrificed. I would rather sacrifice those interests than the interests of the victims of adversity and those who may come under the aegis of our various insurance measures.'[19]

This challenge, to their credit, was accepted by those in the union world who had the most to lose from it — the officials who ran the unions' own approved societies. They, for the most part, were willing to go so long as social insurance as a whole were recast.[20] Some went further: Ernest Corbey wanted the approved-society system eliminated irrespective of what happened elsewhere. As the long-standing Secretary of the National Association of Trade Union Approved Societies, he dedicated his life to the 'nationalization' of NHI.[21]

The insurance agents, however, did not share his idealism and, through their unions, they made their views known to the leaders of the TUC. That, combined with opposition posed by the powerful National Union of Railwaymen (then led by the conservative J.H. Thomas), forced the General Secretary of the TUC, Walter Citrine, to retract.[22] Throughout the 1930s, Citrine and his colleagues had to move cautiously where the approved societies were concerned. Even the Labour Party in 1929 could not commit itself too strongly to their abolition out of fear of losing votes.[23] Not until the Second World War began did the climate of opinion change, but then it brought the nation as a whole down against the approved-society system.

Unions seek impartial specialist care

By the time negotiations on the Health Service began, therefore, TUC as well as Labour Party opposition to the approved-society system had hardened but, where the doctors were concerned, the unions were more pliable. Though they wished to see the medical-care system as a whole revamped, they attached more importance to the reform of the hospital world than of general practice. Victims of industrial accidents generally required hospital attention — particularly where the larger claims were concerned — and that led the insurance industry to direct its favour to consultants. Consequently, when the unions came to consider the kind of Health Service they wanted, they had only one priority — to bring the voluntary hospitals under state control.[24] Once that was done, specialists could be paid for their work and would no longer have to look elsewhere for largesse.

So strongly did the unions feel on this subject that they established a voluntary hospital of their own. For this innovation, Dr Morgan was responsible. In a memorandum he prepared for Labour's Advisory Committee on Public Health in 1920, Morgan scolded the unions for scattering their donations over so many voluntary hospitals that 'they have absolutely no control or voice' and urged them to confine their contributions to selected hospitals. In London, this would permit them 'to have a voluntary hospital of their own, subject to their policy, influence and control, manned by their specialists and sympathisers combined with an efficient ambulance system for bringing their trade union members from any district'.[25]

Almost immediately, the unions complied: through the Industrial Orthopaedic Society, they concentrated their funds on Manor House Hospital (which eventually made its home in Hampstead). To this day, it remains under effective union control despite the advent of the Health Service. In 1948, all (or nearly all) the other voluntary hospitals lost their independence but the unions insisted on retaining control of Manor House in order to carry on the compensation fights expected under the Industrial Injuries Act.[26]

Unions need GP aid on industrial disease

Though interest in hospital management dominated TUC attention between the wars, it did not stifle union concern for general practice. The unions still needed GP aid to extend the list of industrial diseases scheduled under the Workmen's Compensation Act.[27] Once that happened, two advantages followed: the disabled worker received higher benefits since payments were more liberal under the Workmen's Compensation Act than NHI; and approved society funds were strengthened because once the injured worker won the right to workmen's compensation, he lost his claim to NHI's sickness benefit.[a]

Such advantages were open to all insured persons and approved societies but, within the NHI world, the unions had the most to gain from the scheduling of industrial disease. This was because only their members were associated with specific industries or occupations; the insurance offices and the friendly societies, by contrast, enrolled everyone far and wide. Some unions, however, benefited more than others: it all depended on whether the disease was directly connected with the industry or occupation in which their members were employed. In relation to the amount of compensation paid, occupational disease (as two experts on the subject put it in 1941) 'resolves itself mainly into the problem of disease in mines'.[28]

But neither the miners nor any other workers found it easy to have diseases scheduled under the Workmen's Compensation Act. In 1906, when scheduling first began, only 6 diseases were listed. Though 18 more were added the following year, by 1918 the total still amounted to only 30,[29] and one included in that year — silicosis — had taken 50 years to get there.[30] Where coal-miners were concerned, the scheduling of silicosis took even longer: not until 1943 was it added to the coal industry's list under the name of pneumoconiosis. Before then, only a small number of miners were eligible for compensation under a scheme set up in 1928. Medical support was needed before the Government

a   See p. 228 above.

would go further and even as enlightened a scientist as Professor J. S. Haldane ruled out silicosis as a risk for coal miners.[31] The Medical Research Council, therefore, did nothing.

In 1933, the unions condemned it for refusing to act until 'a sufficient number of men had been murdered in this industry'.[32] That, apparently, persuaded the Council to start a study but the work took 6 years to complete. Finally, in 1942, the Council issued a report which acknowledged that the disease was more prevalent in the coal industry than had been thought.[33] Though pneumoconiosis was promptly scheduled, the experience did not endear the Medical Research Council to the unions. Ernest Bevin also had reason to complain because the Council took 6 years (1928-34) before it would undertake a study of the health of London busmen, and that report was not published until July 1937.[34]

From this we can see how reluctant the authorities were to act where industrial disease was concerned and their behaviour was understandable since employers fought scheduling every inch of the way. The unions badly needed help not only from GPs but from their own approved societies — yet, despite the benefits that scheduling held out for union members, few bothered to enrol in the society their union created.[35 a] The rest, as one angry union official complained, flocked to the insurance offices: 'They talked about worker's control of industry, and then gave their insurance to the Prudential and other companies.'[36]

Why this paradox? The main answer lay in the superior selling techniques the offices employed, but there was a subsidiary reason as well: most workers did not want their employers, their unions, or even themselves, to know that they had contracted an industrial disease. For them, dying on the job was better than living on the dole. Not even the more liberal benefits associated with the Workmen's Compensation Act were enough to convince them otherwise. Nor did the situation change after the advent of the Industrial Injuries Act in 1946. As late as 1950, one union leader felt constrained to urge periodic medical examinations for foundry workers on the following grounds: 'These people must be saved from themselves. There are thousands of people, from my experience, who would rather die from this abominable disease of silicosis than know they had it.'[37]

Growth of union interest in social insurance

With apathy like this in their ranks, few union leaders paid attention to NHI work. Their concern lay on the industrial side where the more dramatic demands of collective bargaining would win them the applause (and votes) of members. The only officials who showed interest in the subject were those who belonged to the National Association of Trade Union Approved Societies, but they lacked status in the movement as a whole. Of the 375 unions affiliated with the TUC in 1924, less than 100 had bothered to form an approved society and only 78 enrolled in the Association.[38] Such

a   See p. 221 above.

indifference caused the long-serving Secretary of the Association (Ernest Corbey) to complain:

> '. . . nine-tenths of the trade union executive committees considered health insurance a nuisance. If the trade union executive committees were half as much alive to the value of research to improve the standard of health as quibbling over industrial matters, they would get a good bit further than they did.'[39]

Despite this neglect, Corbey and his colleagues were not without influence in labour circles. Not only did they dominate the making of policy on the Party's Public Health Advisory Committee: they spoke for the movement as a whole before the Royal Commission on NHI in 1925.[a] Then, 3 years later, came an even greater boost to their status: the formation of a Social Insurance Department by the TUC. This was the result of a report prepared 4 years earlier by Arthur Greenwood who, as head of the Research and Information Department created by the TUC and the Labour Party, had shown the dangers to union membership arising from the development of social insurance under non-union control.[40] To avert it, he urged the TUC to start a national campaign to bring all union members within their union's own approved society.

Action had to await the appointment of a new General Secretary — Walter (later Lord) Citrine. He not only took up Greenwood's suggestion but created his own Social Insurance Department to implement it. In making this bold move, Citrine was no doubt influenced by his old friend, Jim Smyth, who became the director of the new Department.[41] Once installed, Smyth acted energetically and his Department soon fostered a concern for social insurance over the movement as a whole. By 1930, Smyth could tell Corbey and his colleagues: '. . . he was glad that the day had gone when the Parent Movement considered Health Insurance as being merely a side issue. They now found that they could not touch any industrial question without dealing with Social Insurance questions.'[42]

Unions seek better medical care in industry

It was the depression that made such a development possible. Workers who lost their jobs became concerned about the benefits they could obtain from the state, and their interest did not stop with unemployment insurance: it extended to medical care. Among union leaders, Ernest Bevin was the first to sense this concern and at the 1930 Conference of the TUC, he had much to say about the panel system. His comments were not favourable to the doctors.[b] So bad did he consider their care that he regretted the introduction of NHI. Had Lloyd George not done so, Bevin believed, employers would have been forced to fill the void and they would have created a better factory medical service in the process. That was what had happened in America and, according to the medical adviser of the TUC (Legge), the doctors in charge of the industrial medical corps there were determined, because of the

a   For this, see p. 237 below.
b   See p. 174 above.

better facilities at their disposal, 'to fight tooth and nail against any idea of a National Health Insurance Act.'[43]

Because of the burden imposed by NHI contributions, only the larger employers in Britain could afford to duplicate the American system and they waited until 1923 before they did so.[44] As late as September 1939, there were only 30 whole-time industrial medical officers in the country.[a] The number increased rapidly as a result of the demands made by the war but, because of NHI (and later the National Health Service), industrial medical care in Britain always lagged behind America.[45]

There was, however, one aspect of the American system which Bevin and all good trade unionists deplored: that was the practice of putting doctors directly under employer control. Bevin preferred part-time GPs provided by the state to whole-time specialists appointed by management. GPs might not know as much about industrial medicine, but they were better able to discern the relationship between illness and occupation. Industrial medical officers were rooted to one firm: they could not follow the health of the ageing worker as he changed from job to job. Even worse, they had little desire to detect industrial disease: their employment relationship prevented them from making the effort. If the list of diseases scheduled under the Workmen's Compensation Act was ever to grow, there was only one doctor who could do it — the GP.

Unlike other trade unionists, Bevin's interest in industrial medicine was not ephemeral. In 1932, he accepted an appointment to the Industrial Health Research Board of the Medical Research Council and devoted years to promoting studies of worker health, particularly among London bus drivers.[46] These were not the initial cause of his interest in the subject, however. That came from the introduction of chemical processes which, Bevin suspected, had caused industrial disease among members of his own union, the Transport and General Workers. Neither he nor the approved society run by his union could prove it because the medical records kept under NHI did not attempt to trace the relationship between illness and occupation. Yet this was not the fault of Lloyd George. In 1911, he put an 'excess sick' clause in the Act expressly to promote such studies[47] — but not until the 1930s was anything like it carried out.[b]

How could the cause have been discerned with general practice in the state that it was? Panel doctors knew nothing about industrial medicine — lead poisoning, for example, was described by them as 'gastric trouble'[49] — and they lacked the equipment needed for accurate diagnosis. Speed of diagnosis was also essential since GPs had to make the correct diagnosis within a year from the time the worker left his disabling job if compensation was to be secured for diseases already scheduled. Only under the Various Industries

a   For more on this, see pp. 263-4 below.

b   The most useful application of NHI statistics, as far as the trade unions were concerned, was done by the Cardroom Operatives. In 1938, they managed to have byssinosis scheduled as a disease peculiar to the textile industry by using data provided by their approved society.[48]

Scheme for silicosis were longer periods allowed — 3 years in 1928, 5 years in 1939.[a]

To provide GPs with the equipment they required, Bevin recognized, they would have to work in health centres and they would need groups as large as 12 to 20 to justify the expenditure involved. Yet the approved societies had rejected any thought of GPs doing specialist work in 1926 because they wanted more than the opinion of a 'brother panel practitioner'.[b] The unions had less reason to oppose the idea than the offices or the friendly societies, but there was no way to alter administrative opinion on the subject without a marked improvement in the standard of panel care. Bevin's attack on the doctors in 1930 was no doubt mainly inspired by this consideration: he wanted GPs to raise themselves to the point where the approved society world as a whole would consider them worthy of giving specialist treatment. Like Brackenbury in 1919,[c] Bevin hoped every GP would become a bit of a specialist but, this time, their expertise would cover only a part of industrial health, not the whole of medicine.

That, in the climate of the 1930s, would probably have satisfied the unions if not the rest of the NHI world. They needed specialist care more than the other approved societies in order to relieve their hard-pressed funds and, if it could not be made available to all insured persons, then they were ready to limit it to those whose work exposed them to trades dangerous to health. For that more limited task, the unions had reason to believe, GPs would do. Seven hundred of them, in any case, were already providing a form of industrial medical care as certifying factory surgeons under the Factories Acts. In that capacity, they not only determined the fitness of young persons for work (thereby providing, for a century, the main bulwark in the country against child labour) but periodically conducted examinations on workers engaged in occupations dangerous to health.[51 d]

Otherwise, GP experience in the industrial medical field did not extend very far. Like public health doctors employed in municipal clinics, certifying factory surgeons could not provide treatment.[52] The BMA had placed the same ban in the Factories Acts as in the Maternity and Child Welfare Act: the doctors covered by both statutes were restricted to 'prevention'. The factory service, however, offered greater hope of extension because, unlike most clinic doctors, certified surgeons gave only part of their day to factory work. Only 5 out of a total of 1,771 in 1919 worked whole-time and only 100 devoted more than a few hours per week to the job.[53] The overwhelming proportion of their day was spent on private (or panel) patients. That, in Legge's eyes, was what made them superior to public health doctors — or even to those who confined their practice to NHI. It was also the reason he gave throughout the 1920s for urging the use of GPs in place of MOHs to supervise the health of workers in factories:

a   Since 1948, the time limit for diagnosing silicosis has been completely removed because of the hardship it caused.[50]

b   See pp. 156-7 above.

c   See pp. 116-17 and 130-2 above.

d   GPs still perform these duties — only now they are called 'employment medical advisers' instead of their former harsher title.

' . . . What I feel is that private practice does stimulate their alertness of mind and their power of making quick decisions. It broadens their outlook and brings them into contact with fresh people. The worst of whole-time people is that they become drudges.'[54]

Here was the nucleus from which a specialist service might be built. The panel has held back the growth of medical care in industry but, since it was confined to general practice, could not a case be made for by-passing it where specialism was concerned? This, no doubt, was the assumption underlying the report issued by the Association of Certifying Factory Surgeons at the end of the First World War.[55] It called for the reconstruction of the factory medical service, and, 6 years later, the first Labour Government actually introduced a Bill giving the Home Office power to provide such treatment.[56]

So far as the doctors were concerned, however, the measure left too much control in municipal hands and it also invoked the hated principle of 'selection'. In place of the existing 'open' roll of certified surgeons, 4 'appointed doctors' were to be designated and local authorities, if they wished, could take over completely the job of examining young persons. Legge, who had long helped to fashion the views of factory surgeons, knew that this would never be acceptable.[57] Why not link up industrial medical care with NHI instead? If panel doctors participated, they might be willing to lift the ban on treatment. The same could reasonably apply to selection. If local medical committees made the choice, it might be possible to confine the provision of industrial medical care to GPs capable of rendering it.[a] That, Legge told the Royal Commission on NHI, was the way to by-pass the barrier imposed on factory care by the profession on the one hand and the panel system on the other.[59]

Unions seek GP aid

These, no doubt, were the thoughts that flowed through Bevin's mind when he threw down his challenge to the profession in 1930[b]. Join hands with us, he told the doctors, in order to devise a scheme for the extension of medical benefit.[62] The doctors, however, failed to respond. Negotiations did not begin until 1935 and then they foundered again on the principle of selection.[c] Bevin, in 1937, tried to save the day by making a plea directly to the Annual Representative Meeting of the BMA: 'The B.M.A. would fight against a rigid State medical service, but if it did not want such a service it must offer co-operation somewhere.'[63]

Bevin's eyes, however, were on the wrong target. The doctors did not fear the state so much as their own colleagues. As a leading industrial medical officer put

a   In Legge's eyes, they would come mainly from the ranks of those doctors who did not overload themselves with panel patients. Panel work, he felt, engendered bad habits. It also bred competitive problems which Legge was anxious to avoid.[58]

b   Legge became the TUC's medical adviser just before Bevin issued his challenge.[60] Bevin was also stimulated by the publication of the BMA's General Medical Service scheme in 1929.[61] This led him to believe the doctors were ready for change.

c   See p. 157 above.

The Division in British Medicine

it: 'One of the great difficulties in getting the insurance practitioner into part-time industrial service was the fear of other insurance practitioners that he would steal their patients.'[64]

Bevin, therefore, had to wait until 1940 before he could do more. Then, on becoming Minister of Labour, he issued an order which, for the first time, gave adequate recognition to industrial health.[a] With the aid of the Treasury, industrial medical care spread rapidly during the war: Britain, in this respect, no longer remained a poor cousin of America.[65] But the movement collapsed after 1945 because it did not develop in the way the unions intended. Employers, under Bevin's order, continued to employ their own doctors; all the Government did was help them pay the bill. The idea of using GPs for the work was quietly dropped and was not revived until the 1950s when Dr Stephen Taylor raised it again as a remedy for the weakness of general practice.[66] Bevin, by the time the war ended, did not think factory doctors should be employed by the state; as a Minister in a Government anxious to increase production for war, he had come to believe that control should rest with employers.[67] The unions, as a result, lost interest in industrial health for years thereafter.[68][b]

The unions also had larger considerations in mind: they hoped to create a Health Service that would cover medical facilities as a whole (particularly hospitals and consultants) rather than one confined to industry alone.[70] Workers had never been fond of factory doctors, even when the latter were employed by the state; they preferred to keep the care of their health separate from their place of work. Bevin himself never really wanted a segregated industrial medical service.[71] He issued his 1940 order only because of the necessities of war. Once it ended, he hoped the nation would proceed with the plan he presented to the BMA in 1937.

In pushing that plan, however, the unions could not afford to press their views too strongly on the doctors. Two factors inhibited them. In the first place, the unions needed the profession's aid to remove the insurance offices from NHI. But an even greater restraint flowed from the legal battles associated with workmen's compensation. Who but the panel doctor could help the injured worker with his accident claim?[72] The specialists (except for the few on the staff of Manor House Hospital)[c] were beholden to the insurance companies[d] and even GPs sometimes betrayed a similar tendency. Nothing angered the unions more than the way panel doctors supplied reports to insurance companies without worker knowledge.[75] In them the doctor might indicate that his patient was not really ill; yet this same practitioner might freely grant requests from the same

a   See pp. 263-4 below.

b   Perhaps more to the point, they attached greater importance to compensation than cure. Once the Industrial Injuries Act passed, the unions were willing to accept private development of industrial medical care.[69]

c   See pp. 229-30 above.

d   Their dependence deepened during the depression. Many consultants, particularly in the provinces, came to rely on the retainer fees provided by insurance companies.[73] Some went so far as to move their practice to the company office while keeping a Harley Street address so as to appear independent.[74] As a result of these ties, the network of interests supporting the voluntary hospitals strengthened considerably. Opposition to state control, both within and without the profession, was stronger in 1939 than it was in 1919.

patient for sickness certificates under NHI.

To win medical support for their programme, the unions did all they could to promote a feeling of solidarity between GPs and the working class. Here, the way was led by Fred Kershaw who for years had urged his colleagues in the union approved societies to restrain criticism of panel doctors.[76] During the 1920s, Kershaw was President of the National Association of Trade Union Approved Societies and with his friend, Ernest Corbey, dictated the stand the labour movement took before the Royal Commission on NHI. Kershaw then proceeded to draft the Commission's Minority Report with Gertrude Tuckwell, one of the five labour sympathizers on the body. The report called for equal benefits and the abolition of the approved society system, policies which Corbey had pressed on the unions from the moment the National Association was formed in 1914.[77]

A few years after the Commission's Report appeared, Kershaw set up a legal (and investment) department of his own for the purpose of providing the unions with assistance on compensation cases.[78] Aiding him were a prominent surgeon from Manor House Hospital (Dr Ambrose Woodall, later Lord Uvedale), a former civil servant (Dr George McCleary, who joined Kershaw's department after he retired from the Ministry of Health in 1933),[79] and a GP with experience of fighting compensation cases for pottery workers in North Staffordshire, Dr (later Sir) Barnett Stross. When he began compensation work in 1926, Stross was not interested in politics but, in the process of fighting employers and insurance companies, he became a confirmed socialist. The case that impressed him most involved a man suffering from an occupational disease which the physician hired by the insurance company had tried to pass off as syphilis. Yet, even by the time the case came to court, the physician had not arranged for a Wasserman test. Such experiences put Stross firmly on the side of the unions and gave him a long career in Labour politics, entering Parliament in 1945 and serving as Parliamentary Secretary to the Ministry of Health in 1964-5.[80]

Few GPs, however, were able to follow the route which Stross had taken. Their ignorance of industrial medicine made them unsuitable for the work and the refresher course programme started by the Ministry in 1937 did nothing to alter the situation: no more than an occasional lecture was devoted to industrial medicine.[81] The TUC tried to meet this deficiency by altering the pattern of undergraduate, rather than postgraduate, education. In 1935, as the result of a memorandum submitted by the TUC, the General Medical Council recommended the addition of 8 to 10 lectures on industrial medicine. But only 3 of the 42 medical schools in the country bothered to implement the resolution and none were located in London.[82]

The GPs themselves were responsible for the failure of another approach recommended by the unions. Bevin wanted GPs to acquire the necessary experience by working in health centres established, presumably, under GP control but the doctors proved no more responsive to this than they had to Dawson's health-centre proposal. Again, it was the fear of competition that dissuaded them: GPs who worked part-time in industrial medicine aroused the same anxieties as those who worked part-time in hospital. In both cases, their colleagues were afraid of losing patients to them.[83] [a]

By 1939, it was clear, something more was needed if the profession was to respond and the unions sent Smyth to plead their case. The speech he delivered to the MPU in that year shows just how dependent on GP aid the unions had become:

> ' . . . A doctor should have knowledge of all diseases associated with industry. He was all for the general practitioner. He did not believe in specialisation. With all this specialising it meant depriving people of half their rights. He did not like to see those in the mass production factories fixing on one particular job, on automatic performance, each day and every day. He did not want to see the medical profession reduced to something resembling that. He regarded the doctor and the plumber[b] as the two most important people in the community. Although the general practitioner should have a full knowledge of working conditions he was not the expert he ought to be on industrial diseases. Industry was giving rise to certain diseases... Doctors should be ready to expose everything that gave rise to ill-health irrespective of vested interests. To do that they had to be a first-class public service. . . If security was aimed at, the greatest insurance policy was a salaried service to the nation, a decent income, consistent with the profession, and with a full public service.'[85]

This statement contains the full thrust of union policy before the war. Its aim was to separate the profession and put GPs in health centres, where with the stimulus of group practice and the security of salary, they would acquire the competence needed to nullify specialist subservience to the insurance companies. Job-oriented doctors with expertise in industrial medicine: that, above all, was what the unions wanted from general practice.

a   See pp. 235-6 above.

b   Smyth was a plumber by trade and had earlier been the Assistant General Secretary of the Plumbers Union.[84]

24

The BMA-TUC Alliance and the Beveridge Report

GPs may have turned a deaf ear to union demands but BMA leaders did not. Even before the MPU threat materialized in 1935,[a] they were anxious to establish a close relationship with the TUC but the BMA's company status seemed to rule out formal affiliation.[b] The Llanelly dispute, however, provided the chance for a looser tie.[c] As Brackenbury frankly admitted in 1935: 'The Association wanted to come into contact with the TUC, because it was believed that not only in Llanelly but in other areas where contract practice was in question it would be highly advantageous in making arrangements to have the sympathetic cooperation of that important body.'[1]

From this informal tie, a joint standing committee emerged in 1936,[2] and the connections between the two organizations did not stop there. Bevin was not only asked to address the Annual Representative Meeting in 1937[d] — he and Smyth were made Vice-Presidents of the BMA's Medical Sociology Section.[3] Even more important, Morgan found a place on the BMA's Council and stayed there until the end of the war.[4]

BMA criticizes fracture treatment

TUC leaders promptly responded to these moves by endorsing the BMA's maternity policy;[e] they expected even more in return. What they wanted was BMA aid in a joint attack on the Workmen's Compensation Act, using that as a lever for the reconstruction of social insurance as a whole. The impetus for such action came from a horrifying report on fracture treatment which the BMA had compiled in 1935: over half the fractures treated each year were maladministered and 37% of the patients involved in one sample had been disabled for the rest of their lives.[5]

The cause of such treatment lay in the paucity of effective facilities available. Specialized clinics were needed since they reduced the incidence of permanent disability from fractures to only 1%. Even among the prestigious

a   See pp. 182-3 above.

b   For the consultants' opposition to any attempt to turn the BMA into a trade union, see pp. 14-15 above.

c   See pp. 155-6 above.

d   See p. 235 above.

e   See pp. 218-20 above.

teaching hospitals of London, however, such clinics were missing: only 4 out of 12 hospitals contained them.[6] Elsewhere, the situation was worse: due to the dearth of hospital provision, 3 out of 4 fractures over the country as a whole had to be treated mainly at home.[7] Yet few doctors were encouraged to make themselves competent in the subject because there was 'no money in fractures' outside the hospitals.[a] Before 1911, that did not apply: insurance companies had to pay GPs for treatment whether it was carried out in hospital or not. The NHI changed all that: it made panel treatment free for all accidents, even those which occurred at work, and that destroyed the incentive of GPs to perform effectively in the field of orthopaedics.[8]

This accounts for the disturbing situation BMA leaders found when they prepared their report on fracture treatment. Mr (later Sir) Henry Souttar, the chairman of the committee that conducted the study, said he was 'absolutely astounded at the results placed before us'.[9] He was a surgeon of considerable standing but the orthopaedists who served with him on the committee — like Mr (later Sir) Reginald Watson-Jones — were not. They had long suffered neglect in the hospital world and that was why they, almost alone among consultants, welcomed proposals for state control of the voluntary sector. Before 1948, the orthopaedists were the 'radicals' of the medical profession.[b]

The orthopaedists made it clear, in an appendix to the report, where they thought the main responsibility lay. The insurance companies, they maintained, did not welcome the establishment of fracture clinics because that would reduce the amount of premium they could charge and the profit they could earn. Their interest lay in the promotion of quick — and cheap — settlements along lump-sum lines.[10]

That, the doctors suggested, was also why so little progress had been made with rehabilitation. Physical insecurity bred financial insecurity and the insurance companies had a vested interest in the termination of treatment before patients recovered.[11] Was that also why, despite repeated pleas from the voluntary hospitals, the companies had refused to make payments for compensation cases?[12] In this respect, they had shown themselves to be more niggardly than the approved societies — yet when cars, as opposed to human beings, were involved, their generosity knew no bounds. Thus as Professor Hey Groves put it, when a road accident occurred: 'The car is sent to the works and the man to the hospital; the car is paid for, but the man's bones have to be mended as a matter of charity.'[13] Not until 1934 did the doctors receive assurance of payment in road accident cases. Then an Act was passed setting forth the fees to be allowed, but as late as 1939 some doctors complained about their failure to receive them.[14]

The BMA report on fractures appeared in February 1935, and had an immediate impact on Whitehall. The Workmen's Compensation Act, the

a　See p. 159 above.

b　For a good indication of this, see the statement by Professor Hey Groves (one of the leading orthopaedists on the committee) below. Morgan and his colleagues at the Manor House Hospital were equally committed to the nationalization principle, but they were not given a place on the BMA Committee because it would have prejudiced the case the doctors wanted to make against the insurance industry.

doctors had shown, did not fulfil the purpose for which it was intended: instead of enabling injured workers to live with their disabilities, it turned them into invalids, dependent on charity or the Poor Law for subsistence. The Government's response was to form two official committees: one, the Delevingne Committee, to study 'the rehabilitation of persons injured by accidents';[15] the other, the Stewart Committee, to investigate 'certain questions arising under the Workmen's Compensation Acts'.[16]

Royal Commission on Workmen's Compensation

The former endorsed the BMA's call for fracture clinics but the latter, evading the issue because of the unions' own inhibitions on the subject, failed to condemn the practice of lump-sum settlements.[17] The unions, nonetheless, demanded legislation and, through their representatives in Parliament, brought pressure on the Government which was too strong to ignore.[18] In June 1938 it created a Royal Commission on Workmen's Compensation. This, however, was no mere deflective manoeuvre: not only Smyth but others sympathetic to the union cause were appointed to the body. These included two well-known union leaders (William Lawther and George Isaacs), the Controller in charge of NHI (Edgar Hackforth), an academic who had once been a research officer of the TUC and Labour Party (Barbara Wootton) and, as chairman, an academic with a long record of devotion to social reform (Hector Hetherington).

Here was the chance the unions had been waiting for.[a] Earlier they had found it prudent to withhold criticism of lump-sum settlements because of the popularity of the payments. The full burden of the attack had been left to the BMA.[20] Now the unions joined hands with the doctors and presented a heated indictment of the insurance companies for the way they had administered the Act.[21] Nor did they stop with workmen's compensation: they brought NHI under pressure as well. Smyth, from his position on the Commission's rostrum, repeatedly condemned various aspects of the approved-society system, particularly its failure to provide statistics on industrial disease.[22]

In the midst of the hearings, the question of hospital provision inevitably intruded: the nation could no longer tolerate a situation where damaged cars were paid for but broken bones were not.[23] Something had to be done to supplement the limited aid provided under the panel, and extension could not be limited to workmen's compensation alone. There were several reasons for this. In the first place, too many injuries were sustained outside the confines of factory gates: of the total number of fractures the country experienced each year, only some 10% fell within the provisions of the Compensation Act.[24] The rest had to be treated and, since most of the injuries were sustained by insured persons (roughly half the total), the majority of people

---

a   Smyth was angry when the Royal Commision was first announced, considering it to be
      just a delaying action on the part of the Government, but he changed his mind after the
      members and terms of reference became known. He then realised that the Commission
      would put all the social services 'in the melting pot', not just workmen's compensation.[19]

suffering fractures could clearly not afford to pay.[25]

Beyond that, the panel had to be extended for reasons of its own: it could not function effectively as long as it was restricted to GP care. But the furore over fractures demonstrated how close was the involvement of NHI with workmen's compensation. The time had come to amalgamate the two, at least where medical benefit was concerned. Hackforth strove hard to persuade the Commission to adopt this view.[26] As Controller in charge of NHI, his voice carried great weight and, had he felt able to speak freely at all times, no doubt he would have gone further: like the unions, Hackforth always wanted to eliminate the approved-society system.[27] But the presence of his old chief in the Ministry had kept him silent before (except on the few occasions when he had the chance to address the unions).[28] Sir Walter Kinnear, the former Controller, was a hard-hearted insurance man devoted to contributory principles; not until he retired from office in 1937 did Hackforth secure freedom to help the union cause.

That cause lay in the process of amalgamation and, once it began, who knew where it would stop? Cash benefits, in time, might be covered too, and, from there, the merger movement might proceed to the point where it embraced all the state had to offer. At that moment, the unions would have realized their dream of 'all-in insurance' but, surprisingly, they did not take kindly to Hackforth's efforts in this direction. The reason lay in their long-standing objection to the contributory principle.[29] Bad as it was, workmen's compensation was at least financed by employers; if it were merged with NHI, then workers might have to contribute, too. That, in turn, might strengthen the approved-society system — which was the last thing most of the unions wanted to do. Only if the Government held out hope of removing the insurance companies from social insurance would the unions agree to a wider application of the contributory principle. Until then, they felt, it was better to leave workmen's compensation to the state — and the same applied to medical care. The resources of the Exchequer were needed to supply the enormous funds required for hospital and specialist treatment. The time had come to bring the voluntary hospitals under central — not local — government control.

Here union ranks were split. Those close to the SMA tended to favour its policy of municipal administration. Morgan was the leader of this group but even he aimed mainly at the abolition of the voluntary hospital system. As long as the hospitals were brought under state control, he did not care greatly whether title rested with central or local government.[30] In the end, therefore, he deferred to the Durham miners and other unions which objected strongly to 'the failure of small local authorities to join together, even in the establishment of a small joint hospital scheme'.[31]

Such was the direction of union thought when the war intervened [32] and the Commission, because of an employer boycott, found it necessary to suspend its hearings. However, the miners and the railwaymen — the two groups of workers most exposed to industrial accidents — refused to give up. At the TUC's Annual Conference in 1940, they introduced a motion calling for the end of the compensation 'offset': accident benefits, they argued, should be added to NHI's sickness benefit, not deducted from it.

The proposal seemed modest enough, but it was not as simple as it appeared. Here was the explanation given by the delegate who introduced it:

> '. . . if we can get this matter referred to the General Council with your approval and support, I have no doubt that the whole question of industrial insurance, a sort of all-inclusive industrial insurance involving an adequate amount being placed at the disposal of the injured or sick worker, will be ventilated. That is really the intention behind this resolution, although we thought that the best way to approach the matter was by bringing to your notice the gross anomaly that exists in regard to compensation cases.'[33]

The Beveridge Committee

The General Council took the hint and conveyed it to the Ministry of Health, asking not only that NHI be overhauled but the social services linked up in one large co-ordinated scheme.[34] At that point, however, the Minister in charge of reconstruction problems intervened. This was Arthur Greenwood, and he had never forgotten how his dream of a national health service,[a] along with other elements of a welfare state, had been destroyed in 1920. Now that a second chance had arisen, he was determined not to lose it.

Foremost in Greenwood's mind was the need to avoid the mistakes the reformers had made during the First World War. Then, a new department had been formed (i.e. the Ministry of Reconstruction) to deal with post-war planning but it had not had sufficient status to command a seat in the Cabinet. As a result, its reports never received the attention they deserved. No similar department was created in the Second World War. Instead, the subject was entrusted to an inter-departmental committee of top-level civil servants with a respected 'outsider' — Sir William Beveridge — in charge. Beveridge, as the father of unemployment insurance in Britain, not only had great expertise in the field, but was eminently acceptable to the unions because of the way his views had been transformed in the 1930s. At one time he had tended to take a stern approach to insurance questions, sounding more like a Poor Law guardian than a social reformer. But in 1934 he had been appointed Chairman of the new Unemployment Insurance Statutory Committee, charged with the duty of managing the insurance fund, and the personal hardships he enountered there (among the unemployed) turned him into a sympathetic administrator.[35] Through this work, also, he came in contact with Jim Smyth of the TUC and the friendship they formed no doubt greatly influenced the nature of the proposals Beveridge made in 1942.[36] Yet, when the social insurance inquiry began, the friendly societies and the insurance offices seemed oblivious to the danger — possibly because they believed Beveridge still clung to the views he expressed in 1924. Then, he had proposed an 'all-in' scheme of reform which not only left the approved societies intact but gave them (and insurance committees) the job of administering workmen's compensation.[37]

If the approved societies were later taken by surprise, so was the Treasury.

a   See p. 50 above.

At the start of the inquiry, it had wanted the meetings to be held in secret so as to avoid giving the impression that the Committee's recommendations might become policy.[38] If it had felt that the proposals (even if given in private) might entail substantial Government expenditure, it would certainly have insisted on a Treasury official being put in charge. Instead, the civil service entrusted secretarial control to a young academic — D. N. Chester, later Warden of Nuffield College — and, though completely new to the field of social insurance, he did much to fashion the report that gave Beveridge his place in history.[39]

Not everything, however, was left to chance: the Government did create a Cabinet committee of its own to deal with reconstruction problems.[40] This, apparently, was Bevin's idea and he seems to have worked closely with Greenwood in planning the strategy of reform at the time.[41] José Harris, in her biography of Beveridge, suggests that Bevin, who at first opposed the creation of the social insurance inquiry, changed his mind only after he saw the chance it offered of removing Beveridge from his place in the Ministry of Labour which Bevin himself had provided. [42] The evidence she offers in support of this thesis, however, is not conclusive: it comes from Beveridge (or people close to him) rather than from Bevin. She also fails to make clear the reasons for Bevin's initial opposition to the inquiry: he opposed it because he was vitally concerned with the plight of injured workmen and he did not think a committee could deal as boldly with the question of workmen's compensation as a Royal Commission. Here, in full, is the explanation given by one of Bevin's own civil servants (Mr Tribe) at the official meeting which Harris repeatedly cites:

> 'Mr. Bevin is particularly interested in the rehabilitation and treatment of injured workmen. He thought that a Committee consisting partly of civil servants and partly of outsiders would be no good, and that so far as Workmen's Compensation was concerned the Royal Commission would be the most suitable body to make the sort of report that was needed. Mr. Bevin would be willing to approach the employers and try to persuade them to given [sic] evidence. He agreed that rehabilitation was closely linked with National Health Insurance and that the Royal Commission would be able to survey only part of the field.'[43]

The last sentence of this statement indicates that Bevin may have changed his mind for a different reason than the one given by Harris. The new committee would be able to cover the whole field of social insurance, not just workmen's compensation, and through it the unions would be able to make the changes they wanted in NHI. But to do this the committee would have to concern itself with policy questions, not just technical details (as initially seemed likely), and Bevin may have wanted Beveridge's appointment not just to get rid of him but to make sure that the inquiry dealt boldly with the whole field of social insurance. Smyth almost certainly took this view because he, it was reported at the same meeting as above, 'was not pressing at all for a Royal Commission report and would be quite content with a Departmental Committee'.[44]

Another factor which had worked against reform after the First World

War had been the timing of the proposals. No sooner did hostilities end than a reaction set in which gathered strength as economic conditions deteriorated.[a] Greenwood, in the Second World War, was determined to have the necessary legislation ready (if not enacted) before the troops returned home.[45] The leaders of British industry, however, did not wish to proceed so fast. Thus, the Director of the British Employers Confederation (Sir John Forbes) urged the Beveridge Committee to delay its report: '. . . we did not start this war with Germany', he angrily declared, 'in order to improve our social services.'[46] Not all his colleagues, however, agreed. While some employers merely saw social reform as a way of rousing the workers behind the war effort,[47] others, like Samuel (later Lord) Courtauld, took a more positive view: they regarded such legislation as a kind of national investment.[48]

In the end, the Beveridge Report by no means damaged British industry. On the contrary, along with the country as a whole, industry benefited in many ways from the heightened sense of security stimulated by the legislation the Report engendered. Also, as a result of the Health Service, employers and insurance companies were relieved of the medical costs stemming from accident claims. They still had their own weekly insurance contributions to meet — but, even here, the burden imposed on them proved to be far lighter than the one placed on employers elsewhere (particularly in France). Because of the country's dependence on foreign trade, the British Exchequer always did its best to relieve industry of social costs.

British industry, in any case, found it difficult to oppose the Beveridge Report because of the way its spokesmen had boycotted the sittings of the Royal Commission on Workmen's Compensation. That, indeed, was said to have been the main reason for setting up the Beveridge Committee.[49] Churchill and his party had little room for manoeuvre on the question of social reform — and they were restricted further by the fervour with which the public welcomed the Beveridge Report.[50] The only major difference between the parties came on the question of timing and even Bevin felt that legislation should be delayed until the war was won.[51]

Within the Government, the Conservative who displayed the strongest opposition to the Beveridge Report was Sir Kingsley Wood.[52] As Chancellor of the Exchequer, he felt bound to speak against a programme which presented formidable financial problems. But before the war, he himself had been a protagonist of social reform.[b] While Minister of Health in 1937, he had asked his Chief Medical Officer (Sir Arthur MacNalty) to prepare a feasibility report on a national health service.[53] Though no action was taken at the time, Kinglsey Wood did more than any other Minister of Health to develop the public health service between the wars. His great achievement was the Midwives Act of 1936 (which created a salaried midwife service under local authority control) and, when it passed, the public-health world had nothing but praise: '. . . in Sir Kingsley Wood we have a Minister of the

a   See Chapter 7 beginning on p. 73 above.

b   For the important part he played in the events that led to the creation of the Ministry of Health see p. 36 above.

Crown who really does put himself out to give the people the services which they desire.'[54]

Greenwood thus had a favourable climate in which to work and the outcome proved more far-reaching than he, in 1941, had reason to hope. Beveridge started the process going with an extensive programme of social reform. His Report recommended not only a wide range of cash benefits but, almost as an aside, a comprehensive health service. This appeared in the Report as the famous 'Assumption B'.[55] Beveridge recognized the importance of the subject but he had to treat it in this cavalier fashion because of the Committee's restricted terms of reference. As Beveridge himself interpreted them, he could deal only with the coverage of medical care (including the way in which it was financed), not with the details of organization.[56]

On the question of a salaried service Beveridge said nothing, but he did imply support by declaring his belief in the need for the health service to prevent disease and control certification.[57] Both objectives had long been associated in the public mind with the aims of those who wanted to pay panel doctors by salary. On this point, however, the Committee's Secretary did not agree. In a memorandum he sent to the Lord President of the Council (Attlee) in August 1943, Chester expressed sympathy for the profession's point of view: GP care, he believed, was of too personal a nature to convert into a bureaucratic salaried service. Even after health centres were established, he felt, the principle of free choice should operate.[58]

Where the rest of the Report was concerned Chester registered no dissent, and there Beveridge moved boldly. The strongest position he took was against the principle of insurance industry participation, excluding it from the administration of all the benefits in the Report — which meant that the offices would lose their place in NHI as well as workmen's compensation. Both were to be administered by the state. In the interest of equal benefits to all, the long-standing approved societies were to go. Only the 'disinterested' types might remain to act as agents of the state and by these, Beveridge took care to explain, he meant only the friendly societies and the trade unions.[59]

In making this bold recommendation, Beveridge was influenced by the Association of Approved Societies as well as the TUC. The Association had been the first to appear before the Committee and its unconditional call for the abolition of approved societies made it easier for Beveridge to adopt the suggestion. Unlike the TUC, the Association did not have a vested interest in the proposal; on the contrary, most of its members (i.e. small societies of one type or another) were likely to be seriously damaged since they had no other work to fall back on. Nearly all ceased operation after 1948, along with the Association itself. For this altruistic gesture, the Association's Secretary (Austin Spearing) deserves much of the credit since he prepared its evidence to Beveridge (as well as to the Royal Commission on Workmen's Compensation) on his own initiative.[60]

Beveridge, however, was not content to stop with what the Association wanted: he attacked the private side of insurance industry work as well. Because of the high costs and other abuses associated with industrial assurance, Beveridge suggested that it be converted into a public service.[61]

What this meant was that a large part of the business of the Prudential and other offices would be nationalized. Here, Beveridge went far beyond the point that anyone expected and, in view of the controversial nature of the proposal, it was not surprising that the civil servants on the Committee decided to let him sign the report alone.[62]

This recommendation was so far-reaching that we must delve deeper into the reasons for it. It should be noted that not even the Parmoor Committee (in 1919-20) or the Cohen Committee (in 1931-3) had had the courage to make it and they, unlike the Beveridge Committee, had been created to deal specifically with the abuses of industrial assurance. Why, then, did Beveridge suggest nationalization? From the Harris biography, we now know that the idea came from the radical economist, John Maynard Keynes.[63] What we still do not know, however, is why Beveridge accepted it, and we are unlikely to discover that until the two missing boxes of correspondence on the Beveridge Report are found.[64]

Meanwhile, we can only suggest possible explanations. One likely contender is that Beveridge hoped the proposal would persuade the insurance offices to let the approved-society system die peacefully. The recommendation, after all, was added almost as an afterthought: it came at the end of a long list of proposals and Beveridge did not consider it essential to his plan. If this, in fact, was the reason, it is ironic because Lloyd George seems to have employed the threat for the opposite reason in 1910: by presenting the offices with the danger of nationalization, he hoped to force them into NHI, thereby overcoming any possible resistance from the friendly societies.

In his Report, however, Beveridge offered another explanation: nationalization, he claimed, was needed not only to cure the evils of industrial assurance but to enable the offices to be used as agents for the administration of social insurance.[65] In doing so, Beveridge knew that he could not hope to confine the agency role to the friendly societies and the trade unions: the offices were too efficient for that. Therefore, if the agency recommendation was to succeed, Beveridge had to save a place for the offices, too.

Whatever the reason for the proposal, no one could deny that it was bold — yet that, surprisingly, did not impede the report's chance of success. It was published in November 1942, and the Government took only 3 months to endorse the bulk of its recommendations. Events moved more slowly after that and, in the case of the Health Service, some backtracking was done — but even the doctors did much to ensure the enactment of the eventual legislation. By supporting the TUC's call for an industrial medical service, they threw the fear of costs into employers and made them support legislation that would cover the community as a whole.[66]

Labour creates a welfare state

Once the war ended, some legislation was sure to follow for even the Conservative caretaker Government that took over in May 1945 had seen fit to put a Family Allowance Act on the statute book.[67] However, the unexpected Labour victory in the ensuing election made the reforms more far-reaching than the

Tories would have allowed: an Industrial Injuries Act, a National Insurance Act and, last but not least, a National Health Service Act — all, in that order, found their way onto the statute book. Greenwood, at long last, had realized his dream of a welfare state. Corbey spoke for both of them when he said he 'had never expected to live to see the measures this Government is proposing'.[68]

The big unions that dominated the TUC also viewed the development with delight, but their interests were somewhat different from those on the left of the Labour Party. When the Beveridge Report first appeared, the TUC proudly described itself as the 'father' of the document,[69] but what concerned it most were the paragraphs on workmen's compensation. The insurance companies were excluded from the administration of that — and, with the end of the approved-society system, had also to give up their place in NHI.

Once that was accomplished, the unions lost interest in the nationalization of industrial assurance. The Government therefore waited until 1949 before it considered action, and then ran into opposition from the labour movement's own Co-operative Insurance Society.[70] The Society was the only insurance office in England without an approved society of its own so it calmly accepted the nationalization of NHI.[71] But industrial assurance was another matter: the Society insisted that Labour adopt a policy of 'mutualization' instead.[72] This, conveniently, left it alone since it was owned by its policy-holders. So happy was the co-operative movement with the outcome that it decided to apply the same tactic to its other institutions whenever the threat of nationalization appeared. As Mr (later Sir) John Bailey, the secretary of the Co-operative Party, put it in 1950: 'In any consultations with the Labour Party we should always be ready to put up the Co-operative alternative to conventional ideas of public ownership.'[73]

That ended any serious thought of nationalization where the insurance industry was concerned. But death benefits by themselves were another matter, and they were also included in the Beveridge Report. Yet, even here, the insurance industry was protected because the benefits, when enacted, were set so low that they required private supplementation. The offices kept their industrial assurance business intact[74] — and the same applied to the funeral funds of the unions.[75] Both groups found it easy to thrive within the framework of the welfare state.

Only the friendly societies suffered a blow from which they never recovered. Beveridge gave them and the unions the chance to administer social insurance on an agency basis[a] but Labour, when it assumed office in 1945, applied the principle only to unemployment benefit and, since that had never been a friendly-society function, the unions alone were given the task.[76] Still, the friendly societies had only themselves to blame. When Beveridge first proposed the agency idea, they rejected it, preferring to join the offices in a campaign to save the approved-society system.[77] That prospect was ruled out even by the Coalition Government in 1944[78] and only then did the societies see the danger before them. Finally, late in 1944, they decided to go it alone[79] and, during the election campaign which followed in 1945, they managed to extract a pledge from Labour in support of the agency idea.[80] But no sooner did the Party gain

a   See p. 246 above.

power than the new Minister of National Insurance (James Griffiths) ruled out the option.[81]

Why did Labour change its mind? One reason lay in union fear of competition from the friendly societies. For over a century, the societies had taken members from them, and the unions wanted to be free of that threat.[82] But the unions took this harsh stand only because of the way the societies had betrayed them. 'Is death-bed repentance always genuine?' asked one union approved-society leader;[83] decidedly not, answered Corbey. He and others in the unions could not forgive the societies for the way they had allied themselves with the insurance offices.[84] The Labour Government, in any case, had little choice in the matter: where sickness benefit was concerned, it would have been difficult to discriminate. How could the offices be excluded from an agency role when they, as the Cabinet's own Committee on Reconstruction Priorities had recognized in 1943, 'were the most efficient of the organisations working in the field'?[85]

By allying themselves with the offices, then, the societies signed what Beveridge himself called their 'death warrant'[86] and the dire prophecy which Kershaw had issued in 1918 was painfully fulfilled.[a] Although the affiliated orders (which always formed the heart of the friendly-society movement) retained ample funds, their membership fell sharply after 1948. By 1962, it had plunged as much as 32% below the 1952 level, and the total prevailing then represented only about 25% of the membership they had had in 1911 when state intervention began.[87]

As for the unions, their delight at the action taken in 1945 knew no bounds. So grateful were they that they finally abandoned all objection to the contributory principle.[88] Even the miners decided that the time had come for them to make some payment towards the cost of industrial accidents. Their feeling on this delicate issue, no doubt, had also been affected by the long-sought victory won where industrial disease was concerned. In 1942, shortly before the Beveridge Report appeared, the Medical Research Council — after years of dithering — had finally decided that pneumoconiosis was an affliction peculiar to the coal industry.[b]

Beveridge, however, left the miners little choice but to accept a contributory scheme because he skilfully exposed the contradiction in their demands. On the one hand, they wanted other industries to share the heavy costs of accidents in coal — yet, on the other, they expected only employers to put up the funds. Why, Beveridge asked, should the burden fall on one side of industry and not the other?[89] The new Industrial Injuries Act imposed charges on employees as well as employers.

Union interest in the Health Service

When it came to the Health Service, the unions displayed similar flexibility and similar concern. Here, as always, they were interested mainly in

a   See p. 36 above.

b   See pp. 230-1 above.

extending the range of care to disabled workers. For that purpose, they had to focus their attention on the hospital world — but they did not ignore the problem of general practice. The unions still wanted GPs to learn more about industrial medicine and to have the independence they needed to deal with employers who ran unhygienic workshops: that, for them, was the alternative to MOH and municipal control.[90] In order to realize it, they wanted GPs to work in groups and accept the salaried service the profession had long abhorred. From that, also, might come the possibility of higher cash benefits, since doctors paid by salary would be able to control sick claims and thus give the Government confidence to set higher allowances under the National Insurance Act.[91]

For all these reasons, the unions endorsed the Labour demand for salary and tried to persuade the BMA to accept it. But because of their overriding need to fight compensation cases, they backed away as soon as the profession objected: the unions, in 1944, could not afford to lose the support of GPs. Free choice, as 30 years of NHI had shown, at least put the panel doctor on the worker's side. Where the Health Service was concerned, then, all that the unions insisted on was the state control of the voluntary hospitals. That, together with the payment of consultants by salary, would provide the conditions needed to accelerate the recovery of disabled workers.[92]

Nor did the passage of the Industrial Injuries Act significantly alter their concern. The statute did remove the insurance companies from administration — but it put a new adversary in their place, the Ministry of National Insurance.[93] The unions soon discovered that they could not do without medical aid.[a] Now, however, with the voluntary hospitals under state control, they found it easier to recruit consultants in place of GPs. Even before the war, the unions had recognized that, where a compensation battle was concerned, it was 'no good putting up a panel doctor against a specialist'.[96] But since so few consultants were available, they had no choice — which was why the unions had been so intent on extending the competence of GPs. But this was linked in union eyes with salary and, when that hope disappeared, union attitudes towards general practice changed, too. Consultants alone, the unions now recognized, would have to fight industrial injury cases and, as the number of specialists under the Health Service grew, the unions made increasing use of them.

GPs would still work on the preventive side, and the unions never lost sight of their potential role in rehabilitating disabled workers. But both these functions placed the family doctor in the community: hospital work would be only a distraction. The GP's main job, in union eyes, was to conduct 'periodical examinations of the men all the time'.[97] These were the words

a   Smyth, in 1943, hoped to remove the doctors completely from compensation cases, leaving the issue to be fought out solely by lawyers.[94] In that way, he wanted to make it possible for the profession to concentrate on the rehabilitation of injured workers rather than, as so often happened, on the amount of compensation they received. But such a separation proved impossible to secure and the unions, in 1946, even had to exclude Manor House Hospital from state control in order to obtain the medical aid they needed.[95]

used by the Minister of National Insurance (Griffiths) in 1946 to stress the medical needs of rehabilitation and the unions agreed with that priority.[98] For such a task, only GPs were suitable because workers would not have allowed their jobs to be imperilled by doctors they did not trust.

When Bevan came to construct the Health Service, then, he heard nothing from the unions about the dangers of dividing British medicine. On the contrary, they left him with the impression that he could make the separation complete.

Part 7
Defeat of Socialist
Medical Association Policy
1940-1948

During the 1930s, the SMA emerged as the leading exponent of the health-centre idea but it developed a model different from Dawson's. Its health centre did not contain beds and it was meant to start a salaried service, not stop one. The SMA also believed strongly in municipal administration and on this issue it refused to compromise because of the dogmatists in its ranks. In the late 1930s, the SMA opened its door to socialists of all kinds and this, by altering its political image, eventually weakened its impact on health policy. Its first defeat came in the field of industrial health: the SMA tried to start a salaried service under state control but employers were allowed to proceed on their own. SMA policy on the Health Service was also defeated after it came in conflict with a new right-wing medical organization opposed to any form of state control. BMA leaders came under pressure and they found it necessary to force a series of concessions before the Service began. All the SMA really managed to salvage from the struggle was the principle of universal coverage.

' . . . What the public needs is a health service maintained by a completely unified profession, operating as a single instrument to bring every aspect of scientific medicine within the reach of every member of the community.'

> — from a letter by SMA leaders in *The Lancet*, 1943, 2, pp. 304-5.

'I believe there has been a tendency to dig too wide a gulf between the general practitioner on the one side and the specialist on the other.'

> — from the remarks made by Aneurin Bevan, Minister of Health, after the Health Service had been created, Parliamentary Debates, House of Commons, 19 October, 1949, Vol. 468, Col. 652.

25
Health Centre Dogma

The trade unions were not the only group in the labour movement that Bevan had to satisfy: the SMA also made demands. Unlike the SMSA which preceded it, the SMA affiliated with the Labour Party and this enabled it to exercise greater influence on Party policy. During the 1920s, the SMSA had found itself outflanked on Labour's Public Health Advisory Committee by the BMA.[a] This prompted the SMA, after it was formed in 1930, to present its proposals directly to the Party Conference and it was aided, after 1932, by the suspension of the Advisory Committee. By 1934, it was evident that the strategy had worked, for in that year Labour endorsed the SMA call for a salaried service.[1] The BMA fought back by way of the TUC[b] but, within Party circles, the SMA reigned supreme. So confident was it there that, in 1938, Hastings had the Public Health Advisory Committee restored (with himself as chairman) and this time no BMA representatives appeared.[2]

During these years the SMA's position on the LCC was also strong. Here, its influence had grown since 1933 when it contributed greatly to the Labour victory in the municipal election. As many as 9 SMA leaders found a place on the body, and Hastings, as chairman of the LCC's Hospitals and Medical Services Committee, directed the development of its health policy.[3] The era was one in which all efforts were concentrated on the expansion of municipal hospitals and that led SMA leaders to become the advocates of an integrated system.[4] Only by bringing GPs and local authority clinics in closer contact with municipal hospitals, they felt, would it be possible to establish a comprehensive service. In pursuing this goal, however, they failed to display the flexibility the situation demanded and that destroyed any chance of realizing the integration ideal.

SMA concept of health centres

During the 1930s, the SMA emerged as the leading exponent of the health-centre idea but, due to the large number of municipal doctors in its ranks, it developed a model different from Dawson's. Though some SMA leaders (including Stark Murray)[c] recognized the need for closer contact between

a   See p. 87 above.
b   See pp. 218-20 and 239 above.
c   See p. 174 above.

GPs and consultants, none saw that as the main aim of the health centre. What they thought it should do was promote co-operation among GPs. Above all, they wanted GPs to work in groups within a communal surgery, as Dawson himself had originally envisaged.[a] But, in contrast to Dawson, SMA leaders did not see how such co-operation could be fostered unless GPs were paid by salary.[5]

Furthermore, like the health centres started by local authorities in the 1930s,[b] those proposed by the SMA did not contain beds and this became the model of the period. Not only the BMA's own Medical Planning Commission but, even more, the Coalition Government's White Paper on the National Health Service called for health centres on the model the SMA had proposed. In the case of the latter, conformity was more complete because the White Paper endorsed the SMA's salary idea too, but the BMA's approval of any health centre at all was remarkable since they had been omitted from its 1938 General Medical Service scheme.[c] For this, no doubt, the 3 SMA representatives on the Medical Planning Commission (Hastings, Stark Murray and Dr Henry H. MacWilliam) were responsible. Without their prodding, it is doubtful if the profession would have adopted the idea in 1942.[6][d]

In developing its health-centre model the SMA departed not only from the concept proposed by Dawson but also from the policies preferred by the organization that had preceded it — the SMSA. Professor Moore and his colleagues had also leaned towards salary,[e] but they had agreed with Dawson that the health centre should serve mainly as a hospital for GPs.[f] One of Moore's disciples at the Walton Hospital in Liverpool tried to carry that message to the SMA.[7] This was Dr Henry H. MacWilliam, author in 1939 of the hospital-oriented Walton plan. By this time, MacWilliam had become a leader of the SMA and he tried to persuade his colleagues to accept the idea of GP and specialist teamwork in hospitals as well as health centres.[8]

For a while, it seemed, MacWilliam might succeed because the SMA, throughout the 1930s, saw group practice mainly as a way of generating the specialists Britain lacked. Indeed, it often used a different term at the start to describe its health centres: it called them 'clinics' — presumably to suggest their affinity to the polyclinics on the Continent.[9] Only later, as it came to place increasing emphasis on the concept of preventive medicine, did the SMA confine itself to the term 'health centre'. By then, the name had an entirely different connotation from the one Dawson had assigned to it.

a   See Chapter 10 beginning on p. 101 above.

b   See pp. 179-80 above.

c   See pp. 145 and 185 above.

d   This, however, raises an intriguing question: why were they ever given the chance to argue their case? The MPU was excluded the Commission's proceedings; could not the SMA have been, too? Perhaps BMA leaders were more attracted to the health-centre idea than they dared to admit.

e   See pp. 54-5 and 86 above.

f   See pp. 106-7 above.

Dawson was horrified by the change the SMA had wrought. His health centre was meant to stop salary, not start it, and he stressed the need to include beds if the standard of general practice was not to fall.[10] By this time (1943-4), GPs had become aroused, too — but they protested not so much against the absence of beds as against the presence of salary and municipal control.[a] For that reason, BMA leaders felt compelled to condemn the Ministry's health centre as nothing more than a communal surgery. By itself, they asserted, it would do nothing to raise the quality of medical care. How could the mere grouping of doctors in one building make any difference in the service they gave? 'It would be a fraud on the public', declared Hill angrily, 'to represent that as a real advance.'[11]

Despite these harsh words, BMA leaders were still receptive to the health-centre idea. They needed health centres, they thought, to meet the threat of municipal clinics and were ready to listen to any proposals the SMA had. As Hill put it to an audience of BMA members:

> ' . . . On the whole there was much that was sound and attractive to the
> health centre conception, but their attitude must be tinged with caution, lest
> a form of health centre, without sufficient experiment, be pushed by those
> who sought in the long run not health centres but a particular form of
> salaried employment under local authorities. (Hear, hear.) Care must be
> taken that this was not the thin edge of the wedge.'[12]

SMA fervour for municipal control

Had SMA leaders been willing to alter their model to suit the mood of the profession, they might have given Bevan freedom to start the reorganization of general practice in 1948. But that flexibility was not forthcoming. The main reason lay in an immutable belief in municipal control: no matter how they tried, SMA leaders could not contemplate any other system. In 1940, they had let the MPU soften their stand[b] — but that applied only to the principle of free choice, not to the method by which a salaried service is governed. For that, they believed, local authorities were ideal: their value had already been demonstrated in London where, thanks to the efforts of Hastings and others, the LCC had developed some of the finest hospitals in the land.[c] Hastings was proud of his achievement and he, more than any other SMA leader, would brook no interference with municipal methods.[d]

Bevan chose to ignore SMA advice on this score[e] and that led Stark Murray, who liked to give the SMA credit for everything, to revise the stand taken by the organization during these years. In his 'official' history of the body (published in 1971), he went so far as to suggest that the SMA was

a   See Chapter 19 beginning on p. 190 above.

b   See pp. 183-4 above.

c   See p. 138 above.

d   See p. 206 above.

e   See pp. 292-3 below.

responsible for the degree of direct representation granted in the 1946 Act.[13] The facts, however, indicate otherwise. The SMA wanted only to relax the ban on municipal elections: doctors employed by local authorities, it suggested in 1943, should be allowed to stand for office even if they worked whole-time.[14] This, however, was not what the BMA meant by direct representation: it wanted to retain the rights it had under NHI and, to that, the SMA was strongly opposed.[15] When Bevan decided to preserve the pattern (through executive councils), the SMA was the first to protest.[16]

Otherwise, SMA leaders recognized the need for municipal reform: they wanted both larger areas of administration and restrictions on MOH powers. Doctors employed in health centres, Stark Murray wrote in 1942, should have the right to govern themselves.[17] When the time came to create the Health Service, however, he and his colleagues were ready to take local authorities as they were: the SMA made no protests when health centres were assigned to them.[18] Not until years later, when the damage was done, did Stark Murray realize how wrong the decision had been.[a]

Only one SMA leader dissented from the course Hastings pursued: this was Brook. He knew from his MPU experience how strongly GPs resented municipal control.[b] Not all local authorities, Brook recognized, were as progressive as the LCC and, as early as 1940, he indicated his willingness to accept central control in order to give the profession the representation it desired.[19]

Three years later, Brook went further after the MPU protested against the fervour within the Labour Party for municipal administration. Not only, Brook admitted to the readers of the MPU's journal, was the charge justified but he left no doubt as to who was responsible: 'The whole trouble with Labour Party Public Health Reports is that they are usually drafted by specialist members of the profession and by lay people who are members of local authorities and whose opinions may be influenced by their Medical Officers of Health who, like other specialists, tend to be too rigid in their views.'[20] One did not have to look far to guess whom Brook had in mind: as chairman of Labour's Public Health Advisory Committee Hastings was all but dictating the stand the Party took in the field of medical care.[21][c]

Marxist influence in the SMA

Hastings, however, was not the only source of SMA thought: another cause of rigidity stemmed from the substantial corps of Marxists in its ranks. To them the health centre had assumed an importance out of all proportion to its

---

a   See p. 297 below.

b   See pp. 182-3 above.

c   Brook, by this time, had given up command of the SMA (see pp. 261-2 below). During the negotiations on the Health Service, he kept his distance from SMA leaders but he never lost his affection for the organization. That probably explains why, in the statement cited above, he did not mention either the SMA or Hastings by name. Only within the confines of a private memorandum (circulated in October, 1943) did he become specific and, there, it was Stark Murray he criticized, not Hastings.[22]

clinical utility. It was not just a communal surgery — it was much more. As the writer in an article in *Medicine Today and Tomorrow* (the journal edited by Stark Murray as a medium for SMA views) put it in 1944: 'To a marxist, the health centre represents a dialectical change, a revolutionary step.'[a] Through it, he declared, GPs would work in groups and develop a new outlook, thereby transforming — by some almost mystical process — 'quantity into quality'. A paler version of this idea must have spread widely in medical quarters for Hill, in the same year, had to warn his colleagues against the notion that the mere 'setting up of a health centre would work some magical effect'.[24]

Marxism can assume many forms and not all who subscribe to it belong to the Communist Party, but no sign of Communist influence was evident in the SMA when it began in 1930. Then, Brook and his colleagues confined their rolls to Labour supporters in order to secure the SMA's affiliation to the Labour Party. That was the main point of difference between it and the SMSA, and the main reason why Hastings (whose accession contributed so much to the growth of the SMA) decided to abandon the older body. During the 1920s, Hastings had become the SMSA's leader — yet he could do nothing to stop its relentless decline. For this, he blamed the SMSA's non-party stance. At the end of 1929, he tried to persuade his colleagues to take a stronger political line in order to take advantage of Labour's victory in the General Election. However, they not only refused to do that — they changed the SMSA's name to the *National* Medical Service Association in order to avoid the connotation associated with the word 'State'. To many, it meant a salaried service under municipal control and some SMSA members were not even sure that one should be run from Whitehall. At that point, there was little to distinguish their policy from the BMA's and the organization disbanded only a year after the SMA began.[25]

Labour Party affiliation was thus considered vital for the development of the new body and, in arranging it, Brook received much help from James S. Middleton, then Acting Secretary of the Party. But the SMA soon found it difficult to live with the restrictions Labour affiliation imposed. Doctors, as we saw earlier,[b] tend to be conservative in politics and few could be found who would join an organization that called itself 'Socialist'. With less than 500 on its rolls, the SMA needed to attract more members if it were to have an impact on health policy.

This, together with the desire to form a united front against fascism, were evidently the main reasons why the SMA in 1936 decided to open its door to any brand of socialist, including Communists. By 1943, judging from the

a   The article, called 'Dialectics of Health Centres', was signed, 'P.D.H.'[23] I have not been able to identify the author and it is possible that he was not a member of the SMA since *Medicine Today and Tomorrow* was not an official SMA organ and Stark Murray had freedom to accept contributions from anyone. Nevertheless, the journal was read mainly by SMA members and the author of the article cited here was clearly trying to rouse the Marxists among them behind the faltering campaign for health centres. It is, therefore, not unfair to use the article as an indication of a Marxist presence within the organization.

b   See pp. 53-4 and 55-6 above.

number of members who read the *Daily Worker*, Communists or Marxists represented as much as one-fifth of the SMA's membership[26] and their influence was greater than this proportion implied. This became evident in 1946 when the SMA, by a vote of 81 to 31, decided to support the Communist Party's application to join the Labour Party.[27] Though the main figures in SMA history — Brook, Hastings, Stark Murray — were not Marxists, they had to learn to live with them in order to create a viable organization.

At the same time that the SMA decided to open its door to Communists, it agreed to admit other health workers and that eventually carried its roll far above the level reached by the SMSA, which had never enrolled more than a few hundred members. At its height in 1944, the SMA attracted over 2,000. Of this total, doctors represented only 43%; the majority came from other professions. Neither of these changes in membership rules are mentioned in Stark Murray's 'official' history of the SMA; they are, however, recorded in Brook's 'unofficial' memoir.[28]

By liberalizing its rules in this way, the SMA was also able to accommodate the medical (and other health worker) refugees fleeing from the Nazis. The early arrivals came for political as well as religious reasons and they needed an organization that would tolerate their continental brand of Marxist socialism, not just the Christian variety that predominated in the Labour Party. In responding to their need, the SMA was true to its traditions because, from the start, the organization had been deeply involved in continental affairs. It owed its origin to a dentist from Berlin, Dr Ewald Fabian; in the summer of 1930, he urged Brook to start the body.[29] As soon as Hitler came to power in 1933, the SMA condemned the dictator's racial policies and, from then on, it became increasingly involved in the provision of aid to refugees.[30] No other medical organization in Britain did nearly so much for those who were persecuted by the Nazis.

Marxist tendencies, however, were found not only among the socialist refugees entering Britain in the 1930s — they appeared also in the ranks of those who helped to form the Labour Party. The Webbs in particular found much to admire in the Soviet Union. To them, it seemed, the depression had demonstrated the failure of capitalism — while, in Russia, an attempt was being made to find a better way.[31] Such feelings were also held by some who came to socialism by way of Christianity and this applied, above all, to the President of the SMA — Somerville Hastings.

Hastings was a son of the manse who described his socialism as 'simply the application of my Sunday school training'.[32] Throughout the 1930s, he was active not only in the SMA but in another group affiliated with the Labour Party: the Society of Socialist Christians. Though it had only 300 members, it was the largest Christian left-wing organization in Britain. Formed at the end of the First World War, it aimed to be a propagandist body like the Fabian Society.[33] From the start it affiliated with the Labour Party, and its President in 1932 was none other than the leader of the Party, George Lansbury.[34] Hastings, who was close to Lansbury at the time, served as Treasurer from 1933 to 1938 (when he was forced to resign due to ill-health)[35] and other SMA members active in the Society's work were Dr Alfred Salter (one of the founders of the MPU) and Dr Frank G. Bushnell (who established a Socialist Workers' National Health Council in 1931).[36]

Bushnell, among the medical members of this group, was the first to show sympathy for Marxist methods. He visited Russia in 1929 and came back an ardent defender of the Soviet system: 'Socialist Christians maintain that Socialism and Communism in their ultimate aims are economic and practical Christianity.'[37] Three years later, Hastings expressed much the same thought. Russia, he wrote in 1932,

> '. . . does not know the law of God, but the greatest of Russians [Tolstoy?] has told her that "where love is, there God is". Russia has already learned the lesson of co-operation for the common good, of the care of the sick and the children, to value a man by what he is and not by what he possesses. She has much yet to learn, but in fundamentals she is right and the other nations are bound to follow her.'[38]

Hastings, who had not been reluctant to criticize the disgraceful way in which the Communists behaved at the Labour Party Conference in 1929,[39] apparently came to this view as a result of the deepening depression. He was greatly affected by the condition of the unemployed and likened it to the ordeal inflicted on the founder of Christianity: 'Today a million Christs are being crucified on the Cross of unemployment, starvation, pain . . .'[40] His sympathy for the Soviet system was also strengthened by a tour of Russia, a visit arranged by a group calling itself the Society for Cultural Relations with the U.S.S.R.,[41] whose Chairman was the editor of *The Lancet*, Sir Squire Sprigge. Throughout the 1930s, Sprigge did all he could to promote understanding between doctors and scientists in the two countries.[42]

In this endeavour, however, *The Lancet* went too far in 1937 when it tried to justify the treason trials in terms of revolutionary psychology.[43] Even before this, the profession had not shown much enthusiasm for the Soviet cause but, for most doctors, the trials were the last straw. They revealed the full horrors of Stalinism and subsequently the campaign conducted by *The Lancet* made no impact on the profession. Cox — who, it will be recalled, had once been a socialist himself [a] — spoke for many doctors when he recounted his own feelings at the time: 'Nothing in my life has given me more painful mental shock than did the return of the Webbs from Russia as convinced Communists.'[44]

All of this had a profound effect on the course of SMA affairs. When the organization began in 1930, it had been able to draw on the aid of the General Secretary of the MPU, even to the extent where Welply had agreed to serve as Treasurer of the body.[b] But when Brook (followed shortly by Morgan) left the Council of the MPU in September 1935,[45] Welply resigned as Treasurer of the SMA[46] and the organization had to look elsewhere for aid. Eventually, in 1938, it found the ideal organizing team — Dr Leslie T. Hilliard (who served as Treasurer) and his wife, Dr Elizabeth Bunbury (who

a   See p. 54 above.

b   See p. 182 above.

became Propaganda Secretary and editor of the SMA's new internal Bulletin).

Under their leadership, membership rose and the SMA developed organizational strength — but, in the process, it acquired a political image which weakened its impact on health policy. Hilliard and Bunbury had 'strong political views'.[47] Though neither were members of the Communist Party, they were sympathetic to Marxist principles and felt the need for socialists of all kinds to work together. Many on the left in the 1930s thought it important to enlist Soviet aid in the fight against Hitler and medical care, because of its beneficent nature, was seen as an ideal way of forming a bridge between east and west. These, no doubt, were among the considerations which led Bunbury to serve as Honorary Secretary of the Anglo-Soviet Medical Council, established in 1941 by the Society for Cultural Relations with the U.S.S.R.[48]

Within the SMA, such policies created no difficulties. Socialists of all kinds mingled harmoniously and the Communists within its ranks acted as democratically and responsibly as those who rejected Marxist principles. But the Labour Party had a policy of excluding Communists from membership and it did not think any of its affiliated organizations should contain them either. This was unfortunate for Brian Kirman, the doctor who became Honorary Secretary of the SMA in 1939. Though a man of the highest ideals and the greatest integrity, he was an open member of the Communist Party. This proved too much for Labour leaders and they asked the SMA to find a new Secretary.[a] Kirman resigned in 1941 and was replaced by the most prestigious doctor the SMA could find — Mr Aleck Bourne, one of the leading obstetricians of the day. Bourne remained in office for only 2 years but that was enough to make SMA influence felt on the Medical Planning Commission.[50] Bourne's position as Secretary did much to make the organization respectable.[b]

Bourne's departure in 1943 again raised doubts about the control of SMA affairs and that, together with other activities in which the organization was engaged, exposed it to the same sort of criticism as it had felt in 1941. The pressure for Kirman's removal, no doubt, came from trade unionists like Bevin who could not forget how the Communists opposed the war before Hitler invaded Russia in June 1941.[52]

So the stage was set for the defeat of SMA policy. Its leaders had the best of intentions but, as we shall see, they did the organization no good by the political image they acquired in the late 1930s.

a   Kirman claims he could have remained in office if he had insisted but he was busy with other matters and was quite willing to resign. In his view Labour Party pressure was not the only — or even the main — reason for his resignation.[49]

b   This was no slight episode in Bourne's life but he failed to mention it in his autobiography. He did, however, cite his membership of the Labour Party during the 1930s — as well as his abiding belief in socialism after leaving it.[51]

26
No Industrial Medical Service

THE SMA met its first defeat in the field of industrial health, a surprising failure since the scheme it proposed had much in common with the one favoured by Bevin and the TUC. To understand why it miscarried, we must first examine the outlook for industrial medical care when Bevin arrived at the Ministry of Labour.

Bevin's initiative on industrial health

In 1940, industrial medical services were lacking everywhere[a] but the gap was more easily filled in the larger factories where doctors could be employed whole-time than in the smaller workshops where medical attention was rarely needed and where, to justify full-time employment, a doctor's services had to be spread over several establishments. Few workshop employers, in such circumstances, bothered to make arrangements; they simply relied on the part-time corps of appointed factory surgeons (most of whom were GPs) to meet statutory requirements. Otherwise, workers in workshops found themselves without medical supervision or even, in many instances, access to emergency care.[1]

The SMA's plan would have filled this void. Its health centre, apart from serving the community generally, would have provided a convenient base from which to cover the smaller workshops.[2] GPs working in groups could have given not only general medical care but the specialist attention that industrial medicine demanded. This involved not merely emergency treatment when accidents arose but the medical supervision needed to avoid them. Prevention was always a primary object of the SMA's plan — and it always made provision for the inclusion of industrial care.[3] In this respect, its health centre differed sharply from the Ministry of Health's for, until Bevin threatened to start an industrial medical service at the Ministry of Labour, the Health Department showed no enthusiasm for the task.[b] In 1924, it even rejected responsibility on the grounds that it had too much to do already.[4] The SMA's health centre, therefore, must have appealed greatly to the

---

a   See p. 233 above.
b   See p. 270 below.

unions for it resembled, in all essentials, the one Bevin presented to the BMA in 1937.[a]

Bevin's appointment as Minister of Labour in May 1940 thus presented the unions as well as the SMA with a great opportunity. For years, they had awaited the development of an industrial medical service financed by the state, but the department to which they looked for direction (the Ministry of Labour) had also shown little interest in the subject. Bevin intended to change all that; in future, he made clear, welfare would be treated 'not as a trimming but as a central part of the Government's labour supply policy'.[5]

One of Bevin's first acts at the department was to bring all industrial health and welfare under his control. This involved the removal of the Factories Acts from Home Office direction and the establishment of a new division at the Ministry of Labour to administer the statutes. Bevin put one of his ablest officials (Godfrey Ince) in charge[b] and gave the unions, through an advisory board, the chance to influence policy. By July, they — and Bevin — had an order ready which, for the first time, gave adequate recognition to industrial health: medical supervision was required in all factories on Government contract which employed 250 persons.[6] 'At last', proclaimed the *Journal of Industrial Welfare,* 'it is realised that care for the human element in industry is not a philanthropic hobby for the successful large employers, or a concession to the frailty of women and children, but a vital necessity for the nation's effort.'[7]

The need was great. Apart from the restricted cover provided by appointed factory surgeons, Britain had virtually no industrial medical service. Over the country as a whole, there were only 30 whole-time and 50 part-time industrial medical officers.[8] That was scarcely sufficient to meet the demands made by the war, and Bevin made sure that he did not have to wait for employers to act. Under the terms of the order issued in July, he not only had power to grant financial aid but he could, if a factory inspector deemed it necessary, appoint doctors on his own.[9] This meant that he could have created a salaried service run by the state: the factories would still be owned by private enterprise but the doctors who worked in them would owe their allegiance to the Minister of Labour.

Revolutionary as it sounds, the move was not without precedent: such a service already existed in the hospital world. It had been created before the war to care for the casualties expected in air-raids and, though (fortunately) far fewer arose than anticipated, the Emergency Medical Service went ahead as planned. Treatment was provided through the medium of voluntary as well as municipal hospitals but — and this was the essential point — all the doctors and nurses involved were engaged by the Ministry of Health. In the beginning, they were even barred from private practice: like the doctors envisaged in the SMA's health centre, they had to devote their whole time to the work.[10]

SMA leaders could not but note the parallel and the Emergency Medical

---

a   See pp. 232-5 above.

b   Bevin first offered this post to Beveridge but the man-power expert lost the opportunity when he displayed signs of hesitation.

Service, as originally conceived, must have appealed greatly to them. But the attraction did not last long.[a] As early as November 1939, the Ministry dropped its ban on private practice (as far as fully-established specialists were concerned)[11] and thereafter consultants within the voluntary hospitals practised much as they had always done — the only difference being that now they were paid for a part of the care they gave. When the change was made, the Ministry displayed a failure of nerve: it tried to make consultants revert to honorary status but the doctors refused to accept it.[12]

Nor was that all SMA leaders had to endure: the service offered little hope of ending the voluntary hospital system. On the contrary, it strengthened it greatly: for the first time in decades, the hospitals had surplus funds on hand.[13] The warning to all was clear — if something was not done soon, the voluntary rather than the municipal hospitals would set the pattern for the Health Service to come.[14]

The SMA's first reaction was to strike back with an emergency scheme of its own and it did so in association with 2 other medical socialist groups thought to be under Communist control. They were the Left Book Club Medical Group[b] and the University Labour Federation (which enrolled medical students); the latter was actually expelled from the Labour Party in 1940 because of its Communist associations.[16] Early in 1940 these 3 groups jointly demanded the creation of a salaried system under municipal direction. The Emergency Medical Service, they told the Ministry, was failing the nation. Not only were the voluntary hospitals refusing to take their fair share of the civilian sick but, because of the way they dominated sector staffing, they were depriving municipal hospitals of necessary doctors. These difficulties could be overcome only by extending the emergency scheme until it covered everyone. That required Exchequer aid but — and this was the key to the SMA's plan —the job of administering it should be left to local authorities. In that way, SMA leaders hoped, the voluntary hospitals would lose their privileged position in hospital planning.[17]

To make sure they did not regain it, the SMA added another point to its plan: it wanted local authorities to offer not only hospital treatment but GP care too.[18] That, for the most part,[c] had been omitted from the Emergency Medical Service and its absence was most noticeable in the air-raid shelters of London. At one — the notorious Tilbury shelter on Liverpool Street — as many as 15,000 people slept each night, yet only 1 doctor (with 3 nurses) was on hand and he received no pay.[19] After Herbert Morrison became Home Secretary in October 1940, clinics (employing whole-time doctors)

---

a   The only one who retained admiration for the service was Brook and what appealed to him was the principle of central control. That, he thought, would enable the profession to secure the representation it wanted and pave the way for the establishment of an extended state system after the war. See p. 258 above.

b   This organization had an especially close link with the SMA because Kirman had been Secretary of the Group before he became Secretary of the SMA.[15]

c   For the exceptions, see pp. 195-6 above.

were created[a] but their work was limited to prevention and emergency treatment. For continuing care, patients still had to consult their panel or private doctor — yet that was difficult to do when they had to work all day and sleep in the shelters all night.[21]

The need for general medical care was felt widely outside London as well due to conscription and the dislocation of population caused by the war.[b] Parts of London may have had too many doctors but, over the country as a whole, there were too few. The profession, in such circumstances, seemed ready to accept salary, and *The Lancet* itself did much to promote the idea: '. . . the doctor who would willingly join a salaried service to look after the health of the soldier cannot logically refuse to join another to look after that soldier's family.'[22]

The challenge was clear but BMA leaders failed to respond to it. The most they would do was think about the kind of service that should come after the war ended and, even then, they had to be prodded by the MPU.[c] The Medical Planning Commission was created as a result and, in an attempt to silence its main protagonist, the BMA offered 3 places on it to the SMA. SMA leaders leapt at the opportunity and did their best to secure support for their programme. But, even before the Commission was formed, they had come to the conclusion that it would not be safe to rely on one tactic alone, however promising it appeared. At the end of 1940, therefore, SMA leaders began to search for other ways to realize their goal of a salaried service.

SMA attempt to start a salaried service in industry

Bevin's order of July seemed to supply it. If a salaried service could be started in industry, then the example might prove so beneficial that it would be applied to the community as a whole. The prospects for such a strategy seemed brightest where TB was concerned: it was a disease associated with work and the outbreak of war had produced a disturbing increase in its incidence.[23] Yet panel doctors found it difficult to deal with because the workers afflicted did not want to lose their jobs. In this field at least, GPs might be willing to let salaried doctors take over.

Local authorities had already noticed such a tendency in GP behaviour as far as the operation of their TB dispensaries were concerned. The whole-time officers working in them found it easier to carry out domiciliary treatment than their counterparts in maternity clinics. The profession rigidly applied the ban on home care contained in the 1918 Maternity and Child Welfare Act but it did not show the same vigilance where TB was concerned. The 1936 Public Health Act also left the door open for local authorities to extend their activities beyond the institutional sphere: Section 173 gave

a   Once the danger of epidemics passed (about May, 1942), the clinics were closed except in shelters used by 500 people or more. That, however, still left some 200 doctors and 400 nurses in the service.[20]

b   See p. 183 above.

c   See pp. 184-5 above.

district councils the power to 'make such arrangements as they think desirable for the treatment of tuberculosis'.[24]

Despite this freedom, many local authorities had failed to act. Not only did they lack the necessary dispensaries, but those that were in operation did not seem to operate satisfactorily. According to statistics culled from post mortem examinations, 1 out of every 10 TB cases defied detection until after the patient died. For this state of affairs, however, the Ministry blamed GPs rather than local authorities. Despite repeated pleas from the department, too many GPs had failed to carry out the sputum tests needed to diagnose the disease.[25] Local authorities, as a result, had been forced to set up clinics of their own which patients could attend directly — but these only confirmed GP negligence in the field. No fewer than 40% of the people examined for the first time were found to have TB.[26] How many others were there unknown to the authorities?

One expert on the subject suggested a way to find out: Dr Philip D'Arcy Hart, director of TB work for the Medical Research Council and an influential member of the SMA. His method of detecting TB was by means of mass X-ray examinations conducted periodically on susceptible groups. These, he thought, would not only help to prevent the spread of TB but would, because of the need for treatment they uncovered, lead eventually to 'a comprehensive health service that would include the detection of pulmonary tuberculosis as merely one of its important functions.'[27]

D'Arcy Hart, who enjoyed considerable status in the profession, made his views known as early as 1937 through the prestigious Milroy Lectures[28] — but he had to wait until 1940 before the time was ripe to try them out. Then, after some 8,000 patients had been removed from sanatoria to make room for war casualties, fear of infection became widespread. As one famous surgeon put it at the time, 'every tuberculous person turned forth is like a bomb thrown among the public'.[29] Lord Horder, in the autumn of 1940, added greatly to the fear. As chairman of a Home Office committee dealing with conditions in air-raid shelters, he issued a report calling attention to the danger of infection.[30]

Horder, however, had reservations about D'Arcy Hart's remedy: before mass X-ray examinations were introduced, he wanted studies carried out to assess their effects. He made this recommendation as chairman of another committee appointed by the Minister of Labour, and Bevin accepted it.[31] The rest of the Government followed Bevin's lead; for the moment at least, the scheme was dead.[a]

The decision did not go down well with doctors in the civil defence programme and that gave the SMA activists among them the chance to broaden the demand: they called for mass X-ray examinations in factories as

---

a   It did not revive until September 1942. Then the Medical Research Council (after making an exhaustive study of the subject) issued a report in favour of mass X-ray examinations and the first civilian unit came into operation in October 1943. The programme, however, was administered by the Ministry of Health, not the Ministry of Labour, and it did not include an industrial medical service. Only limited financial aid was provided and it was not sufficient to overcome worker resistance. By the end of 1945, only 826,000 workers had submitted themselves to examination.[32]

well as air-raid shelters.[33] At this point, opposition arose from a different quarter — the trade unions. Workers, claimed Morgan of the TUC, would not submit to the examinations: they feared the loss of their jobs more than they did TB. The only way to woo them was to offer protection against victimization: in his view, that meant not only the provision of ample cash benefits during treatment but the opportunity, through rehabilitation and training, of securing employment.[34]

With that SMA leaders agreed, but they added a point which Morgan had overlooked: the conditions under which the industrial medical service operated would have to change, too. Worker fear of victimization would never disappear until the doctors who supervised them were appointed by the state. The time had come for Bevin to make use of the powers he had secured in July: such was the essence of the message Kirman delivered to the Secretary of the Labour Party (Middleton) in November 1940.[35]

Support for the idea came from doctors already in industrial employ. Meeting in 1941, the Association of Industrial Medical Officers made no attempt to deny the existence of employer bias; on the contrary, some of its members called for a state service in order to free themselves from dependence on commercial interests.[36] Most took this position, however, not for political reasons but out of concern for job security. Who knew when employers might be forced to curtail industrial medical services due to business conditions? From the time it was founded by Wilson Jameson in 1935, the Association tended to favour state control:[37] all it changed was the method by which this was to be done. At first, strongly influenced by Jameson and other public health doctors in its ranks, the Association preferred municipal employment;[38] later — after 1961 — it opted for a public corporation.[39] For this change, no doubt, union antipathy to local authority rule was responsible.

Industrial medical officers, however, were not the only group of doctors that added their weight to the movement; surprisingly enough, the BMA did, too. In 1941, it issued a report calling for an end to employer control. Henceforth, it said, industrial medical officers should be appointed by a central advisory body and provision should be made for their periodic transfer from one firm to another. Though this could be done without creating a state service (and the report carefully avoided any expression of opinion on that controversial subject), the thrust of the BMA argument tended to support those who thought Bevin should.[40]

Bevin rejects SMA demand

Bevin, nevertheless, rejected the SMA demand. Despite the order he issued in July, he said he had no right to control the doctors employed by industry.[41] [a]

a　The press, however, reported him as moving in the opposite direction. He intended, two newspapers claimed in November 1940, to have resident doctors and nurses on hand in every large factory; only the smaller ones would be exempt.[42] The implication of the report was that he would make the appointments himself (or direct employers to do so) but he apparently decided to leave the initiative in private hands. Just why he changed his mind (if, in fact, he did) cannot be determined.

Nor did he seem anxious to secure the power: as long as firms remained in private hands, he now believed, the people who owned them should retain responsibility.[43] SMA leaders were astonished by the response for it ran counter to the position Bevin had taken in 1937.[a] If the Minister of Health could appoint doctors to work in private hospitals, then why could the Minister of Labour not do the same in private factories?[44] Where workshops were concerned, there was no alternative to state provision. Without doctors to improve health and curb absenteeism, production would fall and the war effort would falter. Was Bevin fearful of making demands on the profession which it could not meet? If so, then the SMA could tell him where he could secure the doctors he needed. Instead of locking up medical refugees on the Isle of Man, the state should release them for service in industry and elsewhere.[45][b]

At this point, however, opposition arose from an unexpected quarter — the MPU. Though Welply had managed to secure assent where a general salaried service was concerned,[c] he could not alter the highly-charged feelings of his followers on refugee questions. These, as we shall see, had been fanned by Bayly before the war as part of a wider campaign directed against Jews.[d] In 1940, the MPU warned Bevin of the fifth columnists he would unleash if he decided to use refugee doctors in the factory service.[47]

Bevin, in any case, failed to respond to the SMA idea. This gave its leaders cause to complain but they did not dare to criticize the Minister in public. Russia, in 1940, had not been attacked and Communists in Britain were not noted for their devotion to the war effort. The SMA was in no position to tell the Minister of Labour how he ought to act when it had, as its Honorary Secretary, a member of the Communist Party.[e] That, no doubt, was the reason why Kirman decided to route his request through Middleton instead of presenting it to Bevin directly.[f] Not until Kirman resigned in May 1941 did SMA leaders secure freedom to act and, even then, they let the radical science correspondent of the *Daily Herald*, Ritchie (later Lord) Calder, speak for them. Calder criticized Bevin for inaction but the gist of his remarks was directed towards the Medical Planning Commission: through it, he told the SMA, it would be possible to create a salaried service that would cover not merely industry but the nation as a whole.[49]

SMA leaders took the hint: for months afterwards they concentrated their efforts on the Commission's proceedings. Only Hastings carried on the fight

a   See pp. 233 and 235 above.

b   Here the SMA merely added its voice to a plea registered on behalf of aliens generally by François Lafitte, then a research officer for Political and Economic Planning.[46]

c   See pp. 182-4 above.

d   See pp. 275-8 below.

e   See p. 262 above. It was also inhibited by an exchange that took place in *Medicine Today and Tomorrow* during 1940. Stark Murray, in March, criticized those who helped Spain but refused aid to Finland because of political considerations. This provoked an angry reply and Stark Murray, in reply, had to point out that his journal was not, strictly speaking, an SMA organ.[48]

f   See p. 268 above.

for an industrial service and he did that in his capacity as Chairman of Labour's Public Health Advisory Committee. In July 1941, the Committee tried to make arrangements with the BMA for a joint approach.[50] Though the deputation would present its demands to the Ministry of Labour, it would ask for administration to be assigned to the Ministry of Health. This had always been the medical position (BMA as well as SMA) and that may also explain why Bevin refused to consider it.

SMA campaigns with Labour Research Department

Interest in the subject did not revive until March 1942, and it took an outside agency to do it. The stimulus came from one of the leading Communist 'front' groups in Britain — the Labour Research Department (LRD).[51] After Hitler's attack on Russia, the LRD completely altered its attitude towards the war effort. During 1940, it had been concerned about the threat the war posed to the Factories Acts[52] but, after June 1941, all it could think of was the need to increase production.[53] For that purpose, it felt, an industrial medical service was indispensable and it persuaded the SMA to wage a joint campaign. If the Minister of Labour would not create one, then the Minister of Health should. Such was the theme of the conference held by the 2 bodies in May 1942.[54]

Shortly afterwards, a third organization began to show an interest in an industrial medical service — the Association of Scientific Workers, a small but highly influential trade union. In May 1942, it formed a Medical Science Committee and started to study the subject. Though no policy statement was issued until February 1944, its leaders said enough in public beforehand to indicate the direction in which they were heading. Three-quarters of the workers in industry, the Association reported in November 1942, were located in factories employing less than 1,000 persons and they were not likely to have the benefit of an industrial medical service.[55] For Bevin, the message was clear: the time had come for the state to fill the gap left by private enterprise.

This pressure at last aroused Bevin: in April 1943, he called a conference on industrial health to determine what action to take. Ernest Brown, who opened the gathering, pleaded with him to leave the subject alone. Negotiations on the National Health Service had only just begun and he, as Minister of Health, was afraid that a separate movement in industry would weaken the chance of success: 'The present need was to bring together in a simple and sensitive pattern all the particular services, and to see them as parts of a total service for health for the nation — for old and young, whether working in a factory, pit, office, or field, whether at school or in the home — a service covering the whole range of advice and treatment from family doctor to specialist and hospital.'[56]

The BMA, by and large, agreed: it opposed municipal administration but it did think that industrial care ought to be incorporated within the Health Service.[57] After all, where the workshops were concerned, how could it be otherwise? Health centres had to be formed before they could be covered.

Bevin decided to pursue that line in the Cabinet. Industrial medical care, he told Brown, needed separate provision; it could not, as some in the Ministry of Health believed, be left entirely to the National Health Service. But on one point he agreed: the 2 systems should inter-lock and the health centre was the medium through which it should be done. The factories, at first, would provide the specialists who worked there but, as knowledge of industrial medicine developed, GPs would be able to take over responsibility. In time, the unions would have the best of both worlds: their members would be given access to competent care but the doctors who provided it would not be tied to industry.

Brown accepted this demarcation but gave it a different emphasis: he wanted GPs to assume responsibility for most factory treatment from the start, thereby enabling them to develop expertise more rapidly. Bevin, on the other hand, did not want them to take over until they had demonstrated their competence. Meanwhile, he thought, the job should be left to whole-time industrial medical officers who, through their work in health centres, would show GPs how it should be done. These officers, Bevin envisaged, would be responsible to the Ministry of Labour and he did not expect them ever to be completely displaced: GPs, in time, might be able to take over most of their work, but not all.[58]

The Association of Industrial Medical Officers, not surprisingly, agreed with Bevin's view[59] — but so, it seems, did the SMA. Stark Murray had even less faith in the potential of GPs than Bevin. He did not think they ever could — or should — take over the work done by industrial medical officers in large factories. There, indeed, he wanted to reverse the displacement procedure: factory doctors would provide *all* the treatment needed, leaving only a home service to promote rehabilitation.[60]

TUC fails to act

With the prospect that Bevin held in view, the TUC was content to wait. Had the unions been more insistent, they probably could have forced the Minister of Labour to act but they chose, instead, to accept the arguments he raised.[61] When the miners proposed to build rehabilitation centres in South Wales, Bevin was swift to stop them. 'Where I think the mistake will be made', he wrote in November 1942, 'is if the miners attempt to do this alone. What is needed in South Wales is a chain of rehabilitation centres that will treat the whole community including miners.'[62]

Nor was that the only consideration: TUC leaders may also have been deterred by the source from which the demand for an industrial medical service sprang. Only a month before its joint campaign with the SMA, the LRD was expelled from the Labour Party and, shortly afterwards, was removed from the TUC too. Because of the strong Communist influence prevailing in the unions, this had only been achieved with difficulty. The proscription (which had been made by the General Council acting on its own) was upheld by only a narrow majority at the unions' annual Congress — 2,210,000 to 1,980,000.[63]

From this, we can see the extent to which Communist influence in the movement had grown and TUC leaders, no doubt, were anxious to avoid any action that might increase it.[64] What must have concerned them were the health sub-committees which the LRD and the SMA included in their programme. These were to be established everywhere under the jurisdiction of joint production committees and such committees, as the creatures of the shop stewards' movement, had become the focal point of Communist activity on the shop floor.[65]

Now we can see why the TUC failed to show enthusiasm for the creation of an industrial medical service during the war. In fact, its leaders seem to have clashed head-on with the SMA over the question. Through Hastings, the SMA had managed to insert a demand for an industrial medical service in the important policy statement issued by the Labour Party in 1943 called 'A National Service for Health'.[66] But in deference to TUC wishes, the document said nothing about who would administer the service. Ever since 1933, the SMA had been in favour of municipal (as well as Ministry of Health) control[67] but Hastings found it prudent to omit any mention of that. Furthermore, despite the inclusion of the demand for an industrial medical service in the policy statement, it was left out of the motions passed by the Labour Party Conference in 1943 and referred to the TUC instead.[68] On this issue, as on so many others regarding the Health Service, it was union opinion that counted, not the SMA's.

The SMA may have put its own position in peril as a result of the joint campaign it waged with the LRD. Its expulsion from the Labour Party was probably prevented only by the protection afforded by the Party's leading inquisitor of Communist activities — Herbert Morrison.[69] The LCC was his domain and, throughout the 1930s, he received continuing aid from SMA leaders. Nor was that the only reason for Morrison's tolerance: the SMA also made itself respectable through its advocacy of local authority control.

Out of concern for Morrison's feelings, it would seem, TUC leaders found it expedient to ignore the SMA challenge which, in turn, made it possible for the Ministry of Health to pass briefly over the subject of an industrial medical service in the White Paper produced in 1944.[70] Then, the only way the SMA could fight back was through the medium of the most prestigious doctor in its ranks — D'Arcy Hart of the Medical Research Council. Because of the high status he held in medical circles, he had been able to play an active role in the Royal College of Physicians and it was certainly no accident that the College committee on which he served produced a report in 1945 calling for the creation of an industrial medical service under the Ministry of Labour.[71] [a] This was contrary to medical policy, but the physicians no doubt endorsed it in the hope of finding some way to keep GPs busy outside the hospital world.[b]

---

a	One by-product of D'Arcy Hart's work for the Medical Research Council should also be noted. He was responsible for the study which led to the scheduling of pneumo-coniosis as an industrial disease in coal-mining[72] and that, as we saw (see p. 249 above), may have paved the way for union acceptance of the contributory principle in the Beveridge Report.

b	For consultant concern with this subject, see pp. 186-8 above.

D'Arcy Hart's move was designed to overcome TUC resistance because the unions had always opposed Ministry of Health control, fearing that it would lead to MOH supervision. The unions asked for factory inspectors to be put in charge and, since the Factory Department was now lodged in the Ministry of Labour, that was where they wanted responsibility for an industrial medical service to rest.[73][a]

Now, however, it was the employers' turn to object: they did not want the state to start any service but, if one had to come, they preferred to see it done through the Ministry of Health rather than the Ministry of Labour.[74] Bevan, to the unions' surprise, came down on the employers' side: he strongly opposed the TUC demand for Labour administration.[75] As he wrote later (1955) in his journal, *Tribune:* 'I regard such a proposal as muddled, inefficient, wantonly extravagant and opposed to the true interest of the worker.'[76]

Yet, as Minister of Health, Bevan was not prepared to act — and neither were the politicians who succeeded him. They, like Bevin, left development to private initiative and even the unions, it seems, were content to let that happen. Not until 1959 was the TUC roused from its lethargy, and it took a flagrant rejection by employers in Halifax to do it. Despite an official plea from the Industrial Health Advisory Committee (a body which Bevin had set up with high hopes in 1943) to create an industrial medical service, the employers there refused to act.[77] Similar resistance appeared elsewhere — so that, even today, Britain lacks adequate provision in the private as well as the public sphere.

What did all this mean in terms of SMA strategy? The implications were clear even before the war ended. In the absence of public provision, private enterprise grew and the medical services offered by employers during the war made increasing demands on the voluntary hospitals. From its narrow concern with air-raid casualties, the Emergency Medical Service expanded until, by the end of 1943, it covered all the manual workers employed by industry (as far as most accidents were concerned).[78] Its scope was so wide that no one could ignore it: even the *New Statesman* called for its extension when uncertainty developed in January 1946 over the outlook for Bevan's Bill.[79]

Thus was the die cast for the future: the voluntary, not the municipal, hospitals would set the pattern for the Health Service to come. Nor was that all: once they were in control, the principle of whole-time employment was bound to go, too. The SMA's dream of a salaried service died in the campaign it waged with the LRD in 1942.

a   See also pp. 218-9 and 263-4 above.

Rise of the Medical Policy Association

The SMA's defeat on industrial care set the stage for its larger set-back on the Health Service as a whole. Here, however, the doctors, and not Labour leaders, were the cause. Not only Morrison but Bevin himself came out whole-heartedly for the health centre model the SMA had devised.[1] Within Labour circles, there was never any dispute about the desirability of that; the difference applied to the principle of central control. By 1945, however, the profession had made it clear that it wanted nothing to do with the model the SMA (and the Ministry) had devised. Though the BMA continued to profess a willingness to condone experiments,[2] its heart was not in it for, to the average doctor, health centres had come to mean not only salary and municipal control — even worse, they spelled socialism and communism. For that, the SMA was only partly the cause. Throughout the war, an anti-semitic group of doctors, calling themselves the Medical Policy Association (MPA), drove the point home. Their role in the creation of the Health Service has never been told before — but, during the negotiations that preceded it, they prevented BMA leaders from playing a constructive part. In this chapter, we shall trace the origin and growth of this strange organization.

Social-credit origins of the MPA

Its leaders came from that section of the social-credit movement identified with the Social Credit Secretariat and led by Major Clifford Douglas, the originator of this theory of monetary reform. In Britain, the other main section was headed by John Hargrave, long associated with a youth organization called Kibbo Kift.[3] A tendency towards anti-semitism had always been evident in social-credit thought because of the Jewish presence among money-lenders and Douglas finally embraced it in 1938.[4] But Hargrave, despite the fact that his beliefs (especially where animals and vivisection were concerned)[a] provided an even greater temptation to blame Jews, managed to resist it.

This difference came to distinguish the two wings of the movement.[5] Douglas became so obsessed with hatred for Jews that he almost abandoned social credit[6] — yet his ideas appealed greatly to the doctors who formed the MPA. After the war began, the doctrines Douglas advocated provided one of

a For the association between anti-vivisectionism and anti-semitism, see p. 169 above.

the few media in Britain for the insertion of Jewish conspiracy theories;[7] fascism, because of its ties with Hitler and Mussolini, had lost the right to a public forum.

One of the MPA leaders, however, did not make his start in public life through social credit; he owed his first office to the ties he had with Bayly and his group in the MPU. This was a London GP by the name of Dr Russell V. Steele and, in 1936, shortly after Bayly assumed control of the MPU, Steele (who had never played any part in the organization before) suddenly appeared as a member of Council.[8] What he shared with Bayly was apparently a distaste for Jews, for after this the refugee doctors fleeing from the Nazis became a target of MPU attack. At one point, the MPU's journal, *Medical World*, not only praised Hitler's eugenic law, barring marriage between Gentiles and Jews,[a] but tried to steer panel doctors in the direction of the British Union of Fascists. Reviewing Mosley's programme in September 1938, the journal commented: 'We are tempted to don black shirts and damn democracy.'[11] [b]

Economic causes of medical anti-semitism

How, in an organization composed mainly of doctors on the left of the political spectrum, was it possible for such views to take hold? Occasional jibes at Jews had appeared in *Medical World* long before Bayly assumed control, the first instance dating from 1918 when Dr Leonard Williams became editor.[14] Even Dr Gordon Ward, writing in 1922 under the name of 'Hereward', had cast anti-semitic aspersions on the Minister of Health, Sir Alfred Mond (later Lord Melchett).[15] But it was not until Bayly appeared on the scene that the attack assumed significant proportions. The opportunity was provided by the financial plight of the profession during the depression. In 1934, one of the oldest members of the MPU Council —Dr T. F. Keenan — raised bitter cries about the economic exploitation of general practice.[16]

No one could deny that a legitimate grievance existed. As the depression deepened, the profession found itself buried under a crushing burden of debt. By 1934, at least one-third of the panel practices in Britain were in the hands of insurance companies or money-lenders.[17] The leading firms involved were not noted for their Jewish connections and it is likely that the bulk of the funds provided came from 'Gentile' sources. But that, in the climate of the

a   The German law also required a medical certificate, covering physical and mental fitness, before marriage was allowed. *Medical World* thought such work would do much to benefit 'an impoverished profession'. The date when this item appeared enables us to pinpoint the time when Bayly probably took control of *Medical World*. It came on 28 February 1936, at the start of a new volume and publishing year.[9] Only one month earlier, by contrast, the journal had taken the opposite position, warning that anti-semitism threatened to impede the progress of medicine in Germany.[10]

b   As early as 1929, the Nazi swastika appeared around several advertisements in *Medical World*.[12] This came only at the start of Bayly's ascent to power but he probably had enough influence even then to arrange its insertion. The same symbol appeared in red ink on the front page of the *Sunday Express* in 1931 but the paper removed it after the Jewish community protested.[13]

1930s, made little difference. Due to the incessant propaganda of anti-semites everywhere, finance capital had become associated with Judaism.[18] In Britain, the connection was made explicit by a GP (and anaesthetist) who wrote detective stories, William Stanley Sykes. In 1931, he published a book called *The Missing Money-Lender* and, in it, not only were the financial problems of general practice portrayed but the villain was a financier named Israel Levinsky.[19]

Nor was that the only influence exposing the profession to anti-semitism: to the burden imposed by the Jewish money-lender at home was added the threat presented by the Jewish doctor from abroad. Medical refugees fleeing from the Continent found a cool reception when they landed in Britain. Panel practitioners during the depression could not afford to be generous and they tended to associate refugees, as a class, with the same money-lenders to whom their practices had been mortgaged. Even socialists in the profession found it hard to be generous: one said he would reject his own relatives if they intended to compete.[20] After the Austrian *Anschluss* in March 1938, the number of doctors seeking asylum rose substantially —but, if all had been admitted to Britain, there was a real danger, as the *New Statesman* pointed out, that English medical men would become 'roaring anti-semites'.[21]

Bayly, nonetheless, did his best to push the profession in that direction. Before 1936, the MPU showed some sympathy for refugees, even to the point where it tolerated the admission of a few.[22] But that changed after Bayly took over: then the MPU became the most bitter opponent of immigration. By 1938 it said it would not accept any more no matter how desperate their plight.[23] Brackenbury and his colleagues in the BMA did not share this view[24] — nor, it seems, did one of the foremost figures within the MPU itself, Dr Edward A. Gregg, President of the MPU from 1924-1932 and a long-standing member of St Pancras Borough Council. Although it was he who first raised (in 1927) complaints in MPU circles about the way financiers were exploiting general practice in the East End of London, that was before the issue assumed racial overtones.[25] When the latter appeared in 1934, Gregg was swift to rise to defend the financiers.[26] He stayed in the MPU for a few years after Bayly's ascendancy but, in 1938, he finally left after having already established himself within BMA circles as Chairman of its Insurance Acts Committee.[27]

Gregg and Brackenbury, no doubt, wanted to take the 500 doctors from Austria that Sir Samuel Hoare (as Home Secretary) proposed to admit in 1938.[28] But Bayly— aided at BMA meetings by a popular doctor from Paignton (Dr Ernest Ward) who repeatedly introduced motions against the admission of refugees[29][a] — made it impossible for the BMA to accept more than 50.

Though few refugees were thus admitted to Britain, those that did gain entry found it hard to forget the medical practices they had learned at home.

a   Though Ward took the same stand as Bayly on the refugee question, there is no evidence
that they acted in concert. Ward did not belong to the MPU and confined his clinical
work largely to TB, but he did have wide experience of general practice and was known
as an advocate of collective research by GPs. This, combined with two books he
published in 1929 and 1930, made him extremely popular with the profession and he
maintained close contact with hundreds of practices throughout the land.[30]

On the Continent, specialists did not wait for referrals: they tended to accept any patient who sought their services. To this was added the plight of the moment: doctors starting afresh could not afford to be particular. Some of the refugees undoubtedly employed methods that went beyond the bounds of medical propriety.[31] The situation was ripe for anti-semites to exploit and a writer in *Medical World* (probably Bayly) did not miss the opportunity: 'All men know that there is one race which is never absorbed, a race to which claims of "business" always come before any consideration for those who are unwise enough to give them hospitality.'[32]

Once the war began, Bayly's propaganda had its effect: doctors were interned on the Isle of Man along with other aliens.[33] The medical needs of the country, however, dictated their release shortly after[34] and, though this gave *Medical World* the opportunity to demand their return home,[35] nothing could be done until the war ended.[a] Medical feeling on the subject of refugees, therefore, slowly defused and, with the nation in conflict with fascism abroad, Bayly could no longer hope to move panel doctors in that direction at home. A new strategy had to be devised and Bayly found it in the Douglas theory of social credit.

From his point of view, the theory had much to commend it. Social credit appealed greatly to the economic class to which panel doctors belonged — small entrepreneurs whose financial condition had deteriorated as a result of the debts they incurred.[36] Through the magic of the 'national dividend' — a cash payment made directly by the Government to consumers, thereby enabling them to make their own arrangements with producers[37] [b] — the profession's plight could be alleviated overnight.

Thus far, Bayly could note, the war had done little to aid doctors; many had actually seen their position worsen.[c] Yet even doctors who joined the armed forces apparently had to meet their mortgage payments when due. That, at least, was the impression conveyed by social creditors like Dr Aubrey Westlake who assailed money-lenders in the columns of *Medical World*. Financiers, he cried, are 'the enemy in our rear';[39] something must be done to remove their power over doctors. The way, he told his colleagues, was by means of the national dividend: through it, the profession could free itself from the grip of money-lenders on the one hand and the state on the other. Social credit was the alternative to a service run by Whitehall; that, rather than salary, was the direction in which the MPU should move.[40]

With that, Bayly agreed — and he also had much in common with Westlake where fringe medicine was concerned. Westlake was an ardent devotee of the subject; he had abandoned general practice in order to pursue it.[d] Social credit also attracted him but he had joined the Hargrave, rather than the Douglas,

a   For the aftermath then, see p. 312 below.

b   As far as NHI was concerned, there was nothing novel about the idea: something like it had existed from 1911, mainly to accommodate insured persons who lived in areas without doctors on the panel.[38] It also bears a strong resemblance to the voucher schemes about which we hear so much today.

c   See p. 183 above.

d   Before this happened in 1937, Westlake had practised in partnership with Dr Alfred Salter,

school and at no point in his attacks on money-lenders did he mention Jews. (Indeed, there is no reason to believe that Westlake had any anti-semitic feelings.)

Bayly needed a doctor who felt no similar inhibitions — as well as one who would be more acceptable to those who practised orthodox medicine. *Medical World* therefore published articles by a follower of Douglas and, in one of the series, a subtle reference to a well-known anti-Jewish forgery (the *Protocols of the Learned Elders of Zion*) appeared: '. . . whether these documents represent the policy of Zion or whether they are spurious documents matters not at the moment. What matters is that there is much wisdom in them'.[42]

The doctor who wrote these articles (Dr J. C. Jones)[a] also outlined an attractive plan of clinical organization which had much in common with the one Dawson had drawn: under it, GPs would finally receive a place in the hospital world.[43] But despite the stimulus such a scheme offered, the panel doctors who belonged to the MPU refused to be drawn: they preferred the security inherent in a salaried service. What they wanted in place of money-lenders was not social credit but a pension. As Dr Gordon Ward put it in 1937: 'At the end of so many years in insurance practice the doctor has a certain capital value in his practice which he can sell. We would gladly surrender that value in return for a pension.'[44] [b]

Nature of MPA propaganda

There was thus a limit to which the MPU could be pushed in an extreme right-wing direction. Not even Bayly and his group could hope to reverse its long-standing sympathy for state control; too many members had benefited from NHI for that.[47] Steele made his dissent from the state medical service idea clear in a letter to the *British Medical Journal* in September 1941.[48] By then, he must have realized that a new medical organization had to be formed and a young Australian doctor named Bryan W. Monahan provided the way. Monahan was active in the Social Credit Secretariat which was then under the direction of Dr Tudor Jones, a biologist with medical qualifications who once served as a Lecturer in Anatomy at the University of Liverpool.[49] Jones as well as Monahan must have had a deep interest in medical affairs for, when Monahan saw a letter from Steele in the *Daily Telegraph*, Monahan wrote to him personally and drew Steele and his brother, Basil (a partner in his

one of the founders of the MPU. Later, in 1944, Westlake prepared a National Health Service scheme for Hargrave's Social Credit Party which was based on the national dividend idea.[41]

a　　From the qualifications listed after his name, this doctor can be identified as Dr John Christopher Jones. His name last appeared on the Medical Register in 1960 but nothing is known about him since no obituary notice can be found.

b　　The panel doctors who belonged to the MPU did not seek compensation for the capital value they would have to surrender. Most of that, they recognized, would go to money-lenders in payment for the debts they owed. What they wanted instead was past credit for the service they had given under NHI.[45] That, however, would not have satisfied doctors who never joined the panel (or who devoted little time to it) and Bevan chose the compensation route instead. He also made provision for pensions but credit was confined to service given after 1948, not before it.[46] For the background to the MPU's interest in pensions and salary, see pp. 182-4 above.

practice), into the social credit movement.[50] There, they joined forces with an ophthalmologist named Andrew Rugg-Gunn whose office on Harley Street was used as the MPA's postal address.[51]

Throughout its work, the MPA kept its distance from the Social Credit Secretariat and operated independently.[52] But the four doctors who formed it accepted the 'Jewish money power' conspiracy theory so popular in Douglas circles and constructed their first bulletin around it. It was issued in the spring or summer of 1943 and was called *The Opponents of the Medical Profession*. Though copies do not seem to be available in any library, a summary of its contents appeared in the *British Medical Journal*.[53]

The bulletin declared the aim of the MPA to be opposition to a state medical service and, in taking this stand, it said it wanted to preserve the freedom of doctors as individuals. It then proceeded to link this struggle 'with a general struggle involving the whole of society'. Here, Dr Tudor Jones was quoted in order to reveal the existence of 'a vast chain of interlocked organisations, possibly, and indeed probably, inspired from a common source, which pursue a long-term policy'. Some agents of this policy were the Fabian Society, Labour Party, London School of Economics and the research group known as Political and Economic Planning (PEP). The bulletin then tried to prove the 'closest connexion between high finance and Socialism' with the aim of those in control of the 'central financial institutions' being ' to replace control through finance by control through law'. When this was realized, the 'personnel in ultimate control will of course be those at present in control of international finance — the Warburgs, Schiffs, etc.'.

Not only Jewish financiers but a Jewish retailer was singled out for attack — Israel Sieff of the Marks and Spencer chain and a prominent figure in the Zionist movement. Sieff was thought to have provided a considerable portion of PEP's funds and PEP, Rugg-Gunn was said to have declared in an interview with the *Evening Standard*, was 'the parent of the idea of a State Medical Service'.[54] Apparently because more than Jewish financiers were involved, the bulletin saw fit to refer thus to the *Protocols of the Learned Elders of Zion*: 'There is no doubt that they are *effective* plans (i.e. for the complete domination of the world) written with deep understanding of human psychology'.[55]

In a letter to the *British Medical Journal,* Rugg-Gunn declared the article on the bulletin to be 'a fair analysis of its contents'.[56] But he and his colleagues repeatedly denied the charge of anti-semitism. Thus, when interviewed by the *Evening Standard,* they are reported to have said: 'We are not against the Jews. We are against Jewish fascism — international financial control by Jews.'[57] Rugg-Gunn denied that he and his colleagues had used the term 'Jewish Fascism'[58] but he himself employed it in a book published that same year by the Douglas press called *British Medicine and Alien Plans*. In it, however, 'Jewish Fascism' was described as 'Marxian Socialism, or Communism, or Bolshevism'.[59]

Dr Morgan, for one, was not satisfied with the denial MPA leaders had given and in Parliament he tried to persuade the Home Secretary to take action. But Morrison refused: 'This document appears to introduce, quite gratuitously, certain arguments which may be regarded as having an anti-semitic bias but it affords no grounds for prosecution or for any other action on my part.'[60] The Minister of Information (Brendan Bracken), however, proved more responsive. When queried on the same subject in Parliament a few months later, Bracken condemned MPA leaders for 'prostituting the name of a great profession'.[61]

Following its first bulletin, the MPA stopped referring to 'the origins of the threat to freedom' and concentrated on the details of medical politics.[62] Here, its attack centred on the principle of state (or central) control and the extent to which BMA leaders had been seduced by it. Bulletin after bulletin appeared and they were widely distributed.[63] By 1944, the MPA had compiled a mailing list of 7,000 readers[64] and, although everyone who received the bulletin could not be considered a supporter, this suggested a following greater than the MPU enjoyed at the time. (By December 1944, MPU membership had fallen to 3,913 from a height of 5,857 in 1938.)[a] In 3 areas, MPA influence was strong – so much so that it was said to have captured control of the BMA Divisions there. These were Guildford, Maidstone and Cumberland.[65] No fewer than 10,000 doctors, furthermore, responded to the questionnaire sent out in 1943 and 77% of them supported the stand it took against the principle of central control.[66] One BMA leader (Dr A. Talbot Rogers) tried to dismiss the importance of this response but the long letter he sent to the *British Medical Journal* in September 1944, rebutting an MPA attack on BMA policy, revealed the extent to which BMA leaders had become unnerved by the MPA challenge.[67]

Impact of MPA propaganda

From all of this we may assume that the MPA made a significant impact on the profession – yet one searches in vain for any mention of the organization in the many accounts that have been written on the Health Service. Only one, to the writer's knowledge, even cites the MPA and that was a brief memoir in the medical newspaper, *Pulse*, in 1969.[68]

Part of the MPA's popularity may have been due to the anti-semitic feelings still felt by many in the medical world[69] — but few doctors could have been seduced by the conspiracy theory it spelled out in its first bulletin. The fantasies which Douglas conceived were too absurd to inspire belief: by 1943, he even had Hitler acting in accordance with Jewish interests.[70] Yet that was the year when reports began to appear in the press about the millions of Jews who had died in concentration camps.[71] The MPA's decision to drop the Douglas line probably owed as much to the criticism it aroused from the profession as to the ridicule it provoked from the press and Parliament.

With the stand it took against the principle of central control, the MPA enjoyed much greater success. But even here its impact was limited. Though many doctors endorsed the cry, they were never sure just what it meant.[72] Was the MPA against the idea of any state service — or did it merely object to one directed from Whitehall? If the latter, then not many doctors agreed for they vastly preferred that to the one the Ministry proposed — a salaried service under municipal control.

a　　See p. 169 above.

In reality, however, the MPA did not want to have *any* service run by the state: it desired simply to distribute the national dividend social credit offered. That would enable patients to make their own arrangements for medical care, leaving the profession completely free from regulatory control. The idea, no doubt, appealed to many doctors but they knew it did not have much chance of success. Those who had worked under NHI were not even sure that it was desirable. For 30 years, the panel system had carried them in the opposite direction and they had come to like the security it provided. When NHI started in 1912, the doctors had protested strongly against the capitation method of payment, desiring to replace it with the attendance (or fee-for-service) system that the social credit scheme implied.[73] But by 1943, they recognized, such a change would destroy the capital values which had taken so long to acquire. The doctors, therefore, showed no enthusiasm for the alternative plan the MPA proposed.

Where they did respond was to the attack made on the SMA and the identification of its ideas not only with socialism but with the concept of a state service. Here, it seems, MPA leaders chose to maintain a stony silence; in the bulletins and extracts available, no reference to the SMA was made. The attack, rather, was left to BMA members who were attracted by MPA propaganda. As early as 1941, one such doctor (Dr E. U. MacWilliam) started a correspondence on the subject in the *British Medical Journal*.[74] Later he became a fervent MPA supporter[75] and the appeal its propaganda had for doctors like him caused the *Journal* to wonder in 1944 whether 'the formation of such bodies as the M.P.A. may be the inevitable reaction to the existence and activities of the Socialist Medical Association'.[76]

What worried doctors most about the SMA plan was that it seemed to put the freedom of the profession at stake.[77] This was due not merely to the salaried method of payment or the degree of municipal control; far more worrying was the demand the SMA made for whole-time service. That, combined with universal coverage, left little scope for private practice. If everyone had the right to use the state service, and if the doctors employed in it had to work full-time, there would be no room for medicine outside. The SMA plan seemed to aim at nothing less than the nationalization of the profession — and that was only the beginning. Stark Murray himself had said that the socialization of the nation (i.e. industry as a whole) would follow.[78] In this respect as in so many others, medicine would lead the way.

BMA leaders under pressure

As part of the reaction against these ideas, BMA leaders came under suspicion. Had they not given the SMA a place on the Medical Planning Commission?[79] To many doctors, it seemed, the profession's own policy was tainted with socialism. Here was the secret of the MPA's success: it derived its strength from the way SMA policy became associated with the leaders of the BMA.

The latter, it seems, were alive to the danger for, even before the MPA campaign began, they had tried to put themselves at a distance from the SMA. Thus, when the Ministry proposed a health centre similar to the one advocated by the SMA, Hill reacted angrily: 'It is not the time to develop a "Socialist" cell within a "Capitalist" organism.'[80] And, a few months later, the Secretary of the BMA (then Dr G. C. Anderson) published a paper called *Evolution, Not Revolution* in which he proclaimed the BMA's undying opposition to the principle of whole-time service.[81] Some experiments, he conceded, might be made with salaried employment in health centres but on no account should they be combined with a ban on private practice. That, he believed, would be disastrous for the profession since the doctors who worked in health centres would be cut off from their colleagues outside.

These efforts notwithstanding, medical suspicions mounted. The reason, it seems, lay mainly in the bargaining tactics BMA leaders felt it advisable to pursue: in order to promote their image with the public, they thought it necessary to declare their willingness to accept a service that would cover the nation as a whole. As Anderson put it in 1943: 'If we try to fight it [i.e. the principle of universal coverage] we are likely to lose the sympathy and goodwill of the public, and our subsequent moves will be regarded with suspicion and branded as self-interested. We shall in the end gain more by reserving our strength for negotiating the terms and conditions of service.'[82]

This explanation failed to satisfy the rank and file; they saw it as further evidence of SMA influence on BMA policy. What made them so suspicious was the way that policy had changed during the war. Before it began, the BMA had not been in favour of the '100% idea'; it wanted to cover only 90% of the population,[83] and that was the stand endorsed by the Medical Planning Commission in 1942. NHI, at the time, embraced only half the population and the doctors wanted to extend it so that it covered dependants and others in the working class. The latter were so numerous that their addition would have raised the total to 90% leaving only the 10% in the middle and upper classes outside[84] — but the profession wanted to save these fee-paying patients for private practice. Only one BMA leader before the war felt differently on the subject: that was Brackenbury. In 1939 he told the public-health world (which had objected to the income limit in the BMA's General Medical Service scheme) that he personally favoured 'the inclusion of everybody'.[85]

Here he was at one with the SMA and shortly after the Medical Planning Commission held fast to the 90% rule, those SMA members who managed to secure a place at the BMA's Annual Representative Meeting campaigned for more. To the astonishment of the nation, they pushed through a motion for universal coverage by the narrow margin of 94 to 92.[86] The deciding factor behind their success, however, was not sympathy among doctors for the SMA cause. It stemmed from the profession's desire to eliminate the need for local authority clinics along the lines which the

MPU had proposed.[a] Nor was that the only consideration; yet another arose from the doctors' desire to eliminate the approved-society system. Though tensions had eased since the 1920s,[b] the doctors still did not want the approved societies around. Yet there seemed to be no way to remove them as long as the right to medical benefit was dependent on insurance principles. Only by establishing a service that covered everyone could the profession's separation be assured. Not until the Beveridge Report appeared did this consideration weaken because then it seemed that the approved societies would go, no matter what action was taken with regard to medical care.[c]

In the BMA's acceptance of the principle of universal coverage was the main source of the profession's suspicions, and the MPA, once its bulletins began, made sure they did not subside. One year later (in the summer of 1943), the Representative Body changed its mind[87] and, with that reversal, the Chairman of Council went, too. Souttar gave way to Dain and the Medical Planning Commission over which he presided never met again.[88] In a desperate attempt to regain confidence, the BMA brought back the ageing Dawson as President[89] — but his brief this time was to save the doctors from salary (and the MPA), not to close the gap that divided GPs from the hospital world.

a   See pp. 174-5 and 184-5 above.

b   See p. 219 above.

c   See p. 246 above.

28
Bevan's Concessions

Dawson's appointment provided only temporary relief for BMA leaders. They came under pressure again in the spring of 1944 when they issued a secret document on the Government's White Paper. Though the action was intended merely to keep medical deliberations private, it enabled the MPA to sow further suspicion and, this time, it was aided by a consultant in Parliament who, as a champion of the voluntary hospital system, strongly opposed the idea of a Health Service. He was Sir Ernest Graham-Little, MP for the University of London from 1924 to 1950 and long a thorn in the side of BMA leaders.[1] From the moment the Medical Planning Commission was formed, Graham-Little fought it[2] and, throughout the course of the struggle over the Health Service, he worked in tandem with the MPA.

This alliance was most apparent at a medical meeting in Guildford (an MPA stronghold) in March 1944. Graham-Little delivered the opening address[3] and, a few weeks later, he developed the comments he made there in the columns of *Truth,* an extreme right-wing journal which served as a clearing-house for the forces that were opposed to the welfare state.[4a] Here, as at Guildford, Graham-Little cast aspersions on BMA leaders. The referendum held on the White Paper, he suggested, could not be trusted; it showed an unusual degree of support for the health-service idea, whereas the MPA's poll had indicated the opposite.[b] Though Graham-Little did not refer to the latter directly, the implications of his remarks were clear: the BMA had manipulated the vote. Such was the state of the medical mind at the time that not only were many doctors ready to accept this — they thought their own negotiators (not the Ministry) had been responsible for the plan produced in the White Paper. The BMA had to revamp its bargaining team and, on the new body it formed, many militants were found.[6]

Inflexibility of the SMA

At that point, if the health-service idea was to succeed, the SMA had to alter

---

a   It was then edited by Collin Brooks and, in 1944, he appointed a former fascist to help him, A. K. Chesterton.[5] The latter, after the war, became one of Britain's leading anti-semites, linked with the Douglas social credit group through a journal published in Taunton called *Sovereignty.*

b   For details of the BMA's referendum, see p. 285 below; for the MPA poll, see p. 280 above.

its stand. Dawson, in a letter to *The Times* in September 1944, pleaded with the 'ideologues' to cease their agitation for a salaried service.[7] Even Morgan of the TUC agreed: as a member of the BMA's Council, he knew what effect SMA tactics were having on medical policy. Not only health centres but the '100% idea' was in danger and Morgan pleaded with his socialist colleagues to refrain from criticizing the BMA where that issue was concerned.[8]

SMA leaders, however, refused to listen. Their stand on medical policy hardened — so much so that, as the year 1944 progressed, they showed themselves to be even less flexible than the Marxists who ran the Communist Party.[9] Both bodies sought salary and municipal control, but, whereas the Party made allowance for what the doctors wanted, the SMA stuck rigidly to the municipal model Hastings revered. As early as March 1943, the SMA sent a memorandum to the Ministry in which it said: 'We do not believe that the profession as a whole has strong views on the need for representation on local authorities.'[10] And 10 months later, at the start of 1944, it went so far as to advise Willink in these terms:

> '. . . It is contrary to democratic principles and to the interests of the profession to suggest that scientific and medical advice should be given by a small group of doctors serving on a Regional Health Committee,[a] whether they have voting powers or not. A Regional Health Committee must be a body reflecting the political outlook of the Regional Council of which it is a part, and the balance of power within it cannot be maintained if outside groups, such as the medical profession, are allowed direct representation on it.'[11]

This was the position to which the SMA adhered throughout the negotiations on the Health Service — which suggests that, where principles of medical administration were concerned, Christian socialists were made of sterner stuff than Marxists.[b] What made SMA leaders so intransigent was their misreading of medical opinion: they thought they knew better than the BMA what the profession wanted. To support their claim, they said, one had only to look at the results of the referendum conducted by the BMA. Though the majority rejected the White Paper as a whole, only half the profession responded and from this, Stark Murray concluded, 'we can safely assume that nearly all the remaining 50 per cent agreed with and accepted the certainty of the Government scheme'.[13] Nor, he stressed, was that all: those who had answered showed a surprising degree of support for important parts of the White Paper — such as its provision for health centres (by a vote of 68% to 24% for the profession as a whole) and establishment of the principle of universal coverage (60% to 37%).[14]

These points were made by Stark Murray not only in 1944 but also in

---

a   For 'regional' here insert the term 'local authority'. The SMA used a different word simply to indicate its desire for larger areas of local government where the administration of health services was concerned.

b   This became even more apparent after the Health Service began. During 1955, the Marxists in the SMA realized that a new initiative was needed on health centres and one of them did his best to soften the SMA's stand on salary. For this, however, he was branded a heretic and he actually had to defend himself against the charge that he was an enemy of health centres.[12]

1971 when, reviewing the course of the whole conflict, he had the chance to correct the misjudgment the SMA had made. But instead of doing that, Stark Murray came to the same conclusion as he did when the dispute occurred: 'Had the Minister of Health been a socialist he would have had at this point a mandate from the profession to go right ahead.'[15]

In fact, however, no such mandate existed — as Bevan, when he himself came to power, was the first to recognize. The doctors might have been willing to accept a salaried service if it were divorced from municipal control — but that neither the Ministry nor the SMA were willing to do.[a] On this key issue, medical opinion was clear: whenever a question in the referendum raised the spectre of local authority direction, the doctors disapproved[b] — and, where the use of joint authorities for hospitals was concerned, they made the rejection overwhelming (78% to 13%).[17] This, above all, explains why the profession rejected the White Paper as a whole and, despite the naïve assumption made by Stark Murray, there is no reason to believe that the doctors who failed to participate would have voted differently.

Medical policy, in any case, was not then — nor has it ever been — decided by referendums. The key decisions were (and are) made by the internal organs of the BMA and the local medical committees attached. Any Minister of Health who wants to introduce a salaried service must first win the approval of the doctors at all levels who make up the organization known as the BMA.

Doctors accept universal coverage

It was there, in fact, that SMA leaders turned their attention as soon as the referendum was concluded and, by the end of 1944, they were joined in a struggle with the MPA for the control of medical policy.[18] Both had adherents within the BMA's Divisions: the SMA, mainly in the City; the MPA, mainly in Guildford. In both places, key personalities evolved — Dr P. Inwald for the SMA and Dr G. H. Steele for the MPA.[19] Taking advantage of an attack that appeared in *The Spectator* in September,[20] the *British Medical Journal* tried to stop the fight but, by concentrating its fire on the SMA, the *Journal* showed which side was causing the most embarrassment. 'The real issue', it had said a few months earlier, 'is . . . whether the medical profession is to be socialised'; ' . . . it is upon this issue that opposition must be unshakably offered in the coming months.'[21]

The editor of the *Journal* at this time was Dr Norman Horner, but most of its comments on the Health Service were probably written by the man who succeeded him in 1947 — Dr Hugh Clegg.[22] For all who could read between the lines, the message was clear: if the SMA wanted to see a Health Service

---

a   See p. 190 above.

b   They also rejected the idea of central administration by the Ministry (51% to 35%)[16] — but this was probably due to their preference for a corporate body at the head (on which they could be represented) rather than a Government department. If the doctors had been forced to make a straight choice between the Ministry and local authorities, there is no doubt about how the decision would have gone: they would have voted overwhelmingly for the former.

enacted, then it had better stick to essentials and restrain its criticism of the BMA on such matters as salary and municipal control. Only Inwald, however, responded:[23] like Morgan, he knew from his intimate contact with BMA affairs the difficult situation its leaders were in. Stark Murray, on the other hand, only succeeded in making matters worse: the SMA, he wrote in a letter to the *British Medical Journal,* merely wanted to convert the BMA to socialism.[24] He and his colleagues then sent the wrong man to represent them at the critical Annual Representative Meeting held in December 1944. The doctor they chose to plead their case for health centres was Dr C. K. Cullen, a municipal chest physician well-known in public life as a member of the Communist Party.[25] Needless to say, the motion was defeated and, with it, went all hope of realizing a salaried service.

From that point, the BMA fell increasingly under the sway of doctors opposed to state intervention and they concentrated their attack on the issue where they thought it most vulnerable — the principle of universal coverage. Here, they attracted much support because, as a result of Brown's (and the SMA's) plan, many doctors had come to associate that principle with a salaried service and municipal control. BMA leaders did their best to separate the two: thus, a member of the negotiating team (Dr Frank Gray)[a] introduced a motion calling for a 100% service 'in matters of personal health'.[26] But this, too, went down to defeat at the meeting held in December. In its place, the doctors resurrected their pre-war programme — the extension of NHI alone — only this time, they made clear, hospital and specialist services must come before dependants.[27]

In the months that followed, the whole health-service idea was in doubt. PEP tried to dismiss the alternative scheme proposed by the BMA as 'an elaborate device for excluding 10% of the population'[28] — but, to the doctors who conceived it, it represented much more: it was their way of saying 'no' to municipal control. Willink understood that and, by making the necessary concessions, he persuaded the doctors to think again.[b] This time, it seems, they were ready to listen to what their leaders had to say and the latter gave them the same advice in 1945 as Whitaker had offered in 1910 when he was Secretary of the BMA: 'The profession had no right to say that the State should not create a new system, but it had a right to say that it would work on certain terms.'[29] With that the doctors agreed, for the Representative Body, at its meeting held in May 1945, finally acknowledged that 'the 100 per cent issue was one for Parliament to decide'.[30]

In coming to this decision, the BMA differed sharply from its American counterpart because, until recently, the AMA always acted as if it were the arbiter of action in the medical sphere.[31] But the deference shown by the profession in Britain was not due solely to recognition of its proper place: even more important was the doctors' fear of resurrecting the approved-society system. That, in accordance with Beveridge principles, was

a   For more about Gray, see p. 189 above.

b   See p. 213 above.

scheduled to go but, if NHI continued as the BMA envisaged the December before, the profession's old *bête noir* might win a new lease of life.[32]

Whatever the reason, the doctors' decision meant that Bevan would not have to start afresh: when he assumed office in July 1945, he knew what he had to do to put the Health Service across. The middle class in Britain was not excluded from the benefits of the welfare state; Bevan, who had an obsessive fear of fascism,[33] did not intend to let the nation repeat the mistakes made by German Socialists in the Weimar Republic. Nor, indeed, would his advisers have let him for they, too, shared the same concern. This applied particularly to one of his closest advisers, Dr Stephen Taylor. While at the Ministry of Information during the war, Taylor wrote a memorandum to Attlee (then Lord President of the Council in Churchill's Coalition Government) urging coverage of the middle class at least for costly hospital and specialist care: 'The evils resulting from a disgruntled and impoverished middle class in other lands are too obvious for us to miss the lesson.'[34]

This, however, was not the only factor behind Bevan's concern for universal coverage. Equally important was his dislike of the contributory principle (where social insurance was involved) and his fear that an income limit might perpetuate the double standard of treatment that had developed under the panel between the wars. Despite the contrary arguments raised by some American friends, Bevan insisted on a non-contributory scheme covering everyone.[35]

The same determination was not evident where the organization of general practice was concerned: because of the damage done by the SMA in 1944, Bevan found it difficult to carry out meaningful reform. He did abolish the sale of practices and introduce 'negative' controls over the location of doctors, but neither had much effect on the quality of care: the panel system, after 1948, went on virtually as before.[a] Because of the need to bring consultants into the Health Service, and the demands made by the BMA during negotiations, Bevan's energies went into the hospital side rather than general practice.

BMA turns intransigent

The year 1944 thus marked the end of SMA influence on BMA policy. Few of its members managed to attend Annual Representative Meetings thereafter and even Morgan, in 1946, lost his seat on the BMA's Council.[b] BMA leaders, however, still had to contend with the MPA and they were crippled by the attacks it made from the rear. As Hill (who became Secretary of the BMA after Anderson died in 1944) later admitted: 'We

a   Abolition of the sale of practices did end the money-lender problem and doctors no longer have to go in debt as they did between the wars. But some goodwill is still sold under the cover of partnership agreements,[36] and some areas of the country still lack sufficient GPs despite 3 decades of 'negative' controls over location.[37]

b   Morgan did manage to retain a place on two lesser committees (one dealing with the General Medical Council, the other with rehabilitation) but neither offered entry to the portals of BMA power.[38]

were spokesmen, not leaders. I had none of the power of a general secretary of a trade union. Always we entered negotiations with no power to negotiate without reference.'[39]

As a result, he and his colleagues not only had to present demands that were hard to satisfy — they had to do everything they could to prevent Bevan from succeeding. Each time the Minister disposed of one grievance they raised another. Eventually, all their complaints were rolled into one — 'an attack on the huge potential powers of the Minister'[40] — and this bore a striking resemblance to the warning the MPA had raised earlier about the danger of central control.[a] 'Multitudes of doctors', Bevan's biographer observed, 'had swallowed whole the charge that the all-powerful Minister was engaged in a dastardly attack on medical freedom.'[41] All this left the doctors with but one simple object: 'The clear aim of B.M.A. leaders *was* to make an Act of Parliament unworkable.'[42]

Only one of the BMA's consultant radicals had the courage to dissent: that, to his credit, was Souttar. He returned to office in 1945 as President of the BMA, but resigned in disgust in 1946 because of the blind opposition shown by his colleagues.[43] Watson-Jones, on the other hand, stayed on, making a great show of militance. In 1946 he told Attlee and Bevan directly: 'I will not be a Civil Servant' — but, just before the Health Service began in 1948, he changed his mind and counselled acceptance.[44]

What effect did this have on the expectations of SMA leaders at the time? When the BMA first presented its demands to Bevan in 1945, Stark Murray and his colleagues did not think they would 'exert much influence on the Minister'.[45] They expected him to return to the salaried service Brown had proposed, which bore such a strong resemblance to their own programme. But Bevan not only rejected that because 'it contained too much of the element of regimentation'[46] — he was forced to make 'a long series of concessions' without one, in return, being offered by the profession.[47] Like Johnston before him,[b] Bevan put 'quantity' first: almost any sacrifice was offered to obtain the goodwill of GPs.

Bevan, in fact, went further than Johnston — for, whereas Johnston drew the line when it came to the doctors' demand for direct representation,[c] Bevan conceded even more than Willink. He not only gave GPs a place in administration,[d] he did the same for some consultants: those in teaching hospitals won the right to appoint one-fifth of the seats on the separate boards of governors set up to supervise them.[48] (Willink had earlier conceded only the former, not the latter.)[e] Bevan also made liberal provisions for private practice in the hospital world and these affected all consultants, not just those in the teaching sector. But both these concessions, it is important to recognize, were partly for 'quality' reasons: Bevan hoped they would attract the best brains

a   See p. 280 above.

b   See pp. 197-8 above.

c   See p. 207 above.

d   See pp. 292-3 below.

e   See p. 213 above.

to the Service and give it the necessary prestige to make it universally accepted.[49]

The hospitals are nationalized

Otherwise, Bevan refused to compromise on 'quality' where the hospital service was concerned. There, he went far beyond his predecessors and brought all hospitals under Ministry control. At first, the teaching hospitals did not figure in his plan. No doubt in response to the arguments raised by Lord Moran, he decided to exempt them 'partly on the ground of their exceptional standing in the hospital and medical world, partly because it is a good thing in itself to keep separate a field for innovation and independent experiment in method and organisation (for which purposes teaching hospitals are excellently suited), partly because it is undesirable to introduce a full and direct State control and regulation into the educational field (determining what and how the medical profession should be taught).'[50]

His Scottish colleagues, however, could not afford to grant such an exemption. More than 25% of the voluntary hospital beds in Scotland were located in the teaching sector and the country could not exclude them without undermining its hospital service.[51] In deference to Scottish wishes, then, Bevan brought the teaching hospitals into his nationalization plan: the voluntary sector, with only a few exceptions (like Manor House), was taken over whole.[52]

Not even the SMA had considered such a bold stroke. Its leaders probably shied away from the idea because of the disappointments they had suffered with the principle of central control under the Emergency Medical Service.[a] Yet, once Bevan decided to nationalize the voluntary hospitals, Stark Murray not only hailed the decision but, in his characteristic fashion, tried to give the credit to the SMA.[53]

Against this decision, surprisingly, the voluntary hospitals made little protest: the financial help (and freedom) they had received from the Emergency Medical Service removed their fear of state intervention.[54] Nor did consultants register greater dissent: most, in fact, accepted the decision with relief because it at last erased the spectre of municipal control.[55] Only a few die-hards from the voluntary spectre resisted and some (like Graham-Little) had ulterior motives for expressing disapproval.[56]

The same could not be said of the municipal world: MOHs could not bear to see their hospital empires go. This applied even to one who had just retired — Sir Frederick Menzies, former MOH of the LCC. Just before the Health Service began in 1948, he started 'an imposing correspondence' in *The Times* calling for its postponement on the grounds that it was 'quite impossible' for the Minister to provide the facilities.[57] The leader of the Labour Party on the LCC, on the other hand, took the loss gracefully. Earlier, he had been hostile to nationalization[b] but, once his Party came to power, Lord Latham loyally supported Bevan's decision, recognizing that it would do much to promote the integration of the hospital service.[58]

a   See pp. 264-5 above.
b   See p. 199 above.

Morrison was not so understanding. Nothing, in his view, could justify the loss of municipal control and he forced Bevan, within the Cabinet, to wage his 'biggest battle on this issue — the most crucial in the whole fight for the Health Service'.[59] There, surprisingly, he received support from Arthur Greenwood, then Lord Privy Seal and chairman of the all-important Cabinet Committee on the Social Services. Greenwood, at this point, was intent on the passage of legislation giving effect to the cash benefit side of the welfare state and he was afraid that Bevan's Bill, involving as it did difficult and protracted negotiations with the profession, might block it.[60] He therefore endorsed Morrison's call to delay the Health Service,[61] but Bevan refused to give in. For the sake of efficiency, he insisted, the hospitals had to be integrated and he showed no patience with those who defended the smaller ones 'on grounds of intimacy and local patriotism'. 'Although I am not myself a devotée of bigness for bigness' sake', Bevan told Parliament, 'I would rather be kept alive in the efficient if cold altruism of a large hospital than expire in a gush of sympathy in a small one.'[62]

Bevan ignores quality in general practice

When it came to general practice, Bevan failed to show the same interest or determination. The family doctor, he was later to write, constituted the most important part of the Health Service[63] — but that was not the impression his actions presented when he created it. All his concern for quality went into the hospital sector and the excellence of the service there, it seems, was supposed to make up for deficiencies elsewhere.[64]

The only point at which Bevan showed an interest in the quality of GP care was when he talked about the need to secure a more even distribution of doctors.[65] But this was mainly a rationale for a more vital change — abolition of the sale of practices — and that he wanted to achieve for moral as well as medical reasons. To Bevan, such a custom was 'an evil thing', and he was not offended when the doctors accused him of running a 'Ministry of Morals' rather than a Minstry of Health.[66] No matter what the cost, he was determined to stop the purchase of patients without their consent.[67] Even more to the point, he probably wanted to end money-lending in medicine, because only in that way could the influence of organizations like the MPA be removed from the medical world.

Otherwise, Bevan left GPs in the same state they had been in and this lack of concern contrasted sharply with the stand he took on housing. That subject, until 1951, remained under the jurisdiction of the Minister of Health — yet, despite the pressing need for more homes, Bevan refused to compromise on building standards.[68] Quality, however, is harder to measure in the field of medical care.

Though they did little to resist, all this was apparent to BMA negotiators. Bevan, one of them (Dr A. Talbot Rogers) recalled in 1971, did not see the need for radical change in general practice: 'All that seemed to the Minister essential was to ensure that everyone should have a general practitioner able to provide a service matching that of the club doctor, but enhanced in content because of the availability of a hospital-based diagnostic service. For this an NHI type of administration appeared adequate and it was adopted.' The conclusion Rogers reached was not flattering to the Minister: 'I sometimes wonder whether the progress of general practice was not set back a whole generation by the conditioned reflexes of Mr. Aneurin Bevan.'[69]

So the stage was set for the profession's demands, and Bevan ended up by making a surprising series of concessions. Bit by bit, the SMA saw its expectations eroded so that by the time the Health Service began, it had little to cheer except the principle of universal coverage. That, however, was not how Stark Murray saw it in 1946: then, he claimed, all the SMA's basic principles had been secured except the establishment of whole-time salary for general practice.[70] In his enthusiasm for the Act Bevan passed, Stark Murray forgot the importance his organization had assigned to an integrated service. Nor was that all he missed. To see just where SMA policy failed, let us now take up the four areas in which its programme was decisively rejected.

Doctors win direct representation

The first to go was Hastings' beloved system of municipal administration. In place of that, Bevan gave the doctors the direct representation they had long demanded. Here he simply followed what Willink had done and resurrected the NHI pattern of insurance and local medical committees. But the doctors had never been content with the share this had given them: they held only 10% of the seats while the approved societies held 60%. On the larger insurance committees (30 to 40 members), the doctors did not even enjoy this proportion. They could not appoint more than 2 members on their own so that when more doctors were called for (in order to maintain the profession's nominal 10% share), the third (on committees of 30) was selected by the local authority involved and the fourth (on committees of 40) by the Ministry.[71] Since the chemists had no direct seats of their own (representation for them being allowed only through the Ministry), the two professions involved in NHI were hopelessly outnumbered: the lay majority against them was almost 9 to 1.

Despite this handicap, the doctors eventually did manage to dominate insurance committee affairs.[72] By the 1930s the approved societies had lost almost all influence over medical benefit.[a] Had it not been for the MPA challenge and the threat of municipal control, it is doubtful if the doctors would have insisted on a change in insurance committee composition.

Insist they did, however, and Bevan gave it to them. Following exactly what Willink had done,[73] he agreed to equalize the proportions between the opposing sides, leaving only a chairman to break deadlocks.[74] The changes were as shown in table opposite.

The concessions made to the doctors were even more generous than these numbers suggest. Among the lay members, no more approved-society representatives were found. Thanks to James Griffiths and his National Insurance Act, they had been finally removed from medical affairs. In their place came the municipal and Ministry appointees who, in the struggle for control of medical

a   See pp. 166-7 above.

	Insurance Committee (20-40 members)	Executive Council (25 members)
Laymen	60% approved societies 20 local authorities 10 Ministry* —— 90%	– 32% local authorities 16 Ministry* —— 48%
Professions (direct rep.)	10% doctors 0 chemists —— 10%	28% doctors 12 dentists 8 chemists 0 opticians —— 48%
		4% chairman (lay or professional)**

* Includes chemists under NHI; opticians under the Health Service.

** First appointed by the Minister — afterwards, by executive councils. Under NHI, insurance committees always chose their own chairmen from among their own members and, usually, a layman was selected. Not until the Health Service did medical chairmen become more evident.[75]

benefit, had always been considered 'neutrals'. Unlike the approved-society members, they had no financial stake in the provision of medical care. Their attendance at NHI meetings had been perfunctory and it did not improve after the Health Service began. The professions, even when a layman occupied the chair, often found themselves in an embarrassing majority.[76]

Bevan tried to justify the arrangement by invoking principles of workers' control: if it were right for miners, he told his Labour colleagues, how could it be wrong for doctors?[77] But he had doubts and one of his closest advisers, Dr Stephen Taylor, explained why to Parliament: 'A real danger he saw in the Bill was that it gave the doctors too much freedom, and he feared that we might impose on ourselves a medical dictatorship.'[78]

Change in disciplinary procedure

Bevan also changed the disciplinary procedure, making it more foreboding. This must have annoyed his civil servants since they thought the old procedure cumbersome[a] but, because of the universal coverage provided by the Act and the heavier penalties entailed by dismissal, Bevan decided to give the doctors additional protection. Between the new executive council and the Minister, he put an independent tribunal. Now, before a doctor could be dismissed, the decision had to be made by 3 rather than 2 bodies.

The doctors, however, failed to appreciate the value of what Bevan had done. They wanted him to go further and provide an appeal to the courts. But this was a concession no Minister could make — it was, Bevan discovered, 'constitutionally impossible'.[79] The doctors, therefore, had to live with the procedure he constructed and, by 1953, their leaders realized it was too good to let go. As Dain put it: '. . . the great value of the complaints procedure was that it presented an opportunity of airing complaints and getting rid of them, and in that way it was

a   See pp. 207-10 above.

frequently more protective of the doctor — the person complained against — than punitive.'[80]

Private practice allowed within the Health Service

Next came the concession the SMA most deplored: within the framework of the Health Service, Bevan made room for private practice.[81] He also deplored the provision: nothing, in fact, 'caused him more anxiety and heart-searching' than this.[82] At first, he tried to restrict its application by barring private practice from health centres — but even that limitation disappeared in 1949.[83] The privilege, nevertheless, affected GPs only peripherally: few patients, after the Health Service began, felt the need for private attention where GP care was concerned and many family doctors found those ready to pay fees too demanding. GPs preferred to limit their work to the less critical patients from the public sector.

The concession, therefore, was mainly designed to please consultants and, by making it possible for all 'senior' hospital doctors to treat private patients in Health Service beds,[84] Bevan revolutionized SMA attitudes towards GP access. Henceforth, it aimed to keep hospital work as restricted as possible: if consultants needed medical men to help them, they should rely on registrars (and other 'juniors' who were barred from private practice)[a] rather than GPs.[85] To the delight of the Royal Colleges, the SMA threw its weight strongly behind the development of the 'firm' idea. This, in some instances, came to include as many as 6 assistants working under consultant supervision — a senior registrar, 2 registrars, a senior house officer and 2 house officers.[86] The idea was not new — 'firms' had long existed in voluntary hospitals[87] — but the practice developed under the Health Service to the point where it covered nearly every consultant in the land. In this respect, it deserves to rank as the one great change in practice organization made by the Health Service — but it was not without its drawbacks. The system meant that appointments to consultant posts occurred infrequently, and as a result many junior hospital doctors chose to emigrate to America and elsewhere in order to secure the full specialist status they thought they deserved.

The problem might have been avoided if GPs had been used in place of part of the junior hospital corps but that idea never appealed to those responsible for staffing the hospital service.[b] No one was more pleased by their decision than Stark Murray of the SMA (himself, it should be noted, a consultant in the field of pathology). In 1942, he had been foremost among those who sought to bring GPs into hospital[c] — but this was at a time when

a　This ban, however, did not stop junior hospital doctors from working for the emergency night call services that grew up after the Health Service began. This represented a technical violation of their contracts but neither the Ministry nor the SMA were concerned because the doctors involved made no attempt to conduct private practice on their own. Had they done so, consultants would have been the first to protest and that would have stopped the violation.

b　For their reasons, see pp. 302-3 below.

c　See p. 174 above.

the SMA hoped municipal hospitals would form the base of a salaried service. Once Bevan removed the hospitals from local authority control, SMA policy changed. By 1950, Stark Murray had emerged as the leader of those who wanted to keep GPs in the community. Private practice, he now claimed, was the motive that underlay GP desire for beds.[88] Later he modified his stand — by 1973 he was willing to consider GP entry to hospitals if the profession demanded it. But before the proposal could be accepted, GPs would have to abandon their right to private practice — by agreeing to serve in health centres on a whole-time salaried basis.[89]

Ban on salary in general practice

Last came the concession Bevan was most anxious to avoid: a statutory ban on salary in general practice. This was a subject on which Lord Moran offered much advice. He warned Bevan about the danger the Health Service presented to general practice. Because of the sharp division it created between GPs and consultants, the Act was 'going to take the milder degree of specialization out of the general practitioner's hands, and therefore deprive his life of interest'.[90] In the long run, Moran believed, there was only one remedy: 'We have to make up our minds to bring the general practitioner into the work of the hospitals.'[91] Until that could be accomplished, some kind of incentive was needed and Moran argued strongly for the capitation system. The alternative of salary he wished to avoid at all costs: '. . . unless there is an adequate incentive . . . to keep men on their toes . . . a whole-time service would be an incalculable disaster.'[92] Only in the hospital world, he believed, was it safe to try salary and, even there, Moran insisted on a system of merit awards before the experiment began.[93a]

In general practice, no similar protection existed for, once a doctor left hospital, all organizational restraints disappeared.[95] Capitation, therefore, had to be preserved and even it, Moran warned, was only a temporary palliative: 'I am less happy about the general practitioner service planned in this Bill than I am about the hospital service.'[96]

Bevan listened to what Moran said: he decided to pay GPs everywhere by capitation. Nor, he claimed, was this merely a tactical manoeuvre: he ruled out the whole-time principle because it could not be reconciled with free choice of doctor and that, at the moment, was the only safeguard the patient had against poor service.[97] To his left-wing critics in Parliament, however, Bevan hinted at something different. When challenged as to his reasons for rejecting a salaried service, Bevan replied: 'I do not believe that the medical profession is ripe for it.'[98]

No matter how much Bevan later tried to disavow these words the doctors

---

a   The experiment was also needed to move consultants to the periphery. 'At present', Moran told Bevan, 'the consultants are all crowded together in the large centres of population. You've got to decentralise them.'[94] The only way to do it, in his view, was to give them the security of salary. Uneven distribution was also a problem in general practice, but the shortages that existed there had been alleviated by 30 years of the panel. To complete the task, Bevan hoped, only 'negative' controls over location would be needed.

could not get them out of their heads. Nor did the Minister help matters by adding a basic salary (£300) to the capitation payment Moran recommended.[99] That, he explained, was needed only to help young doctors start practice but, to a profession already paralysed with fear, the proposal appeared like the 'thin end of the wedge'.[100] Moran himself called upon Bevan to drop it but the Minister held fast in the hope that the doctors would give in.[101]

Bevan, after all, had his own left-wing critics to consider: having conceded so much on salary, he could not afford to give away any more. Two of his closest advisers had doubts about the incentive a capitation system would offer. Addison (then, leader of the Labour Party in the Lords) had become completely disillusioned with it[102] — while Taylor thought additional protection was needed in the form of inspection.[103] Later, however, Taylor changed his mind and, by 1954, was even hailing capitation as 'a great social invention'.[104] Hastings also abandoned his opposition to capitation once it became clear that the sale of practices would go.[105] That, he believed, would eventually induce the profession to accept salary[106] but, for a Christian socialist like him, the moral reform of medicine always took precedence over its clinical regeneration.

Bevan's decision to preserve a salary element, nevertheless, proved to be a gross miscalculation because it forced BMA leaders to come back with a demand they themselves had been anxious to drop: the right to sell practices.[107] Only by retaining property interests in the patients they owned, GPs believed, could they hope to protect themselves against the salaried service Bevan intended. Surprisingly enough, even Cox from retirement spoke up in favour of the demand[108] — but this was one that Bevan under no conditions would concede.[a] That left him only one choice: he had to ban a whole-time service by statute and even the basic salary provision had to be abandoned before the profession would give in.[109] [b]

Still, that was enough to save the face of BMA leaders and enable them to accept the start of a service which they always knew would come.[111] Dain went so far as to say in *The Times*: '. . . the profession would do its utmost to make the new Service a resounding success.'[112] This, no doubt, indicates how he really felt about the 1946 Act. He and Hill had to fend off the MPA, but there was certainly a point beyond which they would not go.[113]

The same, in all probability, applied to the eminent physician who emerged as the leader of the doctors opposed to the Act — Lord (Thomas) Horder. Though he never ceased to criticize the Health Service, he himself had been in favour of the '100% idea' before the war as far as general practice was concerned.[114] And while the Bill was being debated in the Lords, he came close to wishing it well: 'I have committed myself to the belief that the doctors of this country will do their utmost to work this Bill be it good or bad.'[115]

a   See p. 291 above.

b   Bevan, however, managed to save part of the idea to help ease the shortage of GPs in under-doctored areas. The profession agreed to let a fixed annual payment be made to young doctors starting out in practice as well as to others who might need or desire this form of remuneration.[110]

Later (in 1949), Horder went all the way to America to declare his opposition to the Health Service[116] — but even that had a beneficial effect. It showed doctors on both sides of the Atlantic how free speech could flourish within the framework of a system run by the state. Perhaps the best clue to Horder's real feelings lay in his refusal to sponsor any amendment that would give GPs the right to sell practices. Hill, for the BMA, privately asked him to do so but, 'This one', Horder replied, 'is not a starter.' Yet when the Bill was debated in the Lords, Horder condemned the ban on sale (along with other provisions) as a gross infringement of personal liberty. Hill found the experience 'very puzzling'.[117]

Health centres under municipal control

The Health Service thus weathered the storm brewed by the MPA but, by the time Bevan finished making concessions, only one point of the SMA's administrative plan remained — the placing of health centres under local authorities. In time, Stark Murray came to regret even that. The decision, he admitted in 1971, was a mistake 'because reactionary County Councils joined with reactionary doctors to make the building of any Health Centres virtually impossible'.[118]

Yet who was responsible for giving them control? Stark Murray, unbelievably, tried to pin the blame on the BMA: this was the only point, he claimed, at which it did not object to municipal administration. The facts show otherwise: no sooner was Bevan's Bill published than the BMA protested. Health centres, it argued, should be administered by regional hospital boards, not local authorities.[119] Bevan, however, had Morrison to contend with and Stark Murray forgot how strongly the SMA backed his stand on local authority administration.[120] With the hospitals passing under national control, Bevan could not afford to remove any more duties from municipal purview. He decided to give health centres to local authorities as a form of compensation. 'Hospital function', he told Parliament, 'had been taken away from local authorities and he thought it a wise provision that they should be given this new function.'[121] With this, it seems, the voluntary hospitals agreed for, as early as 1941, one of their spokesmen (C. E. A. Bedwell) had recommended the same division of duties: '. . . local authorities might be more easily reconciled to the surrender of their hospital control to a regional authority if they would retain their general care of the public health, for which a personal knowledge of the needs of the people and of their manner of living is essential.'[122]

Looking back over the course of negotiations as a whole, nothing was more striking than the way SMA leaders succumbed to the compromises Bevan made. The Minister's main accomplishment, in fact, was not so much the creation of the Health Service as (in the words of one Labour MP) 'the way he applied the anaesthetic to supporters on his own side, making them believe in things they had opposed almost all their lives'.[123]

Why, when they had been so dogmatic before, did SMA leaders become so pliable when a socialist sat in the ministerial chair? Their faith in Bevan and the charm of his personality provided only part of the answer. Far more important was the intensity of their belief in the '100% idea'. That took precedence over everything else[124] and once it was realized, they believed, the rest would follow. Free access to all would lead inevitably to salary[125] and the reform of general practice would have to wait until then. Their reasoning, as the years unfolded, proceeded something like this: the only way to raise quality was through group practice[126] and group practice was no good without health centres.[127] But health centres, they believed, would not work without salary,[128] and thus a mere change in the method of payment became the panacea for everything.[129] Salary, in the minds of SMA leaders, is now synonymous not only with socialism but with quality too.

Only one ancillary thought survived to complete the obsession: SMA leaders (Stark Murray, in particular) never forgot their detestation of private practice.[130] On this score, they eventually won the resounding support of the unions[131] and so, as recent (1975) events have shown, this has become the dominating motif of Labour policy.[a]

In the process, the movement lost sight of the need to integrate the medical world. Labour, at the end of the First World War, strongly supported Dawson's move to bring GPs into the hospitals[b] — and even the SMA, before it became so enamoured of the hospital 'firm', saw its health centres as the breeding ground for specialists.[133] Sidney Webb, in 1918, made it clear to GPs that he wanted them to have access to all branches of medicine: 'There had in the past been too much separation, too much segregation, and too much virtual extinction.'[134] And Charles Brook echoed the same theme 15 years later. 'The only way of combining the various branches of work in the profession', he told the panel doctors who belonged to the MPU, 'was by provision of a co-ordinated medical service.'[135]

This view, however, swiftly disappeared after the Health Service began. Then, dominated by union interest in rehabilitation and socialist concern for the 'underprivileged sick' (the aged, mentally ill, and chronic sick), Labour policy turned towards ways of keeping GPs in the community. Led by Stark Murray, the SMA even began to see health centres as a way of keeping GPs out of the hospitals rather than putting them in.[136]

---

a   It was, however, only a subsidiary point in a Green Paper prepared for the Labour Party in 1973. I was a member of the Working Party that wrote the report and I do not recall the subject ever being discussed. We merely added a brief statement covering it at the end of a long report.[132] This was subsequently blown up by the press out of all proportion to the importance we assigned to it.

b   Indeed, in this respect as in so many others, Labour (and the SMSA) *anticipated* Dawson. See pp. 86-8 and 105-7 above.

Part 8
The Separation
of the Profession
1948-1968

GPs were administratively separated from the hospitals when the Health Service began and this made it easy for consultants to exclude them despite the manpower shortage that existed in the hospital world. 'Firms' of junior hospital doctors were developed instead. In the process, a viable referral system emerged but it formed a sharper point of division than had been envisaged by those who started the movement. This was due mainly to the poor work done by GPs before 1948 in the field of surgery. In Britain, the GP in hospital came to be regarded as a menace — whereas, in America, the opposite attitude prevailed. During the 1960s, a chance arose to bring GPs into hospital in order to avoid periodic manpower problems but consultants, backed by the Ministry, opposed it. They preferred to keep GPs in the community where MOHs needed their aid to deal with the aged, the chronic sick and the mentally ill. A new corps of GPs arose dedicated to this view and their feeling was shared by the medical refugees who were used to staff the Health Service. German experience had shown how important it was to preserve the humanity of medicine and, in this task, GPs had a vital role to play. The separation of the profession was thus the result of many factors but the doctors failed to use the opportunity presented by the Health Service to make a fresh start. GPs as well as consultants must share responsibility for the division in the medical world that exists today.

'. . . Believe me, there is no one in the world who can build up Chinese walls around themselves better than the members of the medical profession, unless administrators take a hand.'

— from the remarks made by Aneurin Bevan at the opening of the new health centre at Harold Hill near Romford in Essex, 15 October 1954, as reported in the *British Medical Journal,* 1954, 2, Supp., p. 152.

'The plain fact is — it repels and fascinates the older doctor — that a hostility exists between two sections of the profession. The conception of the "colleague" . . . is dying, if it is not already dead.

'This is a tragedy for the profession; it is a tragedy for the public; it is a tragedy for the National Health Service. . .'

— from an article on a conference held between GPs and hospital doctors in 1971 written by the medical journalist (and brother-in-law of the late Hugh Gaitskell), Dr Hertzel Creditor, in *Pulse,* 20 November 1971, p. 6.

29

Consultants Reject GPs

In creating the structure for the administration of the Health Service, Bevan unwittingly set the stage for the further division of British medicine. The profession as a whole wanted freedom from municipal control but, instead of putting GPs under regional hospital boards as BMA leaders wanted him to, Bevan gave GPs their own executive councils.[1] The Health Service was thus split 3 ways instead of 2.

GPs separated from hospital administration

On this issue, the profession had mixed views. Both the Council and Annual Representative Meeting of the BMA voted for regional administration of general practice so as not to divide it from the hospital world,[2] while the Annual Conference of Local Medical Committees opted for local administration in order to give GPs the same protection they had under NHI.[3] Here we see the difference between those GPs who still had a foot in the hospital world and those who did not. The former tended to dictate the decisions taken by the BMA's older policy-making bodies, while the latter — mainly panel doctors from industrial areas — controlled the choices made by local medical committees.[a]

The reasons for Bevan's decision have not been revealed, but it seems likely that he separated GPs from hospital administration for bargaining purposes: he wanted to avoid making concessions to one branch of the profession which he had to offer to the other. Thus, while he had to ban salary from general practice, he did not have to do so from the hospital world: fixed incomes were needed to correct the uneven distribution of specialists since they would not move from London to Cornwall unless they could be sure of their income.[4]

Similarly, while GPs expected the same right of direct representation as they had under NHI, consultants (outside the teaching hospitals)[b] did not: all they wanted was freedom from municipal control.[5] In return for the right to

---

a   After 1948, the difference between these groups disappeared. Once all (or nearly all) GPs were removed from the hospital world, they tended to favour the view formerly held by panel doctors. This became evident when the Health Service was reorganized in 1974. Only the hospital and municipal sectors gave way to the new area health authorities; GPs insisted on their own family practitioner committees.

b   For the direct representation given to consultants in teaching hospitals, see p. 289 above.

treat private patients in Health Service hospitals, consultants accepted the terms of service Bevan offered. Unlike GPs, they had little choice: without access to beds, they could not survive and, once all (or nearly all) voluntary hospitals passed under state control, they had to enter the Health Service to stay in specialist practice.[6]

Bevan thus had good reason to break with the hospital plans his predecessors had made and, in so doing, he secured far more unity in hospital administration. But unification there came at the cost of compartmentalization elsewhere: hospital authorities were not responsible for general practice and, almost without realizing it, made decisions detrimental to its welfare. The joint boards conceived earlier could not have acted in this way: since they covered the whole of medical care, they could not have reorganized the hospital world without taking account of the effects on general practice.[7]

Bevan soon became disturbed by the damage he had done and tried to repair it. At the start of negotiations on the Health Service, he was anxious to establish a clearer distinction between consultants and GPs.[8] The profession had too many pseudo-specialists in its ranks and the surest way to eliminate them was to deny access to beds. Bevan, therefore, wanted *all* consultants to work in hospital, even those (like psychiatrists, paediatricians and geriatricians) who might have been better based in the community.[9] This may also partly explain why he was willing to let them treat private patients there.[10] But Bevan never intended to put the doctors in separate clinical departments and, even before the Health Service began, he pointed out the means by which they could work together. Health centres, at first, were to supply the medium[11] and, after that possibility faded, Bevan tried to make room for GPs in the hospital world.[12]

A lost opportunity

Those in charge of hospital policy, however, failed to respond to the challenge. With the start of the Health Service, they had a magnificent opportunity to undo the damage which decades of separatism had done. With only 13,100 hospital doctors on hand (as opposed to 18,615 GPs),[a] British hospitals were severely short-staffed.[14] Instead of using GPs to overcome the deficiency, consultants developed 'firms' of their own. They did whatever they could to close down the smaller, cottage hospitals open to GPs,[15] and they also made it difficult for con-scientious GPs to visit patients who had been admitted to hospital wards. The old, friendly relations that used to exist between some consultants and some GPs turned distant and cold. In their place, what has been called 'an antiseptic barrier' arose between the two branches of the profession.[16]

Why did this happen? Financial considerations were clearly a primary factor. As two angry GPs put it in 1949: 'Now that the consultant is being paid largely by the State, the GP as a source of private work has fallen in

---

a   These figures apply only to England and Wales; comparable data for Scotland is not available. By the late 1960s the proportions were reversed and, since then, the totals for hospital doctors have exceeded those for GPs by an increasing number each year. By 1974 (and these figures now apply to Great Britain as a whole), there were 31,473 hospital doctors and only 25,849 GPs.[13]

importance.'[17] The Health Service, in this way, produced a revolution in consultant attitudes.

But there was more to it than money: consultants also had pride in their work and they wanted to create conditions in hospital where the highest standards would be upheld. GPs who refused to accept selection for midwifery were not likely to possess the critical faculties needed. Nor would they be ready to accept direction from specialists who knew more about a subject than they did. For many consultants, Bevan's failure to hold the line on obstetrics was the last straw;[a] if GPs were not willing to uphold standards there, they were unlikely to do so elsewhere.

Obstetricians reacted even more strongly — they could not forgive GPs for the damage they had done to their specialty. Ever since 1936, when midwives were brought into municipal employ, the obstetricians had managed to develop a unified service — but that, they believed, was destroyed both by the intrusion of GPs and the tripartite division of the Health Service.[18] Had GPs been willing to accept minimal standards, their presence might have been tolerated but even the conditions they had rejected (for qualification as a 'general practitioner obstetrician') were not felt to be sufficient. The President of the Royal College of Obstetricians and Gynae-cologists (Sir Eardley Holland) had dismissed them as 'an absolute sham' and 'a misuse of the word "obstetrician" '.[19]

The many demands on GP time provided another reason for consultants to exclude them. Doctors who had to keep themselves on call in the community would find it hard to accept the rigours of hospital routine. Their failings in this respect had been all too evident in the operation of municipal clinics.[b] Consultants, therefore, had little difficulty persuading hospital authorities to ignore the circulars Bevan issued. Few GPs found a place in the new order established by consultants.

The realization of a referral system

In this almost accidental way, the Health Service completed a process which had long been the goal of those concerned with the ethics of British medicine —the development of a viable referral system. Here, the pioneering work had been done by a BMA leader we have encountered before — Dr Lauriston Shaw, a prominent physician and former Dean of Guy's Hospital Medical School.[c] As far back as 1918, Shaw had said:

> '. . . The essential classification of medical attendants in order to
> secure efficient division of labour must be a primary division into
> *general practitioners and specialists.* But to be effective such division
> must be complete. It will not be altogether popular with either section of
> the profession, nor, perhaps, in the first instance, with the public. But in
> the national interest it must be secured. Without it, confusion,
> overlapping, and inefficiency are inevitable.

a   See p. 177 above.

b   See p. 139 above.

c   See p. 55 above.

'The role and ambition of the general practitioner should be to know
something of everything, the role and ambition of the specialist to
know everything about something. Each must recognise the advantages
and limitations of his position. The work of each is of vital necessity to
the community. Neither must encroach upon the other's province. The
general practitioner only must undertake independent practice. The
specialist must frankly accept the position of consultant to the general
practitioner.'[20]

For Shaw, these were not mere words. From the turn of the century, he
had worked for the establishment of a viable referral system as Chairman of
the BMA's Central Ethical Committee.[21] The idea of dividing the profession
grew out of that experience and no one knew better how closely the ethical
and economic factors were entwined. As Shaw put it in 1910: 'Just as a
dishonest consultant steals a patient, so a dishonest general practitioner
keeps a patient to himself long after he has discovered that he cannot without
further advice on diagnosis or treatment do the best possible for such a
patient.'[22]

As long as most doctors felt compelled for financial reasons to practise the
whole of medicine, there was no hope of persuading them to restrict their
work to a part. Only by giving them a sufficient number of patients could
they afford to confine themselves to one branch or the other. The 1911 Act,
by enabling a large number of doctors to practise solely as GPs, offered just
such an opportunity and that was why Shaw risked his medical-political life
to support it.[23] In the process, he suffered much abuse[24] and lost his place in
the BMA but Shaw never withdrew his endorsement of the panel system. On
the contrary, he favoured its extension in order to establish a more pervasive
distinction between specialists and GPs. Like Brackenbury,[25] Shaw wanted
everyone to have a family doctor — although the reasons in his mind sprung
more from ethical than social considerations. At that point, the separation of
the profession would be complete and the work for which he had sacrificed
so much would be done.

Shaw did not live to see his dream fulfilled. He died in 1923, but the
movement he had started went on. Between the wars it gathered momentum
as a result of the clashes that erupted within the profession. The battle was
first waged over surgery but spread to other specialties in the 1930s partly
as a result of the problems caused by the medical refugees fleeing from the
Nazis.[a] In Germany and Austria, the profession had not been divided as it
partly was in Britain. NHI began there much earlier — in 1883 instead of
1911 — but the doctors were paid by item for service rather than capitation.
This forced most of them to practise both as GPs and specialists.[26] As one
writer has recently observed: 'The item for service system provides incentive
for the GP to specialise rather than refer, and GPs build up their reputation
on their particular minispecialty.'[27]

The German doctors who came to Britain in the 1930s found it difficult to
alter the methods they had followed and the referral system — which, in any
case, had never functioned as Shaw intended — broke down (particularly in

a   See pp. 141 and 276-7 above.

London). The doctors who suffered most were consultants rather than GPs. As long as GPs could count on 'guaranteed' capitation fees, they did not have to worry unduly about patients lost to refugee 'specialists'.[a] But consultants did not have this protection and that was why, when the Health Service began, they were so intent on splitting the profession into separate compartments. As one leading surgeon (Mr Arthur Dickson Wright) put it in 1944: 'In contract practice in Germany patients had nothing to do with general practitioners: they went straight to consultants, and in Berlin a group of specialists grew up outnumbering the general practitioners by 4,000 to 3,000. Not only must the doctor-patient relationship be preserved but also the general practitioner-consultant relationship.'[28]

Neither Wright[29] nor Shaw, however, wanted to exclude GPs from the hospital world. Shaw, as the Dean of Guy's Hospital Medical School, had an educational reason for wanting them in: the hospital was the centre of medical advance and only through continuous contact with it could GPs be kept abreast of the latest developments. But their participation, he argued, was needed for another reason — to secure continuity of care. Even the slightest variation in home conditions or financial circumstances could necessitate hospitalization and, if GPs did not have access to beds, then capricious variations in treatment might occur.[30]

Shaw, therefore, never envisaged the kind of division that developed under the Health Service. On the contrary, he had before him the vision of a united profession and the hospital, he believed, was the institution in which it would be realized. This goal was set clearly before his colleagues in a paper he published in 1910: 'A united profession might well be expected to secure that hospitals should be a bond of union instead of a bone of contention amongst its members, and that the experience gained within their walls should be the privilege of the many rather than the prerogative of the few.'[31]

Shaw's opposition to a salaried service[b] was largely dictated by the same concern: he feared that it would divide the profession, too — this time, between doctors for the rich and doctors for the poor.[32] He did not see how the nation could — or should — construct a salaried service that would cover everyone. The BMA leaders who followed him took the same position and that was why their 'radicalism', when it appeared, extended only to the principle of universal coverage: they considered it more important to provide a family doctor for everyone than to change the way in which GPs were paid.

Far from being a 'separatist', then, Shaw longed for the day when all doctors would work together; yet, under the Health Service, the referral system for which he laboured so long came to serve a purpose exactly opposite to the one he intended. Here, indeed, is one of the great ironies of British medical history.

GP-surgeon causes concern

The responsibility for this development did not rest with the specialists from

---

a   This did not, however, make them any more generous where the question of admitting refugees to Britain was concerned; the panel covered too few patients for that. See p. 276 above.

b   See p. 55 above.

whose ranks Shaw emerged — the physicians. It lay, rather, with the surgeons. Yet the leaders of the Royal College of Surgeons had to move warily on the subject because so many of its Members and Fellows practised part-time as GPs. The tension that arose over the issue appeared clearly at a meeting of the Fellows held in May 1944 to consider the White Paper on the National Health Service. The GP-surgeons present expressed concern about the threat posed to the smaller hospitals in which they worked; many, they feared, would 'degenerate' into convalescent homes without surgical patients. To calm them the President of the College — Sir Alfred (later Lord) Webb-Johnson — had to give assurance of support but he was careful to confine it only to those hospitals that were 'doing good work'.[33] The others, he implied, would lose their operating theatres — as, indeed, many did.

As this exchange suggests, it was surgery above all that attracted GPs to cottage hospitals. Before the war, it was estimated, GPs performed as many as $2\frac{1}{2}$ million operations per year.[34] For the GP corps as a whole (about 18,000 doctors), this represented an average of 2 or 3 a week but, if the computation is continued to those with access to beds (about 3,000 to 4,000 doctors), then the average is much higher — about 14 operations a week or almost 3 a day.[a]

Not only did the mechanics of surgery fascinate GPs but they thought they had to undertake it to maintain status with the public. Dr Joseph Collings (an Australian doctor who conducted an extensive study of general practice in 1949) claimed that he 'actually met doctors who believe that they must do a certain amount of major surgery or lose the respect or "faith" of their patients'.[36] Even the efficiency of cottage hospitals tended to be gauged by the number of operations they performed. The reason for this attitude, according to the leader of the cottage-hospital bloc (Dr Charles Flemming), was 'natural because the results of surgery are generally more immediately manifest, more dramatic, than are those of medical treatment'.[37]

Had the operations been competently performed, then the surgeons could have had no cause for complaint but, as one leading MOH (Dr R. H. Parry of Bristol) observed, they were not. In 1946 he claimed that 'more people are killed than cured' in cottage hospitals[38] — a charge which, though no doubt exaggerated, showed how strong feeling in the medical world against the GP-surgeon had become. Nearly every impartial study of the hospital service before 1948 came to the conclusion that cottage hospitals should go.[39]

Contrast between America and Britain

Thus, when the question of using GPs in hospitals arose, consultants could think only of the GP-surgeon; any other role was forgotten. The GP in hospital came to be regarded as a menace in Britain — whereas, in America, the opposite attitude prevailed. There, he was seen as a safe doctor because he was

---

a   These are only rough figures and they no doubt include many minor operations (such as the removal of sebaceous cysts) since GPs did not have enough beds for anything more ambitious. Across the country as a whole, there were only about 3 beds per doctor working in cottage hospitals. (The total number of beds in cottage hospitals amounted to about 10,000.)[35]

subject to the restraints and stimuli of the hospital world.[40] Before GPs were admitted to American hospitals, however, they were subject to a network of controls which one British doctor said had 'to be experienced to be believed'.[41] American specialists, as a result, lost some of their own 'freedom' because they had to subject themselves to the same restraints. Yet this, they felt, was a small price to pay in order to raise the quality of GP care and give the profession the protection it needed against the competition of unqualified practitioners.

British doctors, on the other hand, found their security in a state service confined to registered men. The main purpose of the Health Service, Bevan proclaimed in 1946, was to provide free care for everyone — but he also wanted to make the service so good 'that nobody would want to buy anybody else'.[42] To do that, GP aid was essential since they, alone, handled 90% of the complaints patients presented. But quality considerations, in the end, did not apply to them: only consultants received merit awards; GPs were paid mainly on the basis of the amount of work done. In that way, hospital practice was left 'free': British consultants did not have to make the same sacrifices as American specialists. It was easier simply to exclude GPs.

The arrangement, nevertheless, preserved the nation's huge corps of GPs: they did not disappear like those in America.[43] Specialists there had to join forces to replace them[44] — which explains why group practice in America took such a different form. In both countries, group practice was originally designed to meet a shortage of specialists, especially in rural areas — but the movement in America was undermined by the growth of community hospitals between the wars.[45] Hospital entry became a substitute for group practice[a] and many GPs passed completely into the specialist category. At that point (the 1940s), groups of the opposite form arose — specialists who joined together to make up for the deficiency of GPs, particularly in the larger cities.[46] That is why group practice in America is now largely an urban phenomenon whereas the earlier movement (as in Britain) drew its strength from rural areas.

Even before the war, however, groups in Britain did not specialize as they did in America: the panel system, together with the shortage of hospital facilities, forced the members of most groups to function mainly as GPs. After 1948, this tendency became more pronounced as a result of the divisions created by the Health Service. Group practice and partnerships spread widely in Britain during the 1950s and 1960s, but they developed for different reasons than before and the GPs who formed them made hardly any attempt to specialize.

However, it would be wrong to exaggerate the effect in Britain of the exclusion of GPs from the hospital world. It did restrain the growth of specialist tendencies among GPs, but the main reason lay elsewhere: panel doctors in Britain did not have to become specialists as American GPs did because, from 1911 on, they could be sure of sufficient earnings from general practice. The nation managed to preserve its GP corps not because GPs were excluded from the hospital world but because they received enough aid from the state to enable them to avoid specialization.[47]

State intervention, in fact, made possible the best of both worlds because,

a See pp. 110-111 above.

with the creation of the Health Service, the kind of co-operation Dawson (and Shaw) envisaged at last was at hand.[48] GPs, after 1948, no longer had to fear competition from consultants; their capitation fees were paid no matter how many patients they referred. Nor, after the prospect of additional income was withdrawn,[a] did surgery any longer interest them. After 1948, it was the specialty of medicine that attracted them since that was the field where the most dramatic developments took place.[51]

A community role for GPs

By the 1950s, then, the conditions which had forced GPs to withdraw from the hospital world no longer applied. Was it time to bring them back? Every departmental committee that considered the subject said yes. Not only would it aid GPs[52] but it might also help the hospitals to solve their manpower problem.[53] First, during the 1950s, they found themselves with too many registrars; then, during the 1960s, with too few.[54] This fluctuation was due to the very 'firm' concept which the hospital world prized. Every consultant, until retirement at 65, trained between 5 and 6 registrars, and the only way all could expect promotion was through the expansion of the hospital service. Not until the 1960s, however, did sufficient openings arise. The only way the hospitals could hope to avoid a repetition of this problem was to hire doctors without consultant ambitions — and ones, preferably, who could be used elsewhere in the Health Service should the need arise.[55]

GPs were ideal for the task but still consultants baulked, mainly through fear of the damage they would do to the 'firms' which had greatly raised the quality of hospital care. GPs would have been tolerated only in wards of their own and, even there, the experience that midwifery offered deterred many consultants. Many GPs had been drawn to this work after the Health Service began[b] but, with the trend moving strongly towards hospital confinements, they needed beds to practise it. The result, according to one doctor in 1961, was that the maternity services had become 'primarily a battleground for GPs and consultant obstetricians in their struggle for power, and the safety of mother and child is of secondary importance'.[56] No one in the hospital world wanted to see the 'battle of the beds' extend beyond obstetrics.

Few consultants had the courage to reject GPs on these grounds. It was more diplomatic to raise the old prevention-treatment dichotomy argument which the physicians had tried before.[c] In hospital, consultants argued, GPs had little to offer but who else could co-ordinate the care given in the community? Without GPs to guide them, patients would drift from specialist to specialist as they did in America and many, in time, would end up in the hands of

---

a   Under the Health Service, extra fees are allowed only for midwifery, not surgery. Special payments are also made for cottage hospital work but the amounts are low and these cover general duties, not surgery specifically.[49] In America, on the other hand, surgery pays handsomely — much more per hour than general practice — and that is why so many doctors there do it.[50].

b   See p. 177 above.

c   See pp. 186-8 above.

unqualified practitioners.[57] GP attention was needed to keep orthodox medicine humane. As the Chief Medical Officer of the Ministry (then Sir George Godber) put it in 1961: 'The general practitioner is the patient's main insurance against the effects of over-specialisation.'[58]

All this applied with particular force to the chronic sick. Their care, according to the hospital surveys made during the war, 'requires complete and revolutionary change'.[59] Only a few of the chronic sick could afford hospital treatment — which meant that the vast majority, when they needed bed care, had to obtain it through the Poor Law hospitals. But, although these hospitals had passed under municipal control in 1929, bed provision for the chronic sick remained as sparse as before. Local authorities, for the most part, chose to concentrate their resources on the acutely ill; only in that way could municipal hospitals hope to attain the reputation won by their rivals in the voluntary sector. The consultants who worked in the latter never had time for the chronic sick: such cases, they claimed, lacked 'interest' and could not, where medical students were involved, be used for teaching purposes. Bed provision for the chronic sick, then, tended to be found in the old Poor Law hospitals and workhouses which had not been upgraded by local authorities.

It was hoped that this would change once the Health Service came into being. No one would then have to worry about charges (or means tests) for hospital care and more beds, after the voluntary hospitals were taken over, would be available. But, instead of conditions improving after 1948, they worsened.[60] The distaste for the chronic sick which so bedevilled the voluntary sector spread over the hospital world as a whole. Consultants who worked in upgraded Poor Law hospitals acted no differently than their colleagues elsewhere: all preferred 'interesting cases' and those, in their minds, meant the acutely ill.

The patients who had always suffered the most from this attitude were the aged, and their position, in some respect, even deteriorated after 1948. Under the old Poor Law (as well as the 1929 Local Government Act), they at least had the right to a bed if they could pass the means test imposed. No similar entitlement existed under the Health Service.[61] Patients gained entry to hospital beds only if consultants accepted them, and few consultants, where the aged were concerned, felt so inclined. By 1953, the plight of the old had become serious and some concerned with their care proposed to appoint special officials to help them. Nor was that all: to make sure that sufficient beds were available, they called for the construction of temporary, pre-fabricated buildings. To his credit, however, the Minister of Health (then Iain Macleod) refused to entertain the idea: 'Short-term solutions might remain longer than was intended, and it would be the final irony of the Welfare State if all they could find to solve this immensely difficult problem was to bring back the relieving officer and rebuild, in whatever form, the workhouse.'[62]

Macleod decided, instead, to study the subject in detail and, when the investigation was completed in 1957, the department found that beds alone would not solve the problems posed by the elderly and chronic sick. In fact, its report suggested, additional provision might only generate 'stagnation and apathy'.[63] The solution in its view lay in the extension of community care, and there GPs had a key role to play.

For consultants plagued with GP demands for maternity beds, the report could not have been better timed. Had they not been saying for years that the place of GPs lay in the community? Bevan had tended to support their view but the decisions he made had been more the result of tactics than design. Now, however, consultants had Ministry officials on their side: the separation of the profession became the future aim of department policy. During the planning that was done in the 1960s, one assumption above all predominated: consultants should stay in hospital; GPs in the community.[64 a]

The new alliance between MOHs and GPs

In time, there arose a new network of interests firmly committed to this view. At its heart lay the medical directors of the old public-health world: with their hospital empires gone, MOHs had no outlet but in community medicine. After 1948 their attitude towards GPs underwent a revolutionary change: whereas before they had done all they could to keep GPs out of public-health work, now they did all they could to bring them in. What prompted this change was the new pattern of maternity care that emerged under the Health Service. Not only were institutional confinements removed from municipal purview but an alternative system of ante-natal clinics arose under hospital direction. Women could now go directly from GP to obstetrician once pregnancy began; they no longer had to pass through their gestation period under the care of public-health doctors. If municipal clinics were to survive, MOHs soon realized, they would have to make peace with GPs.

Their new attitude emerged clearly before a departmental committee created in 1956 to investigate maternity services. Not only did MOHs seek more beds for GPs, but they demanded more home confinements. They also opposed any attempt at unification under hospital control; if the maternity services could not be combined under municipal direction, MOHs preferred a divided administration.[66] All of this contrasted sharply with the position they had taken before 1948.

Thus did a new era of 'peaceful co-existence' begin.[67] GPs soon forgot the battles of the past and some even felt sympathy for doctors who, like themselves, had been transformed into 'the poor relation of the consultant'.[68] The way for a wider partnership was open but, with hospital confinements becoming more and more the usual thing, it needed a field with greater scope than midwifery. The means were found in social medicine, particularly as applied to the aged and mentally ill. Our Society, MOHs proclaimed, is really a College of Social and Preventive Medicine; if general practice is to win the status it deserves, GPs will have to join with MOHs rather than consultants. 'At last', went one hopeful prediction by MOHs in 1959,

a	This did not apply in Scotland. There, under the lead of a different Chief Medical Officer (Sir John Brotherston), the department strove to integrate the profession, particularly at Livingstone where a bold attempt was made to bring GPs into the hospital world.[65] Brotherston, however, retired in 1977 with the results of the experiment still uncertain.

'general practice is coming to be seen as a discipline in itself, as important as the specialist disciplines which have for so long arrogated to themselves the right to define the shape of Medicine.'[69]

In the face of such flattery, GPs found the social medicine appeal hard to resist — particularly in view of the role MOHs had fashioned for them. GPs, in their community work, were to be at the head of wide-ranging teams embracing district nurses, midwives, health visitors and social workers — all of whom would be ready to relieve them of the more menial tasks required. In hospital, on the other hand, they could never hope to be more than junior members of closely-confined specialist firms, called upon to discharge duties that their senior colleagues deplored and liable to instant criticism for any weaknesses displayed. It did not take long for many GPs to decide which role they preferred: as one of them (Dr J. S. Norell) put it in 1965, 'he would rather be recognised as the most versatile of medical-social workers than the least of medical men'.[70] In short, most GPs preferred to be seen as 'senior social workers' rather than 'junior consultants'.

No GPs came down more strongly on the side of social work than those who had developed an interest in psychology. Their numbers had grown steadily since 1948. When the College of GPs was formed in 1952, it tended to attract doctors from rural areas with access to beds.[71] They were able to practise medicine at its fullest and, consequently, the standards they set tended to be wider and higher than those elsewhere. It was thought that the best GPs came from the country; in large cities like London, standards were lower.

All this changed as the Health Service developed. With the decline of surgical work in cottage hospitals, the ranks of the old GP-specialists thinned and their place in the Royal College (as it was called after 1967) was taken by others — mainly those with access to maternity beds but partly by GPs who had completed the 2-year course in practical psychiatry offered by Dr Michael Balint at the Tavistock Clinic.[72] Though less than 1% of GPs had undergone this training by 1974,[73] they exerted an influence far out of proportion to their numbers. Some — like Dr J. S. Norell — held leading positions in the College and the stand they took was supported by others who were anxious to establish general practice as an independent specialty.[a]

Psychiatry had always lacked status in British medicine because of the stress its leaders put on physical ailments but that did not deter GPs since the specialty was one that could be practised with ease. Not only were no hospital or other costly facilities required but psychiatrists welcomed their aid.[75] Mental hospitals were overloaded with patients and, with the aid of GPs, many could be returned to the community.

Unlike midwifery then, psychiatry offered the chance to form close links with consultants and its status rose rapidly in Royal College circles. The 'best' GPs now strove to distinguish adolescent instability from developing schizophrenia[76] — whereas their predecessors from the cottage-hospital

---

a   The influence of the National Association for Mental Health should also be noted. Starting in 1958, it held 2 weekend courses a year and many GPs, through that experience, developed a strong interest in the subject.[74]

world had been satisfied with the detection and removal of an incipient cancer. Psychology replaced surgery as the mark of distinction in general practice and it was GPs with an interest in this specialty who responded most swiftly to the role MOHs offered.

Refugee aid to British medicine

Only one other group in the medical world shared their intensity of feeling. These were the doctors from all disciplines who had fled to Britain before the war to escape Nazi oppression. To understand why they felt so strongly on the subject, we must first go back to 1946 and see how they became involved in the Health Service.

By the end of the war, some 3,000 medical refugees had entered the country and, under the terms of a temporary register established in 1940, they were allowed to practise until the end of 1947.[77] After that, their future was uncertain but, as soon as the war ended, the organizations which spoke for refugees as a whole (lay as well as medical) made it clear that their followers did not want to return home.[78] At that point, anti-semitic feeling made itself felt once more, and a series of demonstrations was held demanding their expulsion.[79] Bayly and his group in the MPU were quick to join the attack[80] and this time the lead was taken by Dr James Burnet, a medical teacher from Edinburgh who, despite strong anti-vivisectionist sympathies, had managed to win considerable prominence in the profession. Though *Medical World* itself took care to denounce the Nazi atrocities,[81] it did not hesitate to print letters from Burnet and others displaying the old anti-semitic allusions.[82] Thus, one of Burnet's most outspoken allies (Dr R. E. Illingworth) went so far as to say:

'. . . It is time that we in this country realised that, so far as British medicine is concerned, a position is arising in this country analogous to that which existed in Germany in 1930. One loathes Hitler and all he stood for, but there can be no doubt that there was in Germany a question which demanded a drastic solution.'[83]

This time, however, such tactics did not work. The horrors of the concentration camps were being exposed daily in the press and British doctors reacted strongly against the anti-refugee campaign. One woman doctor spoke for many when she said: 'I am 100 per cent English, 100 per cent Gentile, and yet my soul sickens when I read these letters.'[84]

Burnet's campaign marked the last gasp of anti-semitism within the MPU. Welply, who retired from office in 1948, found the ideal candidate to replace him, Dr Bruce Cardew. Cardew was not only a socialist but, even more important, he was the grandson of a prominent anti-vivisectionist (Sir Frederick Cardew) who, like Bayly himself, had spoken out strongly against the research provisions in the 1911 NHI Bill.[85] With such credentials, Cardew was bound to be approved by Bayly — and no sooner was he appointed than Cardew began a long campaign to sterilize the MPU of its anti-semitic and anti-science tendencies. In this task, Cardew received much aid from a medical member of the Communist Party, Dr Hugh Faulkner. Though the two split in 1964 for reasons which are still not clear, they did not do so until after Bayly had gone.[86] He died in 1961 after having spent a decade trying to live down his past and, from that day to this, no sign of anti-semitism has reappeared in the organization.[87]

All of this, however, was far in the future. Bevan, in 1946, had to contend with the reality of Burnet's tactics but he was rescued from the difficulty by the healthy reaction of MPU members, and that gave him the freedom he needed to use refugee doctors. Without them, Bevan might not have been able to start the Health Service. The hospitals had great need of their aid since many (if not most) of the refugees were specialists. Because of the shortages inherited from the past, the country had to double its consultant personnel.[88] As the *Manchester Guardian* put it in 1947: 'The case for giving them [alien doctors] a permanent status, strong as it is on ethical and humanitarian grounds, becomes incontestable when considered in the light of our present and prospective shortage of men qualified to staff the specialist branch of a national health service.'[89]

The refugees were given permanent status[90] and all became British subjects, rendering invaluable aid to the nation. But they never forgot the lessons they learned on the Continent. German medicine, because of its specialist orientation, was harsh in the extreme. As Dr George Adami (then vice-chancellor of the University of Liverpool) observed in 1920:

'. . . Here [in Britain] the human being is the first consideration, in Germany and Austria hospital patients might altogether too often be so many animals. Heedless of modesty and natural emotion, man, woman, maiden and child are ordered to expose this part or that to the crowd of students, are subjected to this or that test. They might be a herd of cattle or a company of Prussian privates.'[91]

From this, it is tempting to think that only GPs in Germany commanded the respect of the public. Yet even they must have lost favour in the 1920s as financial difficulties drove them into the specialist sphere. An orgy of operations and abortions ensued which no nation had witnessed before;[92] indeed, only America today — where 30% of the profession perform surgery to some degree[93] — has surpassed it. To the doctors of Germany, it was the acute case that mattered, and the more they could do to the patient the better it was for them financially.

In the process, the conscience of the profession weakened and German doctors sank swiftly from one moral plane to another. By 1940, they were even ready to accept the 'final solution' Hitler ordered. As Dr Leo Alexandre observed in his study of medicine under the Nazis: 'From the attitude of easing patients with chronic diseases away from the doors of the best types of treatment facilities available, to the actual dispatching of such patients to killing centres is a long but nevertheless logical step.'[94]

If medicine in Britain was not to go the same way, general practice had to be preserved. Nothing in the nation gave the individual a greater sense of security than the realization that he could, in time of need, turn to his family doctor. The stability of society — as well as the reputation of orthodox medicine — depended on the GP's presence in the community. That was the message the refugees and their consultant colleagues delivered to GPs in order to justify their exclusion from the hospital world. As one leading physician (Dr W. McAdam Eccles) put it as far back as 1918:

> '... Thirty three years of practice had convinced him that they were not going to have the best if they forfeited the human touch as between doctor and patient. That had been one of the greatest assets of the British medical profession. They had admired the organisation and teaching in connexion with medical work in Germany, but it was disappointing to find in that great country the lack of human touch.'[95]

30
A Shared Responsibility

The rejection by consultants of a hospital role for GPs set the stage for the further separation of the profession that occurred under the Health Service. As the years passed, more and more GPs came to like the role which not only consultants but they themselves had fashioned, preferring to spend the whole of their day in the community rather than a part of it in hospital. The health centres that eventually did emerge were not of the type Dawson envisaged. They did not contain beds and few made provision for consultant out-patient sessions. Most of the centres contained only GPs and local authority clinics. Instead of providing a means of unifying the profession, the health centres established after 1948 tended to divide it further. GPs, today, are more isolated from hospital than ever before.

A review

The process, as covered by this study, began with the development of club practice. That tended to confine GPs to a narrow sphere and made it difficult for them to obtain hospital appointments. At the same time, it enabled GPs to obtain the assurance of some income from general practice, thereby lessening their need to attempt specialist procedures. The lesson was not lost on consultants who came to see the extension of club practice as a way of preserving their privileged place in the hospital world.

The NHI Act provided the means through which that extension came. Lloyd George, in 1911, did his best to free GPs from the financial bonds which the friendly societies had placed on them but he did nothing to widen the care they gave. Under the panel system, GPs were able to prescribe drugs more freely but they had no more clinical facilities than before. Dawson, in 1920, tried to provide the necessary equipment in a way that would ensure the safety of the public. He offered GPs hospital-type health centres but, by placing consultants alongside them, he hoped to prevent them from attempting specialist services beyond their competence.

Neither the profession nor the authorities, however, were ready for the radical solution Dawson proposed. GPs did not want to work with consultants and, for ideological as well as financial reasons, the policy-makers at the Ministry of Health did not want to build Dawson's kind of health centre. They preferred to extend GP interest in the direction of community medicine and that, for them, meant that the benefits of the panel system should first be extended to the people who had been excluded in 1911 — the wives and children of insured persons.

The depression beginning in 1921, however, ruled out that possibility — while other, more modest, extensions of the panel system had to be excluded for other reasons. GPs who wanted to widen the care they gave thus had an incentive to do so only for their private patients. To supply it, furthermore, they had to gain entry to hospital or install the necessary equipment in their surgeries.

Hospital development had proceeded rapidly by the end of the nineteenth century and some GPs had found a place not only in the small cottage hospitals that arose but also, due to the shortage of consultants, in the larger voluntary hospitals built in provincial towns. The nation, nevertheless, did not have a sufficient number of beds to satisfy GP needs and this led, during the 1920s and 1930s, to a restoration of the same kind of tension within the profession as had existed before the panel system began. Now, however, the conflict was attenuated by the greater financial security NHI offered over club practice.

Between the wars, GPs made repeated attempts to enter the hospital world but they were defeated by the opposition not only of consultants but also of MOHs who wanted to raise the standards of the new municipal hospitals falling under their control. In the end, most GPs gave up the attempt and reconciled themselves to the narrow range of care provided under the panel system. When the debate on the Health Service began, their concern was centred on the competition presented by municipal clinics rather than on the need to gain entry to the hospital world.

The question of hospital privileges for GPs hardly arose during the negotiations and Bevan ended up making the same kind of changes in general practice in 1948 that Lloyd George had made in 1911. He improved the financial position of GPs, but he did not give them the facilities they needed to widen the range of care. Once again, the means of doing that were left to the hospitals but consultants made sure GPs were barred. After 1948, the separation of the profession became virtually complete.

Reasons for GPs' indifference to hospital access

In reviewing this development, we can see that state intervention had the effect of widening only the kind of people GPs served, not the range of services they gave. GPs, today, can refer patients more easily to hospital, but they have no more right to work there than club doctors did in the nineteenth century. None of this, however, need necessarily have happened if GPs had been more insistent about hospital entry when the debate on the Health Service began. How can that indifference be explained?

Part of the answer lies in the demands of the war and the debate about health centres. GPs were in short supply and not many had time to think about medical planning. Those that did had their attention absorbed by the threat of a salaried service in health centres. This both repelled and attracted them. On the one hand, they did not want to fall under municipal control — but on the other, they did want access to the diagnostic facilities which health centres seemed to offer. The need, as they saw it, was to separate health centres from municipal control. If that could be accomplished, hospital access would be almost superfluous.

That, however, still leaves unexplained the fact that, even before the war, GP interest in the hospital world had faded. For this, no doubt, the growing specialization of medicine was partly responsible. That made it increasingly difficult for GPs to keep abreast of new techniques and intensified their reluctance to expose themselves to consultant review. Life was easier and more comfortable in their surgeries. By the 1940s, many GPs were content to confine themselves to general practice in the community.

Yet American GPs faced the same advances in medical science and that did not deter them from seeking access to hospital. On the contrary, as specialization increased, so did their desire for beds. Other factors, therefore, must have been at work in Britain and the most important stemmed from the panel system. One the one hand, it tended to demoralize GPs because it did not give them the opportunity or incentive to develop skills; on the other, it tended to promote a feeling of security among panel doctors because they could count on some income from NHI. Both influences undermined the desire of GPs to enter the hospital world — the first, by intensifying their inferiority complex; the second, by weakening their economic incentive.

American doctors were subject to different pressures. They were totally dependent on private practice and knew that they would lose patients to specialists if they did not gain access to hospital. No referral system existed there; patients in America were as free to consult specialists as GPs. This gave GPs an incentive to extend their range of care as wide as possible and, with that, came increasing self-confidence. The process was not without its danger to the public; many GPs provided services which they were not competent to offer. But the fact remains that American GPs did not display the same reluctance to enter the hospital world as their colleagues in Britain.

Added to this was the financial penalty that went with hospital practice in Britain. In most of the larger voluntary hospitals, medical work was either poorly paid or not paid at all and, whenever GP-specialists insisted on payment, they found themselves losing patients to consultants. Only in the smaller cottage hospitals were payments both adequate and secure — yet not enough of such hospitals existed to accommodate more than a minority of GPs.

In America, by contrast, a strong community hospital movement emerged between the wars, backed with substantial funds from philanthropic sources and with charges set high enough to cover both an element of depreciation and repayment of debt. This ensured the construction of a sufficient number of smaller hospitals to give a majority of GPs access to beds. In the larger hospitals, furthermore, less charitable work was done — which meant that doctors everywhere tended to be adequately compensated for the services they supplied in the hospital world. American GPs thus had a much stronger incentive for seeking hospital privileges than their British counterparts.

Reinforcing this economic motive was a social one, stemming from the absence of class distinctions in American society. GPs and specialists in America all felt themselves to be members of a united profession — the bond between them arising from the nature of the work they did. Few were concerned about the social origins of their colleagues. In Britain, on the other hand, social class exerted a powerful influence on choice of career and GPs tended to come from a lower class than consultants. To reach the pinnacle of the hospital world before 1948 one had to go through a long, largely unpaid, apprenticeship and not many medical students could afford it. This was enough to keep the consultant class small and exclusive. Those who could not finance the process had to become GPs and that led them to regard the hospital world as something separate and distinct.

In this way, the medical profession in Britain came to acquire somewhat the same attributes as those which applied to the legal profession. GPs were separated from consultants in the same way that solicitors were separated from barristers. Both were denied access to the main centres of professional work — the hospital in the case of GPs, the courtroom in the case of solicitors.[a] In America, by contrast, no such division existed: all doctors, like all lawyers, tended to enjoy the same professional privileges.

Beyond this was the influence exerted by differences in leadership and finance. In Britain, few medical leaders arose who were committed to the ideal of hospital privileges for GPs, and they did not receive the financial aid needed to make the dream a reality. Even the larger voluntary hospitals in Britain had to accept state aid and control in 1948. Nor did the state itself provide sufficient funds to expand the hospital service materially until the 1960s.

In America, by contrast, AMA leaders were united in their demand for hospital privileges and they received enough aid from private philanthropy to permit the growth of community hospitals between the wars. Not until 1945 did this source of finance falter and then, when the state did step in (with financial aid, not complete control), it provided enough funds to permit the continued development of hospital facilities. In the process, America ended up with too many beds and too few GPs — but at least it had enough hospitals to give nearly the whole profession access.

The separation of the profession in Britain was not the result of a simple process. Many factors were involved — the most basic arising from social class differences and the growing specialization of medicine. But the attitude of the profession was also important and that was strongly influenced by the economic conditions under which doctors worked. The competitive pressures of private practice forced doctors apart — yet they also induced GPs to seek the same privileges as specialists in order to retain the patients they served. By freeing them from the influence of financial forces, state intervention gave the doctors the chance to make a fresh start but, instead of using that opportunity to work closer together, they drifted further apart. The profession as a whole, then, must share responsibility for the division in the medical world that exists today.

---

a   Solicitors, however, do appear in Magistrates' Courts and in some County Courts.

Epilogue

'. . . I have no doubt that what I am saying is highly controversial and probably many consultants will differ completely, but I believe that in time the pick of the general practitioners must follow their patients into hospital and will become part of the staffs of those hospitals. I know it will be said that the standard of those hospitals will go down, but I do not think that that should happen if we see that the general practitioners are properly integrated with the consultants already on the staff of the hospitals. It is the bond between these two that will decide the success of this experiment. I shall not myself live to see it carried out, but I believe that it is the most important administrative move in the next decade. If that is not done, with a discontented profession, efficiency must wither, whatever the remuneration.'

– Lord Moran in Parl. Deb., Lords, 2 July 1958, Vol. 210, Col. 469.

Appendix

Biographies of Key Figures

Addison, Christopher (Lord Addison) (1869-1951)

Addison was the medical politician who devised the strategy needed to reconcile the doctors to the idea of state intervention.

He started his career as a lecturer (later professor) in anatomy but soon realized that the problems facing his profession would not be solved in a university. Abandoning the academic world in 1910 (at 41) he entered Parliament where he stayed for nearly the rest of his life. No one did more to influence the course of medical politics as regards state intervention. Lloyd George, as well as Aneurin Bevan, found him indispensable for dealing with the doctors. In 1912 he hit on the brilliant idea of forming a mobile panel of willing doctors (2,000 in all) to break the medical strike and, when it succeeded, his political career was made. Thereafter, he held many offices but the most relevant here are Parliamentary Secretary to the Board of Education in 1914, and at the Ministry of Munitions in 1915; then Minister of Munitions in 1916, Minister of Reconstruction in 1917, President of the LGB in January, 1919, and then first Minister of Health in June, 1919, until he left office in 1921. Though not directly concerned with the Ministry of Health after that, Addison played an important role (as leader of the Lords) in starting the Health Service in 1948, using the same tactics he had employed in 1912.

Sources
> Minney, R. J., *Viscount Addison: Leader of the Lords,*
>   Odhams, 1958.
> *DNB*, 1951-60, OUP, 1971, pp. 3-7.
> *The Times*, 12 Dec. 1951, p. 8.
> *BMJ*, 1951, 2, pp. 1525-7.
> *Lancet*, 1951, 2, pp. 1186-7.

Bevan, Aneurin (1897-1960)

A man of immense charm and great imagination, Bevan was the poet in politics who coaxed, cajoled and pushed the doctors into the National Health Service — only to find when he had finished that he had not done enough to aid general practice.

The son of a Welsh coal miner, Bevan had little formal education but he learned more from life than most people do from years in school. He entered the mines at the age of 14 and did not leave until he was 21. For the next 7 years he found it necessary to live mainly on the dole, but he did enough in the way of trade union and community work to keep busy. Finally, in 1922, he managed to start the political career he wanted by winning a seat on the local urban district council. This was followed, 6 years later, by a place on the Monmouthshire County Council and, in 1929, he won election to Parliament itself — where he stayed for the rest of his life.

There, the remarkable speaking powers he possessed, together with his fierce commitment to socialist ideals, brought him to the attention of the leaders of the Labour Party. Nevertheless, he had to wait until the war ended in 1945 before he was given office. Attlee then made him Minister of Health and he proved to be the man of the hour, for it is doubtful if anyone else in British politics could have turned negotiations round from the parlous state in which Willink had left them. Bevan put the Health Service Bill across and, in so doing, he placed the nation, as well as his Party, eternally in his debt — but the political conflicts which followed prevented him from rising to the leadership heights to which he aspired. In 1951, having moved to the post of Minister of Labour, he resigned from the Government over (among other factors) the charges the Chancellor of the Exchequer introduced in the Health Service — and, 4 years later, the same man (Hugh Gaitskell) beat him in the contest that determined who would be Attlee's successor. Bevan, therefore, never became leader of the Labour Party and he died, in 1960, without even having had the chance to hold office again.

Sources

Foot, Michael, *Aneurin Bevan, Volume 1: 1897-1945,* MacGibbon and Kee, 1962 (Four Square Edition, 1966); *Volume 2: 1945-1960,* Davis Poynter, 1973 (Paladin Edition, 1975).

Brome, Vincent, *Aneurin Bevan,* Longmans, 1953.

Krug, Mark M., *Aneurin Bevan, Cautious Rebel,* Thomas Yoseloff, 1961.

DNB, 1951-60, OUP, 1971, pp. 99-102.

Bevin, Ernest   (1881-1951)

Bevin was the moving spirit behind the trade union drive for the creation of a National Health Service.

From a poor family, he left school at 11 and did a number of odd jobs in the Bristol area before joining the Dockers Union as an organizer in 1910. His rise in the union hierarchy was rapid, aided by the training he had received as a Baptist lay preacher (providing yet another example of the extent to which the Nonconformist tradition contributed to the growth of the labour movement in Britain). In 1920, he leapt into the national limelight as the 'Docker's K.C.' because of the impressive way he performed before the Shaw Inquiry into the pay of his members. The success he scored made his selection as General Secretary of the union inevitable after it amalgamated with another to form the Transport and General Workers Union. Today, this union is the most powerful in Britain and it was Bevin who made it that way. With Walter Citrine (who became General Secretary of the TUC in 1925), he dominated the making of TUC policy during the 1930s and it was largely the concern he showed for industrial health that made it possible for BMA leaders to form the alliance they sought with the unions.

Bevin left his union in 1940 to become Minister of Labour and from that vantage point, he and Arthur Greenwood paved the way for the social legislation that followed the war. Though Bevin showed no enthusiasm for the Beveridge Report (largely, it seems, out of personal dislike for Beveridge himself), he had no reservations when it came to the Health Service. Bevin pushed strongly for it in the Cabinet discussions that preceded the end of the war and, when the Labour Government was formed in 1945, he stood firmly behind the new Minister of Health.

During the 1930s, Bevin had done his utmost to foster the health-centre idea and he must have been greatly disappointed when it failed to materialize after 1948. By then, however, he faced other problems since he became Secretary of State for Foreign Affairs and held that office until just before his death in 1951.

Sources

Bullock, Alan, *The Life and Times of Ernest Bevin: Volume 1: Trade Union Leader, 1881-1940, Volume 2: Minister of Labour, 1940-1945,* Heinemann, 1960 and 1967.

Harris, José, *William Beveridge, A Biography*, OUP, 1977, pp. 370-7, 383.

DNB, 1951-60, OUP, 1971, pp. 102-10.

Brackenbury, (Sir) Henry Britten   (1866-1942)

Brackenbury was the main spirit behind the social-work concept of general practice which so influences policy-making today.

A man of great culture and learning, he was the wisest leader and best speaker the BMA ever had. His father, a Methodist minister from an old Lincolnshire family, gave his son as good an education as his ill-paid post would allow. Brackenbury, after qualifying in 1887, spent 5 years working in hospital before entering general practice in Hornsey in 1892. Over the next half century, he gave himself more fully to public life than any doctor has ever done. Education as well as public health were his specialties and he gave service to the county (Middlesex) as a whole as well as to his borough in particular. Hornsey, in gratitude, made him Alderman, Mayor (1905) and Freeman (1930) — and this was capped with a knighthood in 1932.

Before 1914, Brackenbury played little part in medical politics but, thereafter, he held every important post within the BMA, dominating the making of medical policy between the wars. His only failure came in national politics (losing two Parliamentary elections in the process) but he accomplished more in the BMA and local government than most Ministers do over a lifetime in office.

Sources
   BMJ, 1942, 1, pp. 398-9.
   Lancet, 1942, 1, p. 369.
   Medical Officer, 1942, 1, p. 92.
   Hornsey Journal, 20 March 1942.
   Cox, Alfred, *Among the Doctors*, Christopher Johnson, 1950, pp.
      105-6.

Cox, Alfred   (1866-1954)

Cox was the medical trade unionist *par excellence* who gave the profession the
organizational strength needed to make its demands felt.

A GP of working-class origins, Cox rose to the most influential office in the
field of medical politics. He entered the profession by way of an apprenticeship
but secured a medical degree at the University of Durham before settling down to
practice at Gateshead for 17 years (1891-1908). During this period, he emerged
as a militant leader of club doctors, advocating trade union action to fight the
friendly societies. The movement he headed was responsible for the reform of the
BMA in 1902 and when his colleague, Dr Smith Whitaker, became Medical
Secretary, it was only a matter of time before Cox followed him — first, as
Deputy Secretary (1908) and then as Medical Secretary in his own right from
1912 until he retired in 1932.

No man did more to strengthen the profession's position under NHI and Cox
lived to see his dreams fulfilled when the approved societies were abolished in
1948. He deserved a knighthood for his efforts but the most he received was an
OBE.

Sources
   Cox, Alfred, *Among the Doctors*, Christopher Johnson, 1950.
   BMJ, 1954, 2, pp. 597-9, 648-9, 706-7, 758.
   Lancet, 1954, 2, pp. 556-7.

Dawson, Bertrand (Lord Dawson)   (1864-1945)

Dawson was a prominent physician best known for the health-centre idea. As
chairman of a Ministry committee in 1920, he produced the famous Dawson
Report in which the idea first received official sanction.

Born into a middle-class family, Dawson never encountered any difficulty in
his career. By the time (1900) he married the daughter of a wealthy shipbuilder
(Sir Alfred Yarrow), he was on his way to an appointment as physician (1906) at
the London Hospital (where he spent his entire working life). Soon even the King
became his patient and Dawson was rewarded with a knighthood in 1911.

Such respectability made him the ideal man to launch the medical movement
for a Ministry of Health, particularly since he had not become embroiled in the
1911 dispute over NHI. Until the war, he showed little interest in the larger
problems facing his profession but a few years on the battlefield changed
all that. Inspired by the teamwork he found in the army, he returned with a

desire to reorganize civilian practice and that, in his view, required the creation of a Ministry of Health, 'the most pressing of all reconstruction problems'.

The widely-reported Cavendish Lectures gave him the chance to propogate his views (in July, 1918) and they immediately fired the imagination of the public if not the profession. Dawson did, however, manage to stir the doctors by showing them how they could combine the protection offered by an extended state service with greater control over administration. Medical support proved crucial in the later stages of the struggle over the Ministry and Dawson was rewarded first with a peerage (1919) and then with the pre-sidencies of the BMA and the Royal College of Physicians (the latter for an unprecedented 7 years).

Through these honours, he managed to exert a continuous influence on medical politics even after the Medical Consultative Council which he chaired came to an untimely end (in 1921). Ironically, just before his death, he launched an attack on his own creation, health centres, because (through the White Paper on the National Health Service) they had become linked with a proposal which he abhorred and which the health centres were originally designed to thwart — a whole-time salaried service.

Sources

Watson, Francis, *Dawson of Penn*, Chatto and Windus, 1950.
DNB, 1941-50, OUP, 1971, pp. 201-4.
The Times, 8 March 1945, p.7; 10 March 1945, p. 7.
BMJ, 1945, 1, pp. 389-92.
Lancet, 1945, 1, pp. 353-6.

Hastings, Somerville (1878-1967)

Hastings was a respected teaching hospital consultant who led the SMA in its fight for a Health Service, but he made the mistake of imposing on its policy a rigid adherence to municipal control.

A son of the manse, Hastings was born in Wiltshire and educated at Wycliffe College in Gloucester but, from the time he entered university until the day he died, he lived in or near London. His medical training was obtained at University College, where he was a medallist in botany, and at the Middlesex Hospital, where he qualified in 1902. This was followed, 4 years later, by an FRCS, and in the same year (1910) that he joined the Webbs in their campaign for the reform of the Poor Law, he was appointed to his old hospital, the Middlesex, as an aural surgeon. This was no mean feat because few hospitals, at that time, were willing to appoint socialists to their staff. The Middlesex never had any cause for regret. Hastings stayed there until he retired in 1945, doing much useful work along the way.

It was as a politician, however, that his main reputation was made. Hastings came from a deeply religious home and he always saw socialism as the application of his Christian beliefs. He joined the SMSA when it began in 1912, and during the 1920s, when the ardour of all his colleagues had cooled, Hastings alone kept the organization going. In that decade also he made his first entry into

Parliament, holding a seat on two occasions (1923-4 and 1929-31) as Labour MP for Reading.

Hastings lost his seat in the 1931 election, and for the 14 years that followed he confined his attention to local politics in London. The way here was opened by the new socialist medical organization that Dr Charles Brook formed in 1930. Brook had close links with the London Labour Party and, when Hastings decided to throw his lot in with the SMA, he found himself (along with Brook and others) a candidate for the LCC too. He won a place as the representative of Mile End and victory here proved to be more permanent than in Reading. After Labour gained control in the 1934 election, Hastings became Chairman of the Hospital and Medical Services Committee — which gave him the opportunity, over the next decade, to build up the finest municipal hospital service in the land. So grateful were his colleagues for the work he did that they made him Chairman of the LLC as a whole in 1944.

During this period the goals of the SMA were never out of his mind and, as early as 1934, he persuaded the Labour Party to accept its call for a Health Service. From then on Hastings worked vigorously to have the policy implemented, finding the Party's Public Health Advisory Committee (which he revived in 1938) an effective medium to press his views. By 1944, SMA policy, for the most part, had become Labour policy, but it was tied, like Hastings himself, to the concept of local authority control. The SMA leader thus made the same mistake as Newsholme had done 3 decades earlier: he failed to appreciate how much the doctors detested municipal administration.

Bevan, when he came to power in 1945, was forced to accept a different plan from the one the SMA had proposed but Hastings took great pride in the Health Service that was formed. The same year (1945) also saw the offer of a safe seat in Parliament. For 14 years he represented Barking and, when he retired in 1959, the Borough made him a Freeman in gratitude for the work he had done. Child welfare also received much attention at his hands. This was a subject for which he had long shown concern and, in the years 1946-8, he was one of the most active members of the Curtis Committee. Despite failing eyesight, he continued to devote many hours to the LCC (on which he served as Alderman from 1946) as well as to the SMA (even after he retired in 1951 from the presidential chair which he had held since the organization was formed in 1930). Those who studied under him at the Middlesex Hospital, it was true, sometimes found his surly treatment of patients too much to bear but those who met him outside never had reason to doubt his concern for the welfare of the public at large. He died without honours but this, no doubt, was only because he did not think they were appropriate for one who believed in the socialist cause.

Sources
> *The Times*, 8 July 1967, p. 12.
> *BMJ*, 1967, 3, p. 182.
> *Lancet*, 1967, 1, p. 161.
> *Socialism and Health*, Nov., 1970, p. 3.
> *Medical World*, March, 1953, pp. 365-9.
> Personal knowledge.

Hill, Charles (Lord Hill) (1904-   )

Hill became known as Bevan's great antagonist in the fight over the Health Service but he deserves to go down in history as the doctor who, in collaboration with Jim Smyth, forged the BMA-TUC alliance that made the welfare state possible. Though he later became a leading figure in the Conservative Party, his heart was always with those on the left of the political spectrum.

His father, a piano maker from East London, died when Hill was only 2, leaving his mother with few resources to raise 3 young children. However, she managed well and Hill received a good grammar school education which took him to Trinity College, Cambridge, but he never had a pool of funds on which to draw. It was this background, no doubt, that led him to join the Labour Club at Cambridge, and radical tendencies were evident in his work throughout most of the years he spent with the BMA.

Coming from a non-medical background, Hill had no burning desire to be a doctor. However, he qualified in 1927 after receiving his training at the London Hospital, and for 2 years did a variety of locum jobs (mainly in London) before deciding to enter the public-health world, first (1929) as deputy medical superintendent of a mental hospital in Nottingham and then (1930-2) as deputy MOH of the City of Oxford. It was this municipal experience, no doubt, that made his qualifications so interesting to Brackenbury and, when Hill applied for the post of Assistant Secretary to the BMA in 1932, the elder statesman made sure he was chosen.

For the next 18 years, Hill gave his life to the BMA, becoming Deputy Secretary in 1935, and after his chief (Dr G. C. Anderson) died in 1944, Medical Secretary. Even before 1944, however, Hill wielded more influence than his position implied since Anderson lacked the ability to make decisions. The alliance the BMA formed with the TUC was largely Hill's doing and he tried to steer the unions as well as the doctors in the municipal direction that Brackenbury desired. But though he was later forced to change course, he undoubtedly felt greater sympathy for the Health Service ideal than he dared to display. Nevertheless, good officer that he was, Hill did not let this stop him from doing all he could to satisfy the demands of those who employed him. Bevan, during the negotiations over the Health Service, faced no greater opponent than Hill of the BMA.

Even before this task was done, Hill's thoughts had turned to politics and, though he failed to win a place in Parliament as an Independent in the 1945 election, he did manage to do so as a Conservative in 1950. For this success, however, his BMA association was only partly responsible; even more important was the publicity he had received as the 'Radio Doctor' of the BBC, and that also made him a suitable candidate for Government office. No sooner did Hill enter Parliament than he was offered a succession of posts — and he received others equally eminent after he left political life (with a peerage) in 1963.

It is still not clear why Hill became a Conservative in 1950. Perhaps, as the leader of a profession that fought so hard against a Government under Labour control, he did not think it right to enter Parliament on the socialist side — and with this, no doubt, his BMA employers concurred. But if it had not been for

BMA leaders like Hill, it is doubtful whether any Government — Labour or otherwise — would have had the chance to create the Health Service that Bevan did in 1948.

Sources
> Hill, Charles, *Both Sides of the Hill — The Memoirs of Charles Hill, Lord Hill of Lutton*, Heinemann, 1964.
> *Who's Who*, 1977.

Jameson, (Sir) William Wilson   (1885-1962)

Jameson was the chief inheritor of Brackenbury's mission in the medical world and he did his utmost to ensure that the BMA leader's concept of general practice prevailed when the Health Service began.

Like so many medical leaders of his day, Jameson came from a deeply religious background. His father died when he was only 6 so that his mother exerted the main influence in his life — but the family on both sides were strong Presbyterians. They were, moreover, Scots, and Jameson passed the whole of his educational career in Aberdeen.

As soon as he qualified in 1909, Jameson moved to London and there he stayed, for the most part, for the rest of his life. After a spell in general practice (which he heartily disliked), he turned to public health and so impressed his teacher at University College (Professor H. R. Kenwood) that he was asked to join the staff. Then came the First World War. Jameson spent 4 years in the army and, after it ended, secured his first MOH appointment at Finchley. This was followed, 5 years later, by the same office in Hornsey and there he came in contact with the man who no doubt had a great effect on his life — Sir Henry Brackenbury. Jameson must have made a deep impression on the BMA leader for, in 1928, we suddenly find him elevated to the Chair of Public Health at the new London School of Hygiene and Tropical Medicine. Kenwood was largely responsible for this move but it is doubtful whether he could have offered the post to Jameson unless others (like Brackenbury and Newman) had also been impressed with the young MOH.

Once appointed, Jameson more than vindicated his selection and, in 1931, he was asked to become Dean of the School. He held that position throughout the 1930s and, during this decade, he completely dominated the academic world of public health. When Newman retired from the Ministry in 1935, he wanted Jameson to succeed him but this could not be done without wounding his deputy, so the appointment went to Sir Arthur MacNalty. The latter did not live up to the task and, when the outbreak of war forced the civil service to drop all decorum, MacNalty was given the same chance to 'retire' at 61 as Newsholme received in 1919. Jameson became Chief Medical Officer of the Ministry of Health.

He stayed there for 10 years — throughout the negotiations on the Health

Service — and no one did more to ease the anxieties of the profession. A selfless man, completely without guile, Jameson acted as an 'honest broker' between the politicians and the doctors. Later, Bevan himself paid tribute to the good work Jameson had done. For the wounds suffered by general practice, however, Jameson also had to share part of the blame. His public-health background must have made him extremely sensitive to MOH feelings about the loss of municipal hospitals and it was probably he, more than the local authorities themselves, who pressed Bevan to put health centres under MOH control. It also seems possible that GPs might have been assigned to the care of regional hospital boards, as BMA leaders desired, if this idea had not so conflicted with the concept of general practice that Jameson and Brackenbury held.

After Jameson left the Ministry, he spent another decade working for the King Edward's Hospital Fund. In 1953 he also helped to set a new direction for health visitors by chairing an official working party on the subject. For such a lifetime of service, he deserved a peerage — but, like Newman, all he ever received was the knighthood given in 1939.

Sources

Goodman, Neville M., *Wilson Jameson, Architect of National Health,* Allen and Unwin, 1970.
The Times, 20 Oct. 1962, p. 10.
BMJ, 1962, 2, pp. 1131-3, 1265-6.
Lancet, 1962, 2, pp. 889-91.

Kershaw, Fred (Lord Kershaw)   (1881-1961)

Kershaw was one of the main architects of Labour policy on social insurance between the wars.

Born into a working-class family in Prestwich, he began his insurance career as an official for the Sons of Temperance Friendly Society, leaving it in 1914 to head the approved society section of the National Federation of Women Workers. Here he joined Mary Macarthur and Margaret Bondfield who widened his horizons, making him a socialist as well as a social reformer. His work here also opened his eyes to industrial insurance abuses, since his society competed with the offices for female members, and in 1931-3, he served on the Cohen Committee that investigated the industry. In 1920, the Federation merged with the National Union of General Workers and Kershaw left a few years later to form his own department, offering financial and legal advice to union-approved societies. This gave him wide experience of social insurance and, for 20 years, he served as chairman of the Courts of Referees under the Unemployment Insurance Acts. Municipal affairs also attracted his interest and since his local authority (Hornsey) happened to be the same as Brackenbury's, Kershaw was well-placed to foster the alliance that developed between the doctors and the unions.

Though his views changed in the 1930s, Kershaw had been among the foremost advocates of equal benefits, driving the unions in the direction of state administration. He no doubt played a large role behind the scenes between 1942 and 1948. His career, however, did not end with the abolition of the approved-society system. Rather, the peerage he received in 1947 gave him the chance to vent his views in the Lords as well as to hold high office in industry.

Source
   The Times, 7 Feb., 1961, p. 13.

Lloyd George, David (Lord Lloyd George)   (1863-1945)

Lloyd George created the NHI system that led to the development of the welfare state in Britain. It was a feat of immense proportions since even the workers who stood to benefit from the Bill did not want it and Lloyd George risked his political life pushing it through Parliament.

   The son of a schoolmaster who died shortly after his birth, Lloyd George was raised by a deeply religious uncle (a shoemaker who was also a Campbellite Baptist lay preacher) who instilled within him the tenets of Nonconformity as it operated in North Wales at the end of the nineteenth century. This, combined with a distaste for the landed gentry class that ruled the rural society in which he was raised, made Lloyd George a radical bent on social reform and he used the practice of law as a springboard for a career in politics. After qualifying as a solicitor in 1884, he entered Parliament on the Liberal side in 1890 and rose, by dint of his immense political skill and spell-binding oratorical powers, to the leadership of the radical wing of his Party, becoming first President of the Board of Trade (1905-8) and then Chancellor of the Exchequer during the period when he pushed the NHI Bill through Parliament.

   After the First World War began, Lloyd George moved to offices in which his great talent for getting things done were needed, serving first as Minister of Munitions (1915-16) and then as Secretary of State for War (1916) before becoming Prime Minister. For 6 difficult years, he led the nation, attempting to build a coalition of forces that would, after the war, enable him to complete the programme of social reform which he had started before 1914. In the end, however, he was defeated by a combination of economic and political circumstances that proved impossible to overcome and, in 1922, he returned to the back benches, destined never to hold office again.

   Those who had been hurt (or discarded) by him were glad to see Lloyd George go and it was true that he pursued his goals with ruthless disregard for the feelings of others. But such qualities are sometimes needed in politics to get things done. Lloyd George, above all else, was a master of the moment and it is doubtful whether any other politician could have pushed the NHI Bill through Parliament as he did in 1911. For that alone the nation owes him an immense debt.

Sources
   du Parcq, Henry, *Life of Lloyd George*, Caxton, 1912.
   Thomson, Malcolm, *David Lloyd George*, Hutchinson, 1948.

Jones, Thomas, *Lloyd George*, OUP, 1951.
George, William, *My Brother and I*, Eyre and Spottiswood, 1958.
Morgan, Kenneth O., *David Lloyd George*, University of Wales
    Press, Cardiff, 1963.

Macdonald, Peter (1870-1960)

Macdonald was the architect of the bargain that underlay the creation of the Health Service: in exchange for 'extension' (i.e. the principle of universal coverage), the Labour Party offered the doctors 'freedom' (meaning, in this context, no salaried service and as much medical influence in administration as circumstances would permit). Macdonald, a socialist as well as a medical leader, acted as the broker between the opposing sides, showing his colleagues in both worlds how such an agreement might be reached.

A son of the manse, Macdonald was Scottish by birth and received his medical education at Aberdeen University (1890-4). But he spent his whole professional life in York, practising first as a GP and then, after NHI began, as a specialist in ophthalmology and otolaryngology. There he met his Quaker wife, a member of the eminent Rowntree family, and Macdonald served as Medical Officer of the famous chocolate firm from 1904. Allied to this association, no doubt, was Macdonald's interest in politics for he joined the Independent Labour Party at a time (1898) when the two great Quaker families of the Rowntree's and the Cadbury's were doing all they could to create a pressure group on the left of the Liberal Party. Macdonald became a friend of Keir Hardie and stood for Parliament as a Labour candidate in the 1918 General Election. Though his failure then ended his political career, he maintained ties with the labour movement, serving first on the Party's Public Health Advisory Committee in 1924 and then on the joint BMA-TUC Committee in 1939.

A paper Macdonald wrote on 'The Future of the Medical Profession' probably had a great effect on the shaping of Labour policy. In it, he set forth the difference between a salaried State Medical Service (which many socialists at the time desired) and a National Medical Service that offered freedom from bureaucratic control (which the profession was likely to accept). This paper, which was published in the *British Medical Journal* just before the 1918 General Election, brought Macdonald prominently before the members of the BMA. Until then, he had acted through the MPU, serving on its executive committee in 1917, but his political foresight, together with his competence in mathematics (a subject which he taught before he studied medicine), made him too valuable a recruit for BMA leaders to ignore. In 1918, he was one of 6 doctors appointed by the BMA to work with an actuary on the formulation of a central pool method of payment for panel doctors. From then on, Macdonald rose swiftly in BMA circles, dropping his MPU ties in the process.

Between the wars, he served most actively on the Hospital Committee, doing what he could to prepare his colleagues in the specialist world for the coming National Health Service. The first step was taken in 1929 with the establishment of a National Eye Service (as an additional benefit under NHI) and, in helping to form it, Macdonald worked with his fellow ophthalmologist, Bishop Harman. In 1942, all of this preliminary work came to fruition with the publication of the 'radical' report by the BMA's Medical Planning Commission and Macdonald directed the discussions that followed in his capacity as Chairman of the Annual Representative Meeting. In 1945, however, his term of service came to an end and, probably because of the right-wing reaction that affected BMA affairs, he did not play a prominent part in the negotiations that followed. Nevertheless, the creation of the National Health Service must have given him great satisfaction and, though he retired from practice in 1951, he lived long enough to see it win the profession's approval.

Sources
 BMJ, 1918, 2, pp. 435-6; 1933, 1, Supp., p. 110; 1938, 2, Supp., p. 165;
   1960, 2, pp. 809-10.
 Medical World, 13 Dec. 1918, p. 377.
 Labour Party, *Minutes of Jt. Com. of Gen. Council of TUC and Nat.*
   Exec. Com. of Lab. Party, Feb. - Sept., 1924, p. 47r.

Maude, (Sir) Evelyn John   (1883-1963)

Maude, as Permanent Secretary of the Ministry of Health during the Second World War, had the best chance of anyone to create a unified Health Service, but he let the opportunity slip by because he did not understand the depth of medical distaste for local authority control.

Born into a family of means, Maude received an education appropriate to an Englishman of his class. Rugby was followed by Oxford but then, after being called to the Bar at Lincoln's Inn in 1908, he joined Morant in 1912 and devoted his working life to the administration of NHI. With the legal training he had, it was only natural that he should enter the solicitor's department after the Ministry of Health was created in 1919 and, by 1926, he had risen to the highest post this section had to offer. That, to many of his colleagues, seemed about as far as he would go but, 8 years later, when the Permanent Secretary of the department (Sir Arthur Robinson) retired, Maude unexpectedly was transferred to the administrative side and made Deputy Secretary of the Ministry as a whole. Then when Sir George Chrystal retired in 1940, Maude succeeded to the highest civil service post the Ministry had to offer — Permanent Secretary.

During the next 5 years, Maude did his best to create the unified Health Service he desired but, in developing department policy, he made the mistake of basing all on municipal administration. A similar attempt along more modest lines had been made in the late 1920s and Maude should have learned from that experience how much the doctors disliked the thought of local authority control. He paid the price for his error by an early retirement in 1945: he was then eased out of the Ministry with an appointment as Deputy Chairman of the Local Government Boundary Commission. There, no doubt, he finally learned what he should have realized before — that municipal administration of the Health Service could not be effected until the geographical areas which local authorities covered were enlarged. This he made clear in the reservation he wrote to the

Guillebaud Report that appeared a decade later — and he also took care to stress how important it was to give the doctors control over discipline before unification (through local authority administration) was again attempted. How different the history of the Health Service might have been if these lessons had been learned earlier!

Maude made NHI his life's work, and was rewarded with a knighthood in 1937, but this does not erase the fact that his mind was too legalistic for the administrative challenge with which he was confronted.

Sources
> *The Times,* 7 Feb. 1963, p. 14.
> *Report of the Committee of Enquiry into the Cost of the National Health Service,* HMSO, Cmd. 9663, 1956, pp. 274-86.

Morant, (Sir) Robert   (1863-1920)

Morant was a social reformer who used his position within the civil service to lay the basis of a national health policy in Britain.

An Oxford graduate, Morant became tutor to the royal family of Siam before entering the civil service in 1895 as an education specialist. His rise was rapid and no one did more to steer the great 1902 Education Act through Parliament. After it passed, he became Permanent Secretary of the Board of Education but left it in a storm over the Holmes Circular in 1911. He then succeeded W. J. Braithwaite as the leading civil servant at the NHI Commission until his untimely death in 1920.

Morant's influence on public-health policy was profound. It began long before 1911, having sprung initially from an interest in medical education and research. Morant understood, as few laymen do, the delicate unity of medicine — the extent to which the quality of treatment depends on the climate of research and education in which doctors practise. As early as 1908, he saw the need for a Ministry of Health and wanted to move to the LGB to create one. Though he went to the NHI Commission instead, Morant remained in close contact with the colleague he left behind — George Newman — and yearned for the day when they could work together again. This personal attachment helps to explain not only why Morant exerted so much effort on behalf of the Ministry but also why Newman became Chief Medical Officer instead of Newsholme.

Sources
> Allen, Bernard M., *Sir Robert Morant*, Macmillan, 1934.
> Newman, George, *The Building of a Nation's Health*, Macmillan, 1939, pp. 451-72.
> Newman, George, *Diaries* (on file at the Library of the Department of Health and Social Security, London), 17 Aug. 1913, letter from Morant.
> Markham, Violet, *Friendship's Harvest*, Reinhardt, 1956, pp. 167-207.
> *DNB*, 1912-21, OUP, 1927, pp. 386-8.
> *BMJ*, 1920, 1, pp. 419-20.

Newman, (Sir) George   (1870-1948)

Newman was one of the main architects of public-health policy in Britain, striving through state intervention to develop a social role for GPs.

Born into a prominent Quaker family, Newman never lost his deep-rooted religious interest in the Society of Friends. He entered the public-health world in a unique manner — by way of bacteriology — and thus had a stronger tie to medical science than many MOHs. After serving in Bedfordshire (1897-9) and Finsbury (1900-7), he became Chief Medical Officer of the Board of Education and held that post until his retirement in 1935. In 1918, he took over the same post at the LGB just before it was absorbed by the Ministry of Health and held that, too, until 1935.

At the start of his civil service career, Newman followed Newsholme, his elder, but their tactics diverged over the years. Newman became more influential because of his flexible pragmatism and his genuine belief in the value of the general practitioner. The clue to his thinking — crucial for understanding the development of public-health policy in Britain — lay in the 3 principles he enunciated in 1909: gradualism, expediency and unification (in administration). The last is self-evident but the first 2 reveal his approach to all problems in government. In face of the clash of vested interests, Newman recognized the need for compromise and caution — particularly where fiercely individualistic GPs were concerned — moving slowly towards the improvement of public health services, while retaining the confidence of both GPs and MOHs.

Sources
    Newman, George, *Diaries*, 1907-48.
    DNB, 1941-50, OUP, 1959, pp. 624-5.
    BMJ, 1948, 1, pp. 112-13.
    Lancet, 1948, 1, pp. 888-9.
    Public Health, Feb., 1909, pp. 160-1; May, 1956, pp. 196-7.
    Newman, George, *The Building of a Nation's Health*, Macmillan,
        1939, pp. 427-9.

Newsholme, (Sir) Arthur   (1857-1943)

Newsholme was an influential public health planner who let his passion for municipal control blind him to the wider opportunities offered by state intervention in medicine.

Newsholme began his career as a private practitioner and club doctor in Clapham (1883-8), but soon entered the public health service — first as a part-time MOH, then whole-time at Brighton for 20 years (1888-1908). This long period in local administration made him unfit for service at the national level. It cast his mind in a mould and led him to see the MOH, rather than the GP, as the pivot of medical service. His main aim in public health was to put all personal care under MOH control. He therefore wanted unification first, extension only later. The Webbs listened to him but, fortunately for the nation, Lloyd George did not. NHI passed Newsholme by and he never learned to live with it.

He went to the LGB as Chief Medical Officer in 1908 but, 10 years later, he was forced to retire at the age of 62. He would have been happier at the General Registry Office where he originally wanted to go for he was essentially an epidemiologist, not an administrator. His whole approach to medicine was statistical rather than scientific and he never shared Newman's feeling for medical research — or his understanding of the delicate art of medical politics.

Sources
  DNB, 1941-50, OUP, 1959, pp. 625-6.
  BMJ, 1943, 1, p. 680.
  Lancet, 1943, 1, p. 696.
  Newsholme, Arthur, *Fifty Years in Public Health*, Allen and Unwin, 1935; *The Last Thirty Years in Public Health*, Allen and Unwin, 1936.
  Newman, George, *Diaries*, 18 Dec. 1913.

Smyth, James L.   (1882-1966)

Smyth was the trade union official who forged the alliance between the unions and the doctors that produced the welfare state in 1946.

Of Smyth's early life, nothing is known but he was probably of Irish descent and raised in Liverpool. By the time he reached the age of 34 in 1916, he was working as an official of the United Operative Plumbers and Domestic Engineers Association. Four years later he became its Assistant General Secretary and, at that point, he formed a friendship that was to alter the course of his life. Working also in Liverpool was a trade union official named Walter Citrine and, as Assistant General Secretary of the Electrical Trades Union, he served with Smyth on the Federation of Engineering and Shipbuilding Trades. From that tie, a close friendship was formed and, when Citrine moved to London in 1928 as General Secretary of the TUC, Smyth went with him as Director of its new Social Insurance Department.

Smyth, because of the injustices he had seen under the workmen's compensation system, had developed a hatred of insurance company administration and the main task in his new job, as he saw it, was to remove its influence from the field of social insurance. The doctors, for reasons of their own, had come to the same conclusion and, during the 1930s, Smyth skilfully fostered an alliance between the BMA and the TUC. In 1939, as a forceful member of the Royal Commission on Workmen's Compensation, he made sure their joint views were heard —and he did the same, 3 years later, in the evidence he presented to the Beveridge Committee on behalf of the TUC. Beveridge, by then, had come to respect Smyth greatly; the two had formed close ties as a result of Beveridge's long-standing service (from 1934) as Chairman of the Unemployment Insurance Statutory Committee. When Smyth spoke, Beveridge listened and he later acknowledged the debt he owed his TUC friend for the recommendations he proposed in the report that made history.

When Labour came to power in 1945, the realization of Smyth's long-standing campaign was assured and he resigned from the TUC in order to help the Ministry of National Insurance develop the new system. Before he left, however, he did the doctors one more service: as a member of the official Spens Committee that dealt with their pay, he made sure that their earnings would rise once the Health Service began.

Once these tasks were done, Smyth's life-work was completed and he retired from office in 1952, at 70, a much-satisfied man. No one did more to promote the growth of the welfare state — yet, disdainful of the honours the country normally bestows, he refused all recognition for the contribution he had made.

Sources

The Times, 1966: 23 April, p. 12; 27 April, p. 14.

TUC, *Annual Congress Report*, 1966, p. 382.

Journal of Plumbing Trades Union, June, 1966, p. 307.

Labour Magazine, 1932-3, Vol. 4, p. 96.

Citrine, Walter, *Men and Work*, Hutchinson, 1964, pp. 72, 76.

Beveridge, William H., *Power and Influence*, Hodder and Stoughton, 1953, pp. 226, 301.

Whitaker, (Sir) James Smith   (1866-1936)

Whitaker, as a BMA leader in 1911, secured the conditions necessary to ensure the profession's participation in NHI and then entered the ranks of those administering the Act in order to make sure the new system did not fail.

Born into a middle-class family in Lancashire, Whitaker had a talent for mathematics and entered Manchester Grammar School with the intention of studying at Cambridge. His father's sudden death, however, forced him to leave school to save the family firm (a small knitted goods business) but his classical education apparently did not fit him for business administration. The firm failed and Whitaker went back to school — this time, with the aim of becoming a doctor. He secured his medical qualifications at Manchester University in 1891 and entered general practice in Great Yarmouth.

Over the next decade he established himself as a leader of the militant club doctors who demanded the reform of the BMA, and, when the task was partly completed in 1902, Whitaker became the organization's new Medical Secretary. In that capacity, he led the profession in the 'battle of the clubs' — the fight with the friendly societies for the control of club practice. When all efforts failed, he found it necessary to turn to the only alternative — the creation of a state system which would give the doctors the protection they had failed to secure through the medium of private enterprise. Whitaker skilfully prepared the profession for that move and nothing more reveals the subtlety of his mind than the report he wrote in 1911 on *The Organization of Medical Attendance on the Insurance Principle*. It became the basis of the panel system that followed and Whitaker (after much hesitation) was persuaded to take a place on the NHI Commission so as to ensure its success. The move, however, was misunderstood and many in the profession never forgave him for the way he changed sides.

Whitaker, nevertheless, served the profession and the public well during the 2 decades he spent in the civil service, and he was honoured with a knighthood in 1931. No one within the Ministry of Health was more intent on raising the standard of panel care and, when he retired in 1932, a force went out of GP administration which has never been replaced.

Sources

BMJ, 1911, 1, Supp., pp. 81-122; 1936, 1, pp. 669-70.
Lancet, 1936, 1, pp. 809-10.
Cox, Alfred, *Among the Doctors*, Christopher Johnson, 1950, pp. 75-9, 81, 93-4.
Interview with Whitaker's son, Dr Allen J. Whitaker, 13 March 1962.

Wilson, Charles McMoran (Lord Moran) (1882-1977)

Moran was the consultant leader who helped Bevan find the concessions needed to satisfy the profession in 1948. In the process, he laid the basis for a vast improvement in the hospital service but, despite the damage this development did to the pattern of general practice (which Moran foresaw), he did nothing to correct it.

The son of a Yorkshire GP, Moran worked all his life at St. Mary's Hospital in Paddington. Qualifying there in 1908, he returned after the war as an assistant physician and, shortly afterwards, became the (unpaid) Dean of the Medical School. Though only 37 at the time, Moran had impressive administrative talents and it was these his colleagues recognized. Their selection was justified, for Morant developed the School to the point where a new building was opened in 1933.

His ability as an educator also became evident since it was Moran who introduced the clinical unit system that started in the 1920s. Here, no doubt, he ran into opposition from a colleague on the St. Mary's staff, the dermatologist-politician, Sir Ernest Graham-Little. The latter's political power depended on the easy-going, part-time teaching habits that consultants enjoyed and the whole-time clinical units which Moran introduced threatened to upset the pattern.

From the struggle that ensued, Moran emerged the victor. In 1941, he was elected President of the Royal College of Physicians and there he stayed throughout the negotiations on the Health Service. Bevan turned to him for advice and Moran did much to overcome the political problems that were encountered.

For his long service to medicine he received many honours — notably, a knighthood in 1938 and a peerage in 1943. He had the good fortune to live to the advanced age of 94 and thus could derive much satisfaction from seeing the development of the Service he had done so much to form.

Sources
The Times, 13 April 1977, p. 14
BMJ, 1977, 1, p. 1088.
Lancet, 1977, 1, p. 915.

Wood, (Sir) Howard Kingsley   (1881-1943)

Wood did more than anyone to channel and control the power of the industrial insurance industry so that it could be used in a great programme of social reform.

The son of a prominent Methodist minister with a long record of mission work among the poor, Wood developed a social conscience which he never lost despite a lifetime in Conservative politics. After qualifying as a solicitor in 1903, he spent eight years building up his law practice before serving on the LCC from 1911 to 1918. Though he represented the insurance offices during the negotiations on the 1911 NHI Bill, he did not win national recognition until he drafted the approved society scheme for a Ministry of Health in 1917. This proved to be his passport to Parliament in 1918 (together with a knighthood) and a long career in Conservative Governments, becoming a most able Minister of Health himself (1935-8) after having earlier held the two junior appointments there (Private Parliamentary Secretary, 1919-21, and Parliamentary Secretary, 1924-9). He conducted himself equally well as Chancellor of the Exchequer in Churchill's Coalition Government, introducing budget reform along Keynesian lines in 1941. In that capacity, also, he passed financial judgement on the Beveridge Report but he died in 1943 before the issue it raised could be resolved.

Wood's law firm (Wood, Williams and Murphy) advised the insurance offices throughout the entire NHI period. For many years, Wood was also closely associated with Percy Rockliff, the colourful leader of one group of approved societies, and, between them, they exerted an enormous influence on the policy of the approved society world as a whole.

Sources
DNB, 1941-50, OUP, 1959, pp. 971-3.
The Times, 22 Sept. 1943, p. 8.
Addison, Paul, *The Road to 1945,* Jonathan Cape, 1975, pp. 101-2, 170-1, 220-1, 233-6.

Source References

Guide to Source References

All books published in London unless otherwise indicated.

Books are listed in full on first appearance as source reference; afterwards, by surname of author and year published.

Journals are listed by their full title on first appearance as source reference, thereafter by abbreviations.

Government reports are listed in full on first appearance as source reference; afterwards, by surname of chairman of body that produced it and year published.

Private Government papers are designated according to the letter and numbering system used in the Public Record Office:

CAB — Cabinet
MH — Ministry of Health
PIN — Ministry of Pensions and National Insurance
RECON — Ministry of Reconstruction

Introduction: The Division in British Medicine

1 For a good indication of the way these specialties grew between the Wars, see Stevens, Rosemary, *Medical Practice in Modern England*, Yale University Press, 1966, pp. 38-52.
2 No study, to my knowlege, adequately describes the pattern of medical care prevailing throughout the world but for a good attempt at an overview, see the chapter by Prof. Brian Abel-Smith, 'The History of Medical Care', in Martin, E. W. (editor), *Comparative Development in Social Welfare*, Allen and Unwin, 1972, pp. 219-40.
3 Hodson, Mark, *Doctors and Patients*, Hodder and Stoughton, 1967, p. 70.
4 *Journal of Medical Education*, January, 1951, pp. 16-27, article by Dean Stanley Dorst, College of Medicine, University of Cincinnati.
5 For this difference between the two countries, see Stevens, Rosemary, *American Medicine and the Public Interest*, Yale University Press, 1971, pp. 92-4, 231-5.
6 Hodson (1967), p. 73.
7 See Ministry of Health, Central Health Services Council, *Report of Committee on General Practice within the National Health Service* (Cohen Report), HMSO, 1954, pp. 2-3, para. 12. See also Ministry of Health, Central Health Services Council, Standing Medical Advisory Committee, *The Field of Work of the Family Doctor* (Gillie Report), HMSO, 1963, pp. 9-10, para. 21-3.

8   Abel-Smith in Martin (1972), pp. 232-3.
9   *Lancet,* 1969, 1, pp. 715-18.
10 For a summary of the early history of the profession, see Carr-Saunders, A. M., and Wilson, P. A., *The Professions*, Oxford, Clarendon Press, 1933, pp. 65-75.
11 For the development which follows, see Horner, N. G., *The Growth of the General Practitioner of Medicine in England*, Bridge & Co., 1922; Carr-Saunders and Wilson (1933), pp. 75-83; Hamilton, Bernice, 'The Medical Profession in the 18th Century', in *Economic History Review*, 1951, Vol. IV, No. 2, pp. 141-70; Parry, Noel and José, *The Rise of the Medical Profession*, Croom Helm, 1976, pp. 104-30.
12 Abel-Smith, Brian, *The Hospitals, 1800-1948*, Heinemann, 1964, pp. 1, 16, 102; Parry (1976), p. 136.
13 Parry (1976), pp. 133-4.
14 Abel-Smith (1964), pp. 19-20.
15 *Ibid.*, pp. 101-18.

Chapter 1: The Panel System

1   For the development of medical services under the Poor Law, see Hodgkinson, Ruth G., *The Origins of the National Health Service: The Medical Services of the New Poor Law, 1834-1871,* Wellcome Historical Medical Library, Monograph No. 11, 1967.
2   For summary of the changes made in NHI between 1911 and 1948, see Canadian Department of National Health and Welfare, *Health Insurance in Great Britain, 1911-1948*, Ottawa, 1952, Social Security Series, Memo. No. 11.
3   *Ibid.*, pp. 34-5, 143.
4   For the best guide to the benefits described here, showing all the legal interpretations and qualifications, see Comyns Carr, A. S., Garnett, W. H., and Taylor, J. H., *National Insurance*, Macmillan, 1913.
5   Abel-Smith (1964), pp. 352-3.
6   For the proportions of insured persons covered by each of these additional benefits in 1938, see Canadian Department of Health, *Health Insurance in Great Britain, 1911-1948,* 1952, pp. 49-55.
7   For the 1913 estimate, see *Medical World,* 18 Sept., 1913, pp. 248-51. For the estimate made in the 1930s, see *British Medical Journal,* 1931, 2, Supp., pp. 54-5. This was later confirmed by an official report, for which see Ministry of Health and Department of Health for Scotland, *Report of the Inter-Departmental Committee on the Remuneration of Consultants and Specialists,* Spens Report, HMSO, 1948, Cmd. 7420, pp. 17-25.
8   Abel-Smith (1964), pp. 133-51, 189, 339.
9   For the growth of these schemes, see *ibid.*, pp. 135-7, 311, 323-7, 385-7.
10 *Ibid.*, p. 200.
11 For the number of district medical officers in 1910, see Webb, Sidney and Beatrice, *The State and the Doctor*, Longmans, 1910, pp. 11, 16.
12 Abel-Smith (1964), pp. 200-16.
13 *Ibid.*, pp. 119-32.
14 For a summary of the rough statistics applicable to the Act, see Gilbert,

Bentley B., *The Evolution of National Insurance in Britain*, Michael Joseph, 1966, pp. 437-9.

15 No adequate study of club practice has appeared, but for a book which covers part of the early history, see Gosden, P. H. J. H., *The Friendly Societies in England, 1815-1875*, Manchester University Press, 1961, pp. 138-49. See also the long report on contract practice that the BMA prepared in 1905. *BMJ*, 1905, 2, Supp., pp. 1-96.

16 *BMJ*, 1912, 1, Supp., p. 355 (Maclean). See also article by Dr. Adolphe Smith, 'The Medical Opposition to the NHI Bill', in *National Review*, 1911, Vol. 57, pp. 1055-68.

17 Gilbert (1966), pp. 165-7. To the estimates he makes there, I have added data to include the groups he excluded — working women and young men between the ages of 16 and 19. Both were later covered by NHI and therefore it seems appropriate to include them in any estimate made of the proportion covered by the friendly societies before 1911.

18 *BMJ*, 1905, 2, Supp., pp. 1-2.

19 *Manchester Medical Guild Quarterly*, 1900: Jan, pp. 1-2 and April, pp. 1-3.

20 For the dispersion of rates as found by the BMA, see *BMJ*, 1905, 2, Supp., p. 35. For an example of a society which held fast to a 2s-3s. rate from 1833 down to the end of the nineteenth century, see *Medical Magazine*, 1900, p. 237.

21 The BMA, in its study of contract practice, found free choice existing in less than 10% of the friendly society club appointments surveyed (211 out of 2,300). *BMJ*, 1905, 2, Supp., pp. 6, 35-6.

22 *Lancet*, 1896, 1, p. 1170.

23 Note the friendly societies' own recognition of this in *BMJ*, 1909, 1, Supp., pp. 69-76; 1910, 1, Supp., p. 271 (para. 76-7).

24 *General Practitioner*, 1901, pp. 7-8, 29.

25 *Lancet*, 1901, 1, p. 121 ('GP').

26 *Gen. Prac.*, 1901, pp. 7-8, 29, 45, 198, 393-4. *Lancet*, 1904, 1, pp. 239-40; 1907, 2, p. 1116; 1911, 1, pp. 176-7; 1911, 2, pp. 919-20. *BMJ*, 1902, 2, Supp., pp. 98-101; 1907, 2, Supp., p. 92; 1910, 2, pp. 121-4; 1911, 1, pp. 978-81.

27 *Lancet*, 1907, 2, pp. 302-3.

28 *Lancet*, 1895, 2, p. 1004 (Stretton). See also *ibid.*, pp. 1256-7.

29 *Lancet*, 1906, 2, pp. 15-18; *Medical Press & Circular*, 1913, 1, p. 297.

30 For the complaints of club doctors about this, see *Med. Mag.*, 1893, pp. 117-18, 121-3; 1897, pp. 582-8; 1900, pp. 468-75. *BMJ*, 1899, 2, pp. 1501-3; 1901, 1, Supp., p. 14 (Cox).

31 *BMJ*, 1900, 1, pp. 54-6, 116; 1900, 2, pp. 189-91; 1901, 1, Supp., pp. 1-48; 1901, 2, pp. 301-6; 1902, 1, pp. 1633-51, 1902, 2, pp. 183-97. See also Cox, Alfred, *Among the Doctors*, Christopher Johnson, no date (but 1950), pp. 48-79.

32 *BMJ*, 1907, 2, Supp., pp. 252-4; 1908, 1, p. 1420-2.

33 *BMJ*, 1906, 2, pp. 1821-5.

34 *BMJ*, 1911, 2, Supp., p. 699 (Horsley).

35 *BMJ*, 1905, 2, Supp., pp. 106-9; 1906, 1, Supp., pp. 109-37; 1906, 2, p. 41; 1906, 2, Supp., pp. 26, 89-91; 1907, 1, Supp., pp. 145-82; 1908, 1, pp. 1379-80; 1908, 1, Supp., pp. 307-44; 1908, 2, pp. 276, 1883; 1908, 2, Supp., pp. 65-7, 124-5; 1909, 1, p. 971; 1910, 1, Supp., p. 260 (para. 51-2 of Council Report); 1910, 2, pp. 31, 121-4; 1911, 1, Supp.,

p. 263 (para. 29-30 of Council Report); 1911, 2, Supp., p. 212; 1912, 1, Supp., pp. 240-1, 452 (para. 34 of Council Report); 1912, 2, Supp., pp. 595-6; 1913, 1, Supp., pp. 370-1 (para. 26 of Council Report); 1913, 2, Supp., pp. 15-18 (App. X of Council Report).

36 *BMJ,* 1913, 1, pp. 733-4.

37 *BMJ,* 1911, 2, Supp., pp. 222-3 (Horsley).

38 For a good guide to the provisions of the panel system, see Harris, R. W., and Sack, L. S., *Medical Insurance Practice*, BMA, 1922, 1924, 1929, 1937.

39 Gilbert (1966), pp. 411-12.

40 *Ibid.,* p. 440. See also *Lancet,* 1913, 2, pp. 431-2 (Hardwicke).

41 For a clear indication of this, see the memoirs of the civil servant who helped Lloyd George frame the Bill, William J. Braithwaite, in Bunbury, Henry N. (editor), *Lloyd George's Ambulance Wagon,* Methuen, 1957, p. 183.

42 Comyns Carr and others (1913), p. 46. See also the comments by Lloyd George in Parl. Deb., Commons, 12 July 1911, Vol. 28, Cols. 425-9.

43 Note, for example, the statement by one friendly society leader (Marlow of the Foresters) in *BMJ,* 1911, 2, p. 385. See also Gilbert (1966), p. 370.

44 *BMJ,* 1911, 2, Supp., pp. 521-2 (Whitaker).

45 Gilbert (1966), pp. 349-50.

46 *Shepherd's Magazine,* 1911, pp. 146, 290-4.

47 For examples of approved society outbursts over the years, see *Oddfellows' Magazine,* 1913, pp. 210-13 (Warren). *National Insurance Gazette,* 1919, p. 519; 1921, p. 257 (Barnes); 1923, pp. 271, 275.

48 *Nat. Ins. Gaz.,* 1934, p. 597 (Lesser).

49 Gilbert (1966), pp. 350-1.

50 For this, see the article by the social insurance expert, W. H. Dawson, 'Social Insurance in England and Germany — A Comparison', in *Fortnightly Review,* 1912, Vol. XCII, pp. 304-20.

51 International Labour Office, *Compulsory Sickness Insurance*, Studies and Reports, Series M (Social Ins.) No. 6, Geneva, 1927, pp. 432-7.

52 *BMJ,* 1921, 2, Supp. pp. 147-8 (Mond); 1922, 1, Supp., pp. 96-9 (Robinson); 1923, 2, Supp., p. 173 (Robinson).

53 For the details of how this worked, see International Labour Office, *Compulsory Sickness Insurance*, 1927, pp. 502-8.

54 For the German system, see Dawson in *Fort. Rev.*, 1912, Vol. XCII, pp. 304-20. See also *The Times*, 1911: 22 May, p. 9; 23 May, p. 7; 15 June, p. 17; 21 June, p. 15; 4 Aug., p. 5. See also *Transactions of Life Assurance Medical Officers' Association*, 1908-9, p. 93; 1914-15, pp. 85-114.

55 *New Statesman,* 14 March 1914, Spec. Supp., p. 11; 20 June 1914, pp. 330-1; Association of Approved Societies, 'Enquiry Into Medical Benefit', 16 July 1914, on file at British Library of Political and Economic Science, LSE.

56 *The Times,* 7 Nov. 1912, p. 4.

57 *BMJ,* 1923, 1, Supp., pp. 105-6.

58 Canadian Department of Health, *Health Insurance in Great Britain, 1911-1948,* 1952, pp. 48-56.

Chapter 2: The Division in Health Administration

1 Keebel, T. E. (editor), *Selected Speeches of the Late Rt. Hon. The Earl of Beaconsfield*, Longmans, 1882, Vol. 2, pp. 511-12.
2 For the history of the General Board of Health, see Finer, S. E., *The Life and Times of Sir Edwin Chadwick*, Methuen, 1952, and Lewis, R. A., *Edwin Chadwick and the Public Health Movement*, Longmans, 1952. For the history of the LGB, see Lambert, Royston, *Sir John Simon 1816-1904 and English Social Administration*, MacGibbon and Kee, 1963, and Brand, Jeanne L., *Doctors and the State*, Baltimore, Johns Hopkins Press, 1965.
3 For the best short review of this, see *BMJ*, 1920, 1, pp. 56-7. For the area in which the LGB did manage to make a significant contribution (ie control of infectious disease), see Brand (1965), pp. 37-64. For an attempt (in my view, unconvincing) to shift the blame from the LGB to the Treasury, see the paper by Roy M. MacLeod, 'The Frustration of State Medicine, 1880-1899', in *Medical History*, Jan., 1967, pp. 15-40; and by the same author, *Treasury Control and Social Administration*, Occasional Papers on Social Administration, No. 23, G. Bell, 1968.
4 Rumsey, Henry W., *Essays on State Medicine*, Churchill, 1856, p. 62. *BMJ*, 1911, 1, pp. 1217-81. *Medical Press*, 1912, 2, p. 445. MH 62/36, Meetings and corr. between Morant and General Medical Council, Nov. 1913, to Feb. 1914.
5 *BMJ*, 1920, 2, Supp., p. 19.
6 Keebel (1882), pp. 532-3. See also Boyle, Edward, *Tory Democrat*, Conservative Political Centre, 1950, pp. 11, 30-1, 47. Smith, Paul, *Disraelian Conservatism and Social Reform*, Routledge, 1968, p. 159.
7 Newman, George, *The Building of a Nation's Health*, Macmillan, 1939, p. 462.
8 *Assurance Agent's Chronicle*, 1906, p. 577.
9 Newman, George, *Infant Mortality*, Methuen, 1906, pp. 6-7, 18.
10 *Med. Press*, 1917, 2, p. 26. During the war, however, the infant mortality rate fell sharply, for which see the paper by J. M. Winter, 'The Impact of the First World War on Civilian Health in Britain', in *Economic History Review*, Aug. 1977, pp. 487-507.
11 *Maternity and Child Welfare*, March 1938, pp. 453-4. Colville, Cynthia, *Crowded Life*, Evans Bros., 1963, pp. 148-57. See also *Medical Officer*, 1917, 1, p. 79-80; *New Witness*, 3 Sept. 1920, pp. 348-9.
12 For the full list, see *Med. Press*, 1917, 2, p. 26.
13 *BMJ*, 1917, 1, Supp., pp. 14-15, para. 2e.
14 Lambert (1963), pp. 557-8.
15 Royal Commission on Poor Laws, Min. of Ev., 1910, Cd. 5068, Q. 92,842 and p. 836, para. 15.
16 Webb, S. and B., *English Poor Law Policy*, Longmans, 1910, pp. 211-19. *BMJ*, 1910, 1, Supp., pp. 123-5. For a complaint about the separation of indoor and outdoor medical relief, see the paper by Dr Robert Lyster in *Crusade*, March 1911, pp. 43-7.
17 *BMJ*, 1905, 2, pp. 414-15.
18 Royal Com. on Poor Laws, Min. of Ev., 1909, Cd. 4684, Q. 22,940-50. Abel-Smith (1964), pp. 123-7.
19 Gilbert (1966), pp. 117-31.

20 *Nat. Ins. Gaz.,* 1919, pp. 141-2.
21 *Odd. Mag.,* 1910, pp. 150-3. See also the Webb proposals on NHI as explained by Dr Robert Lyster in *BMJ,* 1911, 1, pp. 507-8.
22 Royal Com. on Poor Laws, Min. of Ev., 1909, Cd. 4625, Q. 2867, 10,311-16, 10,475-89, 10,758-74; Cd. 4684, Q. 21,193. Webb, S. and B., *English Poor Law Policy,* 1910, pp. 120-1, 211-19. *BMJ,* 1910, 1, Supp., pp. 123-5.
23 Royal Com. on Poor Laws, Min. of Ev., 1910, Cd. 5068, Q. 92,776-800.
24 Newsholme preferred this policy in any case. See *BMJ,* 1908, 2, pp. 56, 566-7, 1119-22; and Newman *Diaries,* entry for 15 April 1908 (on file at the Library of the Department of Health and Social Security in London).
25 Gilbert (1966), pp. 133-43.
26 *BMJ,* 1914, 2, pp. 677-8. Newsholme, Arthur, *The Last Thirty Years in Public Health,* Allen and Unwin, 1936, pp. 196-7.
27 For the details of what follows here, see Honigsbaum, F., *The Struggle for the Ministry of Health,* Occ. Papers on Social Admin. No. 37, G. Bell, 1970, pp. 20-3.
28 For an indication of Newsholme's feelings here, see Newsholme (1936), pp. 103, 109-19. For Newman's critical comments of Newsholme's view, see Newman (1939), p. 397.
29 These expense figures are based on data contained in International Labour Office, *Compulsory Sickness Insurance,* pp. 230, 310, 362.
30 For the details of the process intended here, see Honigsbaum (1970), p. 25.
31 Note the comments on this strategy by Addison in CAB 24/23, GT 1724, 13 Aug. 1917. See also Waldorf Astor in *Med. Press,* 1917, 2, pp. 372-4.

Chapter 3: Unification or Extension?

1 MH 78/81, report of local authority deputation to Hayes Fisher and Addison, 9 Jan. 1918, p. 18 (Addison).
2 RECON 1, 41/33, LGB Memo. by Walter Long, Oct., 1916, pp. 4-6.
3 Note the periodic tributes paid to Burns for his harsh administration of the Poor Law in Poor Law District Conference Reports: 1907-8, pp. 311-12; 1910-11, pp. 71, 516; 1911-12, pp. 331-2.
4 Addison, Christopher, *Four and a Half Years, Volume 1 (1914-1916),* Hutchinson, 1934, pp. 34, 37.
5 Parl. Deb., Commons, 4 May 1914, Vol. 62, Cols. 75-83. *BMJ,* 1914, 1, pp. 1029, 1140-1. *Nat. Ins. Gaz.,* 1914, pp. 513-14, 521. Addison (1934), pp. 13-18.
6 *Post Magazine and Insurance Monitor,* 1914, pp. 560-4 (Thompson).
7 LGB Medical Officer's Report, 1913-14, HMSO, 1914, Cd. 7612, pp. XIX-XXII.
8 For evidence in support of this view, see *Med. Press,* 1917, 2, pp. 324-5; *Mat. and Child Welf.,* Jan. 1918, p. 20. See also Mackenzie, W. Leslie, *Scottish Mothers and Children,* Dunfermline, Carnegie U.K. Trust, 1917, pp. 69-89.
9 *BMJ,* 1915, 2, pp. 101-2; *Mat. and Child Welf.,* May 1917, p. 205.

10 McCleary, George F., *Maternity and Child Welfare Movement*, P. S. King, 1935, pp. 17-18, 56.

11 Women's Coop. Guild, *Maternity*, Bell, 1915, pp. 200-8.

12 *National Health*, Aug., 1914, pp. 47-54.

13 *New States.,* 14 March 1914, Spec. Supp., p. 29; 16 May 1914, Spec. Supp., whole issue devoted to 'Motherhood and the State'.

14 Parl. Deb., Commons, 8 July 1915, Vol. 73, Cols. 617-31, 783-804.

15 Parl. Deb., Commons, 8 March 1917, Vol. 91, Cols. 645-6.

16 *Nat. Ins. Gaz.,* 1917, pp. 67, 125, 127, 163, 374-5, 540; 1918, p. 195.

17 For recognition of this, see Addison's Memo. to War Cabinet, CAB 24/23, GT 1724, 13 Aug. 1917. See also MH 78/80, Conf. with Reps. of Health Ins. Orgs. on Estab. of Min. of Health, 28 Jan. 1918; and Minute from Heseltine to Addison, 4 March 1918.

18 CAB 24/18, GT 1268, 20 July 1917. See also Parl. Deb., Commons, 24 June 1918, Vol. 107, Cols. 812-30.

19 *The Times*, 1916: 25 April, p. 2; 12 June, p. 3; 13 June, p. 3; 16 June, p. 5; 14 Oct., p. 3; 28 Oct., p. 15; 18 Nov., p. 5; 28 Nov., p. 7; 29 Dec., p. 3. See also Wilson, Robert MacNair, *Doctor's Progress*, Eyre and Spottiswoode, 1938, pp. 184-9.

20 *Medical World*, 7 Aug. 1913, pp. 16-18, 21; 10 Nov. 1916, pp. 568-9 (Salter). *Lancet*, 1918, 1, pp. 741-2.

21 *The Times*, 25 Oct. 1916, p. 9 (Cox). *BMJ*, 1916, 2, pp. 731-2.

22 Royal Com. on Poor Laws, 1910, Cd. 5068, Q. 92,934-5.

23 For recognition of this, see *BMJ*, 1917, 2, pp. 156-7.

24 *Lancet*, 1913, 1, p. 123. *BMJ*, 1916, 1, pp. 241-2.

25 *BMJ*, 1915, 1, Supp., pp. 229-33; 1915, 2, Supp., p. 62; 1916, 1, pp. 241-2; 1919, 1, pp. 171-2 (Craig).

26 *BMJ*, 1916, 1, pp. 385-7, 597; 1916, 2, pp. 115-16, 185-6; 1920, 2, pp. 38-40 (Linnell).

27 For the details here, see Honigsbaum (1970), p. 33.

28 RECON 1, 41/37, LGB Memo. by Edmund Bourke, 7 Nov. 1916, *Med. Press*, 1916, 2, pp. 551-2. *Nat. Ins. Gaz.,* 1916, p. 377 (Cardale).

29 *The Times*, 23 March 1917, p. 3. *BMJ*, 1917, 1, Supp., pp. 102-3.

30 For the scheme the BMA prepared on a Ministry of Health, see *BMJ*, 1917, 1, Supp., pp. 102-3.

31 For an indication of this, see *Med. World*, 25 May 1917, pp. 567-8.

32 For the details here, see Honigsbaum (1970), pp. 34-7.

33 CAB 24/22, GT 1662, 9 Aug. 1917. Parl. Deb., Lords, 18 July 1918, Vol. 30, Col. 984 (Peel); 29 July 1918, Vol. 31, Col. 8 (Haldane).

34 For the details here, see Honigsbaum (1970), pp. 38-45.

35 *Insurance Magazine*, Dec., 1917, pp. 184-5.

36 *Son of Temperance Magazine*, 1918, pp. 169-70.

37 *The Times*, 1917: 3 Aug., p. 9; 11 Oct., p. 4.

38 *Nat. Ins. Gaz.*, 1917, pp. 497-8, 503-5, 509-16.

39 *The Times*, 1918: 14 Jan., p. 11 (Astor); 15 Jan., p. 7 (Broadbent). *Mat. and Child Welf.,* Jan., 1918, p. 20. Parl. Deb., Commons, 24 June 1918, Vol. 107, Cols. 812-14.

40 For the details here, see Honigsbaum (1970), pp. 42-3.

41 Lloyd George Papers, F/11/1/3 (formerly on file in Beaverbrook Library, now in Library of House of Lords).

42 CAB 24/32, GT 2688, 20 Nov. 1917. *BMJ*, 1917, 2, p. 664; 1917, 2, Supp., pp. 110-11; 1918, 2, p. 49.

43 *BMJ*, 1917, 1, Supp., p. 144 (para. 5-6).

44 *BMJ*, 1917, 1, pp. 653-4; 1917, 1, Supp., pp. 89-90 (para. 75-6); 1917, 2, pp. 559-60, 802-3; 1918, 1, Supp., pp. 2-3.

45 Ministry of Reconstruction, Local Gov't. Com., *Report on the Transfer of Functions of Poor Law Authorities in England and Wales* (Maclean Report), HMSO, 1918, Cd. 8917.

46 *BMJ*, 1917, 2, pp. 726-8, 865-6. *Nat. Ins. Gaz.*, 1918, pp. 53, 55, 164-5. Addison, C., *Politics from Within*, Hutchinson, 1924, Vol. 2, pp. 223-4. Addison (1934), p. 478. Newman (1939), pp. 120-1.

47 Webb, S. and B., *English Poor Law History: Part II: The Last Hundred Years*, Longmans, 1929, Vol. 2, p. 581.

48 For the lead taken in this opposition by Rev. P. S. G. Propert, the Rural Dean of Fulham (which was Hayes Fisher's own constituency), see *Fulham Chronicle*, 1918: 5 April, p. 5; 26 April, p. 5; 17 May, p. 3.

49 For the details here, see Honigsbaum (1970), p. 46.

50 For Hayes Fisher's demand on this score, see CAB 24/51, GT 4533, 13 May 1918. For the assent of the Home Affairs Committee of the Cabinet, see CAB 26/1, Minutes of Meetings, 18 July 1918 (no. 3).

51 *Nat. Ins. Gaz.*, 1918, p. 393. See also *ibid.*, pp. 282, 413-14 (Rockliff).

52 For the details here, see Honigsbaum (1970), pp. 49-52.

53 For the details here, see Honigsbaum (1970), pp. 52-4.

54 Parl. Deb., Commons, 7 April 1914, Vol. 61, Cols. 478-557. *Abolitionist*, Aug., 1914, pp. 191-3.

55 Parl. Deb., Commons, 26 Feb. 1919, Vol. 112, Cols 1832-3. See also LGB (by Addison), *Memorandum on Ministry Bill as to the work of the Medical Research Council*, HMSO, 1919, Cmd. 69.

56 Parl. Deb., Commons, 21 March 1919, Vol. 113, Cols. 2455-9. See also *Animal's Defender*, 1919: April, p. 89; May, pp. 3-9.

57 Parl. Deb., Commons, 27 June 1919, Vol. 117, Cols. 511-54. See also *Med. Press*, 1919, 2, p. 5.

58 *Med. World*, 31 Jan. 1919, pp. 69-70. *Public Health*, March 1919, pp. 61-2.

59 For Newsholme's own recognition of failure here, see Newsholme (1936), p. 95.

60 Newman (1936), pp. 102-16.

61 *Nat. Ins. Gaz.*, 1919, p. 142.

62 MH 78/68, Memo. of conference with Min. of Health Com. of Royal Colleges, 4 Sept. 1918, pp. 3-4.

Chapter 4: Movement for a Salaried Service

1 *BMJ*, 1918, 2, pp. 259-60; 1919, 1, Supp., pp. 87-8; 1920, 1, pp. 581-2.

2 *Public Health*, Feb., 1919, pp. 52-5. *BMJ*, 1937, 1, Supp., p. 54. *Med. Off.*, 1943, 2, p. 161.

3 Ministry of Health Act, 1919, 9 and 10 Geo. 5, Ch. 21.

4 *Med. World*, 7 Feb. 1919, pp. 92-3. See also *ibid.*, 25 Jan. 1924, p. 501.

5 See Section 15 of the 1911 NHI Act and Section 11 of the 1913 NHI Act, both reproduced for convenient reference in Comyns Carr and others (1913), pp. 87-94.

6 *Lancet*, 1946, 2, pp. 719-20.

7 PIN 2/16, NHI Jt. Com., Report of proceedings of Advisory Committee

(regarding medical benefit), 2nd Meeting, 17 May 1912, p. 10 (Morant).

8 McCleary (1935), pp. 17-18.

9 For all these figures, see Newman (1939), pp. 134, 207, 247, 304, 310, 415.

10 Lab. Party, Annual Conf. Reports: 1909, p. 88; 1910, p. 96; 1911, p. 106; 1913, p. 106. See also the paper by Prof. Arthur Marwick, 'The Labour Party and the Welfare State in Britain, 1900-1948', in *American Historical Review*, 1967, Vol. LXXIII, pp. 380-403.

11 *Railway Review*, 2 Jan. 1920, p. 1.

12 TUC Annual Report, 1912, pp. 229-30 (Chandler). See also *Assur. Agent's Chron.*, 1908, pp. 399-400. Medical-Legal Society, *Transactions*, 1910-11, pp. 53-4.

13 Derived from data in the Beveridge Report. See Beveridge, William, *Social Insurance and Allied Services*, HMSO, 1942, Cmd. 6404, p. 25.

14 *Nat. Ins. Gaz.*, 1918, p. 378. See also *Med. World*, 8 Nov. 1918, pp. 297-9.

15 For an anticipation of this change in policy, see *Vote*, 7 Dec. 1917, pp. 68-9. See also *Common Cause*, 8 Nov. 1918, p. 347.

16 Parl. Deb., Commons, 9 April 1919, Vol. 114, Cols. 2111-12.

17 Abel-Smith (1964), pp. 200-1.

18 *Kensington News*, 17 July 1914, p. 2.

19 *Charity Organisation Review*, April, 1918, pp. 165-6. See also Chance's paper, 'Unsolved Problems of the English Poor Law', in Dawson, Wm. Harbutt (ed.), *After-War Problems*, Allen and Unwin, 1917, pp. 291-310.

20 *BMJ*, 1917, 2, pp. 587-8.

21 *Vote*, 6 Dec. 1918, p. 4. See also *Common Cause*, 1 Nov. 1918, p. 233. *Labour Woman*, May, 1919, pp. 6-7. *Women's Industrial News*, April, 1919, p. 5. Occasional Paper of National Union of Women Workers (later called National Council of Women), Sept., 1918, p. 11.

22 Wilson, Robert MacNair, *Wife: Mother: Voter — Her Vote. What Will She Do With It?*, Hodder and Stoughton, 1918, p. 74.

23 *Vote*, 4 April 1919, p. 143.

24 *The Times*, 4 Feb. 1919, p. 5. MH 73/29, Consul. Council on Gen. Health, 1919: Heseltine to Morant, 10 May; Heseltine Memo., 6 June; Lady Rhondda to Addison, 29 May; Morant to Lady Rhondda, 3 June; Heseltine Minute, 9 July.

25 *Common Cause*, 1919: 17 Jan., p. 473; 28 Feb., p. 551; 7 March, p. 556. *Vote*, 7 March 1919, p. 108. *The Times*, 1919: 4 Feb., p. 5; 12 Feb., p. 7; 13 Feb., p. 5.

26 *Lab. Woman*, 1919: March, pp. 23-4; April, p. 34; May, p. 43. MH 73/30, Consul. Council on Gen. Health, CC. No. 392, 5 Nov. 1920, H. S. Syrett, *Report of Work of Consumer's Council of Min. of Food*. MH 73/31, Minutes of Meetings, 19 Nov. 1920 (no. 19).

27 Parl. Deb., Commons, 1919: 26 Feb., Vol. 112, Col. 1874-6; 9 April, Vol. 114, Col. 2109-20. MH 73/29, Consul. Council on Gen. Health, 1919: Heseltine to Morant, 10 May; Heseltine Memo., 6 June. *Common Cause*, 1919: 2 May, p. 27; 25 July, p. 186; 3 Oct., p. 306. *Vote*, 27 Feb. 1920, p. 514. *The Times*, 14 Feb. 1920, p. 16.

28 MH 73/30, Consul. Council on Gen. Health, Minutes of Meetings, 28 Nov. 1920 (No.10), *Report on Improved Provision of Med. and Allied Services*, para. 7. This paragraph, part of which did not appear in the final

report, was prepared by Greenwood. For evidence of this, see MH
73/31, Minutes of Meetings, 7 Dec. 1921 (No. 24), document entitled
'Observations by Greenwood on First Draft Report', para. 6.

Chapter 5: Doctors Attempt to Influence Ministry Policy

1   For an indication of medical fear about power being concentrated in the
    hands of one man, see *BMJ*, 1920, 1, Supp., pp. 20-1 (Garratt).
2   *BMJ*, 1917, 1, Supp., pp. 89-90 (para. 75 of Council Report).
3   *Lancet*, 1922, 2, p. 931.
4   *BMJ*, 1918, 2, pp. 23-6.
5   *Observer*, 27 Oct. 1918, p. 2.
6   BMA, *A Ministry of Health*, 1918, pp. 14-16. For the background to this
    policy change, see *BMJ*, 1917, 1, pp. 653; 1917, 1, Supp., p. 124; 1917,
    2, pp. 865-6.
7   *New States.*, 29 Sept. 1917, p. 604. The article from which this quotation
    was taken had no signature but it clearly reflected Webb's views at the
    time. Only a few months later, he made speeches and wrote papers in
    which the same arguments were presented.
8   Webb, B., *Our Partnership*, Longmmans, 1948, pp. 396-7.
9   For this, see the lecture delivered by Geo. Bernard Shaw the day before
    the Poor Law Reports were published. *Trans. of Med.-Legal Soc.*,
    1908-9, pp. 202-28. See also Webb, B., (1948), p. 381.
10 Webb, S. and B., *The State and the Doctor*, 1910, pp. 252-9.
11 *Ibid.*, pp. 207-8.
12 Royal Com. on Poor Laws, 1905-9, Majority Report, HMSO, Cd. 4499,
    1909, p. 300.
13 *Ibid.*, Minority Report, p. 889.
14 Abel-Smith (1964), p. 232.
15 Gilbert, Bentley B., *British Social Policy, 1914-1939*, Batsford, 1970,
    pp. 11-12.
16 *New States.*, 23 Nov. 1918, p. 150. See also *BMJ*, 1917, 2, pp. 626,
    801-2; 1918, 1, p. 265; 1920, 1, pp. 229-30. *Lancet*, 1918, 1, pp. 27-8,
    441-2. Cole, Margaret I. (ed.), *Beatrice Webb's Diaries, 1912-1924,*
    Longmans, 1952, pp. 122, 140. Henderson, Arthur, *The Aims of
    Labour*, Toronto, McClelland, Goodchild and Stewart, 1918, p. 115.
17 *Gen. Prac.*, 1908, pp. 362-3, 420-1, 728-9; 1909, pp. 395-6. *Social
    Democrat*, 1908, pp. 447-56. *New Age*, 1908: 23 May, p. 79; 4 July, p.
    185. For Eder's role in the formation and dissolution of the League, see
    Justice, 8 July 1911, p. 6.
18 For Cox's activities in the Independent Labour Party, see his autobio-
    graphy, *Among the Doctors*, 1950, pp. 66-8. See also *Labour Leader*,
    1903, pp. 367, 399; 1904, p. 307; 1905, p. 327; 1908, pp. 311, 782. See
    also the *Annual Reports* of the ILP: 1904, p. 59; 1906, p. 6. Cox did not
    mention his membership of the Fabian Society or the Socialist Medical
    League in his autobiography — but for evidence of that, see *Fabian News*,
    Nov. 1907, p. 91; July 1908, p. 63. See also *Lab. Leader*, 1908, p. 322.
19 *Justice*, 15 Oct. 1910, p. 4.
20 For a brief account of the rise and fall of the SMSA, see Stark Murray,
    David, *Why a National Health Service?*, Pemberton, 1971, pp. 1-19.

21 *Med. World*, 7 Aug. 1913, p. 5. For an address Webb delivered to the SMSA shortly after its formation see Stark Murray (1971), p. 12.
22 Stark Murray (1971), p. 9. See also SMSA Minute Book, pp. 30, 46.
23 For the 145 figure (which was apparently the maximum), see SMSA Minute Book, p. 46.
24 *Ibid.,* pp. 22-6.
25 For the resignation of the most prominent, Dr H. H. Mills, see *Med. World*, 29 Jan. 1914, pp. 177. See also SMSA Minute Book, p. 126.
26 SMSA Minute Book, pp. 172-4.
27 *BMJ*, 1912, 2, Supp., pp. 662, 693-5. *The Times*, 14 Dec. 1912, p. 8.
28 *BMJ*, 1912, 2, Supp., p. 726. *The Times*, 24 Dec. 1912, pp. 5-6.
29 *BMJ*, 1912, 2, Supp., pp. 719 (Buttar), 727 (Buttar); 1913, 1, Supp., pp. 93 (Helme), 145 (Shaw).
30 For this, see *Med. World*, 16 July 1914, pp. 85-7.
31 For a clear indication of this, see *Med. Press*, 1916, 2, p. 192 (Hamilton).
32 For the formation of the MPU and the stress it placed on political action in its early years, see *Med. World*, 9 July 1914, pp. 61-2; 16 July 1914, pp. 88-93; 16 June 1916, pp. 768-70.
33 *BMJ*, 1918, 2, p. 558.
34 *Med. World*, 1918: 15 Feb., pp. 110-11; 28 June, pp. 399-400, 402.
35 *Med. World*, 1 March 1919, pp. 135-6.
36 *Med. World*, 26 July 1918, pp. 59-60. See also Webb's reply one week later, *ibid.*, 2 Aug. 1918, pp. 74-5.
37 See, for example, the novel by Cronin, A. J., *The Citadel*, Gollancz, 1937. See also the paper by Cox in *BMJ*, 1920, 2, Supp., pp. 73-6.
38 For one doctor who *did* make the distinction, see *Med. World*, 16 Jan. 1920, p. 81 (Pirie).
39 Morgan, H. B. W., *Trade Union Advisory Medical Officers*, Memo. No. 53, Joint Research and Information Dept., Labour Party and TUC, no date (1923?), p. 8, italics underlined in original.
40 *BMJ*, 1918, 2, pp. 609, 634. Cole (ed.) (1952), pp. 122, 140.
41 Webb, S., *The Future Organisation of the Medical Profession*, 1918, on file in the Brit. Lib. of Pol. and Econ. Science, LSE.
42 Webb, S., *Ministry of Health*, 1918, address to Association of Approved Societies, 20 April 1918, on file at Brit. Lib. of Pol. and Econ. Science, LSE.
43 *BMJ*, 1918, 2, Supp., pp. 26-8.
44 Cole (ed.) (1952), p. 64.
45 *BMJ*, 1953, 1, Supp., p. 148.
46 Dawson, B. *The Nation's Welfare*, Cassell, 1918, pp. 5-6.
47 *Ibid.*, pp. 8-9.
48 *BMJ*, 1918, 2, pp. 301-2.
49 BMA, *A Min. of Health*, 1918, pp. 11-12. See also *BMJ*, 1917, 2, Supp., p. 14; 1918, 2, pp. 550-1.
50 *BMJ*, 1920, 1, pp. 743-5; 1920, 2, p. 750. MH 73/48, Med. Council, letter from Dawson to Robinson, 17 Sept. 1921.
51 MH 73/37, Memo. of Proposals as to Constitution of Med. Council under Clause 4 of Min. of Health Bill, 1918. MH 78/68, Memo. of Conf. with Min. of Health Com. of Royal Colleges, pp. 5-6.
52 *BMJ*, 1919, 1, p. 249; 1919, 1, Supp., pp. 43-4.
53 Dawson (1918), p. 5.

54 CAB 57/8, Com. of Imperial Defence, Sub-Com. on Man-Power, 8 June 1923, p. 13. See also *BMJ*, 1923, 1, pp. 24-9 and Cox (1950), pp. 109-22.

55 *National Medical Journal*, 1917, pp. 1-2, 17-21, 25-6, 52; 1918, pp. 25, 33-5; 1919, pp. 25-9.

56 *Med. World,* 1918: 8 March, pp. 154-5; 28 June, p. 389 (Adams); 13 Sept., p. 165.

57 *BMJ*, 1918, 2, p. 724; 1919, 1, Supp., pp. 3-4, 27-8.

58 *BMJ*, 1919, 1, pp. 522-3.

59 *Med, World*, 28 Feb. 1919, pp. 145-51 (Angus). See also *BMJ*, 1919, 2, Supp., pp. 148-9 (Benson).

60 *Med. World*, 19 April 1918, pp. 246-51 (Stancomb). See also MH 62/124, Remun. of Ins. Pracs., Papers A, no date, para. 7-8. For recognition that war work did cut into the BMA's other activities, see *BMJ*, 1917, 1, pp. 21-2.

61 *BMJ*, 1915, 1, p. 260; 1917, 1, Supp., p. 92; 1918, 2, Supp., p. 22; 1919, 1, Supp., pp. 80-1; 1919, 2, Supp., pp. 146-7; 1920, 2, Supp., pp. 113-15.

62 *BMJ*, 1919, 1, p. 249; 1919, 1, Supp., pp. 43-4.

63 MH 73/37, Revised Proposals of Min. of Health Com. of Royal Colleges, 26 March 1919.

64 MH 73/37, Report of Deputation from Min. of Health Com. of Royal Colleges to Addison, 7 April 1919. See also *BMJ*, 1919, 2, Supp., p. 2 (para. 245 of Council Report); 1920, 2, Supp., pp. 126-8 (Addison), 157.

65 *BMJ*, 1913, 1, Supp., pp. 25-34.

66 Addison (1934), pp. 26-7.

67 *BMJ*, 1918, 2, pp. 379-82; 1919, 1, Sup., p. 79 (para. 127 of Council Report). *Med. World*, 16 Aug. 1918, p. 101. *Lancet*, 1919, 1, pp. 185, 345-6, 351, 801-2, 808-11.

68 *BMJ*, 1918, 2, pp. 420 ('Politicus'), 449 (Harman); 1919, 1, p. 159-60, 250; 1921, 1, p. 322 (Ward). *Lancet*, 1919, 2, p. 121-3; 1920, 2, pp. 1177-9; 1921, 1, pp. 47-8 (Mummery), 460; 1921, 2, p. 157; 1922, 1, pp. 859, 1215-16; 1923, 1, pp. 512, 1192; 1924, 1, pp. 1321-2. See also all issues of *Health* (Journal of the Fed. of Med. and Allied Societies), 1921-2.

69 MH 73/34, Dep. from Society of MOH's, 17 July 1919, pp. 5-6 of folder.

70 *BMJ*, 1921, 2, Supp., pp. 42-3.

71 See Brackenbury's own complaint about this in *Med. World*, 19 May 1922, pp. 293-311.

72 *Med. World*, 7 Nov. 1919, pp. 462-8, italics underlined in original. For a BMA rejoinder, see *BMJ*, 1919, 2, Supp., pp. 133-4.

73 *BMJ*, 1919, 1, p. 590; 1919, 2, pp. 212, 434-5, 443-5; 1919, 2, Supp., pp. 2-3 (para. 244-50 of Council Report); 1920, 1, Supp., p. 114 (para. 101-3 of Council Report).

74 MH 73/27, Consul. Council on Local Health Admin., Minutes of Meetings, 16 July 1920 (no. 6). See also *BMJ,* 1919, 1, pp. 39-43.

75 MH 73/48, Dawson to Robinson, 17 Sept. 1921.

76 MH 43/42, Newman to Robinson, 14 and 26 June 1920. For the actual words quoted here, see para. 2 of the 14 June Minute and para. 1 of the 26 June Minute.

77 *Lancet*, 1919, 2, pp. 617-18.

78 MH 43/42, Newman to Robinson, 26 June 1920, para. 4 (iii).
79 *Ibid.*, 14 June Minute, para. 5.
80 *Ibid.*, 14 June Minute, para. 2 (iii).
81 *Ibid.,* 14 June Minute, para. 4 (1v).
82 *Ibid.*, 14 June Minute, para. 3.
83 *Ibid.*, 14 June Minute, para. 5.
84 *Ibid.*, 26 June Minute, para. 3.
85 *Ibid.*, 14 June Minute, para. 5.
86 *Ibid.*, 26 June Minute, para. 5.
87 MH 73/49, Med. Council, Minutes of Meetings, 1920: 11 June (no. 18), 18 June (no. 19), 30 July (no. 20). MH 73/46, Med. Council, Conf. Coms., Minutes of Meetings, 28 Oct. 1920 to 12 Feb. 1924 (nos. 1 to 6). See also *BMJ*, 1919, 2, Supp., pp. 2-3; 1920, 2, Supp., p. 22 (Brackenbury). Watson, Francis, *Dawson of Penn,* Chatto and Windus, 1950, pp. 156-7.

Chapter 6: The Dawson Report

1 *BMJ,* 1919, 2, p. 575.
2 For the Minutes of Council Meetings, see MH 73/49.
3 Min. of Health, Consul. Council on Med. and Allied Services, *Interim Report on the Future Provision of Medical and Allied Services* (Dawson Report), HMSO, 1920, Cmd. 693. The report was reprinted in 1950 by the King Edward's Hospital Fund for London.
4 MH 73/45, Med. Council, Minutes of Meetings, 5 Feb. 1920 (no. 11). See also MH 73/45, Heseltine to Barter, 14 April 1920.
5 For the motives behind the Dawson initiative, see *Med. Press,* 1918, 1, p. 78; 1918, 2, pp. 1-2. See also the statement by Dawson in *BMJ,* 1919, 1, p. 162.
6 *BMJ,* 1918, 1, pp. 456, 653-4, 673.
7 *BMJ,* 1918, 2, p. 59.
8 *Hospital,* 20 July 1918, pp. 345-6.
9 Note the comment on this by Dr Dewar in *BMJ,* 1920, 1, pp. 850-1.
10 A copy of this pamphlet is available at the Brit. Lib. of Pol. and Econ. Science, LSE. For a contemporary comment, noting the wisdom of the change in title, see *Med. Times,* Oct., 1918, p. 299. See also *BMJ*, 1918, 2, p. 348.
11 *Hosp.,* 3 May 1919, p. 98.
12 *BMJ,* 1918, 1, p. 456. See also *ibid.,* 1918, 2, pp. 467-8; 1919, 1, p. 162. See also the reference to Dawson's view by Prof. Henry (later Lord) Cohen, 'A Comprehensive Health Service', in *Agenda,* Feb. 1943, pp. 25-44.
13 *BMJ,* 1913, 2, Supp., pp. 472-3.
14 *Med. World,* 4 July 1919, pp. 13-24.
15 *BMJ,* 1920, 1, pp. 743-5.
16 *BMJ,* 1919, 2, Supp., pp. 44-5.
17 Dawson Report (1920), p. 18, para. 71. MH 73/38, 'Memo. on Function of General Practitioner in an Ideal Scheme of Service', no signature and no date but classified as CC/M/16/1/32. Dain can be identified as the author in Minutes of the Council's proceedings for 16 Jan. 1920. See MH 73/49, Med. Council, Minutes of Meetings: 24 Oct. 1919 (no. 2), pp. 4-5; 16 Jan. 1920 (no. 8), para. 15.

18   MH 73/8, Memo. by Dr C. J. Bond to Consul. Council on Med. for 24 Oct. 1919 meeting, 'The Position of the General Practitioner in an Improved Scheme of Medical Service for the Community.'

19   MH 73/49, Med. Council, Minutes of Meetings, 1920: 30 Jan. (no. 9), para. 19; 13 Feb. (no. 10), para. 5, 7, 9, 12; 5 March (no. 14), para. 6; 19 March (no. 16); 5 Nov. (no. 21); 19 Nov. (no. 22), para. 9, 10, Annex 2; 3 Dec. (no. 23), para. 15, 17.

20   Dawson Report (1920), p. 6 (para. 7). See also pp. 5 (para. 4), 13 (para. 47), 18 (para. 69-72), 19 (para. 73).

21   MH 73/49, Med. Council, Minutes of Meetings, 17 Dec. 1920 (no. 24), para. 10.

22   *Labour Bulletin*, 1921, pp. 184-6.

23   Dawson Report (1920), pp. 6-7, 11-19.

24   *BMJ,* 1918, 2, pp. 23-6, 56-9.

25   Lab. Party, Memos. by Adv. Com. on Public Health, *The Organisation of Preventive and Curative Medical Services and Hospital and Labour Systems Under Min. of Health,* 1919, p. 5, italics in dark print in original.

26   *Lancet,* 1944, 1, pp. 131-2; 1947, 1, pp. 152-3. See also Abel-Smith (1964), p. 286, n. 4; Morgan, Gerald, *Public Relief of Sickness,* Allen and Unwin, 1923, pp. 158-86; Davis, Michael M., *Medical Care for Tomorrow,* New York, Harper, 1955, p. 176. See also the paper by Milton Terris, 'Hermann Bigg's Contribution to the Modern Concept of the Health Center', in *Bulletin of History of Medicine,* Oct. 1946, pp. 387-412.

27   *BMJ,* 1911, 2, Supp., pp. 429-30 (Keay); 1920, 2, pp. 83-6. *Med. World,* 7 Aug. 1913, pp. 6-7. *Lancet,* 1919, 1, p. 145. Dodd, F. Lawson, *A National Medical Service,* Fabian Tract No. 160, 1911. Stark Murray (1971), pp. 1-15.

28   MH 73/49, Med. Council, Minutes of Meetings, 5 Nov. 1920 (no. 21).

29   MH 73/31, Consul. Council on Gen. Health, Minutes of Meetings, 16 June 1920 (no. 11), p. 3, para. 8.

30   Abel-Smith (1964), p. 322.

31   MH 73/49, Med. Council, Minutes of Meetings, 2 Jan. 1920 (no. 7), p. 12. Dawson Report (1920), pp. 12 (para. 39-41), 13 (para. 48), 14 (para. 51), 26-33. *BMJ,* 1920, 1, pp. 743-5.

32   *BMJ,* 1920, 2, pp. 83-6.

33   Abel-Smith (1964), pp. 238-9, 250, 252-83, 276-8, 295.

34   *Ibid.,* pp. 296-7.

35   *BMJ,* 1948, 1, pp. 264-7.

36   *BMJ,* 1920, 2, Supp., p. 20.

37   *BMJ,* 1918, 2, pp. 23-6. See also Watson (1950), p. 152. See also *BMJ,* 1918, 1, p. 673; 1920, 1, pp. 743-5.

38   *BMJ,* 1920, 2, p. 86.

39   *BMJ,* 1918, 1, p. 673.

40   MH 73/48, letter from Dawson to Robinson, 17 Sept. 1921.

41   Dawson Report (1920), p. 14, para. 50. See also *BMJ,* 1918, 2, p. 26.

Chapter 7: The Failure of Reform

1 *BMJ,* 1919, 2, p. 575. For an indication of Addison's desire to have the council move even more swiftly than it did, see MH 73/45, Med. Council, 22 Jan. 1920, Heseltine to Morant; MH 73/49, Med. Council, Minutes of Meetings, 30 Jan. 1920 (no. 9).

2 *Public Health,* March, 1918, pp. 61-2.

3 *Charity Org. Rev.,* May, 1909, pp. 7-8 (Bailward).

4 Honigsbaum (1970), p. 30. See also *Local Government Journal,* 5 June 1920, p. 355.

5 For a clear indication of what the Ministry wanted, see Morant's address to the Medical Council. MH 73/49, Med. Council, Minutes of Meetings, 2 Jan. 1920 (no. 7), pp. 8-9.

6 *The Times,* 16 Jan. 1920, p. 13.

7 MH 73/29, Heseltine to Morant, 26 Jan. 1920.

8 MH 73/45, Heseltine to Morant, 22 Jan. 1920.

9 MH 73/49, Med. Council, Minutes of Meetings, 19 Nov. 1920 (no. 22), para. 10 and Annex 2, *Extension of Medical Benefit to Dependants,* words in capital letters as in original. This Memo. was prepared after the report but showed what was in Dawson's mind earlier.

10 Dawson Report (1920), pp. 21-3, para. 92-104.

11 MH 73/49, Med. Council, Minutes of Meetings, 2 Jan. 1920 (no. 7). See also 5 Dec. 1919 (no. 5); 19 Dec. 1919 (no. 6); 19 March 1920 (no. 17). Before an MOH audience, Morant spoke more openly on the subject. See *BMJ,* 1919, 2, p. 542. See also Newman's paper in *BMJ,* 1920, 2, pp. 33-6.

12 *BMJ,* 1920, 2, Supp., pp. 21-2.

13 *Municipal Journal,* 30 Nov. 1917, pp. 1103-4.

14 MH 73/27, Consul. Council of Gen. Health, Minutes of Meetings, 1920: 28 July (no. 7), 2 Dec. (no. 9). *Local Govt. J.,* 5 June 1920, p. 355.

15 MH 73/31, Consul. Council on Gen. Health, Minutes of Meetings, 12 Feb. 1920 (no. 1).

16 *Ibid.,* 31 March 1920 (no. 5). For the Report, see MH 73/29, *Interim Report on Med. and Allied Services for Mothers and Infants.*

17 MH 73/30, Consul. Council on Gen. Health, *Report on Improved Provision of Med. and Allied Services.*

18 *Ibid.,* para. 9.

19 *Charity Org. Rev.,* Oct. 1918, pp. 101-4. See also Bailward, W.A., *The Slippery Slope,* John Murray, 1920, pp. 172-83.

20 For evidence, see Hayes Fisher's remarks (as Lord Downham) to the Central Poor Law Conf. in 1919. Poor Law Dist. Conf., 1918-21, pp. 20-1.

21 For an account of this whole campaign, see Drage, Geoffrey, *Public Assistance,* John Murray, 1930.

22 *Charity Org. Rev.,* Nov. 1918, p. 111. See also Lewis, W. G., *The Devoted Work of the Guardians,* 1918, p. 65 in particular.

23 *Charity Org. Rev.,* March 1913, pp. 115-16. See also Drage's book, *State and Poor,* Collin's Clear-Type Press for Nation's Library, 1914.

24 *Charity Org. Rev.,* April 1933, p. 55.

25 For the League's move to Denison House in 1916, see *Vaccination Inquirer,* Sept. 1916, p. 209.

26 *National Opinion* (organ of National Party), 1918-23.

27 Harmsworth, Harold Sidney (Viscount Rothermere), *Solvency or Downfall?*, Longmans, 1921.
28 *Nat. Opinion,* Sept. 1920, p. 2; Jan. 1921, p. 3.
29 Gilbert (1970), p. 30.
30 *Local Gov't. J.,* 9 April 1921, p. 211.
31 MH 73/28, Consul. Council on Local Health Admin., Minutes of Meetings, 7 July 1921 (no. 12), *Report on Economies in the Cost of Local Government Services.*
32 *Poor Law Officers' Journal,* 1920: 6 Feb., pp. 128-9; 11 June, pp. 573-4; 17 Dec., pp. 1221-2.
33 *The Times,* 28 May 1920, p. 13.
34 *BMJ,* 1920, 2, Supp., pp. 17-18. *The Times,* 29 June 1920, p. 18.
35 *BMJ,* 1920, 2, p. 952 (Todd-White). For another critique of the primary health centre on grounds of cost, see *ibid.,* 1920, 1, pp. 850-1 (Dewar).
36 *The Times,* 1920: 20 Oct., p. 11; 8 Nov., p. 9; 2 Dec., p. 12; 4 Dec., p. 7; 15 Dec., p. 13; 16 Dec., p. 13.
37 MH 73/42, Newman to Robinson, 26 June 1920, para. 3.
38 MH 73/29, Heseltine to Barter, 24 March 1920; Barter to Heseltine, 26 March; Rhondda to Addison, 31 March; Addison to Rhondda, 12 April. MH 73/31, Consul. Council on Gen. Health, Minutes of Meetings, 30 June 1920 (no. 12).
39 MH 73/30 Consul. Council on Gen. Health, W.A.R. (Robinson) to Addison, 21 Nov. 1920; Greenwood to Heseltine, 6 Feb. 1921; Heseltine to Robinson, 7 March and 1 June 1921.
40 *BMJ,* 1920, 1, Supp., pp. 67-74.
41 Gilbert (1970), p. 46.
42 MH 73/30, Consul. Council on Gen. Health, Heseltine minutes for Gen. Health meeting, 10 Dec. 1920. MH 73/31, Minutes of Meetings, 10 Dec. 1920 (no. 20).
43 Gilbert (1970), pp. 33-50, 132-61. See also *BMJ,* 1921, 1, p. 535.

Chapter 8: Doctors Resist Salary

1 MH 73/49, Med. Council, Minutes of Meetings, 24 Oct. 1919 (no. 2), pp. 5-6. See also p. 51 above and Dawson Report (1920), p. 14, para. 52.
2 *BMJ,* 1912, 2, Supp., pp. 433-9; 1913, 1, Supp., pp. 25-34.
3 *Med. Press,* 1918, 2, p. 473.
4 *Ins. Mag.,* Feb. 1914, p. 18; *BMJ,* 1914, 1, Supp., p. 28.
5 *Nat. Ins. Gaz.,* 1920, pp. 173, 200-1. *Iron and Steel Trades Confederation Journal,* 1920: Feb., pp. 44-6; April, pp. 118-19.
6 *Nat. Ins. Gaz.,* 1913, pp. 51, 64-5. For his work in the Fabian Society, see *Fabian News,* Feb., 1912, p. 19; April, 1912, p. 34; April, 1920, p. 13; Jan., 1923, p. 2; Dec., 1923, p. 45; Nov., 1926, p. 59.
7 For a profile of Blizard, see *Domestic News,* June, 1916, p. 3.
8 Assoc. of Approved Socs., *Enquiry Into Medical Benefit,* 16 July 1914.
9 *Domestic News,* Feb. 1916, p. 3
10 For Jenkins' control of the Association, see *Steel Smelters Monthly Journal,* March 1917, p. 204.
11 *Nat. Ins. Gaz.,* 1920, pp. 173, 200-1.
12 *BMJ,* 1920, 1, pp. 800-2.

13 MH 62/116, *Memo. on Developments Necessary for Provision of Complete Medical Service for Insured Persons,* no date, no author (but probably Whitaker), italics underlined in original.

14 *Star*, 29 May 1919, p. 2. For a similar statement by a contemporary politician (and one which shows that the department still hopes to implement a salaried service), see the interview with Michael Alison during the period that he served as Parliamentary Under-Secretary for Health in *Gen. Prac.,* 20 July 1973, pp. 10-11.

15 Abel-Smith (1964), p. 279.

16 *Nat. Med. J.,* 1917, pp. 1-2, 17-21, 25-6, 52; 1918, pp. 25, 33-5.

17 For complaints about this, see *BMJ*, 1916, 2, pp. 694, 767; 1917, 1, pp. 86-90; 1918, 2, pp. 661-2. *Lancet,* 1918, 2, pp. 649-50, 722; 1919, 1, p. 45.

18 *BMJ,* 1917, 1, pp. 21-2; 1918, 2, p. 501. *Hosp.,* 1917, pp. 113-14 (10 Nov.); 1918, pp. 357-8 (27 July), 379-80 (3 Aug.).

19 *BMJ,* 1917, 1, pp. 86-90.

20 *BMJ,* 1917, 1, Supp., pp. 143-8 (para. 5); 1917, 2, pp. 156-7; 1917, 2, Supp., pp. 43-4. See also *Hosp.,* 4 Aug. 1917, pp. 349-50.

21 *BMJ,* 1918, 1, p. 327. See also *Lancet,* 1917, 2, pp. 165-6.

22 *BMJ*, 1914, 2, pp. 289-90; 1917, 2, Supp., p. 41 (Buist); 1921, 1, Supp., pp. 186-7 (Haslip). MH 73/49, Med. Council, Minutes of Meetings, 17 Dec. 1920 (no. 24), Memo. by Haslip, *General Practitioner Clinics.*

23 For Hall's participation in the formation of the Soc. Med. League, see *Soc. Dem.,* Oct. 1908, pp. 447-56. For his change of view on a salaried service, see *Med. World,* 7 Jan. 1927, p. 392.

24 *Med. World,* 7 Aug. 1914, pp. 5-7. SMSA Minute Book (in hands of SMA), pp. 20, 122-4, 136, 146. See also the article on this by Stark Murray in *Med. World,* Dec. 1972, p. 2.

25 Webb, B., 'Source Notes to Article on Prof. Org.', Vol. 8, Sec. 7 (ii), p. 34, letter from McCleary, 18 Jan, 1916, on file at Brit. Lib. of Pol. and Econ. Science, LSE. For Dodd's role in the Fabian Society, see Cole, Margaret, *The Story of Fabian Socialism,* Heinemann, 1961, p. 141, n. 1.

26 *Med. World,* 1914: 13 Aug., pp. 244-6; 20 Aug., pp. 276-7; 27 Aug., pp. 299-300; 3 Sept., pp. 325-7; 10 Sept., pp. 350-2; 17 Sept., pp. 372-5.

27 *Med. World,* 8 Nov. 1918, pp. 297-9. See also the article by Hall in *ibid.,* 11 Jan. 1918, pp. 24-6; 21 March 1919, pp. 204-5.

28 For indications of this, see *Med. World,* 1918: 1 March, pp. 143-4; 21 June, p. 379. See also his obituary notice in *ibid.,* 24 June 1938, p. 642.

29 For references to the canvass conducted by the MPU, see *Med. World,* 1918: 27 Sept,. p. 198; 4 Oct., p. 222 (Parker); 6 Dec., Supp., pp. I-IV (Macdonald). See also *Hosp.,* 21 Sept. 1918, pp. 527-8: 11 Jan. 1919, pp. 310-11.

30 *Med. World,* 1918: 11 Jan., p. 11; 25 Jan., pp. 61-2; 1 March, p. 141; 16 Aug., p. 100.

31 Comyns Carr and others (1913), pp. 96-7.

32 *BMJ,* 1917, 1, pp. 171-2 (Craig). See also Assoc. of Approved Socs., *Enquiry Into Med. Ben.,* 1914.

33 *BMJ,* 1920, 2, Supp., p. 131 (Worth).

34 For an NMU critique of the Ministry's data, see *Nat. Med. J.,* 1920, p. 84.

35 *BMJ*, 1919, 1, pp. 201 (Gosse), 658 (Hodgson); 1919, 1, Supp., pp. 6-7 (Cooper); 1920, 2, Supp., pp. 70-1 (Taylor).

36 *BMJ*, 1920, 2, pp. 83-6.

37 *Public Health*, Aug., 1920, pp. 175-6; Feb., 1921, pp. 77-8.

38 *Med. Off.*, 1919, 2, p. 122.

39 Dawson Report (1920), pp. 21-3, para. 92-104.

40 *Public Health*, July, 1920, pp. 155-7.

41 *Med. Off.*, 1920, 1, pp. 192, 210.

42 *BMJ*, 1920, 2, pp. 94 (Davison), 142 (Heaney); 1920, 2, Supp., pp. 13-16 (Heaney).

43 For GP earnings before NHI, see the Plender Report in *BMJ*, 1912, 2, Supp., pp. 89-91. For GP earnings in 1919, see MH 62/118, Cox to Minister, 17 Nov. 1919, para 11; 1919, para. 11; MH 62/119, R. W. H. (R. W. Harris), Memo. on Pay, 24 Oct. 1919; *ibid.*, 'Notes on Remun. of Ins. Pracs.' (no signature and no date but follows Memo. from Whitaker to Newman, 25 Oct. 1919). For comparisons between GP and public health doctor pay, see *Public Health*, Nov. 1921, pp. 30-1; Aug. 1922, p. 294; Aug. 1923, pp. 293-4.

44 *Public Health*, Jan., 1923, pp. 85-6.

45 *Ibid.*, Dec., 1919, pp. 35-6.

46 *BMJ*, 1914, 1, p. 260; 1918, 2, pp. 39-40.

47 *Ibid.*, 1920, 2, Supp., pp. 13-16.

48 For evidence of Buchan's activities here, see *BMJ*, 1921, 1, p. 171 (Paterson); 1921, 1, Supp., pp. 86-7; 1921, 2, Supp., pp. 199-201; 1922, 1, Supp., pp. 4-6, 14-15. *Lancet*, 1921, 2, pp. 974-5, 1293-4; 1922, 1, pp. 46 (Dawson), 605, 751-2; 1922, 2, pp. 132-4. *Public Health*, Dec. 1921, pp. 55-6.

49 *BMJ*, 1923, 2, Supp., pp. 35-41. See also *Public Health*, Nov. 1921, pp. 30-1; July 1922, pp. 277-80.

50 *Public Health*, Jan. 1923, pp. 85-6, 112-13; Aug. 1923, pp. 293-4; April 1924, pp. 153-4.

51 *BMJ*, 1909, 2, pp. 805-6, 1296, 1565-6; 1910, 1, pp. 1340-2; 1910, 2, p. 1985.

52 *Ibid.*, 1914, 1, pp. 1372-3; 1917, 2, p. 703.

53 *Ibid.*, 1920, 1, pp. 803-4; 1921, 1, p. 399; 1921, 1, Supp., p. 132 (para. 245); 1921, 2, pp. 83-4. *Public Health*, Aug. 1921, pp. 204-5. *Lancet*, 1928, 2, pp. 764-5.

54 *BMJ*, 1920, 2, pp. 33-6, 635. See also 1919, 2, pp. 502-3; 1921, 2, pp. 189-90. *Lancet*, 1920, 2, pp. 79, 91-4, 111-14. Newman, George, *An Outline of the Practice of Preventive Medicine*, HMSO, 1926 (first published 1919), p. 134.

55 *BMJ*, 1918, 2, pp. 113-15, 117-18; 1920, 1, Supp., p. 191.

56 *Ibid.*, 1921, 1, Supp., p. 186.

57 *Ibid.*, 1921, 1, p. 469; 1921, 1, Supp., pp. 86-7.

58 *Lancet*, 1935, 2, p. 949.

59 *Lancet*, 1938, 2, pp. 39-40.

60 *Public Health*, 1921: Feb., pp. 77-8; June, pp. 159-60; Dec., p. 55.

61 *Lancet*, 1917, 1, pp. 199-200. MH 78/82, Parker to Addison, 1 Jan. 1918.

62 *Lancet*, 1918, 1, pp. 844-6.

63 *Lancet*, 1918, 2, pp. 85-7. See also *BMJ*, 1920, 1, p. 158.

64 *Nat. Med. J.,* 1915, pp. 101-3; 1916, pp. 85-6; 1917, pp. 82-9; 1918, p. 17; 1924, pp. 309-10.
65 *Lancet,* 1918, 2, pp. 182-3 (Parker).
66 Lab. Party, Memos. of Adv. Com. on Public Health, 1919, p. 2.
67 MH 78/82, Parker to Addison, 1 Jan. 1918.
68 Lab. Party, Memos. of Adv. Com. on Public Health, 1919, p. 10.
69 *BMJ,* 1920, 1, p. 158.
70 *BMJ,* 1918, 1, Supp., p. 39.
71 Interview with Somerville Hastings, 12 Feb. 1962.
72 *Nat. Med. J.,* 1923, pp. 280-4.
73 *BMJ,* 1919, 1, pp. 312-15.
74 *BMJ,* 1927, 1, pp. 253-4.
75 *BMJ,* 1924, 1, Supp., pp. 200-1.
76 *Observer,* 12 Jan. 1919, p. 11.
77 *BMJ,* 1920, 2, pp. 38-40. See also 1921, 2, Supp., pp. 126 (para. 54-5 of Ins. Acts. Com. Report), 166.
78 *St. Bartholomew's Hospital Gazette,* Nov. 1918, pp. 11-13. See also *Nat. Ins. Gaz.,* 1919, p. 279; *Lancet,* 1919, 1, p. 1031.
79 *BMJ,* 1920, 2, pp. 87-8.
80 *BMJ,* 1913, 1, Supp., pp. 25-34.
81 *BMJ,* 1920, 1, pp. 612, 647; 1920, 2, pp. 327-8, 527, 552-3, 750-1 (Dawson), 753-4; 1920, 2, Supp., pp. 126-8; 1921, 1, pp. 535, 747-8; 1921, 2, pp. 193-4 (Buchan). *Lancet,* 1920, 2, pp. 955-6, 1287-94. MH 78/74, whole folder deals with Misc. Prov. Bill. Abel-Smith (1964), pp. 299-302.

Chapter 9: The Ministry of Health Under Attack

1 *BMJ,* 1920, 2, Supp., pp. 18-19.
2 *BMJ,* 1920, 1, pp. 800-2; 1920, 2, pp. 83-6. *The Times,* 29 June 1920, p. 18.
3 For Wilson's use of this term, see *The Times,* 17 Dec. 1920, p. 12.
4 *The Times,* 1920: 10 Nov., p. 12; 15 Nov., p. 13; 19 Nov., p. 11; 24 Nov., p. 13; 27 Nov., p. 11; 1 Dec., p. 13; 7 Dec., p. 13; 14 Dec., p. 13; 15 Dec., p. 13.
5 For the main source of the information which follows here, see PIN 5/44, Ins. Med. Records Com., 'Medical Records for the Insurance Medical Service', Memo. from Min. of Health, 1919. Additional references will be given as needed.
6 *Med. World,* 15 Jan. 1914, pp. 94-9 (Collie). See also *Ins. Mag.,* Feb. 1914, pp. 19-27.
7 MH 62/130, Memo. from Whitaker to Newman, *'Medical Records for the Insurance Medical Service. Obligations Under Regulations',* 15 Nov. 1919.
8 *BMJ,* 1917, 1, Supp., p. 147, para. 28 of Ins. Acts. Com. Report. MH 62/130, Memo. from Newman to Morant, 19 Nov. 1919.
9 MH 62/118, R. W. Harris to Morant, 4 Sept. 1919, para. 7.
10 MH 62/130, Morant to Mackenzie, 24 Dec. 1919.
11 For the official biography, see Wilson, Robert MacNair, *The Beloved Physician,* John Murray, 1926. For a more recent life, see Mair, Alex,

SirJames Mackenzie, MD: General Practitioner, 1853-1925, Churchill Livingstone, 1973.

12 Flexner, Abraham, *I Remember,* New York, Simon & Schuster, 1940, pp. 133-57. See also the paper by Dr Joseph H. Pratt, 'Recollections and Letters of Sir James Mackenzie', in *New England Journal of Medicine,* Vol 224, 2 Jan. 1941, pp. 1-10.

13 See the paper by Mackenzie, 'The Position of Medicine at the Beginning of the Twentieth Century Illustrated by the State of Cardiology', in *New York Medical Journal,* 18 Jan. 1922, p. 13. See also Mackenzie, James, *The Future of Medicine,* Henry Froude (also Hodder and Stoughton and OUP), 1919, pp. 40-8.

14 MH 62/130, Dr James Pearse, 'Notes on Mackenzie's "Future of Medicine" ', Jan. 1920.

15 *Ibid.,* Newman to Morant, 8 Jan. 1920.

16 *Ibid.,* Mackenzie to Morant, 28 Dec. 1919 and 3 Jan. 1920. Mackenzie Memo., 8 Jan. 1920. See also Wilson (1926), pp. 285-7; Mair (1973), pp. 296-7, 305-7.

17 *The Times,* 21 May 1932, p. 6. See also the support given to the record-keeping programme by Brackenbury in *BMJ,* 1920, 1, Supp., pp. 155-7.

18 For the Report of the Committee, see Interdeptl. Com. on Ins. Med. Records, Report (Rolleston Report), HMSO, 1920, Cmd. 836. For the minutes of committee meetings, see PIN 5/44.

19 MH 62/130, Whitaker to Newman, 15 Nov. 1918, p. 8.

20 Rolleston Report (1920), pp. 16-20. See also the paper by Prof. Alex Mair, 'Mackenzie on Records in Insurance Practice', in *BMJ,* 1961, 1, pp. 1331-3.

21 MH 62/117, NHI Com., Contin. of Prelim. Discussions, 6 March 1919.

22 *The Times,* 1920: 26 Nov., p. 12; 24 Dec., p. 10; 28 Dec., p. 4; 29 Dec., pp. 5, 9; 30 Dec., p. 6; 31 Dec., p. 8. *The Times,* 1921: 1 Jan., p. 10; 3 Jan., p. 10; 4 Jan., p. 10; 12 Jan., pp. 10-11; 13 Jan., p. 12; 15 Jan., p. 10; 19 Jan., p. 11; 22 Jan., p. 10; 25 Jan., p. 10; 4 Feb., p. 8; 5 Feb., p. 8; 12 Feb., p. 10.

23 *BMJ,* 1920, 2, pp. 864-5.

24 *The Times,* 30 Dec. 1919, p. 12.

25 Wilson (1938), pp. 171, 199.

26 *The Times,* 26 Aug. 1920, p. 14.

27 *The Times,* 24 July 1920, p. 14. See also 13 March 1920, p. 17; 22 March 1920, p. 13.

28 *The Times*, 26 Nov. 1919, p. 12.

29 Wilson (1926), pp. 285-7. See also *The Times,* 12 Jan. 1921, p. 10.

30 For a full description of the procedure followed by regional medical officers, see Min. of Health, *Standing Instructions to Regional and Deputy Regional Medical Officers* (available from the regional medical staff of the Dept. of Health and Social Security, London).

31 *Lancet,* 1932, 1, pp. 1274-5 (Anderson). *BMJ,* 1937, 2, Supp., p. 268 (MacCarthy). See also Min. of Health, *Standing Instructions to Reg. Med. Off.,* 1932, para. 332.

32 *Med. World,* 15 July 1921, p. 1907 (Bliss). Min. of Health, *Standing Instructions to Reg. Med. Off.,* 1932, para. 311.

33 For an indication of one instance in which this actually was done, see the letter from Lord Russell of Liverpool in *BMJ,* 1937, 2, Supp., p. 29.

34 MH 62/133, McCleary to Whitaker, 15 Aug. 1932.

35 For references to the kind of studies conducted, see *BMJ,* 1934, 2, Supp., pp. 13-14 (para. 133, 150-1 of Report on Scottish Health Services); 1935, 2, Supp., p. 197; 1937, 2, Supp., p. 139 (para. 58 of Ins. Acts Com. Report); *Med. Off.,* 1943, 2, pp. 141-3.
36 *Med. World,* 9 July 1926, pp. 391-2.
37 *The Times,* 16 May 1932, p. 11. For the rebuttal made by the Secretary of the BMA (Anderson), see *ibid.,* 21 May 1932, p. 6.
38 *BMJ,* 1937, 1, Supp., p. 312 (para. 5-9).
39 *Ibid.,* pp. 317-22 (para. 22-8), 351-4.
40 *BMJ,* 1937, 2, Supp., pp. 1-2, 37-8 (Montgomery), 78 (Edwards), 105 (Chalmers).
41 MH 62/133, McCleary to Whitaker, 15 Aug. 1932.
42 *BMJ,* 1939, 2, Supp., p. 232.
43 MH 63/133, McCleary to Whitaker, 15 Aug. 1932.
44 Martin, J. P., *Social Aspects of Prescribing,* Heinemann, 1957, p. 55. Note also the comments on this development by Prof. Titmuss in his foreword on p. xi.
45 MH 62/133, Memo. by Whitaker, 13 June 1932.
46 *The Times,* 24 Nov. 1920, p. 13; 16 Dec. 1920, p. 13; 14 March 1921, p. 13; 2 April 1921, p. 18; 4 April 1921, p. 10; 12 May 1921, p. 11.
47 *The Times,* 1920: 28 May, pp. 9, 13; 24 May, p. 10; 15 July, pp. 11, 15.
48 *The Times,* 1920: 24 Jan., p. 12; 9 April, p. 11; 14 April, p. 11; 28 April, p. 13. *BMJ,* 1920, 1, pp. 105-11, 119. For a review of five years of work at St. Andrew's, see Mackenzie, James, *The Basis of Vital Activity,* Faber & Gwyer, 1926.
49 *BMJ,* 1920, 1, p. 783.
50 *The Times,* 1920: 7 May, p. 15; 11 May, p. 13; 24 Aug., p. 14; 26 Aug., p. 14.
51 *The Times,* 1920: 10 Nov., p. 9; 2 Dec., p. 12; 4 Dec., p. 7.
52 *BMJ,* 1920, 2, pp. 57, 709.
53 Newman, *Outline of Practice of Preventive Medicine,* 1926 edition, p. 138, para. 167. Newman (1939), p. 142.
54 MH 73/42, Newman to Robinson, 26 June 1920, para. 3. Note also the handwritten comments by Robinson and Newman in the margin, acknowledging that the Med. Council had only been asked to project an ideal scheme.
55 Min. of Health, *Report of Post-Graduate Committee.* (Athlone Report), HMSO, 1921. For criticism of the report on the grounds that it denied GPs in urban areas access to hospital, see *Med. World,* 1 July 1921, pp. 1841-3, 1863 (Gregg).

Chapter 10: Doctors Reject Collective Surgeries

1 *BMJ,* 1918, 2, pp. 23-6.
2 For recognition by the profession that the collective surgery represented the heart of Dawson's original programme, see *Med. World,* 26 July 1918, pp. 59-60.
3 MH 73/49, Med. Council, Minutes of Meetings, 24 Oct. 1919 (no. 2), pp. 6-8.
4 Darwin, Bernard, *A Century of Medical Service, The Story of the*

Great Western Railway Medical Society, 1847-1947, Swindon, 1947.

5   See the article by Dr Robert Sanderson, 'War Lessons As Applied to Civilian Practice', in *BMJ,* 1919, 2, pp. 71-2.

6   *Med. World,* 11 May 1917, p. 517.

7   McKail, David and Jones, Wm., *A Public Medical Service,* Allen and Unwin, 1919, pp. 18-20. See also *Med. World,* 17 June 1915, pp. 751 (Richmond), 755. *BMJ,* 1917, 1, pp. 200-1; *Lancet,* 1919, 2, pp. 699-50. For a later study of the geographical overlap in general practice see *Lancet,* 1955, 1, pp. 146-7.

8   *BMJ,* 1918, 1, Supp., p. 33. See also MH 62/117, NIH Com., 'Contin. of Prelim. Discussions', 6 March 1919, pp. 11-12, para. 24-9; CAB 57/8, Com. of Imperial Defence, Sub-Com. on Man-Power, Proceedings, 8 June 1923, testimony of Dr Alfred Cox, pp. 20-2, 46-7.

9   *Nat. Med. J.,* 1917, p. 42.

10 *BMJ,* 1918, 2, pp. 23-6.

11 *BMJ,* 1912, 2, pp. 325-6. See also MH 62/123, Doctors, Terms of Service, Discussion Papers, Cox to Braithwaite, 19 June 1912, enclosing Memo. from State Sick. Ins. Com. of BMA, para 10; PIN 2/19, NHI, Report of Proceedings of Adv. Com., 20 June 1912, p. 21 (Whitaker).

12 *Lancet,* 1913, 1, p. 1676.

13 *Lancet,* 1915, 2, p. 610.

14 *BMJ,* 1918, 2, pp. 529-30 (Mears).

15 London Panel Com., Minutes, 24 Sept. 1918, p. 60 (available at the office of the London Local Med. Com. in Tavistock Square).

16 *Lancet,* 1913, 2, pp. 1129-30; 1916, 1, pp. 415-16; 1916, 2, pp. 758-9.

17 *BMJ,* 1917, 1, Supp., p. 146 (para. 19 of Ins. Acts Com. Report). See also *Med. World,* 22 Sept. 1916, pp. 375-6; 1 June 1917, pp. 584-6.

18 *BMJ,* 1918, 2, pp. 23-4.

19 Dawson Report (1920), p. 11, para. 37.

20 MH 62/116, Memo. on Development Necessary for Complete Med. Service for Ins. Persons, no date or signature, pp. 7-8, para. 23.

21 *BMJ,* 1914, 1, pp. 729-80, 1029; 1914, 1, Supp., pp. 191-2; 1914, 2, pp. 139-40. *Med. World,* 12 Feb. 1914, pp. 253-5; 19 March 1914, pp. 458-9; 4 June 1914, p. 897. Addison (1934), pp. 14-18.

22 *Med. World,* 26 March 1914, p. 501; 9 July 1914, pp. 57-9; 24 Sept. 1914, p. 398 (Forman); 10 Dec. 1914, p. 666; 3 Nov. 1916, p. 566 (Price); 25 May 1917, pp. 569-70 (Angus); 1 June 1917, pp. 584-6; 3 May 1918, pp. 273-8. London Panel. Com., Minutes, 22 May 1917, Memo., pp. 4-5, Section IX (8) (g).

23 *BMJ,* 1920, 1, pp. 189-93.

24 Newman, George, *Public Opinion in Preventive Medicine,* HMSO, 1920, p. 30. See also *BMJ,* 1918, 2, pp. 26-7 (Biggs).

25 *Lancet,* 1914, 1, pp. 1068-9.

26 *Med. World,* 8 Jan. 1914, pp. 53-4. See also leader on p. 63.

27 *Lancet,* 1913, 2, pp. 176-7.

28 *Med. World,* 13 Oct. 1916, p. 470. MH 73/49, Med. Council, Minutes of Meetings, 7 Nov. 1919 (no. 3).

29 Stark Murray, David, *Health For All,* Gollancz, 1942, p. 121. See also *Lancet,* 1942, 2, p. 616 (para. 115 of Med. Plan. Res. Report); 1947, 1, pp. 228-30.

30 *BMJ,* 1919, 1, p. 162.
31 Dawson Report (1920), pp. 7-8, para. 16. For more on Martin's plan, see *Med. Off.,* 1917, 1, p. 41; 1930, 2, pp. 249-52; *County Council Association Gazette,* Feb. 1919, p. 13; Dec. 1919, pp. 231-2; *BMJ,* 1920, 2, pp. 84-5, 87-8, 916.
32 *BMJ,* 1920, 1, pp. 800-2.
33 *Med. Off.,* 1918, 2, p. 109.
34 For this, see *Lancet,* 1911, 1, pp. 1716-18 (Richards); 1912, 1, pp. 1612-13 (Lister); *BMJ,* 1911, 2, Supp., pp. 429-30 (Keay); 1918, 2, pp. 26-7 (Biggs); 1943, 2, Supp., pp. 81-2 (Camps); *Med. World,* 8 Jan. 1914, p. 63 (Hay); *Public Health,* June 1939, pp. 261-5. See also the article by Dr Wm. A. Brend, 'The Case For A National Medical Service', in *19th Cent.,* June 1914, pp. 1234-56. For an earlier version of the collective surgery idea as applied to the Poor Law, see the paper by Dr Ruth G. Hodgkinson, 'Poor Law Medical Officers of England, 1834-1871', in *Journal of the History of Medicine,* July 1956, p. 325.
35 *BMJ,* 1912, 1, p. 931; 1912, 1, Supp., pp. 402-3, 431-2; 1913, 1, Supp., pp. 273-4; 1914, 1, Supp., pp. 38-9.
36 Rhodes, Milson Russen, *A National Medical Service,* Didsbury (Manchester), 1912. See also Murray (1971), pp. 10-12. Another doctor advocating a similar scheme was Dr J. E. Esslement. *BMJ,* 1912, 2, Supp., p. 454. The paper reported here was later published by the SMSA under the title, *The State Medical Service Scheme.*
37 Parker, Charles A., *Panel Doctors and the Insurance Act,* SMSA, 1913. (The pamphlet is not dated but it is based on two articles that appeared in *Med. World* in that year. See the 18 and 25 Sept. issues, pp. 248-51, 291-5.) See also Stark Murray (1971), pp. 9-10. (Stark Murray here claims that Parker's pamphlet appeared in 1912 but that is not correct. *Med. World* did not begin publication until 7 Aug. 1913.) See also Parker's article on a state medical service in *Fort. Rev.,* May 1913, pp. 962-74; and another (with Prof. Moore) in *Lancet,* 1918, 2, pp. 85-7.
38 Lab. Party, Memo. of Adv. Com. on Public Health, 1919, p. 5.
39 *BMJ,* 1919, 1, p. 162; Dawson Report (1920), pp. 11 (para. 37), 13 (para. 46), 30-2 (para. 134-44), 36 (Type 2), 37 (Type 3).
40 *BMJ,* 1920, 1, pp. 800-2.
41 Lab. Party, Memo. of Adv. Com. on Public Health, 1919, p.5.
42 Pearse, Innes H. and Williamson, G. Scott, *The Case for Action,* Faber, 1931. Pearse, Innes H. and Crooker, Lucy H., *The Peckham Experiment,* Allen and Unwin for Sir Halley Stewart Trust, 1943.
43 *Homoeopathic World,* Feb. 1923, p. 50. See also *British Homoeopathic Journal,* Oct. 1943, pp. 80-91. See also *Health and Life,* Jan. 1950, pp. 15-18.
44 *BMJ,* 1964, 2, Supp., pp. 131-2. *Pulse,* 21 Sept. 1974, pp. 2-3.
45 See, for example, the letter in *BMJ,* 1920, 1, p. 784.
46 See, for example, the letter by Todd-White in *BMJ,* 1920, 2, p. 842.
47 *Ibid.,* pp. 83-6.
48 See, for example, *BMJ,* 1919, 2, pp. 91, 151.
49 *BMJ,* 1920, 1, pp. 746-7.
50 *Med. World,* 14 Nov. 1919, pp. 484-8 (Deakin). See also *BMJ,* 1919, 2, Supp., p. 34 (Brackenbury).
51 *Med. World,* 28 Nov. 1919, pp. 546-50 (Clark).

52 *BMJ,* 1920, 2, Supp., p. 95, para. 18; 1921, 1, Supp., pp. 154-5. See also 1920, 2, p. 94 (Harford).
53 Dawson Report (1920), p. 9, para. 21.
54 *BMJ,* 1949, 2, Supp., pp. 131-2. For an earlier study, showing proportions of single-handed practice by area, see Ministry of Health, Report of Interdepartmental Committee on the Remuneration of General Practitioners (Spens Report), HMSO, 1946, Cmd. 6810, pp. 19-21. For other studies, see *Lancet,* 1935, 2, p. 512; and Pol. and Econ. Planning, *Report on the British Health Services,* 1937, p. 143.
55 *Lancet,* 1936, 2, pp. 939-41; 1939, 2, pp. 945-51; 1943, 1, pp. 342-3; 1944, 1, pp. 511-13; 1947, 1, pp. 420-1; 1951, 1, p. 910; 1964, 2, p. 360 (Evans). See also Stevens (1966), p. 55.

Chapter 11: GPs Exclude Consultants from Health Centres

1   *BMJ,* 1920, 1, pp. 800-2.
2   *Med. World,* 11 May 1917, pp. 521-4.
3   This quotation is taken from an article by Goldwater that first appeared in *Modern Hospital,* April, 1933, pp. 4-6. It was later reprinted in a book by Bachmeyer, Arthur C., and Hartman, Gerhard, *The Hospital in Modern Society,* New York, Commonwealth Fund, 1943, pp. 22-30.
4   For a clear indication of this, see *BMJ,* 1920, 1, pp. 800-2.
5   *Hosp.,* 22 Nov. 1919, p. 156.
6   MH 62/85, Whitaker at Conf. with Minister on evidence to Royal Com. on NHI, 12 June 1925. For Whitaker's recognition of the same problem in 1919, see MH 62/119, Whitaker to Newman, 25 Oct. 1919, pp. 5-7.
7   *Observer,* 11 Feb, 1917, p. 11.
8   *Poor Law Off. J.,* 1917: 2 Feb., p. 107; 11 May, p. 414 (Tarpley).
9   *BMJ,* 1919, 1, pp. 312-15. For a similar admission by Brackenbury, see *ibid.,* 1920, 1, Supp., pp. 17-20.
10 Dawson Report (1920), pp. 13-14, para. 49.
11 *Med. World,* 3 May 1918, pp. 273-8.
12 *Med. World,* 28 March 1919, pp. 227-9.
13 Note, in particular, the statement by one such GP-specialist (Dr Peter Macdonald) to Lord Rhondda in *Med. World,* 1 June 1917, pp. 591-2.
14 For the growth of the importance of beds, particularly in private practice, see Abel-Smith (1964), pp. 188-9, 200, 205, 217, 264, 303-4, 338.
15 *BMJ,* 1918, 2, pp. 23-6. See also Dawson's remarks in *ibid.,* 1918, 1, p. 456; 1919, 2, Supp., pp. 44-5. See also *Lancet,* 1918, 1, p. 844.
16 *Lancet,* 1922, 2, pp. 1015-17.
17 The threat GPs posed to physicians had been recognized as early as 1906. See *BMJ,* 1906, 2, pp. 883-4. For an indication in 1920 of the stronger opposition posed by physicians to GP entry than surgeons, see *The Times,* 26 Aug. 1920, p. 14.
18 *Lancet,* 1932, 1, pp. 462-3. See also *Med. World,* 15 June 1928, p. 345. For the early history of the Clinic, see Graham Harvey, *A Doctor's London,* Allan Wingate, 1952, p. 17.
19 Abel-Smith (1964), pp. 188-9.
20 *Med. World,* 23 Dec. 1938, pp. 687-9.
21 *BMJ,* 1920, 2, pp. 750-1. *Lancet,* 1922, 1, pp. 188-9.

22 *Lancet,* 1921, 1, pp. 46-7 (Muir).
23 *Ibid.,* p. 200 (Bruce).
24 *Ibid.,* pp. 259-63 (Stewart), 276-7 (Bruce).
25 *Ibid.,* p. 1086.
26 *BMJ,* 1922, 1, Supp., p. 166. See also *Med. World,* 1921: 18 Feb., p. 1391; 25 Feb., pp. 1436-7; 4 March, pp. 1449-51. See also Abel-Smith (1964), p. 314.
27 *BMJ,* 1920, 2, Supp., pp. 126-8.
28 *Hosp.,* 16 Oct. 1920, pp. 53-4.
29 *BMJ,* 1920, 2, pp. 835-7.
30 *BMJ,* 1917, 2, pp. 89-90; 1920, 2, pp. 982, 987-9.
31 Dawson Report (1920), pp. 13 (para. 46), 16 (para. 59), 20 (para. 81-6). *BMJ,* 1920, 2, pp. 982, 987-9. *Lancet,* 1920, 2, pp. 1287-94, 1313-14; 1921, 1, pp. 259-63, 276-7. *Poor Law Off. J.,* 1920, pp. 128-9, 1272. *Hosp.,* 29 May 1920, p. 214.
32 Dawson Report (1920), pp. 6-7, para. 11.
33 *Ibid.,* p. 17, para. 66-7.
34 *Ibid.,* pp. 15-16 (para. 58), 24-5 (para. 106-11)
35 *Hosp.,* 1920: 3 April, p. 20, 24 April, pp. 77-8.
36 *BMJ,* 1920, 2, p. 84.
37 MH 62/85, Conf. with Minister on evidence to Royal Com. on NHI, 12 June 1925.
38 *Lancet,* 1919, 1, pp.129-33. Pearse made the same points in a memo. to Whitaker on 15 Nov. 1915. See MH 58/237B, pp. 7-8. See also *BMJ,* 1919, 1, pp. 312-15; 1919, 1, Supp., pp. 71-2 (para. 23-35 of Council Report).
39 MH 58/26, Brit. Post-Grad. Hosp. and Med. School, Com. on Post-Grad. Med. Ed., Minutes of 1st and 2nd Meetings, Memo. from Herbert J. Paterson, Hon. Sec. of Fellow. of Med., 21 Feb. 1925.
40 MH 58/42, Post-Grad. Ed. Athlone Com., Memos., 1920-21, No. 52, para. 5. See also Memo. No. 12 by Dr Edward Gregg, then active in the MPU but later a leader of the BMA.
41 *Lancet,* 1918, 1, p. 844. *BMJ,* 1920, 1, pp. 743-5.
42 For Moran's classic remark, see Royal Commission on Doctors' and Dentists' Remuneration, Minutes of Evidence, Days 3-4, HMSO, 1958, Q. 1023.
43 *BMJ,* 1920, 2, pp. 75-6. See also MH 62/116, Report of Conf., 6 Feb. 1919, p. 5 (remarks by Brackenbury and Dawson).
44 *BMJ,* 1920, 2, pp. 64, 75-6.
45 Newman (1926), p. 138, para. 167.
46 *The Times,* 22 March 1920, p. 13.
47 *BMJ,* 1920, 1, Supp., pp. 155-7. See also Mackenzie (1919), pp. 222-3.
48 *Med. World,* 28 March 1919, pp. 227-9.
49 *BMJ,* 1920, 2, Supp., pp. 17-20. See also *ibid.,* p. 95, para. 15-16 of Med.-Pol. Com. Report.
50 Dawson Report (1920), p. 33, para. 147. For the Welsh Report, see Min. of Health, *First Report of the Welsh Consul. Council on Med. and Allied Services in Wales,* HMSO, 1920, Cmd. 703. For a summary of the Report, see *BMJ,* 1920, 2, Supp., pp. 101-2. A second report, dealing with administrative areas, appeared in 1921 but that does not concern us here.
51 *BMJ,* 1920, 1, Supp., pp. 155-7.

52 *Med. World,* 19 March 1914, pp. 458-9, 501. See also *BMJ,* 1914, 1, pp. 1082-3.

53 *Med. World,* 10 Dec. 1914, p. 666.

54 MH 62/116, see report of conf. held on 6 Feb. 1918.

55 *BMJ,* 1919, 2, p. 142.

56 MH 62/116, Memo. on Develop. Necessary for Prov. or Complete Med. Service for Insured Persons, pp. 2-5. See also MH 62/117, Conf., 6 March 1919, p. 12, para. 29.

57 MH 62/117, Conf., 6 March 1919, p. 13 (last page of Memo.).

58 *Lancet,* 1918, 2, p. 252 (Shaw).

59 *Med. World,* 1922: 3 Nov., pp. 221-3; 10 Nov., pp. 243-5. *Lancet,* 1929, 2, p. 933.

60 *BMJ,* 1914, 2, Supp., pp. 88-90.

61 *BMJ,* 1919, 2, pp. 141-2.

62 *BMJ,* 1921, 1, Supp., pp. 154-5.

Chapter 12: Extension of Care - To Dependants or Specialists?

1 *BMJ,* 1920, 1, Supp., p. 155. See also *Med. World,* 1 Aug. 1919, pp. 117, 120.

2 For the fullest expression of Brackenbury's views here, see Brackenbury, Henry, *Patient and Doctor,* Hodder and Stoughton, 1935, p. 173.

3 *BMJ,* 1920, 1, Supp., pp. 126-8. For other indications of Brackenbury's views here, see *ibid.,* 1930, 2, Supp., pp. 39-43, 46-57. See also Abel-Smith (1964), pp. 413-14.

4 *BMJ,* 1919, 2, Supp., pp. 44-5.

5 *BMJ,* 1920, 1, pp. 800-2.

6 *BMJ,* 1933, 1, Supp., p. 144.

7 MH 73/49, Med. Council, Minutes of Meetings, 19 Nov. 1920 (no. 22), Annex 2, Memo. by Dawson, 'Extension of Med. Ben. to Deps.', words in capital letters as in original. See also *ibid.,* 13 Feb. 1920 (no. 11), para. 12; and MH 73/48, letter from Dawson to Robinson, 11 Aug. 1921.

8 In fact, the point was raised in a Memo. prepared for the Chairman of the NHI Joint Committee. See MH 62/116, Memo. on Develop. Necessary for Complete Med. Service, pp. 10-11, para. 29.

9 The costing here was not carried out fully until it was done by the Royal Commission on NHI in 1926. See Report of the Commission, HMSO, 1928, Cd. 2596, pp. 135 (para. 296), 161-2 (para. 366-70).

10 MH 62/116, Memo. on Develop. Necessary for Complete Med. Service, pp. 3-5, para. 11-17.

11 *BMJ,* 1916, 2, pp. 496-8.

12 Gray, Alexander, *Some Aspects of NHI,* P. S. King, 1923, pp. 25-8.

13 MH 62/116, Memo. on Develop. Necessary for Complete Med. Service, p. 11, para. 30. See also MH 62/117, Memo. on Contin. of Prelim. Discussions, 6 March 1919, p. 7, para. 15.

14 MH 62/119, Whitaker to Newman, *Remun. of Ins. Pracs. Suggested New Scheme,* 25 Oct. 1919, p. 4, para. (d).

15 *BMJ,* 1911, 1, Supp., p. 94, para. 65.

16 *BMJ,* 1913, 2, pp. 832-3 (Ward). *Med. World,* 4 Dec. 1913, pp. 701-3.

17 *BMJ,* 1914, 2, pp. 368-70, 513-14, *Med. World,* 1914: 13 Aug., p. 252-3, 259; 8 Oct., p. 449 (Mundy).

18 *BMJ,* 1917, 1, Supp., pp. 144 (para. 5-6), 145 (para. 15).

19 *BMJ,* 1921, 1, Supp., p. 103. *Med. World,* 4 Feb. 1921, p. 1351. See also MH 58/41, Statements to Athlone Com., 1920-1, no. 2 (Dill Russell), para. 2.

20 MH 77/26, Office Com. on Post-War Hosp. Policy, 'Salaried Med. Service', note by Mr Pater, no date but other documents in file dated 1942, p. 2, para. 7.

21 *Public Health,* May, 1918, pp. 94-6.

22 *BMJ,* 1912, 1, Supp., p. 91 (Parker and others).

23 *Lancet,* 1921, 1, pp. 293-5. *BMJ,* 1921, 1, pp. 244-5.

24 *BMJ,* 1916, 2, pp. 416-17.

25 *Hospital and Health Review,* 1922, p. 194. See also *BMJ,* 1920, 1, Supp., pp. 17-20 (Addison).

26 *Med. World,* 13 June 1919, p. 492.

27 MH 62/118, Ins. Acts Com. of BMA, Report on Revision of Conditions of Service under NHI, labelled 'M.25', no date but issued June, 1919, para. 50-8. See also MH 62/116, Ins. Acts Com. of BMA, Memo. on Questions of Conditions of Service Apart from Remun., 5 Dec. 1918, para. 9-23.

28 *Med. World,* 13 June 1919, p. 492

29 MH 62/116, Memo. on Develop. Necessary for Complete Med. Service, pp. 7-8. para. 23.

30 *Med. World,* 4 July 1919, pp. 19-20 (Hodgson).

31 PIN 5/44, Ins. Med. Records Com., Memo., *Provision of Additional Services for Insured Persons,* 9 April 1919, para. 6, 25. MH 62/117, Memo. (considered 2 April 1919) attached to letter to Combined Conferences, 17 April 1919, para. 101.

32 London Panel Com., Minutes, 27 March 1917, p. 25.

33 *BMJ,* 1921, 1, Supp., pp. 122-3 (para. 161-2), 154-5. For an earlier indication of the turn of medical opinion against dependant coverage, see *BMJ,* 1919, 2, Supp., pp. 143-4; 1919, 2, Supp., pp. 41-5.

34 This point was made by the unofficial Lytton Com. in 1914 of which Cox was a member. Assoc. of Approved Socs., *Enquiry Into Med. Ben.,* 16 July 1914. Brackenbury made the same point in *BMJ,* 1917, 1, pp. 88-90.

35 *BMJ,* 1944, 2, Supp., p. 11.

36 Official Reports of Central Poor Law Conferences, 1923, pp. 11-23. See also *ibid.,* 1920, p. 41 (Walker); 1921, pp. 48-72 (Cleaver); 1922, pp. 67-73 (Lipscomb); 1924, pp. 39-55 (Coster). See also *BMJ,* 1921, 2, p. 196 (Walker); 1924, 1, Supp., p. 138 (Sunderland).

37 *BMJ,* 1917, 2, p. 836.

38 *BMJ,* 1917, 2, Supp., pp. 373-4 (Brackenbury).

39 *BMJ,* 1919, 2, Supp., pp. 138-9.

40 *Ibid.,* pp. 132-3.

41 CAB 24/94, C.P. 296, Austen Chamberlain rebuts Addison, 14 Dec. 1919.

42 MH 62/118, Morant to Addison, 28 Oct. 1919, italics underlined as in original. See also *ibid., Extract from Draft Letter to Treasury,* no date but written by Morant (appears on a Minute Sheet following correspondence from Ministry to Cox, 21 Nov. 1919).

43 *Ibid.,* Whitaker to Morant, 25 July 1919, para. 9-13.

44 MH 62/119, Whitaker to Newman, 25 Oct. 1919, pp. 4-5, para. (f).

45 CAB 24/94, C.P. 258, Memo. by Addison, *National Health Insur-*

ance, 5 Dec. 1919; C.P. 296, Chamberlain rebuts Addison, 14 Dec. 1919; CAB 21/181, Minutes of Conf., 8 Jan. 1920; Memo. by Thomas Jones, *Health Insurance Committee,* 21 Jan. 1920; CAB 23/20, C.P. 477, Memo. by Thomas Jones, *Health Insurance,* 21 Jan. 1920 (p. 91 of volume). See also CAB 21/181, Minutes of Highlands and Islands Committee, 17 Dec. 1919; and CAB 27/54, Minutes of Highlands and Islands Com., 18 Dec. 1919, p. 10.

46 MH 62/119, 'Supplementary Notes of Med. Remun.', no date or signature (follows 'Ins. Doctors' Remun', 10 Oct. 1919), pp. 2-3, italics underlined as in original. See also R. W. H. (R. W. Harris), Memo. on Pay, 24 Oct. 1919.
47 *BMJ,* 1920, 1, Supp, p. 19.
48 *Ibid.,* p. 46.
49 *Ibid.,* p. 47, para. 3 (ii).
50 *Ibid.,* p. 50, para. 24-5.
51 *BMJ,* 1919, 2, Supp., pp. 26-9.
52 *Ibid.,* pp. 99 (para. 16-17), 101 (para. 18), 122 (para. 16).
53 *BMJ,* 1920, 1, Supp., pp. 61-2 (para. 49).
54 *Ibid.,* pp. 65-6.
55 *BMJ,* 1923, 1, Supp., pp. 162-3, italics underlined as in original. See also *ibid.,* 1922, 2, Supp., p. 74 (Leighton).
56 *Med. World,* 25 July 1919, p. 95.

Chapter 13: GPs Excluded from Hospital

1 Dawson Report (1920), pp. 7-8 (para. 16), 13 (para. 46). See also *BMJ,* 1920, 2, pp. 87-8, 93-4 (Marshall), 952 (Todd-White).
2 *BMJ,* 1920, 1, Supp., pp. 155-7. See also *ibid.,* 1918, 1, Supp., p. 50; 1920, 2, Supp., p. 21.
3 For the danger facing GPs here, see the paper by Dr Alfred Linnell (a member of Dawson's Council) in *BMJ,* 1920, 2, pp. 38-40.
4 *BMJ,* 1920, 2, p. 769 (Larking).
5 *BMJ,* 1920, 2, Supp., pp. 20-1 (Dain).
6 *Ibid.,* p. 842 (Todd-White).
7 *BMJ,* 1921, 1, Supp., pp. 226-7 (Stich). See also *Med. World,* 15 April 1921, pp. 1586-7 (Newton).
8 Scot. Bd. of Health, Consul. Council on Med., Interim Report, *A Scheme of Medical Service for Scotland*, Edin., HMSO, Cmd. 1039, 1920, p. 6, para. 11.
9 *BMJ,* 1921, 1, Supp., p. 171 (Ward); 1921, 2, Supp., p. 174. *Med. World,* 15 April 1921, pp. 1586-7; 29 April 1921, p. 1633; 15 July 1921, p. 1921; 3 Aug. 1923, pp. 597-8; 11 Jan. 1924, pp. 468-73.
10 *BMJ,* 1935, 2, Supp., pp. 7-8; 1936, 1, Supp., p. 114. Harris, R. W., and Sack, L. S., *Medical Insurance Practice*, BMA, 1937, pp. 19, 312-13.
11 Abel-Smith (1964), pp. 344-5.
12 *BMJ,* 1930, 1, Supp., pp. 234-5 (Jones). For an example of a cottage hospital which started (in 1927) on an open staff basis and later switched to a closed staff, see *BMJ,* 1930, 1, p. 965.
13 *Lancet,* 1929, 1, pp. 29-30; 1929, 2, pp. 933, 1086.
14 For leading articles favouring GP-hospital integration, see *Lancet,* 1949, 1, p. 571; 1950, 1, pp. 27-8. For an early indication of a change in

policy, see *ibid.*, 1953, 2, pp. 659-60. For a fuller sign, see the paper by Fox, 'The Personal Doctor and His Relation To The Hospital', *ibid.*, 1960, 1, pp. 743-60.

15 *BMJ*, 1933, 1, Supp., p. 46 (Beattie). For a later letter by this same doctor on the same theme (recalling events of the 1930s), see *ibid.*, 1961, 2, Supp., p. 148.

16 Abel-Smith (1964), pp. 372-7. See also London County Council, *London County Council Hospitals*, 1949.

17 *BMJ*, 1933, 1, Supp., pp. 142-3.

18 MH 77/22, Post-War Hosp. Policy, Forbes to Maude, 9 Feb. 1941.

19 *BMJ*, 1928, 2, Supp., pp. 44-6.

20 *The Times,* 3 April 1928, p. 17. See also *Med. Off.*, 1928, 1, p. 162.

21 *Public Health,* June 1943, pp. 101-3.

22 *Public Health,* July 1936, pp. 342-9.

23 *Public Health,* June 1938, pp. 267-71.

24 *Public Health,* Dec. 1934, pp. 90-4.

25 *Med. Off.,* 1939, 1, p. 87.

26 *Lancet,* 1934, 1, pp. 598, 637-8. *Med. Off.,* 1934, 1, p. 151. *Public Health,* Dec. 1934, pp. 90-4.

27 *Public Health,* Jan. 1939, pp. 97-101.

28 *Public Health,* Oct. 1931, pp. 7-11. *Med. Off.,* 1934, 2, p. 64.

29 *Med. Off.,* 1926, 2, p. 140 (Hill).

30 *Med. Off.,* 1938, 2, p. 48.

31 *Public Health,* March 1940, pp. 115-17.

32 *BMJ,* 1928, 2, pp. 27-9; 1928, 2, Supp., pp. 77-81.

33 *Public Health,* Dec. 1930, pp. 70-1.

34 *BMJ,* 1933, 1, Supp., p. 46 (Beattie). See also Abel-Smith (1964), p. 394.

35 *Lancet,* 1931, 1, p. 1410.

36 *BMJ,* 1926, 2, pp. 1002-3, 1011-13, 1020, 1078-9. *Med. World,* 10 Dec. 1926, p. 291; 28 Jan. 1927, p. 479.

37 *BMJ,* 1926, 2, pp. 1143-4. *Lancet,* 1930, 1, pp. 1050-1 (Groves).

38 *BMJ,* 1929, 2, Supp., p. 136 (Graham). *Med. World,* 9 Jan. 1931, p. 499.

39 *Lancet,* 1929, 2, p. 933.

40 *BMJ,* 1928, 2, Supp., p. 80; 1930, 1, Supp., pp. 140-2 (para. 130-40 of Council Report). See also Abel-Smith (1964), pp. 344-5.

41 For Dawson's stand here, see *BMJ,* 1933, 1, Supp., p. 144.

42 Abel-Smith (1964), pp. 343-4. See also pp. 313-14.

43 For these, see *BMJ,* 1935, 1, Supp., pp. 9-10, 274-5 (para. 173-4 of Council Report); 1935, 2, Supp., pp. 82-4; 1936, 2, Supp., pp. 87-8; *The Times,* 1 May 1939, p. 10.

44 *BMJ,* 1928, 2, pp. 317, 319-21, 510-11; 1933, 2, pp. 80, 124-5, 169-70, 211, 314, 545-6, 1139-40; 1935, 2, p. 1010. Abel-Smith (1964), pp. 384-404.

45 *Med. World,* 17 Feb. 1939, pp. 997-8.

46 For a hint of this, see Abel-Smith (1964), p. 391.

47 *BMJ,* 1937, 2, pp. 626-7. Abel-Smith (1964), p. 390.

48 *BMJ,* 1933, 1, Supp., pp. 270-2 (Cox). Abel-Smith (1964), p. 400.

49 *BMJ,* 1930, 1, Supp., pp. 140-2, para. 130-7. See also Abel-Smith (1964), p. 332.

50   *BMJ*, 1933, 1, Supp., p. 26. Abel-Smith (1964), pp. 106, 108-9, 137-8, 310, 313-16.
51   *BMJ*, 1931, 2, Supp., pp. 228-9 (Lloyd).
52   Abel-Smith (1964), p. 218.
53   *Ibid.,* pp. 305-7.
54   *Ibid.*, p. 118.
55   *Ibid.*, pp. 311, 317.
56   *Ibid.*, pp. 388-91.
57   *BMJ*, 1931, 1, Supp., pp. 1-2, 38, 246-8, 264 (para. 152 of Council Report); 1931, 2, Supp., pp. 289-90; 1932, 1, Supp., pp. 39-40, 136-8; 1932, 2, Supp., pp. 77-8 (Macdonald), 208; 1933, 2, Supp., pp. 300-2; 1934, 2, Supp., pp. 100-2 (Gray). Abel-Smith (1964), pp. 391, 400-1.
58   Abel-Smith (1964), pp. 345-7.
59   *Ibid.,* pp. 339, 343.
60   *BMJ*, 1938, 2, Supp., pp. 3-6. Abel-Smith (1964), p. 341.
61   Abel-Smith (1964), pp. 339-42, 395.
62   *BMJ*, 1928, 2, pp. 317, 510-11 (Fothergill); 1928, 2, Supp., pp. 266-7.
63   *BMJ*, 1930, 2, p. 58 (Bone); 1931, 2, Supp., p. 255 (Cox). Cox (1950), p. 100.
64   *BMJ*, 1928, 2, pp. 510-11; 1928, 2, Supp., pp. 38-41. Abel-Smith (1964), p. 376.
65   *BMJ*, 1929, 2, Supp., pp. 42-3; 1930, 1, Supp., pp. 257-8; 1930, 2, Supp., pp. 46-57. Abel-Smith (1964), p. 347.
66   *BMJ*, 1935, 1, Supp., pp. 222, 241-2. Abel-Smith (1964), p. 397.
67   *BMJ*, 1929, 2, Supp., pp. 204-5; 1930, 2, Supp., pp. 195-6.
68   For Brackenbury's support of GP claims on the hospital and specialist world, see *BMJ*, 1927, 2, pp. 575-82; 1929, 1, Supp., pp. 153-4; 1931, 2, Supp., pp. 321-4. See also Abel-Smith (1964), pp. 314, 316.
69   For a good paper by Cox on this subject, see *BMJ*, 1922, 1, Supp., pp. 69-73.
70   *BMJ*, 1926, 2, Supp., p. 141. See also *ibid.*, 1928, 2, p. 804.
71   *BMJ*, 1937, 2, Supp., pp. 104-5 (Cox).
72   *BMJ*, 1934, 1, Supp., pp. 146-7, 179-81 (para. 86-7 of Council Report); 1934, 2, Supp., p. 295; 1938, 1, Supp., pp. 58, 214-15 (para. 21 of Council Report).
73   *BMJ*, 1933, 2, Supp., pp. 88-9.
74   Brackenbury (1935), p. 80.
75   *BMJ*, 1933, 1, Supp., p. 72.
76   Brackenbury (1935), p. 75.
77   Abel-Smith (1964), pp. 140-2.
78   *BMJ*, 1930, 1, Supp., pp. 144 (para. 152-4 of Council Report), 165-82.
79   For the home hospital idea as it appeared in the 1929 version, see *BMJ*, 1930, 1, Supp., pp. 174-5, para. 50-2; for its appearance in the 1938 version, see BMA, *A General Medical Service for the Nation*, 1938, pp. 31-2, para. 65-8.
80   *BMJ*, 1929, 2, Supp., p. 273.
81   BMA (1938), pp. 31-2, para. 69-71.
82   *BMJ*, 1929, 1, p. 1181 (Dix).
83   *BMJ*, 1935, 1, Supp., pp. 35-6.
84   *BMJ*, 1937, 2, Supp., pp. 51-3; 1938, 1, Supp., p. 58; 1938, 2, Supp., pp. 57-8; 1939, 2, Supp., pp. 105-7.
85   *BMJ*, 1937, 2, Supp., pp. 104-5, italics underlined in original.

Chapter 14: Range of Care Narrows

1   *Med. World*, 4 March 1921, pp. 1442-3 (Gregg); 9 May 1924, pp. 221-6; 15 Aug. 1924, p. 542; 27 Feb. 1925, p. 613; 17 April 1925, pp. 176-80; 15 May 1925, pp. 249-52; 7 Aug. 1925, pp. 506-18; 9 July 1926, pp. 305-402; 27 July 1928, pp. 450-60 (Gregg); 3 Aug. 1928, pp. 469-70 (Rees); 14 Sept. 1928, p. 5.

2   *Med. World*, 3 July 1931, pp. 446-54. See also *BMJ*, 1937, 1, Supp., pp. 4-6.

3   *Lancet*, 1928, 2, pp. 56-7. Abel-Smith (1964), p. 392.

4   *BMJ*, 1932, 1, Supp., pp. 145-8.

5   See, for example, *BMJ*, 1936, 2, pp. 828-32.

6   *Med. Off.*, 1946, 1, p. 95.

7   *BMJ*, 1938, 2, Supp., p. 367 (Neville).

8   Abel-Smith (1964), p. 391.

9   *BMJ*, 1931, 1, Supp., pp. 246-8.

10 *BMJ*, 1933, 2, Supp., p. 93.

11 *BMJ*, 1931, 1, Supp., pp. 246-8.

12 *BMJ*, 1933, 2, Supp., p. 93; 1934, 1, Supp., p. 185.

13 *BMJ*, 1935, 2, Supp., p. 72 (Burgess).

14 Abel-Smith (1964), p. 392.

15 *BMJ*, 1934, 1, Supp., pp. 101-2. Harris and Sack (1937), pp. 72, 169-78.

16 *BMJ*, 1931, 2, Supp., pp. 156-7 (para. 65 of Ins. Acts Com. Report), 242, 314; 1933, 2, Supp., p. 133 (para. 68 of Ins. Acts Com. Report). *Nat. Ins. Gaz.*, 1931, pp. 559, 569 (Cox), 571, 580 (Rockliff), 595, 605 (Rockliff).

17 Royal Com. on NHI, 1925, Min. of Ev., Q. 1170 (Brock), 1096 (Whitaker), 22,039-40 (Corbey), 22,845 (Lesser), 22,882 (Lesser); App. to Min. of Ev., No. 99, para. 11.

18 *BMJ*, 1938, 1, Supp., p. 393 (Stanley-Jones).

19 *BMJ*, 1931, 2, Supp., p. 80; 1933, 1, pp. 23-4; 1937, 2, Supp., pp. 1-2. Abel-Smith (1964), p. 333.

20 *Lancet*, 1944, 2, pp. 743-5 (Layton).

21 Royal Com. on NHI, App. to Min. of Ev., 1925, No. 48, para. 56.

22 *BMJ*, 1929, 2, Supp., pp. 204-5; 1930, 2, Supp., pp. 195-6.

23 *Public Health*, May, 1965, pp. 209-13.

24 *BMJ*, 1938, 1, Supp., p. 184.

25 *Lancet*, 1901, 2, pp. 1766-7.

26 *Med. World*, 24 April 1931, pp. 187-8. See also Stevens (1971), pp. 145, 184-6.

27 *BMJ*, 1937, 1, Supp., pp. 269-71; 1938, 2, Supp., p. 264 (Brackenbury).

28 *BMJ*, 1938, 2, Supp., p. 7; 1946, 1, Supp., pp. 54-5.

29 Interview with Dr T. R. Davies, 6 Dec. 1964.

30 *BMJ*, 1935, 1, Supp., p. 137 (Dain).

31 *Ibid.*, p. 36. For the evolution of this dispute from the profession's point of view, see *BMJ*, 1934, 1, Supp., pp. 115-16, 262, 338; 1934, 2, Supp., pp. 91, 184 (para. 136-8 of Ins. Acts Com. Report); 1935, 1, Supp., pp. 45-6, 159-60 (para. 77-81 of Council Report); 1935, 2, Supp., pp. 173-4, 236-7. For the dispute from the miners' point of view, see *New Leader*, 24 Aug. 1934, p. 6; 27 Sept. 1935, p. 6.

32 *BMJ*, 1933, 2, Supp., p. 19 (Picton).

33 Royal Com. on NHI, Report (1928), p. 133, para. 290.
34 *Ibid.*, pp. 131-2, para. 282-5. *Lancet,* 1926, 1, pp. 501-2.
35 *BMJ*, 1928, 1, Supp., p. 270 (Bolam); 1929, 2, Supp., pp. 202-4 (Bolam).
36 *Med. World*, 26 March 1926, p. 98.
37 For this, see Honigsbaum, F., 'Unity in British Public Health Administration: The Failure of Reform, 1926-9', in *Medical History*, April 1968, pp. 109-21.
38 *BMJ*, 1928, 1, pp. 1117-18. For a rebuttal by the approved societies, see *Nat. Ins. Gaz.,* 1928, p. 211.
39 *BMJ*, 1935, 1, Supp., pp. 35-6 (Brackenbury); 1938, 1, Supp., pp. 359-60; 1938, 2, Supp., pp. 237-8. *Nat. Ins. Gaz.,* 1936, pp. 3, 659, 671; 1938, p. 246. National Association of Trade Union Approved Societies, *Annual Report*, 1938, pp. 8-13.
40 Royal Com. on NHI, *Report* (1928), pp. 45-6, para. 92-3.
41 *BMJ*, 1929, 1, Supp., pp. 122-5 (para. 20-2 of Council Report). However, see *ibid.*, 1928, 1, Supp., pp. 165-9 (para. 32 of Council Report).
42 *BMJ*, 1934, 1, Supp., p. 184 (para. 108 of Council Report); 1938, 1, Supp., p. 65 (Hamilton). *Med. World*, 26 Jan. 1934, p. 647.
43 *BMJ*, 1937, 2, Supp., pp. 380-1 (Jape).
44 *BMJ*, 1935, 1, p. 385 ('Z'); 1936, 2, Supp., pp. 82-4 (McIlroy); 1942, 2, pp. 184-5. *Med. World*, 6 March 1936, pp. 39-40; 15 Oct. 1937, pp. 286-90 (Ward).
45 Joint Committee of the Royal College of Obstetricians and Gynaecologists and the Population Investigation Committee, *Maternity in Great Britain*, OUP, 1948, pp. 78-9. For the medical opposition to its use by midwives, see *BMJ*, 1939, 2, Supp., pp. 73-6.
46 *BMJ*, 1935, 1, pp. 371-3; 1950, 1, pp. 598-602; 1953, 2, pp. 721-2. See also Jt. Com. of Royal Coll. of Obs. and Pop. Invest. Com., 1948, pp. 66, 68.
47 *Ibid.*, pp. 48-9.
48 *Ibid.*, pp. 65-8.
49 *BMJ*, 1937, 1, pp. 479-80; 1937, 2, Supp., pp. 34, 382-3 (Walker). Kerr, J. M. Munro, *Maternal Mortality and Morbidity*, Livingstone, 1933, p. xiv.
50 *BMJ*, 1937, 1, pp. 365-7, 425-6, 479, 949.
51 *BMJ*, 1944, 2, Supp., p. 100.
52 Jt. Com. of Royal Coll. of Obs. and Pop. Invest. Com., 1948, pp. 67-8.
53 *BMJ*, 1927, 2, p. 695; 1928, 2, pp. 993-5 (Groves). *Lancet*, 1931, 1, p. 1410; 1935, 1, pp. 383-4.
54 *Public Health*, Sept. 1932, p. 359.
55 *Ibid.*, Dec. 1932, pp. 91-2.
56 Interim Report of Interdept. Com. on Rehab. of Persons Injured by Accidents (Delevingne Report), HMSO, 1937, p. 9.
57 *BMJ*, 1935, 1, Supp., p. 141.
58 *BMJ*, 1931, 1, p. 760.
59 *BMJ*, 1938, 2, Supp., pp. 176-7 (Dyke).
60 *BMJ*, 1937, 2, Supp., pp. 269-70.
61 *Med. World*, 1926: 30 April, pp. 200-1; 4 June, p. 295. Royal Com. on NHI, Report, 1928, p. 134, para. 293-4.
62 *BMJ*, 1928, 2, Supp., p. 152 (para. 101-3 of Ins. Acts Com. Report);

1931, 2, Supp., 157 (para. 66-72 of Ins. Acts Com. Report). *Med. World*, 7 Nov. 1930, p. 233.
63 *BMJ*, 1939, 2, Supp., p. 19.
64 *Lancet*, 1927, 2, pp. 1139-40.
65 *BMJ*, 1927, 2, pp. 139-40; 1929, 1, Supp., p. 279; 1932, 1, Supp., pp. 151 (Dain), 189-90 (para. 111 of Council Report); 1932, 2, Supp., pp. 110, 151.
66 *BMJ*, 1938, 1, Supp., pp. 214-15 (para. 21 of Council Report).
67 *BMJ*, 1931, 1, p. 760; 1931, 1, Supp., pp. 132 (para. 16 of Council Report), 183-5.
68 *BMJ*, 1914, 1, pp. 1096-7 (Harford).
69 *Med. World*, 13 June 1919, pp. 490-3. See also NHI Commission Departmental Committee Report on Sickness Benefits Claims under the National Insurance Act (Schuster Report), HMSO, 1913, Cd. 7687, Min. of Ev., Q. 30,311-21 (Cox), 30,812 (Cox), 34,199 (Balding).
70 *BMJ*, 1920, 1, p. 407.
71 Addison (1934), pp. 14-15, 18.
72 *Med. World*, 19 May 1922, pp. 269-71.
73 *BMJ*, 1932, 1, Supp., p. 70 (Dickinson). *Nat. Ins. Gaz.*, 1937, p. 11 (Morgan). Newsholme, Arthur, *International Studies on the Relation Between the Private and Official Practice of Medicine*, Allen and Unwin, 1931, Vol. 3, p. 142.
74 Home Office, Departmental Committee on Certain Questions Arising under Workmen's Compensation Acts (Stewart Report), HMSO, 1938, Cmd. 5657, pp. 62-3, para. 128. See also Wilson, Arnold, and Levy, Hermann, *Workmen's Compensation*, OUP, 1939, Vol. 1, pp. 223, 227-43.
75 *BMJ*, 1934, 2, Supp., p. 263 (Halliday).
76 For the number in the regional medical corps., see *BMJ*, 1932, 2, p. 125. For the number of doctors on the panel in 1936 (roughly the same as 1932), see Political and Economic Planning, *Report on the British Health Services*, 1937, p. 142.
77 *Lancet*, 1948, 1, pp. 888-9. For similar criticism from the public health world, see *Med. Off.*, 1948, 2, p. 1.
78 CAB 87/77, Interdeptl. Com. on Social Ins. (Beveridge Com.), Minutes of Meetings, 6 May 1942 (no. 9), Q. 2665 (Stack). See also the comments of Prof. Hermann Levy, an expert on the international aspects of social insurance, in *Lancet*, 1943, 2, pp. 516-18, and in his book, *National Health Insurance*, CUP, 1944, pp. 332-5.

Chapter 15: The Anti-Vivisectionist Attempt to Divide the Profession

1 *Med. World*, 2 July 1926, pp. 363-4.
2 *Med. World*, 1923: 25 May, pp. 315-16; 22 June, pp. 384-94.
3 TUC and Lab. Party, Jt. Adv. Com. on Public Health, *National Health Insurance Medical Benefit*, no date (but 1923), pp. 4 (para. f), 14-15. This report was prepared by Cox and G. W. Canter, a trade union approved society official, both of whom were members of the advisory committee at the time. Brackenbury and Percy Rockliff (another approved society leader), however, assisted them. For evidence of this, see *Nat. Ins. Gaz.*, 1923, pp. 158, 200, 235.

4 *BMJ*, 1923, 2, Supp., pp. 58-60.
5 Harris and Sack (1937), pp. 52-61. For a list of the services ruled outside the range of panel care in London in 1935, see *Lancet*, 1936, 1, p. 573.
6 Levy (1944), pp. 125-6. For the actual testimony given by the Association before the Commission, see Royal Com. on NHI, App. to Min. of Ev., 1926, App. XLV, p. 439, para. 5; Min. of Ev., 1926, Q. 14,265-346, 14,412-33.
7 Royal Com. on NHI, Report, 1928, pp. 184-5, para. 431. See also Min. of Ev., 1926, Q. 992 (Brock), 14,824-42 (Brackenbury and Dain).
8 For a review of the whole experience, see Lees, D. S., and Cooper, M. H., 'Payment Per Item-of-Service, The Manchester and Salford Experience, 1913-28', in *Medical Care*, July-Sept., 1964, pp. 151-6.
9 *Journal of Chartered Society of Massage*, June 1930, pp. 330-1; Nov. 1933, pp. 113-14, 127-9.
10 *British Journal of Physical Medicine*, Sept. 1941, pp. 118-23.
11 Wicksteed, Jane H., *The Growth of a Profession — History of the Chartered Society of Physiotherapy, 1894-1945*, Edward Arnold, 1948, pp. 123-4. See also *Lancet*, 1926, 1, pp. 741-2; 1928, 1, p. 933; 1928, 2, pp. 142-3, 685.
12 *Med. World*, 3 July 1936, pp. 607-8; 1 July 1938, p. 664; 14 Oct. 1938, pp. 326-8 (Leeson). See also the paper by Dr. C. B. Heald, 'Menace of Quackery to Physical Medicine', in *BMJ*, 1932, 2, pp. 512-15.
13 Inglis, Brian, *Fringe Medicine*, Faber, 1964.
14 *Med. Press*, 1941, 1, pp. 321-2.
15 For the fullest biographical data about Bayly, see *Vegetarian Messenger*, Jan.-Feb. 1952, p. 20. See also his obituary notice in *World Forum*, Oct. 1961, p. 38.
16 *Med. World*, 1923: 13 July, p. 476; 5 Oct., pp. 134-5.
17 *Abolitionist*, 1924: Oct., pp. 121-2; Dec., pp. 145-51. See also Kidd, Beatrice E., and Richards, M. Edith, *Hadwen of Gloucester*, John Murray, 1933, pp. 274-316.
18 Note Whitaker's comments on this in MH 62/105, Revision of Disc. Procedure, Minute from Whitaker to Brock, 22 Sept. 1926.
19 *BMJ*, 1925, 1, Supp., pp. 122-3. (Here, Harvey was referred to only as 'Dr Z'.)
20 MH 62/105, Minute by Brock, 4 Sept. 1926, p. 8.
21 *BMJ*, 1925, 1, pp. 566, 665-6.
22 MH 62/105, Minute by Brock, 4 Sept. 1926, pp. 15-19. See also the comments on this by the Royal Com. on NHI, Report, 1928, pp. 190-1, para. 447.
23 MH 62/105, Minute by Brock, 4 Sept. 1926, pp. 1-2; Minute from Whitaker to Brock, 22 Sept. 1926, pp. 1-14.
24 *Med. World*, 12 June 1925, p. 355. For a brief review of both cases, see MH 62/99, Minute to Brock, 6 Feb. 1926.
25 Note the comments on this in Robson, William A., *Justice and Administrative Law*, Macmillan, 1928, pp. 256-8.
26 MH 62/99, Cox to Robinson, 11 June 1925.
27 *Ibid.*, Brock to Newman and Robinson, 22 May 1925; and reference to Brock Minute, 6 Oct. 1925.
28 *Ibid.*, Welply to Chamberlain, 30 April 1925; Veale (for Chamberlain) to Welply, 7 May 1925; Welply to Chamberlain, 12 May 1925.

29 *Ibid.*, Robinson note (attached to Minute from Newman to Robinson, 28 May 1925).

30 *Ibid.*, Brock to Robinson, 30 June 1925.

31 *Med. World*, 3 July 1925, p. 411.

32 *Med. World*, 6 Nov. 1925, pp. 157-64; 13 Nov. 1925, pp. 174-5; 19 Feb. 1926, pp. 472-3; 22 Oct. 1926, p. 125.

33 *The Times*, 18 March 1925, p. 15; 25 March 1925, p. 15. For earlier attacks along the same lines, see 18 Aug. 1921, p. 8; 4 April 1922, p. 15; 21 Oct. 1924, p. 15. For later attacks, see 3 May 1928, p. 17.

34 *Solicitors' Journal*, 1 Nov. 1924, pp. 64-5. *The Times*, 1 May 1928, p. 17 (Morgan). Hewart, Gordon, *The New Despotism*, Ernest Benn, 1929, pp. 50-1.

35 MH 62/99, Welply to Chamberlain, 4 March 1926.

36 For the key changes, see *BMJ*, 1926, 2, Supp., pp. 173-4 (Robinson); 1927, 2, Supp., pp. 107-9.

37 Rudolph Klein, in his study of the subject, has failed to recognize the significance of these events. See his *Complaints Against Doctors*, Charles Knight, 1973, pp. 75-88.

38 *BMJ*, 1925, 1, p. 631. See also *Med. World*, 14 Aug. 1925, pp. 532-5; and MH 62/105, Whitaker to Brock, 22 Sept. 1926, pp. 15-19.

39 *Abolitionist*, April 1925, pp. 49-50.

40 *Med. World*, 1925; 28 Aug., p. 577 (Dukes); 4 Sept., pp. 16-18 (Allan).

41 Kidd and Richards (1933), pp. 303-4.

42 *Med. World*, 1928: 30 March, p. 95; 15 June, pp. 328-34.

43 *Med. World*, 27 July 1928, p. 458; 8 Aug. 1930, p. 639; 3 July 1931, p. 452; 14 July 1933, p. 404; 27 July 1934, p. 616. *Anti-Vivisectionist Review*, March-April, 1930, pp. 46-59 (Bayly).

44 *Heal Thyself*, Oct. 1936, pp. 720-2.

45 *Med. World*, 10 Oct. 1943, p. 266.

46 Bayly, Maurice Beddow, *The Failure of Modern Research*, Health Education and Research Council, 1936. Note the review in *Med. World*, 26 June 1936, p. 596.

47 *Med. World*, 24 July 1936, pp. 711-12.

48 For profiles of the two anti-vivisection leaders, see I. me, E. Douglas, *The Mind Changers*, Michael Joseph, 1939, pp. 207-13; and West-acott, E., *A History of Vivisection and Anti-Vivisection*, Rochford, C. W. Daniel, 1949, pp. 189-96, 505, 509. For Bayly's ties with them, see *Progress Today*, March-April 1931, pp. 68-9; April-June 1932, p. 65; Jan.-March 1936, p. 47.

49 *Anti-Vivi. Rev.*, May-June 1930, p. 86. See also Niven, Charles D., *History of the Humane Movement*, Johnson, 1967, p. 90. For a full list of Council members, see *Progress Today*, Jan.-March 1937, p. 25. See also *ibid.*, Oct.-Dec. 1937, p. 179.

50 For background information on Stancomb, see his obituary notice in *Med. World*, 22 May 1942, p. 278; and *Abolitionist*, July-Aug. 1942, p. 45.

51 *BMJ*, 1939, 1, pp. 783-4. See also Picton's obituary notice in *ibid.*, 1948, 2, pp. 960, 1041-2.

52 Thus, Arthur Greenwood aided the osteopaths as early as 1924. See Streeter, Wilfrid A., *The New Healing*, Methuen, 1932, pp. 215-17.

53 *Lancet*, 1935, 1, pp. 955-60; 1935, 2, pp. 213-14. For the testimony given to Parliament on this subject, see Sel. Com. of Lords on Registration and

Regulation of Osteopaths Bill (29) (130) in House of Lords Sessional Papers, 1934-5, Vol. 6.

54 For the first supplement, see *Med. World*, 1 July 1938, p. 664. For Bayly's attempts to steer GPs in the direction of fringe medicine, see *ibid.*, 25 Sept. 1936, pp. 139-40; and 14 July 1939, pp. 743-9.

55 *Jewish Chronicle*, 1891; 13 Feb., p. 7; 20 Feb., p. 7; 27 Feb., pp. 6-7; 6 March, p. 7; 7 Aug., p. 6. See also Ruben, Morris, *Anti-Vivisection Exposed, Including a Disclosure of the Recent Attempt to Introduce Anti-Semitism into England*, Part 1, Bombay, Ed. Soc's. Steam Press, 1894 (on file in British Museum).

56 *The Britons*, Britons, 1952. Benewick, Robert, *Political Violence and Public Order*, Allen Lane, 1969, pp. 42-4. For Clarke's place in the homoeopathic world, see the issue dedicated to him when he died in *Homoeo. World*, Jan. 1932.

57 For recognition of this association (without, however, an attempt to trace the historical reasons for it), see Roth, Julius A., *Health Purifiers and Their Enemies*, New York Prodist, 1967, p. 32.

58 Cross, Colin, *The Fascists in Britain*, Barrie and Rockliff, 1961, pp. 22-3, 179-80, 187. See also Benewick (1969), pp. 114, 273-4, 294.

59 Letter from Dr Charles W. Brook to the author, 30 Oct. 1974.

60 *Med. World*, 22 May 1938, pp. 488-92.

61 *Daily Herald*, 21 Jan. 1935, pp. 1, 8.

Chapter 16: GP Indifference to Hospital Access

1   For the development of this service, see the article by Dr Stephen Taylor in *Lancet*, 1939, 2, pp. 945-51. Titmuss, R. M., *Problems of Social Policy*, HMSO, 1950, pp. 54-86. Dunn, C. L., *The Emergency Medical Services*, HMSO, 1952. Abel-Smith (1964), p. 426-39.

2   Dunn (1952), pp. 424-32.

3   Titmuss (1950), pp. 189-91.

4   For one example, see Taylor, Stephen, *Good General Practice*, OUP, 1954, p. 335.

5   Titmuss (1950), pp. 191-2.

6   CAB 87/77, Beveridge Committee, Min. of Meetings, 24 June 1942 (no. 20), Q. 4960, 5081-4, 5091. For the Report itself, see CAB 87/80, Bev. Com., Memos., No. 60, Nuffield Coll. Social Recon. Survey, 5 June 1942, pp. 4, 6, 10. For a rebuttal by Muriel Ritson of the Scot. Dept. of Health, see CAB 87/81, Bev. Com., Memos., No. 114, 20 July 1942.

7   See, for example, the joint statement submitted by the Labour Party and the TUC to the Royal Com. on NHI, App. to Min. of Ev., 1925, No. 92, pp. 614-22 para. 76.

8   For a clear indication of Labour concern with surgery premises, see Royal Com. on NHI, App. to Min. of Ev., 1926, No. 92, para. 85.

9   TUC, Annual Report, 1930, pp. 321-3. See also *Lancet*, 1930, 2, pp. 646-7.

10 *Lancet*, 1940, 1, pp. 222-4.

11 Lab. Party, *National Service for Health*, 1943, p. 9, italics underlined as in original.

12 Lab. Party, *Annual Report*, 1945, pp. 138-40.

13　Stark Murray (1942), p. 18. See also *BMJ*, 1946, 1, pp. 101-3; 1949, 2, p. 55 (Scott). *Lancet*, 1947, 1, pp. 114-16.

14　This policy was established at the last conference held by the MPU before the outbreak of the Second World War. For a full report of the conference, see *Med. World,* 21 July 1939, entire Supp. See also the article that appeared the following week, 28 July 1939, pp. 851-2; and the report that appeared in *Lancet*, 1939, 1, p. 1404. (The quotation reproduced here is taken from *The Lancet* report.) For a reproduction of the scheme itself, see *Med. World*, 11 June 1943, pp. 401-12.

15　For the Report itself, see *BMJ*, 1942, 1, pp. 743-53. For the establishment of the Commission and its internal organization, see *Lancet*, 1941, 1, p. 45; 1942, 1, p. 739. See also Ross, James Stirling, *The National Health Service in Great Britain*, OUP, 1952, pp. 78-81; and Abel-Smith (1964), pp. 444-51.

16　*BMJ*, 1942, 1, pp. 759-61. See also the letter from a prominent pathologist (Dr S. C. Dyke) recalling Dawson's message at the start of the Commission's proceedings in *BMJ*, 1965, 1, pp. 651-2.

17　*Med. Off.*, 1941, 2, p. 34.

18　*Public Health*, July, 1941, pp. 195-6.

19　*BMJ*, 1942, 1, Supp., pp. 1-2, 23-4, 41-2, 55-6, 69-70.

20　Note, in particular, the papers by Prof. John Ryle and Dr (later Sir) Harold Himsworth in *BMJ*, 1942, 1, Supp., pp. 33-5, 47-9.

21　*BMJ*, 1943, 2, Supp., p. 53 (Souttar).

22　*BMJ*, 1942, 2, Supp., p. 45 (Souttar).

23　*BMJ*, 1942, 2, Supp., p. 46. For Macdonald's resignation from the Hospital Committee, see *ibid.*, 1943, 1, Supp., p. 6.

24　*Lancet*, 1940, 1, p. 389 (Craig).

25　*Lancet*, 1943, 2, p. 203; 1943, 2, pp. 422-6. See also the article by the BMA's secretary (then Dr G. C. Anderson), in which he advocated GP beds in some experimental health centres, *BMJ*, 1943, 2, Supp., pp. 29-34.

26　MH 77/26, National Health Service — Policy, 2nd meeting with small committee of the profession, 3 June 1942, pp. 8-9. Dain maintained a consistent position on this issue throughout his long life. For other examples of his support for the GP-hospital idea, see *BMJ*, 1929, 2, Supp., p. 64; 1959, 2, Supp., p. 100.

27　*BMJ*, 1943, 2, Supp., pp. 63, 79-80, 85, 102-3; 1944, 1, Supp., pp. 57 (Hartley), 88 (Montgomery), 142-3 (Cunningham); 1944, 2, Supp., pp. 108, 131, 137, 139, 149; 1945, 1, p. 97 (Waddington); 1945, 1, Supp., pp. 23, 33, 44; 1946, 1, Supp., pp. 134-6, 160; 1946, 2, Supp., pp. 50-1.

28　*BMJ*, 1945, 2, Supp., pp. 26-7; 1946, 1, Supp., pp. 59, 77, 101-3.

29　*BMJ*, 1944, 2, p. 794-5; 1944, 2, Supp., pp. 109 (Wood), 155-6, 159, 161 (Wright), 170; 1945, 1, Supp., pp. 48-9, 60-1, 130; 1945, 2, pp. 296-7; 1945, 2, Supp., pp. 26-7, 30; 1946, 1, Supp., pp. 133, 141 (Davies). *Lancet*, 1945, 2, p. 506. *Med. World*, 7 Dec. 1945, p. 519. See also Eckstein, Harry, *The English Health Service*, Cambridge, Harvard Univ. Press, 1958, p. 114, n. 4.

30　*Lancet*, 1947, 2, pp. 101, 105-6.

31　*BMJ*, 1947, 2, Supp., pp. 30-1; 1948, 1, pp. 742-4 (question 12); 1948, 1, Supp., pp. 55, 64-6. *Med. World*, 18 June 1948, pp. 517-18.

32　*BMJ*, 1948, 1, pp. 1086-7; 1948, 1, Supp., pp. 149-51, 155-6

(Douglas); 1948, 2, p. 112 (Hastings and Bevan). *Lancet*, 1948, 1, p. 880.

33 *BMJ*, 1949, 2, pp. 1031-2. For an earlier expression of GP interest in hospital for midwifery reasons, see *ibid.*, 1946, 2, Supp., p. 51 (Arthur).

34 MH 77/26, 'National Health Service', 2 March 1943 (confidential Memo. circulated to members of Ministry's Med. Adv. Com.). See also in same file, 'Notes on Terms and Conditions on which Pracs. might be invited to participate in new Health Service', April, 1943, particularly App. A and B.

35 *Lancet*, 1944, 2, pp. 743-5. See also *BMJ*, 1946, 1, p. 696 (Orr-Ewing).

Chapter 17: Ministry Desire for a Salaried Service

1   Newman (1939), pp. 470-1.

2   *Lancet*, 1946, 1 pp. 471-3.

3   *Lancet*, 1943, 2, p. 56 (Batten).

4   MH 77/26, Draft of a paper by Sir John Maude for Ministers on a proposed Gen. Prac. Service, Nov., 1942, p. 10, para. 3.

5   *Public Health*, May 1948, pp. 144-6.

6   For the clearest indication of the Ministry's policy here, see Min. of Health and Dept. of Health for Scot., *A National Health Service* (White Paper on National Health Service), HMSO, 1944, Cmd. 6502, pp. 29, 38.

7   For evidence of Jameson's belief in the Brackenbury school of general practice, see *Public Health*, May, 1930, pp. 253-60; Dec., 1932, pp. 91-2; *Lancet*, 1930, 1, pp. 24-5; 1938, 2, pp. 211-12. For evidence of personal ties between the two men, see *Hornsey Journal*, 20 March 1942; and *Med. Off.*, 1942, 1, p. 92.

8   Goodman, Neville M., *Wilson Jameson*, Allen and Unwin, 1970, pp. 80-2.

9   MH 77/26, Nat. Health Service Policy, 2nd meeting with small com. of prof., 3 June 1943, p. 5.

10 MH 77/26, Post-War Med. Policy, GP Service, Sept., 1942, p. 5; Draft of paper by Maude on GP Service, Nov., 1942, p. 7.

11 MH 77/26, E. J. M. [Maude], 'Note on Sal. Service v. Pay by Cap. Fees for GPs', 12 March 1943, p. 2. For the rationale which underlay this belief, see *ibid.*, Post-War Med. Policy, GP Service, March, 1942, pp. 3-4, para. 9. See also *Lancet*, 1943, 1, pp. 813-15.

12 MH 77/26, Nat. Med. Service, Whole-time v part-time service, March, 1943, p. 2.

Chapter 18: The Profession's Deceptive Radicalism

1   Stark Murray (1971), pp. 25-6. For the SMA's original scheme, see SMA, *A Socialised Medical Service*, 1933. For the evolution of its ideas as indicated by Somerville Hastings, see *Lancet*, 1931, 1, p. 1115. *Med. Off.*, 1935, 1, pp. 105-7. *Medicine Today and Tomorrow*, July 1938, pp. 3-6.

2   *Med. World*, 27 July 1928, p. 458.

3   Brook, Charles W., *Making Medical History*, Percy B. Buxton, 1946, pp. 3-4.

4   *Med. World*, 14 July 1933, pp. 406-9; 6 July 1934, p. 532; 12 Oct. 1934, pp. 205-15.

5   Lab. Party, *Annual Report*, 1934, pp. 214-15, 256-8.

6   Brook (1946), pp. 7-8.

7   *Med. World*, 5 July 1935, pp. 734-6.

8   *Labour Magazine*, 1935: Feb., pp. 138-9; March, p. 164.

9   *Med. World*, 1935: 22 Feb., p. 775; 10 May, pp. 394-6.

10 *Med. World*, 1937: 14 May, pp. 396-8 (Ward); 21 May, pp. 424-6; 4 June, pp. 482-95; 10 Sept., pp. 72-83 (Ward).

11 *Med. World*, 17 June 1939, p. 14-4. See also pp. 6-8 of the Supp. to the 21 July 1939 issue for a full discussion of the subject at the MPU's annual conference.

12 *Med. World*, 22 March 1940, pp. 129-33; 28 Jan. 1944, pp. 630-1.

13 *Med. World*, 13 March 1942, pp. 70-1; 4 May 1945, pp. 374-8.

14 *Med. World*, 6 Sept. 1940, p. 68. The scheme itself was not published in *Med. World* but a similar one did appear 3 years later. See *ibid.*, 11 June 1943, pp. 401-12.

15 *Med. World*, 18 Oct. 1940, pp. 198-9. For the SMA plan, see SMA, *Whither Medicine*, 1940.

16 TUC, *Annual Report*, 1940, pp. 349-50. See also *Med. World*, 29 Nov. 1940, pp. 344-5.

17 *Lancet*, 1941, 1, pp. 260-1.

18 *Med. World*, 10 May 1940, p. 288. The MPU maintained a steady stream of criticism throughout the war. For other examples reminiscent of those it had raised before, see *ibid.*, 29 Aug. 1941, pp. 31-3; 12 Sept. 1941, p. 76; 5 Dec. 1941, p. 341.

19 Hill, Charles, *Both sides of the Hill*, Heinemann, 1964, p. 81.

20 For the effect of MPU action of the formation of the Commission, see *BMJ*, 1941, 1, p. 132 (McCall). For the BMA's Secretary (Anderson) as the prime mover, see *ibid.*, 1944, 1, p. 87 (Dawson). For other references to the Commission's origin, see *Lancet*, 1940, 1, p. 761; 1941, 1, p. 45.

21 For a full list of Commission members, see *Lancet*, 1941, 1, p. 63. When the members were first announced, the MPU did not complain since it was happy to see SMA representatives on the body; *Med. World*, 24 Jan. 1941, pp. 536-8. Later, however, it criticized the BMA for not appointing anyone from the MPU; *ibid.*, 30 May 1941, pp. 338-9. For the SMA representatives on the body (namely, Stark Murray, Hastings and MacWilliam), see Stark Murray (1971), p. 46.

22 For the MPU's efforts to call the profession's attention to this point, see *Med. World*, 21 Aug. 1942, pp. 16-18.

23 *BMJ*, 1942, 1, pp. 743-53.

24 *BMJ*, 1942, 2, p. 516.

25 *Public Health*, April, 1942, p. 142.

26 MH 77/26, 'Post-War Med. Policy, GP Service', Sept. 1942, para. 3. This paper compares the major proposals in an earlier Ministry paper (the one shown to Anderson of the BMA) with those in the Commission's report and finds much similarity between them. For the earlier Ministry paper, see *ibid.*, 'Post-War Med. Policy — GP Service', March, 1942.

27 *BMJ*, 1942, 2, pp. 35-6. See also *Lancet*, 1943, 2, p. 56 (Collier).

28 *Med. Off.*, 1945, 1, p. 93. See also *BMJ*, 1943, 2, Supp., pp. 29-34;
    1944, 1, Supp., pp. 41-3, 52-3 (para. 50-4), 59-60.
29 *Med. World*, 17 July 1942, p. 434; 8 Oct. 1943, pp. 212-18.
30 *BMJ*, 1942, 1, pp. 744 (para. 18-19), 748 (para. 63). Compare this,
    however, with the stress put on the GP-local authority clinic tie when a
    model health centre is actually described; *ibid.*, pp. 749-50 (para. 69).
31 *Lancet*, 1943, 1, pp. 752-3. For the official report, see Parl. Deb., Lords,
    June 1943, Vol. 127, Cols. 747-53. See also *ibid*, 16 April 1946, Vol. 140,
    Cols. 863-6.
32 *BMJ*, 1944, 1, Supp., pp. 142-3 (Cunningham).
33 *Lancet*, 1942, 1, pp. 343-7.
34 *Lancet*, 1943, 2, pp. 546-7, 553.
35 Association of Industrial Medical Officers, *Transactions*, July 1952,
    pp. 63-4 (Tryrer).
36 *BMJ*, 1944, 1, p. 154.
37 *Lancet*, 1946, 2, p. 683. For an earlier expression of the same view by
    the leaders of the British Paediatric Association, see *BMJ*, 1942, 2, p.
    647.
38 *Lancet*, 1940, 1, pp. 993-6. See also *BMJ*, 1942, 1, pp. 429-33.
39 Royal College of Obstetricians and Gynaecologists, *Report on a National
    Maternity Service*, 1944, pp. 33-4. See also the article by Mr (later Sir)
    Eardley Holland (the Chairman of the College Committee that produced
    the Report) on 'The GP and a Midwifery Service', in *Practitioner*, Jan.
    1945, pp. 1-5. For the heated reaction of GPs to the Report, see *BMJ*,
    1945, 1, Supp., p. 82 (para. 32 of Council Report); 1945, 2, pp. 294-6;
    1945, 2, Supp., pp. 34-5; 1946, 1, Supp., pp. 80, 94 (para. 66 of Council
    Report); 1946, 2, Supp., p. 47; 1947, 2, Supp., pp. 30-1. See also Shaw,
    Wm. Fletcher, *Twenty-Five Years: Story of the Royal College of Obstet-
    ricians and Gynaecologists, 1929-1954*, Churchill, 1954, pp. 149-51,
    170.
40 See the paper by a leading obstetrician, Prof. James Young, in
    Edinburgh Medical Journal, 1943, Vol. 50, pp. 474-90. See also his
    letter in *Lancet*, 1940, 2, p. 23.
41 *BMJ*, 1947, 2, Supp., p. 35 (Vaughan Jones).
42 *BMJ*, 1948, 2, Supp., pp. 56-7 (Thwaites).
43 *BMJ*, 1950, 2, Supp., pp. 85-7. For earlier remarks by Gray on the same
    theme, see *ibid.*, 1946, 1, Supp., p. 77; 1947, 2, Supp., p. 108; 1948, 2,
    Supp., pp. 56-7; 1949, 2, Supp., pp. 206-7. For the reference to Gray as
    the leading proponent of this philosophy in England, see *Lancet*, 1945, 1,
    pp. 633-4.
44 *Lancet*, 1942, 2, pp. 598-622.
45 *Ibid.*, p. 616, para. 119-20.
46 *Ibid.*, p. 616, para. 117.
47 For one example of dissent, see *Lancet*, 1944, 1, p. 550 (Cochrane and
    others).

Chapter 19: Medical Fear of Municipal Control

1 MH 77/26, Post-War Med. Policy — GP Service, Sept. 1942, pp. 7-8,
   para. 7; Draft of paper by Maude on GP Service, Nov. 1942, pp. 2-3, 8-9.
2 MH 77/26, Note of Meeting between Min. of Health and Under-Sec. of

State for Scot. and Rep. Com. of Med. Prof., 17 May 1943; 2nd Meeting with small Com. of Med. Prof., 3 June 1943, pp. 2-4.

3 CAB 87/13, Min. Memo., 'National Health Service', 28 July 1943, para. 37.

4 *BMJ*, 1939, 2, Supp., pp. 111-13. For another demand for a salaried service from BMA quarter (in this case, emanating mainly from the Glasgow and Kensington divisions), see *ibid.*, 1938, 2, Supp., pp. 99-100. See also Abel-Smith (1964), pp. 420-3.

5 *BMJ*, 1942, 2, Supp., pp. 34-5.

6 *BMJ*, 1944, 2, Supp., pp. 27-8 (answer to questions 26 and 28), 57-9. For suspected MPU influence on the poll, see *Med. World*, 25 Aug. 1944, pp. 53-4 (Gregg).

7 *BMJ*, 1942, 1, pp. 749-50, para. 69.

8 MH 77/26, Draft of paper by Maude on GP Service, Nov. 1942, p. 7; Note on Sal. Service v. Payment by Cap. Fees for GPs, by E. J. M. [Maude], 12 March 1943, pp. 1 (para. 3), 2 (para. 4).

9 *Med. Off.*, 1943, 2, p. 130.

10 *Lancet*, 1943, 1, pp. 243-4.

11 *Med. Off.*, 1918, 1, p. 185.

12 *BMJ*, 1944, 2, Supp., p. 28, answer to question 27.

13 Hill (1964), pp. 46-50.

14 *Public Health*, Feb. 1937, pp. 145-50.

15 *Med. Off.*, 1930, 2, pp. 227-8. For the excellent record of the service, see *BMJ*, 1940, 1, pp. 562-5.

16 For a verbatim record of the inquiry, see *Public Health*, Feb., 1938, pp. 137-55. For the Tribunal Report, see *ibid.*, March, 1938, pp. 179-82. (This was published by the Ministry as a White Paper, for which see Min. of Health, *Croydon Typhoid Inquiry*, HMSO, 1938, Cmd. 5664.) For a more critical judgement of Holden's behaviour by the former chief medical officer of the Ministry, see Newman's *Diaries*, page opposite entry for Dec. 1937.

17 *Med. Off.*, 1938, 2, p. 275; 1939, 2, p. 221.

18 *Med. World*, 14 July 1939, p. 752. For the difficulties encountered by this experiment, see *Public Health*, March 1946, pp. 81-4.

19 *Public Health*, 1938: Feb., pp. 530-1 (Chrystal); March, p. 183. See also *Med. World*, 10 Feb. 1939, pp. 962-4. For Croydon's prompt compliance with the Ministry's advice, see *BMJ*, 1938, 1, Supp., p. 366; 1938, 2, Supp., pp. 233-4, 368 (Genge).

20 *Public Health*, March 1938, pp. 159-61.

21 For earlier outbursts, see *Public Health*, April 1929, pp. 213-15; *BMJ*, 1933, 1, Supp., pp. 142-3.

22 *The Times*, 22 Nov. 1937, p. 13. For the ensuing correspondence, see *ibid.*, 1937: 24 Nov., p. 15; 25 Nov., p. 10; 26 Nov., p. 12; 2 Dec., p. 15.

23 *Public Health*, June, 1938, p. 275, para. 40 (b). *BMJ*, 1938, 2, pp. 367-8; 1938, 2, Supp., pp. 95-6 (Miller).

24 *BMJ*, 1938, 1, p. 644 (Kershaw).

25 For the background to this, see *BMJ*, 1929, 1, Supp., p. 252 (para. 145-7 of Council Report); 1929, 2, pp. 1213-14; 1929, 2, Supp., p. 91 (Brackenbury); 1930, 1, Supp., pp. 143-4 (para. 145-51 of Council Report); 1933, 1, Supp., pp. 249-50, 278 (para. 142 of Council Report); 1934, 1, Supp., p. 175 (para. 73 of Council Report).

26 *BMJ*, 1936, 2, Supp., pp. 258-9.

27 *BMJ,* 1935, 2, Supp., p. 205.
28 See, for example, *Med. Off.,* 1932, 1, p. 171; 1933, 1, p. 121; 1935, 1, pp. 165-8.
29 *BMJ,* 1938, 1, Supp., pp. 60-1. See also *Public Health,* Feb. 1938, pp. 119-21.
30 For the report of the Public Health Committee meeting during which the Croydon incident was presumably discussed (but of which no mention appears), see *BMJ,* 1938, 1, Supp., pp. 44-5.
31 *Public Health,* June 1938, p. 275.
32 *Public Health,* Dec. 1938, Supp., p. 8. See also *BMJ,* 1938, 2, pp. 367-8.
33 *Med. Off.,* 1937, 2, pp. 222-3.
34 *Public Health,* Feb. 1938, pp. 120-1. See also Holden's complaint about this in *Med. Off.,* 1938, 2, pp. 226-7.
35 See, in particular, the statement on this subject in his important paper, 'The Essentials of a National Medical Service', in *BMJ,* 1933, 1, p. 73.
36 *BMJ,* 1938, 1, Supp., p. 193.
37 BMA, *General Medical Service for the Nation,* 1938, pp. 45-6, para. 99.
38 *BMJ,* 1930, 2, Supp., pp. 65-6.
39 BMA (1938), p. 46, para. 101-2.
40 *Ibid.,* p. 46, para. 100.
41 *BMJ,* 1930, 2, Supp., pp. 144 (para. 153 of Council Report), 173 (para. 44 of 1929 Gen. Med. Service scheme).
42 For indications of the evolution of policy here, see Dawson Report (1920), p. 23, para. 103-4; *Med. Off.,* 1930, 1, p. 230; BMA (1938), p. 46, para. 102.
43 *Public Health,* Dec., 1938, pp. 78-80. *BMJ,* 1939, 1, Supp., pp. 195-6 (para. 119 of Council Report). For the background to the move, see *Public Health,* 1934, p. 107; Jan. 1935, p. 143 (Buchan); Oct. 1936, pp. 25-6; Nov. 1938, p. 45 (para. 11 of Council Report), 79-80. For complaints about consummation of the agreement without referral to the branches of the Society of MOH's, see *ibid.,* March 1939, pp. 186-7 (para. 25).
44 *Public Health,* Jan. 1939, pp. 89-91. See also *ibid.,* Feb. 1939, pp. 148-9 (Ash).
45 Mackintosh, J. M., *Trends of Opinion about the Public Health, 1901-51,* OUP, 1953, pp. 89-90. Mackintosh does not mention the Croydon incident but another historian did — without, however, any appreciation of the wider repercussions. See Frazer, W. M., *A History of English Public Health, 1834-1939,* Ballière, Tindall and Cox, 1950, pp. 460-1.

Chapter 20: Evolution of Ministry Planning

1 MH 77/22, Pater, J. E., 'Notes on Post-War Hosp. Policy', no date (but precedes Paper A, 'Outlines of Proposals', 11 June 1942). CAB 87/12, Com. on Recon. Priorities, Minutes of Meetings, 30 July 1943 (no. 16); CAB 87/13, Memos., Min. of Health and Sec. of State for Scot., 'A Comp. Med. Service', 2 Feb. 1943, PR (43) (3).

2   MH 77/22, Post-War Hosp. Policy, Memo. by Mr de Montmorency, 'Suggestions for a Post-War Hosp. Policy', Aug. 1941, para. 2.
3   MH 77/22, Post-War Hosp. Policy — Dep. Sec's Paper, E.?? to Maude, 20 Jan. 1941. See also the Memos. in the same file from Muriel Ritson, 12 Sept. 1936; from A. N. Rucker, 6 Feb. 1941; from Mr Pater, no date but for meeting on 5 April 1941 (entitled, 'Sal. Med. Service'); from de Montmorency, Aug. 1941; from Dept. of Health for Scot., 20 Sept. 1941. These papers are the ones in which the basic thinking for a comprehensive service was laid.
4   Brook (1946), pp. 38-43. See also Brook's letter in *Med. World,* 7 May 1943, pp. 287-8.
5   *Med. World,* 22 Dec. 1939, pp. 463-4.
6   Titmuss (1950), pp. 189, 227.
7   *Med. World,* 27 Dec. 1940, pp. 437-8.
8   Abel-Smith (1964), p. 453.
9   Addison, Paul, *The Road to 1945, British Politics and the Second World War,* Cape, 1975, pp. 211-28. See also Abel-Smith (1964), pp. 454-7.
10 MH 77/25, Office Com. on Post-War Hosp. Policy, Note by Wrigley, 'Hosp. Policy and Regionalisation', no date but precedes notes by Rucker, dated 6 Feb. 1941. For the health service charges provided in the Beveridge Report, see Beveridge Report (1942), pp. 158-63.
11 White Paper on Nat. Health Service, 1944, pp. 8-12, 46.
12 MH 77/26, Welply to Brown, 1 Sept. 1942. MH 77/40, circular letter from Welply enclosing MPU Memo., 'Transition to a State Med. Service', Aug. 1942.
13 CAB 87/13, Com. on Recon. Priorities, Memos., Sec. of State for Scot., 'National Health Service', 12 Oct. 1943, PR (43) (76). See also *ibid.,* Memo. dated 29 Oct. 1943, PR (43) (88).
14 CAB 87/13, Com. on Recon. Priorities, Memo. by Min. of Health, 'GP and Clinic Services', 10 Sept. 1943, PR (43) (55), para. 5, italics added.
15 BMA (1938), p. 7, para. 4.
16 *BMJ,* 1942, 1, p. 748, para. 56-9. See also BMA (1938), pp. 142-5, para. 93-8. See also MH 77/26, Post-War Med. Policy, — GP Service, Sept. 1942, pp. 1-2, para. 4.
17 CAB 87/13, Com. on Recon. Priorities, Memos., Brown and Johnston, 'A Comp. Med. Service', 3 Feb. 1943, PR (43) (3).
18 *Lancet,* 1921, 1, pp. 276-7 (Bruce).
19 *BMJ,* 1942, 1, p. 748, para. 57-60. See also MH 77/26, Post-War Med. Policy, — GP Service, Sept. 1942, pp. 1-2, para. 4.
20 White Paper on Nat. Health Service, 1944, pp. 12-13. *BMJ,* 1944, 1, pp. 643-52, para. 39-40.
21 *BMJ,* 1943, 2, Supp., pp. 29-34.
22 CAB 87/13, Com. on Recon. Priorities, Sec. of State for Scot., 'Gen. Prac. Service', 14 Sept. 1943, PR (43) (60).
23 See his obituary notice in *The Times,* 6 Sept. 1965, p. 10.
24 CAB 87/13, Com. on Recon. Priorities, Memos., Sec. of State for Scot., 'Nat. Health Service', 29 July 1943, PR (43) (45), para. 5; Sec. of State for Scot., 'Gen. Prac. Service', 14 Sept. 1943, PR (43) (60). See also *ibid.,* Minutes of Meetings, 1943: 30 July (no. 16), 18 Aug. (no. 17), 8 Sept. (no. 18), 16 Sept. (no. 19). White Paper on Nat. Health Service, 1944, pp. 42-6, 68-74.
25 See Honigsbaum, F., 'Unity in British Public Health Administration:

The Failure of Reform, 1926-9', in *Med. History,* April, 1968, pp. 114-15.

26 The fullest discussion of this problem appeared in the White Paper on Nat. Health Service, 1944, pp. 14-17, 39, 77-9. For the background, see MH 77/27, Memo. summarizing interview with Maude from non-county borough dep., 19 May 1943; Memo. to Min. from Urban Dist. Council Assn., 7 June 1943; Memo. to Lees, 23 June 1943. MH 77/26, Pritchard to Maude, 28 May 1943; Minutes of 4th Meeting between reps. of local authorities and Min., 23 June 1943. CAB 87/13, Memos., Min. of Health, 'Nat. Health Service', 13 Aug. 1943, PR (43) (48). MH 77/42, Mitchell to Willink, 21 Dec. 1943.

27 *Med. Off.,* 1942, 1, pp. 202-3; 1942, 2, pp. 130, 186.

28 CAB 87/13, Com. on Recon. Priorities, Memos., Min. of Health, 'GP and Clinic Services', 10 Sept. 1943, PR (43) (55), para. 6. See also his earlier Memo., 'Nat. Health Service', 28 July 1943, PR (43) (46).

29 From an article that appeared in the *Star,* 12 Aug. 1941 and filed in MH 77/25, Post-War Hosp. Policy, after note from Maude to Barlow, 26 Sept. 1941. See also *London News,* Oct. 1941, p. 1. See also the Memo. from Sir Allen Daley, MOH of the LCC, entitled, 'Hospital Policy', 28 Feb. 1941, in MH 77/22. See also his letter to Rucker, 4 March 1941 in the same file. For the strength of feeling among local authorities outside London, see MH 77/42, Mitchell to Willink, 21 Dec. 1943.

30 MH 77/22, Forber to Maude, 9 Feb. 1941.

31 *Public Health,* April 1957, pp. 2-3; Nov. 1966, pp. 16-21.

32 CAB 87/13, Com. on Recon. Priorities, Min. of Health, 'Nat. Health Service', 28 July 1943, PR (43) (46). See also White Paper on Nat. Health Service, 1944, p. 15.

33 MH 77/25, Post-War Hosp. Policy, Memo., 18 Dec. 1939 (but year probably wrong since '1940?' was written on top of Memo.), point 10. MH 77/22, Memo. by Mr de Montmorency, 'Suggestions for a Post-War Hosp. Policy', Aug. 1941, para. 9. MH 77/26, Draft of paper by Maude on GP Service, Nov. 1942, p. 10, para. 5. CAB 87/13, Com. on Recon. Priorities, Memos., Min. of Health, 'Nat. Health Service', 13 Aug. 1943, PR (43) (48). For an excellent review of the whole cancer service, see *Lancet,* 1948, 1, p. 797.

34 For the chaos that emerged in maternity care, see Min. of Health, *Report of Maternity Service Committee*, HMSO, 1959, pp. 74-6.

35 White Paper on Nat. Health Service, 1944, pp. 40, 60. In Willesden, cancer clinics were established as early as 1929. *Public Health,* Jan. 1947, pp. 72-3.

36 For the evolution of the joint board idea, see MH 77/22, Note by Mr Wrigley, 'Hosp. Policy and Regionalisation', no date (but documents following it dated Feb-March, 1941). MH 77/26, Post-War Med. Policy, — GP Service, March 1942, p. 7, para. 19 (a); *ibid.,* Sept. 1942, pp. 1-2; Notes on general admin. structure, for discussion with medical profession's representatives, March 1943, pp. 2-3. CAB 87/13, Com. on Recon. Priorities, Memos., Min. of Health, 'Nat. Health Service', 13 Aug. 1943, PR (43) (48). White Paper on Nat. Health Service, 1944, pp. 14-19, 77-9.

37 CAB 87/13, Com. on Recon. Priorities, Memos., Min. of Health, 'Nat.

Health Service', 28 July 1943, PR (43) (46), para. 5 (1). See also *ibid.*, Min. of Health and Sec. of State for Scot., 'Gen. Prac. Service', 9 Oct. 1943, PR (43) (72).

38   Dept. of Health and Soc. Sec., *Health and Personal Social Service Statistics for England, 1975,* HMSO, 1976, p. 32.

39   Stevens (1971), p. 181.

40   White Paper on Nat. Health Service, 1944, pp. 38-9, 62-3.

41   *Lancet,* 1941, 1, pp. 763-5; 1942, 2, pp. 382, 397; 1944, 1, pp. 26-9, 279-80; 1946, 1, p. 471. *BMJ,* 1942, 1, Supp., pp. 41-2. See also Stark Murray (1942), p. 18 and Stark Murray (1971), pp. 42-3, 64.

42   CAB 87/13, Com. on Recon. Priorities, Memos., Min. of Health, 'GP and Clinic Services', para. 9. See also Brown's address to the Assoc. of Welsh Insurance Committees in *BMJ,* 1943, 2, Supp., p. 56.

43   MH 77/26, Draft of paper by Maude on GP Service, p. 10, para. 3. See also Maude's reservations to the Guillebaud Report. Min. of Health and Sec. of State for Scot., 'Report of Committee of Enquiry into Cost of National Health Service', HMSO, 1956, Cmd. 9663, pp. 278-9 (para. 12), 285-6 (para. 28).

44   *Lancet,* 1943, 2, p. 464.

45   This suggestion emerged strongly from the Memos. Brown submitted to the Cabinet in Aug. and Sept. 1943. CAB 87/13, Com. on Recon. Priorities, 13 Aug. 1943, PR (43) (48); 10 Sept. 1943, PR (43) (55).

46   *BMJ,* 1942, 1, pp. 749-50, para. 66-9; 1942, 2, Supp., pp. 35-6; 1943, 2, Supp., pp. 29-34. See also BMA (1938), pp. 38-9, para. 80-3.

47   MH 77/26, Post-War Med. Policy — GP Service, Sept. 1942, pp. 2-3 (para. 5); Draft of paper by Maude on GP Service, Nov. 1942, p. 3, para. 9.

48   MH 77/26, Post-War Med. Policy — GP Service, Sept. 1942, pp. 1-2.

49   MH 77/26, Draft of paper by Maude on GP Service, Nov. 1942, p. 4, para. 4.

50   *BMJ,* 1945, 1, Supp., pp. 60-1.

Chapter 21: Doctors Demand Direct Representation

1   *BMJ,* 1913, 1, Supp., pp. 501-2 (Brackenbury).

2   *Public Health,* Jan. 1939, pp. 261-5.

3   MH 77/26, Draft of paper by Maude on GP Service, Nov. 1942.

4   MH 77/26, E. J. M. [Maude], 'Note on Salaried Service v. Payment by Capitation Fees for GPs', 12 March 1943, p. 5, para. 12 (5).

5   White Paper on Nat. Health Service, 1944, pp. 41, 79-80.

6   MH 77/26, Note of meeting between Min. of Health and Under-Sec. of State for Scot. and Rep. Com. of Med. Prof., 17 May 1943. See also *BMJ,* 1942, 2, Supp., p. 32.

7   *BMJ,* 1944, 1, Supp., pp. 59-60. See also pp. 131-3; 1944, 2, pp. 409, 697-8, 794-5.

8   *BMJ,* 1942, 1, pp. 573-4. See also 1944, 2, p. 409.

9   *BMJ,* 1942, 1, p. 750, para. 71. See also MH 77/26, Post-War Med. Policy — GP Service, p. 7, para 7.

10   BMA (1938), p. 19, para. 32.

11   *Municipal Journal,* 30 Nov. 1917, pp. 1103-4.

12   CAB 87/12, Com. on Recon. Priorities, Minutes of Meetings, 16 Sept.

1943 (no. 19). See also Honigsbaum, F., 'Unity in British Public Health Administration: The Failure of Reform, 1926-9', in *Med. History,* April 1968, pp. 110-11.

13   *BMJ,* 1918, 2, pp. 437-8.

14   MH 77/26, Minutes of 2nd Meeting between Rep. Com. of Med. Prof. and Officers of Min. of Health, 15 April 1943, pp. 4-7.

15   CAB 87/13, Com. on Recon. Priorities, Memos., Home Sec. and Min. of Home Security, 'Admin. of the new National Health Service', 17 Aug. 1943, PR (43) (49). See also *ibid.,* Min. of Health, 'Nat. Health Service', 28 July 1943, PR (43) (46), para. 16.

16   *Med. Off.,* 1938, 2, p. 48.

17   *Public Health,* Sept. 1942, pp. 197-8.

18   MH 77/26, Minutes of 2nd Meeting between reps. of local authorities and Min., 29 March 1943; Minutes of 3rd Meeting, 16 April 1943. See also the references in 15 above and *Lancet,* 1945, 1, pp. 60-1 (Bourne); *Med. World,* 12 Jan. 1945, pp. 676-7.

19   *Med. Off.,* 1939, 1, pp. 75-6. See also *Lancet,* 1945, 1, pp. 71-5. Hastings' influence can also be seen in Lab. Party, Public Health Adv. Com., Memos., RDR 272/Sept. 1944, 'The Health Services White Paper'; and (on the LCC) in Abel-Smith (1964), p. 470.

20   MH 77/26, Minutes of 2nd Meeting Between Rep. Com. of Med. Prof. and Officers of Min. of Health, 15 April 1943, pp. 4-5.

21   *BMJ,* 1944, 1, pp. 643-52 (para. 42-8 of Council Report); 1944, 2, pp. 697-8. See also CAB 87/13, Com. on Recon. Priorities, Memos., Min. of Health, 'Nat. Health Service', 28 July 1943, PR (43) (46), para. 5; Min. of Health, 'Nat. Health Service', 13 Aug. 1943, PR (43) (48).

22   CAB 87/13, Com. on Recon. Priorities, Memos., Sec. of State for Scot., 'Nat. Health Service', 29 July 1943, PR (43) (45), para. 4.

23   MH 77/26, Post-War Med. Policy — GP Service, Sept. 1942, pp. 1-2, para. 4. See also *ibid.,* 'Nat. Health Service', 2 March 1943, para. 8; 'Local Admin.', May 1943.

24   MH 77/26, Draft of paper by Maude on GP service, Nov. 1942, p. 5; Notes on the general admin. structure, for discussion with the med. prof.'s reps., March 1943, pp. 3-4.

25   MH 77/26, Minutes of 1st Meeting with the med. prof.'s reps., 25 March 1943, pp. 3-4; Minutes of 2nd Meeting with local authority representatives, 29 March 1943; Notes (for discussion with reps. of local govt. bodies on 16 April 1943) on org. of main and local committees of new health bodies, April 1943; Minutes of 3rd Meeting with reps. of local authorities 16 April 1943; Minutes of 2nd Meeting with med. prof.'s reps., 15 April 1943. CAB 87/13, Min. of Health, 'Nat. Health Service', 28 July 1943, PR (43) (46), para. 15-16.

26   CAB 87/13, Com. on Recon. Priorities, Memos., Min. of Health, 'Nat. Health Service', 13 Aug. 1943, PR (43) (48), para. 7. For Morrison's protest, see reference 15 above.

27   MH 77/26, Draft of paper by Maude on GP Service, Nov. 1942, pp. 4-5, para. 4. Note also Maude's remarks to the doctors in *ibid.,* Minutes of 3rd Meeting with small com. of med. prof., 28 June 1943. See also CAB 87/13, Com. on Recon. Priorities, Memos., Min. of Health and Sec. of State for Scot., 'A Comp. Med. Service', 2 Feb. 1943, PR (43) (3), App. 11, Note on a GP Service, para. 4. The Ministry's dissatisfaction here went back many years. For earlier expressions of the need for reform, see

MH 62/116, Memo. on Develop. Necessary for Provision of Complete Med. Service for Insured Persons, no date, no signature (but probably by Whitaker in 1917), p. 12, para. 32; MH 77/22, Ritson Memo., 12 Sept. 1936, p. 5, point (c).

28   For a detailed description of the complaint procedure as it worked under NHI, see Harris and Sack (1937), pp. 179-206. For a study of its development and a description of how it operates today, see Klein, Rudolf, *Complaints Against Doctors,* Charles Knight, 1973.

29   Statistics on complaints cases were reported each year in the annual reports of both the Minister of Health and the Chief Medical Officer of the Ministry. The latter are more convenient to use because they covered both England and Wales and were reported on a calendar year basis.

30   Royal Com. on NHI, Min. of Ev., 1926, Q. 14,628 (Cardale). For similar statements by other bodies, see *ibid.,* Report, 1928, pp. 33-6.

31   Parl. Deb., Commons, 28 June 1923, Vol. 165, Col. 2601.

32   *Med. Off.,* 1939, 1, pp. 75-6.

33   MH 77/26, Post-War Med. Policy — GP Service, March 1942, p. 3, para. 8 (c), 9.

34   Bunbury (1957), pp. 165-6, 182.

35   *Nat. Ins. Gaz.,* 1922, pp. 67-70.

36   Bunbury (1957), pp. 299-306.

37   *Med. World,* 3 March 1922, p. 15.

38   *Nat. Ins. Gaz.,* 1925, p. 54. For the controversy surrounding his departure and the change in the regulations it caused, see *BMJ,* 1925, 1, Supp., pp. 53-4 (Pring); 1925, 2, Supp., p. 125.

39   MH 77/26, Draft of paper by Maude on GP Service, Nov. 1942. p. 6, para. 6. See also *ibid.,* Post-War Med. Policy — GP Service, March 1942, pp. 8-10.

40   For the genesis of the central medical board idea, see MH 77/26, Post-War Med. Policy — GP Service, March 1942, p. 9, para. 22(2); Notes on general admin. structure, March 1943, pp. 1-2.

41   MH 77/26, Post-War Med. Policy — GP Service, March 1942, p. 11, para. 22 (3) (k).

42   *Lancet,* 1932, 1, p. 589. Parl. Deb., Commons, 21 July 1950, Vol. 477, Cols. 2715-16 (Bevan).

43   *BMJ,* 1945, 2, Supp., pp. 16, 41; 1946, 1, Supp., p. 3.

44   *Med.-Legal J.,* 1951, Part 2, pp. 53-4 (Forbes). *BMJ,* 1964, 2, Supp., p. 40.

45   MH 77/26, Post-War Med. Policy — GP Service, March 1942, p. 3, para. 8 (a).

46   MH 77/26, Notes on gen. admin. structure, March 1943, pp. 1-2.

47   MH 77/26, Draft of paper by Maude on GP Service, Nov. 1942, p. 6, para. 6. See also, *ibid.,* 1st Meeting with small committee of rep. body of med. prof., 24 May 1943. For the 3-month notice period, see Hill's attack on the Government's proposals in *BMJ,* 1943, 1, Supp., pp. 61-2.

48   CAB 87/12, Com. on Recon. Priorities, Minutes of Meetings, 12 Oct. 1943 (no. 24). For the development of the central medical board idea, see MH 77/26, Post-War Med. Policy — GP Service, pp. 9-10, para. 22, Notes on gen. admin. structure, March 1943, pp. 1-2; 1st rough outline of a scheme for a comp. health service, no date, no signature (but probably by Hawton in 1943), pp. 5-6, para. 6-7; White Paper, 1944, pp. 36-7.

49 MH 77/26, 3rd Meeting with small com. of med. prof., 28 June 1943.
50 Parl. Deb., Lords, 16 March 1944, Vol. 131, Col. 104.
51 *Ibid.,* Cols. 81-2.
52 Parl. Deb., Commons, 16 March 1944, Vol. 398, Col. 501. See also *Lancet,* 1944, 1, pp. 405-6.
53 Parl. Deb., Commons, 10 June 1943, Vol. 390, Cols. 966-70.
54 *BMJ,* 1944, 1, pp. 95-8. See, however, the strong defence of the board idea in *Lancet,* 1945, 1, pp. 538-9.
55 *BMJ,* 1943, 1, Supp., pp. 61-2. See also Eckstein (1958), pp. 140-3; Abel-Smith (1964), pp. 458-9.
56 *BMJ,* 1944, 1, pp. 41, 367. For Hill's initial attempt at Parliament as an Independent in Cambridge, see *BMJ,* 1945, 1, Supp., pp. 93-4. For his later career as a Conservative, see Hill (1964), pp. 122-255.
57 White Paper on Nat. Health Service, 1944, pp. 26-38. For the profession's objection to local authority control here, see CAB 87/13, Com. on Recon. Priorities, Memos., Min. of Health, 'Nat. Health Service', 28 July 1943, PR (43) (46), para. 25-8.
58 White Paper on Nat. Health Service, 1944, pp. 32-3.
59 For the profession's insistence on this, see MH 77/26, Minutes of 1st Meeting with small com. of rep. body of med. prof., 24 May 1943. *BMJ,* 1944, 2, Supp., pp. 93-4; 1945, 2, p. 833; 1946, 2, p. 555 (Fleming).
60 White Paper on Nat. Health Service, 1944, pp. 31-2, 34-5. Compare this with the Ministry's bold plan for whole-time service set forth in MH 77/26, Nat. Med. Service, Whole-time v. part-time service, March 1943.
61 *BMJ,* 1943, 2, Supp., p. 209; 1944, 1, Supp., p. 103, para. 5 of Council's Report.
62 White Paper on Nat. Health Service, 1944, pp. 14-20.
63 *Ibid.,* pp. 17-19, 31. For the dep.'s earlier plan to put health centres under joint boards, see MH 77/26, Notes on gen. admin. structure, March 1943, p. 3.
64 *BMJ,* 1944, 2, Supp., p. 27, answer to question 9. See also 1944, 1, Supp., pp. 59-60; 1944, 2, pp. 794-5; 1944, 2, Supp., pp. 147-65; *Med. World,* 30 June 1944, pp. 575-81.
65 *BMJ,* 1944, 2, Supp., pp. 147-65; 1945, 1, Supp., p. 8 (Proctor).
66 *BMJ,* 1944, 1, pp. 643-52, para. 42-8 of Council Report.
67 *Lancet,* 1944, 1, pp. 667-8.
68 For a good review of the transformation in the profession's attitude towards health centres, see *Lancet,* 1947, 1, pp. 25-6.
69 *BMJ,* 1944, 1, pp. 293-5.
70 *Public Health,* March 1944, pp. 61-2.
71 MH 77/30A, Progress of Nat. Health Service since White Paper, Min. of Health, 'Nat. Health Service' (draft for Cabinet), no date but probably end of 1944; 'Progress with Proposals for a Nat. Health Service', Confidential Proof to be presented to Parliament in June 1945 (but never published). The author has in his possession a copy of the report on negotiations presented by the BMA Council to the Special Representatives Meeting held on 3 and 4 May 1945.
72 *BMJ,* 1944, 1, pp. 643-52, para. 54-6 of Council Report; 1944, 2, Supp., pp. 93-4; 1945, 2, Supp., pp. 28-9. For the relevant section of the White Paper, see White Paper on Nat. Health Service, 1944, pp. 35-6.
73 *BMJ,* 1944, 2, Supp., pp. 28-9, answer to questions 33-4.

74 MH 77/26, Minutes of 3rd Meeting with small com. of med. rof., 28 June 1943. See also *BMJ*, 1944, 1, Supp., p. 151; 1944, 2, Supp., pp. 103-10, 147-65.

Chapter 22: Trade Unions Versus Insurance Offices

1 *Med. World*, 6 July 1945, p. 647.
2 For the progress of this issue in the Recon. Com., see CAB 87/10, Memo. by Willink on sale and purchase of prac., 5 March 1945, R (45) 32; Memo. by Johnston on sale and purchase of prac., 6 March 1945, R (45) 33; Minutes of 12th Meeting of Recon. Com., R (45), 12 March 1945, pp. 3-6; Memo. by Woolton, Willink and Johnston on sale and purchase of prac., 17 March 1945, R (45) 35; Minutes of 13th Meeting of Recon. Com., R (45), 20 March 1945.
3 Lab. Party, *Annual Report*, 1945, pp. 138-40.
4 Titmuss, R. M., *Commitment to Welfare*, Allen and Unwin, 1968, p. 207-17. For his overriding concern with 'equality', see *ibid.*, pp. 113-204. For Tawney's classic statement on the subject, see Tawney, R. H., *Equality*, Allen and Unwin, 1931.
5 *Lancet*, 1942, 2, pp. 623-4.
6 Nat. Assn. of Trade Union Approved Socs., *Report of Annual Meeting*, 1939, p. 25.
7 For a good indication of what female unionists expected from the Health Service, see Spring Rice, Margery, *Working-Class Wives*, Pelican, 1939, pp. 28-68, 197-200.
8 Family Endowment Society, *Monthly Notes*, June 1930, p. 10. Lab. Party, *Annual Report*, 1942, pp. 132-7. *Nat. Ins. Gaz.*, 1946, p. 399. Rathbone, Eleanor, *Family Allowances*, Allen and Unwin, 1949, p. 279 (from chapter by Eva Hubback). Clegg, Hugh, *General Union*, Oxford, Blackwell, 1954, pp. 290-1, 315.
9 Int'l. Lab. Org., *Factory Inspection*, Geneva, 1923, pp. 24-32. Tillyard, Frank, *The Worker and the State*, Routledge, 1923, pp. 243-7. Mess, H. A., *Factory Legislation and Its Administration, 1891-1924*, P. S. King, 1926, pp. 160-1. Djang, T. K., *Factory Inspection in Britain*, Allen and Unwin, 1942, pp. 41-5.
10 *Public Health*, Jan. 1930, p. 108. See also Legge's paper in *Journal of Industrial Hygiene*, June 1920, pp. 66-71.
11 *BMJ*, 1944, 2, pp. 474-5.
12 *Med. World*, 7 Aug. 1942, pp. 498-9 (Ward); 15 Feb. 1946, p. 5.
13 *BMJ*, 1938, 2, Supp., pp. 8-9. TUC, *Annual Report*, 1938, pp. 138-41.
14 *Ibid.*, pp. 324-33 (Marshall).
15 *Med. Today and Tomor.*, July 1938, pp. 7-8.
16 Lab. Party, Public Health Adv. Com., Minutes of Meetings, 23 Nov. 1938.
17 TUC, *Annual Report*, 1944, pp. 381-5. *BMJ*, 1944, 2, Supp., p. 32.
18 For Ministry recognition of the TUC's 'somewhat colourless' views on the Health Service, see MH 77/73, Memo. from Tyas to Pater, 20 Dec. 1944.
19 TUC and Lab. Party, *Social Insurance and Trade Union Membership*, 1924, p. 10.
20 *Shepherd's Mag.*, 1913, pp. 10-11

21 Nat. Assn. of Trade Union Approved Socs., *Report of Annual Meeting,* 1927, p. 8.
22 *Ibid.,* 1939, p. 23 (Newrick).
23 *Ibid.,* 1932, p. 5; 1934, pp. 11-14; 1939, pp. 18-19, 28, 35. *New Dawn,* 1931, pp. 183-4 (Yerrell). *Health Insurance News,* June 1941, p. 5. Lab. Party, *Annual Report,* 1934, pp. 214-15.
24 For the Prudential's discouraging experience with sickness benefit between 1859 and 1864, see Plaisted, H., *The Prudential: Past and Present,* Layton, 1917, pp. 32-3. See also Webb., S. and B., *Industrial Democracy,* Longmans, 1902, p. 101, footnote.
25 Money, L. G. Chiozza, *Insurance Versus Poverty,* Methuen, 1912, p. 18.
26 TUC and Lab. Party, *Social Insurance and Trade Union Membership,* 1924, p. 8. Here, a proportion of 26% is cited. For a later study, indicating a slightly higher proportion (30-35%), see Nat. Assn. of Trade Union Approved Socs., 'Special Report Submitted by Nat. Exec. on Membership Propaganda', 1933.
27 These percentages are derived from data in Beveridge Report (1942), p. 25.
28 For a clear example, see *Typographical Circular,* Sept. 1915, pp. 10-11. Typographical Association, *Reports of Delegates Meetings: 1930,* pp. 92-6; 1939, pp. 7-9. Musson, A. E., *The Typographical Association,* OUP, 1954, p. 462.
29 TUC and Lab. Party, *Social Ins. and Trade Union Membership,* 1924, pp. 6-8. Nat. Assn. of Trade Union Approved Socs., 'Special Report Submitted by Nat. Exec. on Membership Propaganda', 1933.
30 For one example, see *New Dawn,* 28 May 1927, p. 248.
31 For a good description of the tactics used by the offices and agents at the start of NHI, see Gilbert (1966), pp. 425-7.
32 *Health Ins. News,* Sept. 1945, p. 4. For the exact terms under which juveniles were admitted, see Can. Dept. of Health, *Health Ins. in G. B., 1911-1948,* 1952, p. 30.
33 Wilson, Arnold, and Levy, Hermann, *Industrial Assurance,* OUP, 1937, pp. 120-3.
34 TUC, *Annual Report,* 1941, p. 240.
35 *Health Ins. News,* Sept. 1945, p. 4.
36 For the Prudential's membership in 1946, see *Nat. Ins. Gaz.,* 1947, p. 220. For the union total in 1938 (1,480,000), see Beveridge Report (1942), p. 25. No later figures for the unions are available but the total probably fell during the war.
37 For this memorable phrase, see the article by Sidney Webb in *Crusade,* Feb. 1913, p. 255. Then, however, it was the friendly societies, not the trade unions, which Webb saw as the main victim of insurance office tactics.
38 *New Dawn,* 1936, p. 76.
39 *Labour Leader,* 1911, pp. 343, 345. Fabian Soc., *The Insurance Bill and the Workers,* June 1911. *Fabian News,* 1911: April, p. 34; Aug., p. 66; Sept., pp. 73-4. Lab. Party, *Annual Report,* 1913, pp. 104-6. Pease, Edward, *The History of the Fabian Society,* Fifield, 1916, pp. 223-5. Cole (1961), pp. 141-2.
40 *The Eye-Witness* started publication on 22 June 1911 with a slashing attack on NHI and kept it up week after week. Belloc remained editor

until June 1912 when he turned direction over to Cecil Chesterton. In November 1912 Chesterton changed the title to *The New Witness* and filled the journal with endless diatribes against Jews. Orage attacked NHI in *The New Age*, a socialist journal which he acquired in 1907. For an example of the way he tried to use the unions to destroy NHI, see the issue for 20 June 1912, pp. 169-70.

41 For leading articles on 'The Prudential Plot', and 'The Insurance Plot', see *Daily Herald*, 1912: 12 Aug., p. 1; 13 Aug., p. 1. For the anti-semitic overtones (introduced by Belloc and directed against the insurance firms owned by Rothschild and Sassoon), see *ibid.*, 1912: 5 July, p. 4 (Belloc); 16 Aug., p. 1 (L. S.); 25 Sept., pp. 1, 10.

42 Levy (1944), pp. 11-12, 215-20, 336-7.

43 Nat. Union of Life Assur. Agents, *Monthly Circular*, May, 1892. *Assur. Agent's Rev.*, 1906, pp. 99-100. *Insurance Truth*, 1911, pp. 691-2 (Kirsopp), 828-9 (Brown).

44 Bunbury (1957), pp. 205-6, 208-10, 214-15.

45 *New States.*, 14 March 1914, Spec. Supp., pp. 20-1.

46 Bunbury (1957), p. 289.

47 TUC, *Annual Report*, 1912, pp. 200-3; 1917, pp. 368-70. *Lab. Leader*, 1912, p. 586.

48 *Nat. Ins. Gaz.*, 1933, pp. 337-8. See also Beveridge Report (1942), p. 32, para. 70.

49 CAB 87/77, Bev. Com. Min. of Ev., Day 9, 6 May 1942, Q. 2246.

50 Morrah, Dermot, *A History of Industrial Life Assurance*, Allen and Unwin, 1955, pp. 19-25.

51 Plaisted (1917), pp. 28-32, 67-81. See also *Assur. Agent's Rev.*, Nov. 1890, p. 135.

52 *Commercial World*, 1884, p. 288. *Agent's Journal*, 1886, pp. 1-2, 15, 21-3.

53 *Agent's J.*, 1886, pp. 37-9.

54 *Agent's J.*, 1890, p. 507. TUC, *Annual Report*, 1890, p. 56.

55 *Assur. Agent's Chron.*, 24 Feb. 1890 (Sheard); 24 Oct. 1891; 19 Dec. 1891; 1905, pp. 378-9; 1906, p. 547 (Sheard). For the importance of trade councils in agents' strategy, see *Prudential Staff Gaz.*, 1914, pp. 106-7.

56 For example, see George Horne and E. R. Hartley (both worked for the Liverpool Victoria Collecting Society) in *Lab. Leader*, 1899, p. 362; 1902, p. 6.

57 As part of his 'White Slaves of England' series, Hardie issued 'The Pru in the Pillory' in which he condemned the company's exploitation of agents. *Lab. Leader*, 1898, p. 309 ff. The following year, Hardie sponsored a conference between the two agents' unions to promote federated action. *Assur. Agent's Chron.*, 1899, p. 52.

58 *Assur. Agent's Chron.*, 1891, p. 531.

59 Parl. Deb., Commons, 25 May 1911, Vol. 26, Col. 475. See also *Daily Herald*, 13 Aug. 1912, p. 1 (Simpson).

60 *Daily Herald*, 3 Sept. 1912, p. 4. See also TUC and Lab. Party, *Social Ins. and Trade Union Membership*, 1924, p. 21.

61 TUC, *Annual Report*, 1911, pp. 163-5.

62 TUC, *Annual Report*, 1912, pp. 290-1 (Horne). For the opposition to nationalization from agents in the rival Prudential Staff Federation, see

Prudential Staff Gaz., Jan. 1911, pp. 56-7; March 1911, pp. 98-100; Sept. 1912, pp. 188-91.

63   *Prudential Staff Gaz.*, July 1923, pp. 167-90 (Jones).

64   Nat. Amal. Union of Life Assur. Wkrs., *Nationalisation of Insurance*, Manchester, 1926.

65   TUC, *Annual Reports:* 1911, pp. 163-5 (Knaggs); 1912, pp. 200-3, 290-1.

66   *New States.*, 13 March 1915. For discussions of the Report, see Wilson and Levy (1937), pp. 82-7 and Morrah (1955), pp. 78-81.

67   For a long (but, by no means, complete) discussion of this interlude, see Gilbert (1966), pp. 318-43. See also *Agent's J.*, 1911, p. 374.

68   For the agents' fear of the NHI method of collecting contributions, see *Prudential Staff Gaz.*, Aug. 1912, p. 177. For their reaction to the Fabian Report, see *ibid.*, April 1915, pp. 115-16.

69   Webb., S. and B., *History of Trade Unionism*, Longmans, 1920, p. 621. For an indication of the extent to which the unions provided funeral benefit between the wars, see the paper by Rosemary Hutt, 'Trade Unions as Friendly Societies, 1912-1952', in *Yorkshire Bulletin of Economic and Social Research*, March 1955, pp. 69-85.

70   TUC, *Annual Report*, 1931, pp. 346-7 (Hill).

71   CAB 87/77, Bev. Com. Min. of Ev., Day 9, 9 May 1942, Q. 2308 (Wolstencroft). See also *ibid.*, Q. 2389-90 (Smyth). See also TUC, *Annual Report*, 1942, pp. 223-6 (Allen).

Chapter 23: Trade Union Interest in General Practice

1   *Cotton Factory Times*, 28 May 1915, p. 2 (Davies). *Iron & Steel Trades Confed. J.*, March, 1922, pp. 77-9. *New Dawn*, 1930, pp. 457-8. Nat. Assn. of Trade Union Approved Socs., *Annual Reports:* 1931, pp. 20-4; 1934, pp. 11-14.

2   For the growth of approved society interest in a salaried service, see *Nat. Ins. Gaz.*, 1928, p. 342 (Rockliff); 1938, p. 627. For union interest in the same solution, see Nat. Assn. of Trade Union Approved Socs., *Annual Reports:* 1931, pp. 20-4 (Walker); 1934, p. 8; 1938, pp. 8-13 (Yerrell).

3   For a good summary of the rates prevailing between the wars and the conditions attached, see Can. Dept. of Health, *Health Ins. in G. B., 1911-1948*, 1952, pp. 7, 43-7.

4   *Nat. Ins. Gaz.*, 1930, p. 463; 1937, pp. 450-1 (Hackforth), 457.

5   Royal Commission on Workmen's Compensation, 1939-40, Min. of Ev., Q. 12,826 (Griffiths).

6   Wilson, Arnold, and Levy, Hermann, *Workmen's Compensation*, Vol. 2, OUP, 1941, pp. 121, 133-4, 232.

7   *Ibid.*, p. 130. Beveridge Report (1942), p. 36, para. 79 (iv).

8   Royal Com. on Work. Comp., 1939-40, Min. of Ev., Q. 1686 (Spearing).

9   Wilson and Levy (1939), pp. 258-62. See also Wilson and Levy (1941), pp. 296-303.

10   Wilson and Levy (1941), p. 129.

11   Royal Com. on Work. Comp., 1939-40, Min. of Ev., Q. 9880-5. See also Papers No. 35 (Prudential), pp. 967-8, and No. 36 (Nat. Amal.), pp. 969-71.

12 *Ibid.*, Q. 5508-9, 5911-13, 9021, 11,896, 11,900. See also Royal. Com. on NHI, Report, 1928, pp. 256-9.
13 For the rates applicable to workmen's compensation between the Wars, see Wilson and Levy (1939), pp. 133, 241-2.
14 *Women's Trade Union Review*, July 1911, pp. 7-14.
15 Pru. Staff Union, *Annual Report*, 1945, pp. 18-22.
16 Royal Com. on Work. Comp., 1939-40, Min. of Ev., Q. 9550-8, 9907-8.
17 *Nat. Ins. Gaz.*, 1928, p. 591. See also Smyth's article in *Industrial Review*, April, 1928, pp. 4-5.
18 Clegg (1954), pp. 290-1, 293.
19 TUC, *Annual Report*, 1929, pp. 376-7.
20 Nat. Assoc. of Trade Union Approved Socs., *Annual Reports:* 1929, pp. 21-2; 1930, pp. 20-3; 1931, pp. 25-7; 1932, pp. 11-12.
21 See Corbey's review of the Association's work from the time it was formed in 1914 in Nat. Assoc. of Trade Union Approved Socs., *Report of Special Conf.,* 1943, pp. 17-21.
22 *Nat. Ins. Gaz.*, 1928, pp. 601-2; 1929, pp. 13, 19, 20-1, 27, 41, 43, 55, 63, 67, 73-5.
23 *Ibid.*, p. 163.
24 Nat. Assn. of Trade Union Approved Socs., *Annual Reports*: 1934, pp. 22-3; 1937, pp. 9, 47; 1938, p. 38; 1939, pp. 14, 26, 30-2; 1941, pp. 11, 36.
25 Morgan, 'Trade Union Adv. Med. Off.', Labour Public Health Adv. Com. Memo. No. 53, 1923, p. 9.
26 TUC, *Annual Reports:* 1924, pp. 488-9; 1933, pp. 136-7, 357. TGWU, *Record:* Feb. 1923, p. 9; April 1928, p. 264; Jan. 1930, p. 181; March 1930, p. 237. *BMJ,* 1948, 1, p. 265. Woodall, Samuel J., *Manor House Hospital*, Routledge, 1966. For a recent (and fruitless) attempt by some unions to bring the Hospital into the Health Service, see *Sunday Telegraph,* 28 Dec. 1975, p. 3.
27 For the intense interest of the unions in this subject, see *Labour Magazine,* 1935: Feb., pp. 138-9; March, p. 164. Nat. Assn. of Trade Union Approved Socs., *Annual Report*, 1935, pp. 18-19. TUC, *Annual Report*, 1945, pp. 307-10.
28 Wilson and Levy (1941), pp. 69-70.
29 Tillyard (1923), p. 280. For the full list of diseases scheduled under the 1925 Act, see Collier, Howard E., *Outlines of Industrial Medical Practice*, Arnold, 1940, pp. 421-3.
30 Wilson and Levy (1941), p. 81.
31 *Ibid.*, pp. 86-7. See also the excellent paper by Dr A. Meiklejohn, 'History of Lung Diseases of Coal Miners in G. B., Part III, 1920-52', in *British Journal of Industrial Medicine*, July 1952, pp. 208-20.
32 TUC, *Annual Report*, 1933, p. 354-5.
33 *BMJ*, 1942, 1, pp. 43-4. For an excellent review of the subject, see Hugh-Jones, P., and Fletcher, C. M., *The Social Consequences of Pneumoconiosis among Coalminers in South Wales*, Med. Res. Council Memo. No. 25, HMSO, 1951, pp. 1-2. See also the paper by J. B. Atkins, 'Pneumoconiosis in Coal', in *Journal of Royal Sanitary Institute*, 1948, pp. 516-25.
34 Bevin, Ernest, *The Job To Be Done*, Heinemann, 1942, pp. 166-71. See also the paper by R. S. F. Schilling, 'Industrial Health Research Board', in

Brit. J. of Ind. Med., July 1944, pp. 145-52; and Bullock, Alan, *The Life and Times of Ernest Bevin,* Vol. 1, Heinemann, 1960, pp. 602-3.

35 Nat. Assn. of Trade Union Approved Socs., *Annual Report,* 1933, 'Special Report by Nat. Exec. on Member. Prop.'. See also the Association's 'Twelve Good Reasons why all Trade Unionists should be members of a Trade Union Approved Society', 1934, p. 8.

36 TUC, *Annual Report,* 1933, p. 350 (Manson).

37 TUC, *Annual Report,* 1950, p. 389 (Wigglesworth). See also Wilson and Levy (1941), pp. 67, 205.

38 Nat. Assn. of Trade Union Approved Socs., *Annual Report,* 1927, p. 8. For a full list of those affiliated in 1924, see TUC and Lab. Party, *Social Ins. and Trade Union Membership,* 1924, pp. 27-8.

39 Nat. Assn. of Trade Union Approved Socs., *Annual Report,* 1927, p. 7.

40 TUC and Lab. Party, *Social Ins. and Trade Union Membership,* 1924.

41 TUC, *Annual Report,* 1927, p. 413. For Citrine's friendship with Smyth, see Citrine, Walter M., *Men and Work,* Hutchinson, 1964, pp. 72, 76.

42 Nat. Assn. of Trade Union Approved Socs., *Annual Report,* 1930, pp. 24-5.

43 Royal Com. on NHI, 1925, Min. of Ev., Q. 13,749. See also Legge's paper in *J. of Ind. Hyg.,* June, 1920, pp. 66-71; and his address to the Nat. Assn. of Trade Union Approved Socs., *Annual Report,* 1930, pp. 15-19.

44 *Ibid.,* pp. 15-19. See also Royal Com. on NHI, 1925, Min. of Ev., Q. 13,909-12.

45 For an excellent review of industrial health provision in Britain, see the paper by R. S. F. Schilling, 'Developments in Occupational Health During the Last 30 Years', in *Journal of Royal Society of Arts,* Nov. 1963, pp. 933-84.

46 TGWU, *Record:* Oct. 1928, p. 75; Jan. 1935, p. 133; May 1937, p. 267; Aug. 1937, pp. 20-1. See also the references in 34 above.

47 Bunbury (1957), pp. 136-8, 220-1. Royal Com. on NHI, Report, 1928, pp. 259-60.

48 *Health Ins. News,* March 1939, p. 1. See also Home Office, *Report of Departmental Committee on Dust in Card Rooms in Cotton Industry,* HMSO, 1932; Home Office, *Report of Departmental Committee on Compensation for Card Room Workers,* HMSO, 1939.

49 TGWU, *Record,* Oct. 1928, p. 75. For an admission about medical ignorance in this field, see *BMJ,* 1940, 1, pp. 1060-1.

50 Collier (1940), pp. 418-20. Hugh-Jones and Fletcher (1951), pp. 44-5. Meiklejohn in *Brit. J. of Ind. Med.,* July, 1954, pp. 198-212.

51 Royal Com. on NHI, 1925, Min. of Ev., Q. 12,745 (Legge). For a full list of the duties performed by factory surgeons, see Collier (1940), pp. 401-7. For a short history of the work done by factory surgeons, see the paper by S. Huzzard, 'The Certifying Surgeon: Child Labour and Industrial Disease', in *Bulletin of Society for Social History of Medicine,* 1975, No. 16, pp. 5-6.

52 Royal Com. on NHI, 1925, App. to Min. of Ev., No. 42, pp. 424-8, para. 10.

53 Royal Com. on NHI, 1925, Min. of Ev., Q. 13,755-6 (Legge).

54 *Ibid.,* Q. 13,762. See also Legge's paper, 'Medical Supervision in Factories', in *J. of Ind. Hyg.,* June 1920, pp. 66-71.

55 Association of Certifying Surgeons, *Annual Reports,* 1914-19, pp. 9-10. See also *BMJ*, 1919, 1, p. 109.
56 Assn. of Cert. Surg., *Annual Report*, 1924, p. 7.
57 For the opposition of factory surgeons, see *ibid*.
58 Royal Com. on NHI, 1925, Min. of Ev., Q. 13,762, 13,812-30, 13,834, 13,917-21. See also Legge's address to Nat. Assn. of Trade Union Approved Socs., *Annual Report*, 1930, pp. 15-19.
59 Royal Com. on NHI, 1925, Min. of Ev., App. 42, pp. 424-8, para. 20-3.
60 TUC, *Annual Report*, 1930, pp. 87, 136.
61 *Ibid.*, 1931, pp. 151-3.
62 *Ibid.*, 1930, pp. 321-3.
63 *BMJ*, 1937, 2, pp. 341-2, 610-2.
64 *Ibid.*, p. 343 (Lockhart).
65 Min. of Lab., Conf. on Ind. Health, 9 April 1943, *Report of Proceedings,* pp. 43-6.
66 *BMJ*, 1952, 1, Supp., pp. 49-50. *Practitioner*, Aug. 1958, pp. 133-42. See also the leader in *The Times*, 4 Aug. 1958, p. 7.
67 TUC, *Annual Report*, 1945, p. 73.
68 For explicit recognition of this, see Association of Industrial Medical Officers, *Transactions*, July 1960, pp. 37-8.
69 TUC, *Annual Report*, 1947, p. 145.
70 *Med. Off.*, 1940, 2, p. 56.
71 For a hint of this, see *BMJ*, 1940, 2, pp. 291-2.
72 For a good description of the array of forces involved in compensation battles, see Memo. submitted by a union lawyers (W. H. Thompson) to the Royal Com. on Work. Comp., 1940, Min. of Ev., Paper No. 38, pp. 1006-7, para. 58-67. For the conduct of a typical court case, see *BMJ*, 1936, 1, pp. 913-14.
73 Interview with Barnett Stross, 2 April 1962.
74 Royal Com. on Work. Comp., 1939-40, Min. of Ev., Paper No. 38, p. 1004, para. 39-43.
75 TUC, *Annual Report*, 1928, p. 372.
76 League of Nations Union, *Social Insurance*, Faber & Gwyer, 1925, p. 73. See also Nat. Assn. of Trade Union Approved Socs., *Annual Reports:* 1930, p. 8 (Lowe); 1934, pp. 22-3. See also Nat. Assn. of Trade Union Approved Socs., *Provincial Centre Minutes,* 20 July 1943 (Corbey).
77 Nat. Assn. of Trade Union Approved Socs., *Annual Reports:* 1925, pp. 7-10; 1926, pp. 11-14. *Lab. Mag.*, 1926-7, pp. 159-61. *Contemporary Review,* June, 1926, pp. 150-5.
78 Nat. Assn. of Trade Union Approved Socs., *Annual Report*, 1929, pp. 10-11. *Health Ins. News*, June 1941, p. 1.
79 Nat. Assn. of Trade Union Approved Socs., *Annual Report*, 1933, p. 18.
80 Interview with Barnett Stross, 2 April 1962.
81 *BMJ*, 1937, 2, Supp., pp. 3, 96, 153, 211, 233 (para. 82-7 of Ins. Act. Com. Report); 1938, 1, Supp., p. 156; 1938, 2, Supp., p. 143; 1939, 1, Supp., p. 207 (para. 192 of Council Report). See also Robson, William A. (editor), *Social Security*, Allen and Unwin, 1945, pp. 96-7.
82 TUC, *Annual Reports:* 1936, p. 148; 1944, pp. 69-70; 1945, pp. 309-10 (Morgan).
83 *BMJ*, 1937, 2, p. 343 (Lockhart).

84 *Lab. Mag.*, 1932-3, p. 96.
85 *Med. World*, 21 July 1939, Supp., pp. 6-8.

Chapter 24: The BMA-TUC Alliance and the Beveridge Report

1 *BMJ*, 1935, 2, Supp., pp. 236-7.
2 *Ibid.*, 1937, 1, Supp., p. 52. TUC, *Annual Report*, 1937, p. 130.
3 *BMJ*, 1937, 1, Supp., p. 285; 1939, 1, Supp., p. 147.
4 *Ibid.*, 1938, 2, Supp., pp. 119, 163.
5 *Ibid.*, 1935, 1, Supp., pp. 53-62.
6 *Ibid.*, 1939, 2, p. 402.
7 Delevingne Com., Interim Report, 1937, p. 14. See also Wilson and Levy (1941), p. 271.
8 Delevingne Com., Interim Report, 1937, p. 9. Wilson and Levy (1941), pp. 267-72.
9 *Journal of Industrial Welfare*, May 1936, pp. 26-8.
10 *BMJ*, 1935, 1, Supp., pp. 60-2. See also the strong attack on the insurance companies by Reginald Watson-Jones, one of the 'radical' orthopaedists on the committee in *ibid.*, 1936, 1, p. 899.
11 See the excellent paper on this subject by Watson-Jones in *Chartered Physiotherapist*, Jan. 1944, pp. 72-5.
12 Royal Com. on Work. Comp., 1939-40, Min. of Ev., p. 829, para. 99-101 of paper by Accident Offices Assn. See also Wilson and Levy (1941), p. 279.
13 *BMJ*, 1935, 1, pp. 813-17.
14 *Ibid.*, 1934, 2, pp. 213-14; 1939, 1, pp. 137-8.
15 This Commmittee issued two reports — an interim one in 1937 and a final in 1939.
16 Stewart Report, 1938.
17 *Ibid.*, pp. 84-107.
18 TUC, *Annual Report*, 1938, pp. 142-9. See also TUC Gen. Council, *Trade Unions and Workmen's Compensation*, 1939, p. 3.
19 Nat. Assn. of Trade Union Approved Socs., *Reports of Annual Meetings*: 1938, p. 37; 1939, p. 18. See also Lawson, Jack, *Labour Fights for Workmen's Compensation*, Lab. Party, 1939.
20 Stewart Report, 1938, p. 94, para. 206, 208.
21 Royal Com. on Work. Comp., 1939-40, Min. of Ev.: TUC, p. 416-17, para. 44-56 and Q. 3921-31; BMA, pp. 1223-5, para. 47-55 and Q. 12,774-9, 12,783-8, 12,802-6, 12,825-9. See also Wilson and Levy (1941), pp. 149-50.
22 Royal Com. on Work. Comp., 1939-40, Min. of Ev., Q. 538-41, 1198-1218, 1149-65, 1857-80, 5555-70, 8877-906, 9208-11, 10,186-271.
23 Royal Com. on Work. Comp., 1939-40, Min, of Ev., pp. 1063-5 (King Edward's Hosp. Fund), 1078-91 (Brit. Hosp. Assn.).
24 *Ibid.*, Q. 12,764.
25 *Ibid.*, Q. 12,161.
26 *Ibid.*, Q. 11,041-56, 11,867, 12,185-6, 12,441-56.
27 Interview with Spearing, 10 Aug. 1962.
28 Note his address to Nat. Assn. of Trade Union Approved Socs., *Report of Annual Meeting*, 1930, pp. 19-20.
29 Royal Com. on Work. Comp., 1939-40, Min. of Ev., Q. 4292. See also objections raised by Mineworkers' Fed. on pp. 649-50, para. 174-6.

30 For the evolution of Morgan's views here, see Nat. Assn. of Trade Union Approved Socs., *Report of Annual Meeting*, 1939, pp. 30-2. SMA *Bulletin*, May-June 1944, pp. 4-6.

31 Nat. Assn. of Trade Union Approved Socs., *Report of Spec. Conf.*, 1941, p. 11. See also Smyth's intervention in Royal Com. on Work. Comp., 1939-40, Min. Ev., Q. 927-36.

32 For the best indication of union thought at the time, see the Memo. approved in Sept., 1941, by Nat. Assn. of Trade Union Approved Socs., *Coordination of Social Services.*

33 TUC, *Annual Report*, 1940, pp. 347-8 (Balfour).

34 TUC, *Annual Report*, 1941, pp. 114-15. See also Addison, (1975), pp. 168-9.

35 Harris, José, *William Beveridge, A Biography*, OUP, 1977, pp. 353-61.

36 Beveridge, W. H., *Power and Influence, An Autobiography*, Hodder and Stoughton, 1953, pp. 226, 301.

37 Beveridge, W. H., *Insurance For All and Everything*, Daily News, 1924, p. 32.

38 Harris (1977), pp. 383, 386.

39 I am indebted to Austin Spearing (former Secretary of Association of Approved Societies) for pointing out the significance of Chester's appointment. Interview with Spearing, 10 Aug. 1962. For an interesting series of memoranda by Chester after the Beveridge Report appeared, see CAB 21/1588, Com. on Recon. Priorities — Misc. Corr.

40 For files dealing with establishment of Recon. Com. and Recon. Sec., see CAB 21/1583-6. For later changes in name and personnel of Com., see Addison (1975), pp. 221, 236.

41 Note Bevin's remarks in TUC, *Annual Report*, 1940, p. 324. See also Strauss, Patricia, *Bevin and Company*, New York, Putnams, 1941, pp. 101-10, 210-34.

42 Harris (1977), pp. 376, 383.

43 PIN 8/85, 'Work. Comp. and Social Ins.', 16 May 1941.

44 *Ibid.*

45 Strauss (1941), pp. 101-10. See also Harris (1977), pp. 381-2.

46 CAB 87/77, Bev. Com., Min. of Ev., Q. 2854. See also Q. 2849, 2853.

47 *Ibid.*, Q. 2859.

48 Courtauld, Samuel, *Ideals and Industry*, Cambridge, CUP, 1949, pp. 100-7. See also Addison (1975), pp. 214-15.

49 CAB 87/77, Bev. Com., Min. of Ev., Q. 632 (Lowther). Note Beveridge's own comments on this in Robson (1948), p. 419.

50 Addison (1975), pp. 217-18, 223-4, 233.

51 Beveridge, Janet, *Beveridge and His Plan*, Hodder and Stoughton, 1954, pp. 130-43. See also Addison (1975), p. 225.

52 Addison (1975), pp. 220-5.

53 Cooke, A. M., *A History of the Royal College of Physicians*, Vol. 3, OUP, 1977, p. 1083.

54 *Med. Off.*, 1936, 2, p. 149.

55 Beveridge Report, 1942, pp. 158-63.

56 CAB 87/76, Bev. Com., Min. of Meetings, 8 July 1941 (no. 1); 11 March 1942 (no. 5); Q. 1253, 1351.

57 Beveridge Report, 1942, p. 162, para. 437.

58 CAB 21/1588, Chester to Lord. Pres., 'Nat. Health Service', 17 Aug. 1943.
59 Beveridge Report, 1942, pp. 23-48.
60 CAB 87/76, Bev. Com., Min. of Ev., 26 Nov. 1941 (Q. 291 in particular). Assn. of Approved Socs., *Conf. Proceedings:* 1942, pp. 17-25, 34-5, 46-57; 1947, pp. 25-6. Interview with Spearing, 10 Aug. 1962.
61 Beveridge Report, 1942, pp. 72-6, 249-76.
62 Harris (1977), pp. 387-8.
63 *Ibid.*, pp. 408-9.
64 *Ibid.*, 'A Note on Sources' (page opposite 'Contents').
65 Beveridge Report, 1942, pp. 73 (para. 184), 274-6 (para. 83-8). See also Beveridge, W. H., *Voluntary Action,* Allen and Unwin, 1948, p. 80.
66 *BMJ,* 1943, 1, pp. 514-15. For recognition of employer desire to shift health costs to the community, see paper by Dr Howard Collier in *Journal of Royal San. Inst.,* Nov. 1937, pp. 265-70.
67 For this, see the Epilogue by Beveridge in Rathbone, Eleanor, *Family Allowances*, Allen and Unwin, 1949, pp. 269-77.
68 Nat. Assn. of Trade Union Approved Socs., *Report of Special Conf.,* 1945, p. 26.
69 TUC, *Annual Report,* 1943, p. 237 (Rowlandson).
70 Co-operative Party, *Monthly Bulletin*, 1949: May, pp. 4-7; June, p. 7.
71 Beveridge Report, 1942, p. 72, para. 182. For a protest by Society agents against the handicap this imposed, see *Co-operative Insurance Society, Quarterly Review*, 1924: 2nd quar., p. 18; 3rd quar., pp. 38-9.
72 Lab. Party, *Annual Report*, 1949, pp. 200-8. Lab. Party, *The Future of Industrial Assurance*, 1950. *Insurance Mail Yearbook*, 1950, pp. 15-18, 20-30. *Pru. Staff Gaz.,* Dec. 1949, p. 169; Jan. 1950, p. 4.
73 Co-op. Party, *Monthly Bull.,* May 1950, p. 15-16.
74 *Ins. Mail Yrbk.,* 1946, pp. 76-83; 1947, pp. 39-42; 1951, pp. 118-24. *Nat. Ins. Gaz.,* 1946, pp. 420-1.
75 Hutt in *York. Bull. of Eco. and Soc. Res.,* March 1955, pp. 69-85.
76 *Nat. Ins. Gaz.,* 1945, p. 451. Musson (1954), pp. 531-2.
77 *Nat. Ins. Gaz.,* 1943, p. 454. For the development of this alliance against the Beveridge Report, see *ibid.*, 1942, pp. 472-3, 475, 487, 519, 523, 531-4; 1943, pp. 55, 167, 171-2, 236-7, 239, 427.
78 *Nat. Ins. Gaz.,* 1944, pp. 463, 487, 537.
79 *Ibid.*, pp. 534-5, 540-1.
80 *Nat. Ins. Gaz.,* 1945, pp. 343, 367, 604-5. For the actual wording of the pledge, see *ibid.*, p. 567.
81 *Ibid.*, pp. 565-7, 570-1, 583, 619; 1946, pp. 119, 123, 177, 259, 272, 277, 291, 315. See also Lincoln, John A. (editor), *The Way Ahead — The Strange Case of the Friendly Societies*, Nat. Conf. of Friendly Socs., 1946.
82 For a clear indication of this, see the remarks made by a leader of the Durham Miners in *Nat. Ins. Gaz.,* 1947, p. 519.
83 Nat. Assn. of Trade Union Approved Socs., *Report of Spec. Conf.,* 1945, pp. 9-10 (Lowe).
84 *Ibid.*, pp. 30-1. Assoc. of Approved Socs., *Conf. Proceedings*, 1943, p. 32 (Canter). See also Kershaw's comment in *Nat. Ins. Gaz.,* 1947, pp. 15, 18.
85 CAB 87/12, Com. on Recon. Priorities, Minutes of Meetings, 17 May 1943 (no. 9). See also *Nat. Ins. Gaz.,* 1946, p. 45.

86 *Nat. Ins. Gaz.*, 1943, p. 454.
87 Gilbert (1966), p. 429.
88 TUC, *Annual Report*, 1945, pp. 55-7.
89 Beveridge Report, 1942, pp. 13, 41-2.
90 For the best guide to union expectations here, see the review of the subject in Assn. of Ind. Med. Off., *Transactions*, July, 1952, pp. 50-1.
91 CAB 87/77, Bev. Com., Min. of Ev., Q. 414-16, 489, 498, 572. See also Smyth, J. L., *Social Security*, Post War Discussion Pamphlets No. 1, Odhams, 1944, p. 6.
92 TUC, *Annual Reports:*, 1942, pp. 235-6; 1943, p. 235; 1944, pp. 68, 381-5; 1945, pp. 80-92.
93 For an early indication of union dissatisfaction with Ministry adminstration, see TUC,*Annual Reports:* 1951, pp. 152-4, 386-8, 392-6; 1954, pp. 146-50. See also TGWU, 'Experiences Under the Industrial Injuries and Workmen's Compensation Acts', internal union memo. prepared with the aid of its solicitors, Nov. 1959.
94 Min. of Lab., Conf. on Ind. Health, 9 April 1943, *Report of Proceedings*, pp. 35-8.
95 *BMJ*, 1946, 2, pp. 725-6.
96 Wilson and Levy (1941), pp. 193-4.
97 Parl. Deb., Commons, 18 Feb. 1946, Vol. 419, Cols. 983-5. *BMJ*, 1946, 1, pp. 374-5.
98 *Daily Herald*, 17 March 1942. See also Smyth's testimony in CAB 87/77, Bev. Com., Min. of Ev., Q. 401. For indications of union interest in prevention, see TUC, *Annual Reports:* 1946, pp. 80-92; 1947, pp. 389-91. See also Nat. Assn. of Trade Union Approved Socs., Executive Committee Minutes, 30 Jan. 1946.

Chapter 25: Health Centre Dogma

1 Lab. Party, *Annual Reports:* 1932, pp. 269-70; 1934, pp. 214-15. For the dissolution of the Party's Public Health Advisory Committee, see Nat. Assn. of Trade Union Approved Socs., *Annual Report*, 1933, pp. 1-2.
2 Lab. Party, Public Health Adv. Com., Minutes of Meetings, 23 and 30 Nov. 1938 (on file at Lab. Party headquarters in Transport House, London). See also Lab. Party, *Annual Report*, 1938, p. 52.
3 *Socialist Doctor*, May 1934, p. 8. Stark Murray (1971), pp. 24-5.
4 For clear indications of this, see *Lancet*, 1940, 1, pp. 375-6 (Hastings); 1944, 1, pp. 26-9 (MacWilliam). See also Stark Murray (1942), p. 18; Stark Murray (1971), pp. 42-3.
5 *Med. Today and Tomor.*, Sept. 1942, p. 9; March 1946, p. 5. SMA, *Bull.*, May-June 1944, pp. 4-7; March-April 1946, pp. 2-3.
6 *Med. World*, 30 Jan. 1942, p. 522. Stark Murray (1971), pp. 46-9.
7 MacWilliam, Dr Henry H., *Memories of Walton Hospital*, Liverpool, 1965. See also *Med. Today and Tomor.*, Nov.-Dec. 1965, pp. 2-4.
8 *Med. Today and Tomor.*, March 1939, pp. 1-11. *Lancet*, 1944, 1, pp. 26-9. Stark Murray (1971), pp. 38-9.
9 Lab. Party, *Annual Report*, 1934, pp. 256-8. Note, however, that the SMA used the term 'health centre' in the very first plan it published, *A Socialised Medical Service*, 1933, pp. 8-10. For a clear attempt at a later

date to create a distinction between 'clinics' and 'health centres', see *BMJ*, 1944, 1, Supp., p. 45 (Belfrage).

10   Parl. Deb., Lords, 1 June 1943. Vol. 127, Cols. 738-47; 16 March 1944, Vol. 131, Cols. 101-10.

11   *BMJ*, 1944, 1, Supp., pp. 41-3. See also 1946, 1, pp. 494-6.

12   *BMJ*, 1944, 1, Supp., pp. 41-3.

13   Stark Murray (1971), pp. 64-5.

14   SMA, *Bull.*, May-June 1944, pp. 4-6; Jan.-Feb. 1946, pp. 2-4.

15   MH 77/63, letter from Stark Murray to Willink, 13 Jan. 1944, enclosing SMA Memo., 'Administration of Health Services', para. 9.

16   *Med. Today and Tomor.*, March 1946, pp. 1-2. See also *Lancet*, 1947, 2, p. 150.

17   Stark Murray (1942), pp. 125-39. See also *Med. Today and Tomor.*, Dec. 1943, pp. 3-14. SMA, *Control of Health Services*, 1945, p. 2 (on file in British Museum).

18   *Med. Today and Tomor.*, March 1945, pp. 1-2. SMA, *Bull.*, Dec. 1946, pp. 1-4. See also Stark Murray, D., 'Your Health, Mr. Smith', *Today and Tomor. Publ.*, 1946, p. 24 (on file in British Museum).

19   *Med. Today and Tomor.*, June 1940, pp. 2-8.

20   *Med. World*, 14 May, 1943, pp. 310-11. See also 26 March, p. 134; 14 May, p. 302; 11 June, pp. 399-400. For Party policy at the time, see Lab. Party, *National Service for Health*, 1943.

21   Abel-Smith (1964), p. 452.

22   Brook (1946), pp. 38-43.

23   *Med. Today and Tomor.*, Dec. 1944, p. 11.

24   *BMJ*, 1944, 1, Supp., pp. 57-60.

25   SMSA Min., pp. 190-4, 200, 216-18, 220-8. *Med. World*, 12 April 1929, p. 110 (Rees). Interview with Hastings, 15 Feb. 1962. Stark Murray (1971), pp. 15-19.

26   SMA, *Bull.*, July, 1943, p. 1.

27   *Ibid.*, June, 1946, p. 4.

28   Brook (1946), p. 3. SMA, *Bull.*, July, 1943, p. 1. Stark Murray (1971), pp. 8, 65.

29   Stark Murray (1971), pp. 20-1.

30   *Ibid.*, pp. 30, 41.

31   For the Webbs' admiration of the Soviet Union, see their *Soviet Communism: A New Civilization?*, Longmans, 1935. The question-mark was removed when the second edition was published in 1937. For comments on the interest shown by the Webbs and other left-wing intellectuals in Communism, see Wood, Neal, *Communism and British Intellectuals*, Gollancz, 1959, pp. 42-5.

32   *Med. World*, March 1953, pp. 305-9.

33   For the history of the Society, see *Socialist Christian*, May-June 1942, pp. 4-5; Spring 1957, p. 15. For its size and influence, see *ibid.*, Jan. 1937, p. 6; Winter 1952, p. 1.

34   *Ibid.*, Nov. 1932, pp. 167-8. In 1936 no less than 13 members of the Society held seats in Parliament. For the list, see *ibid.*, Oct. 1936, p. 161.

35   *Ibid.*, July 1933, p. 54; Nov. 1938, p. 72.

36   For Salter's role, see *ibid.*, Nov. 1932, pp. 167-8. For Bushnell's, see *ibid.*, Sept. 1932, p. 48. For Bushnell's Health Council, see *Med. Off.*, 1931, 1, pp. 119-20 and Stark Murray (1971), p. 23.

37   *Soc. Christ.*, June 1930, p. 84.

38 *Ibid.,* March 1932, p. 103; Jan. 1933, pp. 1-2.
39 *Ibid.,* Nov. 1929, pp. 217-18.
40 *Ibid.,* March 1932, p. 103.
41 *Lancet,* 1936, 1, p. 1261.
42 For the publicity given to some of these tours, see *Lancet,* 1931, 1, pp. 256, 887, 1113; 1931, 2, p. 1222; 1932, 1, pp. 700-1.
43 *Ibid.,* 1937, 1, pp. 331-2.
44 Cox (1950), p. 221.
45 For the months when Brook and Morgan resigned, see the return the MPU made to the Friendly Societies' Registry Office for the year 1935, on file at the Public Record Office under the shelf-mark FS 12/232.
46 *Med. Off.,* 1935, 2, p. 173.
47 Stark Murray (1971), p. 40.
48 *Lancet,* 1941, 2, p. 344; 1942, 2, p. 674. *Brit. J. of Phy. Med.,* Sept-Oct. 1943, p. 129.
49 Interview with Hilliard, 20 Jan. 1962. Phone conversations with Kirman and Hilliard, 20 Sept. 1978.
50 Stark Murray (1971), pp. 50, 63. See also Bourne, Aleck, *Health of the Future,* Gollancz, 1942.
51 Bourne, Aleck, *A Doctor's Creed,* Gollancz, 1962, pp. 66-8.
52 Henderson, H. W., *When the 'DW' Was Banned,* I.R.I.S. (Industrial Research and Information Services), 1961. See also Laski, Harold, *The Secret Battalion,* 1946 (statement by Chairman of Lab. Party rejecting Communist plea for unity); and Cockburn, Claude, *Crossing The Line,* Macgibbon and Kee, 1958, pp. 82, 141-2.

Chapter 26: No Industrial Medical Service

1 *BMJ,* 1943, 1, pp. 79-80.
2 *Med. Today and Tomor.,* Sept. 1941, pp. 4-8. Stark Murray (1942), pp. 84-5. For an earlier anticipation of the idea by a leading industrial medical officer, see *BMJ,* 1938, 2, Supp., p. 378 (Lockhart).
3 See Hastings' first presidential address to the SMA in *Lancet,* 1931, 1, p. 1115; and his paper in *Med. Today and Tomor.,* July 1938, pp. 3-6. See also the SMA's first plan, *A Socialised Medical Service,* 1933, pp. 15-17: and Stark Murray (1942), pp. 18, 77, 84.
4 Royal Com. on NHI, 1925, Min. of Ev., Q. 24,181-3 (Brackenbury).
5 Bullock, Alan, *The Life and Times of Ernest Bevin: Volume Two, Minister of Labour, 1940-1945,* Heinemann, 1967, p. 23.
6 *Ibid.,* pp. 78-9. See also *Lancet,* 1940, 2, p. 233; and Fact. Dept., Min. of Labour, 'Memo. on Med. Super. in Factories', 1940.
7 *J. of Ind. Welf.,* Sept. 1941, p. 272.
8 Bullock (1967), p. 79. For a higher estimate of the number of whole-time officers, see *BMJ,* 1941, 2, pp. 762-5.
9 *BMJ,* 1940, 2, p. 291.
10 Abel-Smith (1964), pp. 426-7.
11 *Ibid.,* pp. 429-30, 438-9. See also *Lancet,* 1940, 1, pp. 514-15, 666 (Hastings), 717 (Walton), 807 (Hastings).
12 *Med. World,* 20 Oct. 1939, pp. 214-16.
13 Abel-Smith (1964), pp. 432-3, 437-8. See also Titmuss (1950), p. 456.
14 *Lancet,* 1940, 1, pp. 514-16. Lab. Party, Public Health Adv. Com.

Memos.,R. D. R. 16/Nov., 1941, Hastings, S., 'A Scheme for a State Med. Service'; R. D. R. 50/Dec., 1941, Subcom., 'First Steps Towards a Full State Med. Service'. See also Addison (1975), pp. 179-80.

15 For Kirman's position in the Left Book Club, see *Lancet,* 1939, 1, p. 1126. See also *ibid.,* 1941, 2, p. 1126. For this era in Left Book Club affairs and the concern it caused to leaders of the Labour Party, see *Left,* Dec. 1940, pp. 350-1.

16 Pelling, Henry, *The British Communist Party,* Black, 1958, p. 115.

17 Jt. Med. Soc. Com., 'War and Med. Services', LRD, 1940. See also *Lancet,* 1940, 1, pp. 329-30; *BMJ,* 1940, 1, pp. 313-14; *Med. Today and Tomor.,* Sept. 1939, pp. 1-13.

18 See also the paper by Hastings in *Lancet,* 1940, 1, pp. 375-6.

19 Donoughue, Bernard, and Jones, G. W., *Herbert Morrison, Portrait of a Politician,* Weidenfeld and Nicolson, 1973, p. 283.

20 *Med. World,* 29 May 1942, p. 294.

21 *Med. World,* 27 Dec. 1940, pp. 437-8; 31 Jan. 1942, p. 558. Calder, Ritchie, *Start Planning Britain Now,* Kegan Paul, 1941, pp. 55-7.

22 *Lancet,* 1940, 2, p. 45. See also *ibid.,* 1940, 1, p. 969; and *Med. World,* 22 March 1940, pp. 129-33.

23 Ferguson, Sheila, and Fitzgerald, Hilde, *Studies in the Social Services,* HMSO and Longmans, 1954, p. 255. See also *Med. Today and Tomor.,* June 1941, pp. 2-11.

24 Wilson, Norman, *Municipal Health Services,* Allen and Unwin, 1946, pp. 5-61.

25 *Med. World,* 13 March 1936, p. 79.

26 Kayne, G. Gregory, *The Control of Tuberculosis in England — Past and Present,* OUP, 1937, pp. 135-41.

27 *Lancet,* 1937, 1, pp. 1117-18.

28 For the full text, see *ibid.,* pp. 969-73, 1033-5, 1093-1100.

29 Ferguson and Fitzgerald (1954), p. 254. See also *ibid.,* p. 151 and *Lancet,* 1940, 2, pp. 593-4.

30 *BMJ,* 1940, 1, pp. 457, 495-6, 709, 790-1, 873-5. Home Office, Com. on Conditions in Air Raid Shelters, *Report,* HMSO, Cmd. 6245, Dec., 1940. See also Ferguson and Fitzgerald (1954), p. 255.

31 *Lancet,* 1940, 2, p. 28; 1941, 2, p. 203. *Med. World,* 15 Aug. 1941, p. 600.

32 Ferguson and Fitzgerald (1954), pp. 251-83. See also *Lancet,* 1942, 2, pp. 99, 457-8; 1943, 1, pp. 587, 593-4; 1943, 2, p. 607. Med. Res. Council, *Mass Miniature Radiography of Civilians for the Detection of Pulmonary Tuberculosis,* Spec. Report no. 251 by P. D'Arcy Hart and others, HMSO, 1944.

33 *Lancet,* 1940, 1, p. 263; 1940, 2, pp. 78, 84 (Ellman), 593-4, 611-12. See also SMA, *The War, Tuberculosis and the Workers,* 1942.

34 *Lancet,* 1940, 2, pp. 246-7.

35 SMA, *Bull.,* Jan. 1941, p. 2.

36 *BMJ,* 1941, 2, p. 745. See also pp. 762-5 and *ibid.,* 1943, 1, pp. 79-80.

37 *BMJ,* 1935, 2, pp. 645-6; 1938, 1, p. 38. *Brit. J. of Ind. Med.,* Jan. 1945, p. 63.

38 Assoc. of Ind. Med. Off., *Transactions,* April 1951, pp. 29-31.

39 *Ibid.,* July 1961, pp. 96-8.

40 *BMJ,* 1941, 2, pp. 783-5. *J. of Ind. Welf.,* Dec. 1942, p. 233. See also Hill's address in Min. of Lab., Conf. on Ind. Health, 9 April 1943, *Report*

of Proc., pp. 43-6. For a good report of the conference, see *Lancet,* 1943, 1, pp. 500-2.

41 SMA, *Bull.,* Jan 1941, p. 2.
42 *Med. World,* 6 Dec. 1940, p. 366.
43 TUC, *Annual Report,* 1945, p. 73.
44 *Med. Today and Tomor.,* Sept. 1941, pp. 4-8.
45 SMA, *Bull.,* Jan. 1941, p. 3. *Med. Today and Tomor.,* March 1941, p. 16. *Lancet,* 1941, 1, p. 834.
46 Lafitte, François, *The Internment of Aliens,* Penguin, 1940.
47 *Med. World,* 7 Feb. 1941, pp. 586-8.
48 *Med. Today and Tomor.,* Dec. 1939, pp. 22-3; March 1940, pp. 1, 15.
49 SMA, *Bull.,* Aug. 1941, pp. 3-4.
50 Lab. Party, Public Health Adv. Com., Minutes, 22 July 1941.
51 SMA, *Bull.,* 1942: Jan., p. 3; March, p. 2. For Communist control of the LRD, see Pelling (1958), p. 17. Wood (1959), pp. 77-9. See also *The Communist Solar System,* IRIS, 1957, pp. 59-61.
52 *The Factory Acts in Danger,* LRD, 1940. See also *Labour Research,* Nov. 1940, pp. 166-7.
53 *Lab. Res.,* 1941: Aug., pp. 114-16; Oct., pp. 150-1.
54 *Lab. Res.,* July 1942, pp. 85-6. SMA, *Bull.,* 1942: Oct., p. 4; Nov., p. 7. See also the three reports published jointly by the LRD and SMA during the war: *Health and the War Worker,* 1942; *New Weapons Against TB,* 1943; *Health and Safety Committees in Industry,* 1945.
55 *Science Worker* (Journal of Association of Science Workers), June 1942, p. 22. *BMJ,* 1943, 1, pp. 79-80. *Lancet,* 1943, 1, pp. 26-7; 1944, 1, p. 220. See also Assn. of Scien. Wkrs., *Planning of Science,* Proc. of Conf., Jan. 1943, pp. 104-5.
56 *The Times,* 10 April 1943, p. 2. See also Min. of Lab., Conf. on Ind. Health, 9 April, 1943, *Report of Proc.,* pp. 5-9.
57 *Ibid.,* pp. 43-6.
58 MH 77/26, Nat. Health Service Policy, Bevin to Brown, 9 June 1943; Brown to Bevin, 24 June 1943; Bevin to Brown, 14 July 1943; Brown to Bevin, no date (draft reply). MH 77/27, Nat. Health Service Policy, Maude to Phillips, 22 Nov. 1943; Phillips to Maude, 8 Dec. 1943.
59 Min. of Lab., Conf. on Ind. Health, 9 April 1943, *Report of Proc.,* pp. 50-4.
60 *Med. Today and Tomor.,* Sept. 1941, pp. 4-8. Stark Murray (1942), pp. 84-5, 116-17.
61 TUC, *Annual Report,* 1945, p. 73. See also Lab. Party, Public Health Adv. Com., Report on White Paper by TUC Sub-Com., 9 March 1944.
62 Bullock (1967), p. 218
63 *Lab. Res.,* 1942: May, pp. 49-50; Oct., pp. 129-30.
64 Pelling (1958), pp. 135-7.
65 For a direct exchange between Stark Murray and Smyth on this issue, see Lab. Party, Public Health Adv. Com., Minutes, 8 Nov. 1943. See also *ibid.,* 15 Dec. 1943, report of meeting with TUC's Work. Comp. and Fact. Com. For the jt. prod. coms. as a focal point of Communist activity, see Marx House, *Educational Commentary on Jt. Prod. Coms.,* 4 Nov. 1942. See also *Scien. Wkr.,* June 1942, p. 18; Nov. 1942, pp. 60-1; March 1943, report of Jan. Conf., *Planning of Science.* See

also LRD and SMA, *Health and Safety Coms. in Ind.,* 1945. For Bevin's attempt to cope with the problem, see *J. of Ind. Welf.,* March 1942, pp. 37-8. For Citrine's attempt, see Int'l Lab. Org., *British Jt. Prod. Machinery,* Series A, No. 43, Geneva, 1944, pp. 7-25, 52-5.

66 Lab. Party, *Nat. Service for Health,* 1943, p. 21.
67 SMA, *A Social. Med. Service,* 1933, p. 15.
68 Lab. Party, *Annual Report,* 1943, pp. 14, 144 (Gould).
69 For Morrison's vigilance where Communists were concerned, see Donoughue and Jones (1973), pp. 225-32, 298-9, 383-4, 433-4.
70 White Paper on Nat. Health Service, 1944, pp. 10, 57, 66-7. See also Mackintosh (1953), pp. 173-4.
71 *Lancet,* 1945, 1, pp. 150-1. *BMJ,* 1945, 1, p. 194. *Brit. J. of Ind. Med.,* Jan 1945, pp. 48, 51-5.
72 *Brit. J. of Ind. Med.,* July 1954, pp. 198-212. For the study itself, see Med. Res. Council, *Chronic Pulmonary Disease in South Wales Coalminers,* Spec. Report no. 243 by P. D'Arcy Hart and E. A. Aslett, HMSO, 1942.
73 TUC, *Annual Report,* 1944, pp. 69-70. See also *ibid.,* 1953, pp. 150-3, 324-9, 334-6; 1962, p. 145.
74 For a good review of employer and union differences on this subject, see *Lancet,* 1959, 1, pp. 923-4.
75 TUC, *Annual Report,* 1946, pp. 80-92. *Lancet,* 1946, 1, p. 147.
76 Quoted in *Med. Today and Tomor.,* July-Aug. 1955, p. 7.
77 TUC, *Annual Report,* 1959, pp. 161-2. For the creation of the Ind. Health Adv. Com., see Bullock (1967), p. 240.
78 Titmuss (1950), pp. 469-70. Abel-Smith (1964), p. 434.
79 *New States.,* 5 Jan. 1946, p. 3. See also *Med. World,* 8 Feb. 1946, p. 805.

Chapter 27: Rise of the Medical Policy Association

1 Addison (1975), p. 241.
2 *Lancet,* 1947, 1, pp. 25-6.
3 For the background, see Macpherson, C. B., *Democracy in Alberta: Social Credit and the Party System,* Toronto, Univ. of Toronto Press, 1962, pp. 93-153, 179-92; and Finlay, John L., *Social Credit: The English Origins,* McGill-Queen's Univ. Press, 1972.
4 *Jewish Chron.,* 9 Sept. 1938, p. 22.
5 *Dynamic America* (Amer. social credit journal), July 1940, pp. 26-8. *Message from Hargrave,* 1944, Nos. 319, 352; 1945, No. 385. See also Tom Driberg, 'A Touch of the Sun', in *Cornhill Magazine,* 1944, pp. 57-65.
6 Neither Macpherson nor Finlay deal with this subject adequately: both attempt to excuse or explain away Douglas's anti-semitism. For recognition of his obsession, see the remarks of one social crediter in *The Sun* (organ of Company of Free Men, a social credit group), Winter, 1953-4, p. 5.
7 For an indication of this, see *Men First* (Amer. social credit journal), 7 March 1942, No. 76, commenting on report in *New York Times,* 5 Feb. 1942.

8   *Med. World,* 10 July 1936, pp. 655-6; 9 July 1937, pp. 666-7; 1 July 1938, p. 669. See also his letter in *ibid.,* 4 Nov. 1938, p. 446.
9   *Ibid.,* 28 Feb. 1936, p. 8.
10 *Ibid.,* 31 Jan. 1936, p. 728.
11 *Med. World,* 23 Sept. 1938, pp. 171-2. See also the statement by Dr F. Reynolds in *ibid.,* 21 July 1939, Supp., after p. 780.
12 *Med. World,* 1929: 25 Jan., p. 356; 27 Dec., p. 289.
13 *Patriot,* 21 Jan. 1932, pp. 50-1.
14 *Med. World,* 20 Sept. 1918, p. 180; 26 Dec. 1919, p. 660.
15 *Med. World,* 20 April 1922, p. 175. See also 1 April 1921, p. 1561.
16 *Med. World,* 1934: 6 July, pp. 531-2; 30 Nov., pp. 421-6.
17 *BMJ,* 1934, 1, Supp., pp. 260-1; 1934, 2, Supp., p. 127 (para. 14-15 of Ins. Act Com. Report); 1936, 2, Supp., p. 127 (para. 12-16 of Ins. Act Com. Report). *Lancet,* 1933, 2, pp. 1324-5; 1934, 2, pp. 277, 1363-4; 1935, 2, p. 1372 (Leighton). MH 62/97, Mortgage on Prac., 1933: Memo. by H. W. Townley, 29 Nov.; letter from J. A. Speed, 30 Nov.
18 For the classic statement of this idea by an economic historian who later became a Nazi sympathizer, see Sombart, Werner, *The Jews and Modern Capitalism,* New York, Collier Books, 1962, note pp. 386-7 in particular. (This book was first published in 1911.)
19 Sykes, Wm. Stanley, *The Missing Money-Lender,* Penguin, 1936, pp. 15, 70-1, 143, 151, 166-7, 174-83, 209-17. For Sykes's obituary notice, see *BMJ,* 1961, 1, pp. 1258-9.
20 *Med. World,* 5 Aug. 1938, p. 862 (de Swietchowski). See also *Lancet,* 1938, 1, pp. 808 (Goodwin), 865 (Endean), 914-15 (Lysaght). *BMJ,* 1939, 1, p. 89 (Robinson).
21 *New States.,* 23 July 1938, p. 144. See also the reply from Welply the following week, *ibid.,* 30 July 1938, p. 183. See also Sherman, A. J., *Island Refuge — Britain and Refugees from the Third Reich, 1933-1939,* Elek, 1973, pp. 48, 88-94, 123-4, 259-67.
22 *Med. World,* 1 Dec. 1933, p. 333; 29 June 1934, p. 490. See also *BMJ,* 1933, 2, Supp., pp. 165, 323 (Blonstein). However, for some MPU opposition to the entry of refugees before 1936, see *Med. World,* 7 July 1933, p. 372.
23 *Med. World,* 1938: 30 Sept., pp. 213, 220; 18 Nov., pp. 510-11; 25 Nov., pp. 539-40; 2 Dec., pp. 601-2. See also *Jewish Chron.,* 15 July 1938, p. 19.
24 For a clear indication of this, see the views expressed before the London Jewish Hospital Medical Society by Dr Robert Scott Stevenson, then a sub-editor of the *BMJ,* and a spokesman for the Council of the BMA. *Med. World,* 6 Jan. 1938, p. 784. See also *Jewish Chron.,* 23 Dec. 1938, p. 19. *The Lancet* also supported refugee entry, *Lancet,* 1938, 1, pp. 951-2; 1939, 1, pp. 274-5.
25 *Med. World,* 30 Dec. 1927, p. 396.
26 *Med. World,* 6 July 1934, pp. 531-2.
27 For a tribute to Gregg for his work in the MPU, see *Med. World,* 17 March 1933, pp. 54-6. For his election as Chairman of the Ins. Acts Com. and his subsequent resignation from the MPU, see *BMJ,* 1937, 2, Supp., p. 321; 1938, 1, Supp., p. 118. For the MPU reaction to his resignation, see *Med. World,* 4 Nov. 1938, p. 441.
28 *BMJ,* 1938, 2, pp. 79, 155, 268-9. *New States.,* 23 July 1938, p. 144. Angell, Norman, and Buxton, D. F., *You and the Refugee,* Penguin,

1939, pp. 240-2. Hoare, Samuel, *Nine Troubled Years,* Collins, 1954, pp. 239-41. Sherman (1973), pp. 123-4.

29 For Ward's relentless opposition to the admission of refugee doctors, see *BMJ,* 1935, 2, Supp., pp. 81-2; 1936, 2, Supp., p. 63; 1937, 2, Supp., pp. 49-50; 1938, 2, Supp., pp. 54-6; 1939, 2, Supp., p. 61.

30 For Ward's obituary notice, see *BMJ,* 1945, 2, p. 479; and *Lancet,* 1945, 2, p. 513. See also the paper on him by R. M. S. McConaghey in *J. of Royal Coll. of Gen. Prac.,* Aug. 1974, pp. 568-71. For the 2 books he published in 1929-30, see Ward, Ernest, *Medical Adventure,* John Bale, Sons, & Danielson, 1929; and *General Practice,* J. Bale, 1930.

31 *Lancet,* 1938, 1, pp. 951-2. See also *Jewish Chron.,* 1939: 20 Jan., p. 14; 24 Feb., p. 14.

32 *Med. World,* 2 Dec. 1938, pp. 601-2. See also 25 Aug. 1939, pp. 27-8; and *Jewish Chron.,* 9 Sept. 1938, p. 10. For a wider attack on refugee conduct, see Murchin, M.G., *Britain's Jewish Problem,* Hurst and Blackett, 1939, pp. 60-3, 89-104.

33 *Med. World,* 1940: 26 April, pp. 233-4; 19 July, pp. 523-4.

34 For a good review of this whole question, see Dunn (1952), pp. 424-32.

35 *Med. World,* 22 Nov. 1940, pp. 318-19.

36 Macpherson (1962), pp. 93-7.

37 *Ibid.,* p. 97.

38 Comyns Carr and others (1913), p. 94. See also Royal Com. on NHI, 1928, p. 261, para. 640.

39 *Med. World,* 19 July 1940, pp. 528-30. See also 1940: 28 June, pp. 448-9; 5 July, pp. 480-2 (Hayward); 12 July, pp. 504-6 (Clark); 19 July, p. 530 (Hayward); 26 July, p. 552 (Brown); 2 August, pp. 574-6; 9 Aug., pp. 590-2; 16 Aug., pp. 622-4; 23 August, pp. 20-2 (Westlake); 30 Aug., pp. 44-6.

40 *Ibid.,* 5 April 1940, p. 170; 26 April 1940, p. 240; 17 Oct. 1941, pp. 196-8.

41 Westlake, Aubrey T., *Health Abounding,* Social Credit Party, 1944.

42 *Med. World,* 16 Aug. 1940, p. 612. For the series as a whole, see 1940: 2 Aug., pp. 561-6; 9 Aug., pp. 587-90: 16 Aug., pp. 609-13; 23 Aug., pp. 6-10; 30 Aug., pp. 31-4; 6 Sept., pp. 54-8; 13 Sept., pp. 79-83.

43 For this, see *ibid.,* 13 Sept. 1940, pp. 79-83.

44 *Ibid.,* 10 Sept. 1937, p. 81. See also 1940: 13 Sept., pp. 88-9; 24 Oct., p. 218; 21 Nov., pp. 296-7; 28 Nov., pp. 318-19; 5 Dec., p. 341; 14 Dec., pp. 361-2.

45 *Ibid.,* 1943: 8 Jan., pp. 507-9; 2 April, pp. 231-4; 18 June, pp. 431-4.

46 *Ibid.,* 15 Aug. 1947, pp. 773-4. Lindsey Almont, *Socialised Medicine in England and Wales — The National Health Service 1948 — 1961,* Chapel Hill, University of North Carolina Press, 1962, pp. 230-1.

47 For recognition of this by a doctor in the Bayly group, see *Med. World,* 4 Aug. 1939, pp. 839-42.

48 *BMJ,* 1941, 2, p. 68.

49 For information about Jones, see *Social Crediter,* 22 April 1939, p. 1; 13 Oct. 1956, p. 1; 21 Feb. 1953, p. 4; 18 Jan. 1964, p. 8.

50 For this, see the obituary notice of Russell Steele in *ibid.,* 21 Feb. 1959, p. 4.

51 For the tight control exercised by the Steele brothers and Rugg-Gunn over MPA affairs, see *ibid.,* 4 Dec. 1948, pp. 4-5.

52 *Ibid.,* 23 Oct. 1943, p. 5; 4 Dec. 1948, pp. 4-5. Note, however, the

inclusion of the MPA in the brief history of the social credit movement in England during the war in *ibid.,* 13 Oct. 1945, pp. 1-3.

53   *BMJ,* 1943, 2, p. 552.
54   *Evening Standard,* 9 Sept. 1943, p. 2. See also *ibid.,* 23 Sept., p. 2.
55   This quote is directly as it appeared in *BMJ,* 1943, 2, p. 552. Italics as in original.
56   *BMJ,* 1943, 2, p. 623.
57   *Ev. Std.,* 9 Sept. 1943, p. 2. For other denials of anti-semitism, see *BMJ,* 1943, 2, p. 623 (Rugg-Gunn); *The Times,* 10 March 1944, p. 8 (Basil Steele); *Spectator,* 13 Oct. 1944, p. 338.
58   *BMJ,* 1943, 2, p. 623.
69   Rugg-Gunn, A., *British Medicine and Alien Plans,* Liverpool, K. R. P. Publ., 1943, p. 17.
60   Parl. Deb., Commons, 23 Nov. 1943, Vol. 393, Col. 1463.
61   Parl. Deb., Commons, 23 Feb. 1944, Vol. 397, Cols. 833-4.
62   *The Times,* 10 March 1944, p. 8 (Steele).
63   For references to later Bulletins, see *Social Crediter,* 13 Nov. 1943, pp. 6-7; 4 March 1944, pp. 1-6; 10 June 1944, pp. 5-7; 17 June 1944, pp. 6-8. See also Rugg-Gunn (1943), pp. 19-27.
64   *Spec.,* 29 Sept. 1944, p. 285. See also *BMJ,* 1944, 2, Supp., pp. 49-50 (Rogers).
65   For evidence of MPA influence in Guildford and Maidstone, see *BMJ,* 1944, 2, Supp., pp. 54 (Baker), 78. For its influence in Cumberland, see the article by Monahan in *Fig Tree,* June 1954, pp. 5-16. For SMA recognition of MPA influence within the BMA, see *BMJ,* 1944, 2, p. 540 (Stark Murray).
66   *Social Crediter,* 4 March 1944, pp. 1-6.
67   *BMJ,* 1944, 2, Supp., pp. 49-50.
68   See the paper by Dr W. H. Spoor, 'Looking Backward on the National Health Service', in *Pulse,* 26 July 1969, p. 11.
69   Note, for example, the advertisement that appeared in *Lancet,* 1942, 2, p. 132. See also *Med. World,* 5 Feb. 1943, pp. 598-9. For evidence of wider anti-semitic feeling in Britain during the war, see the article by George Orwell in *Contemporary Jewish Record,* April 1945, pp. 163-71.
70   Macpherson (1962), p. 183. See also Douglas, C. H., *Programme for the Third World War,* Liverpool, K. R. P. Publ., 1943, pp. 27-8.
71   *Jewish Chron.,* 4 Dec. 1942, p. 14; 11 Dec. 1942, pp. 1, 8; 25 Dec. 1942, pp. 7-8; 22 Jan. 1943, p. 5.
72   *BMJ,* 1944, 2, Supp., pp. 49-50 (Rogers).
73   *Ibid.,* 1912, 2, Supp., pp. 713, 722-5.
74   *Ibid.,* 1941, 2, Supp., pp. 31 (MacWilliam), 37 (Apsimon), 41-2 (Bourne), 43 (Forrie), 47 (Hastings), 55-6 (Armstrong), 67 (Mac-William), 68 (Steele).
75   *Ibid.,* 1943, 2, p. 693.
76   *Ibid.,* 1944, 2, pp. 506-7. For the angry exchange this provoked between SMA leaders and others, see *ibid.,* pp. 540-1 (Stark Murray and Smith), 609-10 (Wigfield and MacWilliam), 639-40 (MacDougall, Vinter, Leff).
77   Note the papers by Dr Geoffrey Bourne in *BMJ,* 1943, 1, pp. 227-8, 673-4. See also his autobiography, *We Met At Bart's,* Muller, 1963, pp. 217-19, 242-4.
78   *Lancet,* 1941, 1, p. 370. See also Stark Murray (1942), p. 143.

79 For a clear indication that this had been a subject of concern to some doctors, see *BMJ*, 1941, 2, Supp., p. 43 (Fairrie).

80 *BMJ*, 1943, 1, p. 433. For an earlier criticism of the SMA (on this occasion, for adopting a motion in favour of a Second Front), see *ibid.*, 1942, 2, pp. 16-17.

81 *Ibid.*, 1943, 2, Supp., pp. 29-34.

82 *Ibid.*, p. 31.

83 BMA (1938), p. 17, para. 27.

84 *BMJ*, 1942, 1, pp. 743-52, para. 32-49. See also *Lancet*, 1942, 2, p. 699.

85 *Med. Off.*, 1939, 1. pp. 29-30.

86 *BMJ*, 1942, 2, Supp., p. 33.

87 *Ibid.*, 1943, 2, Supp., pp. 54-5, 66-8.

88 *Ibid.*, 1943, 2, p. 458; 1943, 2, Supp, p. 53.

89 *Ibid.*, 1943, 2, Supp., p. 51. See also Watson (1950), p. 304.

Chapter 28: Bevan's Concessions

1 For biographical data about Graham-Little, see *Dictionary of National Biography*, 1941-50, OUP, pp. 315-17. See also his obit. notice in *The Times*, 10 Oct. 1950, p. 8; *BMJ*, 1950, 2, pp. 894-5; *Lancet*, 1950, 2, p. 543.

2 *Lancet*, 1940, 2, p. 666. *Med. World*, 4 April 1941, p. 164.

3 *Surrey Times*, 31 March 1944, p. 4.

4 *Truth*, 28 April 1944, pp. 328-9. See also the letter from the organizers of the Guildford meeting in *ibid.*, 14 April 1944, p. 306.

5 *Truth* was attacked in Parliament shortly after Brooks became editor because its views were thought to be close to the Fascists. *Truth*, 18 Oct. 1941, pp. 309-10. Chesterton began writing for *Truth* in Aug., 1942: *Ibid.*, 28 Aug. 1942, p. 172, but he did not openly identify himself until 18 June 1943, p. 494. For his appointment as assistant editor, see *Jewish Chron.*, 29 Sept. 1944, p. 16. For his fascist background, see Cross (1961), pp. 79-80, 102, 184-5; and *Jewish Chron.*, 7 Sept. 1973, p. 43. For the ejection of Brooks and Chesterton after *Truth* was purchased by Staples Press, see *Truth*, 27 Feb. 1953, pp. 201-2. For the angry reaction of the anti-semitic camp, see *Social Crediter*, 1953: 7 March, p. 1; 21 March, p. 1. See also Britons, *Truth Has Been Murdered*, 1953.

6 *BMJ*, 1944, 1, p. 663.

7 *The Times*, 16 Sept. 1944, p. 5. See also *BMJ*, 1944, 2, p. 409.

8 SMA, *Bull.*, May-June 1944, pp. 4-6. *Lancet*, 1944, 1, pp. 405-6, 413-17. See also Parl. Deb., Commons, 12 June 1945, Vol. 411, Cols. 1555-8.

9 *Lancet*, 1943, 2, p. 773. See also *Med. World*, 28 Jan. 1944, pp. 630-1; 29 June 1945, p. 617.

10 MH 77/63, Memo. to Min. from SMA (follows note to Wrigley from ?, 21 March 1943). The quotation here appears on p. 4. of the Memo.

11 *Ibid.*, letter from Murray to Willink, 13 Jan. 1944, enclosing Memo., 'Admin. of Health Services'. The quotation here appears in para. 9 of the Memo.

12 *Med. Today and Tomor.*, 1955: July-Aug., p. 14; Sept.-Oct., pp. 9-10.

13 *Med. Today and Tomor.,* Sept. 1944, pp. 3-5. See also Stark Murray (1971), pp. 67-8.
14 *BMJ,* 1944, 2, Supp., pp. 25-8, answer to questions 10 and 26.
15 Stark Murray (1971), p. 68. See also his paper in *Socialist Vanguard,* April, 1944, pp. 210-12.
16 *BMJ,* 1944, 2, Supp., p. 26, answer to question 11.
17 *Ibid.,* pp. 26-8, answer to questions 17 and 27.
18 *Truth,* 15 Dec. 1944, p. 473.
19 For Inwald's role in the SMA, see SMA,*Bull.,* June, 1943, pp. 2, 4; May-June, 1944, p. 7. See also *Med. World,* 10 May 1946, pp. 403-5. For Steele's influence in Guildford, see *BMJ,* 1943, 1, Supp., p. 41.
20 This was the article by Gordon Malet, 'Dissident Doctors', in *Spectator,* 29 Sept. 1944, p. 285. See the reply by Rugg-Gunn in *ibid.,* 13 Oct. 1944, p. 338.
21 *BMJ,* 1944, 1, p. 664.
22 *Public Health,* Nov. 1946, p. 41. *BMJ,* 1947, 1, p. 19.
23 SMA, *Bull.,* May-June, 1944, p. 7.
24 *BMJ,* 1944, 2, p. 540.
25 *BMJ,* 1944, 2, Supp., p. 160. For Cullen's political activities, see *Labour Monthly,* Dec. 1935, pp. 741-6; London Municipal Society, *Socialism in Local Government,* 1938, pp. 57-8; McHenry, Dean E., *Labour Party in Transition, 1931-1938,* Routledge, 1938, pp. 244, 248-9.
26 *BMJ,* 1944, 2, Supp., p. 151. See also *Lancet,* 1945, 1, pp. 633-4, 675.
27 *BMJ,* 1944, 2, pp. 794-5; 1944, 2, Supp., pp. 155-6.
28 *Lancet,* 1944, 2, pp. 789-90. For the PEP statement in its original, see PEP, Planning No. 222, 30 June 1944.
29 *BMJ,* 1910, 2, pp. 84-9. For similar statements by Brackenbury and Dain in 1919, see *ibid.,* 1919, 2, Supp., pp. 42-3.
30 Foot, Michael, *Aneurin Bevan, Volume 2, 1945-1960,* Paladin, 1975, p. 111. See also Vaughan, Paul, *Doctors' Commons, A Short History of the British Medical Association,* Heinemann, 1959, pp. 218-19. A leader in the *BMJ,* however, added a qualification — see 1945, 2, pp. 668-9.
31 Burrow, James G., *AMA — Voice of American Medicine,* Baltimore, Johns Hopkins Press, 1963, pp. 146-51, 153-7, 185-227, 291-303, 329-96.
32 *Lancet,* 1945, 1, pp. 473-4, 544-5.
33 Foot, Michael, *Aneurin Bevan, A Biography, Volume One, 1897-1945,* Four Square, 1966, pp. 147, 169-70. See also Cross (1961), p. 131.
34 MH 77/43, Attlee to Willink, 11 Dec.1943, enclosing Memo. from 'A Medical Man' on the White Paper. For the identification of Taylor as the author, see *ibid.,* ? to Rucker, 13 Dec. 1943. See also *ibid.,* ? to ?, 2 Jan. 1944 [reference illegible]. For other factors behind the inclusion of the middle class, see *Lancet,* 1948, 1, pp. 143-6.
35 Bevan, Aneurin, *In Place of Fear,* MacGibbon and Kee, 1961, pp. 98-121.
36 *BMJ,* 1967, 3, p. 53 (Strang).
37 Butler, John R., *Family Doctors and Public Policy,* Routledge, 1973, pp. 7-42, 138-56.
38 *BMJ,* 1946, 2, Supp., pp. 75-8.
39 Foot (1975), p. 115.
40 *Ibid.,* p. 149.
41 *Ibid.,* p. 203.

42　*Ibid.,* p. 176.
43　*The Times,* 19 Nov. 1946, p. 5. *Lancet,* 1946, 1, p. 970; 1946, 2, p. 766. Foot (1975), p. 143. For Souttar's sympathetic view of the Health Service, see *Fort. Rev.,* Oct. 1945, pp. 213-18.
44　*BMJ,* 1948, 1, pp. 848-50. See also Fellowship for Freedom in Medicine, *The Medical Surrender,* 1951, p. 27.
45　SMA, *Bull.,* Jan.-Feb., 1946, p. 7.
46　Foot (1975), p. 181.
47　*Ibid.,* pp. 185-6.
48　Abel-Smith (1964), p. 479.
49　Foot (1975), pp. 130, 136, 152, 186.
50　CAB 129/3, Memo. by Min. of Health, 'The Future of the Hospital Service', 5 Oct. 1945, CP (45) 205, p. 4, para. 14 (2).
51　*Ibid.,* Memo. by Jt. Parl., Under Sec. for Scot., 'National Health Service', 5 Oct. 1945, CR (45) 207.
52　CAB 128/1, Minutes of Cabinet Meeting held on 11 Oct. 1945, CM (40) 45, pp. 158-9.
53　Stark Murray (1971), p. 77.
54　*Lancet,* 1944, 2, pp. 18-19.
55　*Lancet,* 1946, 1, pp. 632-4.
56　*BMJ,* 1946, 2, p. 179.
57　Foot (1975), p. 208. For a wider indication of the MOH reaction, see Mackintosh (1953), pp. 90, 139-40, 161, 174-91.
58　*BMJ,* 1946, 1, pp. 499-500.
59　Foot (1975), pp. 132-3. For the official record of this fight, see CAB 129/3, Memo. by Lord Pres. of Council (Morrison), 'The Future of the Hospital Services', 12 Oct. 1945, CP (45) 227; Memo. by Min. of Health, 'The Hospital Services', 16 Oct. 1945, CP (45) 231; CAB 128/1, Minutes of Cab. Meeting, 18 Oct. 1945, CM 43 (45), pp. 178-80.
60　CAB 128/1, Minutes of Cab. Meeting, 11 Oct. 1945, CM 40 (45), p. 159; CAB 128/2, Minutes of Cab. Meeting, 20 Dec. 1945, CM 65 (45), p. 339.
61　CAB 129/7, Memo. by Lord Pres. of Council and Lord Privy Seal, 6 March 1946, CM 3 (46).
62　Foot (1975), pp. 130-1.
63　Bevan (1961), pp. 102-3.
64　Foot (1975), pp. 130-3. According to Lord Moran, this was enough to justify the creation of the Health Service. Parl. Deb., Lords, 2 July 1958, Vol 210, Cols. 461-3.
65　*Lancet,* 1945, 2, pp. 781-2. See also Foot (1975), pp. 133-5.
66　Parl. Deb., Commons, Std. Com. C., 19 June 1946, Cols. 1619-20. *BMJ,* 1948, 1, pp. 348-9.
67　Foot (1975), p. 180. For evidence of the determination he displayed within the Cabinet, see CAB 129/4, Memo. by Min. of Health, 'Sale and Purchase of Medical Practices', 23 Nov. 1945, CP (45) 298.
68　Foot (1975), pp. 76-80.
69　*Proceedings of Royal Society of Medicine,* Vol. 65, 1972, pp. 109-18.
70　SMA, *Bull.,* Dec., 1946, pp. 1-4. See, however, the long list of points *not* secured in Stark Murray (1971), pp. 85-6.
71　Harris and Sack (1937), p. 13.
72　*BMJ,* 1928, 2, Supp., pp. 38-41 (Dain). Royal Com. on NHI, 1925, Min. of Ev., Q. 15,441-4 (Ward). See also Schuster Com., 1914, Min.

of Ev., Q. 12,221-2 (Appleton). See also Nat. Assn. of Ins. Coms., 1916, *Proceedings,* 18 May (Hurrey).

73 BMA, Spec. Rep. Meeting, 3-4 May 1945, Report on Negot. by Council of BMA (not published but copy in author's possession), p. 10.

74 National Health Service Act, 1946, 9 & 10 Geo. 6, Ch. 81, Fifth Schedule.

75 For an indication of medical influence on Executive Councils and their national associations, see *Nat. Ins. Gaz.,* 1948, pp. 483, 615. See also Exec. Councils Assn., Eng., 1952, *Proceedings,* p. 137.

76 Guillebaud Report, 1956, p. 155, para. 444. See also Exec. Councils Assn., Eng., 1953, *Proceedings,* p. 108 (Macleod).

77 Abel-Smith (1964), p. 475.

78 *Lancet,* 1946, 2, pp. 176-7. See also the fears Bevan expressed in Parliament. Parl. Deb., Commons, 30 April 1946, Vol. 422, Col. 52; *ibid.,* June, 1946, Standing Com. C., Col. 585. See also the concern later expressed by Lord Attlee. *BMJ,* 1957, 2, Supp., p. 179.

79 Foot (1975), pp. 182-4.

80 *BMJ,* 1953, 1, Supp., p. 296.

81 *Med. Today and Tomor.,* March 1944, pp. 3-7. See also *Soc. Van.,* April, 1944, pp. 240-2; and Stark Murray, D., and MacNae, L. C. J., *Now For Health,* St. Botolph, 1946.

82 Foot (1975), p. 136.

83 *Lancet,* 1948, 2, p. 419. *BMJ,* 1949, 2, pp. 990-1.

84 *Lancet,* 1946, 2, pp. 131-2, 163.

85 *Lancet,* 1950, 2, p. 830.

86 For a detailed description of the firm, see Goldman, Louis, *Angry Young Doctor,* Hamish Hamilton, 1957, pp. 8-20.

87 Stevens (1966), pp. 16, 60-1.

88 *Lancet,* 1950, 2, pp. 648-9, 882-3.

89 Stark Murray, D. S., *Blueprint for Health,* Allen and Unwin, 1973, pp. 187-8.

90 Parl. Deb., Lords, 16 April 1946, Vol. 140, Cols. 829-30.

91 *Ibid.,* Cols. 841-2.

92 *Ibid.,* Lords, 8 Oct. 1946, Vol. 143, Col. 42.

93 Stevens (1966), pp. 214-15.

94 Foot (1975), p. 131.

95 Parl. Deb., Lords, 26 March 1952, Vol. 175, Cols. 985-6.

96 *Ibid.,* Lords, 16 April 1946, Vol. 140. Cols. 841-2.

97 Foot (1975), pp. 134, 151.

98 *Ibid.,* p. 151.

99 *Ibid.,* pp. 134, 181.

100 *Ibid.,* p. 196.

101 *Lancet,* 1946, 2, pp. 697-8, 730.

102 *Ibid.,* pp. 654-7.

103 *Ibid.,* pp. 175-8.

104 Taylor (1954), p. 29.

105 *Lancet,* 1946, 1, p. 980.

106 Murray and MacNae (1946), p. 37.

107 Foot (1975), pp. 162, 180.

108 *Ibid.,* pp. 141, 205-6.

109 *Ibid.,* p. 198.

110 Lindsey (1962), p. 61. Butler (1973), pp. 7-9.

111 Foot (1975), p. 203.

112 *Ibid.,* p. 208.

113 For a hint of Hill's true feelings on abolition of the sale of practices, see Hill (1964), p. 99.

114 *Med. World,* 21 July 1939, Supp. (after p. 780), pp. 2-3. Contrast this with his attack on the nationalization of medicine in 1945. *BMJ,* 1945, 1, Supp., pp. 357-60. For his explanation of the apparent contradiction, see Horder, Thomas, *Fifty Years of Medicine,* Duckworth, 1953, p. 19.

115 Parl. Deb., Lords, 22 Oct. 1946, Vol. 143, Col. 514.

116 Horder (1953), pp. 43-9. For the importance of the free speech issue during the negotiations on the Health Service, see Foot (1975), p. 198; and *BMJ,* 1947, 2, pp. 1037-8.

117 Hill (1964), pp. 92-3.

118 Stark Murray (1971), p. 80.

119 *BMJ,* 1946, 1, pp. 489-91; 1946, 2, pp. 612-13.

120 For the strong support given by Labour to municipal admin., see Mackintosh (1953), pp. 165-6, 174-6.

121 *Lancet,* 1946, 1, p. 907. See also *ibid.,* pp. 699-702.

122 *Lancet,* 1941, 2, p. 455. For an indication of MOH feeling on the subject, see *ibid.,* 1947, 1, pp. 228-30.

123 Addison (1975), p. 273.

124 For an indication of this, see SMA, *Bull.,* Dec., 1946, pp. 1-4; and Stark Murray (1971), p. 77.

125 *BMJ,* 1939, 1, Supp., pp. 133-4 (Hastings). Even Brook subscribed to this view. *Med. Today and Tomor.,* June 1940, pp. 2-8.

126 *Lancet,* 1943, 2, p. 592 (Hastings).

127 *Med. Today and Tomor.,* May-June, 1952, pp. 8-9. See also *Lancet,* 1943, 2, pp. 304-5 (D'Arcy Hart and others).

128 *Med. Today and Tomor.,* July-Aug., 1954, p. 12 (Kerr).

129 *Ibid.,* Spring 1951, pp. 1-2; July-Aug. 1952, pp. 3-6 (Stark Murray). See also Stark Murray (1971), pp. 80, 89.

130 Stark Murray (1971), pp. 124, 129. See also the profile of Stark Murray in the *Guardian,* 16 March 1972, p. 11.

131 *The Times,* 1 Oct. 1975, p. 4.

132 Lab. Party, Report of Working Party, *Health Care,* 1973, p. 43.

133 Stark Murray (1942), pp. 17-18, 72, 105-6. *Med. World,* 24 Aug. 1945, pp. 49-56 (Joules). *Med. Today and Tomor.,* June 1946, pp. 4-5 (Hastings). SMA, *Bull.,* June 1946, pp. 2-3 (Doll).

134 *BMJ,* 1918, 2, pp. 301-2.

135 *Med. World,* 14 July 1933, pp. 406-9.

136 See article by Irwin Brown (pseudonymn for Stark Murray) in *Med. Today and Tomor.,* Autumn 1949, pp. 4-7.

Chapter 29: Consultants Reject GPs

1 *Proceedings of Royal Society of Medicine,* 1972, Vol. 65, p. 113. Note also Bevan's statement in Parl. Deb., Commons, Stdg. Com. C., 6 June 1946, Col. 1518.

2 *BMJ,* 1946, 1, pp. 470 (para. 11-12), 472 (para. 22), 489-91; 1946, 1, Supp., pp. 121-2.

3 *BMJ,* 1946, 1, Supp., p. 126 (Stevens).
4 Foot (1975), p. 131. For the need to secure a more even distribution of consultants, see Eckstein (1958), pp. 59-60, 180, 234-6. For the persistence of regional inequalities, see Stevens (1966), pp. 235-6.
5 *BMJ,* 1946, 1, pp. 575-6; 1946, 1, Supp., p. 79.
6 *BMJ,* 1948, 1, p. 17.
7 *Lancet,* 1946, 1, pp. 421-4. See also *BMJ,* 1950, 2, Supp., p. 261 (Sibley).
8 Parl. Deb., Commons, Stdg. Com. C., 16 May 1946, Cols. 1122-4. A convenient summary of this debate appears in *Lancet,* 1946, 1, p. 796. See also the statement by Sir Henry Morris-Jones in Parl. Deb., Commons, 19 Oct. 1949, Vol. 468, Cols. 650-1.
9 Stevens (1966), p. 81.
10 For suggestions of this motive, see Abel-Smith (1964), pp. 449, 480.
11 *Lancet,* 1946, 1, p. 907.
12 *Lancet,* 1949, 2, pp. 703-4, 711-12.
13 For a convenient comparison, showing figures to 1968, see BMA, *Health Services Financing,* 1970, p. 589. For later data, see Dept. of Health and Soc. Sec., *Health and Personal Social Service Statistics for England, 1975,* 1976, p. 30.
14 Stevens (1966), pp. 142-3, 147. See also Min. of Health and Dept. of Health for Scot., Report of Joint Working Party, *Medical Staffing Structure in the Hospital Service* (Platt Report), HMSO, 1961, pp. 6-7; and BMA, *Health Services Financing,* 1970, pp. 589-91.
15 *BMJ,* 1949, 2, pp. 1031-2. See also 1950, 1, Supp., pp. 165-8; 1952, 1, Supp., pp. 268-71.
16 Honigsbaum, F., 'General Practitioner Work in British Hospitals', in *Social and Economic Administration,* April 1967, p. 35.
17 *BMJ,* 1949, 1, Supp., pp. 358-9. See also Titmuss, R. M., *Essays on 'The Welfare State',* Allen and Unwin, 1958, pp. 192-4. See also Abel-Smith (1964), p. 485.
18 *BMJ,* 1950, 1, pp. 392-6.
19 *BMJ,* 1949, 2, p. 150. See also 1948, 1, p. 1154. For a defence of GPs, see 1949, 2, pp. 799-801.
20 *Lancet,* 1918, 2, pp. 87-90, italics underlined in original.
21 For the origins of this movement, see *BMJ,* 1886, 1, pp. 1030, 1114-15, 1124-5. For reports by the BMA's Central Ethical Committee, see *ibid.,* 1906, 2, Supp., pp. 98-101; 1908, 1, Supp., pp. 241-3, 429-32; 1909, 2, Supp., pp. 337-8. See also Stevens (1966), pp. 31-2.
22 *BMJ,* 1910, 1, Supp., pp. 322-6.
23 *Med. World,* 22 Sept. 1916, pp. 375-6.
24 For this, see his obituary notice in *The Times,* 27 Dec. 1923, p. 13.
25 For Brackenbury's interest in the development of a viable referral system, see Brackenbury (1935), pp. 109-10, 276-8.
26 For the prevalence of GP-specialists in Germany and Austria and the attempts made to stop them, see *Journal of American Medical Association,* 27 Feb. 1932, pp. 749-50; 3 Sept. 1932, pp. 1007-8; 13 May 1933, p. 1554; 27 May 1933, p. 1707; 25 Aug. 1934, p. 619; 16 March 1935, p. 936; 27 July 1935, p. 294. See also *BMJ,* 1938, 1, Supp., pp. 389-90.
27 *Gen. Prac.,* 2 May 1975, p. 15.
28 *BMJ,* 1944, 2, Supp., p. 161. See also the remarks by Wright's colleague

in the campaign, Mr A. Lawrence Abel, in *ibid.*, 1945, 1, Supp., pp. 60-1. See also *Lancet*, 1942, 1, p. 343-7.

29 For Wright's defence of the GP-specialist, see *BMJ*, 1948, 2, Supp., pp. 56-7. For similar concern by Abel, see *ibid.*, 1949, 1, Supp., pp. 17-18. See also the same stand by the President of the Royal College of Surgeons (Webb-Johnson) in *Lancet*, 1950, 2, pp. 882-3.

30 *Lancet*, 1918, 2, pp. 87-90.

31 *BMJ*, 1910, 2, pp. 121-4. See also 1911, 1, pp. 978-81.

32 *Med. World*, 7 July 1916, pp. 13-14.

33 Royal College of Surgeons, *Annual Reports of Council*, 1944, pp. 15-17.

34 See the paper by Prof. Bradford Hill, 'The Doctor's Day and Pay', in *Journal of Royal Statistical Society*, 1951, Vol. CXIV, p. 17. See also Stevens (1966), pp. 56-9.

35 Abel-Smith (1964), p. 408.

36 *Lancet*, 1950, 1, p. 572.

37 *BMJ*, 1945, 1, Supp., p. 44.

38 From the *Western Daily Press* and *Bristol Mirror* as quoted in letter from Dr A. Coleridge to *BMJ*, 1946, 1, p. 549.

39 *Lancet*, 1942, 2, p. 618, para. 140 (ii). For a similar view, expressed by a leading surgeon, see MH 77/19, Post-War Hosp. Policy, Surveys — 1942, Memo. by E. R. C. (Sir Ernest Rock Carling), 'Personal Impressions Gained at the Outset of a Survey', 22 Sept. 1942. This antipathy to GP surgery was shared by Min. officials, for which see MH 77/22, Post-War Hosp. Policy, Memo. by Mr Pater, 'Medical Staffing of Hospitals', 24 Sept. 1942. These attitudes were later reflected in the hospital surveys conducted by the Nuffield Provincial Hospitals Trust and the Ministry of Health. For example, see the one for Sheffield and East Midlands, 1945, p. 70. Moran, though a physician, joined the attack on GP surgery. See *BMJ*, 1946, 1, pp. 653-5. For an interesting defence of their work by two GP surgeons, see *ibid.*, 1948, 2, pp. 24-6.

40 For a good indication of the American attitude, see the article by Dr Michael J. Halberstam, 'The Doctor's New Dilemma — "Will I Be Sued?', in *New York Times Magazine Section*, 14 Feb. 1971, p. 33. For the historical background, see Stevens (1971), pp. 51-2, 80-5, 158-64, 185-6, 194, 305-10.

41 *BMJ*, 1963, 1, Supp., p. 93 (Austin). See also *Lancet*, 1969, 1, pp. 715-17. For a full description of the controls over GPs in American hospitals, see *BMJ*, 1971, 2, pp. 516-19. For a dissenting view on their value by an American doctor who prefers the British way of 'input' controls, see *Lancet*, 1975, 1, p. 1086 (Gerber).

42 *Journal of Chartered Society of Physiotherapists*, Feb. 1945, pp. 85-9.

43 For the decline in America's GP corps, see Stevens (1971), p. 181.

44 For specific recognition of this, see the paper by Dr George G. Reader in *Med. Care*, May-June 1967, pp. 194-9.

45 Southmayd, Henry D., and Smith, Geddes, *Small Community Hospitals*, New York, Commonwealth Fund, 1944. (See, in particular, pp. 4, 13-14, 24-5, 37-8, 40-1.)

46 *British Journal of Social Medicine*, July 1948, pp. 77-105. *Lancet*, 1963, 1, pp. 40-2.

47 Stevens (1971), p. 293.

48 For recognition of this, see *Lancet*, 1944, 1, pp. 410-12.

49 *BMJ,* 1949, 1, Supp., p. 336 (Wood); 1952, 1, Supp., p. 160 (para. 36 of Council Report). See also Honigsbaum, F., 'Gen. Prac. Work in Brit. Hosps.', in *Social and Econ. Admin.,* April 1967, p. 42.

50 *Lancet,* 1963, 1, pp. 40-2.

51 Loudon, I. S. L., *The Demand for Hospital Care,* Oxford, United Oxford Hosps., 1970, p. 19.

52 Dept. of Health for Scot., Scot. Health Services Council, Report of Jt. Sub-Com., *The General Practitioner and the Hospital Service,* Edin., HMSO, p. 9, para. 17. See also Cohen Report (1954), p. 41, para. 157-9; and Gillie Report (1963), p. 41, para. 150.

53 Platt Report (1961), pp. 34-7.

54 Stevens (1966), pp. 143-52.

55 Honigsbaum, in *Social and Econ. Admin.,* April 1967, pp. 35-6.

56 *BMJ,* 1961, 2, Supp., pp. 172-3 (Patterson). See also Honigsbaum, in *Social and Econ. Admin.,* April 1967, pp. 41-2.

57 *Lancet,* 1949, 1, pp. 568-9.

58 *BMJ,* 1961, 2, pp. 843-7.

59 *Lancet,* 1945, 2, pp. 681-3.

60 *BMJ,* 1953, 2, pp. 696, 964-6.

61 *BMJ,* 1951, 1, Supp., p. 262. See also Eckstein (1959), p. 108.

62 *BMJ,* 1953, 2, p. 1436.

63 Min. of Health, Summary Report by Dr C. A. Boucher, *Survey of Services Available to the Chronic Sick and Elderly, 1954-1955,* Reports on Public Health and Med. Subjects No. 98, HMSO, 1957, p. 15.

64 Honigsbaum, in *Journal of Royal College of General Practitioners,* July 1972, pp. 442-3.

65 Duncan, A. H., *The Livingstone Project — The First Five Years,* Edin., Scot. Home and Health Dept., 1973, Scot. Health Service Studies No. 29.

66 *Public Health,* July 1957, pp. 151-7.

67 *Ibid.,* April 1959, pp. 41-2.

68 *Ibid.,* Aug. 1957, pp. 161-3.

69 *Ibid.,* April 1959, pp. 41-2.

70 *Ibid.,* May 1965, pp. 209-13.

71 Coll. of Gen. Prac., *First Annual Report,* 1953, p. 6. For the birth of the College as told by one of its creators, Dr John (later Lord) Hunt, see *J. of Royal Coll. of Gen. Prac.,* Jan. 1973, pp. 5-20.

72 *BMJ,* 1958, 2, pp. 585-90. Lindsey (1962), p. 317. For an indication of what the Balint course contains, see Balint, Michael, *The Doctor, His Patient and the Illness,* Pitman, 1964.

73 *Gen. Prac.,* 22 Nov. 1974, p. 26.

74 *Ibid.,* 3 Jan. 1975, p. 16.

75 For a clear indication of consultant interest in using GPs in the field of psychiatry, see Tripartite Committee of Royal College of Physicians, Society of MOHs and BMA, *The Mental Health Service After Unification,* BMA, 1972, pp. 37-8.

76 See the paper by Dr Stephen Barton Hall, 'Treatment by Specialist or General Practitioner?', in 'The Problems of Stress in General Practice', Supp. to *J. of Coll. of Gen. Prac.,* May 1958, p. 22.

77 Dunn (1952), pp. 424-32.

78 *Polish Jewish Observer,* 11 May 1945, p. 1.

79 *The Times*, 18 March 1946, p. 2. *Time and Tide*, 23 March 1946, p. 268. *Truth*, 1946: 29 March, p. 288; 3 May, p. 420. For the growth of this movement, which was led by Mrs Eleonora Tennant (a strong supporter of Franco during the Spanish Civil War), see material published in 1944 by two groups she headed, the Never Again Assn. and Face the Facts Assn. (available in Brit. Lib. of Pol. and Econ. Science, LSE). See also *Hampstead and Highgate Express*, 17 Oct. 1945, p. 1; 7 Dec. 1945, p. 3; 8 Feb. 1946, p. 3.

80 *Med. World,* 1945: 23 March, p. 167; 29 June, pp. 616-17.

81 *Med. World*, 13 July 1945, pp. 679-80.

82 For a strong letter from Burnet on this subject, see *Med. World*, 20 July 1945, pp. 724-5.

83 *Med. World*, 10 Aug. 1945, p. 824.

84 *Med. World*, 17 Aug. 1945, p. 26 (Davies). See also 24 Aug. 1945, p. 58 (Reuben); 31 Aug. 1945, p. 88 (Illingworth); 7 Sept. 1945, pp. 119-20 (Burnet), 120 (Rainer); 14 Sept. 1945, p. 152; 23 Nov. 1945, p. 455; 1 March 1946, p. 70; 26 Sept. 1947, pp. 135, 186-8 (Scott-Eason); 10 Oct. 1947, p. 220 (Burnet).

85 For Sir Fred. Cardew's activities in the anti-vivisection movement, see *Anti-Vivisection Review*, 1910: May, p. 370; June, pp. 378-9; July, pp. 7-8; *Abolitionist,* June 1911, p. 119. For Bayly's part in the 1911 campaign, see *ibid.*, Nov. 1911, p. 251; Dec. 1911, pp. 259-64.

86 For Faulkner's Communist ties, see *News of the World*, 25 Oct. 1964, p. 1. For the split in 1964 (said to be caused by Communist infiltration of MPU), see above article plus *Sun. Times,* 13 Dec. 1964, p. 6. For a short history of the MPU to 1964, see *Med. World News*, Dec. 1964, pp. 20-7. For Cardew's obituary, see *The Times*, 23 June 1971, p. 19.

87 For Bayly's obituary, see *Animals' Defence and Anti-Vivisection News*, July-Aug. 1961, pp. 78-9; *World Forum*, Oct. 1961, p. 38; *British Vegetarian*, Sept.-Oct. 1961, p. 313.

88 *Med. World*, 24 May 1946, pp. 468-70.

89 Quoted in *Association of Jewish Refugees Information*, Feb. 1946, p. 11. See also Bevan's statement in *Med. World*, 23 Nov. 1945, p. 455.

90 *Assn. of Jewish Refs. Info.,* May 1947, p. 35; Sept. 1947, p. 66; Jan. 1948, p. 1. See also Parl. Deb., Lords, 11 Nov. 1947, Vol. 152, Cols. 555-68; Commons, 5 Dec. 1947, Vol. 445, Cols. 696-721.

91 *Lancet*, 1920, 2, pp. 732-5. For a similar indictment of German medicine by the medical authority, Sir William Osler, see *Med. Press*, 1919, 1, p. 403.

92 Liek, Erwin, *The Doctor's Mission*, John Murray, 1930, pp. xv-xxxix (from Intro. by J. Ellis Barker), 38-40, 53-4, 160-77, 190-202. Liek was later discovered to be a Nazi but for statistics showing the sharp increase in obstetric operations in Germany between 1929 and 1931, see *J. of Amer. Med. Assn.,* 20 Jan. 1934, pp. 224-5. See also *Heal Thyself,* April 1933, pp. 145-9; Nov. 1933, pp. 572-6; Oct. 1934, pp. 594-600; Nov. 1934, pp. 673-82; Dec. 1934, pp. 713-19. See also Mosse, Geo. L., *Nazi Culture*, W. H. Allen, 1966, pp. 227-34.

93 *Medical Care Review,* April 1977, p. 389. See also *Newsweek,* 10 April 1978, pp. 53-5.

94 New York Academy of Medicine, Lectures to the Laity, No. XIV, *The Future In Medicine — The March of Medicine*, New York, Columbia Univ. Press, 1949, p. 97. See also *Lancet*, 1945, 2, pp. 820-1; *BMJ*, 1947, 1, pp. 148-50.

95 *BMJ*, 1918, 2, pp. 437-8. See also *Charity Org. Qtrly.*, July 1935, pp. 164-7 (review of Brackenbury's book). For a more recent statement on a similar theme, see *Medical Week*, 22 Feb. 1972, p. 6 (Platt).

Select Bibliography

Full source references are given above. I propose to list here only the main material on which the study is based.

Private papers were of limited use. The only ones which offered notable insight were the Diaries of Sir George Newman (1907-46), located in the Library of the Department of Health and Social Security. The Minute Book of the SMSA was also useful. It can be obtained from the Socialist Medical Association, 9 Poland Street, London.

Much greater benefit was produced by the material in the Public Record Office. The early records of the National Health Insurance Act will be found in the papers of the Ministry of Pensions and National Insurance (PIN series) and the later in those of the Ministry of Health (MH series). The latter are extensive and require prolonged study. They need to be read in conjunction with the papers of the Ministry of Reconstruction (RECON series) and the Cabinet (CAB series) as well as with the published reports listed below.

Also useful were the records of the Labour Party's Public Health Advisory Committee, available in Transport House, London. These need to be read in conjunction with the annual conference reports of the Labour Party, the Trades Union Congress and the National Association of Trade Union Approved Societies. The annual conference reports of the Poor Law Districts (available at the British Library of Political and Economic Science) were also helpful.

The main source material for this study came from the medical press and this literature is overwhelming. The leading journals have been produced weekly or monthly since the nineteenth century and they require intensive reading. The main ones consulted were: *British Medical Journal, The Lancet, Medical World, Medical Press and Circular, Medical Officer, Public Health, Medicine Today and Tomorrow.* The leading journal of the approved society world, the *National Insurance Gazette,* also required prolonged study. As for newspapers, the most useful was *The Times* during the 1919-21 period.

Next in importance were the reports of, and evidence given to, public bodies. The main ones consulted were:

Royal Commission on the Poor Laws and Relief of Distress, Report, 1909, Cmd 4499; Min. of Ev., 1909, Cmd. 4625, 4684, 4755; 1910, Cmd. 5068.

Royal Commission on National Health Insurance, Report, 1928, Cmd. 2596; Min. of Ev. and App. to Min. of Ev., 2 Vols., 1925-6.

Royal Commission on Workmen's Compensation, Minutes of Evidence, 1939-40.

Athlone Report. Min. of Health, Report of Post-Graduate Committee, 1921.

Beveridge Report. Beveridge, William, *Social Insurance and Allied Services,* 1942, Cmd. 6404.

Cohen Report. Min. of Health, Central Health Services Council, Report of Committee on General Practice within the National Health Service, 1954.

Dawson Report. Min. of Health, Consul. Council on Med. and Allied Services, Interim Report on the Future Provision of Medical and Allied Services, 1920, Cmd. 693.

Delevingne Reports. Inter-Departmental Committee on the Rehabilitation of Persons Injured by Accidents, Interim Report, 1937; Final Report, 1939.

Gillie Report. Min. of Health, Central Health Services Council, Standing Medical Advisory Committee, *The Field of Work of the Family Doctor,* 1963.

Goodenough Report. Min. of Health, Report of Inter-Departmental Committee on Medical Schools, 1944.

Guillbebaud Report. Min. of Health and Sec. of State for Scot., Report of the Committee of Enquiry into the Cost of the National Health Service, 1956, Cmd. 9663.

Maclean Report. Min. of Reconstruction, Local Government Committee, Report of the Transfer of Functions of Poor Law Authorities in England and Wales, 1918, Cmd. 8917.

Platt Report. Min. of Health and Dept. of Health for Scot., Report of Joint Working Party, *Medical Staffing Structure in the Hospital Service,* 1961.

Rolleston Report. Inter-Departmental Committee on Insurance Medical Records, Report, 1920, Cmd. 836.

Schuster Report. NHI Commission, Departmental Committee on Sickness Benefit Claims under the National Insurance Act, Report and Min. of Ev., 1914, Cmd. 7687.

Spens Reports. Min. of Health and Dept. of Health For Scot., Report of Inter-Departmental Committee on the Remuneration of General Practitioners, 1946, Cmd. 6810; same for Consultants and Specialists, 1948, Cmd. 7420.

Stewart Report. Home Office, Departmental Committee on Certain Questions Arising Under the Workmen's Compensation Acts, Report, 1938, cd. 5657.

White Paper on National Health Service. Min. of Health and Dept. of Health for Scot., *A National Health Service,* 1944, Cmd. 6502.

Last, we come to the secondary sources and only the main works will be listed. Limited biographic data is included since this is given for the key figures in the profiles above.

Abel-Smith, Brian, *The Hospitals, 1800-1948,* Heinemann, 1964. See also Abel-Smith's paper, 'The History of Medical Care', in Martin, E. W. (editor), *Comparative Developments in Social Welfare,* Allen and Unwin, 1972.

Acton Society Trust, *Hospitals and the State,* 1955-9, 6 pamphlets.

Addison, Paul, *The Road to 1945, British Politics and the Second World War,* Jonathan Cape, 1975.

Armstrong, Barbara, *The Health Insurance Doctor, His Role in Great Britain, Denmark and France,* OUP, 1939.

Baernreither, J. M., *English Associations of Working Men,* Swan Sonnenschein, 1889.

Brabrook, Edward W., *Provident Societies and Industrial Welfare,* Blackie & Son, 1898.

Brand, Jeanne L., *Doctors and the State: The British Medical Association and Government Action in Public Health, 1870-1912,* Johns Hopkins Press, 1965.

British Medical Association, *A Ministry of Health,* 1918; *A General Medical Service for the Nation,* 1929 and 1938.

Brook, Charles W., *Making Medical History*, Percy B. Buxton, 1946.

Brotherston, John, 'Evolution of Medical Practice', in McLachlan, Gordon, and McKeown, Thomas (editors), *Medical History and Medical Care*, OUP for Nuffield Provincial Hospital Trust, 1971.

Bunbury, Henry N. (editor), *Lloyd George's Ambulance Wagon, the Memoirs of William J. Braithwaite, 1911-1912*, Methuen, 1957.

Canadian Dept. of Health and Welfare, *Health Insurance in Great Britain, 1911-1948*, Social Security Series, Memo. No. 11, Ottawa, 1952.

Carr-Saunders, A. M., and Wilson, P. A., *The Professions*, Oxford, Clarendon Press, 1933.

Comyns Carr, A. S., Garnett, W. H., and Taylor, J. H., *National Insurance*, Macmillan, 1913.

Dawson, Bertrand, *The Nation's Welfare: The Future of the Medical Profession*, Cassell, 1918.

Donnison, Jean, *Midwives and Medical Men*, Heinemann, 1977.

Eckstein, Harry, *The English Health Service*, Harvard Univ. Press, 1959.

Ferguson, S. M., and Fitzgerald, H., *Studies in the Social Services*, Longmans for HMSO, 1954, U. K. Civil History Series.

Frazer, W. M., *A History of English Public Health, 1834-1939*, Ballière, Tindall and Cox, 1950.

Gilbert, Bentley B., *The Evolution of National Insurance in Britain*, Michael Joseph, 1966; *British Social Policy, 1914-1939*, Batsford, 1970.

Gordon, Alban, *Social Insurance, What It Is and What It Might Be*, Allen and Unwin for Fabian Society, 1924.

Gosden, P. H. J. H., *The Friendly Societies in England, 1815-1875*, Manchester Univ. Press, 1961.

Gray, Alexander, *Some Aspects of National Health Insurance*, P. S. King, 1923.

Hardy, Horatio Nelson, *The State of the Medical Profession in Great Britain and Ireland in 1900*, Dublin, Fannin, 1901.

Harris, R. W., *National Health Insurance in Great Britain, 1911-1946*, Allen and Unwin, 1946.

Harris, R. W., and Sack, L. S., *Medical Insurance Practice*, BMA, 1922, 1924, 1929, 1937.

Hodgkinson, Ruth G., *The Origins of the National Health Service: The Medical Services of the New Poor Law, 1834-1871*, Wellcome Historical Medical Library, Monograph No. 11, 1967.

Hogarth, James, *The Payment of the General Practitioner — Some European Comparisons*, Pergamon, 1963.

Honigsbaum, Frank, *The Struggle for the Ministry of Health*, Occasional Papers on Social Administration No. 37, G. Bell, 1970.

Horner, Norman G., *The Growth of the General Practitioner of Medicine in England*, Bridge & Co., 1922.

Inglis, Brian, *Fringe Medicine*, Faber and Faber, 1964.

Joint Committee of Royal College of Obstetricians and Gynaecologists and Population Investigation Committee, *Maternity in Great Britain*, OUP, 1948.

Kayne, G. Gregory, *The Control of Tuberculosis in England, Past and Present*, OUP, 1937.

Kerr, J. M. Munro, *Maternal Mortality and Morbidity*, Livingstone, 1933.

Labour Party, *The Organisation of the Preventive and Curative Medical Services and Hospital and Laboratory Systems under a Ministry of Health*, 1918; *National Service for Health*, 1943.

League of Nations Union, *Social Insurance,* Faber & Gwyer, 1925.

Levy, Hermann, *National Health Insurance, A Critical Study,* Cambridge Univ. Press, 1944.

Lincoln, John A. (editor), *The Way Ahead — The Strange Case of the Friendly Societies,* National Conference of Friendly Societies, 1946.

Lindsey, Almont, *Socialized Medicine in England and Wales, The National Health Service, 1948-1961,* Univ. of North Carolina Press, 1962.

Little, Ernest Muirhead (editor), *History of the British Medical Association, 1832-1932,* BMA, 1932.

Loudon, I. S. L., *The Demand for Medical Care,* Oxford, United Oxford Hospitals, 1970.

McCleary, George F., *National Health Insurance,* H. K. Lewis, 1932; *The Early History of the Infant Welfare Movement,* Lewis, 1933; *The Maternity and Child Welfare Movement,* P. S. King, 1935.

McKail, David, and Jones, William, *A Public Medical Service,* Allen and Unwin for Fabian Society, 1919.

McKenzie, James, *The Future of Medicine,* Henry Froude, 1919.

McKenzie, W. Leslie, *Scottish Mothers and Children,* Dunfermline, Carnegie U.K. Trust, 1917. Mackintosh, J. M., *Trends of Opinion about the Public Health, 1901-51,* OUP, 1953.

Mair, Alex, *Sir James Mackenzie, MD: General Practitioner, 1853-1925,* Churchill Livingstone, 1973.

Masterman, Lucy, *C. F. G. Masterman,* Nicolson and Watson, 1939.

Morgan, Gerald, *Public Relief of Sickness,* Allen and Unwin, 1923.

Morrah, Dermot, *A History of Industrial Life Assurance,* Allen and Unwin, 1955.

Newman, Charles, *The Evolution of Medical Education in the Nineteenth Century,* OUP, 1957.

Newman, George, *Infant Mortality,* Methuen, 1906; *An Outline of the Practice of Preventive Medicine,* HMSO, 1919 and 1926; *The Building of a Nation's Health,* Macmillan, 1939.

Newman, T. S., *The Story of Friendly Societies and Social Security,* 1945.

Newsholme, Arthur, *International Studies on the Relation Between the Private and Official Practice of Medicine,* Allen and Unwin, 1931, 3 Vols.; *Medicine and the State,* Allen and Unwin, 1932.

Nuffield Provincial Hospitals Trust, *The Hospital Surveys,* Oxford, 1946.

Orr, Douglass W. and Orr, Jean Walker, *Health Insurance With Medical Care, the British Experience,* Macmillan, 1938.

Parry, Noel, and Parry, José, *The Rise of the Medical Profession,* Croom Helm, 1976.

Pinker, Robert, *English Hospital Statistics 1861-1938,* Heinemann, 1966.

Political and Economic Planning, *Report on the British Health Services,* 1937; *Medical Care for Citizens,* 1944; *Medical Group Practice in the United States,* 1947.

Poynter, F. N. L. (editor), *The Evolution of Medical Practice in England,* Pitman, 1961.

Richardson, J. T., *The Origin and Development of Group Practice in the United States, 1890-1940,* Univ. of Missouri Press, 1945.

Robson, William A. (editor), *Social Security,* Allen and Unwin for Fabian Society, 1943, 1945, 1948.

Rooff, Madeleine, *Voluntary Societies and Social Policy,* Routledge, 1957.

Ross, James Sterling, *The National Health Service in Great Britain,* OUP, 1952.

Royal College of Obstetricians and Gynaecologists, *Report on a National Maternity Service,* 1944.

Rumsey, Henry W., *Essays on State Medicine,* Churchill, 1856.

Shryock, Richard H., *The Development of Modern Medicine,* Gollancz, 1948.

Simon, A. M., and Sinai, N. S., *The Way of Health Insurance,* Univ. of Chicago Press, 1932.

Socialist Medical Association, *Whither Medicine?,* 1940; *The War, Tuberculosis and the Workers,* 1942; *Control of the Health Services,* 1945.

Southmayd, Henry J., and Smith, Geddes, *Small Community Hospitals,* New York, Commonwealth Fund, 1944.

Stark Murray, David, *Health for All,* Gollancz, 1942; *Why a National Health Service?,* Pemberton, 1971.

Stevens, Rosemary, *Medical Practice in Modern England,* Yale Univ. Press, 1966; *American Medicine and the Public Interest,* Yale Univ. Press, 1971.

Taylor, Stephen, *Good General Practice,* OUP, 1954.

Thomson, A. Landsborough, *Half a Century of Medical Research, Volume 1: Origins and Policy of the Medical Research Council (UK),* HMSO, 1973.

Tillyard, Frank, *The Worker and the State,* Routledge, 1923.

Titmuss, Richard Morris, *Problems of Social Policy,* Longmans for HMSO, 1950, U.K. Civil History Series; *Essays on 'The Welfare State',* Allen and Unwin, 1958. See also Titmuss's paper, 'Health', in Ginsberg, Morris (editor), *Law and Opinion in England in the Twentieth Century,* Stevens, 1959.

Trades Union Congress, General Council, *Trade Unions and Workmen's Compensation,* 1939.

Trades Union Congress and Labour Party, *National Health Insurance Medical Benefit,* no date (but 1923); *Social Insurance and Trade Union Membership,* 1924.

Vaughan, Paul, *Doctors' Commons, A Short History of the British Medical Association,* Heinemann, 1959.

Waddington, Ivor, 'General Practitioners and Consultants in Early Nineteenth Century England', in Woodward, John, and Richards, David (editors), *Medical Care and Popular Medicine in Nineteenth Century England,* Croom Helm, 1977.

Webb, Sidney, *Ministry of Health,* 1918; *The Future Organisation of the Medical Profession,* 1918.

Webb, Sidney and Beatrice, *The State and the Doctor,* Longmans, 1910; *English Local Government: English Poor Law History: Part II, The Last Hundred Years,* Longmans, 1929.

Westacott, E., *A Century of Vivisection and Anti-Vivisection,* C. W. Daniel, 1949.

Willcocks, A. J., *The Creation of the National Health Service,* Routledge, 1967.

Wilson, Arnold, and Levy, Hermann, *Industrial Assurance, An Historical and Critical Study,* OUP, 1937; *Workmen's Compensation,* OUP, 1939 and 1941, 2 Vols.

Wilson, Norman, *Municipal Health Services,* Allen and Unwin, 1946.

Wilson, Robert MacNair, *The Beloved Physician,* John Murray, 1926; *Doctor's Progress,* Eyre and Spottiswoode, 1938.

Woodall, Samuel J., *Manor House Hospital,* Routledge, 1946.

Index